A HISTORY OF MUSIC

A sixteenth-century painting by an unidentified French or Flemish artist. One girl is singing from a part. Another, with her part-book before her, is playing a cross-flute. The third performer, without any music, is twanging a lute, supplying from memory perhaps the overall harmony. The music they are playing can be identified as Claudin de Sermisy's chanson, *Jouyssance vous donneray*.

A HISTORY OF MUSIC

By

WILLIAM L. SMOLDON
Ph.D. B.Mus. (London)

LONDON: HERBERT JENKINS

First published by
Herbert Jenkins Ltd.,
3 Duke of York Street,
London, S.W.1
1965

© WILLIAM L. SMOLDON 1965

PRINTED IN GREAT BRITAIN BY
BRISTOL TYPESETTING CO. LTD.
BARTON MANOR - ST. PHILIPS
BRISTOL 2

To
DR. REGINALD H. HUNT
in token of a lifelong friendship

AUTHOR'S PREFACE

THIS SURVEY of the development of music in the Western world, while designed to be of sound practical value to whole-time students of music, aims also at being acceptable to the growing body of cultured laymen who, though often not possessing any level of technical equipment, are yet interested in the art and its history.

Some attention has been given to the music of the older civilisations, particularly those of classic Greece and Byzantium, each of which played a significant part in shaping the early course of music in the West. Note has also been taken of the small but valuable debts owed to the art of Islam.

As far as possible a chronological progress has been maintained so that the reader may be aware as to where he is standing in the time-scale. In certain specialised works on music it is often found necessary to pursue an art-form through a long period of its development. While some such concentration has here been given to themes such as the rise and expansion of the symphony or of the operatic art, the attempt has been made always to preserve the overall picture.

There is already in existence a more than sufficient literature concerned with the " lives of great composers ". In this present work biographical details have been confined to those which had an effective influence upon the production of their music.

While, in discussing points in the text, I have made use of printed musical examples where they appear to be necessary, I have also relied a great deal on references to relevant gramophone recordings. Since there is always the question of availability, I have called mainly on the ten sets of *The History of Music in Sound* (Great Britain : *E.M.I. Records Ltd.—" His Master's Voice "* Records. U.S.A. : *R.C.A. Victor*) as being in the libraries of most leading musical institutions and larger schools, as well as being stocked by many county lending libraries. The sets of records are accompanied by a corresponding series of ten *Handbooks*, published by the Oxford University Press. The HMS, as it is familiarly called, is likely also to have a much longer life than most single records on the market. I have made occasional mention of recordings other than those of the HMS, but only where there seems a chance of these having something more than transitory existence.

7

As Rollo Myers says (*Twentieth Century Music, p. vii—Calder*): " . . . the arts have always been a more or less accurate barometer of the social and intellectual climate at any given period in the countries where they flourish. Music, the youngest of the arts, is perhaps the most sensitive to variations in this climate . . ."

For these reasons I have tried as far as possible in this work of modest dimensions to sketch in backgrounds of the historical happenings and the ever-varying social conditions as the chronicle progresses, since these cast so much light on the whys and wherefores of musical qualities and evolutions.

I have from time to time made references to a work that should be of considerable value to the music student—the two volumes of the *Historical Anthology of Music* by Archibald T. Davison and Willi Apel (*Harvard University Press*) which provide printed examples of musical compositions —oriental, medieval, Renaissance, baroque, rococo—up to pre-classical times. Another useful reference work on the same lines is the one-volume *Masterpieces of Music Before 1750 (An Anthology of Musical Examples from Gregorian Chant to J. S. Bach)* by Carl Parrish and John F. Ohl (*Faber*). These examples, in performance, have recently been recorded and issued by the Haydn Society.

Notes on points in the text, together with details of recordings that have been referred to, are placed at each chapter end.

I offer here my sincerest thanks to a number of musical and scholarly friends and acquaintances who have from time to time given me salutary advice and criticism. Among these I venture to mention Dr. Reginald Hunt, Professor R. Thurston Dart, Dr. Egon Wellesz, Mr. Anthony Milner, and from the time of my brief stay on the other side of the Atlantic, as well as from correspondence—Professor Gustave Reese, Dr. Leonard Ellinwood and Mr. Eric Salzman, music-critic of the *New York Herald Tribune*.

In offering my gratitude to the above-named, I beg to stress that all short-comings and errors that may appear in the following pages must be laid to my charge, and mine alone.

I should like also to make thankful mention of the name of Mr. T. A. Baker of the Essex County Libraries, who at times procured the most un-likely reference books for me, and saved me many a long journey to the British Museum Reading Room.

There remains a constant gratitude to my wife for her aid in so many ways, and for her unfaltering patience over the number of years that have gone into the preparation of this book.

WM. L. SMOLDON

CONTENTS

LIST OF ILLUSTRATIONS

ACKNOWLEDGMENTS

For permission to use quotations from texts, musical scores (including transcriptions from manuscripts into modern notation) and other copyrighted material from books and periodicals, acknowledgments are here gratefully made to the following. (The page numbers in parentheses refer to the present volume) :

HARVARD UNIVERSITY PRESS (Mass., U.S.A.)
   Historical Anthology of Music : Willi Apel & T. Davison
      Vol. I : Rondeau (p. 81); Diferencias (p. 136); Ricerare (p. 116).
      Vol. II : Monody—Peri (p. 151); Monody—Caccini (p. 148); Symphonic movement (p. 218).
   Music of the Western Nations : Hugo Leichtentritt (p. 446)
   Sixteenth Century Polyphony : A. T. Merritt (p. 110).

HUTCHINSON & CO. LTD. (London)
   The Interpretation of Music : R. Thurston Dart (p. 104)

ALFRED A. KALMUS LTD.
   Violin Concerto : A. Schoenberg (Ex. 83, p. 411)
   Op. 33a for Piano : A. Schoenberg (Ex. 81, p. 408)

MACMILLAN & CO. LTD. (London)
   An Illustrated History of Music : M. Pincherle (pp. 388, 419)

MESSRS. W. W. NORTON & CO. INC. (New York)
   Music in the Middle Ages : G. Reese (Ex. 10, p. 48; Ex. 11, p. 49)
   Music in Western Civilization : P. H. Lang (pp. 64, 98, 219, 334)
   Music in the Baroque Era : H. Einstein (pp. 314, 345)
   Music in the Romantic Era : H. Einstein (pp. 314, 345)
   Masterpieces of Music Before 1750 : Parrish & Ohl (Ex. 35, p. 93)

NOVELLO & CO. LTD. (London)
   Elgar : Violin Concerto (Ex. 73, p. 400; Ex. 76, p. 402)
   Elgar : The Dream of Gerontius (Ex. 75, p. 401)
   Elgar : 'Cello Concerto (Ex. 74, p. 401)

OXFORD UNIVERSITY PRESS (London)
   New Oxford History of Music, II (Ex. 8, p. 47; Ex. 13, p. 52)
   History of Music in Sound :
      Handbook II (Ex. 21, p. 67; Ex. 23, p. 69). Handbook III (Ex. 29, p. 85)
      Handbook IV (Ex. 48, a & b, p. 175)
   The Structure of Music : R. O. Morriss (p. 112)

ACKNOWLEDGMENTS (*continued*)

YALE UNIVERSITY PRESS (Conn., U.S.A.)
The Rhythm of Twelfth Century Polyphony : W. H. Waite (Ex. 18, p. 59)
THE MEDIÆVAL ACADEMY OF AMERICA (Camb., Mass., U.S.A.)
The Notation of Polyphonic Music : W. Apel (Ex. 27, p. 81)

At various places in the chapters of this book a number of other works
have been mentioned in the course of making brief quotations from them.
In each case precise details of sources have been given, and it is hoped that
these will be held to constitute sufficient acknowledgment.

"Music, the greatest good that mortals know.
And all of heaven we have below."

ADDISON, *Song for St. Cecilia's Day* (1694).

"Education in music is most sovereign, because more than anything else
rhythm and harmony find their way into the secret places of the soul."

PLATO, *The Republic, Bk. III, ch. 12* (c. 375 B.C.)

"Where gripinge grefes the hart would wounde,
And dolefulle dumps the mynde oppresse,
There musicke with her silver sound
With spede is wont to send redresse:
Of trobled mynds, in every sore,
Swete musicke hathe a salve in store."

RICHARD EDWARDS, *A Song to the Lute in Musicke* (1560)

A HISTORY OF MUSIC

NOTE

The superior numbers which appear in the text and at the right-hand side of many music examples refer to the numbered notes at the end of each chapter. These notes give additional information concerning points in the text, music examples and quotations.

An asterisk after the number of a note indicates the availability of a *History of Music in Sound (HMS)* recording.

CHAPTER I

Music in the Ancient Civilisations

THE PURPOSE of this history of music is to consider in some detail the progress of the art within the limits of less than a score of centuries and the regions of Western civilisation. To many people these may seem the only considerations that are of any importance for the understanding of music as we know it, but it is well to recall that the roots of the art lie very far in the past. Music pursued its course among civilised communities in highly organised fashion many millenia before the Christian era.

Our detailed survey will begin from the time when Western Europe was struggling to emerge from the chaos caused by the collapse of the Western Roman Empire. Looking at this period, we discover that the one steadfast feature was the Western Christian Church, respected by the " barbarians ", and continuing its long-established Latin rites in every country of the West, its daily services being chanted to an organised system (eventually acquiring the name of *cantus planus*, or " plainchant "), on which Western music of later centuries was to build.[1] When we seek the origins of this chant we find our path leading back and back through time. Let us follow it for a while, even though we can do so only briefly. It takes us first to the early centuries of Christian struggle and expansion. There seems little doubt that the worship-music of the early Church, i.e. at such centres as Jerusalem, Damascus, Antioch and Alexandria, grew from materials already known to the congregations, of which the ingredients were perhaps music of Greek and Syrian origins, together with the service-chants of the Jewish synagogue. What the proportions were that were taken over for the Western rites and those of the Eastern (Byzantine) Church, and how much the music of the latter affected the West are still matters for research and debate, and in any case cannot be pursued here. The chief point is that the style and modality of the ancient Near-East were transferred to Europe.

Music in Mesopotamia and Egypt

Behind Greek, Syrian and Jewish music lay in turn long traditions, and the shadows of older civilisations yet, those of Mesopotamia and Egypt, which were flourishing five thousand years or more (probably a great deal more) ago. In the Land of the Two Rivers and in the Nile Valley temple-priesthoods carried on their liturgies with the aid of trained choirs and arrays of different instruments, many types of which have survived to this day, while at the royal courts, singers, dancers and " orchestras " played their parts in providing pageantry and pastime. Ranging through the last three millenia B.C. we learn from inscriptions, carvings, paintings and even surviving examples that among the instruments used were many-stringed harps of various shapes, kitharas, lutes, pipes (single- and double-reed, and flute types), trumpets, wooden horns, drums of various shapes and sizes, tambourines, clappers, rattles such as the Egyptian sistrum, and, comparatively late, bells and large cymbals. Depictions of piping shepherds and singing harvesters show us that as well as the music of court and temple there were as ever folk-songs, work-songs and in general the simple tunes of everyday life.

Yet for all the instrumental detail we have not yet discovered how this music — Sumerian, Assyrian, Babylonian, Egyptian, Aegean — actually *sounded*, since except for a single brief Sumerian example which is still a subject of controversy, no musical notation has come down to us. One thing seems certain—like all ancient musics it was based on melody alone, a single-line art—*monophony*. When instruments accompanied a vocal tune they may frequently have varied the melodic line (*heterophony*); also, certain scholars have argued cases for there having been simultaneous soundings of fifths and octaves as occasional accent-chords for harps, and for pipe-drones being used. It is held that the five-note (pentatonic) scale was widely employed in all early music, but that a seven-note scale came into use in due course. Evidence from the construction of both Sumerian and Egyptian flutes seems to point to the establishment of such a scale with a tritone fourth (roughly equivalent to our diatonic octave from F). But all this is as yet unproven.[2*]

Jewish Music

The Old Testament and the Jewish Talmud give much information as to the practice of music in the Temple services at Jerusalem, which, (if we include the interval of the Exile) spanned a thousand years. Early mention of music among the Hebrews is in simple terms—singing, and the playing of " lyres " and " timbrils " (tambourines). But in the great days of Temple music from the age of David and Solomon onwards the Temple " orchestra " included harps, reed-pipes, trumpets and cymbals—some types probably borrowed from Egypt in the first instance. After the destruction of the Second Temple in A.D. 70 instrumental music does not seem to have been revived in the synagogues; only the ritual *shofar* (ram's horn) remained. The chant, however, continued, and of late years research has made it increasingly clear that many of the forms and even melodic patterns of the Byzantine and Western Christian chants were adaptations from the music of the synagogues. Ancient Jewish music knew no system of notation. Comparisons have been effected only by the study of the traditional music of modern but isolated Jewish communities like those of the Yemen and Babylon, which have never been in contact with Christianity.[3*]

Greek Music

The rise of the Greek city-states, the first " democracies ", gave a somewhat different slant to organised music. Before their advent the Homeric poems had pictured a " heroic " age, with the figure of the professional bard chanting epics to an assembled and lordly company (*Odyssey, Book VIII*), and also an amateur like Achilles, amusing himself in the privacy of his tent by singing, and at the same time playing his own accompaniment (*Iliad, Book IX*). But if we may believe tradition the various leading Greek cities had established by the sixth century B.C. public festivals where musicians met in competition. Professional contestants sang to their own lyre accompaniment—poet, composer and performer in one. Furthermore, the ordinary citizen was not only keenly interested in the art, but actually took part in choral competitions. Music was an important feature of everyday life, both for ceremonial and pastime. There were choirs of men, of women, of boys, of girls. Linked closely with music itself were the kindred arts of poetry and dancing. In the fifth and fourth centuries B.C., the hey-day of the city-states, music was an essential part of a young citizen's education. Philosophical writers like Aristotle and Plato stressed the importance of the right kind of musical education, since (and such seems to have been the general belief) this was a vital factor in the development of " virtuous " character. We hear much of the term *ethos* in connection with the music of the period.

The Greeks acknowledged their musical debts to the older civilisations, although they showed no taste for the Near East concerted " orchestra ". They made use of such traditional instruments as the trumpet (Gr. *salpinx*), various kinds of harps, pan-pipes (*syrinx*), castanets, tambourines and cymbals. The *magadis*, a twenty-stringed harp, permitted of playing in octaves; hence the term " magadising ", applied to both playing and singing at that interval. But all these instruments occupied a comparatively small part in Greek musical life. In the main their music was built on three modes of expression, the human voice allied to fine poetry, the string-plucked lyre and the reed-blown aulos. (See Plates 1 and 3.)

The organ (which might be described as a combination of the syrinx and the bag-pipe principles) was apparently a Greek invention. About 250 B.C. Ktesibios of Alexandria produced a practical organ which employed water to increase the wind pressure. Under the name of *hydraulis* it developed into an instrument of great power, and is represented as having three and even four rows of pipes. It was a great favourite in the times of Imperial Rome. Nero seems to have been fond of playing it. Eventually it reverted to straightforward pneumatic principles.

To return to the earlier days of the Greeks and their two favourite instruments—the chief types of lyre were the kithara and the lyra. The kithara, the larger of the two, had a wooden frame that allowed of considerable resonance, and was handled usually by the professional musician. The smaller lyra was more the amateur instrument, in shape more approach-

ing the tortoise-shell and goat's horns design of the Apollo myth. Both had
gut strings, stretched vertically and fastened to a horizontal bar at the top
called the yoke, where the tunings took place. Both were plucked by the
fingers of either hand, or in the case of the right, more usually by a
plectrum. The left hand was frequently employed for stopping. Regarding
this technique—in late antiquity there was a finger-board to the instrument,
and also evidence that this was sometimes fretted.

The aulos is almost always depicted in Greek art in double form—two
separate pipes—with a leather strap over the player's mouth and cheeks to
facilitate forceful blowing. It had finger-holes, and probably a double reed,
this making it an *oboe* type. It is regrettable that modern writers on matters
Greek who ought to know better, still continue to translate the word *aulos*
as "flute". Its tone must have been very unlike that of a flute, and was
probably very penetrating indeed. The Spartans (and others) used it at times
as a military "bugle". No ancient Greek explained the reason for there
being a pair of auloi. Probably the idea was to extend the scalic range, but
it has been suggested that it may have permitted the use of a drone, or
of occasional accompanying notes. Since its pitches depended on exactitudes
of hole-boring, it had less resource and refinement in matters of intonation
than the lyre with its delicate gradations of string-tuning and stopping.
It was the great god Apollo himself who was the patron of music, which in
the Greek meaning of the word included the arts of lyrical poetry and
dancing. Two legendary figures, Terpander and Olympos, were, we are told,
the first masters of lyre and aulos respectively. Actually, the history of both
instruments goes back into a far more distant past.

Two tendencies can be observed in Greek music of the classical period.
There was the lofty cult of Apollo that produced the hymns to the Immortals, the lyric songs and the *paeans* (originally " healing " dance-songs
—cures being wrought by the magic of music). With all these was associated
the lyre, Apollo's own instrument. In contrast was the worship of Dionysos,
the nature god. His praise was celebrated by assemblies who danced and
sang in a circle, accompanied by the instrument devoted to him, the aulos.
Such strophic choruses grew to the *dithyramb*, the form which the celebrated
poet-composer Pindar used in his odes. (Actually, there are records of the
dithyramb being accompanied by the kithara.) The dithyramb had a high
destiny. From the dialogue between leader and chorus there developed the
classical Greek Drama, at its greatest in the fifth century B.C. We must realise
that these works (outstanding among their creators being the immortal trio
Aeschylus, Sophocles and Euripides) were something more than poetic drama
alone. The members of the chorus moved to dance-rhythms, the choric
stanzas had their musical settings, as did the more lyrical portions of the
solo parts. A performer whose presence was essential was the single *aulete*
with his instrument. These dramatic festivals, like the music and dance
festivals already mentioned, were competitions—*agones*. Judges watched the
series and named the winning playwright, who would gain lifelong fame
among his fellow-citizens.

We cannot in a book of this scope follow the history of the development of Greek music in any detail. There is information (often of an uncertain quality) which ranges from the seventh century B.C. to the second A.D., and conditions in any one period can never be taken as typical for very long. Through the centuries improvements in instrumental construction took place. Kitharas of the fourth century B.C. had as many as eleven or twelve strings; auloi up to fifteen holes, together with revolving bands which permitted the closing and opening of holes necessary for a change of scalic intervals. To judge by the comments of contemporary writers the beginning of the fourth century B.C., with its advanced instrumental resources, saw the advent of a virtuoso period, a " new " music of greater elaboration and embellishment, much condemned by supporters of the old order. Its chief exponent was the famous Timotheus of Miletus (c. 450–360 B.C.). He is mentioned by Dryden in his poem " Alexander's Feast " as playing before the great conqueror at Persepolis in 331 B.C.—a sad anachronism. But the impulse, whether for good or evil, does not seem to have lasted. It was the period when, after the suicidal Peloponnesian Wars, the decline of the city-states was beginning. A similar falling-away in the vitality of Greek music seems also to have occurred. The surviving music examples from later times (scanty though they are) appear to indicate a return to comparative simplicity of line and diatonic style, a looking-back to ancient days.

A fair amount of information as to the *theory* of Greek music has survived, given by writers ranging from the fifth century B.C. to well into the Christian era. Much of it is obscure and contradictory—the outlook, often, of mathemeticians rather than practical musicians. The most valuable is that afforded by Aristoxenos of Tarentum (born c. 354 B.C.). The intonations he proposed for one type of diatonic scale seems to approximate closely to our " equal temperament ". One is inclined to wonder how far theory strayed at times from everyday practice, but when we turn to the latter we are again in the position of not knowing much as to what the actual compositions *sounded* like. As in the case of a great deal of ancient music improvisation probably played a great part in the earlier centuries—individual workings of standard melodic patterns. Surviving musical examples are scanty and late, written (in some cases carved on stone) in an alphabetical notation; a practice, it seems, not often employed. Fortunately for us, this notation was explained by Alypios (c. 360 A.D.). Two stone-carved Hymns to Apollo, found at Delphi and belonging to the second century B.C., may perhaps represent " prize " efforts; hence the permanent recording. The first is almost complete; the second fragmentary. Another survival (complete, and also on stone) is the brief " Epitaph of Seikilos for his wife " (first century B.C.—but a later date has been suggested). All three have been interpreted, and all show a relatively simple vocal style, with most of the time only one note to a syllable of text and with no extended flourishes, perhaps representing a feature already mentioned—the deliberate return to a more archaic atmosphere.[4*] A transcription of the Epitaph is here given :

The " letters " above the modern notes are reproductions of the Alypian notation; the dots and the lines, rhythmic and time-value signs respectively (see p. 28f.).

In the main Greek music was a vocal art, and like other ancient music, basically monophonic. Accompaniments for instruments were, it appears, at the unison or octave, but references are met as to the use of heterophony. Independent instrumental music was cultivated, naturally enough, and there were even contests between skilled players of solo instruments. An ancient tradition is that the aulete Sakados of Argos won a musical victory at the Pythian Games at Delphi in 586 B.C., with an extensive composition for solo aulos. This pictured, in five sections, the victory of Apollo over the Python. Such a performance was probably assisted by miming. If the story is true, it constitutes the first example in history of " programme music ". The aulos, in spite of its lesser refinements of intonation, was always more favoured than the kithara as a solo instrument, no doubt because of its greater carrying power.

As to the nature of Greek melody (which in a monophonic art was the chief concern of theory) the subject is a difficult and still controversial one, full of doubts and alternative explanations, lacking the touchstone of plentiful practical examples, and hampered, as we have already noted, by the obscurities and disagreements of the Greek writers. We can here refer only to its more general aspects.

It may first of all be said that the Greek musician, having to rely on the resources of a single line, demanded from the ear more refinements of perception than the modern listener might be able to supply, since this ancient music contained at times deliberately contrived intervals quite foreign to our normal experience. What we call the semitone was not enough—other and smaller fractions were required, and often the larger intervals varied in their ratios, for theorists could not agree as to the best tunings (i.e. the number of vibrations) to be given to what we should call the ordinary tones.

It is clear that in a primitive and purely melodic art singers will continue to sing for quite a long time without troubling their heads as to whys and wherefores, after the manner of the whistling street-boy. Having learned a melody, their only concern would be to render it at a pitch which suited their voice range. But when an instrumentalist undertakes to follow that melody then a welter of problems immediately arises. He has to *know* the pitches of the notes that he is called on to produce, and what his fingers must do in the circumstances; he tends to note the patterns of the intervals, and altogether becomes a theorist perforce. It is not surprising that the Greeks solved most of their musical problems by reference to instrumental strings. For this purpose the kithara was to them what the keyboard is to the modern musician. Several of the names given to the tones of the " Greater Perfect System ", a theoretical " scale " which covered the range of two octaves from A to a', were clearly derived from kithara technique.

In this last paragraph, and henceforward, statements concerning the kithara may be held to apply to the (smaller) lyra type.

The interval that the Greeks thought of as being of basic importance was the perfect fourth. Using modern staff-notation we may safely express it thus,

for it maintained itself firmly among other less fixed relationships. Two inner notes were added, completing the so-called *tetrachord*, and it was on this pattern of four notes that the Greeks based their theory. As we have seen, the two limiting notes were fixed ones, but what happened between them was another matter altogether. Let us consider the octave (made up of two disjunct perfect fourths) which the Greeks thought of as roughly the *vocal* range, e to E—

One way of filling in the intermediate notes, which were called significantly enough " moving tones ", may be approximately expressed thus, in double tetrachord form—

This particular treatment of a tetrachord was termed the *diatonic genus*.

A momentary aside is necessary. It must be mentioned that the span which has been called e to E was in practice probably our c sharp to C sharp, a convenient range for men's voices, for which much of Greek music was written. Another point which has already been exemplified—most of the Greek theorists seem to have thought of their scales as proceeding downwards, from top to bottom.

This matter of the *diatonic genus* will seem straightforward enough, even though we might not have liked some of the " moving-note " intonations, owing to the variations of tuning that were practised—the *chroma* (or "shades"), a feature which has already been mentioned. Let us now venture to state this diatonic vocal octave in terms of modern sol-fa, encouraged by the fact that a Greek theorist has recorded that "solmisation" was used even in Plato's time (fifth–fourth centuries B.C.), the syllables tĕ, to, tê, ta,

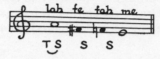

representing the intervals formed by the diatonic tetrachord, and thus being roughly equivalent to lah, soh, fah, me. The octave, then, can be approximately rendered as m' r' d't l s fm.

In the fourth century writings of Aristoxenos (when first the *genera* were analysed) two others were recognised. These altered the "moving tones" in other ways. The first can be approximately rendered thus :

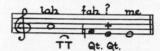

This was called the *chromatic genus*. In sol-fa terms the octave would be roughly, m' de' d't l fe fm.

The last arrangement involved divisions of the semitone—intervals that nowadays are difficult both to appreciate and notate :

This was called the *enharmonic genus*. The *ditone* gap (approximately lah–fah) was as characteristic as the quarter-tones.

There must now be considered another feature of Greek theory, the various arrangements of the central octave, known as "octave-species" of which we have already met one in its diatonic form. This has been expressed in terms of sol-fa as m' r' d't l s fm. These notes represent the intervals T T S T T T S (where T = tone and S = semitone). To this succession, and its variants in the other two genera, Greek theorists in due course applied the term "Dorian octave". It will be clear that melodic variety within the e–E limits could be obtained by, as it were, transferring the first T to the other end of the tonal series and thus obtaining T S T T T S T, or, in sol-fa interpretation, r' d't l s fm r. This was indeed a recognised central octave called the *Phrygian*. Another similar rearrangement, S T T T S T T (d't l s fm r d), gave the *Lydian*. These three octave-species, Dorian, Phrygian and Lydian, were apparently the earliest recognised. Clearly, seven such arrangements are possible, and in due course the other four were listed—*Mixolydian, Hypolydian, Hypophrygian* and *Hypodorian*. Sufficient clue to the tonal successions of each will be given if we say, in modern sol-fa parlance, that they would start respectively with te, fah', soh' and lah' as their topmost notes. Actually, the shuffling of tones that we have suggested is not a factual representation of their origin.

They arose from a theoretical series of two-octave " scales ", called *tonoi*, in the symbol notation previously referred to, built on various degrees of the (theoretical) Greater Perfect System. The subject of the Greek *tonos* is too involved to be embarked on here. It is sufficient to say that from the *tonoi* the various octave-species obtained their names, and the details of their successions of intervals so necessary for the instrumentalist.

It must also be mentioned that even in Aristoxenos' time a " new tuning " was in being, involving a central range of f–F, which bedevilled all the species-names mentioned. The *status quo* was eventually restored. But this concerns only those readers who propose to proceed further in the subject in more learned tomes.

It has no doubt been observed that these octave-species have been presented only in their diatonic form. Each could assume also the chromatic or enharmonic genus. Altogether, it will now be apparent that the possibilities of melodic variety, even in the comparatively small vocal range of little more than an octave were quite considerable.

What was the purpose of the various octave-species? One explanation is to consider the Dorian as being the only true *mode*, and the other species as different aspects of it, existing only to allow melodies of different ranges to be set within the vocal limits. This is one modern view, and probably the most feasible. Other authorities give modal life to octave-species other than the Dorian, after the manner of the Gregorian modes. Certainly we read that in earlier centuries " Dorian " and " Phrygian " music represented strongly contrasted styles, but what exactly was meant by the two terms *in* those times, we have no means of knowing. In the absence of concrete practical evidence the whole question has remained open, even though the " Epitaph " example quoted on p. 24 might suggest independent modal life to the Phrygian octave-species employed there.

It must not be assumed that at the time when the three genera first came under discussion that they existed side by side on equal terms. The diatonic was the oldest (according to Aristoxenos), and around 400 B.C. the chromatic genus was something of a novelty. However, this latter suffered a decline in the Hellenistic, post-Alexandrian world, being used apparently only on rare and formal occasions. (It appears in the second half of the First Delphic Hymn). The diatonic was by that time generally triumphant.

The *ditone* (appr. lah–fah) so characteristic of the enharmonic genus seems to have existed in the archaic style attributed to the legendary Olympus (m′ d′t l fm)—*without* the quarter-tones of the true enharmonic. Whether this represents the latter's ancestry cannot be known, but a late Greek writer suggests that the enharmonic semitone was originally undivided and that " old-fashioned aulos players " could still be heard keeping the semitone whole. There was also the implication that in any case it was only the lower of the two tetrachords which was thus divided.

These quarter-tones were not merely for decorative, *portamento* effect, if we accept the reading of the oldest fragment of Greek music left to us. This is a mutilated scrap of papyrus showing a line or so of Euripides' *Orestes,* together with musical symbols, dating perhaps from 344–338 B.C.

(if it is not a fact that the music is later than the text). In this the *lower* quarter-tone of the enharmonic *pyknon* is approached by leap from a tone outside the tetrachord.

Aristoxenos, writing about 400 B.C., expressed his admiration for the enharmonic style, which to him seemed to represent the nobility of the music of the high classical days that were past. It was, however, already moribund in his time. A later writer, the famous Ptolemy of Alexandria (second century A.D.) mentions it, but his account makes it clear that it was long out of use.

With the knowledge of all these melodic refinements it may be interesting to ponder the problems that faced the kithara player. In the earlier centuries and with a modest number of strings he aspired only to cover the range of the central octave. Curt Sachs (*The Rise of Music in the Ancient World*) has made an excellent case for the assumption that the earlier instruments were tuned pentatonically. Thus a six-stringed kithara would have had for its open notes—e, d, b, a, G, E. (One can play this sequence on the black notes of the pianoforte, moving downward from D sharp.) The missing c and F was no doubt produced by stopping the b and E strings. The oft-mentioned addition of a seventh string may have been that for c. To express some of the problems in modern terms—the diatonic Dorian octave e–E could be played on the piano keyboard as being in the " open key ", but if we wished to obtain the Phrygian and Lydian series of intervals we would need the key signatures of two sharps (*vide* the " Epitaph " example on p. 24) and four sharps respectively. The Greek kithara player was called on to do something analogous in the matter of stoppings of strings. Moreover there were the chromatic adjustments which would be necessary when use was made of the other genera. The reader may care to work out for himself what the " key " analogies would be in the cases of the other octave-species, using the hints already given above on p. 24.[6] In practice the kithara player found that in certain of the octave-species the small divisions of the enharmonic genus were unobtainable, even by stopping, on the instrument tuned as above. The solution was the " higher tuning ", which, as already noted, caused a temporary dislocation of nomenclature for the *tonoi* and the octave-species. The new high tuning on the seven-stringed instrument was probably—f, d, c, b, a, G, E, an arrangement which solved the " enharmonic " problems. By c. 400 the standard number of strings was eleven or twelve, this sufficing to span two octaves. With the fading of the quarter-tone enharmonic genus the need for the higher tuning also faded, and we find that such writers as Ptolemy were using the octave-species names at the old level, with the Dorian restored to its former position.

Brief mention must be made of the " extra " tetrachord *Synemmenon*—the name implying that it was " hooked "—as a sort of spare part to the normal four tetrachords of the Greater Perfect System (which is another feature neglected here). Its four tones were d, c, b flat, A, and practical use was made of it, e.g., in the First Delphic Hymn. The alternative of b flat for b as a melody note reappears in the Gregorian chant system.

Another short reference—the rhythms of the vocal melodies appear to have been very largely dictated by the rhythmic patterns of the verse. A frequent transcription time-signature is $\frac{5}{8}$, e.g., once again the Delphic Hymns. Late in the period signs were used to indicate two, three or even more time-units (vide the "Epitaph" example), while rests and protractions were also provided for.

There are other interesting features of Greek music which cannot here be dealt with. The whole subject may be found expounded to much more generous lengths in such specialised and scholarly works as the previously mentioned *The Rise of Music in the Ancient World* by Curt Sachs; also, *Music in the Middle Ages (Part I—The Music of Ancient Times)* by Gustave Reese; *Grove's Dictionary of Music, Vol. III (article—Greek Music (Ancient))*; and *The New Oxford History of Music, Vol. I.*

Rome

Regarding Roman music, while that great nation in its earlier years had apparently a distinctive native style (Estruscan in origin) for both ceremonial and everyday purposes, in the days of its expansion it suffered permeation from both Greek and Near Eastern sources. What the resultant music was like we have no real means of judging, for once again notational evidence is of the scantiest. Greek virtuosi and teachers of music found highly lucrative posts during the centuries of the Empire, and leading performers became the spoilt darlings of aristocracy and public alike in a manner that fore-shadowed the age of the eighteenth century *prima-donna* and *castrato,* or even some aspects of our own times. We read of gigantic concerts, of massed arrays of instruments (trumpet, horn, woodwind and plucked-string types, together with the powerful hydraulic organ); of huge choruses; of professional jealousies and intrigues; of subsidised "claques" in the audiences. "Chamber music" there was in plenty, if we may give that name to the inevitable professional items that accompanied aristocratic dinner-parties, together with more doubtful entertainment. Always there were swarms of street musicians; also literary evidence that Rome echoed to the sound of popular songs. We may also recall the career of that aspir-ing *kitharodos* Nero. Suetonius' account of the tyrant's artistic activities gives us glimpses of the existence of extensive musical works, classical stories retold in song to kithara accompaniment, such as *The Fall of Ilium,* which he is supposed to have rendered while watching the Roman conflagration. On another occasion, says Suetonius, he performed the song-poem *Niobe* in public. Well-known also is the account of his "victorious" tour of the music-festivals of Greece as a performer.[7]* (See Plate 4.)

A native activity of more dignity was the Roman development of the brass (or more correctly, bronze) instruments. These, inherited from the Etruscans, included the *tuba,* a straight military trumpet of powerful tone;

the *lituus,* with its end curved into a ⌡ shape, pitched higher than

the *tuba*—the "cavalry" trumpet (the *tuba* being that of the infantry); the *cornu* (of horn tone), curving above the player's head in rather more than a half-circle; and the *bucina*, somewhat similar to the *cornu*, but not as powerful. All these were practical military instruments, but were employed on ceremonial occasions. In particular we hear of the use of the *tuba* and *cornu* for the music of the amphitheatre, joined with the hydraulic organ. The surviving remains of such an organ, dating from A.D. 228, show four ranks of pipes, thirteen in each rank. Many-stringed harps were more in favour than in classical Greek times. Auloi (*tibia* was the Roman name for the instrument) were larger, and a particular type, the double " Phrygian " aulos, seems to have been of extraordinary power. As might be expected, percussion instruments were high in favour—several kinds of tambourines and cymbals; even bells. Mention must be made of the *scabellam*, a hinged board worked by the foot—a time-beater. Roman music was making use of a recurring and emphatic stress at equal intervals.

The Roman theatre with its pantomime and decadent drama gave plentiful employment to music, which developed a style that was anything but ethical in tone. The more serious-minded Roman came to speak contemptuously of the art, while the early Christian Church offered it an implacable hostility. In particular all instrumental music was denounced as unfitted for the ears of the Christian neophyte. But the traditions in regard to classical Greek music lived on. Two sixth century Roman philosophers and writers, Boethius and Cassiodorus, Christians both, produced works which purported to give accounts of Greek theory, and their already imperfect understanding of it was transmitted in confused form to medieval Europe. Certain names of the Greek *harmoniai* were transferred to the Church modes—and muddled in the process. Altogether the legend of Greek music retained a considerable hold on men's minds throughout later ages, not for what it was, but for what they thought it was. The enormous respect for its ethical powers expressed by classical philosophers caused medieval and Renaissance musicians to ascribe to it an almost magical quality. The chromatic experiments of the late sixteenth century Italian composers were in part inspired by what they had read of the Greek chromatic genus. Around 1600 certain Florentines were writing a type of simple recitative which they believed imitated the style of delivery used in the great Greek tragedies. They were wrong, but in doing so they stumbled into the beginnings of Italian opera.

NOTES

1   There seems little doubt that in the early stages of Western ecclesiastical chant the primitive neume notation gave indications as to a system of " short and long " rhythmic interpretation. After about A.D. 1000 this tradition was rapidly forgotten. The exact *pitch* of the notes was being fixed through the invention of stave lines, but henceforth the chant was performed in notes of equal length, except at cadences. Hence the term *cantus planus*.

2*   The music of another great and ancient civilisation, that of China, developed independently, and has a fascinating history. Since it does not impinge on Western music no further reference to it will be made. It is treated at length in *The New Oxford History of Music, Vol. I*, together with the music of India, Japan and other Far Eastern peoples. The Indian system and other Asiatic ones, like the Greek, employed, and still employ, small melodic intervals other than the semitone. Arabic-Persian music, a later development, had some effect on the West, and this will be mentioned in due course. It, too, uses chromaticisms strange to Western ears. *The History of Music in Sound, Vol. I* has recordings of numerous examples of Chinese, Japanese and other Eastern musics, ancient and modern, together with excerpts from Islamic countries.

The reader may care also to refer to the *Primitive Music* sections in each of the above-named works, and to that in *Grove's Dictionary*.

3* HMS I has recordings of Jewish chant from the sources mentioned in the text which may well represent survivals of ancient synagogue music.

4* HMS I has recordings of modern renderings by solo voice of the *First Delphic Hymn* and the *Epitaph*. Listeners will note that the beginning portion of the Hymn is "diatonic", but that later it becomes "chromatic". The brief *Epitaph* is entirely diatonic. Regarding the latter, it must be remembered that it belonged to Tralles in Asia Minor, a small Greek inland settlement. How characteristically Greek a melody from ancient Caria might be we have no means of knowing.

5 The transcription of the music of the *Epitaph* is that of Theodore Reinach's (*La Musique Gréque*, p. 193). The original text (in Western alphabet) is as follows:

"Hoson zes phainou, meden holōs sy lypoü. Pros oligon esti to zen, to telos ho chronos apaitei."

The English version offered by the present writer, if not always a word for word translation, conforms with the original in its patterns of single-note syllables and slurrings.

6 The answers will of course be—Mixolydian, one flat; Hypolydian, five sharps; Hypophrygian, three sharps; Hypodorian, one sharp.

7 Roman music as far as we know produced no figure of worth, except perhaps Mesomedes of Crete, Greek kitharodos and composer, who was high in favour with the Emperor Hadrian (second century A.D.). In 1581 certain documents of Byzantine origin were published by the Italian composer Vincenzo Galilei (father of the astronomer). As a result Mesomedes has been credited with the composition of two "Hymns to the Muse", a "Hymn to the Sun" and a "Hymn to Nemesis". Modern scholarship is inclined to accept Mesomedes' authorship of the *poems* of "Nemesis" and "the Sun", but is very doubtful about anything else, including the whole of the dignified music, which is more likely to be of Byzantine origin. Thus recordings of modern performances of these pieces (there are one or two such on the market) must be listened to with these reservations in mind.

Hadrian's successor, Antoninus Pius, seems to have cancelled the pension that had been given to Mesomedes, on the grounds that a musician was not a useful member of society.

* An asterisk after the number of a note indicates the availability of a *History of Music in Sound (HMS)* recording.

CHAPTER II

Monophony in Western Europe

THE characteristic music of the ancient world, that of melody alone, maintained itself in Europe for many centuries of the Christian era. It was the basis of the music of the Byzantine (Eastern Roman) Empire well into the second millenium, but to the West belongs the credit of a revolutionary development. Before A.D. 1000 the Roman Church had laid the foundations of polyphony, i.e. a music which was concerned with the simultaneous soundings of different parts. Present attention, however, will be confined strictly to single-line melody, that is, monophony.

After two centuries of struggle for survival, during which time it gained more and more influence over the minds of men, the Christian Church became so widely and firmly established that the Imperial authorities turned in its favour. In 324 the Emperor Constantine gave the Christian religion official recognition. In 330 he moved his capital to Constantinople (New Rome—Byzantium), an action which, after his death soon led to a division of the Empire. After 364, East and West were never truly united again. In 394 all pagan religions were outlawed, and the Christian Church, East and West, stood triumphant. Under its Eastern "Roman" Emperors Greek-speaking Byzantium developed a culture which endured for more than a thousand years before going down in destruction before the Turks in 1453. In 527 Justinian I became not only Eastern Roman Emperor but head of the Orthodox Church as well, and this he proceeded to reorganise, causing to be built the mighty cathedral of St. Sophia. In the West the weak rule of the later Emperors was ended in 476 by the Danubian leader Odoacer, and for a while there were confused warrings between the "barbarian" kingdoms. But the more important Western rulers were at least nominally Christian, and the authority of the Bishop of Rome, always respected, steadily increased through the centuries. In 800 the Western "Roman" Empire was revived when Charlemagne, King of the Franks, was crowned Emperor by Pope Leo III, a state of affairs reluctantly recognised by Byzantium. In 1050 came the Great Schism. On matters of doctrine Eastern and Western Churches finally broke with each other.

1. Minoan funeral ceremony (c. 1400 B.C.) painted on a limestone sarcophagus in southern Crete. The left panel shows a priestess pouring a libation to the sound of a kithara. The other panel shows a sacrifice about to begin, accompanied by the music of a double aulos. It is of interest to note that this early kithara has seven strings.

2. This stone relief, in the British Museum, represents members of the court orchestra of Elam playing harps, double auloi and a drum (c. 650 B.C.).

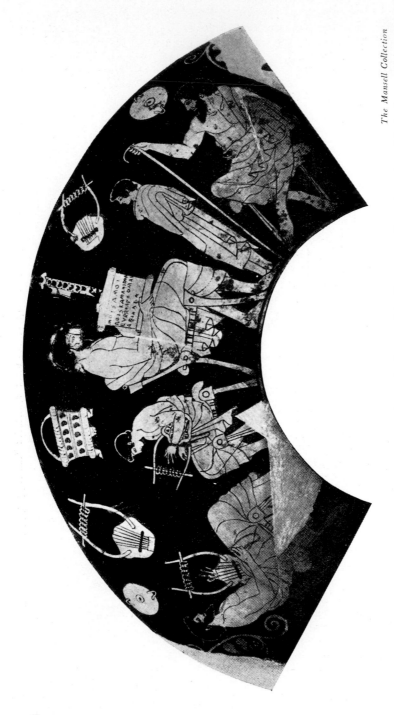

3. The education of an Athenian boy in lyre playing and in literature. Seated to one side is the *paida-gogos*, the family slave whose task was to escort him to and from school. (From a Greek vase-painting).

We recall that the early Christian communities based their service music partly on that of the Jewish synagogue, partly on the music that was extant in their surroundings.[1*] The monophonic, unaccompanied singing, largely congregational at first, seems to have comprised psalms and hymns, probably quite simple melodically, together with alleluias and other jubilant chants in melismatic style. The alleluia was of course borrowed from the Jewish services, as also were chants for the more solemn readings of the scriptures. The singing of psalms, possibly the most important feature of early church music, was at first *responsorial*; a passage sung by a soloist (precentor) was replied to by the choir, or congregation, in brief refrain. When, during the fourth century the Syrian practice of *antiphonal* singing was widely taken up, it involved one choir replying to another, verse alternating with verse. At first this meant men on one hand, and women and boys on the other, but by the sixth century women had ceased to take an active part. The distinctions "responsorial" and "antiphonal" are important, for the contrasting styles were a characteristic feature of Christian Church music.[2*] St. Silvia (Etheria) of Aquitaine, who had journeyed to Jerusalem c. 385, speaks of the music of the Church of the Holy Sepulchre as consisting of psalms, hymns, antiphons and responsories, and of boy choristers singing in the services. While instrumental music of any sort was frowned on by the early Church, surviving documents show that in many parts of the Christian world the value of music attractive to the neophyte was recognised. It may well be that in many countries Christian service-music incorporated something of the folk-song element.

The Music of the Orthodox Church

For long the Church music of East and West was closely linked. Greek was the liturgical language at Rome until nearly the end of the third century. When Latin was officially established it maintained itself all over the West and helped to create a unity such as did not continue in the East, where the churches of Armenia, Abyssinia, Egypt and smaller countries, using their native tongues in ritual, soon ceased to follow the lead of Byzantium. Southern Russia was converted to Christianity from Byzantium about A.D. 1000, and took over the Orthodox ritual together with its music. In 1237 there began the two hundred years of Mongol domination. After Russia had thrown off the yoke there appeared a much more national form of chant.

The Byzantine Orthodox Church, firmly established by the Emperor Justinian, developed its music to a great elaboration. As in the West the daily offices of Matins, Lauds and Vespers were made essential (in Justinian's time Mass was celebrated frequently but not daily), but the trend of Byzantium was towards the creation of a wealth of sacred poetry— hymns and odes, culminating in the eighth century in gigantic musical compositions, *Kanons*, which were each made up of a series of odes, each ode with its own melody. Ceremonial, especially at the mighty St. Sophia, was the richest imaginable, but the music was wholly vocal and monophonic. No instrument, not even an organ, was permitted.[3] A great deal of the music

C

was rendered by skilled soloists, though trained, permanent choirs were also employed. The organ, a portable, pneumatic type, was used only as a secular instrument. We read of choirs of the different political parties in the Hippodrome, singing each to their own particular organ accompaniment. Aulos and kithara continued in use at popular festivals. The Emperor had his Imperial band of trumpets, horns, pipes and cymbals for processional occasions, and at ceremonial receptions he was greeted by specially prepared choral compositions known as " acclamations ". Examples of both Church and ceremonial music have come down to us in a Byzantine notation which has been successfully interpreted. This notation was unequivocal only from the twelfth century. It depended on a system of signs which indicated the pitch relationship between one note and the next. Other signs gave exact rhythmic values to the units, and nuances of expression, even, were indicated.[4*]

The subject of Byzantine music is too extensive, and the period of its continuance too long for adequate treatment here.[5] Mention should be made of the *okto echos* (="eight sounds") which Byzantium seems to have taken over from Syrian music. The name immediately suggests a system of "modes", but they seem to have been, at least at first, merely a series of eight groupings of melody-types. It has been established, however, that in later Byzantine music they developed characteristic starting-notes and finals, and appear to have links with the Gregorian modes (see p. 36f.).

The Music of the Western Church

As already noted, Greek was the language of the Western services until towards the end of the third century. (*Kyrie eleison* represents a Greek survival in the present day Roman liturgy.) Eastern influences on ritual and music continued for much longer, even into the eighth century, perhaps owing to a series of Greek and Syrian Popes. The bishopric of Milan was one of the most important in the West, and it was at Milan that St Ambrose introduced the Syrian practice of hymn singing in the fourth century. He himself also wrote hymns, the texts of which were examples of the growing use in Latin poetry of *accent* instead of the old classical *quantity*. Again, the West owes to him the introduction of antiphonal singing of the psalms (or at least, so tradition has it). The diocese of Milan was a vital force. Later, when central authority was imposing uniformity of chant on the West, Milan's was the only successful resistance.

At Rome, Damasus I (Pope—366–84) introduced the liturgical order of Jerusalem into the Roman ritual, as well as adding to the Mass the Alleluia with its melismatic flourishes. A later Pope (Boniface) is supposed to have achieved a complete chant for the whole year. In these early centuries of the era the dominant position of the Bishop of Rome was recognised in all Western countries, but, particularly at Milan, in France and in Spain, there were systems of chant that probably differed a good deal from that of Rome (Ambrosian, Gallican and Mozarabic respectively).

The true history of the development of the chant during the second half of the first millenium seems a matter of some uncertainty. Its reshaping and codification has been traditionally associated with the name of Pope Gregory I (590–604), the great reformer. Modern research, however, has tended to show that the unification took place rather in the period of the Franco-German (" Roman ") empire under Pepin, Charlemagne and their successors, and represents a fusion of Roman and Frankish elements which in due course returned to Rome and spread through the Western Church. The Mozarabic chant survived until the eleventh century, while the Ambrosian, at Milan, developed in its own way.

With the expansion of the Church and of Western civilisation generally from the Carolingian age onward the chant entered a further period of development to meet the needs of new feasts and extended ceremonies. Early in the eleventh century, however, complaints were being made as to corruptions of texts, faulty copyings and the carelessness of singers. The period of general decay had begun. The art of polyphony eventually overshadowed the chant, and the beauty of this monophonic music was not again fully appreciated until in modern times the researches of the Benedictines of Solesmes restored the original forms of the melodies, and their version of the chant became the official music of the Church of Rome.

To consider very briefly the characteristics of Gregorian chant (a subject upon which whole books have been written)[6*]—we note first its essentially diatonic nature, the austerity of its melodic atmosphere. To use a modern analogy, its vocabulary is the white notes of the keyboard, with B flat as an alternative to B natural. This (reminding us of the Greek tetrachord *Synemmenon*) permitted not only a melodic variation but at times the actual transposition of a passage. Leaps larger than a perfect fifth are very seldom met with, and indeed progressions are more often than not stepwise. There is thus an overall dignity of style.

Modern renderings of the chant have usually followed the methods of " free rhythm " as advocated by the Benedictines of Solesmes; that is, of following the natural rhythms of the Latin prose of the liturgy and the poetry of the hymns. But it has been maintained by some scholars that in the early centuries of the Chant it was sung in a much more definite rhythmic style in accordance with a scheme of signs and letters which can still be studied in certain early manuscripts written in neume notation. It is held by these scholars that the Chant only became " plain " after the year 1000 or thereabouts when the meanings of the original indications of duration began to be forgotten and were left uncopied.[7]

In the simpler chants for choir we find that there is a leaning towards having a single note for each syllable (" syllabic " style). In those of maximum elaboration, intended for soloists, there are frequent flourishes—many notes to a syllable (" melismatic "). An intermediate stage has frequent groups of two, three or perhaps more to a syllable (" neumatic "). One of the techniques of plainchant composition was the employment of various small melodic patterns (an ancient device, as we have seen) which give different flavours to the different modes. In music of a responsorial type great prominence was given to a single note—the " reciting note " or " tenor "—that was pitched above the final. Even in the more melodic antiphonal music this particular note tended to make its presence felt.

The repertory of plainchant is a considerable one. It includes the florid chants of the Proper of the Mass, those (less florid) of the Ordinary of the Mass, the eight tones (or chants) of the Psalms and Canticles, the Antiphons for these, also the Responds, together with much other music, such as the hymns and reading-tones. It may be useful to give some idea of the daily musical requirements of the Roman liturgy. (The forms given here were those achieved and more or less standardised by about the eleventh century.) They are concerned with (a) the Mass—the central rite—and (b) the Canonical Office, a number of separate " Hour " services, i.e. Matins, Lauds, Prime, Terce, Sext, None, Vespers and Compline. Mass is usually celebrated between Terce and Sext. Much of the music of the Hour services is of the nature of psalmody. The music of the Mass is, generally speaking, more elaborate.

The musical requirements of the Mass are concerned with : (a) the Proper, i.e. Introit, Gradual, Offertory and Communion, the texts and the chant settings of these varying from season to season—and (b) the Ordinary, i.e. Kyrie eleison, Gloria in Excelsis, Credo, Sanctus (with Benedictus) and Agnus Dei. These are invariable, although alternative chants are provided. With the development of polyphony these texts were frequently taken over by church composers and set, interspersed with the chant, as individual compositions with various techniques. We shall hear much in later chapters as to " Masses " by numerous composers. These in the main are settings of the Ordinary. As the centuries passed liturgical music became more and more the concern of the trained choir and the still more highly trained solo cantors, to the exclusion of the congregation.

We turn now to the " modal " system on which Gregorian music is assumed to be based. There seems to be no realisation of any such organisation in the early centuries. However, Charlemagne's adviser Alcuin (753–804) makes a passing reference to a Western equivalent of the Byzantine eight *echoi*, as if it were a well-known fact, but further information is fleeting until the time of Hermann the Lame in the eleventh century. As a result of his writings and those of later theorists we are given a more definite picture. The Gregorian modes consisted primarily of four diatonic octave-species founded on the notes D, E, F and G respectively, and termed in medieval times Protus, Deuterus, Tritus and Tetradus. Later, they were also called Dorian, Phrygian, Lydian and Mixolydian, due, as mentioned before, to faulty information concerning the ancient Greek *harmoniai*. These were the *Authentic* modes. Associated with each was a *Plagal* mode (Hypodorian, Hypophrygian, Hypolydian and Hypomixolydian) each also occupying approximately an octave range, but starting a fourth below the corresponding Authentic mode while employing the same final note. Placed above the final, usually at the distance of a fifth in the case of the Authentic mode, was the important note that we have already mentioned, the reciting note or tenor, (sometimes called the " dominant ", a modern and somewhat ambiguous term). The reciting note of each plagal mode was pitched normally a third below that of its authentic partner. The modes were also distinguished by numberings, from I to VIII. The following diagram will serve as a summary :

Mode													
I	Dorian				**D**	E	F	G	*a*	b	c	d	
II	Hypodorian	A	B	C	**D**	E	*F*	G	a				
III	Phrygian				**E**	F	G	a	b	*c*	d	e	
IV	Hypophrygian		B	C	D	**E**	F	G	*a*	b			
V	Lydian				**F**	G	*a*	b	c	d	e	f	
VI	Hypolydian		C	D	E	**F**	G	*a*	b	c			
VII	Mixolydian				**G**	a	b	*c*	d	e	f	g	
VIII	Hypomixolydian		D	E	F	**G**	a	b	*c*	d			

The finals of the modes are shown in bold type, the reciting notes in italics. Regarding the identity of the latter in Modes III and VIII, the note to be expected in each case would be b, but this was avoided, possibly because of its " tritone " relationship with F, and c was substituted. In the course of a Gregorian composition of any length portions of the melody would show characteristics of modes other than the prevailing one. In other words, *modulation* (in the strict sense of the word) would take place.

Actually there are features in the chant that do not always fit comfortably into this theorists' system. Undoubtedly a great deal of the chant was older than the modal strait-jacket. Whether this Western system borrowed from the Byzantine *echoi*; or whether it was established during the reforms effected in the Carolingian period; what alterations were made to the original chant to bring about conformity—these and other questions remain at present unsolved.[8*]

An important achievement of Gregorian chant was that it brought about the invention and development of a system of pitch notation, that of the *neumes*, from which our own modern music notation had evolved. The earliest neume-signs known are found in manuscripts surviving from the 8th century, but the system is undoubtedly older.

This earliest neume notation was a mnemonic one. Singers, already thoroughly grounded in the chant, were *reminded* (that and no more) of the melody they were about to perform by means of the signs that were written above the texts. The origins of these are supposed to be the accent-signs used by Greek grammarians, invented perhaps around 180 B.C., but this has been disputed. The principal ones were the acute (a), the grave (b), and the circumflex (c).

/ \ ∧

(a) (b) (c)

The first indicated a raising of the voice, the second a lowering, the third a raising and lowering. In the Gregorian system the acute sign became the *virga*, a hint to the singer that the note was relatively high. The grave sign implied a relatively low one, but the stroke was soon turned into a single dab, • (*punctum*) by scribes who used reed pens and strict economy of labour. Two notes to a syllable, the first higher than the second, was represented by (d) (*clivis*); the first lower than the second was represented by (e) (*podatus*). Combinations of three notes to a syllable such as (f), (g), (h), (i) should be self-explanatory.

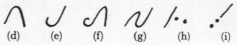

(d)   (e)   (f)   (g)   (h)   (i)

Other neume groupings and certain signs calling for subtleties of performance must escape notice here.

It is clear that this system would be useless for conveying to a singer the exact details of a melody not already known to him. This was of course realised, and by the 10th century manuscripts were showing neumes roughly " heighted " above the text in accordance with the approximate pitch of the notes. Early in the eleventh century came another aid, a pen-scratched line, and later a coloured one, around which the neumes were spaced. There was an understanding as to what the line indicated (usually F at first). A second line, usually intended for C, was soon added, and it became the practice to mark the lines for what they represented—with F or C (or even occasionally D or G). In one region (Aquitaine) there began a breaking-up of the composite neumes into a series of blobs, which gave more or less precise location to individual notes. Similar tendencies towards showing exact pitch were seen elsewhere, and by the thirteenth century the familiar " square " notation had arrived—

etc. The shapes were founded on the technique of the quill pen. The four-line stave was now widely established, together with the alternative C and F clefs. Leger lines were avoided by moving clefs from line to line as necessary. B flat was indicated by the sign ♭ ; B natural by a more angular shape ♮. These were the origins of our " flat " and " natural " signs. The latter shape accounts for the German use of H for B natural. The invention of an exact system of pitch notation had a great effect on the art— for one thing making original composition easier to carry out. It is also contended that it gave the death-blow to the system of *rhythm* which once obtained in the chant, and which had been indicated by certain signs associated with the staveless neumes.

The name of Guido d'Arezzo (995-1050) will always be connected with improvements in notation, even if he did not actually *invent* the stave, as popularly supposed. His work as a teacher and particularly as the developer of a system of sight-singing was of the utmost importance. He taught his choirs to use a " solmisation " method whereby the six notes of a hexachord scale on C received the names " ut re mi fa sol la ". A full exposition of his system cannot be given here, but it may be said that by the device of "mutations" (in modern sol-fa parlance, bridge-notes) which enabled similar hexachords on F and G to be used, the whole vocal range was covered by these syllables. The F hexachord employed, of course, B flat. Guido declared that his system enabled his choir boys to learn in a few days what it had formerly required them many weeks to master.

The low G was written as the Greek *Gamma*, Γ. As the first note of a hexachord it was called *Gamma Ut*, or " Gamut ". Eventually the term was applied to the whole scalic range, and used in this sense long after the modes had faded. Pepys employed the word. Elizabethan musicians (and Shakespeare) were much concerned with solmisation and the Gamut, (see *The Taming of the Shrew III*, i, 64–81).[9]

Another device attributed to Guido is the so-called Guidonian Hand. Various points along the thumb, fingers and the top of the palm of the left hand were allotted to the Gamut, from G (bottom line of the bass clef) to e (4th treble space), together with their solmisation names. The teacher was thus enabled to give practical exercises in solmisation. Here for the present we will leave our consideration of notation. The system arrived at was adequate for plainchant singing, but other demands were soon to be made on it that could not be met without modification and new invention.

Tropes and Sequences

During the revival of Western civilisation that began in Charlemagne's time, one of the manifestations of which was a new splendour in church buildings and ritual, there grew up the practice of adding phrases and sentences to the established liturgy of the Mass and the Hour services. Similar usages in Byzantium and Syria were the probable models. These additions served to expand, explain or comment on the texts and were called *tropes*.

The Alleluia of the Mass afforded a notable opportunity. Already the musical flourish, or *jubilus*, on the last syllable had received extensions. These long melodies were divided into " breath " phrases called *sequentiae*, and each of these was usually marked for repetition, probably to allow for antiphonal singing. In Northern France and in Germany the practice grew up, perhaps as an aid for memorising the lengthy melodies, of fitting suitable words to the neumes, thus eventually forming separate trope compositions that were called *Sequences*. Finally, independent new texts and new music were invented together, and the Sequence became a type of free composition, prose being replaced by rhyming poetry. The traditional inventor of this new form was Tuotilo of St. Gall. The probability is that he was actually the *improver*, and that the Sequence first arose in Northern France. Some of these Sequences found permanent establishment, and include the famous *Victimae Paschali* (? Wipo of Burgundy—eleventh century) *Lauda Sion* (St. Thomas Aquinas and Adam de St. Victor—thirteenth century), *Veni Sancte Spiritus* (thirteenth century), *Dies Irae* (? Thomas of Celano—thirteenth century), and most celebrated of all *Stabat Mater* (thirteenth century), the text of which was the basis of so many later compositions. The sectional and antiphonal repeats of the *sequentiae* account for the musical form of the Sequence, which can be represented thus:

x, aa, bb, cc, dd, (with perhaps more pairs) . . . y.

—there being usually an unpaired line at the beginning and the end.

A veritable passion for Sequence composition arose which spread even to Sweden, Denmark and Finland. There were secular compositions in the same form. Probably the most famous composer of sequences was Adam de St. Victor of Paris (d. 1192).[10*]

The sequence was a specialised form of trope. Tropes were added to other parts of the services, particularly to the *Kyrie eleison*, in a similar internal fashion. Music was invented as well as words, and tropes were also placed before and after liturgical passages. Another favourite location was the Introit of the Mass. In the end the floods of intrusive tropes proved too much an embarrassment to Church liturgy, and with four exceptions they were swept away by the Council of Trent (1545–63).

Church Music-Drama

A certain trope of the Introit of the Mass for Easter Day, the earliest surviving example of which dates from the mid-tenth century, is of great historical importance, since in fact it represents the beginning of the revival in Europe of drama in general. It resembles a dialogue, as between the Marys and the Angel (or Angels) at the empty Sepulchre on the first Easter morning. A transcription and translation of this version, which in both text and music seems to represent original composition, is here given: (See Plate 6.)

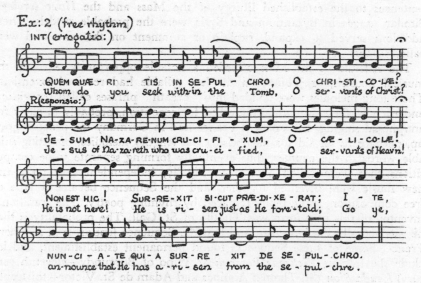

The original is to be found in a manuscript belonging to the monastic library of St. Gall in Switzerland (MS 484, p. 111). Its neume notation had been given various additional signs and letters, undoubtedly indicating note-duration values. The above reading follows Dom Gregory Murray's principles in their interpretation (see p. 43, footnote).

From this simple beginning there developed the Easter music-dramas,[11*] actings within church walls of the Resurrection story, the participants being clerics of various grades, and in some instances even nuns, thus bringing about "mixed" casts. Other sacred dramas arose in imitation, telling of the events of the first Christmas, and eventually embracing other Biblical episodes and stories of St. Nicholas. The rise and full expansion of these music-dramas occupied the tenth to thirteenth centuries, with France and the German-speaking countries, in the main, the regions most interested. After the thirteenth century with the development of the open-air, *spoken* mystery-plays written in the vernacular, the church dramas with their musical settings tended to wither.[12*]

The music of these works makes an interesting study. That of the original dialogue, although perhaps due to an anonymous inventor, is very much a piece of Gregorian chant. Easter liturgical antiphons and responsories, where their texts were relevant, were also pressed into service, but as time went on there came more and more original invention, both words and music. The texts were sometimes in prose, sometimes in rhyming Latin verse. Here is an Easter antiphon of which much early use was made :

Ex : 3 (free rhythm)

QUIS RE-VOL-VET NO-BIS LA-PI-DEM AB HO-STI-O MO-NU-MEN — TI?
Who for us will roll a-way the stone from the entrance of the se — pul — chre?

—and this is its melodious and balanced transmutation, found in one of the more extensive Easter dramas :

Ex : 4

SED NE-QUI-MUS HOC PA-TRA-RE SI-NE AD-JU-TO-RI-O.
But we can-not gain an en-try, if none else the task as-sume.

QUIS-NAM SA-XUM HOC RE-VOL-VET A MO-NU-MEN-TI O-STI-O.
Who for us will roll a-way the stone from the en-trance of the Tomb.

Even what seems to be an early Gregorian-style free invention (the Marys' display of the abandoned grave-clothes)—

Ex:5 (free rhythm)

CER-NI-TIS, O SO - CI - I; EC-CE LIN-TE-A-MI-NA ET SU - DA — RI - UM,
See, O friends, what I dis-play; behold here the linen cloths and the ho — ly shroud,

ET COR - PUS NON EST IN SE - PUL-CRO IN - VEN-TUM.
al - so, the Bo-dy is no lon-ger in the Tomb.

—found a later rhyming and rhythmic metamorphosis in the following terms :

Ex:6 (vivace)

CER - NI - TE, VOS SO - CI - I, SUNT CORPORIS
Friends, the gar-ments that you see, Once wrapp'd the

IS - TA BE - A - TI; LIN - TE - A, QUÆ VA-CU - O,
bles — sed Bo - dy; Left a - bandon'd where He had lain,

JA - CU - E - RE RE - LI-CTA SE - PUL — CRO.
Cast a - side when that He had ris'n a - gain.

Considerations of space forbid any more than two further quotations, of decidedly dramatic yet melodious quality. Here, in one of the St. Nicholas dramas, are the armed followers of a conqueror greeting their king :

Ex:7 (vivace)

SAL - VE, PRIN - CEPS, SAL - VE, REX OP - TI — ME!
all hail, great Lord, all hail, most no - ble King!

QUÆ SIT TU - E VO - LUN-TAS A - NI — ME,
what-so - e - ver may be thy heart's de - sire,

SER - VIS TU - IS NE TARDES DI - CE — RE:
Let thy ser - vants know it with-out de - lay:

SU - MUS QUÆ VIS PA - RA - TI FA - CE — RE.
We will gain for thee all thou dost re - quire.

And here are the King's battle-orders :

Ex: 8 (Vivace)

I - TE ER - GO, NE TAR - DA - VE - RI - TIS,
Go ye forth, then, ma-king no more de - lay,

ET QUAS - CUN - QUE GEN -TES PO - TE - RI - TIS,
And what - ev - er na-tions that ye shall meet,

IM - PE - RI - O ME - O SUB - I - CI - TE;
See that they are forc'd to sub - mit to me;

RE - SIS - TEN - TES VO - BIS OC - CI - DI - TE.
Slay - ing those who will not ac - cept de - feat.

The several recent performances in this country of the twelfth century
Beauvais *Daniel* by the New York Pro Musica, the text almost wholly in
Latin rhyming verse, revealed a remarkable collection of attractive rhythmic
tunes, some of which seem to show secular, not to say, dance origins. But
Daniel is in a number of ways a unique work, and is not typical of the
Easter and Christmas types which make up the bulk of the movement,
although indeed it has already been made clear that other dramas do not
lack fine melodies.

None of the surviving manuscripts of these dramas shows any music other
than the single monophonic vocal line. In one of them only is there rubric
mention of harps being used to support the singing—and this happens to be
Daniel. In some later Easter dramas there are a few rubric calls for the use
of organ during the (unison) final choruses (e.g., *Te Deum, Magnificat,
Victimae Paschali*). Chime-bells (*cymbala*), a feature of medieval church
services, are also given occasional mention.

The question arises as to whether these sparing references to instrumental
accompaniment represent the conditions under which the dramas were performed in medieval times. Remembering that rubric evidence shows that
they were closely linked with the relevant Hour services and sometimes even
with the Mass of the day, it may be useful to examine the situation regarding instrumental accompaniment to the actual liturgy of the medieval
Church. This question has received a certain amount of attention lately,
and the views of the medieval hierarchy can be summed up by the pro-

* The transcriptions, translations and rhythmic renderings of the settings in connection with all the above musical examples from medieval Church drama are by
the present writer, and are derived directly from photographs of the original
manuscripts.

nouncement of Gilles de Zamore, a thirteenth century Franciscan, who declared in his *Ars Musica* that in the singing of its services the Church made instrumental use only of the organ, and this only for " prose, sequence and in hymns, other instruments being commonly rejected because of the abuses of the jongleurs ". (There is evidence enough that to the medieval churchman the jongleur was anathema).

It would seem, then, that Latin church-drama and medieval church-service, as far as surviving evidence can show, were carried out in similar limited conditions in regard to instrumental accompaniments. In my opinion, if any revival of these church dramas is attempted the question of accompaniments should be approached with the utmost caution if false representation is to be avoided.[13]

Too often these Latin church works are confused with the open-air mystery-plays, which, arising from them and later in inception, were performed in the outside, secular world by laymen, and were *spoken* in the vernacular. But there was the occasional song, and as surviving descriptions testify, the fullest use was made of incidental instrumental music of every kind. The professional minstrel, barred from participation in church worship, fairly came into his own. Those moderns who revive the mystery-plays have every justification for employing the whole catalogue of medieval jongleur solo instruments.

Solo instruments eventually entered the church services, at first only occasionally—in processional use and at high festival (shawms, trumpets). It was only with the expansion of the royal and princely chapels in early Renaissance times that single instrumental voices began to play a significant part in liturgical worship perhaps as a result of the co-operation of chaplain and court musician.

A word about the Franciscan, Gilles de Zamore, who was so emphatic regarding the use of instruments in the Church of his time. A learned man, he was employed at the court of the musician-king Alphonzo X (" the Wise "—1252–84), ruler of Castile and Leon, and was the tutor of the King's son and successor, Sancho. Alphonzo was responsible for that remarkable and still-surviving collection, *Cantigas de Santa Maria,* vernacular songs in trouvère style which, though devotional in tone, were clearly intended for secular use. In modern performances of these songs there is, rightly, no hesitation in giving them support by medieval-type instruments, in medieval style. Gilles de Zamore would be hearing plenty of secular music at Alphonzo's court. Hence the value of his statement as to the instrumental dichotomy which prevailed.

The Organ

Though the Roman Cassiodorus makes mention of organs, such instruments seem to have been rare in the Christian West after Imperial times to judge by the notice taken of organs from the East sent as gifts to King Pepin and to Charlemagne. However, in the latter's time the construction of small organs seems to have begun. They appear at first to have possessed only some seven or eight notes, but this range was soon increased. In church their sole use appears to have been to help with the chant at the unison, which was indeed all that they would be capable of doing. A tenth century poem by a Winchester monk tells of a giant organ in the Cathedral there with four hundred pipes, and seventy men employed on the wind supply. If the picture is not wildly exaggerated it must have been something in the nature of a freak, for the usual organs of the period were of a very modest size, and rare in incidence. At first the notes were controlled by the manipulation of slides, a slow and clumsy method. But by the early thirteenth century, after a good deal of fumbling, the principle of a keyboard, with springs to return the units to normal after pressure, was established, or rather, re-discovered, for the Romans had previously had the device. But a very long path of evolution lay ahead.

Medieval Secular Music

Most of the music put into writing in medieval times was that of worship, composed by men with a larger purpose in view. But there existed at the same time (as in every age) work-songs, dance-songs, ballads, songs of love— the music of everyday life and the lay folk. It was on record only in the minds of those who sang, played and listened, and it relied on tradition for its preservation, too often in vain.

The professional bard of earlier ages lived on in the medieval *jongleur*,[14] sometimes a wanderer, sometimes, if more than usually competent, employed by some lordly patron. Eventually a higher circle of minstrels evolved. In England, and elsewhere, they formed themselves into guilds, and sometimes used trades-union methods against non-members. One of the most famous of early minstrels was Taillefer, who was in Duke William of Normandy's service and who led the van at Hastings singing the "Song of Roland", having had the Duke's permission to strike the first blow. Unfortunately for music a Saxon battleaxe struck the second. A popular feature of the jongleur's repertoire was the lengthy *chanson de geste,* which related epic stories, both chivalric and religious. The musical setting of a *chanson de geste* was confined to a simple brief tune of one or two motives, continually repeated, and used also as an instrumental interlude between sections. Only a few fragmentary examples of the kind of melody used have survived. The *lai*, a secular adaptation of the sequence form, was also used. The favourite instrument of the jongleur seems to have been the bowed *vièle*, prototype of the viol and violin. A good jongleur was expected to be able to play a variety of instruments. These might be lute, guitar (both from Arab sources, as was the bow), harp, psaltery and portative organ, besides the ubiquitous vièle.

Travelling minstrels were in no great favour with the authorities of the Church. Of even worse repute were the *goliards*, the "wandering scholars", young men in minor orders who, while supposedly moving from one European university city to another, led frequently disreputable lives on the roads. Their period was from the early eleventh century to the early thirteenth (Pope Gregory IX lost patience with them in 1231). In the course of these centuries certain of them produced a quantity of lyrical poetry of a high order, which, though in Latin, was altogether worldly in tone. There are some gentle love-poems, but the main themes were wine, women and satire against clerical authority.[15] It was *sung* poetry. A great number of texts have survived but very little music. One of the songs complete with music is the (probably tenth century) *O admirable Veneris idolum* ("O lovely image of Venus ") set to an attractive tune in, be it noted, the major mode.[16*] The bulk of surviving goliard poetry is contained in the famous early thirteenth century German manuscript known as *Carmina Burana*, now in the State Library at Munich.

A much more fully documented movement was the "gay science" of the Troubadours[17] and Trouvères, which lasted from about the end of the eleventh century to the end of the thirteenth. It was a highly organised and somewhat artificial lyrical poetry in the (French) vernacular, or rather the two somewhat different vernaculars of Provence and Northern France, each poem with its own, usually strophic, tune. The creator of the poetry was often the composer of the melody. "Arranger" might sometimes be the better word, for many of the tunes were clearly adapted from Church sources (particularly from sequence and hymn), some were probably folk-songs or dance tunes, while there are occasions where two or more poems are found to have made use of the same melody, modifying it as necessary. But we must allow for a great deal of free composition, together with much subtlety of musical construction. The movement began among the cultivated upper classes of the Provençal civilisation, which included Aquitaine. The Troubadours, the poet-composers, were members of that aristocratic society and their works were intended to be sung to those courtly audiences who alone could appreciate the rarified sentiments expressed. There was a working partnership between the troubadour and jongleur classes. The high-born amateur usually had his professional assistant, who was sometimes the performer of his master's composition (and who knows what hand he had in the framing of the music?). Certain famous troubadours and trouvères definitely sang their own works. The actual troubadour movement went down in blood and fire around 1208, when Provence, long the home of the Albigensian heresy, was invaded by the "crusaders" of Pope Innocent III. The Trouvères, already established in Northern France, produced compositions of a very similar nature. However, it may be fairly said that in addition to the difference of language the trouvère songs tended to show more clearly defined rhythm and structure, together with the invention of new poetic forms. Towards the end of the thirteenth century the changes in social life and the rise of the great commercial cities brought about a climate in which the highly artificial conventions of the movement could not live.

Only a few names among the many connected with the art can receive mention here. Bernart de Ventadorn (d. 1195), perhaps the most famous of troubadours, was exceptional as being of plebeian birth, one of the minority who "rose from the ranks". On the other hand a leading trouvère was Thibaud IV, King of Navarre (d. 1253) whose love-songs are outstanding both for their poetry and melodies.

An example of his work is here given :

Ex:9

1. TUIT MI DE - SIR ET TUIT MI GRIEF TOR - MENT VIEN - NENT DE
2. GRANT PO-OR AI POUR CE QUE TOU - TE GENT QUI ONT VE -

LA OU SONT TUIT MI PEN - SÉ: (2) MÉ SONT SI SOR - PRIS DE BO -
- Ü SONGENT CORS A - CES -

- NE VO - LEN - TÉ ; NES DEX L'AI - ME, GEL SAI A ES - CI -

- ENT : GRANT MER-VEILLE EST QUANT IL EN SUEF - FRE TANT.

The original is to be found in Paris, Bibl. de l'Arsenal, MS 5198, p. 51. The transcription is by Sir Jack Westrup, from Chapter VII of the *New Oxford History of Music, II,* p. 231. The translation there provided reads as follows :

"All my desire and all my bitter grief comes from that source where all my thoughts are fixed. I fear greatly, since all who have seen her, who is fair and beauteous, are overcome by goodwill towards her. God himself loves her, I know it truly : it is a marvel when he suffers so much."

Another late trouvère worthy of special mention is Adam de la Hale (d. 1288), who also wrote *rondeaux* (see p. 66) in polyphonic parts. He was the creator of the famous pastoral play *Le Jeu de Robin et de Marion* (c. 1285), full of charming tunes, a veritable *Singspiel*. Ideas concerning the opera form long antedated the Florentines of 1600.

Troubadour-trouvère poetry concerned itself in the main with the subject of courtly love (usually unrequited), but there were other themes, such as were expressed in songs of "service" (addressed to an overlord), crusader's songs and musical "debates". There were even political satires. Many new poetic forms, with distinctive names, were developed, and for this reason the poet Dante was much interested in the art. They are too numerous for comprehensive mention here but we must take some note of the "refrain" types, founded on the dance-song, since the *rondeau* and its developments, the *virelai* and the *ballade,* were favoured not only by troubadours and trouvères but by composers in general for over two hundred years. They originated from the basic idea of the solo leader of the dance-song being answered by a refrain chorus. This in due course became a matter of soloist and audience and eventually the refrain ceased to have choral obligations.

A common type of *rondeau* had six lines, with half the refrain as the second line and the complete refrain to conclude. While the soloist had to memorise a number of lines of text, the chorus had no more than the invariable two to master. The whole of the *musical* material of the complete *rondeau* was present in the refrain.

There was also the more extensive eight-line *rondeau*, of which an anonymous trouvère example is given below. It is quoted by Gustave Reese (op. cit. p. 222) as from F. Gennrich's *Rondeaux, Virelais und Balladen, I. 26.* The charming translation of the text, conforming exactly with the original patterns, is by Gustave Reese.

Ex: 10

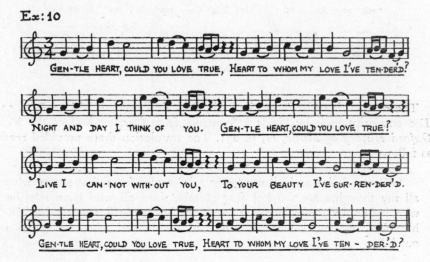

GEN-TLE HEART, COULD YOU LOVE TRUE, HEART TO WHOM MY LOVE I'VE TEN-DERD?

NIGHT AND DAY I THINK OF YOU. GEN-TLE HEART, COULD YOU LOVE TRUE!

LIVE I CAN-NOT WITH-OUT YOU, TO YOUR BEAUTY I'VE SUR-REN-DER'D.

GEN-TLE HEART, COULD YOU LOVE TRUE, HEART TO WHOM MY LOVE I'VE TEN - DER-'D?

(The cadential Fs may well have been sharpened in performance—see p. 75, *Musica Ficta.*)

Designs of text and music can be summarised thus:

Text (refrain chorus underlined):	a	b	c	a	d	e	a	b
Rhymes	1	2	1	1	1	2	1	2
Music (refrain chorus underlined):	A	B	A	A	A	B	A	B

It will be seen that the tax on the musical memory is modest, even for the soloist.

If for the internal refrain-line a new line for the soloist was substituted, the two-unit refrain remaining at the beginning and end, we have the *virelai* form. The internal lines for soloist needed a new and repeated musical unit, together with the refrain music. It can be summarised thus:

4. This badly damaged fresco from Herculaneum shows a Roman concert in progress. The instruments are a kithara (with a considerable sound-box) and a large double aulos. The bulging eyes of the aulos player and the precaution of the cheek straps suggest the force with which the instrument is being blown.

5. King David, inspired by the Holy Ghost, is playing a harp. Meanwhile one attendant juggles, and others play rebec, trumpet and horn respectively. The trumpet is supported on a forked stand. (Cotton MS, 11th century).

British Museum

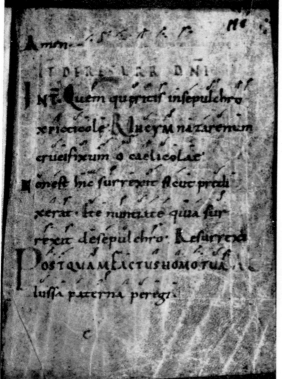

6. St. Gall, Monastic Library MS484 (c. A.D. 950). This earliest surviving example of the *Quem Quaeritis* dialogue, a trope of the Introit of the Mass of Easter, represents the very beginning of Latin church music-drama. Above the text are the *neume* signs, a musical notation which merely reminded the singer of the melody.

Abbey of St. Gall

Text (refrain chorus underlined) : a b c d e f a b
Music (refrain chorus underlined) : <u>A B</u> C C A B <u>A B</u>

By casting even more responsibility on the soloist for new internal material the *ballade* form resulted, of more than one variety. The *musical* designs of three of these are summarised below, once again with the refrain chorus underlined :

(i) <u>A B</u> C D C D E F A B

(ii) <u>A B</u> C D E A B <u>A B</u>

(iii) <u>A B</u> A B C D <u>E</u>

In the last of the three the refrain element is seen reduced to a minimum, often a mere exclamatory phrase or word.

The refrain indeed was found, as a mere poetic convention, in forms other than the dance-song type.

There is no need to imagine any rigidity in the matter of the various forms, even in those that have been reviewed. The practitioners of the " joyous science " tried to follow the principle that no song should be wholly like another in construction, even though differences were often of the slightest. As an example of a somewhat free adaptation of the rondeau form the following song is given, taken from de la Hale's *Le Jeu de Robin et de Marion,* mentioned above :

Ex: 11

The musical material is certainly confined to the A B formula, but with variants, and there is no " half-refrain " in the middle, nor any actual chorus, but the design is " rondeau " in spirit, and entirely satisfactory. The setting is in the F mode and the second rhythmic mode. *Modus* was an overworked medieval term—the term " rhythmic mode " will be presently

D

explained. Owing to the shape of the tune and the particular placing of the
B naturals a modern hearer may get the impression of F major with a
transient modulation to C. This, of course, would not be the outlook of the
period. The example is quoted by Gustave Reese, op. cit. p. 223, as once
more coming from F. Gennrich's *Rondeaux, Virelais und Balladen* (*I, 71*).
The translation is by J. Murray Gibbon.

In general, troubadour-trouvère settings, though relatively simple melodically, of modest range, and almost without *melismata*, show considerable ingenuity of construction and had an effect on the development of a sense
of melodic form. The half-close is frequently found as a mid-cadence, with
the repeat of the phrase giving a full-close (*vide* the Thibaut of Navarre
example above). Regarding tonality, the Gregorian modes are commonly
used (particularly D and G) as might be expected in an age when liturgical
music was all pervading and everyone a frequent church-goer. But a good
proportion of the tunes are in the " wanton " major, implying the influence
of folk- and perhaps instrumental dance-music. As for accompaniment, contemporary illustrations make it clear that instruments were being handled
while songs were being sung, perhaps playing in unison with the voice, or
devising decorations of the melody, or even venturing on brief heterophonic
departures. There seem to have been preludes and postludes. Drones were
perhaps employed. The vièle, with its flattish bridge, lent itself readily to
the device, as did bagpipes and hurdy-gurdy. However, in this matter all
is speculation.

Records of the troubadour-trouvère art are enshrined in the *chansonniers*,
surviving manuscripts that were used at the time by performers. In them
a poem is set out stanza by stanza, a single melody at the head doing duty
for them all. The notation is that of ordinary plainchant, and gives no clue
as to the rhythm. Modern scholars are of the opinion that in practice a
borrowed use was made in many cases of the rhythmic modes. The rhythmic mode scheme is found established (apparently first in France) in the
second half of the twelfth century, being employed in connection with
contrapuntal part-writing. It continued for a long period to be the rhythmic
basis of all polyphonic music in Western European countries.

There were six modes (later amended to five), various patterns of the
" long " and " short " which together, and in that order, make up the
simple triple measure that modern notation could represent by

The " first mode ", which consisted of merely this basic pattern, was
apparently the earliest type used in contrapuntal music, and from this
triple, long-short conception the other modes developed. Only the first three
were of much concern to the monophonic art, but the scheme will be given
in full, since later discussions on polyphony will be concerned with them
all. Modern notation is employed for illustration :

Ex:12

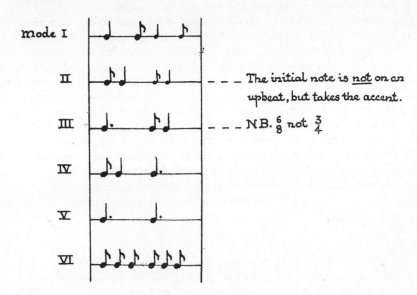

mode I

II ----- The initial note is not on an upbeat, but takes the accent.

III ----- N.B. $\frac{6}{8}$ not $\frac{3}{4}$

IV

V

VI

Some modern transcribers prefer to render Mode III as being binary:

on occasion (that is, in monophony). Binary rhythm seems to have been used freely enough in the thirteenth century (and in any other century) in circles not connected with church music and theory.

We are asked to imagine that a poem with its melody new to the performer would be scrutinised by him and the most suitable rhythmic mode decided upon, the criterion being the correct placing of the accents, especially the rhyming accent. No doubt there was a great deal of rhythmic licence in actual performance, while some melodies are better considered as being in free rhythm.

About 270 troubadour, and about 1,700 trouvère melodies have been recovered—enough for a fair amount of generalisation to be made concerning them.

Lyrical arts akin to those of the troubadours and trouvères arose in other countries. In Germany the aristocratic *Minnesinger* (singers of love) flourished from the second half of the twelfth century into the fourteenth, learning from the trouvères but developing their own national ways. Their praise of the eternal feminine tended to be general rather than particular. Regarding their melodies, there are even more uncertainties as to their rhythmic interpretation than in the cases of their French counterparts, since evidence that would justify the application of the rhythmic modes seems somewhat slender. In transcription binary rhythms are sometimes given as being the more likely, but once again we must bear in mind the probable rhythmic freedoms practised in performance. As for the tonality, once again the major scale holds its own among the Church modes.

One of the most favoured of the many poetic forms taken over from the trouvères was an AAB structure, called by the Germans the *Bar*. It consisted of two similar stanzas (*Stollen*) and an "aftersong" (*Abgesang*), the design, in fact, recommended by Hans Sachs to Walther von Stolzing for his Prize Song, in Wagner's opera. Wagner's knightly minstrels Tannhauser and Wolfram von Eschenbach, together with the Landgrave Hermann and his Tournament of Song, are firmly historical, while Wolfram's epic *Parzival* was the basis of the great composer's last libretto. Contemporary with these two *minnesinger* was the greatest figure of the movement, Walther von der Vogelweide (d. circa 1230). Below is given an example of his work, a song associated with the Sixth Crusade of 1228. The melody is a fine Dorian one, and the form a modification of the *Bar* mentioned above, an additional feature being the employment of musical material from the *Stollen* as a final cadence.

Ex:13

Nu al-erst leb' ich mir wer-de Sint myn sun-dich ouge er-sicht das he-re lant und ouch die er-de Dem man vil der e-ren gicht. Mir ist ge-schen als ich je bat: Ich byn ko-men an die stat Da got me-n[i]s-li-chen trat.

The transcription is by Sir Jack Westrup, from Chapter VII of the *New Oxford History of Music, Vol. II (p. 253)*. The translation of the text there provided reads as follows:

"Now at last life begins for me, since my sinful eyes behold the Holy Land, the very soil which men hold in honour. My prayer is answered: I have come to the land where God in human form set foot."

A different rhythmic reading but equally attractive, will be found on p. 234 of *Music in the Middle Ages* by Gustave Reese.

Outside the period with which we are dealing is the citizen art of the *Meistersinger* (fifteenth–sixteenth centuries), which grew from *Minnesinger* traditions. Hans Sachs (d. 1576), the worthy cobbler-poet, was the greatest figure of the movement, which, however, seems to have been almost as "bourgeois" and uninspired as Wagner represents. It may, however, have aided towards the widespread love of music among the German masses, a state of affairs which bore such fruit in later centuries.

In Italy began the *Laudi Spirituali*, religious in origin but popular in practice, devotional poems set to rhythmic, often very attractive tunes. The movement was given great impetus through being taken up by the Franciscan brotherhood. It was a feature also of the fanatical activities of the Flagellantes. *Laudi* singing continued into Renaissance times, and had much to do with the beginning of oratorio.

In Spain and Portugal similar lyrical arts arose. The most notable survival is the remarkable collection (already mentioned in this chapter) known as *Cantigas de Santa Maria*, and assembled by the Spanish king-musician Alphonzo the Wise. As the title indicates, the songs are mostly devoted to praise of the Virgin. Some of the settings are in measured notation, and seem to confirm the conclusions of the rhythmic-mode transcribers.

England, in spite of its Angevin rulers, one of whom was the trouvère Richard Coeur de Lion, showed little interest in the Continental art. The few monophonic songs that survive, the most notable being *Worldes blis ne last . . .*, have something of an Anglo-Saxon gloom, unlike other vigorous examples of native music of the period, e.g. the polyphonic *Sumer is icumen in* (c. 1240), and some sprightly instrumental dance-tunes.[18*]

NOTES

1* A parallel between a Jewish cantillation of Psalm 8 and the first Gregorian psalm-tone is recorded in HMS I.

2* Examples of ancient antiphonal psalmody are recorded in HMS II.

3 Actually, there were some rare and very special occasions when instrumental accompaniments were permitted to Byzantine church-singing; exceptions that proved the rule.

4* HMS II records some examples of Byzantine church music.

5 The fullest exposition of this subject is given by Egon Wellesz in his *History of Byzantine Music and Hymnography—second edition. (Oxford University Press, 1961)*.

6* HMS II gives a number of recordings of Gregorian excerpts. There are numerous other recordings on the market (e.g. in the *Archive* series).

7 Two important and recently published works dealing with the question are: (a) *Rhythmic Proportions in Early Medieval Ecclesiastical Chant*, by J. W. A. Vollaerts, (*E. J. Brill, 1960*); and (b) *Gregorian Chant According to the Manuscript*, by Dom Gregory Murray (*L. J. Cary & Co., 1963*). Vollaerts' views have been opposed by Dom Eugène Cardine in *Études Grégoriennes* (1963), pp. 7-38 (" Le Chant grégorien est-il mesuré?")

8 As research continues it is becoming more and more apparent that Byzantium played a major part in the early shaping of Gregorian music. HMS II con-

tains recordings of several striking parallels between Byzantine and Western Church music.

9 The solmisation system continued to be employed, with modifications, through the centuries. Many of its features are apparent in the practice of modern sol-fa. When, later in medieval times, the syllables were employed for the seven-note scale, the syllable *si* was allotted to the leading note, and *do* substituted, in most countries, for the somewhat unvocal *ut*. Possibly Guido was inspired by the tetrachord solmisation of the Greeks. As for the supposed derivation of his syllables from certain syllables of a Latin hymn, together with a full exposition of the system, see Reese, op. cit. p. 150, or the articles on SOLMISATION in *The Oxford Companion to Music*, and in *Grove's Dictionary*.

10* HMS II has a recording of a rendering of a Sequence (*Sancti Spiritus*).

11* HMS II has a recording of a very brief Easter Sepulchre drama (the "Winchester Troper" version), the music transcribed by the present writer. Later than many examples of the trope dialogue already mentioned, it is the earliest *surviving* version to show evidence of being *acted* (c. A.D. 980). The manuscript is now in the Bodleian Library, Oxford.

12* HMS has a recording of an excerpt from the Beauvais *Daniel* drama—the "Lament". A revival of the whole work, as edited by Mr. Noah Greenberg (*Oxford University Press*) was achieved in 1959 by the New York Pro Musica, and this has revealed its remarkable dramatic and musical value. A "study" edition, a plain transcription and translation of the original manuscript by W. L. Smoldon, is published by the Faith Press. Oxford University Press have also published recently (1964) an acting-edition of the twelfth century Easter Sepulchre drama from Fleury, under the title of *Visitatio Sepulchri*, also by the present writer. The work has been performed at Coventry Cathedral and at St. Paul's, London. Instrumental accompaniment was confined to what would have been permitted by the church practices of the period. The present writer has also joined hands with Mr. Greenberg to produce in New York (December, 1963) a twelfth century *Play of Herod*.

13 Relevant articles by the present writer are: *Medieval Church Drama and the Use of Musical Instruments* (*Musical Times* for December, 1962) and *The Music of the Medieval Church Drama* in the New York *Musical Quarterly* for October, 1962.

14 *Jongleur*—from *joculator* (=jester). The usual jongleur, apart from his singing and playing, commanded other, more popular lines of entertainment; hence "juggler". He was in particularly bad odour with Church authorities.

15 See *The Wandering Scholars* (Helen Waddell; Pelican Series).

16* HMS II has a recording of this song. In the original manuscript solmisation letters were used to notate the music.

17 *Troubadour*—possibly from *trobar* (=to find), just as *trouvère* might be from *trouver*, with the same meaning; ("Such as found out musical tunes and recited verses in writing"—*Ecclesiasticus, XLIV, 5*). But it is also maintained that the name is derived from *tropus* (=trope), since it was from Church tropes and sequences that many a secular tune was adapted.

18* HMS II has a number of recordings concerned with secular monophony— several troubadour and trouvère songs (including *Tuit mi desir*, by Thibaut of Navarre, mentioned in the text); two Spanish examples, from the *Cantigas de Santa Maria;* two *laudi spirituali* from Italy; a German song in praise of the Virgin by "Frauenlob" (Heinrich von Meissen—d. 1318), a famous *minnesanger*; and the English song, *Worldes blis ne last,* mentioned in the text.

There are also recordings of the Reading Rota, *Sumer is icumen in,* and instrumental renderings of four thirteenth century English dances.

CHAPTER III

The Rise of Polyphony

THE scanty records of written music in the ancient world and the notation of the Christian Church up to the early tenth century point to
systems that relied for their effects on melody alone. But during the latter
period there appeared in treatises and service books of the West evidence
of what seemed a new feature, the deliberate employment of simultaneous
sounds at different pitches. We must be cautious about thinking of this as
something revolutionary, the first general realisation of a harmonic sense.
Churchmen were almost the only writers of the early Middle Ages, and
were interested mainly in their own records and practices, while there is
much to be said for the belief that a rough and ready polyphony existed
in primitive folk-music since time immemorial. It has been maintained that
in untrained folk-singing, if a mixed group of people attempted to render
a melody in unison, differences in voice ranges might cause intervals to be
employed other than that of the octave. This is only one of several theories
that have been advanced regarding the development of spontaneous part-
singing among untutored peoples, but the subject cannot be pursued further
here. A useful summary of the " several theories " referred to above will be
found in Gustave Reese's *Music in the Middle Ages,* pp. 249-51. We may
note some references to such practices in the latter part of the first millenium
A.D., and in connection with our own islands. In the seventh century the
Anglo-Saxon Bishop Aldhem makes somewhat obscure mention of what may
be folk-polyphony, as does Johannes Scotus in the ninth century. Much
later, Giraldus Cambrensis (1147-1220), Court chaplain to Henry II and a
much-travelled man, refers to singing in Wales as consisting of " as many
different parts as there are performers " (this sounds like " round " singing)
and also mentions two-part singing among the folk of the north of England.
Polyphony was already well established in the Church in Gerald's day, but
he speaks as if British part-singing was an ancient custom, derived from
the Danes and Norwegians. Similar practices may well have existed in
other parts of Europe. Of late the Russians have been investigating a very
early folk-polyphony belonging to Georgia.

Organum

Whether or not polyphony was indeed " in the air " in the tenth century, it is certain that the Church at this time was beginning to make use of two-part music. About A.D. 900 a treatise called *Musica Enchiriadis* (Handbook of Music), written probably by Abbot Otger of Tornières, gives the first exposition of the process known as *organum*.[1] While the chant is proceeding in one voice, he asserts, another voice will sing the same melody a fifth below. He gives an example :

This was " simple organum of the fifth ". Another type, " composite organum of the fifth ", was to be obtained by doubling the original voice (*vox principalis*) at the octave below, and the added voice (*vox organalis*) at the octave above, thus :

A third type, " simple organum of the fourth ", was achieved by a two-part arrangement of parallel fourths, such as is represented by each of the pairs of voices given above.

Yet another type is described, " *free* simple organum of the fourth ", exemplified thus :

This third example is significant. No longer is there the monotony of the continuous fourth or fifth. It proceeds from a unison and finishes on one. It uses a second, a major third and even consecutive unison.

The official explanation regarding the use of free organum was that it

avoided any occurrence of the tritone fourth in two-part writing. It has been
pointed out, however, (see G. Reese, op. cit., pp. 255–6) that this method
of proceeding from and arriving at a unison, very convenient for practical
performance, *may* represent the borrowing of an already existent secular
two-part practice—with the theoretical justification for the technique as an
afterthought.

The notation of all these examples, it may be added, was the so-called
Dasiean, a " letter " type that had no very long existence but which had the
advantage of giving exact pitch at a time when unheighted neumes were
in general use.

More than a century later (c. 1040)—slow progress, we may think—
comes Guido d'Arezzo's *Micrologus,* which also pays attention to free
organum, allows the major third, uses contrary motion, and actually crosses
the parts. Meanwhile, the " Winchester Troper ", an English service book
of the early eleventh century, now in the Bodleian Library, Oxford, shows
a large number of two-part organa, mostly for tropes, sequences and responsorial chants. These, however, are written in neumes that do not show
the exact pitch of the notes. A significant innovation, however, is that the
added organum is placed *above* the given part, a position henceforth maintained. About 1100 two works, the *Musica* of John Cotton, possibly an
Englishman, and the anonymous *Ad Organum Faciendum* (How to make
Organum), between them supply much more information. Two or three
notes were now permitted in the organum part against the single note of the
principal part. Also the use of B flat is seen as a means of avoiding the
tritone interval between F and b. Other early twelfth century treatises point
to the growing interest in polyphony. Although the freer style was now
established, parallel organum of the fourth and fifth did not die out, and
continued, especially in Germany, until considerably later. Incidentally the
Greek term *diaphony* and its Latin equivalent *discantus* are also found as
synonyms for *organum.* Eventually *discantus* acquired a special meaning in
connection with measured music.

The practice of organum, associated at first largely with trope and
sequence, may have arisen from the same promptings that brought into
existence the tropes and sequences themselves—the desire to embellish the
liturgical chant. Undoubtedly a great deal of organum singing was of an
improvisatory nature and was never written down. Since some treatises provided guidance for such spontaneous efforts the practice must have been
widespread. Not always with the happiest results to judge by one contemporary critic, who says unkindly that performers " howl, shriek and
bark like a dog "; this in spite of the fact that organum singing was the
privilege of the soloist. The body of the choir sang only the single-line
plainchant. This distinction must be remembered as continuing throughout
medieval times. Polyphonic singing was a matter for the trained experts.

France took a leading part in the development of polyphony from the
early twelfth century onwards, and at the beginning of that period the
monastery of St. Martial, near Limoges, was one of the chief musical centres
of Western Europe. The various new factors—the plainchant melody in the

lower voice, free use of contrary motion and the crossing of parts, several
notes of the organum to one of the given part, led to the counter-melody
being more and more highly organised and independent, while the given
plainchant part grew longer and longer in note-value by comparison,
developing towards the drone-like Tenor (*tenere*—to hold). An example
from one of the St. Martial tropers of a trope with organum is given below :

Ex:17

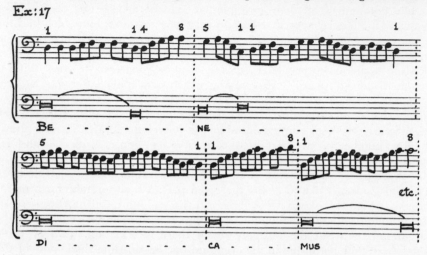

This example, a short passage from a troping of *Benedicamus Domino*, is
taken from a transcription by F. Ludwig (Adler G. : *Handbuch der Musik-
geschichte*, I. 179). Free rhythm is intended. As the transcriber shows in his
vertical placings, each melisma in relation to its tenor note begins and ends
on a " consonance " (as then understood) i.e. a unison, octave, perfect fifth
or fourth—as indicated by the editorial figures placed above.

The style spread to other countries. In Spain the celebrated *Codex Calix-
tinus* (c. 1140) contains twenty similar examples. One of these, *Congaudeant
catholici*, a pilgrims' song, is the earliest extant example of three-part
writing, with its top part much more rapid than the other two and entirely
independent rhythmically.[3*] Lacking any scheme for measuring the duration
of notes, singers must have found a certain difficulty in performing such
works. The need for some system of representing " measure " in music
must have become more and more apparent, even though the eye of the
performer was assisted by the lay-out of the voices, which in these compositions was usually written in score.

The Notre Dame School
In the progress of polyphony some individual names at last emerge,
connected with the Cathedral music of Paris. Concerning Albertus, a *maître-
de-chapelle* in the mid-twelfth century, little is known except that he had
a very high reputation among his contemporaries. He may have been the
composer of the three-part *Congaudeant catholici* mentioned above. The
post was soon after held by Leoninus (Leonin), who flourished between 1160

and 1180. His surviving work, the *Magnus Liber Organi*, consisted of a cycle of more than eighty two-part organa, for use in place of the solo parts of the responsorial Gradual and Alleluia of each of the chief feasts throughout the year. These settings were of two types (a) rapid vocalised organum against extremely long notes in the tenor, which consisted of a portion of plainchant, and (b) *clausulae*—episodes where the two parts move mainly note against note. Leonin's writing was very smooth, melodic leaps seldom exceeding a major third. At times *glissando*-like passages occur, covering an octave or more. Compared with the somewhat aimless wanderings of the St. Martial organa, his melody shows interesting patterns, and at times sequences. Below is a modern transcription of a short organum passage from the *Magnus Liber* (*Audi filia*), which illustrates some of the points mentioned above. The organa line alone is given, since the tenor for the whole of the eighteen " bars " consists of a long drone on C.

Ex: 18

This example is quoted from *The Rhythm of Twelfth Century Polyphony* by W. H. Waite (Yale, 1954), p. 65. In this volume the whole of the *Magnum Liber* will be found transcribed in modern rhythmic notation. In the example above the editorial square brackets over the notes indicate the neume groupings in the original MS. The significance of these groupings is discussed on p. 61 below. In " bars " eight and eleven, the short stroke to the penultimate quaver represents the use of a light note called a *plica*, in this case filling in between the D and B flat. The *glissando*-like passage of " bars " fourteen to fifteen marked with a slur is an example of a *conjunctura* (see p. 62).

Another and most important point is that the whole of the *Magnus Liber* was written with a technique that indicated *rhythm*, the first of the " rhythmic modes ", and the earliest instance that is known of such a use. The method employed is demonstrated below (see p. 61). Whether Leonin was the actual inventor of this technique cannot be known; probably it had been hatching for some years. Certainly the " rhythmic mode " ideas were quickly taken up at this time, and Perotin, Leonin's successor as *maître-de-chapelle*, employed other modal rhythms in his compositions. Leonin's work was probably done at the old Cathedral, for the choir of the then-building Notre Dame was not completed until about 1183.

Perotinus (Perotin), who flourished probably between 1190 and 1220-30, was a composer of great significance in musical history. He revised his predecessor's *Magnus Liber* and made important innovations, refashioning most of the *clausulae*. He often added a third part (*triplum*—hence " treble "), and occasionally a fourth (*quadruplum*). His organa " reveal an astonishing grasp of the problems of formal balance and contrast, the use of imitation and rhythmic variety, the development of melodic kernels and the repetition of thematic material, and—not the least of Perotin's achievements—the writing of an extended piece of music. Some of them may take more than twenty-five minutes to perform "—(*Grove's Dictionary, I, p. 230; article*—ARS ANTIQUA). Other Parisian composers followed the same paths. There is no doubt that the Notre Dame School played a very significant part in the development of polyphony.[4*]

The Polyphonic Conductus

Perotin also composed polyphonic conducti, quite a new type of composition.[5] Such conducti were settings, in two, three, or occasionally four parts, of Latin devotional poems, and an important characteristic was that the voices, all of which sang the words, moved in *chordal* fashion, mainly note against note. Another and even more striking feature was that the tenor (the lowest and most important part) more often than not represented free invention, and not a borrowing. Franco of Cologne (fl. 1280), who advocated such a practice, advised the composer of a conductus to make his tenor " as beautiful as he can ", and then add a *duplum*. Only after that was completed was the *triplum* to be added (if one were needed). Parts were not supposed to be conceived simultaneously, it seems.

Some conducti (Perotin has examples) contain passages of a melismatic nature where words are abandoned and the music probably vocalised. These *caudae,* as they were called, are found at various points in the course of a conductus, and also sometimes at the end. Conducti were apparently made use of in association with the liturgy. Secular types developed, but these also were serious in tone. An example of a somewhat light-hearted conductus is the famous *Prose of the Ass* used in twelfth century Beauvais (and elsewhere) during Christmas festivities.[6*]

Although the Conductus represented the first medieval instance of original composition applied to polyphony (the composer being able to give entirely free rein to his invention), neither the type nor the technique maintained themselves for long. In the Motet form which soon developed the emphasis was rather on *polymelody*, i.e. the parts added to the original plainchant material were most likely to be other melodies, derived from various sources, shaped and amended (one feels inclined to say at times " hacked ") in order to combine passably with the other voices. Strange as it may seem to us, in the writing of the thirteenth century motet this type of technique was held to be superior to that of mere *invention* of parts.

The Beginnings of Measured Music

Before considering the polyphonic form that dominated thirteenth century music, the Motet, we must give some attention to the notational devices that made possible a representation of the rhythmic weaving of its parts. With the progress of organum composition the need for representing " measure " in music became increasingly acute. We have already mentioned the approximations afforded by the vertical alignment of notes in score, but as elaboration grew this was not sufficient. The solution may seem very obvious to us, in possession of proportional notes (semibreve, minim, crotchet etc.) time-signatures and bar-lines, but all these devices represent many centuries of evolution from the stage with which we are now concerned.

The rhythmic modes, which have been set out on p. 51, were the first answer to the problem of fitting together parts with different rhythms, and at the same time making it clear to the performers what these different rhythms were. Though the system found ways of indicating subdivisions of the note-values of the rhythms, it did of course restrict rhythm to certain formal patterns, and was constantly ternary in outline. In due course other ways were found of allowing for greater rhythmic freedom, but for the time being the rhythmic mode system was the best practical method available for polyphonic composition, the twelfth century musician having only the non-mensural Gregorian pitch-notation at hand for the task. In this notation, it will be recalled, notes could be written either singly (for one syllable) or in groups (where more than one note was used for a syllable). These groups we have so far referred to as " neumes ", but in polyphonic music they are always termed " ligatures ". The first graphic methods of indicating rhythmic patterns were based on a special employment of these ligatures. The troubadours and trouvères made use of the rhythmic modes in their single-line settings by deciding which of them best fitted the *verbal* rhythm of a particular poem, but in the case of a polyphonic church composition no such aid was available. All that this stage of composition could do was to *hint*, by means of any melismatic passage (i.e. one with ligatures) that occurred in a part, as to which rhythmic mode was being employed. This hint was conveyed by means of a characteristic ligature grouping. Thus a succession consisting of the following

(or, expressed in units—3 2 2 2) would be read as being in rhythmic Mode I (trochaic), and as being the equivalent in modern terms to

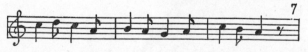

Mode I was almost certainly the first mode to be used, and Leonin's the earliest surviving music to show that use. If the example from the *Magnus Liber* on p. 59 be consulted again, it will be seen that the editorial square brackets indicate groupings on characteristic 3 2 2 . . . lines—with due allowance for any " extra " notes of lesser rhythmic value than those of the pattern. Mode II (iambic) would be indicated by ligature groups which we can represent by the unit numbers 2 2 2 2 3 : Mode III by 1 3 3 3. Details concerning the remaining modes can be found in works that are more technical than this one.

The various parts of the motet type of composition tended to keep each to its chosen rhythmic mode, and consisted of a number of repetitions of the rhythm, of various lengths and divided off by rests. A single presentation of the Mode I rhythm, thus :

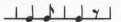

would constitute the first *ordo*; the second *ordo* would be

the third

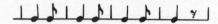

and so on. The other modes were organised similarly.

The monotony of the straightforward patterns was relieved by methods of indicating the breaking up of both the " longs " and " shorts " of the ternary rhythms into notes of smaller values, involving the use of such devices as *fractio modi*, the employment of the *plica*, of *conjuncturae*— complications which cannot be entered into here. The reader is referred to the article NOTATION in Vol. VI of *Grove's Dictionary*, to Vol. II of the *New Oxford History of Music, Ch. X* and to Gustave Reese's *Music in the Middle Ages, Ch. 10* for explanations of these technical terms and methods. He will be introduced to the joys of ligatures " with propriety and perfection ", " without propriety ", " without perfection ", or " with opposite propriety ", and will perhaps wonder how the soloists of the time managed to sing at all ! Another glance at the table on p. 51 will make it clear that on the basis of what we may term a measure of six quavers, the variations of rhythm displayed by the different rhythmic modes were yet permitted to dovetail neatly together in a polyphonic, polyrhythmic composition such as was the usual thirteenth century motet. The reasons for the seemingly odd patterns of Modes III and IV will now be apparent. The respective terms *dactyl* and *anapest* are sometimes attached to these, though of course they are not truly such. Actually the use of Mode IV in polyphonic music was very rare indeed. Mode V, usually in groups of three notes, thus :

was normally employed for the lowest part—the tenor—only. Mode VI, not as often used as the others, was usually in the uppermost part.

These notational practices were expounded in such works as the anonymous *Discantus Positio Vulgaris* (c. 1230–40); the treatise of Anonymous IV (the Englishman who gave so much information concerning the Notre Dame School); the *De Musica Mesurabili Positio* of Johannes de Garlandia (b.

1195); the *De Speculatione Musicae* of Walter Odington (c. 1300); and the *Ars Cantus Mesurabilis* of Franco of Cologne (c. 1280). All these describe the rhythmic mode techniques and the various devices in connection with the lesser note values, these indications being of somewhat ambiguous import at times. Indeed, the skilled modern transcriber, with the writings of these medieval theorists and many examples of the surviving music to hand, is still at times left baffled or in doubt. But the later writers, particularly Franco of Cologne, made progress towards *proportional* notation—towards the idea that the duration of notes should be indicated by their shapes. Franco, in his *Ars Cantus*, codified the practices of the time and established some new principles. Employing the plainchant virga (a) and punctum (b) to indicate *single* notes, at the same time giving them proportional values, he established the sequence (c) (*Maxima*); (d) (*Long*); (e) (*Breve*); and (f) (*Semibreve*).

| (a) | (b) | (c) | (d) | (e) | (f) |

With the exception of the Maxima (*duplex longa*) all note values were normally ternary. The *brevis recta* was the unit of measurement, valued as one *tempus*. The proportions were as follows :

Perfect Long	=	3 tempora, i.e. a " perfection ".
Imperfect Long	=	2 tempora
Breve *recta*	=	1 tempus
Breve *altera*	=	2 tempora
Minor Semibreve	=	$\frac{1}{3}$ tempus
Major Semibreve	=	$\frac{2}{3}$ tempus

Note the anomalous situation of the Imperfect Long and the Breve *altera* each being equal to two tempora.

The conceptions of " Perfection ", " Imperfection " and " Alteration ", which played such a great part in the mensural systems of the thirteenth and fourteenth centuries, arose in fact from the patterns of the rhythmic modes. Although the modal notation did not of course *show* the proportions, the first long of Mode III was worth three breves—the perfect one; the longs of Modes I and II were worth only two breves—imperfect ones; while the second of the pair of breves in Mode III was performed as a note of twice the rhythmic value and was thus " altered ".

Continuing with Franco's system, a dot was used to mark off " perfection ", i.e. ternary groups of notes. The various rests for the various notes were distinguished by vertical lines of different heights.

A wealth of rules regulated the variable values of these notes in practice. For example :

" If a long follows a long . . . the first will be a perfect long, whether the second is a note or a rest."

Again :

> " If two breves stand between two longs (or the corresponding rests) the first breve is *recta* and the second *altera* . . ."

—and so on, to many more and greater complications. As for the ligatures, further attempts were made to clarify time values, but even so a great deal of complexity remained—or so it may seem to us. Pierre de la Croix (? c. 1280), who, according to the *Speculum Musicae* of Jacob of Liège, was the first to divide the perfect breve into four semibreves, also demanded from five to as many as nine subdivisions, using dots (points of division) to mark the limits of a group which equalled a breve in duration. Near the end of the century the Minima (♦) made its appearance, with the value of ½ or ⅓ of a semibreve. In at least one important manuscript notes appear coloured red, to indicate binary instead of ternary subdivision. One cannot wonder that mnemonic rhymes were framed as a help to musicians in interpreting their notation.

However complicated the system, the idea of *proportional* notation had arrived, and was on the right lines. The rhythmic modes and their ligatures gradually faded, bringing about a less rigid style of composition. The basic Franconian principle of a single note bearing a definite relation to another single note is one that underlies the notation of today, which has evolved from it.

The Motet

Having made some mention of the rhythmic techniques that rendered possible the progress of polyphonic composition we return to the early part of the thirteenth century, a period that marked the emergence of that most important form, the Motet, which was dominant in the thirteenth century and had a far-reaching future. It undoubtedly developed from the *clausula* of the organum type of Leonin and Perotin. Words were added to the *duplum* part of the *clausula* which at first were a commentary on the words of the plainchant text, and the name *duplum* was changed to *motetus* (i.e. the " worded " part). Eventually this name was applied to the whole composition. When a *triplum* and, more rarely, a *quadruplum* were added, texts were found for these. The motet was thus originally a composition founded on a liturgical tenor with different words in each of the other parts. It might indeed be described as another stage of troping. As already stated, with the development of the form the added parts were normally borrowings from other compositions. Words and music (with the necessary adjustments) were taken over wholesale : it was the usual, the expected technique.

Listening to the more developed motets, we must cast aside all idea that we are in the presence of a primitive music. Speaking of the type, Professor P. H. Lang says (Music in Western Civilisation, p. 135) :

> " The *modus* could differ in every voice, resulting in an interplay of

independently organised rhythmical patterns of such rhythmic-dynamic intensity as music has never known before or since. . . . There were motets . . . which show (in a modern transcription into measures) four syllables to one bar in the treble, three to a measure in the next lower part, the contratenor, and two to a measure in the lowest part, the tenor; to add to the complexity, the three texts are entirely different, exhibiting unequal verse length and dissimilar strophic construction. The result is a composition of unheard-of complexity in which the rhythmic points of division never occur together in the several parts."

Lang goes on to mention the dramatic situation created by one of the motets of the period in which the inner part utters the idea (in, of course, Latin) that " the pious priests' works shine like stars of the firmament ", delivered in the quiet first rhythmic mode, while above, the *triplum*, in the rapid sixth mode, denounces the " hypocritical, malicious, drunken and lecherous priests, tormentors of the Church . . .". Below this the tenor sustains the verse from the Alleluia of a Mass—the words of Christ, " I will not leave you comfortless . . ."

Only a few decades after the first appearance of the motet came the strange phenomenon of the French motet which used in the upper part (or parts) secular and often amorous words. A great expansion of the form took place after 1250. Three parts being the usual number, the *triplum* became predominant, gaining in speed and independence. The motets of Pierre de la Croix, towards the end of the century, are noteworthy in this respect, for in them he made frequent use of the smaller divisions of the breve, a matter that has already been remarked upon. A more flowing melodic style was being developed. An extract from a modern transcription of one of his " French " motets is given below. What we should consider unsuitably balanced declamation of the text was permitted by the style of the period :

Ex: 19

Aucun – Lonc tans – Annunciantes.

AU-CUN ONT TROUVÉ CHANT PAR U – SA -GE MES A MOI EN DOUNE O – CHOI –

LONC   TANS   ME   SUI

ANNUN[TIANTES]

E

Ex. 19 (contd.)

The passage is quoted from *Polyphonies du XIIIE siècle*, No. 254 (Codex Montpelier, Fac. des Méd. H. 196) ed. by F. Rokseth, 1936–9.

Although France was the original home of the motet, it was quickly established in Great Britain, Spain and Italy. We shall hear much of England later with regard to it.

The secular world took over the motet form with alacrity; many motets of the period are obviously chamber-music. In the latter part of the century the term *cantilena* is frequently met with. This was secular application of the motet polyphony to the favourite dance-forms of *rondeau, virelai* and *ballade* (see pp. 47–50) *Cantilenae* were three-part versions of these, the melody found usually in the highest or middle part, and all voices having the same text. Most surviving examples from the period are anonymous, but half-a-dozen can be assigned to Adam de la Hale. A transcription of a rondeau of his, *Tant con je vivrai,* is given below, set out in the space-saving fashion which the rondeau form permits :

Ex:20

8 *

Jacob of Liège says, near the end of the century, " the moderns use only motets and cantilenae ". This was uttered in tones of regret, for Jacob was still fond of organum forms.

As we have already seen, worldly texts, together with their melodies, found a place in motets designed for church use, while even the hitherto sacrosanct plainchant tenor was sometimes dislodged in favour of snatches of secular tunes. One such motet has the music of a Paris street-cry for its lowest part. Whether the practice of allowing the words of a love-song to be heard within church walls was for a while normal or merely occasional may be a matter for debate, but it seems to have had no very long life. Various ecclesiastical dignitaries thundered against it, as against other mal-practices. A general and culminating denunciation was that of Pope John XXII, whose Bull of 1324–5 attacked the new and " wanton " techniques and banned practically all kinds of polyphony with the exception of organum. The effect was to check the worst excesses; nevertheless the prac-tice of polyphony and the production of motets continued, though perhaps at a lower level of activity for a while. The secular tenor, as a *cantus firmus*, had also come to stay.

Another offence mentioned, one that also survived attack, was the prac-tice of hocketing, whereby the words of a phrase were thrown from one part to another, and chopped by rests—a sort of medieval staccato effect. A brief extract is here given from a modern transcription of the motet *Triumphat hodie*, where the uppermost part sings a Latin text against two lower parts which interchange a portion of an Anglo-French secular song :[9]*

Ex: 21

Polyphonic Music in Britain

Although the British Isles, in common with other Western countries, were under French musical influence, and, as the surviving manuscripts show, were making use of French polyphonic compositions, there is other manuscript evidence for the existence of a worthy school of English com-posers around the end of the thirteenth century. The surviving (anonymous) works, though coming from various parts of the country, seem to indicate Worcester as being a leading centre, a number having been recovered from old bindings and wrappers in the Cathedral library there. The sum total, scanty though it is, reveals a body of church music undoubtedly influenced by France and in some ways old-fashioned, but with certain distinctive features. It was not without charm and in some cases displayed considerable technical skill. Exemplifying both these last virtues is the three-part, bi-textual motet from Worcester, *Puellare gremium* (c. 1300). The tenor is perhaps instrumental, made up of two tuneful phrases which are treated in true *ostinato* fashion (AA, BB—twice more repeated). Significantly enough, in view of the rhythmic reforms which were in the air around 1300, modern transcribers have found it best to render the piece in *duple* time. Against the normal rhythm of the two upper parts the *ostinato* proceeds with its own independent scheme—each " A ", for instance, equally one measure of $\frac{4}{4}$ followed by one of $\frac{5}{4}$. It is a remarkable composition well worth studying from a modern recorded performance.[10*]

As for the " distinctive features " referred to above, one of these concerns certain harmonic practices. We shall see later that these had an important influence on the course of music on the Continent. Even in the twelfth century some examples of English two-part church-music made considerable use of parallel, not occasional, thirds. This developed into a style of writing —the free employment of the " imperfect " consonances (together with frequent crossings of parts), called in the early fifteenth century, *gymel* (=twin-song)—which made the harmonic intervals of the third and sixth a common feature in English music at a time when the Continent, while admitting their use, was more concerned with the older consonances of the unison, fifth and octave. Even more important was the English development of what was later, and in somewhat different circumstances, called *fauxbourdon*—a technique which employed successions of $\frac{6}{3}$ chords. It first arose as a method of *improvising* two voice-parts above a plainchant tenor, this being the only written part in front of the singers. The instructions given by English writers on the subject (the details of which must be omitted here) resulted in each phrase-chain of $\frac{6}{3}$ chords being prefixed and rounded-off by chords in what we should term root position. A notated example from a thirteenth century Cambridge manuscript, a descant on the Te Deum plainchant melody, places on record something like the kind of effect that must frequently have been rendered from a single tenor line in the England of the period. One phrase only is here given :

Ex: 22   II

In te Do-mi - ne spe - ra ———————— vi :

It is possible that in performance the singers of the impromptu parts would have supplied a certain amount of improvised ornamentation at the same time.

This " English discant ", as scholars have chosen to call it, is found in written compositions not only in fairly strict form, as above, but used in snatches during the progress of pieces of normal motet style. It would seem that these chains of $\frac{6}{3}$ chords had a novel charm for their hearers—evidence of an appreciation of harmony *per se*—the *vertical* aspect of music which seemed, aesthetically, to have mattered little so far in musical history.

In spite of the English liking for keeping the *cantus* in the tenor, there is a beautiful example which makes great use of 6 chords while showing the melody in the topmost part. This is the Worcester *conductus, Beata viscera,* of which a few bars of transcription are here given :

BE - A - TA VI - SCE - RA   MA - RI - Æ VIR - GI - NIS,

Another distinctive characteristic of this English choral music was a predilection for the sonorities of four-part writing, at a time when the rest of Europe seemed mainly content with three. There seem also to have been other activities for which we have no clue, but which betray themselves in the famous thirteenth century piece of six-part canonic writing, the Reading Rota, *Sumer is icumen in.* This surely cannot have been an isolated instance of contrapuntal skill. Recently, its established date, c. 1240, has been strongly challenged, and the time of composition advanced seventy years or more. But the original date has been just as strongly defended. Whatever the truth, it may well be described as a musical miracle.[13]* (See Plate 7.)

We know little regarding polyphonic church-music in Scotland at this period. It was apparently in a flourishing state, even though dependent on France. One of the most important of the surviving manuscripts of the century, Wolfenbuttel 677, containing a great deal of Notre Dame music and also some which *may* be insular in origin, was very likely written at St. Andrews.

Instruments

To judge by contemporary evidence, descriptive and representational, the period rang with the sounds of instrumental music in social and public life. Note has already been made of the favoured vièle, the lute, guitar, harp and psaltery. The invention, or rather the rediscovery of a keyboard for the organ in the thirteenth century permitted the construction of small types, the positive or chamber-organ, and the portative, which could be carried about and manipulated by a single person. Also met with were the rebec, organistrum (hurdy-gurdy), recorder, shawm (oboe type), horn (made actually of horn, or wood), bagpipe, panpipes, trumpet, kettledrum, tabor, cymbals, triangle and sets of bell chimes (*cymbala*). Secular musicians had their *estampies* and other traditional dance-tunes, of which the troubadours and trouvères made use, but they seem also to have borrowed church vocal music, e.g. the discant *clausulae,* for use as instrumental pieces. Many of the instruments seem to have been sounded in church on festive occasions, in a world that put parish churches to what later ages would consider extra-ordinary uses. But *not,* it would appear, in the actual chanted *services.* There seems to be very strong contemporary evidence that ecclesiastical authorities in medieval times demanded that for liturgical purposes the organ *only* should be employed. Judging by the complaints of bishops and church councils that are on record there were certainly infractions of these regula-tions, (as there were of most Church taboos).[14] The present writer, investi-gating all surviving examples of the liturgical music-dramas up to and including the fourteenth century, found that apart from a single instance (in the Beauvais drama *Daniel*), where harps were called for, their rubrics indicated similar conditions to those demanded for the services—use only of the organ, and this restricted chiefly to the final unison choruses, together with some mention of chime-bells, but in the main, apparently no accom-paniment at all.

To sum up—there is no doubt that the thirteenth century was one of the most important periods in the history of music, establishing as it did on firm foundations the supremely important art of polyphony. In this France was the prime mover. Other nations were later to make their mark and take leading places, but in this century their contributions, in spite of some distinctive traits, may be referred to with some truth as " French musical art outside the borders of France ".[15]

One final point. Although for music historians the importance of the development of polyphony looms large, it must be remembered that it was practised only on special occasions, by solo specialists, and in its advanced forms only at leading centres. What occupied thirteenth century church singers most of the time were the unison plainsong chants of the services.

NOTES

1 This work, and its companion, *Scholia Enchiriadis* ("Commentary on the Handbook ") were formerly ascribed to the monk-musician Hucbald of St. Amand (c. 840–930). He undoubtedly wrote the famous *De Harmonica Insti-tutione,* which mentions organum but shows no enthusiasm for it.

2* The effects of these passages should not be judged from performances on the keyboard, but from vocal rendering. A number of vocal recordings of early organum are on the market, including those of Vol. II of the HMS.

3* HMS II has a recording of a performance of this piece.

4* HMS II has neglected Leonin and Perotin in its recordings. An excellent American LP record, *Expériences Anonymes,* EA-0021, gives four examples of organa by Leonin and two by Perotin, taken from their respective *Magnus Liber* works.

5 The term *conductus* was also applied to monodic compositions, used at first as tropes in the services to accompany movements from one part of the church to another. The same term was used later for a type of monodic song which, though non-liturgical, was of a serious nature.

6* HMS II has a recording of a four-part performance of the *Prose of the Ass* ("Orientis partibus"); also another conductus apparently popular in the thirteenth century, the three-part *Veri floris*.

7 The example is quoted from the *New Oxford History of Music, Vol. II, p. 323.* The prosody terms "trochaic" and "iambic" have been used for convenience sake, but there is no need to seek an origin for the rhythmic modes in the poetic metres of the Greek grammarians, as some writers have done. The modal scheme probably arose from the purely musical speculations on rhythm by medieval writers, beginning with the *De Musica* of St. Augustine (354–430).

8* From E. de Coussemaker, *Oeuvres complètes du trouvère Adam de la Hale (1872), p. 230,* quoted by HAM I, No. 36.† HMS III has a recording of a performance of the rondeau for solo voice and two instruments—the voice in the middle.

9* The motet *Triumphat hodie* is printed as No. 6 of *English Gothic Music,* ed. Dom Anselm Hughes and Percy Grainger (London, Schott; New York, G. Schirmer & Sons), and is recorded in HMS II. The score, from which the quotation is taken, is printed in the accompanying Handbook (II), pp. 58–60. Incidentally, *hocket* may have been derived from "hiccough", the invention apparently of hostile criticism.

10* A recording of *Puellare gremium* can be found in HMS II. Three other motets —*Marionette douce, Rosa fragrans* and *Alleluia psallat*—all recovered from various English manuscripts, are also recorded in the same volume, together with other examples of thirteenth century English and French polyphony.

11 From G. Reese, op. cit., p. 399, after M. Bukofzer, *Geschichte des Englischen Diskants . . .,* Ex. 18.

12* The conductus *Beata viscera* is printed as No. 3 of *English Gothic Music,* ed. Dom Anselm Hughes and Percy Grainger (London, Schott; New York, G. Schirmer & Sons), and is recorded in HMS II. The score, from which the quotation is taken, is printed in the accompanying Handbook (II), p. 52.

13* A performance of the Rota is recorded in HMS II. The accompanying Handbook gives a facsimile of the original manuscript. The presence of an alternative Latin text, (*Perspice Christicola . . .*) should be noted. The Rota, it seems, had been used not only as a spring-song, but as a devotional piece.††

14 See *The Galpin Society Journal, (X, May 1957),* pp. 40–56: article by Edmund A. Bowles—*Were Musical Instruments used in the Liturgical Service during the Middle Ages?*

15 See Reese, op. cit., p. 330.

† The initials HAM refer to the two volumes of *Historical Anthology of Music* compiled by A. T. Davison and W. Apel (Oxford University Press).

†† In his recent book *Music in Medieval Britain,* Dr. Frank Harrison has cast further light on the subject. The poem *Perspice christicola . . .* celebrates the Resurrection. Dr. Harrison points out that it cannot be a coincidence that the first five notes of the lower of the two *ostinato* bass-parts are those of *Regina caeli,* the special Mary-antiphon for the Easter season. This piece of motet technique seems to support the view that the work was intended in the first place for liturgical use with its Latin text.

CHAPTER IV

Ars Nova and the Music of the Early Renaissance

IT has been made evident that in the last decades of the thirteenth century the progressive liberation of polyphony from the shackles of the rhythmic modes and exclusive triple measure was well under way. A new shapeliness had appeared in melodic invention, and a new freedom in part-writing. Duple division, so long saddled with the slur of "imperfection", was at last being given full scope.[1] There was an increasing demand for rhythmically freer, more picturesque music from the secular, cultured society that was now existing in the cities and courts of Western Europe and Italy around their princely rulers, appreciative of the fastidiously wrought lyrical poetry that was being written in the vernacular. In the new century the composer was finding not only new ways of expressing himself, but increasing opportunities other than those afforded by the Church. It may be that the partial check on the production of church polyphony brought about by the 1324–5 Papal Bull helped towards this new orientation. Anyway, the evidence of surviving French and Italian manuscripts of the fourteenth century is that secular music was given by far the greater attention by composers.

Ars Nova (The New Art)

The notational innovations which had grown up with the freer rhythms of this music found their codification in the treatise *Ars Nova*, written between 1316 and 1325 by Philippe de Vitry (1291–1361), Bishop of Meaux. This work gave its name to the whole movement; *Ars Nova* was the new art in opposition to *Ars Antiqua*, the name given by the modernists of the time to the motet style of the latter half of the previous century. Contemporary with de Vitry, and of like mind, was Jean de Muris (c. 1290–c. 1351), whose *Ars Novae Musica* gives additional and valuable information as to notational theories. The chief of a conservative opposition was Jacob of Liège, whose views were expressed in the *Speculum Musicae* already mentioned. New and influential ideas tend to be ascribed to one prominent name alone, often to the neglect of other contributors. It may be that Philippe, as a leading figure of his age, has attracted some of the credit due

72

to others. But there is no doubt as to his fame. He was a leading churchman, a diplomat, and a composer and poet of European reputation. Petrarch
gave him high praise, while the Englishman, Simon Tunstede, who himself
wrote a valuable treatise in 1351, called him " the flower of all the world
of musicians ". There is also no doubt as to his authorship of *Ars Nova*,
the most important single document dealing with the new trends.

The de Vitry system as first expounded employed the Maxima, Longa,
Brevis, Semi-brevis and Minima, as had *Ars Antiqua*, with the additional
recognition of the *Semiminima* (a). The term MODUS was used to charac-
terise the relationship between Long and Breve. There were two kinds : (b)
represented the PERFECT MODE (let us say " Mood ", to avoid the
further overworking of a sorely tried word); while (c) represented the IM-
PERFECT MOOD. (The name " Imperfect " still survived, even though
the binary relationship now stood on equal terms with the ternary.) The
Breve-Semibreve relationship was termed TEMPUS (Time). (d) represented
PERFECT TIME : (e) IMPERFECT TIME. The Semibreve-Minim relationship was termed PROLATIO (Prolation), with (f) as PROLATIO
MAJOR, and (g) as PROLATIO MINOR.

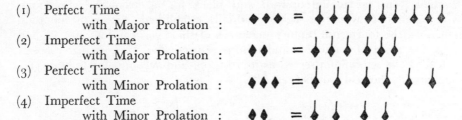

The subdivision of the Minim was binary only. With the introduction of
the smaller note values the longer ones gradually tended to become obsolete.

The invention of the four prolations, i.e. combinations of binary or
ternary time and binary or ternary prolation, was ascribed to Philippe by
later writers. These combinations were :

(1) Perfect Time
        with Major Prolation :
(2) Imperfect Time
        with Major Prolation :
(3) Perfect Time
        with Minor Prolation :
(4) Imperfect Time
        with Minor Prolation :

It is evident that here is the basis of compound and simple time as we know
it; of $\frac{9}{8}$, $\frac{6}{8}$, $\frac{3}{4}$ and $\frac{2}{4}$ respectively.

Free use was made of mensuration signs. Those employed to indicate each
of the four prolations were : (1) ⊙ (2) Ċ (3) ○ (4) C, the last being the
ancestor of our modern " common time " signature. On the occasions when
Mood had also to be considered other symbols were brought in. However, a
more detailed pursuit of this feature is a matter for the specialist. The four
prolations were an important feature of fourteenth century music, and gave

at times some highly interesting rhythmic combinations. In a way, they could be considered as more elastic replacements of the first three rhythmic modes. The famous fourteenth century Montpellier manuscript (H. 196), contains motets in both old and new styles, exemplifying the old modal, and the new mensural notations.

Ars Nova notation continued with the idea that single notes had alternative time values, depending on the nature of the preceding and following notes, on the presence of a dot, or on various other considerations. Thus there had to be the inevitable medieval lists of rules to discover whether a note was perfect, or imperfect, or altered. The dot had a number of different functions. It might be used to mark the end of a group of three beats in triple time, or to add to the time-value of a note (a modern survival). But it was also put to other uses, and theorists displayed no unanimity in the matter. Only gradually were the various anomalies straightened out. Syncopation was now widely used in composition, but the *ars nova* method of indicating it was a somewhat complex one. Signs were employed which called for the augmentation or diminution of the note-values of a passage as written. Diminution (i.e. the performing of a part in the next smaller note-values from those written without altering the proportional relationships between the notes) could be useful when there were any notational difficulties concerning notes of a very small value. (Later generations were to make use of the two devices for other and contrapuntal reasons.) The employment of red ink notation continued, with various implications, e.g. to alter the duration of a note, or to indicate that a passage was to be performed an octave higher—to mention but two of several uses. Later, the practice grew of writing white, i.e. outlined, notes instead of red. The first half of the fifteenth century saw another use for colouration, notes of all values from the semiminim up becoming white. Later in the century the semiminim became black and lost its tail, while black notes of lesser value came more and more into use. The modern principle of white for all values from the minim upward and black for all from the semiminim (crotchet) downward was being gradually established. As for the notation of rests, the fourteenth century made use of short vertical lines, e.g. (a) and (b), for those of semibreve and minim respectively. The original crooked stem of the semiminim served as its rest, (c), and accounts for the modern, apparently illogical crotchet rest (d).

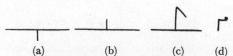

      (a)   (b)   (c)   (d)

The above details represent merely a bare sketch of a system, experiencing periods of considerable confusion, and changing and evolving over a couple of centuries and more, which only the larger modern treatises on notation can expound completely.[2] After 1500, in the period when music-printing began, it was well on its way to becoming standardised, although as yet far from taking on full modern guise.

This discussion of notation has been concerned with the development of the French *ars nova* system, its forms being largely accepted in neighbouring countries. Mention must be made of an independent type of notation (in some ways simpler and more logical) which was widely used in Italy during the fourteenth century, and which was associated with the name of Marchettus of Padua. It was practical enough to survive fully a hundred years before giving way to the developed de Vitry system.

Musica Ficta

The practice of altering a note chromatically, at first confined to the B flat and natural of plainchant, and used in early discant to avoid the tritone interval, was, through the late Middle Ages, gradually applied to other tones for both melodic and harmonic reasons, and also, as Walter Odington admits, " for beauty's sake "—a hint as to the free practices of contemporary composers. In the early thirteenth century J. de Garlandia mentions the possibility of the division of *any* tone into semitones. Since signs for sharpening and flattening were seldom written down, theorists now busied themselves with lists of rules regarding the application of these alterations, rules which singers were supposed to have mastered. (An early name for an accidental was *signum asinorum*!) The system became known as *musica ficta* or *musica falsa*—" feigned " or " false music "—the terms are synonymous. Numerous treatises, including one by de Muris and one (possibly) by de Vitry, dealt with the subject, but certainly not with unanimity, nor, at times, even with clarity. One of the numerous principles laid down may be stated thus—" A sixth expanding stepwise to an octave should be major ". If this was already the diatonic state of affairs,

well and good; if not, the interval had to be altered chromatically :

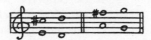

It is clear that such a practice would eventually develop a feeling for the subsemitonal " leading note ", cadence, and thus help to undermine modal differences. Only the Phrygian cadence, with its diatonic major sixth, would remain a " subtonal " one :

About 1400 we have the assurance of an Italian writer that a complete chromatic scale had been achieved, though he informs us that A sharp and D sharp were rarely indicated. Soon after comes the practical evidence of the Robertsbridge manuscript, probably the earliest surviving example of instrumental music for keyboard—six short pieces in two parts, the upper in mensural notation on a five-line stave, the lower indicated by letters. In the course of the music C, D, F, and G all appear sharpened on occasion,

and B and E flattened. Normally, however, no such generous aids were
given in the manuscripts. As a result, modern transcribers, given very doubtful help by the theorists, can never be wholly sure as to the accuracy of
their transcriptions of medieval music, or indeed of any music up to the
end of the sixteenth century, in this respect.

The Music of the French Ars Nova

We have already spoken of the sudden " humanising " of the art, made
possible by the de Vitry innovations. The new vitality, the picturesqueness,
the ingenuity amounting at times to artificiality—all these characteristics
were displayed in the most vivid form by *Ars Nova*'s greatest composer,
Guillaume Machaut. More than half of the surviving compositions of the
period are his. A few other names appear in the manuscripts, such as de
Vitry, contemporary with Machaut (in a handful of motets), and Cordier
and Tapissier as representing the end of the century, but much interesting
music remains anonymous.

Before considering Machaut's compositions we will attempt some generalisations concerning *ars nova* structures and techniques. The old forms of
polyphonic *rondeau, virelai* and *ballade* continued, but with greater rhythmic resource and expressiveness. These were usually in three parts, most
often for single voice with the two other parts played on instruments.
Frequently, no doubt, another instrument doubled the voice, since many of
these compositions were given three-part instrumental preludes, interludes
and postludes. With the new notation had come the possibility of an independent instrumental art. Machaut produced some examples of a type
of double ballade—two voices, each with its own text, together with two
instrumental parts.

There was a certain free and easy attitude regarding the performance
of any kind of vocal composition. An instrument might double or replace a
voice, a vocal composition might be rendered wholly as an instrumental
piece (a German organ arrangement of a French rondeau has survived).
Individual instruments were never specified in the manuscripts; apparently
any one that was available and fitting would do. There must have been a
great deal of instrumental improvisation, for contemporary illustrations show
bell-chimes, drones (on bagpipes), and various percussion instruments being
used in concerted music, but never a part for these has turned up. It is
also likely that vocal lines were embellished impromptu. However, some
fourteenth century pieces were already so intricate in their written forms
that, as Gustave Reese dryly remarks, " if performers may have wished to
modify them, they would hardly have wanted to elaborate them " (op.
cit. p. 353).

Successive entries of parts, and the use of the canonic device are now to
be found, unlike the usual practices of *ars antiqua* (even though some exceptional instances such as the Reading Rota spring to mind). There are
even examples of imitative entry, a device that was to be very wonderfully
developed in the next century. *Ars nova* found a new use for the canon
in the form of the popular two-part *Chace*. Its text described usually some

form of outdoor activity, such as a hunt, in which both the quarry and the initial voice-entry were "chased".[4*] In the mid-century Ivrea MS is found an anonymous and most interesting two-part composition, *Talent mes prus*. The text in translation could be rendered as—"The wish has taken hold of me to sing like the cuckoo". The music is not only a strict canon, but is of the *cancrisans* (crab) variety, that is, the leading voice reverses the melody midway. The work is thus capable of being performed backward, in palindrome fashion. (As a verbal example of a palindrome we may recall the sentence, "Madam, I'm Adam.") This is an extraordinarily early example of the contrapuntal skill that was to develop into the canonic complexities of Okeghem and his school. Apart from this "crab" ingenuity, which is musically barren, there are some artistic exchanges of the cuckoo's minor third in the course of the little work, prophetic of the vocal tone-pictures of the Renaissance.

Here is a modern transcription of the opening, as far as the entry of the second voice :

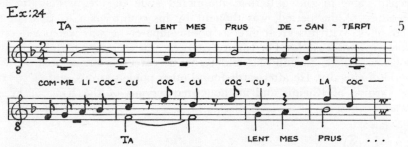

In the French, Italian and English music of the period a cadence unfamiliar to modern ears will frequently be met with. In it the sixth of the scale appears, as a penultimate note, between leading-note and tonic, e.g.

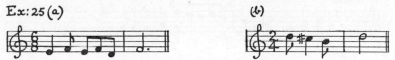

The term "Landini sixth" is sometimes employed with regard to it, but the cadence was actually in use in France before the time of the Italian master of that name, and even before that of Machaut.

A technique new to the fourteenth century, but nevertheless soon widely adopted, was that of syncopation. The earliest mention of it is in an English writing of 1326. Machaut was the first composer to make plentiful and artistic use of it.

Turning to Church music, which received much the lesser attention from *ars nova* composers, we find that a new device has emerged, that of *isorhythm* (i.e. equal rhythm). In a motet a part might consist of a rhythmic pattern of notes and rests, repeated several times (evidently a free development of the rhythmic mode system of *ordres*). Such a pattern was called a *talea* (i.e. cutting). There was no obligation for it to have any connection with any melodic pattern which might be present. More than one *talea* with its repeats might be used in a single part, and other parts might have their own *taleae*. The device turns up occasionally in secular music. France and Britain employed it freely, and it even outlasted the period of *ars nova*. At first glance it appears a purely intellectual trick, but it had the virtue of giving a vague sense of unity to a composition. In motet writing the use of double texts remained, though these were now normally in the same language, and with some subjective relevance between them. Hocketing, very popular in secular music, continued to be employed in the motet, in spite of the Papal ban. Even the few grave and worthy motets of de Vitry which have survived show use of the device. Mention of Mass composition will be made in connection with Machaut, to whom attention will now be given.

Guillaume de Machaut (c. 1300–c. 1377) was a remarkable and famous figure, the greatest composer of *ars nova*. Like de Vitry, he was not only a musician, but priest, poet, scholar and man of affairs. His poetry, entirely secular, and in the glittering, mannered style of the aristocratic love-literature of the period, was thought by his countrymen to rival that of Petrarch's. With his great gifts as poet-composer he was welcomed everywhere in lordly circles. For twenty years he was secretary to John, King of Bohemia, whose adventurous and romantic career belonged to the fading world of chivalry. He afterwards found other noble patrons, ending his days as a canon of Rheims and an honoured servant of the King of France.

[*continued on p.* 79]

Ex: 26

Like John of Bohemia, he showed a certain nostalgia for an earlier epoch; echoes of the trouvères were heard for the last time in his monophonic and unaccompanied *lais* and *virelais*. However, most of his attention was given to "modern", polyphonic settings of *rondeau, chanson-balladée* (which was his term for *virelai*), and *ballade*. The *ballade,* as he shaped it, was his most personal form of expression. We have already taken some note of the usual lay-out and style of performance in connection with these forms, and also Machaut's occasional use of the double ballade. The three-part, single, ballade, with the voice in one (usually the highest) part and with two supporting instruments, the whole freely composed, became the most popular secular form for more than a century.

Whatever preoccupation Machaut may have had with days gone by, he was in the forefront in the matter of the new technical devices—isorhythm, syncopation and even *cancrisans* writing. His mastery of the last two can be seen in his extraordinary *rondeau, Ma fin est mon commence-ment* . . . A translation of the full text would read : "*My end is my beginning and my beginning my end*, and holds truly. *My end is my beginning. My third song three times only reverses itself and thus ends. My end is my beginning and my beginning my end.*" A complete transcription is given on page 78 and 79 (Ex. 26).

The voice sings the middle (tenor) part, with instruments above and below. An examination of these parts will show that the topmost is an exact *reversal* of the voice-part—it begins where the other ends—while the lowest proceeds to its half-way mark and then reverses its own tune. The work being a rondeau, the A, B music pattern is performed *three* times (on the second occasion with repetitions of A). Bearing all these points in mind we must fairly admit that the music illustrates the words most appositely, and the words the music. Machaut was, however, ahead of his age in this exceptionally close linking of text and setting. It may be interesting to compare the work with Adam de la Hale's rondeau, *Tant con je vivrai,* given on p. 66. The stride is clearly a long one.

A strange and unique composition is his *Hoquetus,* "David", written possibly for three instruments. The subtly constructed isorhythmic tenor is founded on a plainchant melody, the two parts above it taking over from each other in an extraordinarily brilliant hocket style.

Although the bulk of Machaut's output was secular, he made some important contributions to church music. There are a number of motets in dignified traditional style, but employing isorhythm, and even diminution of phrases. His most important church work was a four-voice Mass, often called, though without authority, his "Notre Dame" Mass, the first example of a complete polyphonic setting by one composer of the whole of the Ordinary. Though based on the old motet and conductus forms it employs the newer devices of isorhythm and syncopation. There is even hocketing. *Ars nova* had introduced the contratenor voice, interweaving with the tenor, sometimes above and sometimes below. This additional sonority is apparent in the Mass. Perhaps its most startling novelty is the introduction of a short phrase :

which appears with various modifications in each of the movements—a unifying device and a remarkably early example of the *idée fixe*. The dignity and power of this monumental work may still move a modern hearer.[7*]

Machaut's Mass was truly liturgical. However, examples of a renewed
[*continued on p. 82*]

Ex: 27

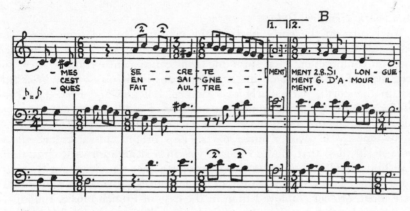

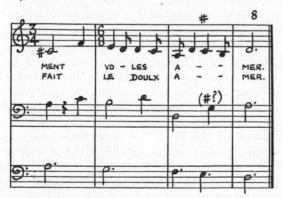

A translation of the text, as given in HAM I, p. 246, is as follows:

(1) *Lovers, love secretly* (2) *If you wish to love long.* (3) Receive this advice: (4) *Lovers, love secretly*; (5) Because who does differently (6) Makes the sweetness of love bitter. (7) *Lovers, love secretly*, (8) *If you wish to love long.*

F

invasion of the secular style may be seen in certain three-part Mass movements (the so-called " *ballade*-Mass " type) found in fourteenth century manuscripts. These had entirely non-liturgical melodies in the topmost part, with two supporting parts below.

The last decade of the fourteenth century and the first of the fifteenth saw the fading of French *ars nova*. At the aristocratic courts for which so much of the music was written it had reached an ultimate state of artificiality and extravagant refinement of rhythm, and went down before a new classicism, the sonority and simplicity of the Burgundian school of Dufay. Some idea of these unparalleled rhythmic complexities may be gained from the example given on p. 81 (Ex. 27), a modern transcription of a rondeau by Baude Cordier, one of the last of the *ars nova* composers, who yet lived to practise the new style. See also Plate 11.

Fourteenth Century Italy

We return to the early part of the century—to the time when Italy, independent for a while in notation, was beginning to display an independence in composition. Her surviving fourteenth century music (we know very little of what went on in the thirteenth) is mainly secular, fostered at first in the north, particularly at Florence, Bologna and Pisa. The Italian gift for melody, springing from the traditions of troubadour music, the laudi, and the conductus form, made itself evident in a flowing, cheerful polyphony, mostly in two or three parts. This bright music, its melodic line more florid than that of the French, was in a straightforward contrapuntal style that relied on no *cantus firmus* prop—a fact significant for the future. Isorhythm made only the rarest of appearances, but canon and imitation were much oftener employed than in the case of French music. Italian composers in the first part of the period still relied much on the traditional consonances of the unison, fifth and octave, but gradually, and probably under French influence, more use was made of the " imperfect " ones.

This *trecento* music flourished between c. 1325 and c. 1425, and was linked with the wonderful period of Italian literature associated with the names of Petrarch and Boccaccio. The part which music played in the aristocratic life of the times is frequently instanced in the *Decameron*.[9] Examples of the work of more than two dozen composers have survived, though very little is known personally about most of them. There were three generations of them. Jacopo da Bologna, Giovanni da Cascia and Vincenzo da Rimini are the best known of the first. The great Francesco Landini dominated the second, which lasted from the middle of the century to its close. Several of Landini's contemporaries—Paolo, Gherardello, Lorenzo, Andrea—are recorded with the appendage " da Firenza," showing them to belong to the brilliant circle which, headed by Landini, made Florence for the time being the city richest in Italian song. The third period, from 1390 onwards, included the names of Matteo da Perugia, Bartolomeo da Bologna and the Belgian-born Johannes Ciconia, the last the most outstanding composer between the times of Landini and Dufay.[10*]

The three secular forms most practised were the *madrigal*, the *caccia*

and the *ballata*. The *madrigal* (the term probably originally denoted "a
poem in the mother tongue") had no links with the sixteenth century form
with the same name. In the earlier part of the period it is usually found
written for two voices only. The text consisted normally of one to four
three-line stanzas, each having the same setting, followed by two concluding
lines (the *ritornello*) with a setting in a different rhythm. There were indeed
some deviations from this pattern. The first line of a madrigal by Giovanni
da Cascia is given below. It illustrates the usual rapid flow of the upper
line and the less florid nature of the lower. The *ritornello* of this piece is
transcribed as in $\frac{3}{2}$ time.

Ex: 28

(The fragment of text above may be translated as—"In the midst of six
peacocks I saw a white one . . .")

Imitation is not seen in this brief extract, but is frequently enough found.
A three-part madrigal by Landini is an extreme example in having its two
lower parts in canon at the beginning, and a three-part canon in the second
section. Another of his, *Sy dolce non sono*, all three parts vocal and "composed throughout", like a sixteenth century madrigal, is a rare Italian
example of the use of isorhythm.

The *caccia*, derived possibly from the French two-part *chace*, normally
employed a strict canonic form, the canon in the two upper voices with a
free instrumental bass below. Like the madrigal it was in two sections, the
second and shorter being a *ritornello*. As in the case of its French counter-

part, it attempted to paint lively open-air episodes, e.g. a fishing scene (a famous example this, by Landini), the bustle of a market place, even the incidents and excitements connected with the putting out of a house-fire. Musically, a *caccia* could be described as a one-strophe madrigal, but one usually of considerable length.

The *ballata*, which was patterned not on the French *ballade* but on the *virelai*, was the most favoured form of the century, often mentioned in contemporary literature. It was of course of dance derivation, and may still have been used for dancing. There are *ballate* with texts for all three parts, or for two, but the form was most frequently a solo song with instrumental accompaniment.

A small quantity of instrumental music survives in the manuscripts— *saltarelli* and *istampite* (=estampies)—single-line melodies which were no doubt given improvised accompaniments in performance. Some of the *saltarelli* have sections which contrast in speed and time signature, a foreshadowing of the "paired" dances (e.g. *pavane* and *galliard*) of later centuries.

We have noted that polyphonic church-music was comparatively neglected. There seems to have been an increase of interest in the later part of the period, but the Mass movements and motets showed plainly enough the influence of the secular forms of madrigal and *caccia*, as in the cases of an extremely florid Gloria by Matteo da Perugia, and a motet by Jacopo da Bologna, *Lux purpurata radiis,* for two male voices and one instrument.

Some further mention must be made of the finest musician of *trecento* Italy, Francesco Landini (1325–97). Though blind from early youth, he trained with Jacopo da Bologna and became a famous organist, a master of improvisation and the leading composer of his age. He spent most of his life in Florence, everywhere admired and respected. Like de Vitry and Machaut he was also an accomplished man of letters. At Venice in 1364 he was awarded a victor's laurel crown, the competition being not in music but in poetry, and one of the "jury" Petrarch himself. He showed a preference for three-part writing rather than two, and brought a new variety and subtlety to Italian counterpoint. The bulk of his surviving compositions are in the *ballata* form (he wrote over 140 examples), in a mingling of voices and instruments. Their beauty is still to be admired. He is known to have written some motets, but he apparently took little interest in church music. A third of all the surviving Italian *trecento* music is his. An important manuscript concerned with the period is the Squarcialupi Codex, named after the Florentine organist who was its first possessor. In it Landini is given pride of place among twelve other composers, and miniature portraits are supplied for all. Landini's represents him as playing his favourite instrument (among the many of which he was master) the portative organ.[12*]

This flowering of Italian *trecento* music faded suddenly after about 1425, though the roots remained. The return of the Papal See to Rome after its Avignon exile brought Northern influences to Italy. These, though overshadowing native music for the time, supplied firm foundations for the later establishment by Italy of the musical leadership of Europe.

Spain and Germany had little of significance to contribute to fourteenth century monody and polyphony but music imitative of France and Italy. Polish and Czech music apparently flourished, but has left scant evidence as to its nature. Both these latter countries seem to have been well acquainted with French and Italian music.

English Music in the Fifteenth Century—Dunstable

It has already been noted in the previous chapter that although native English music did not loom large in the thirteenth and fourteenth centuries, nevertheless it had promises for the future. These began to be fulfilled in the early part of the fifteenth century, when the writing of the famous Old Hall Manuscript preserved for us the names of about a couple of dozen English composers of the time, e.g. Lionel Power ("Leonel" of the manuscripts), Damett, Gervays, Bytterling, Benet, Pycard . . . and quite a generous amount of attractive music. The manuscript contains about 140 compositions—Mass-movements and motets in from three to five parts— apparently for use by the king's Chapel. It seems to date from the reigns of Henry IV and his son Henry V, and to consist of three separate "layers". A Gloria and a Sanctus by Roy Henry contained in it used to be ascribed to Henry V, a warm supporter of the Chapel. Recently Dr. Frank Harrison has brought forward strong evidence in favour of Henry IV as the composer. A contemporary chronicler described him as a brilliant musician. As for the music in general, while it varies in style and achievement, some of it simple in technique, some of it showing imitation, even canon, and the use of iso-rhythm (clearly the result of Continental influence), what is most apparent is its smooth melodiousness, and the frequent use of English discant and the sonorities of triad harmony in general. These characteristic English features we have already remarked upon (see p. 68f). They are well exemplified in an anonymous three-part *Credo* found in the manuscript. The opening portion is here given, the Gregorian *cantus firmus* being in the *middle* voice :

Ex:29

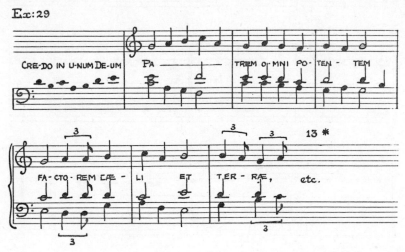

Other English manuscripts indicate that a native and widespread polyphonic activity of the period was the carol. The fifteenth century was its hey-day. Originally processional music, it had both church and secular popularity. In form it resembles the *virelai*—a refrain, followed by a number of stanzas each set to the same music and each rounded off by the refrain, or by another, distinctive to the stanzas. There are Latin examples, but most texts are in the vernacular. They seem mostly to have been intended

[continued on p. 87]

Ex: 30

AL ——————— LE ——————— LU ———————

—————— IA, Now WEL MAY WE MERTH-IS MAKE, FOR US JE-

-SU MAN-HOOD HATH TAKE, ON-LY FOR OUR SIN-NES SAKE, AL-

-LE ——— LU ——— IA   ĀL ——————— LE ———

14*

——— LU ——————— IA.

for ceremonial or festival occasions, and for skilled singers such as would be found at large establishments, but there was no specific attachment of the form to the Christmas season, as was the later tendency. Over 130 carols have survived with their music (there are many other texts without settings). The fifteenth century examples have a smoothness of melodic line, and a mellifluous quality brought about by the frequent harmonic use of the third and sixth, which make them still attractive to hear. One of the best known is quoted on page 86—*Now wel may we merthis make*—an anonymous homage to the Virgin.

Four similar stanzas follow, each with its *Alleluia* burden. It will be noted that successive sixths play a large part in the two-part stanza harmony, and $\frac{6}{3}$ s in the three-part burden. There are two examples of the Landini cadence. The mode would appear to be the "wanton" Ionian. Actually more than half of the carol settings of the period use it—the mode that was to become the major key.

English manuscripts of the period furnish polyphonic songs other than in carol form. *Angelus ad virginem* was the composition which Chaucer's Clerk Nicholas sang to his psaltery accompaniment. The tune, which begins:

Ex: 31

AN- GE-LUS ET VIR - GI- NEM SUB- IN-TRANS IN - CON - CLA - VE,

was well worth singing. It is found in a number of thirteen and fourteenth century manuscripts in various arrangements, and not only in Latin but English, a sign of popularity. A three-part setting which has survived from the early fifteenth century again exemplifies the English predilection for the $\frac{6}{3}$ chain, the melody in this case being in the middle voice. There are even polyphonic (and artistic) drinking-songs to be found. In the same manuscript as contains the well-known two- and three-part *Agincourt Song*, as well as the carol quoted above, is the jolly *Tapster—drinker—fill another ale . . .* with a three-part interlude and postlude for instruments.[15*] (See Plate 15.)

When we turn to the most admired English composer of the period— John Dunstable (c. 1390–1453)—it is surprising to discover that the main evidence as to his great contemporary fame is to be found not in his own land but on the Continent, together with the bulk of the music which confirms it. Little is known of him personally. He was a churchman, and for a time a canon at Hereford. From somewhere, probably the Chapel Royal, he must have received a thorough professional training in music. We read of his being versed also in mathematics and astrology. More important, he was for some years in the service of the Duke of Bedford, brother of Henry V. After the latter's death in 1422, Bedford was Regent of conquered France at Paris until his own death in 1435. Thus Dunstable would have been at the heart of things in musical France, and no doubt was also in touch with the highly-cultivated Dijon court of the Duke of Burgundy, (Bedford's brother-in-law), who for the time being was England's ally. It is also likely that he travelled, and perhaps even resided, in Southern Europe and Italy, since many of his works are found in manuscripts belonging to such places as Modena, Aosta, Bologna and Trent. In France and Burgundy he found musicians who had turned away from the brittle artificialities of the late *ars nova*, and were seeking a new simplicity and directness. Men like Tapissier, Carmen, Grenon and Césaris had gained good reputations, but by the '30's the great names among French and Burgundian musicians were those of Dufay and Binchois. Yet there is little doubt that had it not been for the new musical gospel which came out of England, with Dunstable as its chief missionary, the Burgundian development, and thus the general course of European music, might have been other than it was.

There is contemporary evidence for this (other than the test of actual musical style). A French poet, Martin le Franc, produced in 1441–2 a poem of enormous length, *Le Champion des Dames,* a canto of which was devoted to the arts of his country. In the stanzas dealing with music he mentions various Gallic composers, and finally, in the most favourable terms, Dufay and Binchois. Then follows a quatrain which may be rendered thus :

> " The English guise they wear with grace,
> They follow Dunstable aright,
> And thereby have they learned apace
> To make their music gay and bright."[16]

Even more explicit was the statement of Johannes Tinctoris (c. 1435–1511), the great Flemish theorist, but also composer and master of many other branches of learning. True, he belonged to a generation later, but his knowledge of European music was unrivalled, and posterity owes him gratitude for the twelve treatises which cast such light on the theory and practice of the music of his age. In one of them he says :

> " Thus in our time music took a wonderful flight because it seemed to be a new art which originated with the English under the leadership of Dunstable whose contemporaries in Gallia were Dufay and Binchois."

Some of the attractions of Dunstable's music for these contemporaries we can already realise—the new euphony that avoided the unprepared harshness still to be found in Continental composition, the attractive use of successive $\frac{6}{3}$ chords and of triad harmony generally. There was also the smooth fluid nature of his part-writing, which kept so often to stepwise motion and the smaller intervals, and the striking beauty of his melodies (what part had Italian influence played in this?). Undoubtedly the new suavity of passages such as the following must have impressed Continentals deeply :
(a) (The concluding bars of the three-part motet, *Quam pulcra es*) :

Ex:32

(b) (The opening bars of the three-part motet *Sancta Maria*—the triadic start is typical of Dunstable) :

Ex:33

Part of his strength, however, was that his music was firmly founded on the best traditions of the past. Of the sixty-seven works that have been recovered, scattered over Europe, the bulk consists of Church music—Mass-movements and motets. In these he shows a wonderful blending of old and new in the matter of his varied choice of techniques. Some motets use the simple forms of the ancient *gymel* and the English discant, other the current device of placing the *cantus firmus* in the highest voice, at the same time decorating it freely (a favourite trick of Dufay's). Canon played but little part in his church works—he seemed to associate it more with secular music—but he was a master of the device, and author of a number of examples of the " puzzle " type. When he chose to use other formal techniques he did so in consummate fashion. The style which has already been noted as " English discant " and which involved progressions of $\frac{6}{3}$ chords came to European notice through the consummate use of it made by Dunstable and his English fellow-composers. In this native form the *cantus firmus* was most usually in the lowest voice. But when the technique was later transferred to the Continent the practice was to place it in the highest. The lowest part, deprived of its *cantus* importance, became a " false support ".

Hence the term *fauxbourdon*, which was applied to the device in general as used by the Continentals.

A work of Dunstable's that was known and admired throughout all Europe was the four-part isorhythmic motet *Veni, Sancte Spiritus*, a masterpiece of constructional skill. It is built on a tenor (possibly instrumental) which employs the second and third phrases of the plainsong *hymn* " Veni, Creator Spiritus ". These appear three times, in the form of six isorhythmic *taleae*. On the first appearance the notes are so long as hardly to be recognisable. In the middle appearance the note-values are reduced by one-third, in the final one by two-thirds, when the tune, as it were, emerges against the other parts to make an effective climax. The three other voices, discant, altus and contratenor, are also (independently) isorhythmic, with occasional licences. The discant, mainly free, but making some use of the hymn melody when the tenor is silent, begins with that tune and consists of a setting of the whole of the poem of the *sequence* " Veni, *Sancte* Spiritus ". The free contratenor uses part of the text of " Veni, *Creator* Spiritus ". The altus, on the other hand, sings a *troping* of the sequence poem, an effective revival of an ancient device. Complicated as all this may sound, the work is of a sonorous and impressive unity, and is one that can still be listened to with interest and enjoyment.[19*] Little of Dunstable's secular work has survived. The charming Italian chanson, *O Rosa Bella*, showing some neat imitation, has been ascribed (not at all firmly) to him, but also to the English composer Bedingham.[20*] Apparently a number of other outstanding English musicians found employment on the Continent at this time. Second in general esteem to Dunstable was Lionel Power, whose Church music was sometimes mistaken for Dunstable's. The evidence of his fifty or so surviving compositions show him to be worthy of that esteem. Power also wrote a treatise, in which he forbade the use of consecutive perfect fifths and octaves, an injunction that was already being heeded.

The Burgundian School—Dufay

The Tinctoris passage quoted above has a melancholy continuation as far as English music is concerned. The treatise goes on to say that " the English were compelled to abandon the leadership to the moderns . . ." In other words, the so-called Burgundian School of Northern France and the Low Countries, which came into prominence with the French composers Dufay and Binchois, had learned their lesson from across the Channel, and were forging triumphantly ahead, while musical England, facing the troubled years of the Wars of the Roses, faded into the background for many a year, and awaited a Tudor revival.

Guillaume Dufay (c. 1400–74) was born at Hainault, and had in his younger days a wide musical experience, both in France and Italy. A pupil of Grenon, he served at Italian princely courts, having, we are told, a fine tenor voice. He can exemplify in many ways the attributes and standing of a leading Early Renaissance composer, whose career—whose very existence—was bound up with service to the Church or to some powerful secular court, or, as in the case of Dufay and many another, to both. Such a man would be first and foremost a singer, and would build his career on that foundation.[21] Indeed, at the better centres the training of a singer, as choirboy and choirman, meant a thorough and arduous education in general musicianship, denied to the average instrumentalist. We have already noted the fact that composers like Tinctoris, Dunstable, Landini and Machaut were also men of a wide general culture. While it was quite usual for church singers to be in minor orders, the majority of the leading composers of the time were actually priests. What we may term a worldly advantage arising from this was the fact that their musical eminence could be recognised and rewarded simply enough by the bestowal of livings, prebends and the like, for which residence was not always demanded. Such men were also sometimes confidential secretaries or chaplains, and were sent on responsible missions by their masters, ecclesiastical or secular. Dufay's career covered many such activities. At the height of his powers he returned as a canon to Cambrai Cathedral, the scene of his boyhood training, and ended his days there, writing the greatest of his Masses and motets, and in friendly touch with the Burgundian court at Dijon, where his music was highly appreciated and often performed.[22]

The statements of Martin le Franc and Tinctoris are fully confirmed by the evidence of his compositions. Until well on in the '30's his music still retained something of the angularity of melodic line and casual dissonance characteristic of ars nova. Then, it seems, came the effect of the Dunstable revelations. Thereafter Dufay developed his own individual style—a gentle, mellifluous, almost feminine art of a clarity unknown to past French music, developing the new fauxbourdon technique, and building on a foundation of sonorous triad harmony. There were soon disciples and imitators.

Composition in this new age was no longer a matter of adding successive parts to a single dominating one. The overall effects of the various counterpoints were being borne in mind, even though the idea of one ruling part was still maintained. In Dufay's works and those of his contemporaries and followers can be seen the device of free imitation between the various parts, sometimes in the form of successive voice-entries, fuguefashion, a technique which the sixteenth century was to develop with such virtuosity. Canon was also effectively used, as yet not carried to the extremes practised by the Flemings later in the century. Another important omen can be seen in Dufay's music, the occasional appearance of what we should term a perfect cadence—a V to I, dominant to tonic, progression. The appreciation of tonality was beginning its evolution. Harmonic considerations helped to confirm the contratenor as the lowest part, since the tenor normally carried a fixed tune. However, not until the time of Ockeghem, a generation later, was the real bass range established. Incidentally, this celebrated composer had also a celebrated bass voice (" the best in Europe ", said Tinctoris). In the latter part of the fifteenth century, the contratenor bassus having become the " bass ", there was occasional use of a contratenor altus (high countertenor). From this latter name comes our term contralto. While discussing choral matters we may note here that only from the period of Dufay's maturity do we find the main choir entrusted with part-singing. Before that time polyphony had been the privilege of the more highly skilled solo voices, but thanks to the princely chapels being established (or expanded), everywhere highly skilled singers were becoming more and more numerous.[23]

Dufay wrote a good deal of secular music, including some charming chansons, mostly in three parts, sixty of which are extant. But his main strength was in his church music of which there survive eight complete Masses, two Magnificats, eighty-seven motets and numerous sectional Mass movements. Indeed, the great period of Mass composition begins with Dufay. He continued to write isorhythmic motets in the old style for festival occasions, with a second independent text acting as a commentary on the first, but his " modern " style was a three-part single-text work, the two subsidiary parts showing close similarity of character with the principal. One of his most famous motets (in from two to four parts) is *Ave Regina Coelorum*. He mentioned it in his will, desiring that it should be sung at his passing. Actually, it was performed at his burial.[24]* (See Plate 13.)

His early Masses were of the " Discant " type of the time, the ornamented upper voice being liturgical in origin. The tendency was to keep the material of this discant part more or less similar in the various sections, thus achieving a certain unity throughout. But by the middle of the fifteenth century the so-called Tenor Mass, in four parts, was beginning to make its appearance, and its early development owed much to the work of Dufay. The main theme was (as one might gather) in the tenor, and while this could be a liturgical motif, usually free from ornament, Dufay and his contemporaries soon began to borrow secular tunes for the purpose. Against the set theme the three other parts wove counterpoints. Once more the device was employed of using the same thematic material, with due modification, throughout the Mass. The opportunity for progressively ingenious shapings of imitative patterns is obvious, and for many years the Tenor Mass became the vehicle for the greatest progress of the contrapuntal art. The use of secular themes was undisguised, for Masses derived their distinguishing names from the tunes employed, e.g. *Adieu mes amours, Le bergier et la bergière,* and—greatest favourite of all—*L'homme armé.* As for any profane atmosphere, the themes were usually much altered rhythmically, and in any case it must be remembered that modern distinctions between sacred and profane do not always coincide with the medieval outlook. Alternatively, themes from motets were borrowed in the same way, together with the " text-name ". A composer who, exceptionally, invented his *cantus firmus,* termed his composition *Missa sine nomine,* (Mass without name).

The opening bars of a transcription of the first Kyrie from Dufay's Mass, *Se la face ay pale,* (c. 1450) is given below. The tenor is based on the composer's own chanson of that name (" My face is pale; know the reason is love . . ."), the melody of which begins thus :

Ex:34

SE LA FACE AY PA —————— LE

—written a few years before the Mass, in what we should call the major mode.

Here is the beginning of the Kyrie of the Mass, with this phrase in the tenor; the Mass itself leans towards the Lydian mode :

Ex:35

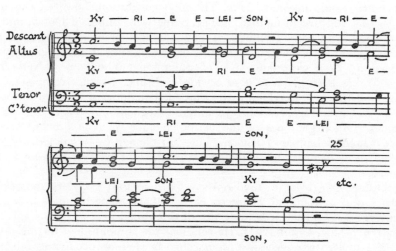

It should be remarked that in the originals of polyphonic works (even printed editions well into the sixteenth century) indications as to the fitting of the syllables of the text to the notes are frequently vague, leaving much for the singer (and the editor) to decide for himself.

Another device which developed in connection with Mass writing was the " head-motif " or " motto-theme ", whereby the same material was employed for a short while at the beginning of each of the sections. A somewhat more startling type which emerged a generation later than Dufay was the parody Mass. The borrowing here was not just the *cantus firmus* but a good deal of the contrapuntal material of the original, which might be a motet but was, as often as not, a cheerful secular chanson. A remarkable sixteenth century example of this procedure was Orlando Lassus' Mass *Puisque j'ay perdu mes amours*.[26*] The four parts of the Kyrie are almost note for note those of the chanson for several of the opening bars. The other movements use modifications. Composers took a pride in showing how they could present the material, reshape it, and then lead away independently for a time. The term had no pejorative import; a parody Mass was as devotional in tone as any other type.

To return to the age of Dufay, upon which the triumphs of the sixteenth century polyphony were built. The only musician comparable with the Cambrai master was Gilles de Binch ("Binchois"—c. 1400–60), who spent most of his life at the Burgundian Court, and, for all that he was in holy orders, mainly in the composition of secular music. His chansons, of which over fifty have survived, were more famous even than those of Dufay. A hearing of some of these (as well as examples of Dufay's) is well worth while, for they combine the new style of contrapuntal skill with a joyous and most attractive freshness and ease.[27*]

The Netherland School

Many French composers contemporary with Dufay and influenced by him must remain neglected here. The next generation, however, contained names that still live in musical history. Some were pupils of Dufay, and the more prominent were Flemings. A new intellectual quality began to permeate the Frankish art, a Germanic earnestness that in religious music evolved an even closer-knit style of polyphony. The name "Netherland School" has been given to a succession of Franco-Flemish composers who developed this new trend, and who shaped the course of Western European music for several generations. Johannes Okeghem may be said to be its founder. Other Flemings of the period include Jacob Obrecht, Antoine Busnois and Johannes Tinctoris. The last-named we have already considered as a theorist; his contemporaries thought well of him as a composer.

Johannes Okeghem (c. 1420–95) was born in East Flanders and studied under Dufay at Cambrai. He seems early to have made his mark as a musician, for in 1454 he was holding the distinguished post of first chaplain to the French king, Charles VII. He retained this appointment for the rest of his life, under two successive monarchs, as well as occupying other responsible positions. Another title given him, more descriptive of his actual duties, was *Maître de la chapelle de chant du roy* . . . His effect on his contemporaries was such that he was spoken of as "Prince of Music", apparently in terms of awe. It is necessary to mention the widespread admiration given to him in his lifetime, since many writers of musical history have treated him with far less than justice. He was *not* a dry-as-dust pedant, but an imaginative and progressive composer. His work was *not* "marred by features of positive ugliness", as anyone who has heard any quantity of his music will have realised. The kings of France were able to call the best available musician to their service, and no doubt they did so.

Regarding the legend of empty ingenuity which has attached itself to the period—even in Dufay's and Dunstable's time the fever for canon writing had begun, and the Netherlanders certainly carried the art to highly complicated and sometimes perverse lengths. Some of the inverted, mirror and crab canon-games may have been musically worthless, but a great deal of the canonic writing as applied to Mass and motet was very effective, especially in Okeghem's case. He shared with Bach and Mozart the power of moving in shackles with ease and grace. One of his most astonishing contrapuntal feats is the four-part *Missa Prolationum*. The four prolations $(\frac{2}{4}, \frac{3}{4}, \frac{6}{8}, \frac{9}{8},)$ are employed simultaneously by the voice-parts in a mingling of rhythms, while the work is written throughout in canon, often double canon, with frequent use of augmentation. A transcription of the opening bars of the Kyrie, given below (from Reese, op. cit., p. 135), exemplifies not only the rhythmic intricacies found throughout, but the use of double canon with augmentation:

Ex:36

An even more astounding fact is that this highly-wrought composition is actually attractive music. It is not to be thought, however, that Okeghem's compositions were continuously sown with technical devices. At times his writing was comparatively straightforward, for his great contrapuntal resources were conditioned by liturgical and artistic requirements. In his works and those of his followers the various voices often tended to assume

prominence in turn, progressing towards the sixteenth century ideal of absolute equality of interest, and giving the effect of successive waves of flowing
sound. Already the trick of hiding cadence seams by means of overlapping
new entries had been learned, but Okeghem's continuous use of it established it as a permanent feature of Netherlandish polyphony. We also find
at the time an increasing employment of discords of suspension. The use
of frequent imitation of a distinctive theme in the various parts caused the
older unifying device, that of isorhythm, to drop out of existence.

Many of Okeghem's manuscripts seem to have perished. Only eleven
complete Masses and some ten motets survive, together with a few secular
chansons. The reputation of his compositions among his contemporaries,
however, seems to have been profound. Though his music went a little out
of fashion towards the end of his life (other stars were blazing), all musical
Europe mourned his death. Among the many elegiac tributes paid him,
musical and literary, was a glowing one from the great scholar and satirist
Erasmus, who was not in the habit of suffering pedants gladly.[28*]

The same flowing, undulating religious style is heard in the Masses and
motets of Okeghem's younger contemporary, the Dutchman Jacob Obrecht
(c. 1453–1505), even richer in harmony and melody and more progressive in
their feeling towards tonality. Obrecht filled various music posts in his native
Netherlands, but also travelled in Italy, a fact that may account for the
more exotic features of his style. It was at Ferrara in Italy that he died.
He *may* have been the composer of an early " scenic " Passion according to
St. Matthew.[29] [30*]

Brief mention may be made of Antoine Busnois (d. 1492), a pupil of
Okeghem, who spent most of his life at the court of Burgundy. His secular
and church music was mentioned with approval by Tinctoris, and included
a famous *L'Homme armé* Mass.

Italy in the last quarter of the fifteenth century was looming very large
in the viewpoint of highly trained and often poorly paid Franco-Flemish
musicians at the threshold of their careers. The healing of the Schism which
meant the return of the Papal See to Rome in 1420 has already been mentioned. The Curia after its re-establishment continued to favour Frankish
music and musicians, and as the years passed other Northerners sought the
rewards, both ecclesiastical and secular, that Italian employment offered.
Soon after 1470 something like an invasion began, and Franco-Flemish
composers, with their consummate command of the new dignified counterpoint, were soon taking over the most attractive musical posts. The " occupation " lasted for almost a century, until native musicians learned to beat
the Northerners at their own game, and to produce an even richer art that
carried Italy to the leadership of musical Europe.

Printing of Music

In one important development of the time Italy was already in the van.
This was in the matter of a really practical method of music-printing (from
metal type). In the days of private patronage and before copyright laws the
only gain to the composer was the possibility of a greater diffusion of his

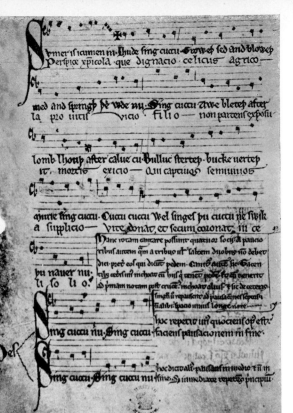

7. The most famous piece of 13th century English music, and the only known six-part piece earlier than the 15th century. Also the only known example of the combination of *rota* (i.e. canon) and *rondellus* (where in two parts one singer repeats the words and melodic phrase of the other).

British Museum

. Secular instrumentalists depicted
y a Flemish artist. In the right
oreground is a portative organ.
pposite are pipe and tabor,
riangle, shawm, straight trumpet,
arp and two lutes. Among the
rowd can be distinguished further
hawms, a psaltery and, possibly,
agpipes.

British Museum

9. An angelic conductor, painted late in the fifteenth century in the
church of SS Apostoli, Rome, by Melozzo da Forli. The baton is being
held in a remarkably modern fashion.

music, but posterity benefited, inasmuch as more music tended to survive. As it is, an enormous amount must have perished. " It has been reliably estimated that about half of all the surviving music written before 1600 is now known only from a single manuscript or printed source." (Thurston Dart, op. cit., p. 136, note). The pioneer printer was Ottoviano Petrucci of Fossombrone, who from 1500 produced at his native town and at Venice, editions of Masses (Obrecht's for example), motets and chansons by composers of the day. Similar enterprises soon started in other European cities, where men like Oeglin of Augsburg and Attaignant of Paris imitated Petrucci in combining the occupations of printing and publishing. Both these latter used improved and cheaper processes, as compared with Petrucci's, but for a long while printed music was an expensive luxury.

More " Netherland" Composers

The international career pursued by the more prominent Netherland musicians of the time is exemplified by the life of Henricus (Heinrich) Isaac (c. 1450–1517), an extremely prolific composer about whose early career little is known, but who as a young man won to the post of household musician to Lorenzo de' Medici, the highly cultured " tyrant " of Florence. He must certainly have been exceptionally brilliant to have satisfied Lorenzo. Isaac provided music of every sort for the Medici court and the Florentines in general for many years, and after the death of Lorenzo and the temporary eclipse of the Medici rule he sought and was given distinguished employment with the Emperor Maximilian, at Vienna, Innsbruck and Constance. He was honoured throughout Europe for the quality of both his sacred and secular music. A notable feat of composition was his *Choralis Constantinus*, a collection of fifty-eight settings (mostly in four parts) of the Proper of the Mass throughout the year, a task that had not been attempted since the time of Perotin, three hundred years before. The earliest version of the famous " Innsbruck " chorale tune is found in his music.[31*]

Alexander Agricola (c. 1446–1506) was another far travelled and highly competent Netherlander. Possibly a pupil of Okeghem, Agricola held posts in France and Italy as a singer and composer, and ended his life in Spain in the service of Philip, King of Castile and Leon. Petrucci printed a number of both his and Isaac's compositions.

Josquin Desprez (c. 1450–1521), a young man from Condé, was chief among the many gifted pupils of Okeghem. His true name was probably Josse van der Weyden, " Josquin " being a friendly diminutive. He had had an early education at Condé Cathedral, and with Okeghem he mastered all the current contrapuntal devices. He probably learned much also from the new melodic, harmonic and generally expressive resources of Obrecht. Then he took the golden road to Italy, where his services were given to various ducal courts, and, from 1486–94, to the Papal Choir at Rome. His earlier work was highly efficient contrapuntally, but was in no way distinguished above that of other clever young Netherland composers. In the South his genius ripened, and in his later work there evolved a simpler, more luminous style, in which harmony, modulation (in the modal sense), and artistic use

G

of discord combine to give his music a quality new to his contemporaries. One of his pupils summed it up in the term *musica reservata*. We hear a great deal from this time onward as to " reservata " music, the subtleties of which, the writers averred, could only be appreciated by cultured audiences. Its full meaning is still not altogether clear. There was a dawning desire at the time, as part of the humanist outlook, to express as fully as possible in terms of music the ideas and emotions of the text, and this Josquin was held to have accomplished as none other had done. One is reminded of an apophthegm of Martin Luther, an admirer of Desprez and no mean musician himself—" Other musicians do with notes what they can, Josquin what he likes ". A further aspect of the " reservata " style was the manner of the musical performance, which needed to be tasteful and sensitive, with the necessary additions of improvised ornamentation. These requirements could be fully met by the Franco-Flemish singers of the period, trained to this style.

The following quotation from Paul Henry Lang's *Music in Western Civilisation* (p. 194) seems to give a succinct summing-up of Josquin's position. It begins with a reference to his earlier works :

" . . . Many of them are somewhat archaic : we find even a polylingual motet, which was rare at this late period. The Netherlandish penchant for complicated canonic construction is also evident in some exceptionally clever virtuoso pieces. Then came Italy, and the sober northerner, already fascinated by the majestic art of Obrecht, forgot the mystical polyphonic flow of his forbears to apply all his great technical wealth to the sublime, clear, well-defined and articulated, emotionally profound and varied music which became the quintessence of Renaissance musical art. Josquin was the creator of the new Mass, the new motet, and the new chanson, and it was in these works that we see the approach of the *a cappella* ideal."

Josquin, the main bulk of his music written, returned to France about 1500 and took service with Louis XII, though there were further travellings to Italy and elsewhere before he retired, as canon of Condé, to the Cathedral of his youth.

Of his compositions, a good quantity has survived in the printings of Petrucci and others. About thirty Masses and over a hundred motets are known. Among the latter is the celebrated *Miserere* for five voices, full of effective devices and still performed. He wrote a large number of French and Italian secular pieces, in which the two styles are clearly differentiated.[32*]

Of lesser but still considerable fame was another pupil of Okeghem, Pierre de la Rue (d. 1518). Born in Picardy, he served the House of Austria in the Low Countries all his life. His royal patrons, particularly Margaret of Austria, seem to have been enthusiastic as to his abilities. His best known work is the low-pitched, dark-toned Requiem Mass, a most effective composition, full of rhythmic subtleties.[33*]

A spate of highly competent Franco-Flemish composers succeeded Josquin, some of them his pupils. One of the latter, possibly the finest of the group, was Jean Mouton (c. 1470–1522), whose music was "in the hands of everyone". Others (a preponderance of French) were Loyset Compère, Antoine Brumel, Antoine de Févin, François de Layolle and Elzéar Genet— mere names to all but the keenest scholars among us, but clearly meaning a great deal to their own generation. For instance, the Papal Choir continued to perform the admired Masses of "Carpentras", otherwise Elzéar Genet, for long years after his death, and it required the stern hand of authority to compel them to abandon them for the new-fangled music of an upstart by the name of Palestrina.

England—The Early Tudor School

The eclipse of English music which Tinctoris noted was no doubt assisted by the troubled social and political situation which, culminating in the Wars of the Roses, was tranquillised only with the establishment of the first Tudor, Henry VII. The most significant musical name belonging to this hiatus that has come down to us is that of Gilbert Banaster (c. 1445–87), an organist, composer and Gentleman of the Chapel Royal who held the favour of a succession of monarchs, and who wrote a five-part motet, still preserved, for the marriage of Henry VII and Elizabeth of York.

Henry gave encouragement to the Chapel Royal, which led a vigorous revival of English composition. The chief treasury of the music of these decades is the famous Eton Manuscript, which seems to date around 1490–1502. Part of it is lost, but it contained originally over a hundred motets and Magnificats. The composers most frequently represented are John Browne (c. 1426–98), Richard Davy (c. 1467–c. 1516), William Cornyshe and Robert Fayrfax. There are other manuscript sources. Another name of importance, not represented in the Eton collection is that of Hugh Aston (c. 1480–1552), a churchman and an early composer of keyboard music. At a later date came John Taverner, the greatest composer of the period that ended with the upheavals (musical and general) of the Reformation in England.

Regarding the Eton Manuscript composers mentioned (together with other worthy names that must remain unrecorded here)—all were in some kind of ecclesiastical employment, Gentlemen of the Chapel Royal, organists or masters of choirs at leading establishments. The music of most of them shows but little acquaintance with the Continental advances. The old English sonority was there, frequently aided by the employment of five, six or even more vocal parts, and by the device of contrasting choral divisions. The Continental head-motif technique is sometimes found, but relatively little use was made of imitation, and the music lacks the spice of the Continental use of discord.

Robert Fayrfax (1464–1521) must be counted as the best of the school, both for the sheer quality of his music, and the fact that he made a deal more use of imitative counterpoint than did his colleagues. Thirty-three works of his are on record. Of these, five complete Masses (all in five parts) survive. One of these, *O Bone Jesu*, is a parody Mass, the material being taken from the composer's own motet of the same name. There are also a dozen surviving motets (some of them unfortunately lacking essential parts) and a few secular part-songs, mostly for three voices. Fayrfax seems to have delighted in the variety afforded by a constant changing, in the course of a composition, of the number of voice parts employed, from two to five. Apparently he headed the Chapel Royal when that body, which included Cornyshe, accompanied Henry VIII to the Field of the Cloth of Gold, where they sang to the admiration of all.[34*]

William Cornyshe (d. 1523) also wrote some worthy church music, but is chiefly remembered for his vigorous three-part songs, that included the celebrated *Hoyda, hoyda, joly rutterkin*. He was versatile in other ways. A favourite of Henry's, he was employed at Court not only as a composer of incidental music, but as a playwright and actor as well. Henry VIII was something of a musician himself, and kept in Court employment a number of French, Flemish and Italian instrumentalists, who must have had some influence on the course of English music. To judge by royal inventories, Henry was the possessor of a fabulous collection of musical instruments.

Fragments of a " scenic " Passion according to St. Matthew, composed by Richard Davy (c. 1500), are in the Eton Manuscript. The liturgical Passions that were (and still are) sung during Holy Week to plainchant suffered some amendment of treatment in late medieval times. The practice began of supplying composed polyphony for the crowd choruses and the utterances of characters other than Christ and the Narrator. This type is usually termed a " scenic " Passion, and Davy's incomplete version was once thought to be the earliest surviving example in Europe. However, two more English examples (St. Matthew and St. Luke) have recently been discovered, seeming to date from c. 1440. They consist only of the polyphonic parts, and are written for three voices. See Grove, Vol. VI; article PASSION MUSIC.[35*]

John Taverner (c. 1495–1545) was the finest technician of the Early Tudor School. Writing with English suavity he yet showed a complete grasp of the Continental style of counterpoint. His background was comparatively obscure. He was trained at Tattershall Collegiate Church in Lincolnshire, and became master of the choristers there. However, he attracted the notice of the Bishop of Lincoln, whose recommendation gained him a similar but more distinguished post at Cardinal Wolsey's newly-founded College at Oxford in 1526. It was at these two places that all his magnificent church music was written, in what might have been only the first part of his career. But in 1530 he was dismissed for heretical opinions, and abandoned music to become an agent of Thomas Cromwell. The rest of his life he spent as a Protestant zealot.

His output includes eight Masses and twenty-eight motets, small in total but significant in quality. His most famous work is the *Western Wynd* Mass, all the movements of which are based on a single secular tune, treated in such masterly and consistent fashion that the composition has been termed " thirty-four variations for four-part choir ".[36*]

Scotland

The Scottish composer Robert Carver (b. c. 1490), a monk of Scone Abbey, produced not only a nineteen-voice motet, *O Bone Jesu*, but also the only British example of a *L'Homme armé* Mass.

Germany

Music in Germany was cultivated by all classes, and we have already considered such earlier movements as those of the Minnesinger and Meistersinger. Though by the middle of the fifteenth century cultured Germany was under the spell of Franco-Flemish polyphony, and was destined in due course to submit to a similar Italian domination, the writing-out (about 1460) of *Lochamer's Liederbuch* shows the existence of a wealth of native German folk-melody. Later in the century and in the first half of the sixteenth a large number of attractive contrapuntal German songs (the principal melody in the tenor) were produced by such men as Heinrich Finck (1445–1527), Thomas Stolzer (1450–1526) and Paul Hofhaimer (1459–1537). Contemporary printings of lute music show that these works were also performed as solo songs for tenor voice, with the original topmost and bass parts rendered as a lute accompaniment. Many of the works in their choral forms have had modern revivals. Early in the sixteenth century appeared a Germanic composer of international stature, Ludwig Senfl (c. 1492–1555), a disciple of Isaac and his successor in Maximilian's service.

However, the time of Germany was not yet, except in all things connected with organs and organ music. Pedal boards had proved a practical proposition for the instruments of Germany and the Netherlands in the fourteenth century, and thereafter Germany had taken the lead in organ-building. By the early sixteenth century there were in Germany organs with two manuals (a third was soon to be added in some churches), independent pedal boards and a variety of stops. France and Spain were not far behind, but Italy, strangely enough, lagged a great deal mechanically. English organs, it was once believed, did not acquire pedal-boards until well into the eighteenth century, but recent research has shown that pedals were not unknown here in the early seventeenth.

The first German organist of European reputation (henceforth such men were steadily recurrent features of the history of music) appeared in the mid-fifteenth century in the person of the blind Conrad Paumann (c. 1410–73). He wrote a treatise, *Fundamentum Organisandi,* on organ composition, and some of his works for organ survive in other manuscripts. There followed Hans Buchner (1483–1538), in whose compositions a considerable advance in technique is seen.[37*]

Instrumental Music in the Fifteenth Century (See Plate 8).

Although a composition of the period, sacred or secular, might be represented only by vocal parts, it is likely both that these parts were frequently doubled or replaced by instruments, and that they were freely treated with ornamentation. Many instruments were capable of sustaining drones, and undoubtedly such effects were used by bagpipes, by the flat-bridged viols of the age with their arched bows, hurdy-gurdies, portative organs fitted with drone pipes, and double recorders. Added to this was the use, as in the fourteenth century, of bell-chimes and a variety of percussion instruments, for which no parts were written, but for the frequent employment of which there is plenty of evidence. Always it must be borne in mind that through medieval, Renaissance and even baroque times improvisation was a highly important factor in all music.

As the fifteenth century drew towards its close we hear less of such instruments as the portative organ, the psaltery, dulcimer, bagpipes and the older " fiddle " types. Tinctoris speaks approvingly of the new kind of viol, in its various sizes, and tells of two skilled players whom he heard rendering chansons very beautifully. Another instrument, from Arab sources, was coming more and more to the front—the lute. Though its technique was a " plucking " one, Tinctoris notes that a skilful player could perform on it in four parts. Sketchily, of course, but, a significant factor, here was an instrument that was developing an advanced *instrumental* technique and not merely reproducing a vocal line. The lute was destined to be for a time the domestic instrument *par excellence,* but other instruments were emerging that were even better able to reproduce the intricacies of contrapuntal music in " chamber " circles.

The problem of fitting a keyboard to instruments of the psaltery and dulcimer type may have been solved as early as the thirteenth century. Certainly some such instrument, called by Machaut *eschaquier d'Engleterre,* was in use by the middle of the fourteenth. In 1360 Edward III presented an " eschaquier " to the captive King John of France. Around 1440 Arnaud of Zwolle produced a treatise that described both (a) the harpsichord, and (b) the clavichord types. Notes were produced in the case of type (a) from the *plucking* of wire strings by metal plectra attached to the key-levers; in the case of type (b) from the strings being struck by metal tangents. The instruments described had ranges of about three octaves. Later, quill plectra were introduced. By 1500 harpsichords with a second register were being made in Italy. Fuller mention of the mechanism and construction of the two types will be made in the next chapter.

England must have had a good deal of interest in such keyboard playing even as early as the beginning of the sixteenth century. Two pieces for virginal (the English type of harpsichord) survive from about 1525, *Hornpype* and *Lady Cary's Dompe,* the first certainly and the second possibly by Hugh Aston (see p. 98). Both show evidence of a real keyboard technique which must have taken some time to develop. There may have been an early school of such composition.

There is plentiful evidence as to the large numbers of professional instrumentalists employed at the courts of great magnates and even by the municipal authorities of the larger cities. It is clear also that the private family was not without its own domestic music-makings. The best reported musical entertainment of the fifteenth century was perhaps that afforded by Duke Philip of Burgundy to his banquet guests at Lille in 1454. It was the occasion when there was presented the celebrated giant pie which concealed

" twenty-eight persons playing on divers instruments ". Chroniclers of the time report a fantastic succession of " turns ", not only from the pie but from a model church. Half of these items were solely instrumental, while various instruments accompanied the singers. The chronicler's description of the affair is too long to be given here, but is readily available. It affords an instructive glimpse of the variety and resource of fifteenth century secular music.[38]

As always, dance music was needed for every walk of life. There have survived fifteenth century illustrations of courtly dance scenes. A Florentine wedding-chest painting of 1420 shows a dance band in action on a raised platform overlooking the open-air dancers, and confirms Tinctoris' description of the usual outdoor combination. It was a " four-piece " one, three instruments of the shawm type and a sackbut.† The nearest equivalents to these in modern colours would be cor anglais and trombone, each probably, much more refined in tone.[39]* A Brussels manuscript of about 1450 supplies not only instructions regarding the two favourite dances of the time, the dignified basse-danse and the quicker pas de Brabant (=saltarello), but gives a clue as to the methods of dance-band playing, for it also sets out a number of tunes in black breves i.e. with no indication as to rhythm. (Several of these have been identified as belonging to well-known chansons.) From other evidence it would seem that these notes represent the step-units of any of the dances, and would be played by the " tenor " instrument, in this case the pommer, the rhythms being varied in accordance with the kind of dance measure needed. The other instruments were subordinate, and supplied improvised counterpoints (or perhaps stock ones). This was haut (=loud) music. Within doors a group of bas (=soft) instruments would be used. These might be (a) treble viol, lute or recorder; (b) shawm or tenor viol; (c) harp or psaltery. Such quiet combinations might indeed accompany a singer in a chanson.

Tablature

Vocal staff notation had by the end of the fifteenth century reached a general state of near-uniformity. But tablatures—systems that indicated not the note but rather how it was to be produced—were still common with regard to instruments, even for harpsichord and organ. Side by side with normal notation organ tablatures endured to the time of Bach. The lute and similar instruments knew no other system. On the whole strings and woodwind were content with staff notation.

† See Plate 14. It would seem that here we have three discant shawms, to the exclusion of a larger shawm-type (pommer) that was frequently included. Of modern instruments the bassoon would be the nearest to the pommer in tone-colour.

NOTES

1 The ternary division had been considered "perfect" because it consisted of a "beginning", a "middle" and an "end". Medieval philosophy, and in particular the dogma of the Holy Trinity, played a great part in contemporary conceptions as to rhythm.

2 The standard work on the subject of medieval and Renaissance notation is *The Notation of Polyphonic Music* (900–1600) by Willi Apel (*The Mediaeval Academy of America*). See also the article NOTATION in Grove, Vol. VI.

3 Thurston Dart observes (*The Interpretation of Music—Hutchinson*, p. 161): "Many early writers encouraged the use of *musica ficta* in plainsong; thus there are some fourteenth century manuscripts of plainsong in which nearly every cadential F, C or G is sharpened, and a Carthusian monk writing in 1500 maintained that in plainsong phrases like D F G or G F G the Fs should always be sharpened. To our ears plainsong handled in this way loses one of its special glories, its modality, but there seems little doubt that in plainsong, as in so much other music, early musicians were less modal than we have often wanted to make them. Accidentals, like ornaments, were often a matter of extemporisation, to be added in accordance with contemporary rules that have long since been forgotten; we may not see them when we look at an early manuscript, but that does not mean that they were equally invisible to a man of the past."

4* HMS III has a recording of a two-part *chace, Se je chant' mains . . .* the text of which describes a hawking scene. The original is found in the mid-fourteenth century Ivrea MS. This modern transcription is that of H. Besseler (1925), but Gustave Reese has pointed out that J. Handschin's version (1949), with a third unison entry of the canon at bar eleven, is more likely to represent the original intention.

5 The whole of the canon is quoted by Gustave Reese (op. cit. p. 336)—after *Die Musikstücke des Prager Kodex XI E 9*, 1931 by F. Kammerer. I have recently been informed by Professor Gustave Reese that Nino Perrotta has shown that this solution of the canon is incorrect. He (Gustave Reese) will be dealing with the matter in his second edition of *Music in the Middle Ages*.

6* This modern transcription of the rondeau is from *De Machaut, Guillaume—Musikalische Werke*, ed. by Friedrich Ludwig, I, 63 (1926). It is quoted in full by Gustave Reese, op. cit., pp. 351–2. It will be seen that the musical pattern is an enlarged version of the normal one, A̲B̲ A A̲ A B A̲B̲ (the "refrain" text-phrases are indicated by underlinings). The actual sentence "Ma fin est mon commencement, et mon commencement ma fin" would have been recognised by medieval listeners as being a familiar "motto".
HMS III has a recording of what is only the first AB of the text, but which of course comprises the whole of the *musical* material. The speed of performance seems rather slow for what is after all an early example of a musical jest.

7* HMS III has a recording of the Benedictus from Machaut's Mass. All the parts are more or less isorhythmic, even the tenor, which derives from the relevant portions of the plainchant of Mass XVII (See *Graduale Romanum*, p. 54*). The two upper parts make use of the hocket.
Machaut's Mass is the earliest known complete polyphonic setting of the Ordinary by a single composer. The so-called "Messe de Tournai" is even earlier in date (the first half of the fourteenth century), but is reckoned to be a collection of numbers by different composers.

A performance of the whole work is recorded on DGG APM 14063. In both this and the HMS recording instruments are used freely to double voice parts.

8   Reproduced from HAM I (No. 48), after the transcription (No. 25) made by W. Apel, *The Notation of Polyphonic Music.* Illustration 11 on p. 81 is a photograph of the manuscript, with its extraordinary notation. In the course of it almost all the mensuration signs belonging to the period are put to use, i.e.

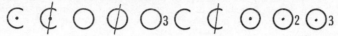

9   e.g., Vol. I, p. 19 (Everyman ed.). Some of the ladies and young men could play and sing "with great skill". All knew "how to tread a measure" to the music of viol and lute. They performed "a stately carol", and then "fell to singing ditties dainty and gay".

10* HMS III has a recording of a chanson by Johannes Ciconia, *O Rosa Bella,* for voice and instruments.

11* The whole of the G. da Cascia madrigal is transcribed in HAM I (No. 50). HMS III has a recording of the work, in which portions of it are treated, in interesting fashion, as instrumental interludes. The original transcription was by J. Wolf—*Geschichte der Mensural-Notation,* III, No. 38 (1904).

12* HMS III has a recording of a three-part ballata by Landini, *Amar si li alti . . .* for voice and instruments; also of a *caccia* by "Maestro Piero", a "first period" composer.

13* This *Credo* is printed in Vol. II of *The Old Hall Manuscript,* ed. Ramsbotham & Collins (Plainsong and Medieval Music Society, 1935), p. 1. It is recorded in HMS III, and a portion of it (from which the quotation is taken) printed in the accompanying Handbook (III), pp. 24–5, (Oxford University Press).

14* HMS III has a recording of this carol, some of the stanzas being omitted. The transcription is from *Early Bodleian Music,* ii, p. 109—J. Stainer.

15* HMS III has a recording of a three-part vocal version of *Angelus ad virginem,* together with renderings of the Agincourt Song and *Tapster—Drinker . . .*

16 Version by Gustave Reese—*Music in the Renaissance,* p. 13.

17 From a Bologna MS., facsimilied by Wooldridge, *Early English Harmony* (pl. 59–60) and quoted in *A History of Music in England*—Walker (rev. J. A. Westrup), p. 29.

18 From HAM I No 62—quoted from *Denkmäler der Tonkunst in Oesterreich, VII, 197.*

19* HMS III has an impressive recording of the whole of this work. It was possibly written for the coronation of the child-king, Henry VI, in Paris.

20* HMS III has a recording of the *O Rosa bella* here mentioned, and gives Dunstable as the composer. cf. the Ciconia setting, also recorded.

21 We read that Philip, Duke of Burgundy, refused to confirm the appointment of a French musician already well known as a composer, since he had found by personal trial that his singing voice was not satisfactory.

22 The principal sources of our knowledge of fifteenth century music are the seven manuscripts known as the Trent Codices (from Trent Cathedral in S. Tyrol) which contain over 1,500 compositions. Dunstable, Dufay and many of their contemporaries, French, Flemish and English, are well represented. There are also works by Italian and German composers.

23 Modern performances of pre-Dufay polyphonic music are frequently rendered by voices in chorus, a practice, from a historical point of view, to be deprecated.

24* HMS III has a recording of the first part of this motet. Attention is called to the sudden and dramatic C minor triad which begins the four-part section.

25 Example as printed in *Masterpieces of Music before 1750* by Carl Parrish and John F. Ohl (Faber & Faber), p. 45, from the transcription by A. Smijers of the Trent Codex 88; Sistine Chapel Lib., 14, 25, and printed in *Algemeene Muziek Geschiedenis*, Utrecht, 1938, p. 101.
In the other movements of the Mass Dufay did not trouble to write out the Tenor part again, merely giving written instructions as to what modifications were to be made regarding its time values in each movement, a common enough labour-saving device at the time.

26* HMS IV has a recording of the Benedictus and Hosanna of this Mass.

27* A characteristic example of Binchois' art is the chanson *Filles à Marier*, recorded in HMS III. With it is the charming Dufay chanson *Pour l'Amour,* showing effective points of imitation.

28* HMS III has a recording of the Kyrie movement from Okeghem's four-part Mass *Fors seulement*. The *cantus firmus* material was taken from a chanson by Okeghem himself; hence the title. The music illustrates well the "seamless texture", the "inexorable flow" and altogether the dignified sincerity of Okeghem's style.

29 See Grove, VI: article, PASSION MUSIC.

30* HMS III has a recording of Obrecht's four-part motet *Si Oblitus fuero . . .* But the opinion of Gustave Reese (resulting from the researches of A. Smijers) is that this motet is by a contemporary of Obrecht's, Ninot le Petit.

31* HMS III has recordings of three pieces by Isaac, clearly vocal in origin, but intended for performance by instruments. Chansons and other vocal pieces were often treated thus. One of the pieces is a version of the famous "Innsbruck" tune, written in canon form.

32* HMS III has recordings of some excellent examples of Josquin's music; (a) part of the Sanctus from the second of his Masses on the secular theme, *L'Homme Armé,* showing a straightforward use of the *cantus firmus*; (b) a short motet, *Tribulatio et Augustia,* full of effective imitation; (c) a racy Italian "part-song" type (frottola), *El Grillo*; and (d) a charming four-part French chanson, *Je ne puis tenir d'aimer.*

33* HMS III has a recording of the Introit of this Requiem Mass, pitched somewhat higher than the original effectively sombre level.

34* HMS III has a recording of Fayrfax's *Regali* Magnificat, the verses in alternate settings of plainchant and contrapuntal chorus. The reader is referred to Grove Vol. III; article, FAYRFAX, for an up-to-date appreciation of that master's work.

35* HMS III has a recording of one of the four-part choruses of the Davy Passion, preceded by a chanted phrase of the Narrator.

36* HMS III has a recording of the Benedictus from Taverner's Mass *Gloria tibi Trinitas*. The name is taken from the text of a Trinity Sunday antiphon, the melody of which is used for most of the Mass as a *cantus firmus*. This antiphon melody is also the stock theme for scores of string fantasias, all termed *In Nomine,* by sixteenth and seventeenth century English composers. The reason for this title has only recently been elucidated, being traced to this particular Benedictus, where in one passage the antiphon *cantus* becomes more than usually prominent, at moments when it is linked with the Mass text "in nomine Domini ".

37* HMS III has recordings of organ pieces by each of these composers.

38 See, for example, Reese, op. cit., pp. 57-8, and Thurston Dart, op. cit., pp. 156-7. The pie was of course "opened" to allow the various performers to emerge and return. Thurston Dart makes the light-hearted suggestion that here is the origin of "Sing a Song of Sixpence". This may well be true, though it would appear that time has taken toll of four of the songsters.

39* Modern equivalents of shawm, pommer and sackbut are used in a HMS III recording of a dance-piece by a Spanish court-musician, inscribed *Alta*—probably equivalent to the *saltarello*. With the *alta* are recordings of two other instrumental ensembles, a chanson by the French composer Compère (clearly humorous), and a German peasant-dance. This latter consists really of two "paired" dances, contrasted in speed and rhythm, an early example of the *Tanz-Nachtanz* type (see p. 132). All three compositions belong to the last quarter of the fifteenth century.

CHAPTER V

The Climax of Polyphony and the Era of the Madrigal

THE period of the sixteenth century, i.e. the Late Renaissance, marked
the climax of the development of vocal polyphony, the last great exponents of which were Lassus, Palestrina, Victoria and Byrd. The weaving
together of different strands of melody was still the prime consideration in
composition throughout this era. But new factors were at work which turned
the attention of musicians more and more towards the consideration of
harmony as an end in itself—a recognition of chords *as* chords. Finally,
approaching the turn of the century a changing outlook is apparent, a movement towards the regarding of the " top-line " melody as the principal
factor, and a composition as being founded on a series of harmonies, which
accompany the melody and are built on the firm foundation of the bass.
But before the coming of these changes the greater composers, who were
in one way or another concerned with church music, still gave most of their
attention to the polyphonic motet and Mass. Let us recall what is meant
by these two forms.

Motet and Mass—Sixteenth Century Technique

A motet was " a short composition for voices intended primarily for unaccompanied singing, written in contrapuntal style upon a Latin text which
is usually liturgical or quasi-liturgical in character ", (Grove). Another name
in published collections for motets was *Cantiones Sacrae*. In England after
the Protestant Reformation we meet the term " anthem ", which is applied
to a composition in motet form, but using an English text. Thus composers
like Tallis and Byrd wrote both motets and anthems.

The musical setting of the Mass was mostly concerned with what is termed
the *Ordinary*, i.e. that part of the rite which remains invariable throughout
the seasons of the year. It usually involved six divisions. These were: (1)
Kyrie eleison (Lord, have mercy), (2) *Gloria* (Glory to God in the
highest . . .), (3) *Credo* (I believe . . .), (4) *Sanctus* (Holy, holy . . .), (4a)
Benedictus (Blessed is he . . .) and (5) *Agnus Dei* (Lamb of God . . .). The
Benedictus text is really part of the *Sanctus*, but was usually given separate

musical treatment. In the later history of Mass settings there are to be found further subdivisions.

Throughout the previous (fifteenth) century the polyphonic motet and Mass had been of the most consummate craftsmanship, in which the devices of close imitation—canon and the like—had been carried to remarkable lengths of human ingenuity. As we have already seen, the Tenor Mass, whereby a single part (*cantus firmus*) sustained a theme around which other parts wove counterpoints, proved a satisfactory way of obtaining a musical unity. For that purpose *cantus firmi* had been borrowed not only from plainchant, but from motets, hymns and even from secular compositions such as chansons and popular tunes in general. The Mass usually admitted, in its title, the origin of the *cantus firmus* material. Variety with unity had often been achieved by modifying the *cantus firmus* as it appeared in one or another of the sections of the Mass, or by using different parts of the borrowed material in the different sections.

In the sixteenth century the practice grew of using a much more flexible technique of imitation. Musical phrases were taken from the "source-composition" and used as short and separate *motifs* for setting the separate phrases or sentences of the verbal text, each voice entering in turn in imitation, and functioning as an equal partner. Such a section would end in some kind of cadence, and could be overlapped by the entry of the next motif with the next portion of the text, thus securing a continuous flow. A very clear-cut example of this procedure can be seen in the Sanctus of Palestrina's Mass *Aeterna Christi Munera* ("The eternal gifts of Christ . . ."). The material of the whole Mass is founded on the ancient Matins hymn of that name. The first three lines of the latter are as follows :

Ex: 37

(A) AE-TER-NA CHRI-STI MU———NE-RA

(B) A-PO-STO-LO-RUM GLO-RI-AM

(C) LAU-DES CA-NEN-TES DE-BI-TAS,

(the last line of the hymn, *Laetis canamus mentibus,* is set to phrase A.)

The Sanctus of the Mass begins with the first line (A), thus :

—to the single word *Sanctus*. For *Dominus Deus Sabaoth*, motif B is used, also imitatively. Later, motif C is employed in the same way for *Pleni sunt coeli*, and motif A returns for the final *Hosanna*. The first *Kyrie* of the Mass, quite brief, contents itself with motif A, in seven imitative entries. The Benedictus uses B and then C, each with its rhythm transformed.

There were naturally many varieties of, and departures from this technique. Time and again in contrast to the contrapuntal style, the chordal (homophonic) passage was used, this helping no doubt to increase the appreciation for pure harmonic effects. Shorter movements might be wholly in homophonic style.

Tonality, the modern "key" sense, was yet to come, and thus, while we readily recognise the chords chosen, the order in which they are placed—their juxtaposition—often sounds strange to our ears. The example which follows, from Palestrina's eight-part *Stabat Mater*, has been quoted often enough, but there is no better illustration in brief terms :[2]

Ex:39

However there are plenty of instances where the progressions differ very little from a modern conception of plain " ordinary " chords. The movement towards modern tonality was at least under way.

Another frequently used technique was the antiphonal effect of one part of the choir replying to another, especially striking when there was something more than the usual number of parts. We have already seen this device employed effectively by the early Tudor school of Fayrfax and his contemporaries. The *Stabat Mater* mentioned above has much expressive writing for two antiphonal four-part choirs, and is mostly homophonic in style.

In spite of these new devices sixteenth century composers continued to write Tenor Masses on occasion, though colouring them with the new tendencies. Another fifteenth century form, the parody Mass, remained in high favour. This, as we have seen, used the device of borrowing not merely a melodic phrase, but *all* the vocal parts making up the opening bars of a motet or even a secular work. The actual notes of the original soon faded as the Mass movement proceeded, but the composer took a pride in permeating all the separate sections of the Mass with suggestions of his borrowed material. The parody technique was not only an accepted but a highly recommended practice. Of Palestrina's hundred or so known Masses, fifty-two are of the parody type. We have already noted (p. 93) Orlandus Lassus' famous parody Mass, *Puisque j'ai perdu mes amours*, a dignified and devout composition which took its title and material from a popular French chanson of that name. Only occasionally did composers of the period invent their own Mass themes. It will be recalled that the use of an original theme was signalised by the title *Missa sine Nomine* (" Mass without name "). The term may indeed have sometimes been used in order to gloss over the identity of the original tune.

The sixteenth century motet shared with the Mass the progressive techniques described above, and was indeed, more than the Mass, the vehicle for still further advanced experiment in the hands of masters like Lassus, Victoria, Byrd and the Gabrielis. An important new attitude was the desire to give due illustration in the music to the meaning and atmosphere of the text. It was the great Netherlander Josquin Despres (d. 1521) who was first noted for his power of word-painting, developing a style to which one of his pupils gave the generally accepted name of *musica reservata* (see p. 97f.). In the fifteenth century, and before, it was the *musical* means employed that gave its shape to a composition. In the world of the Renaissance more and more was it felt that the religious themes of the motet text, and in secular music the word-pictures and emotions of the poet, should all find particular and fitting expression in their musical settings. Thus during the period not only were tonal resources stretched, but composers turned their attention to shaping freer musical patterns, suited to the ideas behind the words that they were setting to music. These objectives, as we shall see, were best realised in the development of the madrigal.

In theory the harmonic resources of the sixteenth century seem slight—that is, as far as dramatic music might be concerned, for the vocabulary, stated in modern terms consisted only of triads, in root position and in first inversion. Considerable colour was obtained, however, by the skilful use of passing notes and the discords of suspension. Furthermore, madrigal, chanson and even motet made more and more use of the chromatic alteration of notes, often obtaining startlingly modern effects thereby.[3*] With the approach of the end of the century harmonic innovations came thick and fast, the English Madrigal School taking a leading place in this respect, and discords began to be used without " preparation ".

Another evolution that the sixteenth century witnessed was the gradual withering of the Gregorian modes (probably owing to the methods of *Musica Ficta*—see p. 75f.) and their replacement by the modern " major-minor " tonalities, which developed from the Ionian and Aeolian modes. The Palestrina Mass that we have quoted from is in the transposed Ionian mode —otherwise F major. Even in the first part of the century a great deal of music, especially chansons and dance tunes, is quite plainly in the major key. Also they sometimes seemed to be making modulations to the dominant key and back—at least, that is how a modern listener would interpret the process. It seems probable that the " major " scale always was in existence in secular music (witness *Sumer is icumen in*), whatever name was attached to it. But modal influences were still apparent, especially in church compositions, well into the seventeenth century.

It may be as well in regard to " modulation " to bear in mind the warning of R. O. Morris (" The Structure of Music ", p. 83—O.U.P.) :—

" Modulation, in the sixteenth century, meant simply cadence and nothing more. For us it means the temporary establishment of a new tonal centre, but such a conception as this would have been quite outside the purview of Palestrina and his contemporaries. It is perfectly correct to speak of ' modulation ' as a feature of sixteenth century music but we must beware of reading into the term a wider significance than it could possibly have had at that time."

One last feature of sixteenth century music must be noticed, one that distinguished it strongly from later periods. This was the rhythmic independence of the part-writing in contrapuntal works. Dance tunes, of necessity, went along with a strong marking of regular rhythm, but no " tyranny of the bar-line " existed in Mass, motet and madrigal. In a polyphonic composition there was an overall beat, or *tactus*, and the placings of the cadences and suspensions were ruled by it, but against it the various parts moved freely and independently, causing frequently the most fascinating effects of cross-rhythm. Referring to the Palestrina *Sanctus* quotation above—if we had continued it further we would have found that the voice entries of " *DO*minus Deus . . ." were on the second, fourth, first and third beats of the respective bars (if there really had been bars). The second Palestrina quotation, from his *Stabat Mater*, is another case in point. The verbal rhythm (indicated by the stress marks) cuts across the time-signature rhythm on the word " dolorosa ". Byrd's great six-part motet *Haec Dies* (This Glad

10. "The Personification of Music", a wood engraving in the "Margarit Philosophica" (Bale edition, 1508). The instruments depicted are harp, lute, chamber organ and recorder. The presence of the scales is probably explained by the single chime-bell and the hammer-shaped beaters. The manufacture of chime-bells (cymbala) was a highly technical process, involving much exact weighing of material.

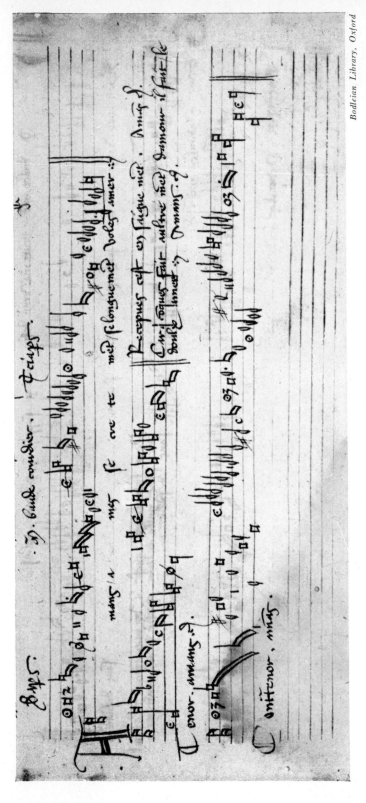

11. Baude Cordier's Rondeau, *Amans ames secretement . . .* of the late fourteenth century. See Ex. 27 for a modern transcription; also Ch. IV, Note 8. The three parts which comprise the rondeau are written separately, and are shown with the mensuration signs of the period, indicating frequent changes of rhythm.

Day) is a study of mingled rhythms of effective and amazing complexity. Even the very minor madrigalist Thomas Greaves, in his *Come Away, Sweet Love*, could obtain, by using cross-rhythms at the phrase " and running in and out ", a perfect little tone-picture of a dance-maze.[4*]

The Netherlanders

Having filled in to some small degree the technical background of late Renaissance music, we will now consider that music and the men who made it in more detail. It has already been seen that the period c. 1450–1550 was " the century of the Netherlanders ". From the time of Okeghem (c. 1425–95) several generations of composers from the Low Countries (the Franco-Flemings, as they are sometimes called) established their polyphonic style, and themselves, in every country in Europe, welcomed for their outstanding musical powers and occupying the most lucrative posts. England was something of an exception. Netherlanders were at royal courts (Henry VIII had a number), but they were never a power in the Chapel Royal.

Roland de Lassus (or Orlando di Lasso—c. 1532–94) was the mightiest Netherlander of them all, and his work, together with that of his contemporary Philippe de Monte, represents the culmination of the great Franco-Flemish period begun by Dufay. Born at Mons, he went early to Italy, where his powers were soon recognised. By his early twenties he had already travelled widely and had acquired a European reputation. He returned to his own land for a while in about the year 1554, but soon moved to Germany to become *Kapellmeister* to the Duke of Bavaria, who at that time maintained the most brilliant musical establishment in Europe.[5] In this post at Munich he remained for the rest of his life, at the head of a large and highly trained body of professional musicians, but free to travel on occasion. For most of his career his outlook was that of the Italian Renaissance, a broadness of interest that expressed itself in many and widely varied ways. The influence upon him of the secular Latin world was tempered by that of Germanic earnestness and serious artistic traditions. As no man had done before he mastered every style and technique of European composition and was able to produce Italian madrigals and villanelli, French chansons and German lieder, stamped with his own personality yet in the authentic atmosphere of each country's art. In this secular music, light-hearted, ironic or more seriously expressive as the case might be, there was always the technical perfection that found more profound uses in his church works. The contrapuntal mastery of his Masses (one of the finest, " Puisque j'ay perdu . . ." has already been mentioned) place them beside those of Palestrina, even if the Roman master has in his something more of the spirit of the Counter Reformation. But in the realm of the motet only the Spaniard, Victoria, reached to the expressive heights attained by the Netherlander. Lassus wrote more than a thousand motets, a number of which by reason of their beauty and dramatic power still maintain themselves in performance. As far as can be reckoned, his total production must have passed well beyond the two thousand mark.

In his later years the new spirit that was affecting Roman Catholic

H

church music caused him to turn almost exclusively to compositions for the Church, in a mood of sombre devotion. Among his last works were settings of the *lagrime* (or " tear ") poetry of Luigi Tansillo.[6*]

Philippe de Monte (1521–1603), born at Malines, had a technical equipment unsurpassed even by Lassus, and like him he was far-travelled and cosmopolitan. One of his journeys in the service of Philip II of Spain took him to England, where he made friends with a promising youth of the name of William Byrd. De Monte spent most of his life as musical director at the Imperial Court at Vienna. Like Lassus, his output was immense; Masses, motets and every type of secular musical form including a wealth of charming madrigals. The last-named, more than twelve hundred of them, are of an individual style more closely knit and polyphonic than the usual Italian type. Also like Lassus (and Okeghem) de Monte was referred to in his lifetime as a " prince of music ". As more and more of his works are becoming restored to performance nowadays it would seem that the title was not undeserved.[7*]

Slightly anterior to Lassus and de Monte were two other famous Flemings, neither of whom served in Italy, Jacob Clemens ("Clemens non Papa "— c. 1500–56) and Nicholas Gombert (c. 1505–c. 1556). The latter, however, spent some time in Spain, wielding an influence there, and was later at the French court.

The Venetian School

Adrian Willaert (c. 1490–1562) is the first name to consider in regard to the work of the Netherlanders in Italy, which had important consequences. Born at Bruges, Willaert studied with Jean Mouton (c. 1475–1522) and was thus the musical grandchild of Josquin Despres. He was early in Italy, and after quickly building up a reputation, he secured what was one of the most coveted musical posts of the age, that of *maestro di capella* at the Cathedral of St. Mark's, Venice. The appointments at St. Mark's were in the control of the proud and powerful Venetian Republic; the *maestro* had under his authority a large body of professional singers, two organs with their highly skilled organists, and a number of players of orchestral instruments. The Byzantine-style St. Mark's was the Doge's own official " chapel ", the year was studded with occasions for state religious festivals, and the *maestro* was responsible for much of the musical side of it all, besides meeting the daily demands of the Cathedral music, which already had a high reputation behind it. Willaert made the most of his opportunities. One of the traditions, aided by the existence of the two fine organs and the galleries on either side of the high altar, was for composition for double-choir. Willaert developed this tradition to spectacular heights, and created the so-called " Venetian school ". He and succeeding composers at St. Mark's, notably the Gabrielis (uncle and nephew), invented choral and instrumental effects new to music—multiple choirs in antiphony and combination, accompanied at times by specially selected orchestral instruments; echo effects; solos and duets with instrumental accompaniment; and even independent orchestral interludes. In addition to his powers as a composer Willaert was a teacher of genius, and among his pupils were such famous musicians as Nicolo Vicentino (1511–72), composer and theorist, who dabbled with the idea of intervals less than the semitone; Philippe Verdelot (d. 1567), and Cipriano de Rore (1516–65), both famous as madrigalists; Andrea Gabrieli (c. 1520–86), organist and almost as progressive a composer as his nephew Giovanni Gabrieli; and Claudio Merulo (1533–1604), the most famous organist of his day, whose playing, we read, packed the Cathedral so closely that doors had to be closed. De Rore, a later *maestro di capella* of St. Mark's, was the last Netherlander to hold that post. He was succeeded by an Italian pupil of Willaert, Giosaffe Zarlino (1517–90) a fine composer and learned theorist. By that time all over Italy the native musicians had completed their pupilage to the North. Zarlino in his writings advocated tuning the octave to " twelve equal semitones ", a view apparently also held by Willaert.

Willaert seems to have been a strict disciplinarian. We read of a singer being dismissed by him for not attending his counterpoint lessons, which, as Willaert declared, "were necessary in the choir ". We may recall here that though the status and pay of a member of a famous choir of the time was comparatively high (the instrumentalist was in a very different category), equally high were the technical standards demanded. A post was obtained only after a rigorous test, not only concerned with the beauty and flexibility of the candidate's voice, but also his general musicianship. We have spoken often enough concerning the improvised ornamentations that solo singers were expected to make.

With regard to the innovations of the Venetian school in choral style, it was the Italian Giovanni Gabrieli (1557–1612) who brought this progress to its highest pitch. His magnificent motet *In ecclesiis* is an excellent example of the technique of the Venetian school at its best, and is still sometimes performed.[8*] It is written for a full choir and a choir of soloists, with passages for separate solos and duets. There are accompaniments sometimes by the organs, sometimes by an orchestra of three *cornetti*, a viola and two trombones, which also plays a short interlude, or *sinfonia*. It is strange to reflect that the younger Gabrieli attained to no higher post than that of first organist. Yet his fame as a composer was European, and students came to him from afar. His innovation in harmony and homophonic style pointed towards the new age, the so-called baroque. Indeed, much of his music might be said to belong to it. He was one of the first composers to make use of that newly developed instrument, the violin. What we have termed a " viola " above was a " viola da braccio ", the (then) highest voice of the new family (see p. 130).

One of Willaert's pupils, the Italian organist Girolamo Cavazzione (c. 1500–1560), produced in his *Intavolatura* volume of 1542 the first significant examples of new instrumental forms called respectively the *canzone francese* and the *ricercare*. The first, as the name shows, was developed from the light and cheerful polyphony of the French chanson. The second derived from the motet, and was usually more serious and closely contrapuntal than the *canzone*. The term *ricercare* implied a " searching ". The composer sought as it were to make the most of the material, fugal fashion. The same type of contrapuntal composition was implied in the term *fantasia*, although this word seems to have some very loose applications. In England the name " fancy " was sometimes employed. These forms were used not only for keyboard but for groups of instruments. Willaert and his pupil Jachet Buus (d. 1565), another St. Mark's organist, wrote some notable *ricercari*, as did later composers of the Venetian school, particularly the Gabrielis.

The first section of a transcription of an instrumental *ricercare* by Andrea Gabrieli is given below, (*Ricercare del 12° tono*). It will be seen that a thoroughly searching use is made of the brief subject. There are three more sections, one in $\frac{3}{4}$ time, and then a repeat is made of the first section. In the second section a new subject is started which is later combined with the first subject :

Ex: 40

The great organist Merulo produced keyboard *toccatas*, in free style, derived from the medieval fanfare. In them we find sections of brilliance contrasted with sustained contrapuntal passages. As the century advanced, more and more were these instrumental forms tending to suit the particular type of instrument for which they were written, and ceasing to be mere transcriptions of vocal pieces.

Church Music. Palestrina and the Roman School

In considering church music after the first three decades of the sixteenth century we must recall the great religious controversy that rent Europe in two. The Church of Rome found itself faced in several countries by a Protestant breakaway. First and foremost came that of Martin Luther in Germany; then appeared Calvin, the inspirer of the French Huguenots. In the England of the boy-king Edward VI, Cranmer with his prayer-book shaped the early course of the new Protestant Church, while further north John Knox, Calvin's disciple, was the first leader of the Reformed Church of Scotland. There were similar movements in other northern countries. In opposition there developed the Counter Reformation, aided in due course by the decisions of the Council of Trent (1545–63). The latter body met periodically over a number of years with the aim of putting the Roman house in order. The Catholic counter-attack resulted in the recovery of some of the lost territory. It is only fair to say that internal efforts towards reform had exercised the Church of Rome even before the drastic Protestant moves.

The Tridentine Council's discussions as to what actions were necessary ranged widely. Church music was one of the subjects, for voices had been raised against such abuses as the musical complication of Mass choral settings (with the consequent obscuring of the texts), their undue length, and the frequent worldliness of the material; also the use of orchestral instruments, a practice which Erasmus had already criticised. Mainly as the result of the findings of a committee led by Cardinal Truchsess certain strictures were made and bans imposed, such as on " all seductive and impure melodies, whether instrumental or vocal . . ." but there was never any real danger, as in past years has been suggested, that polyphonic music in general would be forbidden. Another myth that has taken long to fade was that Palestrina was the saviour of the situation. Cardinal Truchsess had a *kapellmeister*, Jacob van Kerle (1531–91), and it was the latter's fine compositions, produced to order as models of acceptable polyphony, which gained the goodwill of the Cardinal's committee. Palestrina's *Missa Papae Marcelli*, the supposed magic spell, had been written several years before. Yet it displayed the very virtues that the cardinals sought, including the care which the composer gave in his mature works to obtaining in the midst of polyphony as much verbal clarity as possible.

Giovanni Pierluigi da Palestrina (1525–94) was born in the little town, twenty miles or so outside Rome, from which he took his name. After being a child chorister there he received some years of training at Rome in all the disciplines of the Franco-Flemish art, possibly from the famous Netherlander, Jacob Arcadelt (c. 1505–70). While *maestro di capella* in his native town he gained the good opinion of the Bishop of Palestrina. It was the young musician's good fortune that the Bishop should in 1550 become Pope as Julius III and should appoint him director of the Julian Choir, a long established foundation that acted as a training ground for Italian recruits to the Sistine Choir, the Pope's own personal choral body. Furthermore, though Palestrina had no very good voice, Julius proceeded to make him an actual member of the Sistine fraternity, on the strength of his great promise as a composer. This was in spite of the displeasure expressed by that privileged body, who had not been consulted. In any case, Palestrina was a married man, and was for that reason ineligible. After the death of Julius, Palestrina soon found himself ejected and for some years filled other choirmaster posts at Rome. But there was nowhere any doubt as to his eminence as a composer of the kind of music desired by the hierarchy. He returned in 1571 to the directorship of the Julian Choir. Though he was never readmitted to the Sistine Choir Pope Sixtus V gave him the honourable title of *maestro compositore* to that body.

In his music is found the quintessence of the Counter Reformation— otherworldliness, a sense of awe and spiritual elation that contrasted with the uninhibited vigour and brilliance of the Venetian school, yet possesses an inexhaustible flow of melody and a dynamic expressiveness. Too often in the past has the idea been expressed that in it, pure and beautiful as it was, " nothing happened ", that it was lacking in emotion, timeless. This is another of the Palestrinian legends, for though his tonal language is based on what was mainly a diatonic and modal style, it was capable of expressing a wide range of moods, from the Good Friday *Improperia* (reproaches) with its note against note harmony to the ecstatic moments born of wind and fire, of the Pentecost *Dum complerentur*, or the boundless jubilation of *Viri Galilei*. The formidable Pope Paul IV who had dismissed him from the Sistine was so impressed by the *Improperia* that he caused the music to be copied into the choir books for permanent Holy Week performance.

Palestrina's Masses will always be held to be his supreme achievement.[10*] In them he showed his mastery of every known technical device, but always with the sole purpose of serving best the liturgy of his faith. Long after the Tridentine resolutions he wrote a tenor Mass on " L'Homme armé ", and even one on the old hexachord formula (Ut, Re, Me . . .), but the result in each case was a work of complete religiosity.

It is usually held that his motets (nearly 400) did not approach to the standard of his friend Victoria and of Lassus, yet individual examples contain some of his finest moments of vigour and expressive colouring. The 29 motets comprising the *Song of Songs* settings glow with religious passion. There are several eight-part works, such as *Hodie Christus natus est* and the universally known *Stabat Mater* in which he employs two choirs separately and in combination. He was clearly well acquainted with the Venetian style.

His frame of mind was wholly that of a church composer. His madrigals, though the majority were termed " spiritual ", are at a lower level of achievement. The liturgical musician appeared self-conscious in regard to them, since they were published under the pseudonym of " Gianetto ". Yet there can be no doubt that the world of the madrigal which flourished around him played its part in developing the ease and expressiveness of his mature work.

It was Italy and Spain that showed the greatest zeal for the new spirit in Catholic church music. At Rome with Palestrina was a worthy group of Italian church composers which included Felix Anerio (c. 1560–1614) and the elder Nanini (1545–1607). Meanwhile Spanish musicians had cultivated the Franco-Flemish polyphonic art with a skill equal to that of the Italians. The Fleming Nicholas Gombert may have done much to bring the style to Spain, but the whole peninsula was already rich with the inspiration of its own native music. The works of the fine composer Francesco Guerrero (1527–99), including the famous *Passions*, were known and respected in Italy, France and Flanders even during his lifetime. Other Spanish musicians, Cabezón, Milan, de Navaez and Fuenllana will receive later notice. Much remains to be known concerning the music of the sixteenth century Spanish composers who remained at home. But the two leading Spaniards of the age did most of their work in Rome, Cristobal Morales (c. 1500–53) and Tomás Luis de Victoria (c. 1548–1611)—master and pupil. Both employed the consummate contrapuntal style that belonged to the Roman musical incarnation, expressed however in a spirit that was never Italian but passionately Spanish, that of St. Theresa and Ignatius Loyola. Their Masses, motets and Magnificats glow with a mysticism and with passages of dramatic poignancy such as the more temperate Italians did not choose to cultivate.

Morales, a man of broad education though apparently a difficult character, became a member of the Papal Choir in 1535, but after some years returned finally to Spain and to a series of wanderings from appointment to appointment. There is no doubt as to his great contemporary fame as a composer both in Europe and the Spanish New World.

Victoria, sent to Rome as a youth on a grant from Philip II, was early ordained. As a result, his career was that both of musician and priest. He was well acquainted with Palestrina and no doubt learned much from the older man, but two early motets, *O quam gloriosum* and *O vos omnes*, still often performed, show him quickly to have acquired his great expressive powers.[11*] Palestrina in his turn may have gained something from the Spaniard, who made a freer use of chromatic resource and who may have helped to bring about the greater harmonic warmth which can be found in the Italian's motets after 1584.

Victoria's devotion to his faith was intense and single-minded. He wrote no secular work, nor did he ever employ any theme of worldly origin. Like Palestrina, he made use of the techniques of the Venetians in his works for double and triple choirs. He was the first composer to make settings of the hymns for the whole liturgical year. His long years of chaplainship to the ex-Empress Maria took him finally to Spain in 1583. On the death of his patroness he wrote his last and finest work, a Requiem Mass, as great a composition as any of the period.

The usually gentle, even rhythms of the Roman sometimes afford considerable contrast to the style of the Spaniard, who, when in his more dramatic moods (as in moments of *O vos omnes*) makes use of broken, passionate, almost ejaculatory phrases. The art of Palestrina has sometimes been compared in its serene beauty to that of Raphael, and a parallel drawn between the mystical emotion of Victoria and that of El Greco.

Church Music in France

French composers of church music in the period include Clement Janne-quin (c. 1475–1560), Claudin de Sermisy (c. 1490–1562), and later, Claude Goudimel (1510–72), Louis Bourgeois (c. 1510–c. 1561), Claude le Jeune (1528–1601) and Guillaume Costeley (1531–1606). Also at the French court for a time was the Flemish composer Nicholas Gombert, already named. Gombert was a pupil of Josquin Despres, and a past master of the contra-puntal art. But as the century advanced the French technique in church music tended to get less complicated, developing a clarity more characteris-tically Gallic. Goudimel, le Jeune and Bourgeois were later in their careers associated with the Huguenot movement in France, and the first-named died in the St. Bartholomew massacre. We must now consider the effect of the Reformation in general upon music.

Protestant Church Music—Germany

The greatest figure of the Protestant Reformation, Martin Luther (1483–1546), was deeply interested in music, a good tenor singer, a lutenist and very likely the composer of the famous hymn tunes ascribed to him. There is contemporary evidence that he had a respectable command of polyphonic technique. His own favourite composer was Josquin Despres; his friend and adviser Johann Walther (1496–1570), an excellent professional musician, *Kapellmeister* to the Elector of Saxony. Thus it was that under Luther's guidance the changes in the forms of worship established in the German Church did not bear as heavily on music, musicians and musical instru-ments as they did in other Protestant bodies. The Reformation established worship in the vernacular, a principle being that the words should be clearly heard by the congregation, who were to share as much as possible in the service by joining in the singing of hymns and psalms. Yet Luther had no objection to the continued existence of organ playing, and the presence of the trained choir for the performance of the old-style motet and the art-music of the day. Indeed, the Lutherans retained a substantial part of Roman Catholic church music, e.g. the Kyrie and Gloria of the Mass and the Magnificat. The practice of hymn singing developed the splendid musical literature of the German chorale tune, which was a mine of material for the compositions of a gifted line of North German organists, from Michael Praetorius (1571–1621) to Buxtehude and J. S. Bach.[12*]

The Calvinist Movement

Under Calvin, the Swiss reformer, music was not so fortunate, and in the early stages of his régime there was much destruction of organs and music. Calvin forbade even the singing of hymns, these being " man made ". The sole opportunity for music in worship was afforded by the congregational singing, in unison, of metrical versions of the Psalms. For this the cele-brated Geneva Psalter was prepared, the French composer Bourgeois play-ing a leading part in the shaping of its tunes.

In Scotland the ardent Calvinist John Knox established a similar state of affairs, although in the case of the Scottish Psalter which he caused to be issued, part-singing was not frowned on. The Psalter tunes were taken to the hearts of generations of Scottish congregations, but it was not until the nineteenth century that organs were found once more in Calvinist churches.

The Anglican Church

In England the new order began with some violence towards things musical, but destruction was sporadic. Edward VI's Book of Common Prayer established the Services—Holy Communion, Morning Prayer and Evening Prayer, suitable parts of all which composers proceeded to set. One of the first of such settings was the famous though short-lived *The Booke of Common Praier Noted* (1550) by the organist John Merbecke, who narrowly escaped the fire in Mary's time. The single vocal line was based on the old Gregorian plainsong. After the brief reigns of the Protestant Edward VI and his Roman Catholic sister Mary, when the pendulum swung to either extreme, there came the comparative tranquillity of Elizabeth's settlement. The Anglican Church was firmly established, Puritan extremists frowned upon, and colour and choral music restored to Protestant services. At the same time the Anglican chant was adapted from the Gregorian for the singing of the normal prose texts of the Psalms. The motet was largely replaced by the anthem, though Latin motets continued to be produced. The anthem was at first entirely in the contrapuntal motet style, but later took on the new fashion from Italy whereby the chorus was relieved by solo passages, accompanied by organ and sometimes by strings, the "verse" anthem type.

The advanced choral practices of the new Anglican Church here and later mentioned was a matter only for cathedrals, royal chapels and such other foundations as could command the necessary resources. Reformed parish churches in England (in contrast with their Lutheran counterparts) probably had at first little liturgical music except traditional unaccompanied melody, with the psalms in their original prose translations no more than spoken. Yet if a tradition going back to the time of the Lollards is correct it was the practice of sympathisers with the new doctrines to sing together compositions which were in fact metrical paraphrases of the Psalms. Be that as it may, it is certain that Miles Coverdale, who in 1535 produced the first authorised translation of the Bible into English, brought out c. 1539 a book of "ghostly psalms and spiritual songs", with melodies from German sources. It was soon suppressed by order of King Henry VIII. However, better times lay ahead. The famous Sternhold and Hopkins Psalter, "in English Metre", first published in 1549, appeared in 1562 in what might be called a definitive edition ("the whole Psalms, the Evangelical Hymns and the Spiritual Songs") together with over sixty tunes, some borrowed or adapted from Continental sources, some of native origin. There were subsequent issues. At the same time there was printed *An introduction to Learn to Sing*, as an aid for those who wished to master the art of "singing from the book". Already in 1559 Elizabeth had given permission for such singing to take place at morning or evening services. Collections continued to appear, under other editors, for church and private use, and altogether the ordinary churchgoer was now provided with good opportunities for congregational music-making.

The chief English church composers of the mid-century were Christopher Tye (c.1500–73), Thomas Tallis (c. 1505–85) and Robert Whyte (1530–74). Living through the "pendulum" period we have spoken of, their outputs included Masses and Services, motets and anthems. Tye has been called "the father of the anthem". Tallis, organist of the Chapel Royal, teacher and friend of William Byrd, was the greatest of the three, a fine composer, fully trained in the Franco-Flemish contrapuntal technique. His "Dorian Service" is noteworthy, and the dignity and beauty of many of his Latin motets, e.g. *Miserere nostri* and *Adesto nunc propitius*, cause them still to be performed.[13*] His forty-part *Spem in alium*, a motet for eight choirs of five parts each, is a *tour de force* which yet contrives to be good music. Perhaps his finest work is the *Tenebrae Lamentations*, written during his early days at Waltham Abbey, before the Dissolution. Whyte was organist of Westminster Abbey, and was highly thought of by his contemporaries. Morley praises his compositions, among which are many works in the Latin rite. Not enough of his music is yet printed, but closer modern acquaintance with it has confirmed sixteenth century opinion.

In William Byrd (1543–1623) England produced a musician of genius, one of the giants of the art. A pupil of Tallis, he was organist at Lincoln Cathedral for a time, but joined his master at the Chapel Royal, where he shared with him the post of organist. He was a lifelong Roman Catholic, and it is pleasant to note that although he suffered local annoyances on that account he was undoubtedly protected by Elizabeth herself, as one of her domestic musicians, against any more serious action. He was actually favoured, in partnership with Tallis, to the extent of a monopoly with regard to the printing of music paper. In composition, sacred and secular, vocal and instrumental, he adorned all branches. He was perhaps greatest in his motets, and in music of a more serious tinge generally.[14] His volume of *Cantiones sacrae* (1589–91) and his *Psalms, Sonets and Songs* . . . (1588) contain some of his best vocal work. There must also be mentioned his fine "Great Service" (Anglican), and his three unaccompanied Masses, for three, four and five voices respectively. There is a wealth of other Church music, including the monumental *Gradualia*, two volumes of Mass settings and other material of the Roman rite, which were written in his last years and published after his death. There seems little doubt that, as in the case of Tallis, his best vocal work is found in his Latin settings. He was one of the greatest keyboard players of his day—his compositions for the virginals will be later considered. In the words of another excellent Elizabethan composer, Morley, he was "not without reverence to be named of the musitians".

Thomas Morley (1557–1603) is usually thought of as a madrigalist, but a hearing of some of his church music (e.g. his *Agnus Dei* motet) will soon convince a listener that he has other claims.[15*] He was organist of St. Paul's Cathedral and a Gentleman of the Chapel Royal. Like Tallis and Byrd he seems to have been in royal favour, for he took over from them, in succession, the music-printing monopoly. His *Plaine and Easie Introduction to Practicall Musicke* (1597) is one of the most famous books about music ever written.

Many worthy church musicians of the time must escape notice until we reach the last important figure of the age. Orlando Gibbons (1583–1625) was an outstanding composer and a brilliant executant. At the age of twenty-one he was appointed organist of the Chapel Royal. Two years later he was also organist of Westminster Abbey. His life was all too short, but he wrote much fine church music, wholly to English texts—some Services and a quantity of anthems. Of these, some were altogether polyphonic and masterly in their counterpoint, some of the " verse " type, with string accompaniment for the solos. *Behold, Thou hast made my days* is a good example of the latter.[16*] His madrigals and instrumental work, also of importance, will be considered later.

Though, as we have seen, the effect of the Reformation in some countries on church composition was indeed disastrous, the enforced simplicity of writing brought about by the need for suitable congregational music made homophonic methods more and more the practice, and the harmonic point of view more and more the normal one.

Secular Music. The Chanson

In France the chanson had lived on in general esteem ever since the time of the troubadours, and in its sixteenth century form it was more popular than ever. To mention but one printer, Attaignant of Paris, who was publishing between 1528 and 1549—there were issued by him nearly two thousand different chansons. The chanson had become normally a four- or five-part vocal composition, with the melody in the *superius*, the other voices, though frequently contrapuntal, being in general subordinate. It had balanced musical phrases, clearly defined cadences, and an artistic mixture of imitative and homophonic technique. The various forms adopted were usually crystal clear—sometimes just a simple melody, setting a poem strophically in folk-song style, or different musical sections, succeeding in A B C . . . fashion, or more significantly, A B A or AA BB arrangements —the germs of ternary and binary forms, and for longer settings, the rondo —a recurrent refrain with episodes. As we have learned to expect, there was no fixed manner of performing a chanson. It might be wholly vocal, any part might be doubled or replaced by instruments; it might be a solo song accompanied by a group of instruments or by a solo lute.[17] The clarity of form and writing had, as we have seen, caused chansons to be transcribed as pieces for instruments alone, and finally had suggested a type of independent instrumental composition, the *canzone francese*.

All the French composers previously mentioned wrote chansons, some of them hundreds each. Jannequin, the earliest, produced some astonishing examples of considerable length, including *La Bataille* (the battle of Marignano, of 1515, was the reference), and *Le Chant des Oyseaux*, which are in effect descriptive tone-poems, cast in rondo form, and still most attractive in performance. The imitations of bird-song in the latter work are extraordinarily imaginative. The productions of de Sermisy, Costerley and le Jeune are also still able to charm in their melodious vivacity.[18*]

A transcription of a five-part example (*Francion vint l'autre jour*) by a lesser light, Pierre Bonnet, is given below. There is a late sixteenth century air about it, for it relies on top-line melody and chordal accompaniment, rather on any of the graces of counterpoint. However, it illustrates very well, in brief, the continued growth of harmonic resource, and the fact that the different cadences are beginning to suggest different tonal centres.

Ex:41

Two more stanzas follow to the same music.

The chanson spread far beyond French frontiers, and many composers of other nationalities wrote examples. Among these were Lassus and de Monte, who, as might be expected, caught exactly their Gallic spirit.

The Madrigal and Kindred Forms in Italy

It will be recalled that in Italy in the early sixteenth century secular vocal music found popular expression in the *frottola*. This light form of composition was usually in four parts, simple and almost altogether homophonic in style, with the melody in the *superius* and the remaining parts without much individual life. These *frottole*, though patronised by all classes, were most of them ephemeral, appearing from printing presses literally by their thousands and then quickly fading. Their texts were frequently gross, and were seldom of any lasting value. However, many of the surviving examples show a sparkling melodiousness and a lilting charm.[19*] Some Netherlanders, like Josquin Despres, had shared in their production, but in the second decade of the century a reaction had set in against them in more discriminating circles. There had begun at the time a change of literary fashion among the aristocracy, and a more fastidious lyric poetry, with Petrarch as its ideal, was being written at the various Italian courts, the leader of the

movement being Pietro (afterwards Cardinal) Bembo. Musical settings inevitably followed, and the form that proved of the greatest interest to leading composers was the *madrigal*. The word seems to have had a medieval
Latin derivation, and to imply " a rustic song in the mother tongue ". It
was used first, as we have seen, in connection with a fourteenth century
lyrical form bearing no relation to the sixteenth century type. The subjects,
as ever, were chiefly amatory and/or pastoral. What the musicians found
to set was a short poem, seldom more than a dozen or so lines, with no
fixed rhyme-scheme and frequently with a marked irregularity of line-length.
Thus there was no easy solution regarding the form and rhythmic pattern
of the music, as there was in the case of the strophic frottola or the formal
patterns of the chanson. Some of the early madrigals were reminiscent of
frottola style, largely chordal, with the chief melodic importance in the top
part. However, the other parts were usually interesting, and contrapuntal
subtleties soon began to creep in. As the century went on the madrigal
became more and more as it were a laboratory for the trying out of new
and advanced experiments in form, harmony and even tonality.

The Netherlanders (it would perhaps be better to say Franco-Flemings)
took the lead in the first production of madrigals, and we meet once more
the names of Willaert, Verdelot and Arcadelt, together with Jahn Gero
(c. 1518–83) and the Italian Constanza Festa (c. 1490–1545). The first
publication of madrigals was in 1533. Once again it must be said that though
these compositions were written for four voices (soon five voices became
the norm) the single voice with instrumental accompaniment was a frequent
method of performance. Willaert actually arranged and published twenty-
two of Verdelot's madrigals for solo voice and lute. Accounts of court
festivals from the mid-century onwards abound with details of madrigal
performances where the voices were doubled by various groupings of instruments, in astonishing variety. It must be emphasised that in Italy the
madrigal was written essentially for aristocratic tastes (often to order), and
usually performed by professionals.

A sort of second period begins with the madrigals of Cipriano de Rore,
already mentioned as one of Willaert's pupils. The madrigal in the hands
of the Netherlanders, as might be expected, was borrowing much from the
motet technique—equality of parts, the motif in close imitation, the overlapping of sections at the cadences, the alternation of polyphony with chordal
passages, and, as madrigals were now sometimes being written in six parts or
more, choral subdivisions answering each other. In addition, there was a
subtle independence of rhythm in the parts that was so effective on occasion.
(Later composers of motets in the period may have received in return inspiration from madrigal techniques.) The emotions of the texts received progressively more and more attention. Composers endeavoured to frame
musical equivalents for a verbal phrase, and at times for a single word, as
some of them had done in a lesser degree in the motet. The dangers of
exaggeration and musical cliché are obvious, and these occurred in due
course, but chiefly in the days of the madrigal's decline. De Rore brought
to the form a judicious use of chromatic resource, and his works were held

to be models, both in his lifetime and after. So much so, that some years after his death a number of his madrigals were issued printed in score, a most unusual practice at the time. Clearly, they were intended for study use.[20] At the same time as de Rore, Andrea Gabrieli, Baldassare Donato (c. 1530–1603) and others of the Venetian school were making their contributions.

The madrigal had spread to other countries. As already noted, Lassus and de Monte, settled in Germanic lands, produced excellent examples (de Monte wrote at least six hundred). At Antwerp Hubert Waelrant (c. 1517–95), a fine all-round Flemish composer, also published a large number. In Germany native vocal music had still its national style of polyphonic *lieder*, such as had been produced by Finck, Hofheimer, Isaac and Senfl. There was also the *Quodlibet*, a type of vocal composition which consisted of a rough cobbling together of popular tunes.

France, with the treasury of her own chansons, showed no interest in the madrigal. Spanish composers imitated the form, but without much enthusiasm. Spain had a lyric art of her own, a tradition of solo song accompanied by the six-stringed guitar-like *vilhuela*.[21*] England's was a very different story, which will need some special attention later.

Mention must be made of a lighter kind of Italian composition (usually three-part), the *villanella*, deliberately crude in style, which more or less replaced the frottola. There were other similar types, under various names. The last frottola volume had been published in 1531.

The true climax of the Italian madrigal was probably reached in the work of Luca Marenzio (1553–99), who though in high favour at the Vatican, never held any church post. He gave to the madrigal his chief devotion and was termed by his compatriots " the sweetest swan of Italy ". He had technical mastery without pedantry, emotional expression without exaggeration.[22*] His works were freely sung in England, where they were much admired. Italy was now full of highly competent madrigal composers equipped with new harmonic and chromatic resources. The modes were losing ground, and the major-minor tonality was being freely used. " Love " was only one of the themes dealt with. There were scenic and descriptive madrigals, ranging from everyday life in street and country to the terrors of Dante's Inferno, painted in terms of music, and all tending to advance the technical resources of the art. There appeared the strange and unique figure of Gesualdo, Prince of Venosa (c. 1560–1613), whose madrigals and motets were frequently crowded with accidentals, a shifting kaleidoscope of seemingly unrelated harmonies, yet strangely effective at times.

A brief example of his work had better be given, although it goes without saying that a true effect can only be gained from a vocal performance. The following comprises the concluding section of his five-part madrigal *Io pur respiro*. The agonised cry of the poet is—" (let a single blow) give an end to life and great woe ! " Gesualdo's chromaticisms at least illustrate the sentiments :

Ex:42

Of more permanent value was the work of Giovanni Croce (c. 1557–1609), a *maestro di capella* at St. Mark's and a fine composer in all branches, and Luzzasco Luzzaschi (1545–1607), master of the famous Frescobaldi.[23*]

In keeping with the dramatic tendencies that were now everywhere apparent in Italian music Orazio Vecchi (1550–1605), a very competent composer, published in 1597 the extraordinary *L'Amfiparnasso*, a " madrigal comedy ", as he termed it. In a series of fourteen madrigals he gave a presentation (in 1594) of the traditional *commedia dell' arte*—employing the stock figures of Harlequin, Pantaloon etc. As he definitely states, the effects were entirely those of sound. It was *not* opera, but it made clear the fact that opera was " in the air ".

We have already noted the popularity of the *ballata* as a vocal form in *trecento* Italy (see p. 83f.). It enjoyed a revival in somewhat different shape at the hands of Giovanni Gastoldi (c. 1550–1622), who towards the end of the sixteenth century published a volume of five-part *ballati* " for singing, playing and dancing ", as he put it. With their " fa la la " refrains they caught on everywhere and were imitated by other composers, among whom was the Englishman, Thomas Morley.

In the last decade of the century musical taste in Italy was tending to favour the more violent emotions. Though these were very apparent in the highly dramatic and harmonically advanced madrigals of Monteverdi and Luzzaschi, they found even greater scope in single voice compositions, which indeed was what some madrigals had become. The professional singer of advanced technique, whether soprano or *castrato,* was coming more and more into prominence. By the beginning of the seventeenth century the contrapuntal Italian madrigal can be said to be on the way out.

The Madrigal and the Ayre in England

In early Tudor times composers like Fayrfax and Cornyshe had produced secular, contrapuntally accompanied songs of value. An important collection of such songs was published by Thomas Whythorne in 1571, but already the madrigals of Willaert, Verdelot and Arcadelt were known in England. Richard Edwards' famous *On going to my naked bed* (c. 1560) was a near madrigal, but it was only after the publication by Nicolas Yonge in 1588 of *Musica Transalpina* that the flood of English madrigal composition really began. Yonge's collection included madrigals by Lassus, de Monte, Marenzio and other Italians, and two by Byrd. A major contributor was the elder Alfonzo Ferrabosco (c. 1543–88), a famous Italian who spent some years in Eilzabeth's service, and was much admired in spite of his somewhat crooked personality. The volume was an excellent model for the new English movement, which proceeded to do what other countries had not been able to accomplish, create a really national art which was not a slavish copy of Italian prototypes.

The English madrigal was somewhat different in style from the late Italian type (it was flourishing when the latter was in decline), more flowing, less consciously dramatic, and with a true native tunefulness. On the whole the major-minor tonality was prevailing, and there was a great deal of effective experiment in the matter of harmony. The leading English composers were Thomas Morley, " the father of the English madrigal ", William Byrd, John Wilbye (1574–1638), Thomas Weelkes (c. 1575–1623) and almost the last but certainly not the least, Orlando Gibbons. Morley, Byrd and Gibbons have already been noted as church musicians. Close behind the leaders come John Bennet, Thomas Tomkins, Thomas Bateson and quite a number more.

The publication by Morley in 1603 of the famous collection *The Triumphs of Oriana* which honoured Queen Elizabeth after the fashion of

Italian precedents, gave a not wholly representative cross-section of native madrigal composition. About a couple of dozen composers were called upon.[24] There was one foreign name, Giovanni Croce, and several omissions, the most noticeable being that of Byrd. Perhaps his style was thought to be too serious. Morley's own first madrigals appeared in 1593, a volume of *Canzonets* (=light madrigals). In 1595 came *Ballets to Fyve Voyces*, modelled closely, sometimes too closely, on Gastoldi's work. But most of Morley's happy art was quite original, and he was the best-loved English composer of his age.[25*] The madrigal was truly popular inasmuch as it was an amateur, middle-class, cultured-family interest, unlike the Italian, which was always very much an aristocrat affair, and a good deal in the hands of professional performers. For sheer musicianship John Wilbye is perhaps the greatest of the English madrigalists. He was fortunate in being the domestic musician of the rich, cultured and generous Kytson family, and spent his life in household music-making and the composition of madrigals (together with managing the property that his patrons had given him). There were only sixty-five of these madrigals, but the standard, steadily maintained, was very high. Like Marenzio, his taste and judgment were impeccable. *Flora gave me fairest flowers* is possibly his best known madrigal nowadays, but its charms can be paralleled by many more.[26*] In his more serious moments he used powerful harmonic resources to depict deep emotion. Thomas Weelkes was less constant in his artistic standards than Wilbye, but could rise to very great heights, especially when very dramatic music was called for. Passages from his five-part *O, Care, thou wilt despatch me* are frequently quoted as showing the poignancy and daring that the Elizabethan school was capable of in the matter of harmony.[27*] Bennet and Bateson were neither of them far behind Weelkes. Byrd wrote some splendid madrigals, mainly of a serious nature, but his greater inspirations were not in the form. Orlando Gibbons published only one volume, but it was a masterly one, containing the still famous *What is our life* and *The Silver Swan*. Like Byrd, Gibbons' more characteristic note was a serious one. There was very little madrigal publication in England after his death, though mention should be made of a set of ballets and madrigals by that fine composer Thomas Tomkins (1572–1656), brought out in 1622, and quite up to the standard of Morley and Weelkes. After 1630 the madrigal represented an out-of-date form.

The English Ayre

With the fading of the madrigal there came more and more into prominence the *ayre*, which, though the term was sometimes given other meanings in the period, came to be applied to the solo song with accompaniment that was either instrumental or for other and subordinate voices. Song tunes with polyphonic accompaniment had had a long history in England, and Cornyshe and Fayrfax had written some excellent ones. The French chanson had often been performed as for solo voice, with the other part transcribed for lute, and Italian madrigals had been treated in the same fashion. But in the hands of John Dowland (1563–1626), a magnificent

I

lutenist, the ayre took a new turn. His compositions, his lute playing and his fine voice made him a European figure, and for some years he was lutenist to the King of Denmark. Between 1596 and 1603 he published three volumes of *Songes or Ayres* . . . for solo voice and lute accompaniment which gained immediate popularity. Some of them were truly "art-songs".[28*] Not only were the melodies of outstanding beauty, but in these instances the accompaniment had an independent life, sometimes developing its own figures, and on occasion even having the main interest. Certainly in many of the songs the lute part is little more than chordal, and indeed some songs were transcriptions of part-songs or even dance tunes. But in such works as *I saw my Lady weep* and *Flow, O my tears* there is seen a new and more subtle conception. As performed at the time the ayre was sung not only to lute accompaniment but often with the lowest part doubled on a bass viol.

Other prominent ayre composers, though not of Dowland's calibre, were Thomas Campion (1567–1620)—also an excellent lyric poet and lutenist, Robert Jones (b. c. 1575), Francis Pilkington (d. 1638) and Philip Rosseter (1568–1623). In Rosseter's published scores we find bar-lines used in regular fashion in accordance with the time-signature. In the early seventeenth century there is some mention of a new practice of playing accompaniments to solo songs on harpsichord or virginal, a fashion derived from Italy.

Instruments

The sixteenth century witnessed a number of developments in the constructions, techniques and independent life of instruments. The medieval *vièle* had long become the viol, with six gut strings, a rather flat bridge, fretted finger-board and an " archer " type of bow which was slacker than the modern one. There were three usual sizes of viol—treble, tenor and bass, though smaller and larger types than these were known, and sometimes used. As compared with the later violin the tone was quiet and gentle, lacking in dynamics and attack. Like many other solo instruments the viols were now being played in a harmony of the various sizes. Towards the end of the century concerted viol playing became a favourite form of domestic music-making. In Elizabethan England musical families would possess a " chest of viols ", usually two trebles, two tenors and two basses. The usual method of storage seems to account for the name. All sizes were held on or between the knees. We meet the term " consort ", implying any type of instrumental group. A " whole consort " was an ensemble of the same kind of instrument, e.g. viols or recorders or shawms. A " broken consort " implied some sort of mixture, e.g. viols with woodwind and lutes.

Towards the end of the century there emerged a new string type, at first not extending higher than alto range, with the name *viola da braccio*, i.e. " arm-viol ", since, unlike the true viol, it was held at arm level. Only gradually was it received into favour as the advantages of its four strings, high-arched bridge and unfretted finger-board were realised. Praetorius, in 1618, makes it clear that the (treble) *rebichino* or *violino*, constructed in this fashion and tuned G, d, a, e', was the true violin. One of its earliest makers was Bertolotti da Salo (1540–1609) of Brescia. Andrea Amati of Cremona (c. 1520–c. 1578), the first of a famous family, also produced models. The violin was used both by Andrea Gabrieli and Monteverdi, but its development belongs to a later chapter.

The lute, a plucked instrument, had, as we have seen, an ancient and Arabian history, and some mention of it has already been made (see p. 102). It had six gut strings, all except the top one doubled. In the sixteenth century and for a good part of the seventeenth it was an important domestic instrument, and one that professionals developed to a high pitch of virtuosity. An enormous quantity of valuable music was written for it, invariably in " tablature ", a system that indicated not the note-pitches but the strings and fingers to be employed for obtaining the notes. Time values were indicated by the use of note *stems*. The theorbo, a larger size of lute, with extra lower strings for open plucking, was also widely employed. Professional lute players were so skilful that the effect of a number of contrapuntal parts could be " faked " on the instrument with highly satisfactory results.

The gittern was a guitar-like plucked instrument with four gut strings. Not to be confused with it was the more popular cittern (=medieval *citole*) with four wire strings. There was also the pandora, with six double-wire strings, used mainly for accompaniment.

Regarding wind instruments—trumpets and sackbuts (=trombones) were used as freely for ceremonial and open-air purposes as in the previous centuries. The skilled trumpet players at princely courts or in the employ of large cities were of much higher status than the rank and file of professional instrumentalists. The double-reed shawm (early oboe) and its larger relation the bombard or pommer were used mainly for open air and for larger music-makings in church. The wooden cornett, previously mentioned, was often employed as a consort, in the various sizes. Another consort instrument was the recorder, the whistle-flute, which is enjoying a modern revival. In the sixteenth century it was a professional rather than a domestic instrument. The type to which we are more accustomed, the cross-flute, was also played, but not as much as in later centuries.

We have already found that in the fifteenth century Germany had taken the lead in the development of the organ, and this included the establishment of the pedal board, a feature not so soon employed in other countries. By the middle of the sixteenth century there were large organs in Germany with as many as three keyboards and a good variety of stops, including some for the pedals. Other countries lagged behind Germany in this matter, to various extents (see p. 101).

The sixteenth century saw a swift development of the domestic keyboard. We have already noted (p. 102) that the harpsichord and clavichord types can be traced back to the beginning of the fourteenth century or earlier. The harpsichord technique was a plucking one. The key-lever caused a piece of wood called a jack to rise, and a projection (plectrum), made of quill or hard leather, plucked the string in passing. As it fell back an escapement prevented the string from being plucked again. Various names were given to the instrument in various countries (e.g. cembalo, clavecin,

Flügel). Owing to the nature of the mechanism the finger action could make very little difference to the tone, and in the course of the sixteenth and seventeenth centuries various methods were found for providing tonal differences, such as by having alternative strings for each key, controlled by stops, and by an extra keyboard. The body was usually of a triangular "grand piano" shape. By the term harpsichord we nowadays understand this larger, improved type, with strings stretching away at right-angles to the keyboard.

England during the sixteenth and the greater part of the seventeenth century was content with the simpler model, called the virginal(s) (*virgula*= little stick=jack). The frame was usually rectangular, the single set of strings lying parallel to the keyboard. In spite of its simplicity some very fine music was written for the virginal, as we shall see. Somewhat outside the period of this chapter another variation of type is found in England. This was the spinet (? spine=quill plectrum) with wing-shaped body and strings lying at an angle of about 45° to the keyboard. (See Plates 25 and 27.)

The clavichord, less used in the sixteenth century than later, employed a different principle. A brass blade, called a tangent, *struck* the string. Thus it was possible to a certain degree to control with the finger the volume of tone produced, even though that tone was small as compared with that of the harpsichord. The clavichord was thus the instrument for the connoisseur in the privacy of the small room. In the seventeenth and eighteenth centuries the term "clavier" was applied to either keyboard type.

Instrumental Music—Dance Forms

In earlier centuries, apart from the evidence of some brief organ pieces, the only type of independent instrumental music had been that used for dancing. However, by the fifteenth century dance music was beginning to be written down, and a feature to be observed is that such pieces tended to appear in contrasting movements, a slow-quick pairing—pavan-saltarello, pavane-galliard, Tanz-Nachtanz—a slow duple measure followed by a quick triple. It is interesting to note that the same melodic material was often employed in both. At the beginning of the sixteenth century publishers began to issue volumes, especially of lute music, containing these forms. In 1508 Petrucci at Venice brought out a lute book containing the forms *pavan*, *saltarello* and *piva*, set in contrast, in that invariable order. By 1530 Italy had dance groups of up to five contrasting items, and the foundations were laid for the later dance suite. Other countries followed Italy's lead. The *sarabande* came into general use. France developed the *galliard*, *pavane*, *courante*, *basse-danse* and *branle*. The printer Attaignant of Paris published in 1529 a collection of dances, which, though the instrumentation was unspecified, were in four parts, quite homophonic in style, and in regular periods—as dances have to be. In this balance of regular sentences they resembled a type of contemporary French chanson. Though crude and monotonous in harmony, they sketched the shape of things to come, and the major key was freely used. There is little to remark regarding form, except of course the succession of cadenced periods. No attempt was made to balance similar melodic periods except in one instance of ABA. As the century progressed the various dance collections in all countries made more and more use of primitive binary (AB) and ternary (ABA) arrangements. For helping the lute player in his ever-present need for testing his strings the short *priambulum* or prelude was added. In a direct line from the dance groups lay certain chamber-music forms of the succeeding centuries. At the beginning of the seventeenth century the Austrian composer Paul Peuerl produced some string suites—*padouan, intrada, dantz, gallarda* (pavane, courante, allemande, galliard) in which, modified in each movement, the same melodic material was employed throughout.[29*]

Lute Music

Throughout the century leading composers produced a wealth of music for the lute other than in dance-forms. Written in the pseudo-contrapuntal style that professional lutenists had developed were innumerable ricercare, canzoni and fantasias, and arrangements of airs and chansons that were often framed in variation form. There were also examples of programme music after the Jannequin pattern—" battle-pieces " and the like, some naïve, some astonishingly successful. Italy was perhaps the most productive of lute music (French composers were more prominent in the next century). Francesco da Milano (c. 1490 c. 1566) composed brilliant and original fantasias that were models for later composers. Mention may be made also of the blind Giacomo Gorzanis, and Vincenzio Galilei (father of the astronomer). The climax of the Italian lute school came with Simone Molinaro (c. 1565– c. 1613), who wrote in every form with advanced technique, and borrowed from Gesualdo, Prince of Venosa, whose works he edited, some of the latter's extraordinary harmonies.

We have seen that Spain preferred to use instead of the lute the very similar vilhuela. Towards the end of the century this was gradually replaced by the guitar. Among vilhuela composers was Don Luis Milan (c. 1500–c. 1561), Loys de Narvaez (fl. 1540) and later the blind Miguel de Fuenllana. The variations form was practised particularly successfully in Spain at this time.

In Germanic lands the same type of lute music was produced without much individuality. The most famous name of the period is that of Balint Bakfark (1507–76), lutenist to the Emperor at Vienna.

England's important lute period came late. Outstanding was the work of the great John Dowland. Mention can be made of Anthony Holborne (d. 1602), Campion, Rosseter, Pilkington and Francis Cutting. Dowland's lute compositions covered a wide range, but his best remembered work is *Lachrimae . . . seven passionate Pavans*, one of which is a polyphonic elaboration of his song *Flow, O my tears*, while the others make fragmentary references to it. Parts laid out for five viols were also included. After Dowland's death English lute composition languished.

The Viol Consort

Compositions for groups of instruments, unspecified at first but gradually favouring the string group, were produced in all countries, and followed the usual pattern of fantasias, dance movements and arrangements of airs, often in variation style. In England examples survive of instrumental arrangements of hornpipes and jigs by Fayrfax and Cornyshe, but from the time of Taverner onward English instrumental composers favoured most the Fancy (=fantasia). Time and again this would be founded on a certain plainsong theme as found in one of Taverner's Masses, where it set the words " In Nomine . . ." (see Ch. IV, note 36*). For the rest of the century to the time of Purcell and beyond, contrapuntal string fancies labelled " In Nomine " were produced in large numbers. Bull, Morley, Dering, and with special distinction, Byrd, Gibbons and John Coperario (c. 1575–1627) produced beautiful examples of the form. Coperario, whose real name was Cooper, was an excellent musician employed at the courts of James I and Charles I.

Other Instrumental Ensembles

Mention has already been made of the term " broken consort ". In every country were to be found experiments in the combining of the timbres of different instruments. It was not true orchestration, for the various instruments played more or less continuously throughout a piece. Examples of a favourite combination towards the end of the century can be seen in Morley's *Booke of Consort Lessons* (1599) in which he arranged some pieces by various composers (including his own *Now is the Month of Maying*) for treble viol, recorder, bass viol, lute, cittern and pandora. This type of combination was found in the " Musicke roome " of the Shakespearean theatre.

Keyboard Music—Organ

As we have seen, the Venetian school was the pioneer in the keyboard development of the ricercare, canzone and toccata. Throughout the century leading organists in every country composed in these forms. A great name is that of the Dutchman Jan Sweelinck (1562–1621), a church organist at Amsterdam, who may perhaps be termed the last of the Netherland dynasty of composers. He wrote masterly vocal church music in the old polyphonic style, but his keyboard music was pregnant of the future, covering all forms down to secular dances. His single-theme fantasias come very near to being true fugues, and his chorale-variations are the earliest examples of a new form (see Ch. VII, p. 183 : also Ch. VII, Note 16*). He was a brilliant organist and teacher, and was the founder of the great North German organ school. To Amsterdam there came a succession of pupils destined to be the organists and leaders of musical life over a large area of northern Europe. His work was carried on by his best-known pupil, Samuel Scheidt. From his practice of providing music attractive to the morning promenaders in his church he may be considered as the pioneer of the popular organ recital.

With him may be mentioned his friend, the fabulous John Bull (1562–1628) whose early career was in England (at Hereford Cathedral and the Chapel Royal), where his dazzling technique both as organist and virginal player was fully recognised. But he spent much time abroad and after 1613 settled down as organist of Antwerp Cathedral, in which city he died. His best music was probably that written for the virginal, to be mentioned later.

Another *emigré* English organist and composer was Peter Phillips (d. after 1630). His music, both vocal and instrumental, was very famous in his day, and he was organist at the Chapel Royal at Brussels. He wrote a large number of madrigals, which, however, show no particularly English characteristics.

There must be mention of another form that aided the development of the technique of organ composition, the Organ Mass. The practice had grown up in medieval times (perhaps from the early fourteenth century) by which plainchant singing of the Ordinary of the Mass was interspersed with organ playing. In alternate sections of Kyrie, Sanctus and Agnus Dei, and alternate verses of Gloria and Credo the chant was heard, not from the voices but as a *cantus firmus* in the contrapuntal organ passage. Various styles of treatment were essayed and the practice applied, in a lesser degree, to portions of the Proper of the Mass, but the subject cannot be pursued in detail here. A less fortunate result of the device was that a proportion of the liturgical text was never heard by the worshippers, but it certainly constituted a step in the progress of independent composition for organ. The practice was found in all countries, and in the sixteenth century printed organ Masses appeared. In 1531 Attaignant published a volume of them; in 1543 came three notable examples by Girolamo Cavazzoni.

The same alternate treatment was given to Psalm verses, and even to the Magnificat (Cavazzoni published some versions). Organ settings of psalm chants were termed " versets ". Attaignant printed two books of versets, also in 1531. From this practice was derived the chorale variation, developed by Sweelinck and others of the North German school.

Harpsichord and Virginal Music

As the century progressed more and more music for the domestic keyboard was being written in every country, in the usual forms of dance movements, fantasias and air variations. Sixteenth century Spain produced some remarkable composers of keyboard music, and several treatises were published concerned with its technique, notably that of Thomas de Sancta Maria. The most outstanding Spanish keyboard composer of the century was undoubtedly the blind organist and harpsichordist Antonio de Cabezón (1510–66). Recent research has made it clear that he was of the very highest status, and his all-round mastery and originality has suggested the phrase " the Spanish Bach ". Particularly striking is his use of variations (*diferencias*), whereby one variation flows on in unbroken style into the next. He was in royal employment and accompanied Philip II on his journey to England (1554), where he stayed for a year. There he must have made acquaintance with Tallis and the Chapel Royal. His influence may have had something to do with the later high standard of English keyboard technique, and the native skill in handling variations.

Ex:43

(a) [Theme]

[1ST. variation]

etc.

(b) [last variation]

Two extracts from his *Diferencias Cavallero* are given above;[30] (a) the first presentation of the theme, an old Spanish folksong, and (b) the last of the four variations, with the theme in the lowest voice. His characteristic use of linking passages (mentioned above) gives the work an admirable sense of unity .

Towards the end of the century and contemporary with her madrigal school England produced a body of virginal composition that was equally distinguished and national in style, and in the period unrivalled in Europe. Two surviving keyboard pieces from earlier in the century, Hugh Aston's *Hornpype* and the anonymous *Lady Carey's Dompe,* show in their instrumental style that there must have been a good deal of virginal composing and playing in the years before. *The Mulliner Book* (between 1550–1575), a manuscript collection of keyboard pieces by, among others, Taverner, Tye, Tallis, Whyte and Redford, shows a promise of things to come, especially in the brilliant passage work of Tallis. It includes a number of *In Nomine* fantasias. The main wealth of English virginal music appeared at about the turn of the century, chiefly in a number of manuscript collections and one printed volume.[31*] These are :

1. *My Ladye Nevell's Booke*; copied in 1591, and comprising forty-two pieces by Byrd. These included *Sellinger's Round* and the celebrated *Carman's Whistle* variations.
2. *Parthenia* (printed in 1612); a wonderful volume, with eight pieces by Byrd, seven by Bull and six by Gibbons. Most of these are entitled either *Preludium,* or *Pavane* or *Galiardo.*
3. *The Fitzwilliam Virginal Book*; now in the Cambridge museum of that name (Plate 22). The largest of the group, it contains nearly 300 compositions written about 1600.[32] The chief contributors were Byrd, Bull, Phillips and Farnaby, but the names of Morley, Tomkins, Sweelinck and Gibbons, as well as those of less-known composers, are also found. A good proportion of these pieces are in variations form; there are *fantasias* and *In Nomines,* and the usual dances. One of the fantasias by John Bull—*Ut, re, mi, fa, sol, la* (the old hexachord scale), ranges through all the major keys. This suggests a system of equal temperament tuning, even at this early date. There are also a number of charming little miniatures with imaginative titles. One of the best composers of this type was Giles Farnaby (fl. 1590), otherwise obscure. His *Dreame, Toye,* and *Reste* are evergreen.

Belonging to about 1620 is :

4. *Benjamin Cosyn's Virginal Book,* chiefly distinguished in having in it about thirty pieces by Bull and a couple of dozen by Gibbons.

A number of Scottish virginal books survive. A proportion of the pieces therein are found also in one or another of the previously mentioned volumes, but names of Scottish composers also appear, the most distinguished being that of William Kinloch. It is clear from Continental survivals that English virginal music travelled abroad.

NOTES

1* HMS IV has a recording of this particular Sanctus, as well as the second Agnus Dei from another Mass of Palestrina's—*Missa Brevis*. Re the example given—in this (and in all other early music) the bar-lines are editorial. Bar-lines are found in the period, but only in score and placed irregularly, their only purpose being to assist the eye in the vertical scansion of the notes. Not until the next century did they begin to be employed in the modern way.

2 The borrowing here, with its editorial bars and stresses, is from A. T. Merritt's *Sixteenth Century Polyphony* (Harvard), pp. 40 and 42.

3* A truly remarkable example of Renaissance chromaticism is the Christmas motet *Mirabile Mysterium* by the Austrian composer Jakob Handl (1550–91), also known as "Gallus", who was for a time in de Monte's choir. HMS IV has a recording of this work. Certainly a sense of mystery is conveyed, and in a fashion that sounds at times definitely modern.

4* HMS IV has recordings of both the Byrd motet and the Greaves madrigal.

5 The term *Kapellmeister,* sometimes anglicised as "chapelmaster" (It. *maestro di capella*: Fr. *maître de chapelle*), is derived from the word *capella,* meaning a small church building. (Its ultimate derivation from St. Martin's divided cloak (*cappa*) cannot be pursued here.) But the term *kapell* became applied to the body of musicians serving not only a religious establishment, but a secular one. Thus we can assume *Kapellmeister* and its parallels to be the equivalent of "Director of Music".

6* HMS IV has recordings (a) of a motet (*Scio Enim*) by Lassus, and (b) the Benedictus and Hosanna from his Parody Mass, *Puisque j'ay perdu mes amours* referred to in the previous chapter (see p. 93).

7* HMS IV has a recording of the Benedictus and Agnus Dei of de Monte's Mass, *Benedicta es.* The thematic material is taken from a sequence of that name.

8* HMS IV has a colourful recording of *In ecclesiis.* HAM I prints the whole of the score. The two versions differ somewhat in their "resolutions" of the continuo—naturally enough.

9* Extract from HAM I, No. 136. HMS IV has a recording of another instrumental ricercare by Andrea Gabrieli (*Ricercare Arioso*) and one by Willaert.

10* See Note 1 above.

11* HMS IV has a recording of Victoria's six-part motet, *O Domine Jesu.*

12* HMS IV has a recording of a chorale-motet by Praetorius for soloist, chorus and orchestra, founded on a Lutheran hymn.

13* HMS IV has a recording of a performance of Tallis' motet, *Adesto nunc propitius,* which makes use of the melody of the famous hymn *Veni, Creator Spiritus* (cf. Dunstable's setting).

14 Mention has already been made (p. 112f.) of Byrd's six-part Easter motet, *Haec Dies,* a great work, full of striking effects of part-writing and rhythm (see Note 4 above).

15* HMS IV has a recording of Morley's *Agnus Dei* motet.

16* HMS IV has a recording of this "verse" anthem of Gibbons.

17 The reader may recall a sixteenth century picture by an unidentified French or Flemish painter, and usually entitled *Three Musical Ladies*. It is an interior. One of the charming girls is singing from a part. Another with her part-book before her on the table is playing a cross-flute. The other two part-books lie unopened. The third performer, without any music (she apparently " knows her stuff ") is twanging a lute, supplying perhaps the other parts, or the overall harmony. Thanks to the painter's meticulous care, the music they are playing can be identified as Claudin de Sermisy's chanson, *Jouyssance vous donneray*. The picture was the subject of an article by J. A. Parkinson in *Music and Letters*, April 1958, which gave new and interesting information concerning it.

18* HMS IV has recordings of chansons by Costerley, de Sermisy and Passereau, with, at times, instrumental accompaniment. An extremely interesting review of French Renaissance vocal music can be obtained from the two sides of Brunswick (LP) ATXL 1048—Nadia Boulanger and a French vocal and instrumental ensemble (fifteen works). Among other chansons there is included the vivid tone-picture *Le Chant des Oyseaux* by Jannequin.

19* Mention of a recorded example of a frottola, *El Grillo*, by Josquin has already been made on p. 106, Note 32. HMS IV has another— *A che son ormai conducto* —by an obscure Italian composer, Demaphon, and printed by Petrucci.

20 The regular practice of printing compositions in full-score did not begin until much later. How did composers work in those times, and earlier? Thurston Dart (op. cit., pp. 134–5) has shown that owing to the high cost of materials the *cartella* system was used. A *cartella* was a blank sheet of parchment or paper incised with stave-lines. A composition was drafted on it, copied into its parts, and the original washed away to make room for another, this continuing until the material perished.

21* HMS IV has a recording of a Spanish solo song by Luis Milan, with a vilhuela accompaniment.

22* HMS IV has a recording of Marenzio's five-part madrigal, *Scendi dal Paradiso*

23* HMS IV has a recording of Luzzaschi's highly dramatic " Inferno " madrigal, *Quivi sospiri*, full of chromatic harmonies.

24 A recent attempt to identify " Orianna " with Anne of Denmark, James I's queen, has not met with much support.

25* HMS IV has a recording of a performance of Morley's four-part madrigal, *Ho, who comes here?*—a clever piece of descriptive writing.

26* and 27* HMS has recordings of Wilbye's *Flora gave me fairest flowers*, and the first part of Weelkes' *O, Care . . .*

28* HMS IV has a recording of Dowland's song, *Sleep, wayward thoughts*, with lute accompaniment.

29* HMS IV has a recording of a *padouan* and *intrada* from one of Peuerl's instrumental suites.

30 Quoted from HAM I, No. 134.

31* HMS IV has recordings of virginal pieces by Bull, Farnaby and Gibbons. With them is the anonymous *My Lady Carey's Dompe*, previously mentioned (see p. 137).

32 The manuscript has an interesting history, too long for full detail here. It is one of three collections, the other two being of seventeenth century vocal and instrumental music, belonging to and probably copied out by an English musician Francis Tregian, resident for some years in Italy. He died in 1619.

CHAPTER VI

The Baroque Era I

IN reviewing the music of the late sixteenth century one is conscious, especially in the case of Italy, of a rapidly changing outlook. The brilliant choral and instrumental innovations of the late Venetian school, particularly those of the Gabrielis, the daring and dramatic harmonies found in the madrigals of such composers as Gesualdo, Luzzaschi and Monteverdi; the growing vogue of the highly trained solo vocalist; the general tendency of all music to express as dramatically as possible the more violent emotions —all these features were portents of revolutionary change. The leadership of Europe was now firmly in Italian hands, and, in secular music at least, the new age that we are about to consider represented the triumph of dramatic Italian melody over the close-knit counterpoint of the Netherlands tradition. Also characterising the new outlook was the fact that *functional* harmony was being gradually established. Chords were being thought of as separate entities, that is, vertically, and not as happenings which occurred because of the movements of the independent voices. Such a point of view was certainly apparent at times in sixteenth century polyphonic composition, as we have already noted, but part-weaving had been the basic principle. With the new secular music there came at first a violent revulsion against all counterpoint, all horizontal considerations. Such a state of affairs could not last, but when polyphonic part-writing returned generally a new emphasis is apparent. The outlook is now reversed; it is the counterpoint which is conditioned by the *harmonic* frame of the music.

We have termed the whole extensive period the " baroque " era, a name open to criticism since it is a borrowing from the vocabulary of histories dealing with art and architecture. But in default of a better term we shall use it to designate an age which, though it stretched from the closing decades of the sixteenth century to about the middle of the eighteenth, yet throughout had certain steadfast characteristics and techniques. We will consider the more important of these.

Monody

The Italian taste for dramatic declamation took a striking turn about 1600 in the appearance of a new " monody ", sponsored by a group of

Florentine aesthetes. While this was certainly *not* one of the "steadfast" features of the baroque era it was equally certainly the fount and origin of some of them. This use of a single declamatory vocal line in the setting of poetry was a deliberate and violent reaction against the methods of the polyphonic school. The clear delivery of the words being paramount, the instrumental accompaniments of the earliest monodies were framed in the simplest terms, to the exclusion of any counterpoint. A bass line alone was written to the singer's part, and on this foundation the player of a harmony instrument (normally a large lute or a harpsichord) improvised suitable chords. The instrumentalist was guided by the presence of certain numerical figures and accidentals, supplied by the composer. A bass note *solus* meant the use of an ordinary $\frac{5}{3}$ chord; the additions indicated such features as first inversions, suspensions and chromatic alterations. Such an improvisation was called "realising" the bass.[1]

The idea was not altogether new. We learn that as far back as the mid-sixteenth century, in France and Germany as well as Italy, skilled and overworked organists, when faced with the prospect of having to perform large choral compositions with inadequate resources, prepared for the task of filling-in at the keyboard by writing down only the lowest vocal part, and in performance improvised supporting harmonies from it. However, as far as we know, the Italian composers Peri, Caccini and Cavalieri (concerning whom more anon) were the first to use actual *figured* bass in their dramatic works of around the close of the century. Lodovico Grossi da Viadana, well known at the time as a composer, also has some claim in this respect. Possibly its use was more widespread than we know. A greater sonority for the accompaniment was usually achieved through the actual bass-line being doubled by some deep-toned instrument such as a bass-viol, or later, a violoncello. Incidentally, the *absence* of figures from a score did not mean that the bass should not be realised. It meant that the composer was passing on the responsibility to the performer.

Thus emerged the device of BASSO CONTINUO, one of the most characteristic features of the baroque era. Throughout the period the improvised keyboard accompaniment built on the *continuo* line, together with the sustained notes of the string bass, were the necessary features of all concerted compositions. The harpsichord became the normal supplier of the *continuo* in works not specifically demanding an organ, and in all such music we must imagine the incessant twang of that instrument. In bigger works, both continuo instruments might be employed. (A large lute, *theorbo*, sometimes did duty for the harpsichord, especially in the earlier years of the era.) The skilled improvisator filled in the background and remedied any harmonic deficiencies that there might be in regard to the inner parts. While in the earliest monodies the emphasis had been wholly on the vocal line, quite soon in baroque music the very essential bass took on the role of equal partnership with the other outside part, to the comparative neglect of the inside lines, as we have suggested.

The continuo lines of the first monodies were often extremely dull, and while this condition certainly soon improved a formal way was found of treating the bass-part, the device of BASSO OSTINATO (ground bass), which was put into frequent use in compositions of every sort. Such an *ostinato* consisted of a continually repeated bass passage of a few bars' length, and thus it maintained an overall (we should perhaps say, " under-all ") unity, while above, the element of variety would be provided by constantly new aspects of melody, harmony and rhythm. The device bore lasting fruit in the artistic chaconnes and passacaglias that were written, not only in the baroque era but through the later centuries to modern times. There was also the *strophic variation*, sometimes employed when several similar stanzas were to be set. The stanzas all had the same bass-line, but the melody differed with each stanza.

The declamatory monodies have yet another evolutionary claim. The men who produced them applied their principles to dramatic action, and crude and groping as their first efforts were, these gave a beginning to the great arts of Italian OPERA and ORATORIO. The somewhat amorphous and monotonous *stile rappresentativo* (speaking style) quickly became, in more gifted hands, the artistic device of the dramatic RECITATIVE, which, together with the more reflective ARIA, were the chief resources used in the development of opera and oratorio throughout the era.

The Concertato Style

This was another prominent feature of the baroque era. The terms *concertato* and *concerto*, which we find used freely in Italy in the last decades of the sixteenth century, were probably derived from the word *concertare*—to compete. In 1587 was published a joint collection of works by the two Gabrielis entitled *Concerti . . . per voci et stromenti*, and with this meaning the title suited well the particular style of composition, which made the alternation of groups of voices with groups of instruments a dominant feature. Other leading Italian composers such as Banchieri and Viadana used the same term *concerto* for similar works. This " contrast " style, which encouraged the use of large forces and gave brilliant effects, came to be employed generally for larger church compositions without any concerto label. We have already met an example in Giovanni Gabrieli's colourful motet *In ecclesiis* (see p. 115). The style, besides flourishing in Italy, was employed magnificently in the church music of Heinrich Schütz, a pupil of Giovanni Gabrieli, and the first really great German composer. It is seen in less spectacular guise in the verse anthems of seventeenth century England, with their contrasts of solo, chorus and orchestral interlude. Finally, the application of the principle to works for instrumental bodies alone led eventually to the emergence of the CONCERTO GROSSO and the CONCERTO for solo instrument and orchestra. The *Concertato* style produced the baroque Concerto *form*, though this, as we shall see, was not the Concerto form as we now know it.

Further Baroque Characteristics

As at other times of quick-moving musical change there were plenty of writers belonging to the early baroque who were ready to label and dogmatise. The seventeenth century was full of discussions concerning style, for the age was style-conscious in a way that the sixteenth century had never been. The contrapuntal techniques of the latter had sufficed for sacred and also for most secular demands, but the new age spoke of *stile moderno*, and —since it could not altogether discard the sixteenth century when it came to church music—*stile antico*. Monteverdi, like other leading composers of the time, found the need of being a musical bilinguist, writing, as necessity required, in either " first practice " or " second practice " (these were his own terms). Later, writers were maintaining that church, chamber and theatre music had each its own style, a classification which, with the normal meaning to the word, is not always easy to follow in current practice, especially as church music was soon being composed in accordance with the new techniques as well as the old. However, it does indicate that baroque musicians were aware of the need of adapting music to suit the new and more varied calls that were being made on it.

Time and again in discussing medieval and Renaissance music we have noted the necessity of realising that written notes were often merely the framework for the performers' embellishments. This is more than ever true of the baroque era. A modern score is expected to set out a full and exact representation of the music as the composer wishes it to be rendered, down to the smallest mark of dynamics, expression and phrasing. In the baroque era precisely the opposite view prevailed. The notation as the composer wrote it showed not as much as possible, but as *little* as possible of the effect to be heard. The continuo device was but one aspect of the widely held belief that the artistic imagination of the highly trained performers (and performers were indeed highly trained!) must not be fettered by too much notational rigidity. A point to be remembered is that the modern idea as to composer and virtuoso belonging to two separate specialisations did not obtain in the baroque era. To name but a few— Handel, Bach, Domenico Scarlatti, Corelli and Vivaldi were baroque creators and superb performers in one. Thus, while passage work might certainly be written out by the composer, a great deal of further embellishment was definitely expected from the solo performer. A baroque adagio, whether vocal or instrumental, showed in notation a very bare skeleton of notes indeed as compared with what the performing version was expected to be. Only towards the end of the era, and chiefly in the hands of J. S. Bach, do we find figuration written out in a manner that would seem to approximate to the music heard. Actually, Bach was taken to task for this by a contemporary critic, Johann Scheibe, who complained—" All the graces, all the embellishments . . . he writes out in exact notes, which not only deprives his pieces of the beauty of harmony, but makes the melody totally indistinct ". Embellishments had, of course, little place in choral *ensemble* music. We hear of such uses, but the necessary uniformity was obtained by careful rehearsals.

The treatises of the time make it clear that there was much else in baroque performances that depended not on notation but on immediate discretion and taste. We can spare only one further reference—to that of rhythm.

Here, conventions of performance decided that at times notes written as
even values were to be treated as uneven, and vice-versa, while uneven
values were also rendered in degrees of unevenness other than those notated.
Many other matters with regard to baroque performances must escape
notice here.[2]

In the early baroque the very emotional (" affective ") style practised in
solo singing called at times for a disregard altogether of the "beat"—
what earlier times had called the *tactus*. Even Monteverdi marked some of
his recitatives *senza battuta*. But baroque music as a whole, especially in
instrumental works, developed more and more the "bar-line tyranny" of
a long movement in regular unchanging rhythm. The "mechanical pulsa-
tion" of a Vivaldi or Bach concerto movement seems to our ears somewhat
rigid in style—although it may well be that actual baroque performances
were much more elastic and sparing regarding recurrent bar stresses than
some modern versions of the same music are wont to be.

Affection

The term "affective", used above, signalises another baroque preoccupation. The writings of the era are haunted by the term "affection" (or
"affect"), by which was meant the general mood of a verbal text, and
therefore the mood called for in the setting. Mention has already been
made of the *reservata* music of Lassus and his followers which had anticipated this outlook. The madrigalists had had very much the same ideas,
and moreover had at times carried musical illustrations of phrases and single
words to the point of absurdity. But the writers of the early baroque
called such explicit word-paintings pedantry, and insisted that it was the
"affection" of the text as a whole rather than the sense of a single word
that should receive the musical consideration. As Manfred Bukofzer puts it
(*Music in the Baroque Era, p. 5*):

> "Feelings were classified and stereotyped in a set of so-called affections,
> each representing a mental state which was in itself static . . . Accord-
> ing to the lucid rationalism of the time, the composer had at his disposal
> a set of musical figures which were pigeon-holed like the affections them-
> selves and were designed to represent these affections."

It must be added that these musical figures were not meant to be
pictorial. They were, rather, metaphorical, signifying rather than painting
the particular affection (which, in the early baroque, was usually among the
more violent emotions). In the gradually lengthening musical movements
of the middle and late baroque, care was taken that the same affection
should be maintained throughout, whether the piece was an operatic aria
or an instrumental section. There were no "contrasting second-subjects" in
baroque sonatas and concertos.

The Violin

The baroque era saw the full emergence of the violin, and its assumption of leadership as a virtuoso solo instrument capable of the highest artistic results. With it there developed the other members of the family, the viola and violoncello. Gradually the viol consort withered and died, its last stand, a very honourable one, being made in late seventeenth century England. Throughout the era Italy produced violin composers and execu- tants of the highest calibre, and the hour brought the men, e.g. the Amati, Guarnerius and Stradivarius families, who constructed the matchless instru- ments for them to use.

The Baroque Orchestra

In the heterogeneous collection that did duty for the early baroque or- chestra the violin took no dominant place in the mingling of melodic and continuo instruments, but before the middle of the era the *continuo* orches- tra emerged, relying mainly on strings—violins and bass—and the usual " filling-in " by the keyboard player. In the later baroque, contrapuntal writing having returned generally, there was greater equality among the orchestral voices, which were framed polyphonically, especially marked in the case of Bach's orchestra. Thus instruments tended to play more or less continuously throughout the whole of a movement, thereby giving it a colour that was mainly uniform. The actual choice of instruments might be ruled by the particular affection that was being sustained. The whole framework was still held together by the keyboard continuo. Not until the time of Rameau do we get the beginnings of modern orchestration, with its shifting, varying tints.

A Survey

After having considered some leading baroque features, it may be useful to summarise the main developments in the era, which extended from the last decade or so of the sixteenth century to c. 1730. These dates would be Italian ones; other countries were, generally speaking, anything from ten to twenty years behind. We have already made use of the terms early, middle and late baroque, distinguished by some writers, and these divisions we will adopt, with all the reservations mentioned previously.

The first phase, early baroque, may be said to have ended around 1630. It saw the development of the new monody, and the beginnings of Italian opera and oratorio. The old-world modes were still being employed side by side with " major " and " minor ". Thus, while unprepared and striking dissonances are met (together with chromaticisms and dramatic melodic intervals e.g. the augmented fourth) as aids to the violent affections that were favoured, they were not yet attuned to a tonal plan, harmonic lay-outs being still experimental. Movements tended to be short-breathed by our standards, for no satisfactory way of writing longer movements in the new styles had yet developed, except in episodical fashion, e.g. in rondo form. Instrumental music, still less important than vocal, was working out its own independent idioms. The violin, in the hands of Italian soloists, had already before 1630 established many of its characteristic techniques—wide skips, stoppings, *pizzicato*, the use of harmonics, tremolo, even the tricks

K

of *sul ponticello* and *col legno*. Monteverdi, while not the inventor of the devices, made striking orchestral use of the string tremolo and of *pizzicato*, notably in his dramatic scene, *Combattimento de Tancredi e Clorinda* (1624).[3] The violin sonata (solo violin and continuo), with its contrasting movements, was beginning its career, as often as not under the old and overworked name of *canzona*.

In the middle baroque phase, say 1630–80, Italian opera established itself as a highly attractive (and incidentally, commercially successful) art. It used as its two mainstays the devices of accompanied recitative and aria, and its soloists developed the *bel canto* style of singing. Oratorio and cantata were also widely practised vocal forms. The older modes were still evident but fast fading, and the major and minor tonalities were establishing themselves. Contrapuntal techniques were coming back more and more, and constructional devices of a fugal nature allowed for closely knit and more extensive movements, both vocal and instrumental, to be shaped. The " trio " violin sonata (two violins and continuo) became established as a favourite baroque form. The orchestral ensemble, while playing its part in opera and oratorio, found independence in the dance suite. In the development of this latter form Germany began to make some important contributions, both orchestrally and in keyboard music, as did France in an early harpsichord and a late lute school. Instrumental music was now an equal partner with vocal.

We will assume the late baroque to extend from c. 1680 to c. 1730— perhaps to 1750 in countries other than Italy. In it the major-minor tonalities, with considerable resource in the matter of modulation, were wholly established. Tonality as we understand it was not a single invention but its emergence owed much to both the Neapolitan opera and the instrumental music of the famous and long-established Bologna school with which such leading names as Torelli and Corelli were associated. The sense of " key " now ruled chord progressions, treatment of dissonance, and the very layout of the movements,[4] which, with greater constructional resources, were growing to considerable dimensions. Counterpoint was altogether ruled by tonality, but was achieving a high intricacy. Instrumental techniques were distinctively developed in their various idioms, while advanced vocal writing was even borrowing from instrumental figuration. Opera, oratorio and cantata had become stylised, with the soloist supreme. The violin sonata continued its development in church and chamber forms. Keyboard composers produced not only suites of dance forms, but some tentative several-movement " sonatas ". Solo instruments (the violin in the van) combined with orchestra to develop the concerto grosso and solo concerto. The make-up of the late baroque orchestra we have already mentioned.

But by now the continuo age with its revived contrapuntal style had lived a long time. Even before 1730 definite changes of taste were evident. In instrumental music, and even in vocal works, certain composers were writing in a lighter manner, replacing polyphony by comparatively simple, at times artless, harmonic methods. This, the *rococo* style, stood at the threshold of the Classical Age.

The Rise of Opera in Italy

Having broadly surveyed the terrain, it is time for us to consider its features in more detail. We return then to more than a decade previous to 1600, to "monody" and the story of the *Camerata* of Florence. The *Camerata* was one of many learned Italian groups of the time, men of intellect who met to debate matters of interest, these being often enough the principles of poetry and drama, ancient and modern. At the head of the *Camerata*, giving it guest-room, was the gifted Count Bardi. He was later succeeded by his friend Count Corsi. In the circle of scholars, poets and musicians were the Medici-court composer Jacopo Peri; Vincenzo Galilei, learned theorist, noted lute player and a composer well grounded in the old school yet burning to explore new paths; Guilo Caccini, an excellent singer whose training would give him some knowledge of composition; and Ottavio Rinuccini, of the Florentine court, a poet of more than usual ability. There was also the Roman gentleman-composer Emilio Cavalieri. This group was perhaps the most vocal among the enemies of *antico* counterpoint. They revived the ancient charge (one which was made at the Council of Trent) that, since imitative technique caused different words to be sung simultaneously, the result was verbal obscurity. It meant, they said, that the poetry was being "torn to pieces". They maintained that the setting of words should be for a single voice, the text dominating and music the humble handmaid. Bardi, Galilei and Caccini all expressed themselves vigorously in print, in the case of the latter two with examples of the new monody which we have already discussed. Caccini's musical settings of poetic texts survive, first printed in his book *Nuove Musiche* (1601), early essays in the new *stile rappresentativo*, with the new device of a simple *basso continuo* accompaniment. They may indeed be termed "cantatas". Caccini said, in his introduction: "I conceived the idea of composing a harmonic speech, a sort of music in which a noble restraint was placed on singing . . . in favour of the words". The affects, it would seem, were to be much emphasised, with gaspings and grimaces rather in the manner of a modern "pop" singer. Comparative amateurs (except for Galilei) as these musicians were, they had discovered something new—clear, "affective" treatments of the texts, the specially planned embellishments to support these (*gorgia*, we find them called) and the conception of melody being linked harmonically to a supporting bass. There had been solos in plenty in the sixteenth century, but these had been conceived and accompanied in polyphonic style. The invention of the *Camerata* monody seems to be one of the few instances where practice seems to have arisen from a previously imagined theory.

An extract from one of Caccini's "exemplary" works, the aria, *Sfogara con le stella*, which he printed in his second volume (1612) of *Nuove Musiche*, is quoted below.[5] The treble-line "resolutions" of the figured bass are, of course, editorial. One of the *gorgia* of the setting, which will be seen to be labelled, as in the original printing, as a *trillo*, is not a trill as we understand it (that was called a *groppo*) but a rapid measured tremolo on the same note :

Ex:44

A reproduction of a few bars of the original notation of the above extract may be of interest :

Ex: 45

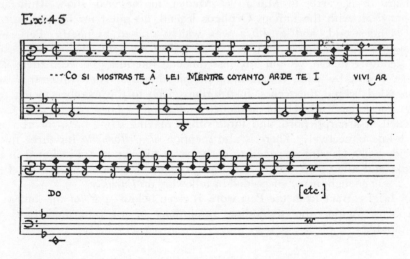

A translation of the text quoted above is as follows :

" . . . So did you show to her
　　As you shine
　　My burning ardours,
　　Would that you would make her with your golden appearance
　　As full of pity as you make me a lover."

The activities of the circle began a spate of " monody-cantata " composition by Italian composers, amateur and professional, some of it extremely crude (it seemed to be a game at which anyone could try his hand), some of it highly original in its daring melodic and harmonic devices, with every sign that a new and vital method of expression had been discovered. Even composers like Monteverdi were joining in.

But the *Camerata* went further. They were deeply interested in ancient Greek drama (we have already seen that Galilei owned some Byzantine manuscripts concerned with Greek music—see Ch. I, Note 7) and they proposed to revive what they imagined to be the style of delivery favoured by Aeschylus and Sophocles in stage works of their own, the *stile rappresentativo* being the basis. We know little enough in modern times concerning the music of the ancient Dionysian drama, but sufficient to realise that the *Camerata's* efforts bore small resemblance. Nevertheless, they were dramatically practical. Under the patronage of Count Corsi, who took over from Bardi in 1592, Rinuccini wrote a libretto poem *Dafne*, based on the Greek myth, which was set by Peri and performed at Corsi's palace in 1597. The invited audience of *cognoscenti* acclaimed it enthusiastically, but no modern assessment is possible since nearly all trace of it has perished. Its success resulted in an important commission for the poet and composer, a work for the Medici court on the occasion of the marriage of Henry IV of France (Henry of Navarre) to Maria de' Medici, in the year 1600. Rinuccini's poem dealt with the famous Orpheus legend, his quest for his lost wife in the Underworld, and *Euridice* was widely praised as poetry. Peri, who himself sang the hero's part, set it in strict *Camerata* fashion, ten scenes of steady recitative without any instrumental interludes between them, and relieved only by a few simple homophonic choruses. The " orchestra " was concealed behind the scenes, instructions given to the members being that they must not " attract the audience's attention ". They consisted of Corsi himself at a harpsichord, and three others playing string bass, theorbo and arch-lute respectively. There is also mention of a *ritornello* for three flutes. Incidentally, Caccini managed to get some of his own music included in the work, and afterwards wrote, and had printed, his own entire setting. Peri, strangely enough, never succeeded in following up *Euridice*.

A brief extract from the Peri work is given below—part of the lament of Orpheus. Again, the treble-line resolutions of the continuo bass are editorial.[6]

A translation of the text above reads :

"Alas, alas! At dawn the sun of my eyes has reached its setting.
Wretch, wretch! and at that hour
That I thought to warm myself in its fair rays,
Death put out the beautiful light . . . ."

Whatever its originality, this type of *dramma per musica* (the term
"opera" is of later date) was a pale sort of art, which had replaced a
musical tyranny by a verbal one. The blood-transfusion that it needed came
from the hands of a man of genius. It was Monteverdi who saw its potentialities, and realised them in a single original work. In 1607 at Mantua

he produced *La favola d'Orfeo*, to another libretto founded on the Orpheus story. It was a masterpiece, and still lives. Let us digress to consider the composer himself.

Claudio Monteverdi (1567–1643) was born at Cremona, and received there a traditional and thorough training in the hands of the well-known composer Ingegneri. From about 1590 to 1612 he served the music-loving (albeit miserly) Duke of Mantua, Vincenzo Gonzago, in various and increasingly important musical capacities. He accompanied the Duke on his travels, which took him as far as Hungary and gave him a wide experience. It was for the Mantuan court that *Orfeo* was written, as well as many of his advanced and highly dramatic madrigals. The licences contained in the latter compositions caused him to be attacked in print by the scholar Artusi, a supporter of the *stile antico*. He also produced much church music, a great deal of which would have escaped Artusi's censure, but some according to the "second practice". In the latter category was his famous *Vesper Psalms*, in *concertato* style and with striking orchestral accompaniments, a work still performed. In 1602 he was made *maestro di capella* to the Duke, but after the latter's death in 1612, he received an abrupt dismissal, and went back to Cremona and temporary poverty. However, in something over a year (1613) there came a dazzling change of fortune. He was elected *maestro di capella* at St. Mark's, Venice, which, as we have seen, was one of the most honourable and coveted of posts, probably on account of his already admired "Vespers". He held the position for the rest of his long life. At Venice he composed an immense amount of church music—Masses, motets and the like, in both practices, as well as a wealth of continuo madrigals, cantatas and monodies. He continued to write operas for the courts of Mantua and Parma until 1630, but their names only have survived. In 1632 he took holy orders. In 1637 the first public opera house was opened in Venice, and though he was over eighty the master's interest in the form was once more aroused. Between 1639 and 1643, the year of his death, he produced a series of works in a new style, and these had their influence on the course of the art. They will be considered later; let us first return to deal with the *Orfeo* of 1607.

The work was in a world apart from *Euridice*. The *Camerata* recitative was expanded into something far more dramatic and powerful. There were melodious solos in strophic variation form. The choruses returned to a contrapuntal attractiveness, and *nuove musiche* was no doubt outraged by the fact that Orpheus and Apollo sang a final duet in canon. The five acts were interspersed with instrumental *sinfonias* of different colourings, some of them more than once employed. There are actually twenty-six orchestral episodes. Monteverdi used no less than thirty-six instruments, not all at once, but so as to give differences of "affect" in different situations. The devices used in the opera by the composer were certainly all known—it was the way in which he selected and handled them that constituted the originality. Actually, the felicities of the work cannot adequately be dealt with in a book of these dimensions. The opera has been more than once revived in modern times, and we can still wonder at its power.[7*] Thanks to Monteverdi's example we find both the melodious *arioso* and the revived contrapuntal chorus taking their places in other operas of the time. Another Mantuan work of Monteverdi's, which attracted widespread attention when produced in 1608, *Arianna*, has unfortunately perished except for the celebrated "Lament of Ariadne", the pathetic beauty of which moved audiences of the time to tears. Nothing else of his early operas has survived.[8*]

Meanwhile opera was developing elsewhere. In the year of *Euridice's* production, 1600, Emilio Cavalieri (d. 1602) brought out his *Anima e Corpo* at the Jesuit Oratory building in Rome. This work is sometimes described as the first oratorio, but if we take the normal definition of the word, oratorio it certainly was not, since it was a *Camerata* stage-work with action and even dancing. It was carried through by the usual means of recitative and primitive homophonic chorus, together with continuo accompaniment. *Dramma sacra per musica* was its contemporary name, and for a time opera could be distinguished from oratorio only by the fact that the former sought to entertain and the latter to instruct and edify. We shall return later to the subject of oratorio; our concern now is for works with the secular outlook. From this time onward in all the greater Italian cities composers were producing operas—still, be it noted, for aristocrat patrons. After 1620 Rome took the lead. Among the many names of composers we can mention only two, Domenico Mazzocchi (1592–1665) and Stefano Landi (c. 1590–1655). Landi's opera, *Sant' Alessio* (1632), was a monumental work with not only fine recitatives and solos, in which characterisation was successfully attempted, but duets and trios. There were eight-part polyphonic choruses, and, most remarkable, comic episodes with rapid *parlando* duets. The accompaniment was for three violins and a number of continuo instruments. It is to be noted that the *sinfonie* before Act II was cast in three sections, an anticipation of Scarlatti's Italian Overture form. Other Roman operas also show the beginning of the comic element, Mazzocchi producing some works that were entirely comic. Regarding *Sant' Alessio*, the librettist was no less a person than the future Pope Clemens IX.

A new phase of opera began with the establishment of public opera houses in Venice from 1637 onward as commercial speculations, a move that was soon imitated elsewhere in Italy. For the rest of the century Venice was the chief centre of what had become a popular entertainment, and around 1700 could apparently fill no less than eleven such establishments. It was during the early years that Monteverdi's last operas were staged, the two surviving examples being *The Return of Ulysses* and *Poppaea*. Monteverdi had perhaps learned something from the Roman school. The recitatives were now more frequently interrupted by song-like passages (*ariosi*) foreshadowing the melodious *bel canto* style soon to come, and comic relief was employed. As ever, the master could summon a dramatic intensity to the serious moments that opera lost thereafter for a while. In company with other commercial operas of the time the accompaniment was an "economical" one, strings and continuo, with other instruments only for special effects.

The subject "Poppaea" (Nero's evil second wife) is significant. Opera having emerged from palaces to become the entertainment of the ordinary citizen, gods and goddesses went out of fashion, and figures from history (of a kind) took their places, displaying human emotions, though chiefly violent ones, restricted mainly to the affects of love and ambition. Since the box-office was now the main consideration, both display and the practice of economy had to be borne in mind. Orchestral forces were modest, choruses small or non-existent. It was the "star" singers, soprano and *castrato*, that gradually became the overwhelming attraction, while as much money as could be spared after the principals' fees had been paid was spent on stylised sets (baroque architecture on the stage), and machines to bring about startling effects of realism. Court opera continued as before, with its large orchestras and polyphonic choral ensembles, together with elaboration of scenic display, costume and stage machinery beyond the resources of the commercial type.

At Venice the leading composer was for a while Francesco Cavalli (1602–76), a pupil of Monteverdi. He wrote at least forty-two operas for the six Venetian opera-houses of his day, and had two performed in the Paris of Louis XIV. In his works monody finally merged into the *bel canto* style of recitative followed by rhythmic, smooth melodious aria, usually in triple measure. He was gradually displaced in public favour by Antonio Cesti (1623–69), even more melodious, and more varied in harmony and instrumentation.[9*] Cesti wrote for both public and court. An Imperial performance of his *Pomo d'oro* at Vienna cost a fabulous sum to produce. Other Venetian opera-composers included Pallavicino, Sartorio, Strozzi and Legrenzi. Giovanni Legrenzi (1626–90) was much more than an opera composer. *Maestro di capella* at St. Mark's, he wrote fine music of every type, was the master of the great violinist Vivaldi, and was admired (and borrowed from) by both Handel and J. S. Bach.

Alessandro Stradella (c. 1645–82), whose life was cut short all too soon, displayed in his melodious operas the growing importance of the set aria. The true *da capo* (ABA) aria is found in his work. He also did much to develop the *basso ostinato* form in effective fashion.[10*]

We now come to a very fine all-round musician indeed, the Neapolitan composer Alessandro Scarlatti (c. 1659–1725). On his work Handel modelled his own operatic style. The ingredients of the more mature Scarlatti operas were the rapid *recitativo secco* (continuo only), the more emotional *recitativo stromentato* with full accompaniment, and the now rounded *da capo* aria. The chorus tended to be neglected, any choral finales usually being sung by the ensemble of soloists.[11*] A successful invention of his, destined for long continued employment, was the "ensemble of perplexity". Some impasse having occurred in the course of the plot the principal characters debate among themselves on the theme "This is terrible! What on earth shall we do next?"—not very high drama, but an excellent opportunity for musical exchanges and the varied minglings of voices. (cf. *The Mikado*—"Here's a how-de-do!")

Scarlatti increased the resources of orchestral colour, and his accompaniments often show subtle detail and rich harmony. All this makes his grace-ful music still a great pleasure to listen to, although the (to us) absurd con-ventions of the libretti cause full performances of his operas to be almost impractical. He established firmly the " quick—slow—quick " three-move-ment form (known to have been already employed) of the so-called Italian Overture—the pattern of the early classical symphony—but it is doubtful if this part of a late baroque Italian opera ever received much attention in a public opera-house.

As time went on the tyranny of the leading singers became increasingly marked. The composer was compelled more and more to defer in various ways to the demands of the *prima donna* and the *castrato*, whose virtuoso aria renderings were the chief attractions for the audiences. Altogether, Italian opera became more and more a type of public concert in costume, in which the solo songs were the only items that were closely followed.

A large number of Italian composers continued the opera tradition of Scarlatti. Many of them were his pupils, and for a generation or so there was maintained what is sometimes called the Neapolitan school. It included Leonardo Leo (1694–1744), Nicolo Porpora (1686–1766), who befriended the young Haydn, Nicolo Jommelli (1714–74), whose works with their fine or-chestral accompaniments were appreciated throughout Europe, Nicola Lo-groscino (c. 1700–63), Giovanni Pergolesi (1710–36) and Tomaso Träetta (1727–79). A late Venetian group were Agostino Steffani (1654–1728), An-tonio Lotti (c. 1667–1740) and Antonio Caldara (1670–1736). From Modena came Giovanni Bononcini (1670–1755), Handel's future rival. At Dresden was Johann Hasse (1699–1783), a pupil of Scarlatti, who, though a German, produced Italian operas, over a hundred of them, and was probably the most popular opera composer of his day, his reputation exceeding even Jommelli's. All the above were gifted men who poured forth not only a wealth of operas, but also oratorios, church music, cantatas and instrumental works. All were admired and praised by their contemporaries in no uncer-tain terms, yet with a few exceptions their works no longer live.

Two names must receive further mention, those of Logroscino and Pergo-lesi. Both excelled in the newly established field of *opera buffa* (comic opera). We have already made note of actual comic operas at Rome, as well as of humorous episodes in the serious ones. The term *intermezzi* came to be applied to these latter, a name borrowed from the musical interludes that gave relief to sixteenth century dramatic works. The Neapolitan opera shaped them into independent under-plots, sketches of contemporary, often low, life, set to sparkling music. These finally won to separate existence. Logroscino was very successful in their composition, while the short-lived Pergolesi's *intermezzo La Serva Padrona* (" The Servant the Master ") created a veritable furore, and swept Europe.[12*] Together with other examples of the *opera buffa* it started the famous " war " (the " Guerre des Bouffons ") that convulsed Paris in 1752, when rival pamphleteers exchanged abuse regarding the relative merits of the dignified styles of Lully and Rameau and the new Italian form. The eventual outcome was the establishment of the French *opéra comique* (with spoken dialogue), and some attempts, notably Gluck's, to reform the serious type.

Some of Hasse's operas showed the earliest settings of texts by Metastasio (1698–1782), the most famous librettist of his age. He was a fine poet, and his twenty-seven " books " were regarded as models of their kind. They were set again and again by leading composers, including Handel and even Mozart. While their literary values were high, their unvarying conventions were partly responsible for the musical formality of serious Italian opera.[13]

Baroque Opera in France

Unlike other countries France refused to succumb to the first spread of Italian *opera seria,* in spite of Cavalli's visit and some other invasion attempts. Early French opera, unlike Italian, remained aristocratic in tone— " court opera "—growing up under the patronage of the young Louis XIV, each spectacular work being prefixed by a musical adulation of the " Sun King ". The first successful essays, e.g. *Pomone* (1671), arose from the association of the composer Robert Cambert with the librettist Pierre Perrin, the latter being the dominant partner. Then a new figure appeared. The stage was taken, quite literally, by Jean Baptiste Lully (1632–87), and it was he who shaped the course of French opera. Ironically enough, he was by birth an Italian, and began his career as Giovanni Batista Lulli, page to the famous Mdlle. de Montpensier. He early ingratiated himself with the young king, and having had a good musical education proved himself not only an amusing companion but an excellent composer of court ballets, in which he shone as a leading dancer. With a natural genius for unscrupulous intrigue as well as music, he succeeded in gaining from Perrin the king's patent for opera production, and he caused the unfortunate Cambert to take refuge in England. This monopoly in opera he guarded jealously for the rest of his career, which was a financial as well as an artistic success. His ascendency established, there began a long series of French operas in which he was associated with the excellent and accommodating librettist Quinault. The latter produced dignified texts, based on a surprising variety of subjects, which exactly suited the current taste, and gave large opportunities for the inevitable ballet. After the initial success of the pastoral, *Amour et Bacchus* (1672), there came the first full-scale opera, *Cadmus et Hermione* (1673), and thereafter operas (Lully's term was *tragédie lyrique*) were produced at the rate of about one a year (e.g. *Alceste, Isis, Amadis, Armide*), a total of about twenty. The majority, but not all, of the texts were by Quinault. Lully was undoubtedly a scoundrel, but he was a fine musician with an excellent sense of drama and construction. His experience as a string player enabled him to train his orchestras to a hitherto unknown pitch of discipline and precision, which became the crisp, strongly rhythmic French style of playing. He established also the French Overture—a dignified opening with plenty of " double-dotted " rhythm, followed by a pseudo-fugal quick movement and concluding with a dance section, or with some reference to the opening material. Handel used this form in his operas and oratorios.

Lully abandoned the *recitativo secco* in favour of a successful accompanied recitative founded on the declamatory style of the French tragic actors, frequently interspersed with short melodious airs of the Cavalli pattern, brief choruses, and of course lively ballets. Stage machinery played a spectacular part, e.g. Phaeton's fall from his fiery chariot in the heavens. There were even some cautious introductions of humour, as in *Alceste*, where the infernal ferryman Charon is shown collecting his fees from the shades, and rejecting the non-payers.[14*] Under Lully there were no troubles arising from the vanity of singers; French opera had but one master. His church music, not lacking in contrapuntal skill, was also much admired by his contemporaries. " Sieur de Lully " was widely respected as a musician, and students from other countries sought the privilege of becoming his pupils. One of these was the short-lived Pelham Humfrey, who transferred his lively style, together with Italian methods, to England and the Chapel Royal, much to the satisfaction of Charles II.

After Lully's death French composers continued the same tradition which culminated in the operas of Jean-Philippe Rameau (1683–1764), a man of great intellect, who comparatively late in his career produced a number of widely acclaimed operas, including *Castor et Pollux* (1737) and *Dardanus* (1739), in which Lully's methods were developed to a much higher technical pitch.[15*] The instrumental writing was much more colourful and illustrative. Flutes, piccolos, oboes, bassoons and trumpets all play their parts on suitable occasions. For the first time the orchestra as well as the singer is speaking in real emotional terms, and some of the independent instrumental episodes are veritable tone-pictures. Unfortunately, his beautiful music was often wasted on poor texts. He was a successful ballet composer, and some of his dance movements are still heard today. He wrote also much fine church and chamber music, and a great number of still vital harpsichord pieces.[16*] He must be remembered as well for his *Traité de l'harmonie* (publ. 1722), the first real attempt to systematise the study of the subject on its new functional basis. Before his death serious French opera was having to contend with the intrusion of Italian *opera buffa*, previously mentioned.

Baroque Opera in Germany

Heinrich Schütz's early venture in German opera (see Note 5) was only feebly followed up by German musicians. The chaotic state of middle Europe for several decades owing to the devastations of the Thirty Years' War (1618–48) must always be borne in mind. In due course, invading forces of Italian singers and composers, together with their operas, established themselves in favour at Vienna and at the courts of the various German minor rulers, where they gained complete ascendancy. In Hamburg, where a public opera-house had been opened in 1678, German opera maintained a precarious existence, kept alive mainly by the exertions of Reinhart Keiser (1674–1739). Keiser, though of necessity producing Italian and French operas, wrote and staged a large number of German ones. He used the familiar technique of the short aria and the *secco* and accompanied recitative. He was an excellent and truly dramatic composer, as his surviving *Octavia* (1705) well shows.[17*] The young Handel played violin and harpsichord in his theatre, and had his own German opera *Almira* performed there in 1704. Keiser's was a brave struggle, but in the end even Hamburg succumbed to the prevailing fashion.

Opera in England

The attempts at musico-dramatic form in the England of the seventeenth century took the form of the aristocratic Masque—acting in costume, singing and dancing, combined with elaborate and highly expensive scenic and stage-machinery effects. In 1617 a court musician, Nicholas Lanier, introduced the *stylo recitativo* into a Ben Jonson masque, while in Commonwealth times Shirley's famous masque *Cupid and Death* was said to have contained recitative, supplied by Matthew Locke (1630–77), which implies that in each case there were musical settings of the dialogues. In 1656 came d'Avenant's *Siege of Rhodes*, which, though cautiously called a " representation " by the author (the Puritans were still in charge), seems to have had its dialogue set throughout in recitative, by Locke and others, and thus may possibly be termed the first English opera. The music is lost; thus evidence is uncertain. Incidentally it must be remembered that the word " opera " was used freely in seventeenth century England, most of the time implying merely a play with incidental music.

There is no doubt as to the nature of Blow's *Venus and Adonis*, a true if miniature opera in a mixture of French and Italian styles. It was written for a private performance (1685) before Charles II. The music is altogether charming, and has a wide dramatic range, including moments of humour. It has stood up well to revival.[18*] John Blow (1649–1708) is better known as a good church composer, organist of Westminster Abbey and teacher of Purcell, who may have learned some tricks from the opera.

Henry Purcell (c. 1659–95) came from a musical family. His father was a member of the Chapel Royal, and Henry was admitted to it as a boy chorister under the régime of Captain Cooke. The latter had restored order out of chaos in the Chapel after the Restoration, and seems to have been a very good choir trainer indeed. That shrewd music-critic Samuel Pepys highly approved of him. The young Purcell was next under Pelham Humfrey, and when his voice broke was retained at the Chapel as a sort of musical odd-job man. Evidently his promise was already noted. In 1679, at twenty years of age, he became organist of Westminster Abbey. Three years later he was made also organist to the Chapel Royal. The rest of his life was a round of composing, playing and teaching, until his untimely death at the age of thirty-six. As we shall see in more detail, his large output included many anthems and other church compositions; secular cantatas; choral works such as the celebrated St. Cecilia and other festival odes; the various " Welcome Songs " written for court occasions; and a multitude of items—songs, choruses, dances and other instrumental pieces—written for stage works; many songs, sacred and secular, independent of the stage; string fantasias and violin trio-sonatas; organ music; harpsichord suites (" lessons ") and single pieces, including rounds and canons for popular use. He was indeed the complete musician.

Some of Purcell's best music was written to supplement play productions, but in 1689 came a true example of the genus " opera ", and a masterpiece at that. Amazingly, *Dido and Æneas* was written for private performance at a London school for " young gentlewomen ", among whom there must have been some considerable talent. It was a work of original genius, though owing something to Blow's pattern. It has been said of it that " in dramatic directness, characterisation, adaptation of means to ends, feeling for climax, as well as actual beauty, the opera is as much alive as are any of Gluck's. Every student is familiar with the poignant farewell of Dido, ' When I am laid in earth ', on Purcell's favourite foundation of a ground-bass; and the succeeding chorus of cupids is hardly less affecting, while the witches' music and all the rest is full of dramatic life and originality ". (Grove, article—HENRY PURCELL).

Much beautiful incidental music can be found in other dramatic works (e.g. *Dioclesian, The Tempest, The Indian Queen*). *The Fairy Queen*, a dramatic re-hash of *Midsummer Night's Dream*, was called an opera, but Purcell set not a line of Shakespeare's. The large amount of music in *King Arthur*, a stage-work by no less a person than Dryden, was again only incidental. We must therefore reject them as true examples. Purcell's short life afforded no further chance of another and larger work on the " Dido " pattern. Thus the opportunity passed for the establishment of real English opera. In 1710 came the Italian-trained Handel to establish an exotic art.

Spain

The seventeenth century found Spain with a national drama of great power in the hands of such men as Lope de Vega and Calderón, and perhaps as a result *opera seria* of the Italian type seems to have held no attractions. Another home-product was the flourishing stage entertainment known as *zarzuela*. This has survived into modern times as a kind of satirical, free-and-easy *opera bouffe*, but in the period, and largely in courtly hands, it partook of the nature of the English masque, always however with a strong element of humour. It thus gave plentiful opportunities for songs, choruses and dancing. Sebastian Durón, though *maestro* at the Chapel Royal at Madrid, was a highly popular composer of such works, as was José de Nebra (c. 1688–1768), also associated with the Chapel Royal. Not until the eighteenth century did Italian opera gain any footing.

Besides a vigorous folk-music there was the popular vocal *villancico*, part-music in strong rhythmic style, but into Spanish music in general there gradually penetrated the basso continuo and the concertato devices. Church music, however, still largely patterned itself on the *stile antico* of Victoria, and contrived to remain national and austere throughout the baroque era. The Spanish colonies, closely controlled by the motherland, reflected in their church music the same conservative outlook.

Oratorio

Oratorio as we know it is a *non*-dramatic setting of a sacred but non-liturgical text for solo voices and chorus with instrumental accompaniment, but the earliest stages of the form, which was of mixed origins, would not have fitted such a definition. Mention has already been made of the devotional *laudi* (see p. 53) which arose in the thirteenth century. The *Laudisti*, a religious confraternity instituted at Florence in 1310, cultivated these works, often sung in parts. In 1556 (St.) Philip Neri founded the Society of the Oratorio (*oratorio*=prayer-hall). At the Oratory building in Rome where he held devotional meetings for Roman youths Philip encouraged the acting of scriptural scenes together with the singing of *laudi*. When the writing of monodies became the fashion religious texts were set as well as secular. There were even dialogues, such as those of Giovanni Anerio (1567–1630). Anerio made use of a "narrator" (*testo*) to carry on the story, and also included contrapuntal reflective choruses. A landmark was the performance at one of Neri's oratorios in Rome of Cavalieri's *Anima e Corpo*, a dramatic work which made use of *laudi*, and which, as we have seen (see p. 153), had some links with the development of opera. Other more or less satisfactory experiments in the setting of religious subjects continued to be made, the best being by Domenico Mazzocchi in the 1630's. Finally the form was crystallised into non-dramatic and satisfactory shape by Giacomo Carissimi (1605–74) in his sixteen or more Latin oratorios, mostly founded on Old Testament stories (e.g. *Jephtha, Jonah*,[19]* *The Judgment of Solomon, Belshazzar*). *Jephtha* was his masterpiece. It is astonishing to note how quickly the composer has learned to shape the essential elements—rhythmic declamatory recitatives for the characters with periods of melodious *arioso*, and reflective or dramatic choruses, welded by the Narrator (*Historicus*) into an effective whole. The "Lament" of Jephtha's daughter, with an echoed refrain by her attendants, and the final six-part chorus that follows, are truly worthy of remembrance.[20]* For accompaniment Carissimi was normally content with continuo, but often two violins were added. In his day the oratorio everywhere became definitely non-dramatic.

Most succeeding Italian composers of the period wrote oratorios. Outstanding were those of Giovanni Colonna (1637–95), a fine church-composer and pupil of Carissimi, and Stradella, whose *John the Baptist* still lives. Alessandro Scarlatti's examples were numerous, and, as might be expected, full of beauties. To the oratorio he transferred his operatic technique of *recitativo secco*, accompanied recitative and formal *da capo* aria, together with, it must be confessed, something of the operatic atmosphere, which was indeed tending to invade Roman church music everywhere.[21]* But at Dresden the Lutheran Heinrich Schütz had earlier practised more austere methods in his *Resurrection of Jesus Christ* (1623). He too made use of a Narrator (*Evangelist*). Only fragments remain of an oratorio by the later composer Keiser. In these a dignified and most effective style is seen.

A specialised form of oratorio was the Passion, a musical setting of the events centred on the Trial and Crucifixion. This theme had been treated musically in a few examples of the medieval Latin church-drama, but the type that was destined to develop into the Passion oratorio was based rather on the liturgical practice, during Holy Week, of chanting by solo voice the

THE BAROQUE ERA I

story as related by each of the Evangelists. The gradual development of the
genre cannot be traced in detail here.[22] We may note however that examples
survive from the fifteenth century whereby the *Narrator* and *Christus* continued with their solo plainchant while independent and polyphonic settings
are given to the utterances of the "crowd" and other characters. A
Passion with a wide vogue was that of Luther's friend, Johann Walther,
written c. 1525. The texts are now in the vernacular, but the solo parts
still use the traditional plainchant (somewhat modified), and the "crowd"
choruses simple four-part harmony. Passions, both in Latin and the vernacular continued to be produced in all Western countries, more especially in
Italy and Germany, but we can pause only at the three by the great
German composer Heinrich Schütz (1585–1672). In these (according to St.
Matthew, St. Luke and St. John) we have the beginning of the oratorio
type. Although the Gospel texts (in German) are used, the words of the narrator (*Evangelist*) and Christ are set to the composer's own recitative. The
utterances of the "crowd" and other speakers are given four-part polyphonic and often strikingly dramatic settings. Schütz was a thoroughly
progressive baroque composer, yet in these Passions, written towards the end
of his life, he appears to be reaching back to the Middle Ages. The recitative which makes up the bulk of each work seems deliberately in its narrow
range, its extreme care for the inflexions of the text and its suggestions as
to the use of a reciting note to be recalling the atmosphere of the Gregorian
chant. The archaism of the style is further emphasised by the composer's
withholding any kind of instrumental accompaniment from his settings.
Modern revivals of these works (in which his *a capella* wishes have been
respected) have confirmed the artistic effectiveness of this seeming asceticism.

But newer fashions were prevailing. In the Passions that followed in the
course of the period, both Italian and German, the tendency was to use
specially written libretto-poems containing a great deal of emotional moralis-
ing, and an operatic style of setting with orchestral accompaniment. The
Passion libretto-poem by the Hamburg senator Berthold Brockes, less taste-
less than some, was the best known of its kind, and was set by Keiser, Telemann, Matheson, Handel and a score of other composers. When J. S.
Bach turned to Passion music he was able in his settings according to St.
John and St. Matthew to bring back a more fitting atmosphere, assimilating and reconciling the incongruous elements. He restored the Biblical
narratives, and even though he made some use of Brockes' verses in the St.
John Passion, he relied on his own shapings and the texts of his friend
" Picander " (the poet, Christian Friedrich Henrici) for his librettos. In each
work his use of a series of German chorales was masterly. Ruling all was
the power of his matchless technique and his spirit of religious devotion.

With the mention of Heinrich Schütz we must give further consideration
to the greatest German composer of the age. He was a man of wide culture,
and though a good Lutheran went to Italy to complete his training, as did
Handel and Mozart and many another German composer. He studied at
first under Giovanni Gabrieli, and later undertook a second course with
Monteverdi. Thus comprehensively equipped he carried on his life-work as

L

Kapellmeister to the Elector of Saxony at Dresden. His *Psalms of David ...* (1619) and *Cantiones sacrae* (1625) employed a blaze of tonal and instrumental splendour in the best Gabrieli tradition, but he showed that with striking dissonances and unusual melodic intervals he could blend the old polyphonic style of masterly counterpoint. His religious sincerity was all his own. Over the years he published a series of motets, the *Symphoniae sacrae*. One of these (1650) was the celebrated " Damascus road " scene, " Saul, Saul, why persecutest thou Me?".[23]* In his *Christmas Oratorio* (1664) each individual and group has for its accompaniment a particular tone-colour. In complete contrast were his volumes of *Little Sacred Concertos* (1636 and 1639) written for small forces, since the Thirty Years' War had at that time temporarily disrupted the Dresden establishment. In them Schütz showed himself as much a master of the solo cantata as of the larger forms. Of late (1963) his great stature is being more generally realised, and his music more than ever performed.

Other German composers of Schütz's day were contributing abundantly to the type of motet that had its place in the Lutheran service. Among them was Johann Schein (1586–1630), whose most important contribution was *Cymbalum Sionium* (1615), a group of thirty motets. Samuel Scheidt (1587–1654) most famous perhaps as an organ composer and teacher, also published church " concertos " in the same style. Though historians speak of the " three S's ", neither Schein nor Scheidt approached the greater master's stature. Regarding these motets, the ubiquitous term " concerto " was the name most frequently given to the form, which was destined with the aid of further Italian influence to develop into the Protestant church-cantata as Bach knew it. We will now trace the path of the cantata form from its first beginnings in Italy.

The Cantata

The term " cantata " implies merely " a composition that is sung ", but we will expand this to " a narrative lyric poem set to music in monodic style ". As we have seen, such works abounded in Italy at the beginning of the seventeenth century, having arisen from the same sources as those of opera and oratorio. Various names were given to the type, even that of " madrigal ", but the term " cantata " was not used until about 1620. After various experiments the form became standardised as one in which a variety of personal emotions were expressed by means of recitative, arioso and aria with continuo accompaniment. Monteverdi wrote some famous monodies which may be regarded as cantatas, but the first leading exponent was the Roman composer Luigi Rossi (1598–1653).[24]* The man who more or less fixed the shape of the Italian cantata for many years was Alessandro Scarlatti. It was now a popular chamber-music form, and Scarlatti poured forth examples to the total of nearly six hundred. Most were in the pattern of recitative, aria; recitative, aria—successively, and they showed as some of his best and most melodious work, being written with greater care than some of his operas. Stradella's cantatas were also celebrated. Indeed, almost every prominent Italian composer of the age had cantatas to his credit.[25]*

Besides the Chamber Cantata (*Cantata da Camera*) for secular use, in tragical, pastoral, or even humorous or satirical vein, there was also the Church Cantata (*Cantata da Chiesa*) with a religious text for libretto and devotional in intention. Carissimi's church cantatas were particularly renowned. Two-voiced cantatas in contrapuntal style (chamber duets) were sometimes written, a form favoured by Handel, and there was the occasional festival cantata for trio and quartet.

The form, as ever, spread to other countries. Southern Germany, thoroughly Italianised musically, took to it readily enough, the North less eagerly, though Keiser produced about a hundred secular examples. It must be recalled that owing to the terrible Thirty Years' War there was a greater division than ever between Catholic South Germany and the Protestant North. In Lutheran Germany the music of the people was largely centred on the local church, and religious music of a national, Protestant temper played a great part in the general life. Thus the development of the Lutheran church cantata, though finally borrowing as Schütz had done, the devices of recitative and da capo aria, was moulded by German composers to a definite German style. In its motet form it was usually based on a Latin Biblical text, which was linked with the Gospel of the day, and thus with the sermon, but, as in the case of the Passion, devotional poetry began to be used, and the later shape owed much to the libretti of Pastor Neumeister, who around 1700 wrote a large number of cantata texts for all the church festivals of the year. These were set by composers again and again. Neumeister shaped his libretti in the form of a succession of recitatives and arias, each pair with its single " affect ", and admitted that his style of cantata " looks like a piece from an opera ". It was he who insisted on the term " cantata " for these Lutheran church works, but the old name " concerto " remained still in use. Bach himself seems to have preferred it, and termed his examples of this form *Kirchenkonzerte* or *Motetten*.

The distinguishing feature of the German type of church cantata was the use made of the chorale, that pillar of the Lutheran service. An example of a chorale motet by Michael Praetorius has already been noted.[26*] Various methods of treating the chorale technically and artistically in vocal forms were used by German composers from Praetorius, Hans Hassler (1564–1612) Schein and Scheidt onwards. At the hands of Franz Tunder (1614–67) the *chorale* cantata began its development. In this type the text of a particular chorale was made the basis of the cantata, perhaps used verse by verse in various ways (chorus, recitative, aria . . .), or partially or wholly paraphrased, or having interpolations of independent material. The chorale melody could play a prominent part or quite a minor one, sometimes appearing only in the plain statement of the chorale which usually concluded such a work, and in which the congregation joined. When use was made of the tune in other items this was found most often in the opening chorus. The church cantata continued its course in the hands of such fine composers as Deitrich Buxtehude (1637–1707), Tunder's successor at Lubeck;[27*] F. W. Zachau (1663–1712), the teacher of Handel; Johann Kuhnau (1660–1722), whom J. S. Bach succeeded as cantor at Leipzig, and reached its climax in the work of Bach himself. In its more developed form use was made in various ways of the resources of dramatic recitative, da capo aria, duet and chorus with accompaniments by orchestra and organ, as well as orchestral introductions and interludes. There was much picturesque colour from a large variety of instruments. As in opera, an aria sometimes had an *obbligato* solo instrument with it. In general there was considerable variety as to the forces employed, church cantatas being written even for single voice. The total production of Lutheran church cantatas in this age must have reached an enormous figure, since it was the routine duty of every competent organist-composer to write them for his services. Bach's total was probably nearly three hundred, but Georg Telemann (1681–1767) seems to have more than doubled this figure. In Bach's case the chorale cantata type found increasing favour in his later years at Leipzig, when he was endeavouring more and more to subdue the secular elements to the devotional spirit. With the help of his poet friend " Picander " he established a unity of text and melody that took the forms, in actual chorale-verse statements or in paraphrase, of chorale-recitative, chorale aria, chorale chaconne and other technical designs, onward to the last plain vocal statement. *Jesu der du Meine Seele* and many others composed around 1740 exemplified his most mature achievements in the sphere of church cantata.

Some mention must be made of solo song in baroque Germany, settings of native poetry that flourished for family use and for such gatherings as those of university students. The first prominent composer of this type, the continuo Lied, was Heinrich Albert (1604–51), cousin and pupil of Schütz. A later name is that of Adam Krieger (1634–66), a pupil of Scheidt. The style was mainly strophic, but with sonorous ritornelli. Small ensembles of soloists were also written for. The advent of opera and the cantata form discouraged the progress of the Lied, but in the late baroque Philip Erlbach (1657–1714) produced some popular collections (he called them *arias*, but they were of the continuo lieder type)—his *Harmonische Freude* of 1697 and 1710. The influence of opera can be seen, however, in their obbligato accompaniments and occasional coloratura style.[28*]

Vocal Music in England

A return will now be made to the beginning of the seventeenth century in order to trace the development of native vocal forms other than the foredoomed English opera. The withering of the English madrigal after the first two decades, and at the same time the flourishing of the ayre has already been noted. To judge by contemporary publications the " catch " and " round " type of choral singing was also vigorously alive, and developed in due course into the popular " glee " of the eighteenth century. Men like Henry Lawes (1596–1662), his brother William (1602–45) and Nicholas Lanier (1588–1666), besides writing charming songs took up the Italian cantata form. Henry Lawes' efforts in the Camerata declamatory style gained him the approbation of Milton, who, in one of his sonnets, somewhat exaggerated his achievements. By the 1630's it is apparent that Italian melodic influences and the use of the basso continuo were fairly established in this country.[29]* Special mention must be made of William Lawes, who was killed fighting in the Civil War. Trained by Coperario, he produced in the course of little more than twenty years a wealth of chamber music, songs, part-songs, stage and church music the high quality of which is being more and more appreciated in the light of modern research.

Meanwhile the Anglican church service in high places continued in conservative fashion in the main, though the verse anthem was clearly imitating Continental *concertato* methods. After the deaths of Byrd and Gibbons, William Child (1606–97) was probably the most prominent composer of church music until the arrival of Humfrey, Blow and Purcell. In 1639 Child showed the new trend in his publication of a set of anthems for two trebles and bass with organ or theorbo continuo—" newly composed after the Italian way ".

In 1643, with the Civil War in full spate, the Chapel Royal was expelled, and everywhere in England churches were defaced and organs and service music destroyed. However, the Puritans permitted secular music and even the masque form to continue, and it seems that the suppression of Anglican church music actually had the effect of increasing the practice of private music-makings and the composition of chamber-music, to a standard unsurpassed at that period by any other country in Europe.

With the Restoration of 1660, Anglican church rites were resumed and the Chapel Royal reassembled, but the recovery was gradual and by then French and Italian influences were even more rife. Blow and Purcell wrote fine contrapuntal anthems at times, but the verse style predominated.[30]* Accompaniments frequently had orchestral aid, together with instrumental ritornelli, while the florid melody and lively rhythms of the Continent were at times very apparent. Even in Purcell's greatest church works the loping dotted crotchet and quaver roulade is frequently found. Yet there is much noble music in such anthems as " I will give thanks ", " My beloved spake " and " The Lord is my light ", the greatest of them being possibly the Coronation anthem of 1685, " My heart is inditing ". An outstanding piece of festival music is his Te Deum and Jubilate in D, with numerous solos, five-part chorus, and accompaniment for strings, trumpets and organ continuo, a spectacular piece of " modernity ". Yet he was still a master of the old counterpoint, and wrote a series of " sacred canons " in the strictest form. Some mention has already been made of his secular works, but further attention must be called to the Odes, which contain some of his finest music, written for large forces—soli, chorus, strings, continuo and various obbligato instruments. There were two main reasons for these Odes (apart from some occasional examples)—Queen Mary's birthdays, and the celebrating of St. Cecilia's Day over several years. These tributes to the patron saint of music are significant as being written for *public* music-makings in several different English towns, a new feature. Purcell wrote a number of " Welcome Songs " in his official capacity, addressed either to Charles or James after Royal returns to London—good music, but marred by the fulsome flattery of their bad poetry.[31]* The composer also contributed an extraordinary number of rounds and catches to the already plentiful material used by the numerous tavern and coffee-house " catch clubs " of the period.

Charles II's preference for the lively Continental style was apparent not only in the music of the Royal chapels but in the steady importation of foreign musicians to the Court. Among the English ones displaced was John Banister, composer and leader of the " King's violins ". In 1672, no doubt from economic necessity, he started what were the first public concerts in England. At his Whitefriars house there was " musicke performed by excellent masters, beginning at four of the clock in the afternoon ". These concerts seem to have continued until the year of his death in 1679.[32] Another concert promoter, a remarkable figure, was Thomas Britton, musical amateur and professional small-coal merchant, who started his famous music-makings over his shop in 1678, attracting " genteel " audiences and some notable performers in the course of their long continuance. Towards their end Handel himself was to be found playing the harpsichord in them.

NOTES

1 To speak here of a " first inversion " is to use an anachronism. Not until the time of Rameau was the idea mooted that chords could be explained as being in " root position ", or in " inversions " of that position. " Figured bass " developed, of course, to much greater elaboration as the era proceeded and harmonic intricacies grew. Long after its performance uses had ceased it remained to plague generations of harmony students.

2 The reader should consult Grove's Dictionary, articles: BAROQUE INTERPRETATION, and ORNAMENTATION.

3 In the *Combattimento* . . . there is also an " affective " orchestral figure that seems to be actually graphical, representing the sound of galloping horses.

4 As Bukofzer puts it (op. cit. p. 219): " Tonality established a graduated system of chordal relations between a tonal centre (the tonic triad in major or minor) and the other triads (or seventh chords) of the diatonic scale. None of these chords was in itself new, but they now served a new function, namely that of circumscribing the key."
It was left to Rameau, more than a generation later, to codify the system in his celebrated treatise.

5 The quotation from the Caccini aria is taken from the transcription printed in HAM II (No. 184). The text translation is from the same work.
One gathers from both the writings and actions of Caccini that there was a good deal of " gasconade " in his make-up, and that he was ruled by an intense jealousy of the better musician, Peri.

6 The quotation from *Euridice* is taken from the transcription printed in HAM II (No. 182). The text translation is from the same work.
The libretto was also used, in translation, by the composer Heinrich Schütz, and became the first German opera. It has unfortunately perished.

7* HMS IV has a recording of part of one of the *Orfeo* scenes, in which Orpheus rashly disobeys Pluto's dictates and loses Euridice for the second time. There is also a recording of an excerpt from the *Orfeo* of the Roman composer Landi

—Charon, the infernal ferryman, singing a bass solo that borders on the humorous.

8* The Archive Productions have a LP recording (APM 14020) of a performance of the Lament (together with a recording of Carissimi's oratorio *Jephtha*).

9* HMS V has recordings of arias from operas by Cavalli and Cesti. The Cesti excerpt is from the above mentioned *Pomo d'oro*, an "infernal regions" scene, the affect maintained throughout by the orchestral colour of oboes, bassoons, trombones and chamber-organ. The stage setting was fantastically elaborate.

10* HMS V has a recording of two short arias from a Stradella opera, illustrating both the *da capo* form and the composer's masterly use of the *basso ostinato*.

11* HMS V has a recording of a graceful aria from a Scarlatti opera, it being divided between the four principals. It illustrates well the felicities of the composer's melody, harmony and instrumentation (strings, continuo and two oboes), and also the use of an effective modulating scheme.

12* HMS V has a recording of an amusing *buffa* aria by Logroscino. Regarding Pergolesi, his attractive *Stabat Mater* still receives occasional performance.

13 Metastasio's real name was Trapassi. He was the son of a Roman shop-keeper, but at the age of 32 he was Court poet to the Emperor at Vienna. His success was due not only to his own genius, but also to discerning and generous patronage. His exotic name was a play on his true one. The Italian word *trapassemente* =transition=the Greek *metastasio*. Undoubtedly his career represented a considerable transition.

14* HMS V has a recording of this "Charon" episode.

15* HMS V has a recording of an air from *Dardanus*.

16* HMS V has a recording of a very effective fugal movement for chorus and orchestra (*Cor meum*) from a Rameau psalm-setting.

17* HMS V has a recording of a highly emotional scene from *Octavia*, that of the demented and dying Nero. The hearer will note how the phrase which sets the words, "Nero is no longer Nero" occurs again and again with powerful effect.

18* HMS V has a recording of a scene from *Venus and Adonis*.

19* HMS V has a recording of Jonah's "Lament" from the interior of the whale —a highly emotional declamation, as might be expected in the circumstances.

20* The previously mentioned Archive LP recording (APM 14020—see Note 8) gives a complete and highly competent performance of this fine work. Novello & Co. publish the vocal score.

21* HMS V has a recording of an excerpt from Scarlatti's motet for soli, chorus and orchestra, *Est Dies Trophaei*, which at times, in its frequent lilting rhythms and its handling of solo voices, is curiously similar to the operatic aria, the recording of which has already been mentioned (see Note 11). To be fair to Scarlatti, a great deal of his church music is in the older *a capella* style.

22 Readers should consult Grove's Dictionary, article—PASSION MUSIC. Mention has already been made above (p. 100) of English Passion settings in Tudor times.

23* HMS V has a recording of this work, for a sextet of soloists, two full choirs, two violins and organ continuo. HAM II prints the score in full (No. 202).

24* HMS VI has a recording of six sections (more than half) of Rossi's cantata *Del Silentio*, for voice and continuo.

25* Secular cantatas more extensive than the Scarlatti type were written by the all-round Venetian composer Benedetto Marcello (1686–1739), for soli, chorus and string orchestra. HMS V has a recording of an excerpt from one of them (" The Weeping and the Laughter of the Four Seasons "). The string writing is noticeably brilliant and imaginative.

26* See p. 138, Note 12. HMS V also has a recording of a motet for double choir. *Ich lasse dich nicht,* by Johann Christoph Bach (1642–1703), uncle of Johann Sebastian in which subtle use is made of a chorale of that name together with the third stanza of a hymn poem by Hans Sach. The work is worthy of the nephew.

27* HMS V has a recording of an excerpt from a church cantata by Buxtehude, a duet for bass and soprano with strings and continuo accompaniment.

28* HMS VI has a recording of a solo song by Erlbach from the 1697 collection (" My sighs and plaints "), in strophic form with ritornelli, accompanied by two violins and continuo, each strophe being a da capo aria.

29* Purcell wrote a number of fine solo songs ranging from the simple strophic type to examples resembling the short cantata. HMS VI has a recording of his *The Fatal Hour* for voice and continuo.

30* HMS V has a recording of a verse anthem by Pelham Humfrey, " Hear, O Heavens ", solos and various blendings of solo voices alternating with four-part chorus.

31* HMS VI has a recording of an excerpt from Purcell's Welcome Song, *What, what shall be done.* The music, for strings, recorders, soli and chorus, is most effective. The libretto is terrible.

32   Recent research has tended to increase the stature of Banister, as being a very worthy composer indeed. He was undoubtedly very shabbily treated. Even those English musicians still in the King's employ sometimes found it hard to live, for salaries were in a chronic state of arrears. Pepys reports in his Diary that the Court harpist, the quite famous Charles Evans, did actually " die for mere want ".

ADDITIONAL NOTE—The *Hemiola* Rhythm

An intriguing rhythmic feature inherited from Renaissance times is the *hemiola*. It was used throughout the baroque age, especially in songs and dance movements. Both Handel and Bach can show examples. It amounted to an alternation between $\frac{3}{4}$ and $\frac{6}{8}$ measure (or $\frac{3}{2}$ and $\frac{6}{4}$). Since each measure can be thought of as six units, then such a succession of rhythms as the following, from a drinking song by Monteverdi, can be written:

No rhythm clues such as are given here in brackets appeared in the original. Indeed, in early baroque the use, for example, of C at the beginning of a stave as an apparent time signature might prove a trap for the unwary, since it had not necessarily a metrical, but rather a mensural meaning. It merely indicated that the *beats* were divided by *two*. The piece itself might be in triple time. The reader is reminded of a fascinating nineteenth century example of *hemiola* rhythm as used by Brahms in the first movement of his String Quartet in B flat major (Op. 67). The rhythms vary not only horizontally but vertically.

CHAPTER VII

The Baroque Era II

Instrumental Music. The Violin

MORE detailed consideration will now be given to the instrumental forms of the baroque era, which were no less revolutionary and fruitful than the vocal. The newly established violin, which at first had been viewed with a certain amount of suspicion as being noisy and blatant, not altogether a "U" type of instrument, now came into its own. Mention has already been made of the "dynasties" of Italian violin makers who aided its progress towards material perfection. The chief individuals were Nicolo Amati (1596–1684), Antonio Stradivari (c. 1644–1737), his pupil, and Guiseppe Guarneri (1698–1744)—all citizens of Cremona in Lombardy. With the violin came also the viola and violoncello, but the latter had long to contend with the continued employment of the bass viol da gamba. As it was, the whole viol family lived on through the greater part of the seventeenth century, albeit precariously. Its chief strength was in England, and English viol music continued to be admired on the Continent.[1] English bass-viol players were frequently to be found employed at German princely courts. The baroque era marked the hesitant evolution of the violin bow from the old concave stick type towards straightness and eventually to the present convex form. The most important name in the development of the modern bow is that of the French bow-maker François Tourte (1747–1835)—somewhat outside the period, of course.

The Sonata, Concerto Grosso and Solo Concerto

The technical possibilities of the new instrument were realised and exploited by Italian violinist-composers with remarkable promptitude in the early part of the seventeenth century. The instrumental form most favoured by these solo violinists was the Sonata, an adaptation, as already mentioned, of the *canzona da sonar*, which had become a free fugal chamber form, with a tendency to fall into contrasting sections of different textures and tempos. The baroque sonata idea first developed in certain cities of northern Italy, where the presence of gifted composers occupying important posts, the existence of long-established instrumental traditions (as in Bologna), the incidence of active publishers, and the nearness of the great violin makers all aided in the production of such compositions, which employed strings with continuo. Keyboard sonatas were of rare occurrence until about 1740.

Baroque violin sonata production in Italy falls into three periods : (1) from c. 1597 to c. 1650; (2) c. 1650 to c. 1700; (3) c. 1700 to c. 1750. In the first period the activities, as yet diverse and innovational in style, were to be found mainly at Venice and Mantua. In the second, Venetian composers continued prominent, but equally important contributions came from the instrumental school of Bologna. Other northern Italian cities such as Ferrari and Modena played their lesser parts. This was the period when major-minor tonality together with its new-style counterpoint was becoming established. It culminated in the mature " church " and " chamber " sonatas of Corelli and his contemporaries. The third period stretches from the European influence of Corelli to the mid-eighteenth century, when later continuo sonatas overlapped the type that foreshadowed the classic era. Meanwhile Italians established in France, Germany, England and other countries, together with native composers, had made the baroque violin sonata an international feature.

What was called a solo sonata, i.e. for a single violin as the melody instrument, was also termed *sonata a due,* in reference to the harpsichord or organ continuo. Yet it was the baroque practice to join with the continuo a string bass or some other such deep-toned instrument, so that such a sonata needed three players for its performance. Similarly, the *sonata a tre* or trio sonata (normally a matter of two violins and continuo, the most popular of baroque forms) involved four players. The exceptional type of sonata for solo violin alone was always marked *senza continuo.* Sonatas were also written for as many as four melody instruments with continuo.

It is not possible to determine who was the first to write a solo violin sonata with continuo and the characteristic technical resources of the instrument which had so soon been developed, but one of the earliest names is that of Giovanni Fontana of Venice (d. 1630). His pupil Biago Marini (c. 1597–1665) was an even more important pioneer, a widely travelled soloist and composer. He commanded a wide resource of technique, transferred a number of the vocal idioms of monody to the violin, and was probably the first to employ the string tremolo in a sonata, and to write a solo violin sonata totally without accompaniment, using the resources of arpeggio and multiple stopping. He made use of the terms *sonata da chiesa* and *sonata da camera,* i.e. church and chamber (or court) sonata, which in these early stages signalised merely that the first was considered suitable for performance in church, the other not. An important contemporary was Salomone Rossi of Mantua (c. 1570–1628), a colleague of Monteverdi's, soloist and composer and possibly the first to write a trio sonata (two violins and continuo). A flood of this type of sonata followed. Technical demands on the two violins were usually less exacting than in the case of the solo form with its ornamental melodic display and high positionings. But the fact of there being two independent lines gave opportunities for contrapuntal dialogue between them. As the type progressed the string bass became more and more a true participant, especially in the matter of imitative entries.

A brief extract from one of Rossi's pioneer efforts is given below. There is simple but effective imitation between the violins, in equal partnership. Even the continuo has some interesting patterns, and some moments of participation in the counterpoint.

Ex:47

Trio Sonata. 1607

The above quotation is reproduced from *Music in the Baroque Era, p. 53* by M. Bukofzer (W. W. Norton & Company, Inc.—New York).

Mention must be made of Carlo Farina (c. 1600–after 1640), another violinist-composer who advanced the technique of the instrument. He was one of Monteverdi's violinists at Mantua, but spent much of his life in Germany. He was at Dresden in 1625, working with the renowned Heinrich Schütz. Using the devices of glissando, *col legno,* tremolo, pizzicato and *sul ponticello* in some of his " programme " pieces he was the first " trick " violinist in history, making opportunities for his instrument to crow, bark and caterwaul. But his serious work had considerable influence on early German violinists such as J. J. Walther. Another fine sonata composer of the period was Tarquinio Merula of Cremona (c. 1595–after 1652). During this first half-century the term *canzona* still survived as implying a violin sonata. The number of movements varied. There were contrasts in tempo and texture, and it can also be said that there was at least one section in fugal style and another in slow dance-rhythm. To a modern hearer all movements would seem very short-breathed.

In the second half of the seventeenth century the baroque sonata moved towards its maturity, at a time when major-minor tonality together with its new-style harmonically-ruled counterpoint was becoming established. That all-round musician Giovanni Legrenzi (1626–90), *maestro di cappella* of St. Mark's, Venice, and experienced opera composer, wrote numerous and important church sonatas.[2*] Trained at Venice also and making sonata contributions were Stradella and Giovanni Bassani (c. 1657–1716). At Modena the chief name was that of the elder Bononcini (1642–78), whose son was Handel's associate and rival. Of great moment were the activities at Bologna, where Maurizio Cazzati (c. 1620–77) was at first the ruling spirit. His pupil was Giovanni Vitali (c. 1644–92), who carefully preserved the distinction between church and chamber sonata on his title-pages, though in fact his compositions were mainly of the first type.[2*] He wrote a number of collections that were labelled frankly as dance music. The vigour, tunefulness and fine contrapuntal resource of his church sonatas gave them international fame. His work, together with that of Cazzati, may have become known to and " justly imitated " by Purcell. Of the same school, the name of Guiseppe Torelli (1658–1709) is remembered more for his contributions to the newly developing concerto form, and that of Guiseppe Jacchini (c. 1727) as being responsible for some of the earliest 'cello sonatas.

We have now reached the period in which the great violinist-composer Corelli flourished, Bologna-trained. Church and chamber sonata had now taken on definite and distinctive forms. The norm for the first was four movements, in the order slow, quick, slow, quick—a solemn chordal introduction, a solid contrapuntal second movement, a third of grave melodiousness and a lively finale in dance measure. Another quick movement was sometimes introduced. The chamber sonata was less systematically organised. After a prelude the movements took on a more dance-like nature, the *allemande* and *courante* type being prominent. Actually the chamber sonata was no more than an Italian specialised version of the dance-suite. Again, four or five movements were the usual number. Often one or more of the dance movements would use the variation form, the melody being repeated more than once with elaborations, each variation being termed a *double*.[3]

Arcangelo Corelli (1653–1713) was the leading figure of his age in the matter of violin playing and composition, and indeed one of the most significant figures in the whole history of those arts. He was the first baroque composer to make systematic use of the sequence as a fundamental means of construction. Also, in his music the major-minor tonality was firmly and fully established, with no more echoes of modality. After his Bologna years and some travel he settled in Rome, fortunate in having the rich and music-loving Cardinal Ottoboni as a good friend and admiring patron. His compositions, comparatively few in number but immense in influence, were published in six volumes. Opp. 1 and 3 comprised twenty-four church sonatas (with organ continuo); Opp. 2 and 4 twenty-four chamber sonatas (with harpsichord continuo). All these were of the trio type.[4*] Op. 5 consisted of twelve solo sonatas. His *concerti grossi* (of which more will be said) were gathered in a posthumous volume, Op. 6. In an age of great soloists he was not an outstanding executant, nor was his music as technically advanced as that of some of his contemporaries. At a time when violinists were using the sixth position and higher still, he never wrote above the third, but the balanced form of his art, its expressiveness, beautiful lyricism and dignity made it a model for all who followed him. Alessandro Scarlatti, who did not always see eye to eye with him, praised the excellence of the performances that he brought about, since he demanded " absolute uniformity in the bowing ". Evidently normal standards of orchestral playing in Italy were not those of Lully in contemporary France, with which Corelli may have had some experience.

Leaving the progress of the sonata for the time being, we will turn to a kindred and significant type of composition that was just emerging, a new form of instrumental concerto. The term " concerto ", which has been met with in the time of the Gabrielis, had been used in relation to either vocal or instrumental groups or to combinations of both, and indeed the last connotation survived in Germany to the time of J. S. Bach, who termed his church cantatas, *Kirchenkonzerte*. The implication was simply that the composition was written in *concertato* (contrast) style. In Italy the name was now being applied to instrumental works alone, in which such contrast technique was employed. " Church concertos " had been produced, single movements for organ and solo instruments which made use of the device. There must be mentioned the " trumpet sonatas " of the early Bologna school (Cazzati, Stradella and G. Vitali), in which the solo instrument was accompanied by full string orchestra. Also there were " concertos " that were wholly orchestral. But though contrasts of sonorities were effected, these did not approach the definite style of the late baroque concerto.

The first decisive step towards this was taken by Corelli in his Op. 6 Concerti Grossi, which, though not published until 1714 were probably in being as early as 1682. He divided his orchestra into two contrasting elements, the tutti (the actual concerto grosso) and the solo group or concertino. Each was given its own continuo. Significantly, his solo group was a string trio, the normal sonata combination now pitted against the orchestra. But there he stopped short, for his overall scheme was that of the church or chamber sonata with its four, five or more brief movements. Eight of the dozen were " church concertos ", the rest (with prelude and dance movements) of the chamber type. As for his differentiation between tutti and concertino, it was still largely a matter of volume of sound, without much distinction between the techniques of the two groups or the treatment of the subject matter. The best-remembered of his concertos is probably the " Christmas " one, with its charming Pastorale. But his lead was quickly taken up by others, and important innovations made by Torelli of Bologna and the Venetian, Tommaso Albinoni (1671-1750), both composers of fine violin sonatas, and both attracting the notice of J. S. Bach. Albinoni must also be remembered for his effective oboe concertos, famous in his time, and which have received modern revivals in recordings and broadcasts. In the solo concerto and the concerto grosso is now seen a distinction in the tutti and solo or concertino exchanges whereby the first contained pregnant thematic material and the second virtuoso figuration. We find also the abandonment of the somewhat inconsistent " sonata " scheme of movements in favour of that of the Neapolitan opera *sinfonia*, a three-movement plan of " fast, slow, fast ". In the quicker movements, particularly in the first, there was established another important innovation, the ritornello form.[5] In this the main musical idea played by the opening tutti returned again and again (in its entirety or in part) between the episodes after the manner of a rondo, but distinguished from the latter by its use of different keys and making a full restatement in the tonic only in its final appearance. Tovey has pointed out that the operatic *da capo* aria as developed by A. Scarlatti, in which the instrumental material, introductory and episodical, alternated with the vocal melody in concertante fashion through various keys, had provided a prototype for the ritornello form of the concerto. The artistic completeness and permanent vitality of the late baroque concerto form can be realised by recalling that Vaughan Williams' *Fantasia on a Theme by Thomas Tallis* and Elgar's *Introduction and Allegro for Strings* are both cast in the concerto grosso, ritornello mould. (See Note 12 for details of a recording of a single movement by the German composer Telemann written in most effective ritornello style.)

The chief concerto composer of the early eighteenth century was the Venetian violinist Antonio Vivaldi (c. 1675-1741), a pupil of Legrenzi. Though a priest of the Church of Rome, a great deal of his life, when he was not travelling, was spent as *maestro de' concerti* at the Ospedale della Pietà, one of the four music schools for orphaned girls established in the city. It is a tribute to the musical standards of Venice and the institutions in particular that connoisseurs from all over Europe came to hear the concerts given by these young girl-musicians, whose technique and orchestral discipline won universal praise. It was for the della Pietà that many of Vivaldi's concertos were written. These reached the astonishing total (concerti grossi and solo concertos) of more than 450.

Vivaldi, building on the work of Torelli, brought the trend of the baroque concerto to its height. His ritornelli themes were more than usually striking and pregnant, and the virtuosity of his solo passages above that of his predecessors. In his solo concertos, written for a large variety of single instruments, he even sometimes indulged in some playful essays in programme effects, while in his concerti grossi he tended to use his concertino group as an ensemble of solo instruments, bringing each to prominence in turn (e.g. in the well-known concerto in B minor for four violins, which J. S. Bach transcribed as for four harpsichords). This practice made the distinction between his concerti grossi and solo concertos rather hard to draw at times. Several other of his concertos were studied and transcribed by Bach. Vivaldi followed Scarlatti in frequently presenting his slow movements in the rhythm of the siciliana, and his finales in rapid triple time.[6*] " Il prete rosso " (Vivaldi seems to have had red hair) enjoyed also a considerable career as a composer of operas. More than 40 of them were produced at Venice or at other Italian cities.

Sonatas and concertos continued to be produced by the numerous other

Italian composer-violinists of Vivaldi's time. These included Francesco Veracini (1685–1750), who made a stay in England; Bernadetto Marcello (1686–1739) of *Il teatro alla moda* fame, who also wrote harpsichord sonatas and whose solo concerto for oboe was admired and transcribed by Bach; Giovanni Somis (1686–1763), a pupil of Vivaldi; Francesco Geminiani (1687–1762), who spent a great deal of his life in the British Isles, and who wrote (in English) the first book on violin method; and Pietro Locatelli (1695–1764), of astonishing technique. The last three were all pupils of Corelli. Jacchini, previously mentioned, wrote what was possibly the first 'cello concerto. Geminiani seems to have been the first to add the viola to the concertino group, making it the familiar string quartet. Composers of wider range such as Caldara, Porpora and Pergolesi also made important contributions. But in much of the Italian violin music attractive melody and harmonic principles were now the considerations, rather than contrapuntal constructions. The " display " concerto was beginning, with the solo instrument dominating instead of contrasting. Particularly in the works of Veracini can be seen traces of the new relaxed style that grew up everywhere side by side with the contrapuntal profundities of J. S. Bach.

One last Italian violinist remains to be mentioned, and a very great one. Guiseppe Tartini (1692–1770) devoted his life to playing, teaching and composing for his instrument. His noble and melodious solo sonatas were still in the baroque style, though showing many of the new " harmonic " tendencies. A good deal of his music is still played, and the " Devil's Trill " sonata does not need the aid of a picturesque story to ensure it a place. A perhaps even better work is the G minor sonata (" Dido Forsaken "). His influence on the art of violin playing was immense, particularly on that of bowing, the technique of which he advanced by his treatise *Arte dell' arco*. His keen ear noted the faint " differential tone " that is produced when two pure tones are sounded strongly together, but he was unable to supply an adequate acoustical explanation.

Meanwhile German court orchestras had fallen completely under the spell of this bright and vigorous Italian concerto music, favouring especially the works of Albinoni and Vivaldi. Yet Germany had already produced an outstanding and individual composer in Heinrich Biber (1644–1704), whose solo and trio sonatas show a high standard of technique and a great liking for double and triple stoppings. As an aid to this practice he followed Marini in employing the device of *scordatura*, whereby the normal string tunings were altered to suit the particular situation. Thus in his D major sonata (1681) the four open strings written for are A, e, a, d'. The printed notes are thus sometimes only a guide to the player's fingers and not those actually heard. e.g. Biber *writes*

Ex:48 a.

but the sounds *produced* are

Ex:48b.

Mention should be made of his sixteen famous " Rosary " Sonatas, purporting to be meditations on " Mysteries from the Life of Mary ". In these the *scordatura* device was extensively used. The last of them is a passacaglia in G minor on a ground-bass for violin solo entirely unaccompanied, a skilled and imaginative piece of work. He was ennobled by the Emperor Leopold I. Two other German violinists of virtuoso rank were Johann Birkenstock (1687–1733) and Johann Pisendel (1687–1755), a pupil of Vivaldi. The German composers of trio sonatas often employed a viol da gamba instead of a second violin, thus obtaining a greater tonal contrast. The famous organists Dietrich Buxtehude (1637–1707, Swedish-born) and Johann Pachelbel (1653–1706), the prolific Georg Telemann (1681–1767), together with other well-known composers such as Johann Krieger (1649–1725), Philip Erlbach (1657–1714) and many more, also contributed to this type of chamber music. The road led straight to the masterpieces of Handel and Bach.

The violin sonata was less favoured in France, but outstanding were the graceful and melodious examples, truly national, of Jean-Marie Leclair (1697–1764). He also seems to have been particularly fond of double stopping.[8*] Late in the period some chamber works by Rameau for two violins and harpsichord show an approach to the classical age, for the harpsichord part is not a continuo, but is fully written out in a brilliant harmonic keyboard style. It takes an equal if not dominating part in the discussion of the thematic material. The famous harpsichordist, the younger François Couperin (1668–1733), was an admirer of Corelli, and wrote some admirable chamber music, including trio and quartet sonatas. Jean Loeillet (1680–1730) was a Netherlands composer who settled in London, and produced a large number of excellent sonatas, mostly for flute and continuo.

The continued existence of viol playing and composition in England for most of the seventeenth century has already been referred to (see Note 1), as well as the " fancies " of a group of early seventeenth century composers, among whom Coperario was prominent (see p. 134). Viol consorts continued to be written for in Commonwealth and Restoration times by, among others, John Jenkins (1592–1678), Locke and Purcell. This in spite of the growing dominance of the violin and the general enthusiasm for such invaders as Veracini, Geminiani and Matteis (the latter came in 1672). Even Jenkins, who was writing austere contrapuntal fancies in Commonwealth times, " afterwards turned reformer with great success " in his violin trio sonatas of 1660, " with a Thorough Bass for Organ or Theorbo ".[9*] Purcell followed a similar course. His early fantasias for viols, in from three to seven

12. A page from the famous early fifteenth century Old Hall Manuscript. It shows the discant part and a portion of the tenor part of John Dunstable's widely known motet, *Veni, Sancte Spiritus.* See Ch. IV, Note 19.

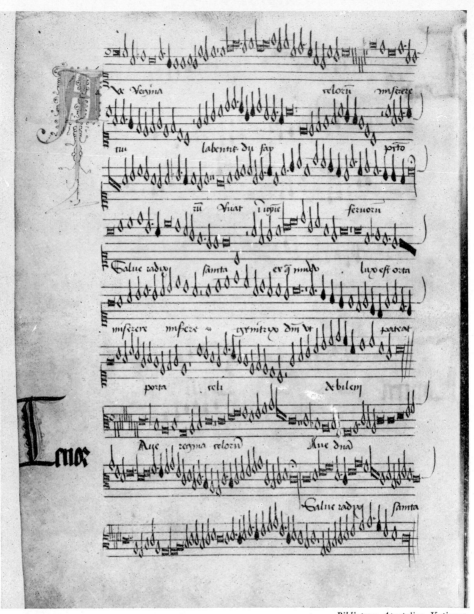

13. A page from Codex B. 80 of the Chapter Library of St. Peter's at Rome. It shows the cantus and tenor parts of the first portion of Dufay's motet *Ave Regina Coelorum*, founded on the liturgical antiphon with that text. The composer wrote it for his own death, and it was sung at his funeral. (See Ch. IV, Note 24.)

parts, actually included an *In Nomine* example (see. p. 134). In 1683 came a change to complete modernity, the set of twelve violin trio sonatas with continuo, which Purcell himself asserts were written " in just imitation of the most fam'd Italian masters ". No doubt Vitali, Cazzati and Matteis had their influences. The patterns were certainly " justly imitated ", with the composer's own individuality and mastery shining through them, even though it would seem that he had not wholly grasped in full the particular idiom of the violin. In 1697 a posthumous set in the same arrangement and written probably about the same time as the first, was published by his widow. Included in them was the so-called " Golden Sonata ", which has been given a perhaps undeserved prominence over the others in modern times.

The publications of John Playford, particularly *The English Dancing Master* (1650), give much information as to everyday English music of the age. Christopher Simpson's *Division Violist* (1659) makes it clear that viol playing, and especially bass-viol playing, was still a widespread practice in his time, and that " playing divisions on a ground ", i.e. improvising variations to an *ostinato* accompaniment—or even a free part above a " thorough-bass "—were continuing to be regarded by amateurs as gentlemanly accomplishments. A special type, the " division viol ", slightly smaller than the usual bass-viol, was the favourite instrument for this style of playing.[10] Later came a last-ditch supporter of viol music in the Cambridge lay-clerk Thomas Mace, who in his *Musicke's Monument* (1676) supplied much technical and useful information as to the art, as well as to lute playing and contemporary music in general. Another important publication was the volume of " Memoires " by the lawyer Roger North (1653–1734). His shrewd comments on matters musical are often quoted.

The Suite

We have noted that in late Renaissance times use was made of dance forms in a variety of instrumental media—keyboard, lute, and various string and wind ensembles. These at first were in contrasting pairs (e.g. pavan, galliard), and then in groups of increasing size as various other dances, characteristic of one or another country but interchanged often enough, were introduced. The adoption of the " prelude " for practical reasons has also been mentioned. The practice of such groupings continued into the seventeenth century and onward, both for ballroom needs and as a convenient form of purely instrumental music. Though not actually termed " suites " until much later, the number of dances included was sometimes quite large, although there is no need to assume that all the pieces of a group were necessarily played at a single performance. The musical effect of a suite was that of contrast in tempo and mood between the movements, together with unity of key throughout, and these features continued until the form died out at the beginning of the classical era, to be replaced orchestrally by the serenade, divertimento and cassation of Mozart's time. In the later stages of the suite there are found mild tonal contrasts between the movements (e.g. relative major instead of minor, etc.). The

M

form was usually binary with sometimes suggestions of tripartite form. Some dances were followed by a couple or so variations of the melody, often labelled " double ". This discussion will confirm what has been previously stated—that the Italian type violin chamber-sonata was nothing more than a special form of suite. But as we have seen, the sonata in due course moved towards a more abstract style, and abandoned any " church " distinction.

In spite of what is sometimes said, there was never a fixed number of movements to the suites, nor any indispensible dance-form. However, in the important developments of clavier composition, France and Germany came to show a great deal of favour in their *ordres* and *partitas* to a nucleus consisting of allemande, courante and sarabande, seen first perhaps in French lute music, borrowed by French harpsichordists like Chambonnières and then taken up in Germany. There, the gigue, after being treated as an optional dance for a time, became the most usual " finale ". (The term " clavier " is used to cover both secular keyboard instruments, the harpsichord and clavichord.)

Among these basic dances were interspersed other types, these dependent on the nationality and also on the taste and fancy of the composer—minuet, bourrée, gavotte, passepied, (in England, the native hornpipe)—and many more, (see Note 2). In due course there were even included movements other than dances. In the late seventeenth century clavier suites ("lessons") of Purcell, while the allemande and courante are found in their normal positions, the gigue, curiously enough, though of English origin, is absent. The French too were often far from orthodox. As R. O. Morris says : " . . . in the *ordres* of Couperin almost anything may turn up."

Most of the independent ensemble music of baroque Germany was based on the dance suite, written often enough for five-part string orchestra, together with wind additions. An early name is that of Johann Rosenmüller (c. 1620–84), whose sets (1667) were each introduced by a *sinfonie*. The clavier developed at the same time, the South German organist Johann Froberger (1616–67) being the first important name. It was he who borrowed the allemande, courante, sarabande nucleus from France for German use.[11] He also carried on the native tradition of the variation suite. We have already considered the beginnings of this type in the *Neue Paduan* of Paul Peuerl (see p. 133), string suites of four contrasting dances in which the melodic material of the first is shaped anew in each succeeding one. The device was used again more elaborately by Johann Schein in his *Banchetto musicale* sets of 1617. Froberger's *Mayerlin suite* is even more intricate. He took a well-known allemande tune, gave it six patterned variations, and then used it with rhythmic modifications as the material of the other dances of the suite, these also having " doubles ". " Variation " was the lifeblood of baroque music. Even in the ordinary dance suite a thematic link is sometimes to be discerned between allemande and courante, and almost any dance was liable to spill a couple or so " doubles ". However, the true variation suite gradually fell into disuse, the late baroque apparently preferring the independent dance forms with their greater contrasts.

Competent composers of suites in later baroque Germany were as plentiful as blackberries. Mention will be made of a few of the leading names, most of whom will have been encountered before—Johann Reinken (1623–1722), the near centenarian whose organ playing was so much admired by the young Bach; Johann Kerll (1627–93), a pupil of Frescobaldi; Georg Muffat (c. 1645–1704); Johann Kreiger; Johann Pachelbel; Philip Erlbach; Johann Ferdinand Fischer (c. 1665–1746); Dietrich Buxtehude, who kept very regularly to an " allemande, courante, sarabande and gigue " pattern; Johann Kuhnau (1660–1722), a celebrated organist and clavier player; and the versatile Georg Telemann.[12*] Johann Fux (1660–1741), who to many represents the dry-as-dust theorist, was actually an excellent composer of light-hearted partitas, besides the wealth of dignified church music which he wrote as *Kapellmeister* to the Emperor Charles VI at Vienna. The seventeenth century English theatre was responsible for a veritable flood of ensemble dance music, and many collections of dances were printed, the publisher Playford taking a leading part. When these were arranged in definite suites (e.g. those of Locke and Benjamin Rogers), we find little heed paid to any fixed order. We shall return to further considerations of the ensemble suite when speaking of Handel and Bach.

The Lute

In the course of the seventeenth century Italy, once the very home of lute playing, allowed it to decline, its place being taken to some degree by the simpler (and noisier) Spanish guitar. In other countries there was a similar withering of interest, although the theorbo (large lute) was occasionally used for accompaniment purposes almost to the end of the eighteenth century. France was the exception. There, a last golden age of lute playing and composition had for its leading figure Denis Gaultier the younger (1597–1672). The technical shortcomings of the lute (which included lack of sustained tone) were brilliantly covered by the " broken style " which made ingenious use of the arpeggio and multiple stop, often producing the illusion of continuous full harmony and counterpoint. An example, a portion of a *Pavanne* by Gaultier, is quoted below; (a) gives the lute notes as implied by the tablature, (b) the approximate effect obtained. (Various " graces " must also be imagined.) Actually, (b) represents a skilful realisation for keyboard (with a few small rhythmic modifications) which was made by the contemporary composer Perrine.

Ex:49 a.

Ex:49 b.

The above quotations are reproduced from *M. Bukofzer : Music in the Baroque Era, p. 166 (W. W. Norton & Company, Inc.—New York).*

This highly skilled professional lute-school developed a very elaborate system of ornamentation, and also cultivated the dance suite, with allemande, courante and sarabande as its chief props, and an optional gigue among the subordinate dances. We have already spoken of the promptitude with which this pattern was taken up by composers of keyboard and ensemble suites, especially in Germany. Much use was made by the lutenists of fanciful titles, without, the hearer may think, there being much apparent substance for them. All these features appeared in the school of French clavecinists (harpsichordists) that was expanding at the time. Before turning to the matter of keyboard music some consideration must be given to a problem that troubled all baroque composers when they wished to make use of the more extreme keys.

Tonality and Temperament

It will be recalled that even in Renaissance music there was movement from the modal scales to those of the major and minor; also that harmonic effects are to be found in the sixteenth century that give the impression, at least to the modern ear, of modulations to the adjacent sharp and flat keys. At the beginning of the seventeenth century the position was still fluid. Composers were still aware of the ancient modes, and the modern key sense was not wholly established. Giovanni Gabrieli can be found playing with the effect of dominant and tonic as if it were a novel one. But as the century advanced the modes altogether vanished, and the modern major-minor system with its new-found power of effective key-modulation became the normal raw material of composition. For most of the baroque era, however, as anyone with a practical knowledge of the music of the period will have noted, the range of key-signatures employed was a modest one. The reason was the system of tuning for keyboard instruments.

The limits of this book do not allow for any prolonged acoustical discussions, and we will therefore confine the mathematics of the subject to a few simple statements.[13] If from the bottom C of a modern pianoforte we proceed to superimpose a series of perfect fifths to carry us to the topmost C, *twelve* in all, we will find that in doing so we have apparently spanned exactly seven octaves. The acoustical truth of the matter is, however, that

the succession C, G, D, A, E, B, F sharp, etc. . . . to B sharp, tuned to
the true vibration ration 2 : 3, places the last B sharp at a slightly higher
pitch than the last C of the seven octaves, tuned to the ratio of 1 : 2—a small
but appreciable interval. This fact was well known to the ancient Greeks,
as the term for it, the " Pythagorean comma " indicates. An octave diatonic
scale consisting of acoustically correct intervals would be said to represent
" just intonation ", and such fastidiousness was possible in the early, comparatively non-chromatic music of the modes, but with the advent of a
greater chromaticism, followed by the appearance of keys and key-modulation, certain tonal troubles began, affecting organs, harpsichords and clavichords, and even such fretted instruments as lutes and guitars. It was found
that even the near-by keys to C major were somewhat out-of-tune, and a
consequent compromise much used in the period was the mean-tone temperament, which can be described roughly as a tuning which kept the major
thirds accurate while adapting other intervals. This permitted comfortable
use of possibly six major and three minor keys, even though eighteenth
century violinists chose to speak scornfully of dull-eared harpsichordists and
their out-of-tune instruments. However, the problem of the extreme keys
still remained. The system that nowadays has been universally arrived at is
that of equal temperament. By equalising all twelve semitones of the octave
and thus causing all diatonic intervals except the octave to be very slightly
incorrect acoustically this tuning makes it possible for all twenty-four keys
of the major-minor cycle to be safely employed. J. S. Bach tuned his harpsichords and clavichords in this fashion, and signalised the fact by writing
his two books, *The Well-Tempered Clavier*, the forty-eight preludes and
fugues contained therein ranging twice through the cycle.[14] There was a
general recognition for the system after this time, though organs tended to
keep to " mean-tone " and the less extreme keys. There were plenty of
mean-tone organs well into the nineteenth century.

Bach has sometimes been spoken of as the pioneer of equal temperament,
but this is far from the truth. Some scholars would give the credit to the
Greek theorist Anaxagoras (b. c. 354 B.C.). We have already seen that
Zarlino, at St. Mark's, Venice, advocated it in 1586, as did Willaert (see
p. 115). But about a hundred years before that time it seems that the
Spaniards were fixing the frets of their guitars in accordance with the
tuning, following the suggestion of Ramos de Pareja in 1482. Reference has
also been made (p. 137) to a virginals piece by John Bull in the Fitzwilliam
book showing modulations that must surely have called for something like
the tuning. A number of other pieces, notably a *basso ostinato* work by J. C.
Kerll which passes through every major key, seem to point to a certain
amount of appreciation of the tuning in the middle baroque. Later, one of
Johann Pachelbel's sets of suites makes use of seventeen of the major and
minor keys. Again, Johann Ferdinand Fischer, writing a collection of
preludes and fugues for organ which omitted only five of the major-minor
key cycle, showed the purpose of the work by entitling it *Ariadne musica
neo-organeodum* . . . (1702). It was to be a guiding thread through the
mazes of the less familiar keys. The pieces are very short-breathed as com-

pared with those of Bach's collection, but oddly enough not only does the scheme, but even some of the themes employed, foreshadow the coming of the " Forty-Eight ".

Clavier Music

The first important name among composers of French clavier music is that of Jacques Chambonnières (c. 1602–72), clavecin (harpsichord) player to the young Louis XIV. Behind him was the tradition of earlier French writers for the keyboard, and the work of the English virginalists was not unknown to him. But in his style is seen also the influence of contemporary lute technique. His music and that of his followers took over many of the artificialities of the Gaultier school of lute composition in its succession of highly-ornamented, fancifully-titled miniatures.[15*] Three of his pupils were named Couperin. Of these, two, Louis (c. 1626–61) and François (c. 1631– c. 1701), became quite noted figures, but it was the son of Charles, the third brother, François Couperin " le Grand " (1668–1733), who gave European significance to the family name. With the elder Couperins may be mentioned Nicolas-Antoine Lebègue (c. 1630–1702) and Henri d'Anglebert (1635–91).

In the work of the younger François Couperin, French clavier composition of the period reached its acme. Although he was one of the organists at Versailles and the composer of worthy church and chamber works, the main bulk of Couperin's music was written for two-manual harpsichord and published in a series of four *Livres*, each made up of a varying number of suites or *Ordres*, twenty-seven in all. In these compositions he followed the practice of brevity of construction, profuse ornamentation of melody and the use of fanciful titles, but all was managed with exquisite taste and a true and individual keyboard style.† Much information regarding clavier technique of the period can be gathered from his treatise *L'Art de toucher le clavecin*. Among his contemporaries were Jean Dandrieu (1682–1738) and Louis Daquin (1694–1772). The latter's little tone-picture *Le Coucou* is still found in popular piano albums. Rameau published several volumes of clavier pieces, mostly belonging to his earlier years, the first appearing in 1706. These showed at times the brilliance that might be expected from a virtuoso of the instrument.

The clavier suite flourished in Germany, the composers of orchestral suites writing also for the keyboard. We may give special emphasis among the names already mentioned to that of the celebrated organist Johann Kuhnau. He was the greatest German clavier player before Bach, and the first German composer to adapt the Italian *church* sonata to the keyboard in his volumes of clavier works. His curious " Bible " sonatas were a series of programme pieces that ostensibly illustrated Biblical episodes—among them the combat of David and Goliath. In them he used all manner of instrumental forms, including even the choral prelude, and supplied also an explanatory preface. The efficient harpsichord " lessons " of Purcell have already been mentioned.

† Couperin's music, though still of the late baroque, yet had characteristics of the succeeding *rococo* in its aesthetic delicacy, belonging to the world of Watteau and the *fêtes galantes*.

The Organ and Organ Music

The baroque era saw the expansion of two important instrumental forms, the chorale prelude and the fugue. In both cases it was the organ which provided the main practical means.

The Chorale Prelude

Note has already been taken of the career of Jan Sweelinck (1562–1621), the Dutch organist, whose compositions link the two centuries.[16*] He was called affectionately "the maker of organists", and his teaching was the foundation of a long tradition of North German organ playing. He wrote much choral church music in the old polyphonic style, but in some of his compositions his influence stretched far into the future. Building on the established practice of allowing organists to play alternate verses of the congregational hymns as solos (which they usually did with added counterpoint) he developed from this the artistic Chorale Variations form. The expansion of this was carried on by the great organist Samuel Scheit, and afterwards by such men as Kreiger, Reinken and Buxtehude. The latter even cast his variations into the allemande, courante, sarabande, gigue sequence— a sort of Chorale Partita. In the hands of the North German organists there developed also the Chorale Fantasy, a rhapsodical type in which the chorale tune made only fragmentary appearances.

More in the nature of a true Chorale Prelude was the Chorale Fugue, similar in method to the late Renaissance motet, which so often consisted of a series of fugal expositions of successive themes, settings of verbal phrases or sentences which overlapped at the cadences. In the Chorale Fugue the opening subject was formed from the first line of the chorale (usually in diminution) and as the exposition proceeded the same line in dignified long notes appeared in one of the parts. The process was repeated with the second line, and so on until the whole chorale was completed. As a variation of this method a single-subject fugue could be maintained throughout, the lines of the chorale striking in as before. As might be expected, other ways of varying the same principles were also found.

Plainer methods of shaping the Chorale Prelude were often used. The chorale could be broken into its separate phrases, the other parts flowing on to fill the breaks, in which case this accompaniment was often founded on some striking and independent figure that maintained itself throughout. (A popular piano arrangement "Jesu, Joy of Man's Desiring", an adaptation of a Bach composition, is readily available to illustrate this type.) Finally the chorale tune might appear itself melodically decorated, in which case care was taken that it was not overborne by too much intricacy in the accompanying parts.[17*]

Most of the fine organ composers of North and Central Germany who were the predecessors of J. S. Bach made their contributions to this great form. Although Bach's examples were the culminating achievements, it cannot be denied that his path had been well and truly lighted.

The Fugue

We have already met the term " fugue ", attached without the modern implications to the device used in sixteenth century motets, Masses and madrigals, whereby a vocal theme in one part was answered in another, at the unison, or at the octave, fourth or fifth above or below (actually, in accordance with solmisation principles). It has also been shown that these methods were transferred to instrumental music, giving rise to the ricercar, the canzona and the fantasia. The derivation of the ricercar from the motet, and the canzona (of a more vivacious texture) from the French chanson, were certainly apparent at first, but as the seventeenth century progressed it becomes difficult to perceive much distinction between the styles and techniques used under the different labels. Ricercar, canzone and fantasia all employed the fugal type of device, and variation played a frequent part.

The important distinction in the matter of future development lay in whether one or several themes were thus treated. Once the principle of using a single subject throughout a composition was established, then the foundations of the true fugue were laid. It was a model baroque texture, for in it one single " affect " was carried through on the principle of continuous expansion. The work of the Italian organist and composer Girolamo Frescobaldi (1583–1643) is important in this respect. While he wrote ricercari with as many themes as there were sections in the work, some of his compositions in this form were founded on a single subject. His *Capriccio sopra un soggetto* (1626) uses the same theme in each of a number of brief fugal sections. However, the theme is modified, sometimes considerably, at each reappearance, and new counterpoints found for it. By contrast, in others of his *sopra un soggetto* works the subject is kept fairly constant. But the sectional nature of the construction is very apparent.[18*]

It was Sweelinck who really established the single-subject, continuous fugue. He himself called such a work a *fantasia*, and in his larger examples a sort of tripartite design is apparent. The theme appears at first against a succession of counter-subjects, which are themselves drawn upon for new material; then the subject is presented in augmentation, and finally in diminution, while stretti and other contrapuntal complexities are in frequent use. Everything was done to build up a concluding climax in a type of composition that achieved an artistic unity.

Johann Froberger, who was a pupil of Frescobaldi, and Samuel Scheidt, who studied with both Frescobaldi and Sweelinck, each continued with the " fantasia " type of single-subject fugue, as did Bernado Pasquini (1637–1710), the Italian clavier player and composer. The seventeenth century canzonas and the fugal movements of the Italian church sonatas were all efforts that were to lead to the finished type. Another important name is that of Jean-Henri d'Anglebert, already mentioned as a harpsichordist, probably the finest French player of the instrument before Couperin le Grand. His five celebrated organ fugues were constructed on the pattern of variants of a single subject, and showed high contrapuntal mastery. It was the late baroque group of German organists and composers, notably Pachelbel, Reinken, J. Ferdinand Fischer and Buxtehude, who shaped the fugue more in the manner known to J. S. Bach. However, we may recall that a toccata and fugue which for a long while had been attributed to John Sebastian (being fully worthy of him) have now turned out to be the work of Henry Purcell! Bach, ever the student, had thought them well worth copying out.

J. S. Bach owed less to his predecessors in the matter of fugal construction than he did in the case of the chorale prelude. Even the monumental fugues of Buxtehude lack the logic and essential unity of Bach's examples. The latter evolved his episodes from the material of his subjects and counter-subjects with a skill that had not been imagined before, and made more consistent and relevant use than his predecessors of such devices as double counterpoint, inversion and stretto.[19*] In other words, the Bach fugue was something new in the history of the art. It represents also the quintessence of the texture. We may also note that, whatever the text-books may choose to lay down in the matter of rules, in so many fugal features his practice was that of infinite variety.[20]

Organ Music in France

In France organ music developed on somewhat different lines from that of Germany. Without such strong traditions as those built up by Sweelinck and his successors, French organ composers showed in their music aspects of a style derived from harpsichord playing, such as a liking for free use of the various types of ornament, and even, (at second hand) the broken arpeggio of the lute. They were also deeply interested in the contrasts of colour brought about by carefully planned registrations. A group of Paris organists, Guillaume Nivers (1617–1714), Nicolas-Antoine Lebègue (previously mentioned as a harpsichordist)—both pupils of Chambonnières—André Raison and Jean-François Dandrieu (another harpsichordist) all published Livres d'orgue. Much explanation is given in their volumes as to the new styles of playing being practised, involving the use of additional manuals and new types of stops. Regarding Raison, we may note that the theme of a Passacaglia in G minor found in his first Livre d'orgue was appropriated by Bach for use in his own great Passacaglia in C minor. In the works of all these organ composers a secular element is apparent in their increasing use of sprightly dance-patterns. Another Parisian, François Rober-day (1620–90), organist of Notre Dame, wrote in a somewhat earlier style, a highly contrapuntal one. His " Fugues and caprices " were of the variation ricercare and capriccio type as modelled by Frescobaldi, but his was the novel device of grouping them in contrasting pairs, the dignified ricercare subject being transformed rhythmically into a vivacious one in the following movement. The organ fugues of Jean-Henri d'Anglebert have already received mention.[21*]

Spain

The strong national sentiment found in Spanish church music was naturally enough reflected in works specifically for organ, expressed in various ricercar types (tientos). The chief name in early baroque times is that of Correa de Araujo (d. 1663), and in the mid-period Juan Cabanilles (1644–

1712). The latter composer wrote prolifically in many forms, and these included groups of national dances.

North America

Music in North America made an inauspicious start at the hands of the Puritan settlers of New England. As in the case of the Scottish Calvinists service-music was restricted to the unaccompanied unison singing of metrical psalms, and some objections were heard even to this practice. Various seventeenth century injunctions against dancing and the use of instruments point to there having been some attempts to cultivate secular music, but the prevailing temper of the early colonists was that attention given to music was a sinful waste of time—and this included any effort to master its notation. It was not until 1698 that an American psalter containing printed music was brought out—psalm settings in two parts. Towards the end of the seventeenth century the regions south of New England began to receive settlers from Germany and Sweden, who brought with them a less arid Protestantism and a love for choral singing and instrumental music. In a church near Philadelphia the first organ in the English colonies was set up. The Teutonic cultivation of music continued to flourish, and even produced a chorale composer in Conrad Beissel (1690–1768). Whatever the New England states might do, other regions made musical progress. Charleston saw a performance of a London ballad opera in 1735. Even earlier Williamsberg (Virginia) was in possession of a permanent playhouse. London's *Beggar's Opera* reached Maryland in 1752. Meanwhile, Carl Pachelbel, a relation of the famous German composer, was able to make a professional life as an organist at Rhode Island and at Charleston, and give public concerts both at the latter town and at New York.

NOTES

1 The chamber music written by English composers for viols and for other domestic type instruments from the middle of the seventeenth century onwards is of unique and admirable quality. This flourishing may be accounted for in part by the Puritan closings of the theatres and the suppression of Anglican church music during the period of the Commonwealth.
The modern double-bass (violon) still retains the characteristic viol build.

2* HMS VI has recordings of church sonatas by Legrenzi and Vitali. Legrenzi's dates from 1665, and shows an earlier stage than Corelli's, nearer to the old *canzona* type. All the same, the work is thoroughly instrumental in style and full of Legrenzi's contrapuntal skill. The Vitali sonata (publ. 1667) is of the slow, quick, slow, quick pattern, and despite its " church " designation has a very lively gigue for its last movement. Both works illustrate what has been said regarding the brevity of most of the movements of these early sonatas.

3 It seems unnecessary in a work of this scope to give details of the characteristics of the various dance-forms. Such information is readily available in the many textbooks that deal with "form", e.g. *The Structure of Music—R. O. Morris* (*O.U.P.*).

4* HMS VI has a recording of Corelli's church (trio) sonata in F minor from Op. 3. In the fugal second movement it will be noted that the bass shares in the little exposition. In the recorded performance the written notes are at times ornamented, as would certainly have been the procedure in baroque times. A later edition (? 1725) of Corelli's works printed passages purporting to be the ornamentations supplied by Corelli himself in " grave " movements. Compared with these the original lines are indeed bare skeletons.

5 *Ritornello* = a small repetition. The term had also been used earlier for the concluding section of fourteenth century madrigals, and for instrumental passages played in operas.

6* HMS VI has a recording of the whole of Vivaldi's concerto grosso in B flat major for oboe, violin and orchestra.

7* HMS VI has a recording of three of the six movements of the Biber D major sonata mentioned in the text, for solo violin and continuo—a slow, very much " stopped " introduction, a presto, and a gigue with two *doubles*. All the movements are brief; the second and third, simple binary form with repeats of each section. The musical examples quoted in the text are taken from the sonata extracts printed in the accompanying Handbook (VI), p. 31 (*Oxford University Press*). In the *Musical Quarterly* for July 1963 there is a valuable article on the " Mystery " Sonatas by David D. Boyden, with much information on the *scordatura* device. The occasion is a reviewing of Cambridge Records Set CRM 811, a recording of the whole work.

8* HMS VI has a recording (complete) of a sonata in G for solo violin and continuo by Leclair, published in 1728. Its form is that of a four-movement church sonata, but the third movement, in ternary form, is clearly a gavotte. The solo part has a great deal of graceful ornamentation. The continuo has at times a strong rhythmic vigour, and also a share in the thematic interest.

9* HMS VI has a recording of a G minor fancy by Jenkins, dating from about 1655, not long before his " reform ". It was written for two viols and string bass, with continuo. The work is in single-movement, canzona form, imitative throughout. Towards the end the time changes from duple to triple, and then back again for the last six bars.

10 In connection with the bass-viol we must bear in mind that as the smaller sizes of viol gradually went out of use, leaving it as the sole survivor, there was a tendency to refer to it as the " viol da gamba ". Actually the term *viole da gamba* (leg-viols) applied to the whole family, since, large or small, they were held downwards, either on or between the knees. It is necessary sometimes to ask oneself in which sense, general or particular, the term *viol da gamba* is being used.

11 It has sometimes been stated that Froberger established the allemande, courante, sarabande, gigue sequence. This is not so. In his manuscripts the gigue, where used, had an internal placing. Its position as a concluding movement is found only in posthumous printings of his works.

12* HMS VI has a recording of a movement of an orchestral suite in E minor by Telemann, the suite being one of a series of three called *Musique de Table* . . . published in 1733 and comprising programmes of music performed at Hamburg during municipal banquets and the like. This particular movement, it will be noted, is in the form of the first movement of a concerto grosso, and was written for string orchestra and a *concertino* of two flutes, two violins and 'cello. The main melody is of considerable vitality and beauty, and the modulations skilfully laid out. Telemann was an extraordinarily prolific composer of every branch. Handel, who knew him well, and who was one of the subscribers to the first edition of " Table Music ", said of him that he could write a motet in eight parts as easily as anyone else could write a letter. Telemann's facility must have been very great to have impressed Handel, himself a master of that quality.

13   The reader who wishes for wider information on the subject should consult the article TEMPERAMENTS in Grove's Dictionary. A briefer and less mathematical exposition can be found in Percy Scholes' *Oxford Companion to Music, p. 923* (*O.U.P.*).

14   Actually, it was the first book only (completed in 1722) that received from Bach the title *Das wohltemperirte Clavier . . .* The so-called " second book " (completed in 1744) was not so named by him.

15*   HMS VI has recordings of four brief harpsichord pieces by Chambonnières. In these miniatures can be seen the influence of contemporary lute technique of which we have spoken. As Gerald Abrahams says, Chambonnières " in effect treated the instrument largely as a lute with greater resources ". Couperin " le Grand ", Rameau, and the late baroque German composers for the clavier developed much more of a characteristic keyboard style.

16*   See p. 133. In HMS IV is a recording of a set of chorale variations by Sweelinck.

17*   HMS VI has some recordings of chorale preludes for organ. The first, a working of the chorale *Dursch Adams Fall*, by Pachelbel, represents a plain version of the melody against a quick-moving but simple counterpoint. Another treatment of the same melody is given, this time by J. S. Bach. Again the melody moves through its length without break, but this time the stern emotion of the words is reflected by the poignant chromatic harmonies, together with a striking and characteristic pedal figure. A third example, by Buxtehude, uses the Christmas melody *In Dulce Jubilo*. This illustrates the device of the tune itself being varied and decorated, the accompanying parts in consequence being less active. Finally, a working of the same melody by J. S. Bach is given—a masterly treatment. The tune is rendered in plain fashion, starting against a running counterpoint, but in the next bar the other voices enter in double canon, which device continues for twenty-four bars, an amazing achievement, which, as is usual in Bach's case, contrives at the same time to be beautiful music. Later, another canon makes its appearance.
      The reader is also referred to HAM II, No. 190, a, b, c, d, where are set out for comparison the treatments given by Scheidt, Buxtehude, Pachelbel and J. S. Bach respectively, to the chorale *Vater unser im Himmelreich*.

18*   Frescobaldi, a pupil of Luzzaschi, was in his maturity Italy's most famous organist, most of his career being spent at St. Peter's, in Rome, where his playing attracted large bodies of listeners. HMS IV has a harpsichord version of the 1626 *Capriccio sopra un soggetto* mentioned in the text.

19*   With the two books of the " 48 " to hand no one need lack examples of Bach's unique mastery of the fugal art. However, HMS VI has a recording of the G minor Prelude and Fugue from the first book, an example of a performance rendered on the clavichord. Bach himself would probably have preferred this quiet instrument for these two pieces.

20   Arising from this point, we have followed Tovey's wise lead in calling the fugue a " texture " rather than a " form ".

21*   HMS VI has recordings of organ pieces by Lebègue, Raison and Dandrieu, which illustrate very well the points mentioned concerned with style, registration and ornamentation. The piece by Raison is the actual passacaglia referred to in the text. All three pieces were recorded on the organ of Saint-Merry in Paris, which still possesses some seventeenth century stops.

The Historical Anthology of Music (HAM), Vol. II, by A. T. Davison and Willi Apel (Oxford University Press) prints numerous examples of the music of baroque, rococo and pre-classical composers.

CHAPTER VIII

An End and a Beginning

ABOUT the middle of the seventeenth century, and perhaps even before, there began to appear in Italy and France evidences of a definitely new musical outlook, that of the " rococo ". The baroque age with its closely woven counterpoint and its basso continuo methods was suffering a dilution by what for the time being was a simpler art, a preoccupation with the single-line melody and the harmonic, rather than the horizontal aspect. As in the case of a previous period, a hundred and fifty years back, there had come a reaction against the elaborations of contrapuntal writing which seemed to be clogging straightforward tunefulness. This tendency had, as we have seen, been apparent in the style adopted by Locatelli, Veracini and other violinists of the Italian " display " school, and by French harpsichordists. In its more artless guise such music has received the name of *style galant*. But before the baroque sunset there came a blaze of glory. The age found its consummation in the music of two men of supreme genius, J. S. Bach and Handel. Both were born in 1685, and both were native to Protestant Germany, but they were destined for widely dissimilar careers.

Johann Sebastian Bach (1685–1750), like most serious musicians of his age, spent the whole of his life under authority; for some periods at princely courts, but in the main as a musician of the Lutheran Church. He was never outside his own native land, and travelled only a few hundred miles within its borders. He was certainly famous during his lifetime, but only in Germany, and chiefly as an incomparable organ virtuoso. Even in the narrow circle in which his compositions were heard their qualities were not fully recognised, and with his death they passed almost into oblivion. Although within a few decades such discerning men as Baron van Swieten, Mozart and C. G. Neefe were making use of such treasures as had happened to be recovered, it was not until well into the nineteenth century that the real revival of his music began, and his true stature proclaimed.

He was born in the Thuringian town of Eisenach, where his father, Johann Ambrosius, was " town musician ". For many generations both before and after Johann Sebastian's day the province and its neighbouring ones were sprinkled with men of that family tree holding musical posts.

189

" The Bachs without intermission were making music in Germany from the age of Luther to the advent of Bismarck ".[1] To the inspiration of such an ancestry Johann Sebastian brought his own genius, and an earnest searching mind that to the end of his days was always eager to learn from others and to build on that knowledge. Left an orphan at ten years of age he was given a home by an elder brother, Johann Christoph (1671–1721), himself an organist and composer. He was also fortunate in his schooling, coming under the influence of an enlightened cantor, Elias Herder. In 1700 his fine soprano voice gained him a place in the excellent choir school at Lüneburg, where he profited by the proximity of the well-known organist and composer Georg Böhm (1661–1733). His own initiative enabled him to make journeys to Hamburg to hear the veteran Johann Reinken, and to the ducal court at Celle, where the orchestra performed French music in the crisp, disciplined Gallic style, and the compositions of Couperin and his school were to be encountered. He was learning fast. His organ playing was already regarded locally as phenomenal, and there were youthful compositions—chorale variations and preludes. Even so, it was his early training as a violinist, first begun by his father, which gained him his first professional post (1703) in the private ducal band at Weimar.

In the same year he moved to Arnstadt, to become organist of a church and master of a fine new instrument. During the next four years he had leisure for both composition and organ practice, laying the foundations of that consummate keyboard and pedal technique that was the chief reason for his lifetime fame. It was in this period that he made his famous pilgrimage on foot to Lübeck, to learn from the playing of Buxtehude, and to listen to the master's *Abend-musiken* concerts, which fascinations caused him to overstay his leave. Back at Arnstadt he was reproved not only for this offence but for the novel complications now to be found in his organ-playing, which were not to the taste of the consistory. After the Lübeck experience he was no doubt trying his wings. At Arnstadt were written the earliest of the wonderful series of church cantatas. He began also his long development of the fugal art in the comparatively immature Prelude and Fugue in C minor and the Toccata and Fugue in C major for organ.

In June 1707 he moved to a larger and more musical city, Mühlhausen, but here, unfortunately, he found a divided community, split by the rivalries of orthodox Lutherism and Pietism. The latter movement, like Calvinism, opposed " art " music of any kind in the services, while the followers of Luther, as we have seen (p. 120) had retained a substantial part of the musical traditions of the Roman Church, including the trained choir, the highly skilled organist, and orchestral instruments, all combining to perform complicated " figural " music, the bane of the stricter sects.[2] Bach's views as to what Church music should be and the part that he had to play in it, had by now hardened into principles. His ruling and life-long passion was for the service of the Deity as he understood it, which was through the orthodox Lutheran form of worship. After barely a year at Mühlhausen he resigned, stating that he sought a position that would give him a " regulated church music in the honour of God ". In the autumn of 1708 he moved to a complete change of atmosphere as Court organist to Duke Wilhelm Ernst at Weimar.

Here he remained for over nine years, one of the liveried servants of the autocratic Duke. There were advantages, however. He was in charge of the small choir of the ducal chapel and the organ—also small, but with a 32-foot stop. His duties were comparatively light, and to this period of relative tranquillity belong many of the masterpieces for organ, e.g. the "Gigue" Fugue, the Passacaglia and Fugue in C minor, most of the mature organ Preludes and Fugues and Toccatas and Fugues, and the "Little Organ Book", a series of seasonal chorale preludes (at least begun at Weimar), which the composer intended as examples of the various possible treatments of a chorale subject.

He was also called upon to take his place (as "chamber-musician") in the court orchestra, where he was ruled by the *Konzertmeister*. Not until 1714 was he given the latter post, while the overall authority of *Kapell-meister* was never his. In the Duke's orchestra and in the cosmopolitan world of Weimar he grew more and more aware of the greatness of Italian music, and as in the days of his youth, we find him learning by transcription and imitation. Instrumental concertos by Vivaldi, Telemann,[3] Marcello and others were studied, and rearranged for organ, for clavier, and in one Vivaldi instance, for four claviers and strings. The Italians could teach him nothing with regard to contrapuntal mastery; what they did instil was a new melodic clarity, together with a greater lucidity in formal construction. His study of Italian sacred music was also fruitful.

It was during this period that his fame began to spread far and wide as a recital organist, since he was given permission to travel in that capacity. His pedal technique, his improvisations and his sight-reading were all re-garded as transcendent. To 1716 belongs the incident, too well known for detail here, of his triumph over the famous French organist Louis Marchand, who seems to have shrunk from a proposed contest.[4]

Bach's post as *Konzertmeister* brought him again the no doubt welcome duties of cantata composition, sacred and secular. In the church cantatas of this period he developed a new modernity of style. Many of his libretti were by the well-known Lutheran preacher Pastor Neumeister, the reflective portions of whose cantata texts were quite deliberately cast in "recitative and aria" form. Bach set them with all the Italian dramatic devices, heightened by his own great powers of emotional harmony. Well might the Pietists exclaim that opera had entered the church. But to the "orthodox" Lutheran Bach it meant that secular forms were being consecrated to the service of God, which was in Lutheran opinion the purpose of all art. In such works he showed plainly enough that had inclination and opportunity led him in that direction he could have become a great opera composer.

In the same year the post of *Kapellmeister*[5] fell vacant, and it must have been one of the greater disappointments of Bach's life that he did not obtain it. His reaction was his acceptance of a *Kapellmeister* offer from Prince Leopold of Anhalt Cöthen.

At Cöthen (1717–23) he found a congenial and musical patron and the

highest salary of his career, but an organ of small scope for such as he, and
no religious employment, since the Cöthen court held Calvinist opinions
and the rather grim chapel heard no sounds of music other than those of
metrical psalms. His duties concerned only the Court orchestra (in which
the Prince played the *viola da gamba*) and chamber music in general. Thus
while he continued to display his powers on organs of other cities, and give
expert advice on them, he devoted most of his attention at Cöthen to the
composition of instrumental music. During this period of something over
four years the bulk of his chamber and purely orchestral music was written.
Included in it were the six Brandenburg Concertos—" courtly entertainment
music at the highest level "[6]—the four Suites (" Overtures ") for orchestra,[7]
the Violin Concertos (the example in D minor for two violins is immortal[8]),
and the Sonatas (church and chamber) for, variously, violin, violoncello,
flute and viola da gamba. The Brandenburg Concertos were written at the
instigation of the Margrave of Brandenburg, who put the scores into his
library, where they long lay forgotten. We have already spoken of Bach's
" line " orchestration, which tended to keep to the baroque tradition of one
" affect " and one instrumental colour-group per movement, but the variety
of the schemes used in the six works was most exceptional. The majority of
the sonatas were for solo instrument and *obbligato* harpsichord, that is, the
keyboard accompaniment was no mere continuo, but was fully written out,
and played the role of an active partner. Six violin and six 'cello sonatas
were for single instrument *solus*, the contrapuntal textures maintained by the
frequent use of multiple stoppings. They are still searching tests for modern
soloists.

The clavier music of the period included the Chromatic Fantasia and
Fugue, the English and French Suites, the first book of the Forty-eight
Preludes and Fugues (see p. 181), the Little Preludes, and the Two- and
Three-Part Inventions. A great deal of all this was written for teaching
purposes, the pupils including members of Bach's own family. Early in his
Mühlhausen period he had married his cousin, Maria Barbara, and he now
had growing children to instruct, among whom were the gifted Wilhelm
Friedmann and Carl Philipp Emanuel. We note that in an age when the light
touch of keyboards permitted the three inner fingers to accomplish the bulk
of the work, that Bach, like Couperin, had his own ideas as to the best
technique, and advocated the consistent use of the whole hand, including
the hitherto neglected thumb. He did not, as is sometimes stated, *invent* the
use of the thumb. The Spaniards employed it long before his time, or
Couperin's.

Returning in 1720 from one of his organ journeys Bach found that his
devoted wife had died suddenly. There followed a period of understandable
restlessness. It may be that he was concerned with his young family; the best
of Lutheran education was not to be found in•Calvinist Cöthen. It may
be that he longed to practise again his true vocation, that of a Lutheran
church musician. Perhaps the marriage of the Prince to a young wife with
a dislike for music also unsettled him. Whatever the dominant reason, after
the death in 1722 of the famous Johann Kuhnau, Cantor of the Thomas-

14.   A fifteenth-century Italian dance-band. The combination seems to
be three shawms and a sackbut (the old name for the trombone type).
Apparently there is promise of refreshment in the background. The
scene belongs to a brilliantly coloured Florentine chest-painting of about
1420, " The Wedding of the Adimari ".

15. The cantus part of a drinking song, *O potores exquisiti*, found in a manuscript dating from about 1450 (Egerton MS 3307), probably written for the Chapel Royal of St. George, Windsor. Most of the contents of the manuscript were of a more serious nature.

British Museum

16. The blind composer Francesco Landini, playing the portative organ. The illustration from the famous Squarcialupi manuscript forms the portrait initial to the first of his compositions written therein. The manuscript is in the Medicea-Laurenziana Library, Florence.

Biblioteca Medicea-Laurenziana, Florence.

schüle at Leipzig, Bach applied for the vacant position. He was successful, but only after the two more favoured candidates, Telemann and Graupner, had each had second thoughts and declined it. He came to Leipzig with a newly-married second wife, Anna Magdalena, who proved as devoted a helpmeet as Maria Barbara had been, and who also produced sons destined for renown (Johann Christoph Friedrich and Johann Christian).

"Cantor" (i.e. chanter) is a term with a long medieval history. It *could* mean the official in charge of the music of a cathedral, second only to the Dean, but a lesser standing was usually attached to the function. In Bach's Germany we find the name given to the musical head (under the Rector) of an educational establishment, whose appointment was often in the hands of the municipal authority, with the result that he was usually called on to undertake outside responsibilities. Such was the nature of Bach's post. As Cantor of the Thomasschüle he was concerned, among other duties, with the music of four of the city's churches—though in the case of two of them only to a small degree. He had no service tasks as actual organist. The post was of course a descent socially from the rank of *Kapellmeister*, which is perhaps the reason why he liked to sign himself "Director of Music". More than a decade later he sought and finally obtained the title of "Court Composer" from the King of Saxony at nearby Dresden. His aim was to increase his status, the better to deal with the annoyances he suffered at the hands of the local authorities, pedagogic and municipal.

For his music-makings he had under his control a body of choir singers consisting of Thomasschüle boys from the age of ten to late adolescence. A proportion of school pupils had been recruited originally as having musical promise. To these were added some grown men, an orchestra (school players and a few "town" musicians) and some musical assistants. As we have seen, Bach's duties were concerned with the weekly service music of the two main churches, but there were frequent special occasions. For all these needs Bach supplied the music, usually his own. As regards the school, he "taught music", while another of his tasks, nominally, was instruction in elementary Latin, but this latter he transferred to a deputy. As time went on he deputed more and more of the routine tasks. His post, as he saw it, was the municipal Director of Music, and it may be that he hoped that by devoting himself to the composition of church music and organising its performance he could succeed in making Leipzig a far-famed Lutheran centre.[9] There came, gradually, a fading of these dreams.

He had rather too many masters. He had to satisfy the Rector (headmaster) of the school, the City Council and the various officials connected with the churches, as well as the authorities of the University, where he had some responsibilities. John Sebastian never suffered opposition meekly, standing firmly, if not always tactfully, for his rights. Thus there were soon clashes. But in spite of all the distractions and difficulties a new and marvellous stream of music began. Bach brought with him to Leipzig his newly completed St. John Passion. In 1729 came the first performance of the immortal Passion according to St. Matthew; the six cantatas of the "Christmas Oratorio" belong to 1734; about 1737 the Lutheran Masses (Kyrie and

N

Gloria only). All these works were for solo voices, chorus (often double chorus), orchestra, continuo organ, and sometimes continuo harpsichord also, and, as musicians well know, call for considerable technical skills. At various times came the four motets, the Psalms, the five Sanctus movements. Continually Bach was meeting the call for the weekly cantata, which took its place in the principal Sunday service and was designed as the musical complement to the Gospel text and the sermon. He wrote nearly three hundred cantatas, most of them for Leipzig, completing the yearly cycle of fifty-nine five times over. During twenty Leipzig years, before the stream dried up, he must have averaged one new cantata each month. Fortunately he had a fluent and complaisant librettist in a local poetaster who wrote under the pseudonym of " Picander ", but we can only marvel how Bach could take in his stride the urgency and strain which must have occurred from time to time, when composition, arrangements for copying, rehearsal and performance had to be compressed into the shortest of periods. And the fact remains that these cantatas, the craftsmanship and beauties of which are perhaps even yet not fully recognised, number among themselves masterpieces. Bach cast them in a variety of forms (almost a quarter of the total are solo cantatas) but the features—dramatic recitative, aria, contrapuntal chorus, rich harmony and subtle orchestral accompaniment—were all designed to serve and underline the religious intentions of the texts. Nearly all employ the chorale proper to the occasion as a conclusion, in vocal harmony, but use is sometimes made in the body of such a work of musical material from the chorale (as in " *Jesus nun sei gepreiset* "). Some attention has already been given in Ch. VII to the frequent use by Lutheran composers, including Bach, of chorale *texts* both in their original forms and in paraphrase as a means of providing the whole, or nearly the whole, of a church cantata libretto. This was the so-called chorale cantata.

For some years Bach found conditions at Leipzig tolerable enough, but after 1729 the changing policy of the City Council towards the Thomasschüle meant that fewer and fewer musical children were becoming available for the calls that he had to meet. He protested bitterly, but there is little doubt that thereafter his musical resources both vocal and instrumental, were considerably diminished. It is sad to reflect that many of his concerted works as heard by him must have suffered quite inadequate performances. The situation had its credit side, however, for it led to the production of a musical masterpiece. We have already noted his application to the King of Saxony in 1733. He supported this by sending also the newly-written Kyrie and Gloria in B minor (in effect a Lutheran Mass). In 1738 he augmented it by the addition of the other, traditional, sections, the music of some of them adapted from earlier works. There are twenty-four movements in all, the standard divisions being subdivided, and thus it became an early and supreme example of the " Concert " Mass, a masterwork containing some of his loveliest and most subtle music, but too gigantic for any liturgical use. It was not performed until long after his death.

As regards his hopes of any development of his establishment, the final blow was dealt by the advent in 1734 of a new Rector, Ernesti, who was actively opposed to music. There were years of janglings, but increasingly, as time went on, Bach deputed his duties, and retired to his own private world as far as composition was concerned. In his last decade only one new church cantata is known to have been written. However, the period had its compensations for him. He made a number of journeys to the friendly court of Weimar and to other cities for the purpose of giving recitals. Everywhere his unique powers as an organist were acclaimed. In 1744 the second book of the " Forty-Eight " was completed, probably, like the first, for the use of growing sons and other private pupils. He continued with his last wonderful organ chorale-preludes, the " Eighteen " and the " Catechism ". In 1742 he printed his " Aria with Thirty Variations ", the so-called " Goldberg Variations ", a commission from his admirer Count Keyserling, the Russian Ambassador, who asked for " cheerful music " to while away the hours of his chronic insomnia. Bach's answer was a work of combined beauty and intricacy (every third variation is written in canon) that has fascinated musicians ever since. The Count's domestic musician was a certain Johannes Goldberg, a famous harpsichordist and a former pupil of Bach's. He had the task of playing the work—hence the name. It is pleasurable to record that for once Bach was generously rewarded for a composition.

Bach's grown-up sons were now occupying prominent posts, Carl Philipp Emanuel being harpsichordist at the Court of Frederick the Great at Potsdam. The King, who was a music lover after his own fashion, and who held regular private concerts at which he performed on the flute, had several times expressed the wish to see " Old Bach ". In the spring of 1747 the journey was made, and the autocrat gave the grand old musician every token of respect and admiration. Bach was asked to try over the new-fangled Silbermann " forte-pianos ",[10] and afterwards the palace organs. One of his improvisations was on a subject given him on the spot by Frederick himself, and with it he built up a six-part fugue. After his return to Leipzig he made a series of workings of the theme—ricercars and canons of incredible ingenuity—together with the tactful addition of a trio sonata for the King's flute, a violin and continuo. He termed this collection of thirteen pieces " A Musical Offering " and sent it to Potsdam. Neither the visit nor the composition seems to have brought any pecuniary acknowledgement from the thrifty Frederick.

Bach's last few years were hampered by failing eyesight. Because of this he was compelled to abandon before completion the monumental " Art of Fugue ", which set out to teach counterpoint and fugue by means of practical examples, all founded on a single theme. It was published after his death by his son, Carl Philipp.

In 1749 he became completely blind, but even then continued to work on a revision of the " Eighteen Preludes ". In July 1750 he died, and was buried in the cemetery of St. John's Church with no monument to mark his grave. The Town Council set about appointing his successor without any motion of regret or any sign that they were aware of the stature of the man they had hampered and cavilled at.

His death was widely mourned in musical Germany, but it was to the technician, the incomparable organist, that the homage was paid. New methods of composition were opening up vistas of promise, with a Bach as the pioneer. Johann Sebastian was thought, by the majority of those musicians who happened to know anything at all about his works, to be an old-fashioned Lutheran church composer, overloaded with dry learning, and speaking a regional dialect in music.[11] Even his sons seem to have held this opinion to some degree. We shall mention in its place the revival of interest shown by van Swieten and his circle (which included Mozart). Later milestones in the rehabilitation were the publication in 1802 of the first biography (by J. N. Forkel), and the revival, by Mendelssohn, of the St. Matthew Passion in 1829. Today, among those who care for the art, the music of Bach is more alive than ever before. The opinion expressed by Alfred Einstein will be echoed by all music-lovers : " Supreme musicianship, the utmost vividness of imagination and the profoundest capacity for emotion were in Bach made one ".

Like Shakespeare, he is " not of an age, but for all time ".

Georg Friedrich Handel (1685–1759) was born at Halle in Saxony, less than a hundred miles from Bach's Eisenach. Yet so basically different were the professional lives of these two musical giants of the late baroque that it is not surprising that they never met. Handel followed a long tradition in rounding off his training in Italy, and he spent most of his mature energies in writing the Italian type of *opera seria* for a dilettante English society, with an eye on the box-office and a finger on the pulse of current taste; the first of musical free-lances, making and losing more than one fortune during his stormy career as a public entertainer.

Unlike Bach, he had no outstanding musical antecedents, but there was quick local recognition of his precocious gifts—enough to overcome the initial opposition of his barber-surgeon father to a musical career. At the age of eight he was training with F. W. Zachau, the famous organist, harpsichordist and composer. Some of the characteristics of the master's music long remained with the pupil, and Handel always remembered his old teacher with respect and affection. In his early 'teens he was already a keyboard prodigy, playing also violin and oboe, and thoroughly trained in composition. His father died in 1697, but Handel honoured a promise to remain in Halle to complete his university studies in law. Then, in 1703, he set out to make his career as a musician—to Hamburg, as a violinist and later harpsichordist in Keiser's opera orchestra (see p. 157f.). Here was valuable experience. Besides Keiser, he rubbed shoulders with other prominent musicians, notably Telemann. In spite of an early success with his youthful opera *Almira* (which owed a great deal to Keiser's influence), and a flourishing teaching practice for which he had written much harpsichord music, he decided that Hamburg was not enough.

In 1706 he set off for Italy, his funds for the journey being perhaps the payments he received for two operas that he did not trouble to wait to see performed. For a while he moved between Florence and Rome, playing at princely palaces and meeting notable composers including Corelli and

Alessandro Scarlatti, studying the music he encountered and himself impressing the Italians. At Rome he found a Papal ban on all opera, which he evaded, as did the native musicians, by composing some highly dramatic chamber cantatas on the Scarlatti pattern, of which *Apollo e Dafne* was an early masterpiece.[12*] In 1707 at Florence his first opera before an Italian audience, *Rodrigo*, was a definite success. About this time he first met Domenico Scarlatti, the son of Alessandro and the most famous harpsichordist in Italy, who recognised " the Saxon " as his equal as a virtuoso.

Italian church music had also received Handel's attention. In 1708, with the encouragement of Cardinal Ottoboni, Corelli's patron, he produced among other church compositions the oratorio *La Resurrezione*—a work in the Carissimi tradition. In 1709 at Venice came his greatest success in Italy, the opera *Agrippina*. In it he showed a thorough grasp of the " Venetian " style of Legrenzi, Caldara and Lotti. As a result of his fame he received two invitations, one to Hanover, the other (from the English ambassador) for a visit to London.

He left Italy in 1710 the polished master of Italian dramatic music, having attained at the early age of twenty-five what was the highest ambition of most musicians of the day, the post of *Kapellmeister* at a princely court—in his case, that of Hanover. Yet after but a few weeks there he obtained leave for a visit to London. He had projects in mind that were wider than the dull round of court duties.

The musical dilettanti of the London of 1710 were ready for such an advent. Italian music, as we have seen, was known and liked, but native composers, of whom only Blow was of any prominence, were unable to meet aristocratic tastes in the matter of operatic entertainment.[13] Within a fortnight Handel had written *Rinaldo*, which was produced with resounding success. The composer returned with reluctance to Hanover and his duties, and continued there for two years, producing various Italian-type chamber duets, much harpsichord music and some oboe concertos. In the autumn of 1712 he was back in Queen Anne's London. This time his leave was very definitely overstayed.

It is a measure of Handel's matchless powers and forceful personality that he, without other influence and a foreigner, could have so impressed himself on the aristocratic and official circle of London in so brief a time as to be given the task of writing the " Utrecht " Te Deum for the peace celebrations of 1713, and afterwards gaining the grant of an annual pension of two hundred pounds from Queen Anne. In the next year the Queen died, and the errant *Kapellmeister* found himself in a situation that later generations have found mildly humorous, since the successor to the British throne also happened to be the Elector of Hanover. The mountain had come to Mahomet.

There is reason to believe that the legend of Handel's disgrace has been much exaggerated, and that the well-known " Water-Music " episode belongs to a somewhat later date. Anyway, the apparently indispensible composer was soon back in favour, his pension confirmed and doubled. For a short while (1718–21) he acted as *Kapellmeister* to the wealthy Duke of

Chandos, a circumstance which produced the twelve Chandos anthems, the dramatic pastoral, *Acis and Galatea* and the masque, *Haman and Mordecai*. He was also appointed music-master to the Royal children, Queen Caroline being always his warm supporter. One of the harpsichord suites of this period contained an *Air and Variations* to which a later publisher attached the well-known but totally unauthorised " Blacksmith " title.

Soon came the opportunity that the composer was seeking. In 1719 there was formed (with the support of the King and various noble lords) a company for the production of Italian operas, with the title of " The Royal Academy of Music "[14] and with Handel as one of its directors. The money was duly found, Handel as chief composer could be relied on to produce the lovely arias, and the only other important ingredient, probably thought to be the most important, was a sufficient supply of famous Continental singers to tickle the ears of an audience who cared little for anything but displays of vocal pyrotechnics. Handel went abroad and returned with, among other soloists, the finest at the moment of the *castrati, Senesino.* On this journey he left Germany just too early to have encountered J. S. Bach.

Thus began Handel's twenty years of opera composing to Italian texts, during which period he produced over thirty such works. The pity is that for all their magnificent music they must count for little in the history of the art. We have already considered the Scarlatti pattern of opera, the " concert in costume " type with its strict conventions as to the number and nature of the arias, its successive alternations of recitative and aria, its disregard, or at the most, sparing use of choral effects. It was always rich in melody, and might have many felicitations of harmony and orchestral colouring, but through its traditional rigidity it was lacking in true dramatic unity and force. The final Italian influence on Handel had been Scarlatti's. He took over the same form and raised it to new heights of beauty without changing its essence, even though he wrote individual arias and orchestra-accompanied recitatives that were charged with high emotion.[15*] It was his misfortune that close after him came Gluck and a little later Mozart, to make the art of opera a far more vital one. As a result, though many of Handel's operatic arias continue to charm us in the concert room, any revivals of a whole work on the stage are something of the nature of offerings at his altar, needing a deal of the sacrificial knife. Modern appreciation is also handicapped by the pitiful quality of most of the libretti. Gluck and Mozart were much better served than Handel, for the latter's customary hacks Rolli and Haym were frequently less than mediocre. Well might Beaumarchais remark that what was not worth saying could always be sung. Very occasionally the composer took advantage of the superior quality of a Metastasio text (see p. 156 and p. 167, Note 13), the opera *Poro* (1731) being a highly successful result.

It is ironic to note that when nowadays it is planned to perform a work of Handel's on the stage, the solution is usually to adapt one of the English oratorios that he wrote late in his career. As most of these, in fact, unfold very dramatic stories, they need little other addition than costume and action to be ready for the theatre, the choruses supplying the "crowd" scenes usually absent from the composer's actual operas. A very successful modern adaptation (1958) was the Covent Garden production of *Samson*. Some decades earlier, (in 1925) a dramatic version of the secular "choral cantata" *Semele* (the libretto by Congreve) was staged at Cambridge. The work contains some of Handel's loveliest music, particularly in the "sleep scene". One of the arias, "Where'er you walk . . .", will be known to everyone. Another recent staging (1960) of an English oratorio was that of *Hercules*, written in 1745 and originally termed by Handel, significantly enough, a "musical drama".

Another handicap to modern revivals of the actual operas is the fact that the leading men's roles were given to *castrati*, whose voices commanded a range and facility of execution that could not nowadays easily be paralleled. The modern world can learn of the characteristic tone quality only by report, but we know that its beauty, flexibility and enormous power seem to have produced a hypnotic effect upon audiences, both Continental and English. Senesino, Farinelli and their like received fabulous salaries and widespread adulation. That kind of popular singer has gone, but not the mass-hysteria of the "fans".

Handel's first period of supplying *opera seria* in a foreign tongue to limited, "subscription", upper-class audiences began with the very successful *Radamisto* in the spring of 1720, and lasted until 1728. If success had depended only on the qualities of the music and the performances his tasks would have been straightforward, but, unfortunately, at the King's Theatre he faced an auditorium in which the more turbulent elements sought to vary their entertainment by splitting into noisy, even riotous factions—whether in support of rival composers, rival singers or rival political parties. Since another well-known opera composer, Giovanni Bononcini (1670–c. 1750) was also being employed by the Academy, there soon began a partisan-battle, too well known probably for detail here, which ended in Handel's favour with the enthusiastic reception of his opera *Otho* in 1723. Bononcini continued with occasional contributions, but the relative statures of the two men had been decided. As for Handel's problems concerning the egotisms and jealousies of singers, these were almost insoluble. He was not averse from using strong-arm methods as a last resort, but on one celebrated occasion (the production of *Alessandro*—1726), having Cuzzoni and Faustina Bordini on the stage together, *prime donne* both, he devised parts for each that were equal in importance and in opportunity for technical display— an instance which certainly reveals how hollow as drama the Italian art could become.

By 1728 audiences were very definitely dwindling in numbers, thanks to the unruly conditions, and to a general public reaction against this exotic form of entertainment. Moreover, a rival stage attraction had appeared, of a very different type, and in English—John Gay's *The Beggar's Opera*, the earliest of the "ballad" kind founded on well-known tunes. Gay's text was a salty satire on political and social conditions, as well as on the absurdities of fashionable opera. London laughed loud and long, and *opera seria* received a decided set-back. Gay's work, joined with Dr. Pepusch's musical *pastiche*, has remained alive to this day, and at the time provoked numerous imitations. In the same year the Royal Academy collapsed in ruin, with nothing of its capital left. Handel himself was not much affected financially, and in typical indomitable fashion was ready in the next year to try the game again as his own master, assisted only by a manager, Heidegger. This time he had to be his own financial backer.

Let us record in passing that with the advent of George II, the composer's annual £400 pension was renewed, together with an annual £200 as payment for the instruction of the Royal children. His later financial distresses, therefore, never rendered him wholly penniless. Among the music which he wrote for George's coronation in 1727 was the anthem *Zadok the Priest*, still used as a ceremonial work. He had already, in 1726, become a British subject.

Even while he continued single-handed the operatic struggle, he had found a new and promising interest. As a birthday compliment to him the Children of the Royal Chapel had revived his masque, *Haman and Mordecai*—renamed *Esther*. When a second, and public, performance was mooted the Bishop of London interposed to place his ban on the *acting* of a Biblical subject. Handel therefore cut down the recitatives, increased the choral element, added new numbers, and then gave a successful rendering at the King's Theatre without stage action (1732). Thus, almost unaware, he achieved the first of his English oratorios on "sacred" subjects. He continued the idea next year with *Deborah* and *Athalia*, having found that oratorio was a useful commercial stand-by in the Lenten season, when opera was discouraged.

In spite of the high musical qualities of some of the later operas (e.g. *Orlando*—1733) where strikingly expressive recitative and rich orchestral colouring brought to the outworn form much characterisation and dramatic power, his operatic projects were going badly. Once more partisan antagonism mounted (Handel was a "King's man"). The Prince of Wales' faction finally set up a rival opera company with the aim of ruining him, calling on the Italian composer Nicola Porpora (1686–1766) to aid them in their purpose. Handel gave up the struggle in 1737, and, crippled in fortune and in health, was forced to go abroad to recover, his only consolation the fact that the rival organisation had followed his to limbo. There was something of the bull in his invincible persistence, for after his return later in the year he began, with a curious and uncharacteristic blindness to the realities of the situation, to launch yet more operas, including one of his best, *Serse* (1738), which contains the celebrated aria, *Ombre mai fu* (Handel's "Largo").

His interest in choral works to English words had been growing. His settings of Dryden's *Alexander's Feast* (1736) and the *Ode for St. Cecilia's Day* (1739) both gained public approval. Also in 1739 there appeared two more oratorios in English, *Saul* and *Israel in Egypt*, the latter almost wholly choral, something new and strange for audiences. He wrote no new operas after 1741.

In 1740 he composed a choral trilogy, *L'Allegro, Il Penseroso and Il Moderato*. The texts were the work of a rich eccentric, Charles Jennens, who had adapted Milton and added a lamentable third part of his own. In the next year Jennens produced an oratorio libretto, which the collaborators termed *Messiah*. It was excellently compiled from Bible and Prayer Book, and a case has been made out for Jennens' secretary, a Rev. Pooley, being the actual arranger. Handel set it in twenty-four days, and a world masterpiece was born.[16] It was enthusiastically received at its first performance at Dublin in April 1742, on the occasion of Handel's stay there. Later, it was heard in London with a coldness that lasted for several years, owing to the religious prejudice against " entertainment " being gained from such a subject.[17*] *Messiah* is, for all its dramatic-sounding choral moments, basically reflective and truly religious in mood.

The early '40's were dark times for the composer. The performance of his *Te Deum* to celebrate the victory of Dettingen gained him some credit, but neither the new oratorios nor revivals of past operas helped his material fortunes. Then in 1745, soon after he had recovered from another serious relapse in health, came a sudden change to better days. The dangerous Jacobite rising had just been defeated. *The Occasional Oratorio* and even more, *Judas Maccabaeus*, both of that year, caught the exultant public mood of the time, (and, incidentally, the valuable support of the Jewish community for the latter). It was a real and a wide public to which Handel was now appealing. He had given up his subscription system and for the first time had thrown open his concerts to all and sundry. The English middle-class taste for choral music—and Old Testament history—now supported him and warmed to the confident virility of his settings. With soloists who were, in the main, amenable native artists, both new and revived oratorios met with increasing success, with citizen rather than aristocratic audiences. There came, among others, *Joshua* (1748), *Susanna* and *Solomon* (both of 1749).[18*] *Messiah* grew to nation-wide popularity, though in Handel's lifetime the proceeds of all performances of it were devoted to charity. With it came the " modern " type of concerts with not only masses of people in the audience, but on the platform also.

In 1751, while engaged on his last oratorio, *Jephtha*, his sight began to fail. The work was finished, but by 1753 he had become totally blind. In spite of this he continued to revise past works and to take part in performances, the last before his death in 1759 being one of *Messiah*.

In the course of his career he naturally enough poured out a flood of pieces for clavier—suites, " lessons ", fantasias and miscellaneous pieces—some for concert purposes, a great deal for teaching use. They include some fine, individual and perhaps unduly neglected fugues. A set of six concertos was marked as for harpsichord or organ; undoubtedly they were played by him as organ concertos in his later concerts. They are not of much significance. His chamber music includes works which are still very much alive, particularly his trio sonatas for two solo instruments and continuo.[19*] There is a wealth of orchestral works including the celebrated *Fireworks Music* suite (1749), and a large number of concertos for various instrumental combinations. Of these the Twelve Concerti Grossi (1739) rank with the Brandenburg set as among the finest orchestral works of the baroque age. Unlike the Bach works they are written for an invariable layout of string tutti against two solo violins and 'cello. Also unlike the Brandenburg set is the variety in the numbers of the movements—four, five and even six. No. 5 in D major, in six movements, could be described as comprising two French overtures joined together. Altogether they represent Handel at his most masterly, and seem to have suffered undue neglect.

As a melodist and a master of the art of writing for the human voice Handel stands very high indeed, with only Mozart to equal him in the latter capacity. J. S. Bach, never commanding the virtuoso type of professional singer for which Handel composed, suffers by comparison regarding his solo writing, which often appears instrumental in its idioms—not that any aspersions need otherwise be cast on his command of inspired melody.

The differing outlooks of the two men are apparent also in their handling of the contrapuntal art. Enough has been said concerning Bach to show that his mastery of the " science " of music was at a superhuman level. His great feats of counterpoint were polished and perfected to the last degree, even though, one suspects, he may have known that but few of his immediate listeners would plumb the full depths. Disregard for appreciation or censure seems characteristic of the man. It was sufficient for him that the task had been accomplished " as well as possible "—as he himself once put it. Handel, similarly master of every contrapuntal device, clearly bore in mind out of his long public experience the limits of the average listener's appreciation when it came to the weaving of polyphonic strands. Counterpoint in plenty there is in his great choruses, but relieved and contrasted by sonorous and picturesque harmonic effects. The most telling strokes in his oratorios are often those of a basic simplicity, the simplicity of genius.

Gluck and the " Reform " of Opera Seria

We have already noted the critical attitude of English audiences towards Italian *opera seria,* one shared by men of letters such as Addison and Johnson. A similar dissatisfaction had long been evident on the Continent, keenest perhaps in the land of its origin. A very early attack on the art and its exponents, a fully informed and professional one, was the vitriolic satire *Il teatro alla moda* (1720), by Bernadetto Marcello, himself a noted composer. The Italian critic Francesco Algarotti, in his *Soggia sopra l'opera in musica,* pictured the deplorable state of affairs as he saw it over thirty years later, in 1755. Although Gluck goes down in history as the first composer to make a practical stand against the current follies and absurdities of the art, a reaction against the well-worn, invariable pattern of recitative alternating with *da capo* aria had already been made manifest in the works of certain Italian composers, notably Niccolo Jommelli (1714–74) and Tommaso Träetta (1727–79). Jommelli anticipated Gluck's dramatic continuity by his skilful use of long stretches of colourfully accompanied recitative. Indeed, his handling of the opera orchestra was in a class by itself among his Italian contemporaries, and he made it an effective aid to characterisation.

Träetta brought back the chorus to play an essential part in dramatic progress, and also anticipated Gluck in the expressiveness and dignity of his settings. Yet the works of these fine composers, in company with, literally, thousands of other tuneful baroque operas, no longer live. It was left to Gluck, who in many ways was less well equipped musically than either, to write effective examples which are still given place in the modern operahouse repertoire in their own right, and not as resuscitations.

Christoph Willibald Gluck (1714–83) was born in the Upper Palatinate, the son of a gamekeeper who found employment with the wealthy and music-loving Lobkowitz family. After a somewhat bleak adolescence he was given the opportunity, thanks to a discerning patron, of four years of training in Italy with the well-known composer Sammartini, now remembered only as a pioneer in the development of symphonic form. Whatever Gluck learned from him, it was not proficiency in contrapuntal writing, nor even complete mastery of some other of the aspects of musical composition. There was an opposite side to the ledger, though, for he quickly proved that he possessed the gift of unusually lucid and attractive melody, which, in the case of a composer of the formal type of Italian opera, was one that covered a multitude of other musical sins. It was to this career that Gluck devoted himself for several years. Then, thanks to his young patron, Prince Lobkowitz, he was given the experience of musical London and Paris. He made the acquaintance of Handel, who afterwards passed a celebrated remark— a comparison between Gluck's contrapuntal knowledge and that of his own cook. Gluck, however, found Handel's music an overwhelming experience, ever after declaring that Handel was his favourite composer. There is no evidence as to what music he heard at Paris, but certainly Rameau was active at the time, and much could have been learned from contemporary French opera. Nevertheless, on his return to his native land he continued his career as a producer of the stock Italian type, some of his libretti being those of that arch-priest of *opera seria*, Metastasio. The climax of his success in these years was his gaining the favour of the Empress Maria Theresa with a particularly tuneful work, and his appointment as *maestro* of the Court opera (1752). The peasant's son was now mingling with intellectual and highly cultured people, and was intelligent enough to learn from such contacts. For several years he continued to produce successful Italian operas, together with incidental music in plenty for the French comedies performed at the Viennese Court, secure in the fact that a rich marriage had made him henceforth financially independent of his art.

Then in 1762 came the fruit of his acquaintance with Ranieri Calzabigi, a man of culture and of letters, and a former diplomatist. Calzabigi had his own ideas as to what an opera libretto should be. Metastasio still reigned as Imperial Court poet, but Calzabigi detested him and all his works and succeeded in swaying Gluck to his views. Having decided to use once more the stock theme of "Orpheus and Euridice" the librettist produced a text as completely unlike the formal, standard Metastasio pattern as was possible. As Donald Tovey puts it: "He reduced the operatic scheme from a complicated plot designed for working in three arias in each act for each of

seven expensive singers, to the simplest possible means of expressing and
concentrating the obvious emotions aroused by a classical myth ".

Calzabigi was indeed returning to something resembling the Camerata
outlook, even in the choice of subject, and in this he received full support
from Gluck, who took over his views with enthusiasm. The emotions expressed by the characters (only three were employed, apart from the chorus)
were underlined by direct and effectively dramatic music which was mainly
a type of declamation, a considerable blunting of the old recitative-aria
division. The *secco* type of recitative was discarded altogether, recitative-like
passages being accompanied orchestrally throughout. Each act progressed
as a musical-dramatic unit, a blending of the ingredients of solo voice,
chorus and dance in a manner that put across the action of the story and
the emotions of the characters without the let and hindrance of the Metastasio pattern. The vocal music, though pruned of unnecessary ornament,
was Italian in style; the lack of formal " display " arias (except for the
famous da capo *Che faro* . . .), and the maximum use of chorus together
with ballet, were French in tradition, but the overall novelty of the work
puzzled the Viennese at first. Nothing quite like the episode in the second
act, showing the gradual subduing of the trombone-accompanied Furies by
the spell of Orpheus' harp music, had been conceived before. Only in the
overture and the final chorus was Gluck perfunctory.

He soon found discerning support for the experiment, but nevertheless,
for court music and in works written for Italian cities returned for a while
to normal Italian methods. But his forward path was inevitable. In 1767
came *Alceste*, a setting of another classical myth (the poem again by
Calzabigi), which Gluck prefaced by his famous manifesto. In this (a) he
condemned halts in poetry and action for any kind of vocal display or unnecessary orchestral interlude; (b) he declared that the overture should be
of such a character as to prepare the listener for the drama that was to
follow (a practice which had already been established by some Italian opera
composers, including the use of themes borrowed from the body of the
work); he demanded also that (c) the character of the instrumentation should
suit the degree of interest and passion in the words, and (d) there should not
be too great disparity between the recitative and air of a dialogue. These
principles Gluck adhered to in *Alceste* and in the later works, but one
statement of his—" I endeavoured to reduce music to the proper function,
that of seconding poetry by enforcing the expression of the sentiment . . ."
which has a Caccini-like ring of music-subservience about it, he fortunately
failed to carry into practice, his music occupying its rightful position in the
partnership. Another " Camerata " resolution—" My chief endeavour should
be to attain a grand simplicity . . . " certainly described the effective quality
of his style.

The overture to *Alceste* was a fitting introduction to a great tragedy; the
whole work a triumphant vindication of his main principles. But though it
was favourably received in Vienna, together with another Calzabigi work
(" Paris and Helen ") which came three years later, neither gained the meed
of appreciation for which Gluck had hoped. Meanwhile he was writing a

new opera on a French text adapted from Racine, and believing that a better atmosphere for it would be found in Paris, he managed to get himself invited there for its production, thanks to the influence of the Dauphine, Marie Antoinette, who had formerly been his singing pupil at the Imperial Court. After six months of rehearsal, during which time singers and orchestral players groaned under the new and stern discipline which the *maestro* imposed on them, the *tragédie opéra, Iphigénie en Aulide* was staged at the Paris Opera in April 1774, and was a success in spite of much hostility, which Gluck had attempted to placate by claiming, with much truth, that his methods were built on those of Lully. (Indeed, in French *tragédie lyrique* there was to be found an effective use of chorus, dignified ballet and accompanied recitative.) The work began with a magnificent overture, one of the finest orchestral pieces of the eighteenth century, and once again Gluck succeeded in creating a dramatically satisfying work. In the same year he produced a revised version of *Orfeo*, the libretto rendered in French, the original " Orpheus " part which had been written for a contralto *castrato*, transposed for a tenor voice, a move which played havoc with Gluck's original modulation schemes. (It should be noted that when the opera is performed nowadays the version normally used is a rearrangement of the 1774 score made by Hector Berlioz in 1859).

But by now the opposition was really warming up. As we have already seen, there was always, at this period, a party in Paris ready to support Italian opera and Italian methods as against native music and the native tongue. A French version of *Alceste* in 1776 caused some conversions, notably that of Rousseau's, but the " war " continued, largely journalist-inspired. A rival to Gluck was found in the Italian composer Piccini, competent enough, but more skilled in the lighter forms. The campaign of rival operas will not be detailed here, except for mentioning that it led to the production of two masterpieces by Gluck—*Armide* (1777), a beautiful setting of an old Quinault libretto, and, as a final death-blow to his rival's pretensions, *Iphigénie en Tauride* (1778), with its " storm " overture and splendid first act. It is ironic to reflect that all unknown to the supporters of Italian *opera seria* there was in Paris at the time a twenty-two-year-old genius by the name of Mozart, sick for the lack of opportunity for writing in the Italian style. No doubt Mozart heard something of Gluck's music, but in his own dignified *Idomeneo* (1781) he followed Italian patterns in his own matchless way. Soon after, Gluck returned to Vienna and, in semi-retirement, wrote little more of consequence except for some Klopstock songs, one of the rare occasions when he chose to set his native tongue. He died in 1787. In his last years he learned to admire the music of Mozart.

He had but little influence on the progress of the art of music. He wrote the best operas of the age that was passing, but he founded no school. Though something of his quality is apparent in the works of Étienne Méhul (1763–1817) and later, Gasparo Spontini (1774–1851) he had no real successor. The best of his music seems to have been called forth by the more finely dramatic moments of the text that he was setting. These periods of inspiration, the attractiveness of his melody, his sound dramatic methods which caused the attention to be gripped throughout a whole scene or even a whole act, and his divine gift of being able to achieve a striking musical effect by the simplest of technical means enabled him to create music dramas that are still good (if occasional) box-office and broadcast attractions.

His work helped to give the mortal blow to the Metastasian type of opera, and for that matter to the classical French *tragédie lyrique* as well. But his triumph in Paris was no more than a personal one. What made *opera seria* out of date was *opera buffa* and the growing fashion in countries other than Italy for opera in the vernacular, singspiel, etc.

Berlioz was a keen admirer of Gluck's orchestral technique, and said that he knew better than anyone before him the colour of each individual instrument. The great baroque composers could always create an appropriate colour for an aria or chorus, choosing their instruments to suit the particular " affect ", but Gluck (*vide* his manifesto) sometimes used his orchestral palette to tint a sudden expression of emotion. For an example let us turn to the opening scenes of *Iphigénie en Aulide*. From Agamemnon we learn that owing to the goddess Diana's displeasure the Greek fleet bound for Troy is becalmed at Aulis, and that Calchas the priest has told the King that the price of Diana's forgiveness is the sacrifice of Iphigenia his daughter, who has been sent for on a pretext. Agamemnon, secure in the belief that his private messenger has prevented her coming, utters at first a defiance both of the goddess and of Calchas. Even as King and priest interchange reproaches, the chorus of Greeks announce the arrival of the princess, and then proceed to extol the beauty of one whom they believe is about to become the bride of Achilles. Against the background of harmonious rejoicing are thrown the horror-stricken exclamations of Agamemnon and the sinister mutter of Calchas (" The victim approaches . . ."). It is during the " defiance " solo of Agamemnon's that there occurs a passage particularly admired by Berlioz. As Agamemnon sings " I hear the plaintive cry of nature sounding in my breast . . ." there comes the simple but effective two-note utterance of the oboe, repeated again and again in a rising sequence, and answered each time by a sustained bassoon note and a pizzicato double-bass, so obvious but yet so moving.[20*] Another imaginative stroke, and another example of dramatic irony, is met with in *Iphigénie en Tauride*, when the remorseful Orestes strives to conceal his horror and despair with the words " Calm is returning to my heart . . ."—to the interval of an augmented second, and even as the agitated violas proclaim the actual truth. We are told that at a rehearsal Gluck had to explain the subtlety to certain literal-minded members of the orchestra, who thought that something must be wrong somewhere.

The orchestra employed by Gluck in his " Tauride " drama had indeed a wide range of colour, consisting as it did of piccolo, two flutes, two oboes, two bassoons, two horns, two trumpets, three trombones, kettledrums and strings. In his " reform " operas he had banished altogether from his orchestra the formerly ubiquitous continuo harpsichord of baroque age. Something was needed to replace the harmonic filling-in which it had supplied. The need was met, by other composers as well as Gluck, by the employment of the French horn, or rather a pair of horns, used particularly for "holding notes", a most effective device, and one still useful in the modern art of orchestration. Not only was the continuo gone, but Gluck wrote out exactly what the orchestra were to play. The old days of baroque improvisation were past.

Gluck may be considered the first of "modern" conductors in his insistence on the strictest observance of every detail of his scores—notation, dynamics and tempo. No variation from his clearly stated intentions was permitted. He seems actually to have terrified his instrumentalists and singers. Orchestras demanded double pay when he was in charge. He in turn insisted on anything up to thirty rehearsals of a work, until his unprecedented standards of perfection had been attained. Jommelli and Handel before him had enforced stern disciplines, and, like him, had curbed the vocal impromptus of egotistical singers, but Gluck's artistic tyranny seems to have been the most effective of his age.

"New Music" for the Harpsichord

Another highly original musician of this transitional period whose fame rests on a single form of activity was Domenico Scarlatti (1685–1757), son of Alessandro Scarlatti. Like his distinguished father, Domenico wrote operas, cantatas and church music, everything of which has passed into oblivion. His harpsichord "sonatas", however, vital, brilliant and original in style, and most of them composed after his fiftieth year, are as alive at the present time as they were in his own. That is, those that are known in the modern concert hall, only a proportion, unfortunately, of the five hundred and fifty odd that are in print. But appreciation of this music may well continue to grow. Written in brilliant fashion for single-manual harpsichord they transfer to pianoforte without much loss of effect. Even nowadays many of them need a more than average pianist for adequate rendering.

We have already noted Domenico's friendship with Handel at a time when the two young men were counted as the leading virtuosi of the harpsichord in Europe. For something over four years (until 1719) Scarlatti was choirmaster at St. Peter's. But his significant work was done in another land. About 1721 he began his employment with the Portuguese Royal House. In 1728 he was music-master to the Portuguese princess Maria Barbara at Lisbon. In 1730 she married the Spanish Crown Prince, and took her harpsichord teacher with her to Madrid. Scarlatti was attached to the Spanish court there until his death nearly thirty years later. As England was to Handel so was Spain to Scarlatti. The far-travelled Dr. Burney admired his music, gathered much information about him from close acquaintances, and said that the composer himself had stated that his harpsichord pieces "imitated the melody of tunes sung by carriers, muleteers and common people . . .", in other words, they were founded on Spanish folk and popular music. In Scarlatti's piquant rhythms, his vivacious melodies and at times far from conventional harmonies we may imagine the stamp and

weave of the Peninsular dance, the clangour of guitar, cymbals and castanets.

A more important consideration is the place of these sonatas in the progress of music. They exploit a wide range of keyboard technique—brilliant
scale-passages, diatonic and chromatic, chains of thirds and sixths, double
octaves, rapid repeated notes, wide keyboard leaps, and characteristic and
novel effects obtained by the rapid crossing of hands. In the period, only
J. S. Bach (e.g. the "Goldberg" Variations) made greater demands on
finger technique. Bach's keyboard style, however, was founded on baroque
counterpoint, while Scarlatti as a technical innovator deserves to be mentioned with Clementi (an admirer of his), Chopin and Liszt.

Equally interesting is the contribution of the sonatas to the development of form. Most of the pieces are in single-movement, binary shape,
many of them of only "two-page" duration. The first half closes normally
in the dominant key, or that of the relative major. Very frequently the
material of the closing bars of this part is used also in the second part,
transposed so as to give a tonic conclusion, a device which had certainly
been previously employed, but which was handled by Scarlatti with particularly good effect. Unlike the usual baroque practice a change of mood
often occurs as the first part proceeds. It is possible to see in these pieces
some glimpse of a "contrasting second subject", and a general foreshadowing of classical "sonata form". Von Bülow's opinion went further, and
distinguished in Scarlatti's sparkling and witty patterns the germs of the
Beethoven scherzo. It is also possible that Scarlatti wished some of them to
be considered as being in contrasting pairs (e.g. Nos. 497 and 500, each in
F major), a matter that has been disregarded in the order of modern
printings.

Fifty-four of these sonatas were published in London between 1738 and
1752. The rest remained in manuscript during the composer's lifetime. He
termed his volumes "Exercises for the gravicembalo", but gave the label of
"sonata" to single movements. If a contemporary affirmation is true that
the works were written *for* (and not merely to be played *to*) the Princess
of Asturias and Queen of Spain, then she must have been an exceptional
royal pupil.[21*]

The same type of sonata was written by a younger Spanish contemporary
(possibly a pupil) of Scarlatti's—Antonio Soler (1729–83), with examples of
novel and colourful modulation that foreshadow the romantic effects of a
later age, as a brief extract from one of them will show; see. Ex. 50, p. 209.

In 1762 Soler produced a technical treatise on the subject (*Llave de la
modulación*). He was in fact the most original Spanish composer of his age,
at a time when the glories of earlier Peninsular music had faded, and Spain
and Portugal, to their national detriment, were falling more and more
under the spell of the Italian style.

Ex:50

etc.

NOTES

The music of J. S. Bach and Handel is of course well catered for in the catalogues of the leading gramophone companies.

1 Quoted from Grove's Dictionary, article, BACH, by C. Sanford Terry, which should be consulted for further information regarding the "Bach tribe".

2 Some of Bach's compositions belong to this tradition—the Latin *Magnificats*, the four "Masses" (*Kyrie* and *Gloria* only), the motets, and other features such as the *Sanctus* settings. By his time the Lutheran use of Gregorian chant and the *stile antico* motet was fading.

3 The concertos of the German composer Telemann followed the Italian style.

4 A contrary theory is that Marchand, secure in his European fame and engaged in touring Germany, found that he just couldn't spare the time to meet this (to him) obscure provincial organist.

5 Let us repeat that the term *Kapellmeister* implied the overall directorship of an important musical establishment, ecclesiastical or lordly, and this might include a great deal of secular musical activity. The social standing of a *Kapellmeister* was comparatively high.

6 The Brandenburg works represent the Vivaldi pattern of the concerto grosso raised to a higher power. Except for the first, which has a minuet with trios as a fourth movement these Bach concertos are all in three-movement form— ritornello or free fugal type for first and third, with middle slow movement. But the selections of concertino instruments show astonishing variation, and thus a wide range of colour; also there is an infinite variety of method in their handling. In the 1st concerto (in F) horns, oboes and bassoon all play a part, but the principal soloist is a *violino piccola*, tuned a minor third higher than the normal violin. In the 2nd concerto there are four soloists—high trumpet (*clarino*), flute, oboe and viola. The 3rd concerto is the well-known G major work for strings alone, in ten parts. The 4th, also in G, has a solo group of one violin and two flutes. The 5th in D uses flute, violin and harpsichord

O

for its very unusual concertino. Finally, No. 6 dispenses altogether with violins, employs two violas as soloists, and brings in also two *viole da gamba*.
Bach's normal orchestra at Cöthen consisted of the usual strings, oboes, bassoons, horns, trumpets and drums, together with the more occasional use of *viola da gamba*, flute, *oboe d'amore* and *oboe da caccia*. The last two instruments could be reckoned as being respectively mezzo-soprano and contralto oboe. In the last part of the seventeenth century great strides had been made in Germany and Italy in the techniques of the trumpet, which in Bach's time was expected to play just as fast as did the oboe, another much improved instrument.

7   The *Badinerie* for solo flute and strings (2nd Suite) and the celebrated (" G string ") *Air* from the 3rd Suite are often performed separately.

8   The "Concerto for Two Violins" or "Double Concerto" as it is sometimes called, is, as Thurston Dart has pointed out, actually a concerto grosso. In Bach's original score the two violin soloists had their own 'cello and harpsichord continuo. Too often in modern performance the same full orchestral accompaniment with continuo is given to both *ripieno* and soloists.

9   This is the view of Prof. A. J. Hutchings—eloquently maintained on pp. 197–8 of *Music and Western Man* (*Dent*).
To present a different opinion—while it is well enough known nowadays that a certain number of Bach's later church works represent transcriptions, adaptations or "parodies" (in the Renaissance sense) of earlier compositions, Prof. Friedrich Blume in a recent paper would change the Leipzig picture a great deal more. He thinks that in due course it will be found that an even greater proportion of the supposed Leipzig church music will prove to be of earlier date; that at Leipzig Bach wrote much more secular music for civic ceremonial and public concert occasions than has at present been recovered; and that he was in fact just as much devoted to the secular side of his art as to the religious. This address to the International Bach Society was reproduced in translation in *Music & Letters* for July, 1963. Many people may be inclined to await more definite evidence before supporting this view.

10   The first practical pianofortes were the invention of the Florentine harpsichord maker Bartolomeo Cristofori, and date from about 1709. The new principles were basically those of the modern instrument and involved the *striking* of a string by a hammer, which then *rebounded* a short distance. While the key was kept depressed the string was clear of its damper and therefore free to vibrate. With the release of the key came the simultaneous damping of the string. Cristofori's name for his instrument, *Gravicembalo col piano e forte*, stressed the variations of tone-volume that were now easily available, since the finger could control the speed at which the hammer was thrown. The actual mechanism was far from satisfactory at first (perfection was indeed a matter of many decades of evolution), but Cristofori and others were soon making improvements. The German maker Silbermann showed J. S. Bach two of his instruments in 1726, but was disappointed by the Cantor's verdict—the treble was too weak, the touch too heavy. Later, another model of his earned Bach's praise, but the latter never acquired one of his own.

11   Johann Scheibe, a Leipzig musician, made more than one attack on Bach's music (see p. 143), describing it as turgid and confused. One of Bach's University friends defended him ably in print. Bach's own retort was in the secular cantata " Phoebus and Pan " (1731), in which Scheibe, as Midas, was given a pair of ass's ears. It appears that the "Italian Concerto", for harpsichord, actually gained Scheibe's approval.

12* A complete performance of *Apollo e Dafne* is recorded on Oiseau Lyre OL 50038. Among the many felicitous passages of orchestral accompaniment are the moments when a solo violin (Daphne) is pursued through the score by a solo bassoon (Apollo).

13   It must be remembered that there was much other musical entertainment in London at the time—English " operas " which, like Purcell's several examples,

were plays with songs, (perhaps choruses) and incidental music—pastorals, pan-
tomimes, masques—serious commercial rival to the "opera" theatre of the
Haymarket. Such attractions, above all the 1728 success of the *Beggar's Opera*,
were some of the reasons for the normally precarious state of Handel's operatic
ventures in the Italian language, which more than once collapsed into financial
ruin. An almost forgotten operatic success in English—and a true opera—was
Calypso and Telemachus (1712), the libretto by John Hughes and the music by
Johann Galliard, a German who came to London ahead of Handel, in 1706.
The work was approved by Burney.

14 Nothing to do, of course, with the present Royal Academy, which was founded
in 1822 for a different purpose.

15* HMS V has a recording of part of a scene from *Guilio Cesare*—a beautiful aria
by Cleopatra ("Lydia"), to the accompaniment of both the theatre and a
back-stage orchestra, and interrupted by a *secco* recitative by Caesar.

16 In setting *Messiah* Handel made some use of previously composed music, four
of the choruses being adapted from a set of Italian chamber-duets which he had
written not long before. Others of his works show similar adaptations. Such a
practice, that of an economical craftsman using up pieces of material that could
be spared from somewhere else, was common enough to the age (Bach's music
can show similar instances). But in the case of Handel there is no doubt that
he was not always above extending such borrowings to other people's compositions, though apparently without earning any particular obliquy. William Boyce,
his contemporary, remarked tolerantly: "He takes pebbles and converts them
into diamonds". There were, of course, no laws of copyright to restrain such
doings—nor the "pirating" of music by printers.

17* The "coldness" towards *Messiah* continued in spite of the oft-related incident
of George II springing to his feet at the first impact of the Hallelujah Chorus.
As for "entertainment", Handel declared that in *Messiah* his object was not
to "entertain" his listeners, but to "make them better"—a perfectly genuine
sentiment, for in character he was basically pious and honest.
Messiah was the original naming, but the title *The Messiah* is in widespread use.
Recordings of excerpts and of the complete work are of course readily available.

18* HMS VI has a recording of the first chorus from *Susanna* ("How long, O
Lord"), one founded on a chromatically moving basso ostinato, reminiscent of
Purcell's "Dido's Lament", and even more of one used by Cavelli. However,
the result that Handel built on it is something quite different, and is indeed
a movement of great power.

19* HMS VI has a recording of Handel's five-movement Trio Sonata in F major for
flute, violin and continuo. To return to the subject of self-borrowings—three
of the movements make use of material found elsewhere in his instrumental
works.

20* HMS VII has a recording of part of the first act of *Iphigénie en Aulide*. It
includes a portion of the scene between Calchas and Agamemnon (in which
occurs the "plaintive cry" of the oboe), and the people's greeting to Iphigenia's
chariot. Another example of a "simple but effective device" is the sudden in-
dignant string unison at Agamemnon's words "cet ordre inhumaine".

21* HMS VI has a recording of a harpsichord performance of a Sonata in B flat by
Scarlatti, its second theme, a lilting *siciliano*, a complete contrast to the head-
long semi-contrapuntal first subject.
A two-album publication of twenty-nine of the sonatas is well known.

CHAPTER IX

The Formation of the Classical Style

IT has already been noted that the second part of the eighteenth century witnessed a remarkable change in instrumental style. It was indeed only one minor example of the effect on the arts in general of the gradual changes in social climate that were taking place. The period of the so-called Enlightenment was setting in, when the discoveries in natural science and the opinions of the philosophical writers were having their effect on the social outlook, and when autocratic rule in Europe was becoming uncomfortably aware of the rising middle classes. The French Revolution was yet at a distance, but the movements that were to lead to great political changes and to the artistic revolution known as Romanticism were already beginning. The first musical effect was the emergence of the more homophonic, rococo style, with lightness, variety and entertainment as its motto, the antithesis of the more grandiose aspects of the baroque. Soon the suite and the concerto grosso fell into decay. The long baroque movement of unrelenting rhythm was succeeded by one of more changeable moods, while the fugue began to be regarded as a Gothic type belonging only to the realm of church music. For a time the leaning was towards *Empfindsamkeit*—" sensibility " (i.e. sentimentality)—this especially a feature of the German rococo.

The type of instrumental composition that was growing more and more popular was the *sinfonia,* the symphony, the Italian three-movement type which had graduated from Neapolitan opera to the concert room to entertain not only aristocratic listeners but the growing body of citizen audiences. This was so not only in Italy but in other European countries. The new style, by adopting sectional, harmonic methods in homophonic fashion, in which subsidiary ideas were contrasted with the principal one in both mood and rhythm, was faced with the problem of shaping such a scheme into some kind of artistically satisfactory form that would fill an extended movement. Over a period of about fifty years a host of worthy composers in their instrumental works were committed to the task. By about 1770, before the later symphonic masterpieces of Haydn and Mozart began to arrive, what was widely regarded as a satisfactory framework had been hammered into shape—one that could be used for the first movements of symphony, concerto, *divertimento,* keyboard sonata and chamber work—and termed in modern text-books " sonata " or " first movement " form.

Before surveying the intervening years let us take some note of what comprises this form, as far as it *can* be defined. In broad detail it was a large ternary type. The first section consisted of a presentation of the thematic material—the text-book " exposition ". The second was a reshaping of some or all of this material—the " free fantasia " or " development "; (in the early stages of progress especially it might not deserve the latter name). The third was a recapitulation of the first section with certain modifications; (in the early stages with perhaps a deal of omission). The exposition section was sometimes preceded by an introduction, derived from and at times reminiscent of the fanfare which often preceded the three-movement Italian opera-overture. " First " and " second subject " materials were usually contrasted—the first more resolute in character than the lyrical second. With the example of the already established binary-form practice, the second subject was normally presented in the key of the dominant, or if the movement were a minor-key one, in the key of the relative major. Secondary material (the so-called bridge passage) linked the two and effected the modulation. Leading on from the second subject some kind of cadential passage rounded off the exposition in the new key.

In the mid-century period of experiment more and more resource was shown in the treatment of the middle (development) section. Modulations such as the baroque overture never knew were employed, and growing skill, especially in Germanic hands, was shown in the presentation of new aspects of the thematic material.

In the recapitulation section, the restatement of the exposition material was of necessity modified (as in the case of simple binary form) so that the movement might close in the home key, effected usually by an alteration of the bridge passage and the presentation of the second subject in the tonic. The idea of some kind of extended closing passage, the coda, is also to be found. Often a reminiscence of the first subject was used, or at least some previous material.

No musical form arises from a vacuum. P. H. Lang has suggested (op. cit. p. 598) that the dualism of the new sonata form owed its origin to the type of first movement as used by Vivaldi in his later concertos. The opening energetic *tutti* was the prototype of the first subject; the less dynamic solo passage that succeeded suggested the contrasting second subject. Vivaldi's mature concertos connected the two by some episodical bars— the new " bridge ". Once the idea had grown up of providing material of a contrasting nature for the second section the new exposition was in being. Possibly opera and folk music played their parts in giving the cantabile characteristics to the second section.

As for the overall plan of the new sonata and symphony—for a time the number of movements was usually restricted to three, the quick-slow-quick of the Italian overture (the concerto has always kept to that number). The middle slow movement inherited its song form from earlier times, but in the developing symphonic scheme we find slow movements written in modified sonata form, or shaped as an air with variations. The final movement soon made use of the " rondo " plan suggested by the *tutti*—episode alternations of the baroque concerto, spiced by the flavour of the vivacious and tuneful Neapolitan opera-finale. The sonata-form of the first movement was also sometimes transferred to the last. Eventually in the hands of Haydn and Mozart (among others) a synthesis took place, the sonata-rondo form. The air and variations also found a place in the finale.

By the date that has been suggested (c. 1770) the *four*-movement, classical type symphony is found firmly established, the addition being that of the minuet (and trio) as the third in the order. This, a baroque dance-form, had been used often enough in the suite, as well as in the overtures and the concert symphonic works of the first part of the century, where it usually appeared as a closing movement. Sammartini of Milan, a pioneer symphonist, made this use of it, and Haydn, even, ended thus in some of his clavier sonatas, including his last example (1794). But it was given the more permanent, third-movement place by composers of the so-called Mannheim school in the mid-forties. It fitted not particularly happily into the symphonic scheme of the time, and some composers, especially Northern German ones, fought shy of it at first. Even Mozart chose at times to write a three-movement symphony.

It is always dangerous to dogmatise regarding any musical " form ". Like the fugue, sonata-form is capable of an endless variety of organisation. Though Haydn, for example, normally presented the usual two subject-groups in his sonata-form movements we find instances, even in his most mature works, where he has chosen to concentrate on one single subject, without appearing to need any other material of significance. Such movements in Haydn's hands were none the worse for that. This material—

Ex. 51

was matter enough for one of his loveliest movements, the first of Symphony No. 104 in D major, the last of the twelve written for his London visits, and his very last symphony. Another single-subject instance is the finale of Mozart's E flat Symphony (No. 39).

The Progress of Sonata Form

A return will now be made to the period of the first emergence of the new style. While prominent Italian opera composers of the Neapolitan school such as Baldassare Galuppi (1706–85) and Giovanni Pergolesi (1710–36) wrote homophonic harpsichord sonatas that were certainly tuneful but not very definite in structure, it was Giovanni Sammartini of Milan (c. 1700–75), Gluck's master, who showed first a distinctly symphonic attitude. His three-movement *sinfonias,* written for concert use in attractive instrumental style, broke new ground in his employment of a variety of rhythms within a single movement. Rinaldo da Capua (c. 1710–1780) was another pioneer in this respect, being as far as is known the first to write a definite contrasting second group in a movement. Let us also bear in mind Domenico Scarlatti. The cosmopolitan musical world of Vienna was in close touch with Italy (Milan was then ruled by Austria), and it was there that the symphonic form began a significant development, a blending of the Italian melodic gift with the more intellectual qualities of the South German and Czech composers. In Vienna, indeed, the influence of French rococo was not as strong as in North Germany, and a good deal of the old polyphonic tradition was still surviving. A list of the composers of various nationalities working within the bounds of the Empire in the second quarter of the century, all concerned with developing the dualistic principle, would be a long one, and only leading names can be mentioned. The Viennese composer Georg Monn (1717–50), with an excellent instrumental style, wrote a four-movement symphony in D major in 1740, one of the movements being a minuet.[1*] The whole question of the evolution of the sonata principle is somewhat complicated by the fact that not enough is known about the early Italian and Viennese efforts in that direction. As more and more works by previously unknown composers, as well as previously unknown works by known ones, come to light, credits tend to be moved further and further back. It is interesting to note that the excellent composer of baroque concertos, Tommaso Albinoni, is now found to have written four symphonies (albeit in the very beginnings of the " courtly " style) which were in *four* movements —allegro, andante, *minuetto,* presto—the minuet being in the " right " place. The greatest master of the Vienna symphony before its emergence to complete classical form was Georg Wagenseil (1715–77), court composer at the capital and probably the first to establish the keyboard concerto on the model of the new sonata. The child Mozart played one of his concertos during his visit to the Court in 1762. In his work, as in that of his contemporary Stamitz at Mannheim, is seen the principle of employing themes containing within themselves motives which could be used separately and in pregnant fashion in subsequent development. The Haydn subject given as Ex. 51 is a later illustration of this feature. The first phrase of four notes and the last two bars of the example each has its independent life in the development.

To follow another phase of symphonic growth we must now leave Vienna and travel to Mannheim, capital of the Palatinate, which was exactly what a number of important Southern German, Czech and Italian composers did.

The Elector Carl Theodor who ruled at Mannheim was himself a good musician, a man of considerable culture and a generous patron of the arts in general. During his reign there (he transferred his Court to Munich in 1778) Mannheim became established as a leading cultural centre. In the early forties a brilliant group of cosmopolitan musicians was gathered at the Court, made up both of leading composers and first-class instrumentalists. As we have seen, in the eighteenth century it was quite usual for the two accomplishments to be combined to a high degree in a single individual. A veritable school of symphony composition began, and the Court orchestra came to be regarded as the finest in Europe. All the "latest" works, e.g. the operas of Jommelli, Hasse and Galuppi, soon found performance at Mannheim.

Johann Stamitz (1717–57), a brilliant young Czech violinist, was appointed to the orchestra in 1741. In 1745 he became *Konzertmeister,* and it was at his hands that Mannheim rose to its musical fame. A master of all the strings of the orchestra, he set himself to train his instrumentalists, both as individuals and as a team, in a manner never achieved before. A tradition of extremely expressive yet highly disciplined and accurate playing was established which survived Stamitz's early death, to be carried on by Christian Cannabich (1731–98). Burney wrote enthusiastically of the Mannheim performances under the latter in 1772, and even to the widely travelled young Mozart, who heard the orchestra in 1777, the fire, precision and expressiveness of the playing came as a revelation. Incidentally, Mozart gives the strength of the orchestra as being " 10 or 11 violins on either side, 4 violas, 4 violoncelli, 4 contrabassi, 2 flutes, 2 oboes, 2 clarinets, 4 bassoons, 2 horns, with trumpets and drums ". He was attracted by the Mannheim clarinets, though indeed the instrument was by then widely known, and he must have met it in London in his childhood, and elsewhere. The curse of faulty intonation, an eighteenth century characteristic of all woodwind, was noted even at Mannheim. Regarding trumpets and drums, parts for these were seldom included in published works, and they may well have been employed at times in orchestral performances without the evidence having survived. One of Burney's ascriptions to Mannheim, the *invention* of the orchestral crescendo, is certainly incorrect. The baroque age knew it, and both Rameau and Jommelli made most effective uses of the device, but there was plenty that was novel or polished out of recognition in the highly drilled Mannheim orchestral style.

Stamitz's place as a pre-classical symphony composer is also a high one, though not so high as once thought, now that it has been more and more realised how much pioneer development had taken place in Italy, Vienna and elsewhere. Like C. P. E. Bach (about whom more anon) he made the subsidiary section of the exposition—the second subject—a living force, often made up of a number of different motives, and clearly contrasted with the first subject, which in his hands was usually extremely vigorous and arresting—the so-called " Mannheim rocket ". The blazing vitality, the explosive force of the Stamitz orchestral first movement was something new to the suave *galant* generation. Its dramatic constructional contrasts were heightened by accompanying contrasts of orchestral colour, woodwind and horns taking their share in the presentation of the themes. The fading of the continuo outlook can be seen in his more advanced use of the middle voices, which contributed their quota of interest to the orchestral web. Only in the later stages of the sonata plan was the classical pattern not achieved. The tonal scheme of | tonic, dominant : dominant, tonic | was firmly adhered to; the embryo development section was signalised by the appearance after the double bar of the first subject in the dominant key; but seldom in the recapitulation does it reappear in the tonic, in its normal classical place. However, Stamitz at least helped to establish the symphonic spirit.

Below, (p. 218), are given a few bars, in condensed form, of the first *Presto* of Stamitz's D major Symphony from the Op. 5 group. It was scored for two each of flutes, oboes, bassoons and horns, with strings and continuo. We may well suppose trumpets and drums to have been added. Even in this brief extract some of the composer's characteristics are apparent—the vigorous fanfare-like opening, the excitement of the string tremolos (an effect somewhat neglected since the days of Monteverdi), the sudden dramatic changes of tone-volume, and, with the fifth bar, the ascent of the " Mannheim rocket " in a gradual crescendo to a double-forte outburst, followed by a quiet echo. Certainly a firm orchestral discipline was needed for the artistic rendering of such a passage. Also given are two bars from a later, contrasting section in the key of the dominant.

Stamitz was one of those who helped to stabilise the position of the minuet and trio as following the slow movement in the four-movement symphony. The life of the minuet was for a time uneasy until later composers learned to disguise its dance-suite origin by using methods of a more symphonic nature in its construction. Stamitz wrote no less than seventy-four symphonies. Among his solo concertos was one for clarinet, possibly the first clarinet concerto ever written.

His pupil, the Mannheim-born Franz Beck (1723–1809), also wrote a number of meritorious and progressive symphonies, but in 1761 he moved permanently to southern France, where his work was continued in relative obscurity, away from the main symphonic stream. Stamitz's disciples and successors at Mannheim, Cannabich among them, wrote in the same style without the spark of their great leader, and the school sank finally to empty imitation, as Leopold Mozart shrewdly noted. The symphonic dominance of Vienna was now being fairly established.

It is time now to turn to a musician who, in the same period and in comparative isolation, was also making important progress in the evolution of the symphonic form, and who was of greater merit as a composer than any of the pioneer symphonists mentioned so far.

Carl Philipp Emanuel Bach (1714–88), the second son of Johann Sebastian, received all his training at the hands of his mighty father, and already in his eleventh year was a masterly performer on clavier and organ, though never a string player. Frederick the Great of Prussia heard him play in 1738, and in 1740 invited him to Potsdam to become Court harpsichordist. In the King's musical establishment there was also the famous flautist Johann Quantz (1697–1773) who did much to improve the mechanism of his instrument, but whose life-task as a composer was to write flute concertos for his Royal master to play—over three hundred of them—in a somewhat outworn genre. Also there were two other well-known musicians, the brothers Graun—Carl (1704–59), the *Kapellmeister* and composer of Italian operas for the Court theatre—and Johann (1703–71), the *Konzertmeister* of the orchestra. C. P. E. Bach, even from the first, was not particularly happy there, and on his father's death (1750) he applied unsuccessfully for the

Ex: 53

4

Leipzig post. However, he had plenty of leisure for composition and study. In 1742 came the six " Prussian " sonatas for clavier; in 1744 the " Wurtemmberg " set. In 1753 there was published the first part of his monumental treatise " The True Art of Playing the Clavier ", which dealt exhaustively with every aspect of the subject, notably with what the author held to be the principles of correct fingering. Many of his views seemed revolutionary at the time, but were ultimately vindicated, for the later keyboard players Clementi, Hummel, Czerny and Cramer followed them and built on them. Thus Carl Philipp may be described as the founder of modern pianoforte technique, though he himself kept to the harpsichord and clavichord, the latter being his favourite instrument.

As a composer of keyboard sonatas he proved himself a pioneer of genius. It is a measure of that genius that he could in composition escape what might have been the overwhelming influence of his great father, whom otherwise he admired greatly. (Strange it is that a Bach should speak of canons as " dry and despicable pieces of pedantry ".) These sonatas had ultimately an important influence, since they were known to Haydn and Mozart. P. H. Lang (op. cit. p. 596) says of the above-mentioned sets that in them " the musical dialect of the classical style was established; they had themes of symphonic pregnancy, developments of sombre intensity, harmonic intricacies of startling modernity, and a humour of disarming bonhomie. There is scarcely another case in the history of music in which prophetic utterances turned into reality only to be forgotten in the very tumult they created ". He goes on to say : " Nothing of such developed and mature symphonic fabric can be found in the Mannheim symphonies or in contemporary orchestral works of any sort ". Though these sonatas may have been neglected in later times, Haydn and Mozart were free in their tributes. The former as a young man based his study of composition on them, and declared that C. P. E. had been his only model. Their dramatic aspects find echoes even in the sonatas of Beethoven. Bach's symphonies, less well known, had, perhaps for that reason, less influence in shaping the classical style. In some ways Carl Philipp was the child of his time. It was the age of *Empfindsamkeit*. The " sighs ", the emotionalism of the period, found deliberate expression in his music, especially in his frequently rhapsodical slow movements. One of his guiding principles was the belief that " it is the special province of music to move the heart ".

In a few bars quoted on p. 220, from the second movement of a clavichord sonata, the drooping fourths, chromatic harmonies and expressive appoggiaturas illustrate some of the methods used by the composer to bring about this atmosphere of emotionalism.

The " prophetic " nature of his work is undoubted, achieved at a somewhat earlier date than that of the symphonic composers of significance at Mannheim and the South. The exposition, with its subject groups contrasted in key and character (sometimes having contrasting sections within the group), was fully matured, but in the succeeding parts the standard form was not yet fully arrived at. The " development " was frequently merely a modified statement of the opening matter in the new key, and

Ex:52

often the reappearance of the tonic key came only with the restatement of the second subject group. Thus the complete classical details had yet to be worked out, even though the main features had been achieved.

To turn once more to Bach's career. In 1767, on the plea of ill-health, he at last succeeded in escaping his service with Frederick, being appointed musical director to the city of Hamburg in succession to Telemann. There he supervised the music of the principal churches, organised concerts and took part as soloist in them, as well as conducting the city orchestra; and there, as leading musician, the rest of his life was spent. Burney, his guest in 1772, found him widely famous (more famous than his father had been) and living in tranquil and comfortable circumstances. The Englishman admired his consummate keyboard improvisations, and noted that his music had no roots in his father's art. C. P. E., he said, expressed his contempt for "learned" music.

Carl Philipp's works have too often been dismissed as those of a " forerunner ". It would be nearer the truth to return to contemporary European opinion, and think of him as a great composer in his own right, a fact which hearings of his music (now fortunately becoming more common) will quickly prove. He wrote at least eighteen symphonies, and his output included over fifty clavier concertos, as well as violin concertos, flute concertos, and sonatas for various solo instruments and clavier. Over two hundred clavier works are known. There were other sets of clavier sonatas besides the two groups already mentioned, as well as fantasias and rondos. Choral works include two oratorios, twenty-two Passions and about two hundred and fifty songs.[2]*

Mention must also be made of Johann Sebastian's eldest son, Wilhelm Friedmann Bach (1710–84). He was regarded in his lifetime as an outstanding organist and clavier player, with much of his father's genius in the art of improvisation. He was also the composer of some powerful and original music, as his surviving sonatas, concertos and cantatas testify. Unfortunately his eccentric manners and a lifelong indolence prevented his gaining the eminence that his great natural abilities might have won for him.

Johann Christian, the " English " Bach (1735–82), the youngest son of Johann Sebastian, has a claim for a leading place in the age. Like his brothers Johann Christian was early a brilliant keyboard player. He was only fifteen when his father died; however, his half-brother Carl Philipp took him under his wing at Berlin. He heard much Italian opera at Frederick's court, and in 1757 went to Italy to learn more about it, mainly at Milan and Naples. He had his father's passion for assiduous study, and, helped by a generous Italian patron, he gradually established himself as a composer of operas and church music. For a while he was cathedral organist at Milan, being the only Bach to exchange his Lutheran opinions for those of Rome. In 1762 he accepted an invitation to London from the management of the King's Theatre, and in London he settled, becoming a fashionable and widely beloved teacher, performer, impresario and composer. The Court of George III, to which contemporary English music owed much, made use of his services and paid him generously. Unlike Handel's, his numerous Italian operas written for London scored almost unbroken successes. Associated with him as close friend and collaborator in concert production was Carl Friedrich Abel (1723–87), composer, keyboard player and the last of the viola da gamba soloists. Johann Christian, besides being a fine musician, seems to have been a man of kindly and most charming character. Mozart had an undying admiration and affection for him, both because of his musicianship and for the friendship and guidance given to him (Mozart) when he came to London as a child prodigy in 1762.

Johann Christian was one of the first to give preference to the rapidly developing " fortepiano " as opposed to the harpsichord. Although nowadays the two instruments are very plainly to be differentiated, the tone of the pianoforte of the mid-eighteenth century was very similar in quality to that of the older instrument. The five-octave pianoforte of the time had single strings and leather-covered hammers, and its tone was if anything smaller than that of the concert harpsichord. Until about 1770 the harpsichord was usually preferred as the instrument for the public performer, but as the new action improved so a reversal of opinion took place. After 1790 the harpsichord began to be thought of as obsolete. Haydn, in London in 1791, directed his symphonies from the pianoforte.

Johann Christian's chief claim for remembrance lies in his compositions for the new instrument. His sonatas, like his brother's, influenced the greater men who followed him. Flowing and richly melodious, they helped to shape the *style galant* towards the more logical classical forms. He was apparently one of the first to play pianoforte duets. We know also that his music in general charmed those shrewdest of critics, the Mozarts, father and son.

The style and some of the characteristic features of the Mozart type of pianoforte concerto can be found in his examples of the form, as well as those of Carl Philipp, and indeed in those of the Viennese composer, Georg Wagenseil. Mozart, in more than a score of pianoforte concertos, must be given most of the credit of establishing the classical type, but he was always ready to acknowledge his debts in the matter. The keyboard concertos of the two Bach brothers can still be listened to with delight, and, for any hearer new to them, with perhaps a sense of revelation.[3]*

The name of Luigi Boccherini (1743–1805) is worthy of remembrance, especially in connection with the increasing brilliance of symphonic string writing. He made his mark on his generation both as composer and solo 'cellist. His chamber music was, in his day, widely esteemed and compared favourably with that of his contemporary Joseph Haydn. But as an Italian his concentration was very much on the melodic aspect, and his comparative neglect of the polyphonic element left him still a rococo composer. However, the beauty of his music is undoubted, and posterity has treated him badly, as did his aristocratic Spanish and German patrons. Little more than a graceful minuet from a string quintet and a 'cello concerto seem to have survived from an enormous industry in composition, which included hundreds of chamber works (quintets, quartets, trios and sonatas) as well as concertos and twenty symphonies.

The work of the Vienna composer Carl Ditters von Dittersdorf (1739–99) has had better fortune, and that deservedly. Born plain " Ditters ", he gained an ennoblement from one of his powerful patrons in the course of a brilliant career both as solo violinist and as composer of every type of music—even Italian oratorio. He toured Italy with Gluck, and became a firm friend of the young Haydn. Undoubtedly the two rising young men learned from each other. His symphonies, concertos and chamber music, approximating to true classical style, were much admired in his lifetime, and examples are still heard in the modern concert hall. More will be said later regarding his position as an opera composer. He had a succession of eminent patrons, but an irregular life affected both his health and full worldly success.

Another Viennese composer of symphonies famous in his day was Leopold Kozeluch (1752–1818). Although Beethoven expressed his contempt for him his works were long in favour. We read that symphonies of his were in the repertoire of the Konvikt orchestra in which the young Schubert played, together with the G minor of Mozart and Beethoven's Second. Like Dittersdorf, he took exception at times to the music of Mozart, and appears to have been something of an enemy to him.

Pre-Classical Chamber Music

The most popular form of chamber-music in late baroque times had been the string trio sonata, which implied, as we have seen, four instruments, since the harmonic deficiencies left by the weaving of the strings were expected to be made good by the harpsichord continuo player. With the advent of the new homophonic style the first violin became the main melody-bearer, the other parts having little else to do but accompany, often in a very mechanical way. It was a state of affairs that could not last. The obvious superfluity of the continuo accompaniment was solved in two different ways. The first was to banish the harpsichord altogether (as was the case eventually in regard to the symphony) and substitute another solo instrument, usually a stringed one. Thus began the new type of string quartet, which served as an important laboratory for the great composers who gradually perfected the classical form. The other way was to treat the keyboard instrument as an equal partner, and not merely as a gap-filling machine. Signs of this attitude were numerous in the late baroque. We have already noted this tendency in some of the delightful chamber works of Rameau, and of course in those of J. S. Bach. However, the eighteenth century development took an odd turn. It would seem that the keyboard had nursed a century-old grievance, and having got its chance, became the tyrant of the new piano trio and quartet. The usual full and interesting keyboard part is often merely *accompanied* by the strings, which are given only few opportunities to shine. Even Haydn at the summit of his career, when his symphonies and quartets were miracles of thematic development shared by all instruments, continued to write such chamber works for piano and strings.[5*]

The string-based chamber music of the time, however, was showing vital development. While Wagenseil and his fellow-composers at Vienna were writing quartets of excellent quality for solo strings, music-lovers in the city—and this meant a high proportion of the population, plebeian and patrician—were showing their appreciation for that type of composition (usually four-part) known as the *divertimento*. This was the mid-eighteenth century replacement of the baroque dance-suite, used for entertainment purposes at both popular and aristocratic gatherings, as often as not in the open air. The call for the composition of such works was continuous. We find the terms *serenade, cassation* and *nocturne* also applied to the type, which consisted of a string of contrasting movements, the number indeterminate—dances of various kinds, marches, slow movements, rondos and the like—of a tuneful, unsophisticated and entertaining nature. They were permeated with the healthy spirit of South German folk-song, and even the most skilled of composers were not above contributing examples, Haydn and

Mozart among them. *Divertimenti* might be scored for any grouping of instruments with any number of players to a part; according to available resources, it would seem. In general, the type seems to be one intermediate between orchestral and true chamber music. With the development of the symphony we find that some *divertimento* movements are actually cast in sonata form. Haydn and Mozart wrote *divertimenti* all their lives, and their more mature examples have real symphonic interest as well as popular charm.[6*] For Haydn the *divertimento* served as the first experimental field for his strivings towards mastery of instrumental writing. It is to this great master that we now turn.

Joseph Haydn (1732–1809) has often enough in the past been claimed as the "father" both of the symphony and the string quartet. Nowadays this view is no longer maintained, for reasons which have already been shown, but we can at least allow that, with Mozart, he played the leading part in bringing up the children the way they should go. Guided by him the classical symphony and string quartet each came to a marvellous consummation.

He was born in the village of Rohrau in Lower Austria, near the borders of Hungary. His father, a wheelwright, though naturally musically inclined was able to give his son no other chance of education, musical or otherwise, than was provided locally by village school and church choir. However, Georg Reutter, the Imperial choirmaster of St. Stephen's Cathedral, Vienna, noted through a chance visit to the village the exceptional soprano voice of the eight-year-old boy, and took him off to Vienna (1740) to the choir school of the cathedral. Here he received less musical education than he had the right to expect (certainly little in composition), and here he formed the lifelong habit of learning for himself by dogged private study and experiment. In 1745 he was joined in the choir by his younger brother Michael, himself destined to do honour to the name as a composer. For several years Joseph was the leading boy soloist, then in 1749 came the inevitable breaking. Not yet seventeen, he found himself on the streets, a youthful escapade giving Reutter the excuse of getting rid of him.

Seldom can a future genius have had such a testing of character. He was a raw adolescent; he was cast adrift in Vienna to earn his bread by his own exertions or starve. His resources were a chorister's practical knowledge of music, and such skill in clavier and violin playing as he had acquired from men no more distinguished than his village schoolmaster and two members of the St. Stephen's choir—plus his own exertions. A friendly loan enabled him to hire an attic room and buy an old clavier. The fees of a few pupils kept him alive, while he gave every spare moment to practise on clavier and violin, together with the study of the "Prussian" sonatas of C. P. E. Bach, as being the latest enlightenment on the art of composition. Afterwards, the theoretical works of Mattheson and Fux *(Gradus ad Parnassum)* were similarly pored over. He began to try his hand at church music, clavier sonatas and the inevitable *divertimenti*. Thus, self-supporting and self-taught, the years of his young manhood were passed. After a while he was lucky enough to gain the notice of no less a person than Metastasio, who brought him pupils. Next came his employment as lesson-accompanist (and shoe-cleaner) by the famous Nicolo Porpora. Through doing some travelling around with him he met Wagenseil, Gluck and the youthful and friendly Ditters(dorf).

In 1755 he was twenty-three years old. At that age Mozart was a famous composer of important works, but Haydn's real achievements lay far ahead. However, in this year his fortunes began to change. Two lesser nobles, Baron von Fürnberg and Count Morzin, successively engaged him as music-director at their country-house establishments, giving him the experience of writing a number of *divertimento*-like works for the limited resources which in each case he found there. While he was with Count Morzin he married—probably the rashest act of his life, for it seems to have been a loveless match. The lady proved a shrew, with a penchant for using her husband's manuscripts for curl papers. Though Maria Anna survived until 1800, Haydn seems to have seen as little as possible of her.

In 1761, with a growing reputation as a composer of attractive music, he gained a far more enviable post, that of second *Kapellmeister* at Eisenstadt, the country seat of Prince Paul Esterhazy, one of the richest landowners in the Empire. Paul died the next year, and was succeeded by his brother Nicolaus, even more devoted to music, and with even more grandiloquent ideas as to a fitting style of living. The palace of Eisenstadt was not enough. An enormous new establishment, Esterhaza, was built in an even more remote countryside; " second only to Versailles ", French visitors remarked. For his own and his guests' entertainment Nicolaus provided not only a highly efficient orchestra, but two private theatres, one for plays and operas, the other for marionettes. In 1766 with the death of the first *Kapellmeister,* Haydn was given full control. Already he had been providing almost the whole of the music, and already his early quartets and symphonies were becoming widely known. He was not so isolated as he sometimes claimed to be. There was the Prince's annual winter season in Vienna; moreover, a constant stream of aristocratic, cultured visitors came to Esterhaza, including the Empress Maria Theresa, and listened with appreciation to the attractive music of " Nicolaus the Magnificent's " private composer. As a result, even by the middle 1760's Haydn's name was well known in other capitals. Publishers were printing his works, and concert promoters, even from Paris, begging for his symphonies. The Age of Patronage justified itself at Esterhaza. Nicolaus, for all his autocracy, was normally a just and appreciative employer. Haydn and his musicians were, by the standards of the time, highly paid, and no composer has ever had more ideal conditions for his work. He could write in peace and quiet and without financial anxiety. He could experiment if he wished in the most advanced style that he knew, for his listeners possessed highly cultivated musical tastes. Having at his beck and call an orchestra which if small (no more than a couple of dozen at the most) was among the most competent in Europe, the composer could instantly try out anything that he had written. Thanks to his own genial, tolerant and kindly nature his subordinates were devoted to him, and were always willing to give their best for " Papa Haydn ". With the

P

same tireless urge that possessed J. S. Bach under very different circumstances he took the fullest advantage of his settled conditions. No wonder that the art of symphonic writing moved from strength to strength in those otherwise uneventful years at Esterhaza. Incidentally, it was not *all* labour. On the estate Papa Haydn gained quite a reputation as a good shot and a fisherman.

Much other work was produced besides symphony, concerto and string quartet—church music, keyboard sonatas, *divertimenti,* and numerous operas for the Palace theatre, for which companies of Italian singers were engaged. Although one of Haydn's youthful successes in Vienna had been the music for one of the earliest German *Singspiel,* his genius was never operatic, and the Esterhaza stage-works have remained largely neglected by later generations, even though, at the time, some were performed in Vienna. Lately, an English revival of the *dramma giocoso, Il mondo della luna* makes it clear that the composer's modesty in not wishing to compete with Mozart in that genre was justified.

The only real outside influence that came to him in his maturity was that of the young Mozart, twenty-four years his junior. They knew each other's instrumental work, and Mozart had profited. When they met in 1781–2 their mutual admiration was manifest. Mozart's six string quartets, finished in 1785, were dedicated to Haydn, who told Leopold Mozart that his son Wolfgang was the greatest composer known to him. Very willingly, in the ensuing years, Haydn learned much from Mozart—greater richness of harmony; greater refinements of orchestration. From Haydn, Mozart learned perhaps a greater subtlety in thematic development. Together, the two masters perfected the classical style.

In 1790 Prince Nicolaus died. His son Anton broke up the musical establishment, except for the chapel musicians. Haydn was generously pensioned, and retained only nominally the title of *Kapellmeister.* At last he was free of all direction. Offers of various sorts immediately came, the most attractive for him being that of the violinist and concert-promoter Salomon of London. In January 1791 he set off on his first long journey, and stayed in London until the summer of 1792. Here the peasant's son became a lion of society—the guest of the King's Court, of the City Fathers and of numerous aristocratic hosts. He was presented with a Doctor's degree at Oxford, where one of his recently composed symphonies was played, and henceforth called " The Oxford ". Six symphonies (nos. 93–98) were produced for Salomon's concerts, which were enthusiastically attended. Here Haydn found a larger orchestra (about forty members) than he had encountered before. As ever, he won their hearts, and the symphonies, among them the " Surprise " and the " Miracle ", represented a new height of achievement.[7]

Another and important new experience was his visit to a Handel Commemoration Concert. The impact on him of large choral forces and Handel's powerful genius was overwhelming. " He is the master of us all " was his comment. Nevertheless, the spirit was not all of humility, for from the hearings there emerged the idea that he had himself something to contribute to the art of oratorio, on similarly monumental lines, an ambition which he later achieved. The British National Anthem also spurred him to emulation. In 1797 he produced the immortal " Emperor's Hymn "—his favourite work, we are told. Salomon persuaded him to return for a second visit in January 1794, which was an even greater success than the first. The six last symphonies (Nos. 99–104) were written and performed. These included the " Military ", the " Clock ", and " Drum Roll " and the so-called " London ". To the usual woodwind choir were now added two clarinets. Much else of his music was heard, and there were offers for him to remain permanently in England. He renewed his acquaintance with Handel's music, and when he returned to Vienna he took with him a poem founded on Milton's *Paradise Lost* which had been prepared for Handel shortly before the latter's death. It was translated into German (with modifications) by van Swieten, the Imperial Librarian, and became the libretto of *The Creation*.

Haydn gained considerably over two thousand pounds as a result of his London visits. His Esterhazy pension had been increased, too, and altogether he was in comfortable independent circumstances. A renewed Esterhazy service—to the second Nicolaus and occupying only summer months, was not an arduous one. At his Vienna home he settled to the composition of the last and greatest of his string quartets (Opp. 76 & 77) and the oratorio *The Creation*. In the latter he showed himself a master of choral writing and orchestral tone-painting. It was finished in 1798 and immediately performed, producing a profound impression. London heard it in 1800, and it was given at the Worcester Three Choirs' Festival in the same year. It is still very much alive. Somewhat against his will the fast-ageing composer was persuaded to undertake another major choral work, the libretto an adaptation by van Swieten of Thomson's *Seasons*. Completed in 1801, it had first a success equal to *The Creation*. Haydn wrote little more of significance. His last appearance in public was at a performance in March 1808 of *The Creation* conducted by Salieri, the Imperial *Kapellmeister,* when the highest in the land paid him homage. He died at his home in May 1809, at a time when Napoleon's troops were in occupation of Vienna.

The Development of Haydn's Instrumental Style

Haydn's perfection of the classical symphonic form has been rightly described as " one of the greatest achievements in the whole history of the arts ". It represented indeed an enormous sweep of individual progress. In the Fürnberg, Morzin and Eisenstadt years his music belonged to the *rococo,* the *style galant,* however individual his lively melodiousness might be. There was a tying together of tuneful motives without much feeling of continuity, with the first violin part monopolising the situation. No sign had yet appeared of the logical construction of his mature movements, nothing of the calibre of Wagenseil or Stamitz. The first dozen string quartets (Opp. 1 & 2) and a few early symphonies belong to the *genus* " divertimento ". Only in some of the Op. 3 quartets (c. 1763–4) do we see the accompanying parts taking some interest in the thematic material. But established at Esterhaza Haydn began to make the distinction between divertimento and string quartet. When he wished to write a divertimento he did so, and called it by that title. The string quartets Opp. 9 (1768), 17 (1771) and 20 (1772) took on the character of a distinctive quartet style. He followed the Viennese scheme of complete recapitulations, and took over definitely the four-movement lay-out. The first movements showed clear-cut themes of which interesting use was made, although he was slow in adopting the dualistic plan. We have already noted that even in the most perfectly balanced and logically developed movements of his maturest works he was at times content to have one dominating theme only. It is significant that in the quartets that we are discussing, contrapuntal devices such as fugue were beginning to be employed. The composer was already groping towards an ideal, an equality of interest in the parts.[8]* Then after 1772 came a strange hiatus. He wrote no more string quartets for nearly a decade. It could be imagined that while continuing his production of symphonies he was awaiting enlightenment as to how a riper style could be developed, for it was the string quartet which he found most congenial for his " laboratory " thinking.

Returning to earlier years for a consideration of the symphonies, we find that the first forty or so represent a parallel period of experiment progress. They were scored in the main for two oboes, two horns and strings, with the occasional appearance of flute and bassoon. (A warning as to possible discrepancies between the instrumentation of printed score and actual performance has already been made.) Many of the early examples were in three movements, but from No. 31 (1765) onward the four movement scheme is normal. Evidence of the competence of the Esterhaza orchestra is seen in the employment of solo parts of advanced technique.[9]*

The decade c. 1770–80, the time of the neglect of the string quartet, was occupied (together of course with much else) by symphonies No. 41 to 70. This was also the time of the emotional *Sturm und Drang* movement in German literature, the impact of which is obvious on the music of C. P. E. Bach and many others. Haydn's was similarly affected. The thirty or so symphonies concerned are much more emotional and subjective in their style than before, possibly the direct influence of C. P. E. Bach's Hamburg style. They are little remembered nowadays, with one exception, the picturesque " Farewell Symphony ", No. 45 in F sharp minor (1772), a good example of Haydn's imagination and humour, composed with a practical aim, tactfully to hint to Nicolaus the keen desire of his musicians for their overdue leave. The candle-extinguishing and gradual retirement of the orchestra in the slow finale make an irresistible bait for modern revival.

In 1781 came what was perhaps the most important landmark in Haydn's musical development, the composition of the six string quartets, Op. 33, called the " Russian Quartets ", since they were dedicated to his admirer the Grand Duke Paul of Russia, who was resident at the time in Vienna. In his printed invitation to subscribers Haydn spoke of them boldly as being composed in an entirely new and particular manner. Indeed, it is in these that the true classical style is at last achieved. The thematic interest is now carried through all the parts, and maintained by the skilled and judicious use of imitative contrapuntal writing. There is now a matchless logic which causes a movement to be as it were cast in a single mould, each section taking its inevitable place in the overall conception. The time coincided with his association with Mozart in Vienna. The latter declared, " It was from Haydn that I first learned the true way to compose quartets ". It is likely that he was referring particularly to the Op. 20 (" Sun ") group. He learned well indeed, for the meeting inspired his own famous six dedicated to Haydn (1785), which in turn produced the latter's well-known declaration to Leopold Mozart.

Onward to the end of his life Haydn continued to compose masterly string quartets. Opp. 76 & 77 (c. 1799), his last eight, represent the ideal balance of the classical style. In No. 2 of the Op. 76 set the composer showed with what ease he could reconcile old and new by writing a delightful minuet in strict two-part infinite canon. It became known as the *Hexen,* or " Witches " Minuet.

The new outlook was inevitably transferred to the symphonies. Nos. 71 to 92 contain many masterpieces, particularly the group of six (1785–6) commissioned for concerts in Paris, which made Cherubini Haydn's devoted admirer. From now on, we may safely say, the composer's close-knit orchestral scorings needed no aid from the formerly inevitable continuo. The climax of his symphonic writing was of course that wonderful last dozen written for London. In them, as in the string quartets of 1799, there arrives a last perfect blend of rich melody with his new and purposeful polyphony, and tightly-knit developments which proceed with a logic of design that leaves no place for anything irrelevant. In all the purely instrumental music of the last period the humour and high spirits that were basic traits of Haydn's character show themselves, not only in the attractive and original themes, but in the unprecedented subtlety of his rhythmic constructions. More than ever in the mature Haydn we find the varied phrase length, the wayward hesitation, the sudden silent bar, the numerous tricks of syncopation and general rhythmic variation. He foreshadowed Beethoven in his love for the sudden sforzando or pianissimo. Altogether one of the charms of a later Haydn movement is its frequent moments of unexpectedness.

Most of the dozen Salomon symphonies show a feature common to others of Haydn's mature period, the slow introduction. What had once been a comparatively meaningless flourish became now a subtle musical brooding, before the launching of the adventure. These introductions had their influence on later composers, including Beethoven. Another feature of the Salomon sets is the great attractiveness and musical quality of the finales. The high spirits of the tuneful peasant dance-rondo are still there, but woven now into the close fabric of the sonata-rondo. The last movement of his very last symphony (No. 104 in D—the so-called London) is surely the quintessence of classical perfection.

A similar perfecting of the classical style is seen in the mature pianoforte sonatas, which are on the whole finer examples of the genre than those of Mozart. On the other hand, his concertos, in spite of the popular examples for 'cello and for trumpet which are still played, do not reach Mozart's highest standard; and this can be said also of his many occasional compositions of the divertimento type.

In *The Creation* and *The Seasons* Haydn showed not only his genius for choral effects but his mastery of orchestral resource for dramatic purposes (even though we may smile at the naïvety of some of the tone-paintings). In his larger Masses are found similarly impressive choral passages, but these works, together with a wealth of other church music, must remain neglected here. Nowadays his sacred music seems to border on the theatrical in style, but as he himself said, he believed in praising the Lord with cheerful voice. Also neglected must be the numerous cantatas, the Esterhaza operas, incidental music in connection with Nicolaus' theatres, a large amount of chamber music other than string quartets, and scores of solo and part songs. Among the last are some notable specimens, widely known in his own day.

He must be counted as one of the major figures in the history of music. His tuneful, wholesome, warm-hearted yet subtly intellectual works will always continue to be given performance, however far the art may choose to remove itself from his dialect and outlook.

The Netherlands composer, Francois Gossec (1734–1829) deserves some notice as an instrumental composer at Paris. Both his symphonies and his string quartets became popular, and he made some novel orchestral experiments, notably in his handling of two orchestras, one of them outside the building, in his *Messe des Morts* (1760). He did much good work in organising music at the French capital, and in raising the standard of orchestral playing. He is also credited with first having introduced the solemn sound of the gong to orchestral music. His own compositions are now mere museum pieces.

The long-lived Bohemian, Adalbert Gyrowetz (1763–1850), was also famous in his day as a composer of symphonies (over sixty), chamber music and operas. Mozart thought enough of one of his symphonies to produce it successfully at a Vienna concert in 1786. He was engaged as a composer in London in 1789, where he met Haydn during the latter's first visit. At Paris he found that some of his symphonies were being played under the belief that they were by Haydn, the best compliment a contemporary composer could receive.

Thus far we have given our main attention to the progress of classical instrumental music. Before turning to another of the giants of all time, Mozart, whose work in opera so much influenced the course of its history, let us review briefly the state of that art in the eighteenth century up to about 1760.

Eighteenth Century Opera Before Mozart

Opera in this age derived, as we have seen, almost wholly from Italy. Every other country, including Britain, was permeated with it. From Italy were exported not only the fascinatingly tuneful works themselves, but their composers, their highly trained singers and skilled instrumentalists. The new symphony, and indeed the new concerto, owed their origins to the styles and features found in Italian opera, particularly those of the lighter Neapolitan type. Leading German musicians such as Handel and Hasse spent most of their lives writing the Italian style of opera to Italian libretti.

However, Italian *opera seria,* with its rigid conventions, was even before the middle of the century suffering a setback, in spite of the successful careers of such exponents as Leonardo Leo, Porpora and Bononcini (to name but a few Italians of the time), Fux at Vienna and Hasse at Dresden. Most *opera seria* composers in Italy wrote also comic operas and *intermezzi;* Pergolesi, with many *opera seria* to his credit, swept Europe with his *intermezzo, La Serva Padrona.* It came to London in 1740. From the *intermezzo* developed the Neapolitan *opera buffa,* a full-scale, three-act type of work in humorous vein, which unlike the *opera seria* with its chains of recitative and *da capo* aria, contained a variety of forms—duet, trio and above all the brilliant concerted act-finale. While making their contributions to serious opera, fine composers like Jommelli, Sacchini, Traetta, Galuppi, Paisiello and Piccinni expanded the *opera buffa,* with its various concerted pieces and its *secco* (harpsichord accompanied) recitative, into a true art-form. Of special importance was their development of the concerted finale to one of several sections, moving to a culmination at the curtain. Eventually, as a foil to the comic characters, two "serious" ones—usually a pair of languishing lovers—were allowed to be added. *Opera buffa* in Italy received increased standing through the libretto contributions of Carlo Goldini, the famous dramatist.

The Italian invasion reached Paris in 1752, and waged war (the *guerre des bouffons*) against French music in the person of Rameau. It will be recalled that Gluck, himself a writer of light-hearted operas at Vienna, took over the cause of the French type of dignified opera and stemmed the tide for a while, but with his departure the sparkling humour of *opera buffa* became once more supreme with French audiences. Meanwhile, France began to flatter the invaders by imitation. An Italian composer, Egidio Duni (1709–75) of Parma, settled in Paris like Lully before him, and assimilating the native style established a French type of light opera, the *opéra comique,* which perhaps owes some part of its origin to the satirical and long-established *vaudeville* of the French fair-theatres. One difference between *opéra comique* and Italian *buffa* was that the French preferred their dramatic action to progress by means of spoken dialogue and not by *secco* recitative. French composers such as François Philidor (1726–95), Pierre Monsigny (1729–1817), André Grétry (1741–1813) and Nicolas Dalayrac (1753–1809) continued enthusiastically with the new and popular type. We will anticipate a later development. In the Revolutionary and Napoleonic period *opéra comique* in the hands of such men as Méhul and Cherubini took on a more dignified, and eventually, a more romantic note. As a result a new name had to be devised for the light, amusing type —in fact a translated one—*opéra bouffe.* Grétry, whose chief gift was attractive and expressive melody, and who was otherwise not a well-trained composer ("One might drive a coach and four between bass and first fiddle ") anticipated this romantic trend in his most successful work, the *opéra comique, Richard Coeur de Lion* (1784). It gained great popularity, and was heard in many European cities, including London (1786). The writings of the far-travelled Dr. Burney (see p. 246f.) continually express admiration for the tuneful Grétry, and Burney, on the whole, had little time for French music.[10]*

The English counterblast to Italian *opera seria*, Gay's and Pepusch's *Beggar's Opera* of 1728, encouraged the writing of other satirical English pastiches, of lesser quality. Some of these actually crossed to Hamburg. Similar works appeared in Germany, and showing native characteristics in the hands of the composer Johann Hiller (1728–1804) became the German *Singspiel*. Dittersdorf helped to develop the type, which, like the French *opéra comique* made use of spoken dialogue, and was destined to have a great future in Germany. His famous *Doktor und Apotheker,* produced in Vienna in 1786, was an immediate success, and then swept the Continent as far as to Moscow. It reached London in 1788 and then travelled to the United States. It still keeps the stage. Dittersdorf wrote a number of other quite successful *Singspiel*, as well as many Italian-style operas.[11]*

There is now to be considered one of the greatest composers of all time. Wolfgang Amadeus Mozart (1756–91) is named among the immortals of music, but his short life ended on a note of worldly failure. In his art he was a genius with transcendant powers; in character he was singularly ill-equipped for the lone fight which he undertook in his mature years for economic survival. It was his father Leopold who so devotedly trained the wonderful composer and executant; it is he also who must bear much responsibility for the shortcomings which helped to bring about the final tragedy. His over-anxious and fussy control of every detail of his son's progress through childhood and adolescence was undoubtedly one of the chief reasons for the lack of practical good sense (in all things but music) which Wolfgang often displayed in his manhood. So frequently has the obtuseness of an unsympathetic aristocratic society been blamed for the untimely cutting-off of a unique creative force that it is as well to bear in mind that the faults were not all on one side.[12]

Wolfgang was the younger of the two surviving children of Leopold Mozart and his wife Anna Maria. Leopold at the time of his son's birth was a violinist in the employ of Archbishop Sigismund von Schrattenbach, the ruler of Salzburg, a provincial town in South Germany. In the same year he published a " violin method " which maintained itself as a standard work over a considerable period and was translated into several other languages. Besides being an excellent violinist Leopold had apparently quite a good reputation in his younger days as an organist. In 1757 he was given the title of court-composer. In 1763 he was appointed Vice-*Kapellmeister* under Johann Eberlin (1702–62), a composer of some standing. He never attained to the premier post. After 1762 the staff included Michael Haydn, the brother of Joseph. In spite of the large number of musicians employed the court music had no very high reputation around the mid-century either for progressiveness or quality of performance. Dr. Burney gave an unfavourable report in 1772, though this was from hearsay.

As soon as the boy Wolfgang began to give evidence of his extraordinary precocious gifts Leopold dedicated his own life to their developments. The girl Marianne (Nannerl), four and a half years Wolfgang's senior, was also displaying talent as a harpsichord player, but the boy's progress was unique. At the age of four he was competent on the keyboard; before he was six he was attempting composition. Leopold's pride in his children reached such a pitch that he determined to exhibit their abilities for the admiration of the world. A great deal of Wolfgang's earlier existence was spent in constant journeyings and concert playings in various countries of Europe. The conditions that travellers had to face in those days being what they were, there were infections and illnesses which may have helped to shorten Wolfgang's life.

Leopold never seems to have had much difficulty in obtaining extensive leave from the kindly old Archbishop (tolerant of all except the Protestants within his borders). The family set off on a concert-giving tour of German cities in Jan. 1762, when Wolfgang was just over 6, its climax being an appearance at the Imperial Court at Vienna, where Wolfgang played a concerto by the famous Wagenseil, the composer turning over for him. A more extensive journey was begun in June 1763, and lasted three and a half years. It took in many leading European cities and lesser courts, and finally Paris and the Court at Versailles. By April 1764 the party were in London, where Wolfgang amazed the thoroughly musical English Royal family. Back to Salzburg and away again, he impressed Vienna once more before he was 12.

We shall be content here to leave the full details of these journeys to the larger biographies, mentioning mainly the musical advantages gained by the phenomenal child from the experiences he underwent and the professional contacts that he made. Throughout the journeys he was playing the harpsichord before critical audiences not only as a soloist in a manner far beyond his years, but as a sight-reader, accompanist and an improvisator on given themes to standards that increasingly impressed professional listeners. At Buckingham House in London he played duets with Johann Christian Bach (the "English" Bach) who took a kindly and admiring interest in him. Wolfgang never forgot the help that he received from Bach, and afterwards (1778) warmly renewed the friendship when they met at Paris. In London he learned a great deal from the music of Johann Christian and that of the then much esteemed Karl Abel, both of whom were "progressive" composers in the *rococo* style. While in Paris he had encountered the gifted and eccentric German harpsichordist and composer Johann Schobert (c. 1720–67). A popular soloist, Schobert was also known for his original clavier sonatas and chamber works with harpsichord, in true *Sturm und Drang* style, romantic and emotional. Wolfgang's musical instincts were already sufficiently developed to profit by this first encounter with "poetic" music. On a number of occasions the opportunity arose for him to show that he already had a considerable command of the organ, pedals and all. Through his life his skill as an organist impressed his hearers no less than did his harpsichord and pianoforte virtuosity. As might be expected from the son of Leopold Mozart he showed also precocious skill as a violinist.

In chronicles of these early tours there is a good deal of mention of the child's own compositions—harpsichord sonatas and variations, even symphonies and choral pieces, but the chief interest in regard to these derivative works is that they could have been written at all by one so young. The earliest may have owed a great deal to a father's editing, but all are proof of an extraordinary power of assimilation. However, in 1768, during one of the visits of Wolfgang and his father to Vienna came a striking gesture of confidence from no less a person that the Emperor Joseph himself, a commission for the boy (aet. 12) to compose an *opera buffa, La Finta Semplice* (The Pretended Simpleton). The work was written, but probably owing to the intrigues which were so often set afoot at such a time, it did not reach the Vienna stage. *La Finta* was no masterpiece, but it was as competent, smooth and tuneful as the average Italian journeyman production, and showed that already Wolfgang could handle the tools of his trade with confidence and ease. After the pair had returned to Salzburg the Archbishop not only brought about a performance of the opera, but appointed Wolfgang his *Konzertmeister* (though without salary). All the time there came compositions, Masses, symphonies and *divertimenti* among them, which now have interest chiefly as progress reports, but which, performed by the Salzburg staff, must have been valuable experience.

In December 1769 there began the most important episode of Wolfgang's adolescent years, the journey with his father to Italy, which occupied about a year and four months. They visited all the principal Italian cities and met most of the leading musicians in Italy, including Sammartini the composer, Farinelli the matchless singer, and Nardini the greatest violinist of the day, all of whom gave the lad advice. At Bologna the famous Padre Martini was sufficiently impressed by Wolfgang's talents to allow him a course of counterpoint lessons, a privilege not easily gained. At such cities as Milan and Venice Wolfgang learned what first-class singing and first-class Italian opera really meant, and for the rest of his life his chief love was for opera and the dramatic power of the human voice. The operatic orchestral accompaniments of his maturity in their beauty, variety and appositeness are a never failing joy to the hearer, yet it is always the vocal music from the stage that is the predominant partner.

Details of certain picturesque incidents of the journey, such as Wolfgang's reproduction after a couple of hearings of Allegri's celebrated Easter *Miserere* (supposedly exclusive to the Sistine Chapel) can be left to the many biographies. Naturally, the lad gained far more than he gave, even though Leopold ensured that concerts were arranged at every opportunity. Italian audiences, aristocratic and public, gave due homage to Wolfgang's compositions, harpsichord playing and powers of improvisation, all of which were recognised as being those of a matured musician. Such was the effect of the universal admiration that he was commissioned to write a work for one of the headquarters of opera, the Scala Theatre at Milan. He returned to the

city in the autumn of 1770 with his *Mitridate* (Mithridatus, King of Pontus
—a stock libretto), and actually directed the presentation, controlling from
the keyboard at the age of near fifteen the largest orchestra in Europe at
the time. It was repeated twenty times, and earned him commissions for
a next-season opera and a serenade (i.e. cantata).

Thanks to his natural genius, his father's conscientious training and the
fact that he had at an early age experienced at first hand so many facets of
European music, Wolfgang was now equipped in extraordinary fashion for
his career as composer and performer. Behind an enormous technique was a
musical brain that must perhaps be considered the most wonderful—certainly the most facile, in the highest sense of the word—that has ever
existed. He seems indeed to have possessed the superhuman power of working out mentally in close detail whole movements at a time, and of retaining them in his memory, complete and settled, until the tiresome necessity
arose of committing them to paper. This seems to be the explanation of
the well-known Don Giovanni Overture story—that it was written in
score in the single night preceding the first performance. Probably it had
been fully imagined before that time; the composer had merely forgotten
to make it available to those whose task it was to translate it into mundane
sound. There is more than one reference in his letters to such initial writings-
down of works already composed. Certainly finished manuscripts show
occasional signs of being corrected and improved; also unfinished manuscripts have survived, but the usual reason for his not rounding off a composition was that circumstances had arisen that would make its prompt
performance unlikely (e.g., two incomplete comic operas come under that
category). Mozart's outlook was thoroughly professional; with few exceptions, the works that he wrote were intended to be fee-earning as soon as
possible.

Throughout his career he poured his music into the currently accepted
moulds of opera and classical symphonic form without imposing any real
strain on their limits. Yet in its maturity it was music of the utmost individuality and beauty. He had no desire to reform either *opera seria* or *opera
buffa*; he merely wrote immortal masterpieces in each genre in his own
natural way. He used the pattern of the *Singspiel,* but set it on a higher
level (" The Seraglio "). He took a fantastic fairy-story intended for small-
theatre entertainment, clothed it with matchless music and unwittingly made
it the root of all subsequent German romantic opera (" The Magic Flute ").

It is with the Italian journey that there begins the series of Mozart's
letters which have afforded posterity vivid pictures of the musical and social
life of the times, and above all of the composer's outlook and character.
Written mostly to members of the family they continue irregularly down
to just before his death. In them can be seen his keen observation and his
outspoken estimates of character. Happily, he was able to transmute into
terms of music his gift of painting a personality verbally, as his mature
operas well show.[13]

Father and son returned to Italy in the October of 1772 for the preparation and performance of the commissioned opera *Lucio Silla*. The always

prejudiced Leopold once more reported a great success, but the fact remains that Wolfgang was never again given an Italian offer.

Meanwhile changes were occurring at Salzburg which were to bring darker days for the Mozarts. The old Prince-Archbishop having died, he was succeeded by a certain Hieronymus von Colleredo. Salzburg received Hieronymus sullenly, for he was a "reforming" churchman, and neither city nor *Kapelle* had any desire to be reformed. Musical history has long cast him for the role of Mozart's malicious oppressor, but there seems to be, as usual, two sides to the picture. Certainly there appears but little excuse for his harsh and ungenerous treatment on occasion of the genius of whose true stature he, like most others, never seems to have been aware. On the other hand, what he needed as an employer was an assistant *Kapellmeister* and a *Konzertmeister* devoted to his service, not a couple who were so frequently desiring leave for the purpose of earning money elsewhere. He annoyed the German music staff by importing Italian soloists, and appointed an Italian to the post of *Kapellmeister* on the death of the previous holder, much to Leopold's disgust. He aimed at greater clarity in the liturgical settings (an age-old pursuit of reformers), and objected to the instrumental compositions which had been permitted to replace portions of the sacred texts, and which in some cases were church-sonatas by Wolfgang. Over the years these reforms were gradually established, to the elimination, among other compositions, of a great deal of the young Mozart's very beautiful and elaborate Mass-music, and its replacement by settings composed by Michael Haydn, which to modern ears (and apparently to those of the Archbishop) approximated more to the simplicity and clarity desired.[14*]

Brief space must be spared for Michael Haydn, of whom we have made previous mention. After 1762 he spent the rest of his life at Salzburg, holding various posts, including that of Cathedral organist—this in spite of friendly urgings by brother Joseph to make a career in Vienna. He developed a considerable reputation as a composer of dignified church music, including a number of Masses (one of them commissioned by the Empress Maria Theresa), and Graduals for the whole of the ecclesiastical year. He also wrote several operas and much instrumental music. His effective contrapuntal style, like that of old Eberlin's, was certainly admired and imitated by the young Wolfgang, until in later years the latter met with more inspired models. Haydn's career was undoubtedly handicapped by his addiction to the flowing bowl.

For four years after *Lucio Silla* Wolfgang was once more *Konzertmeister*, at £14 a year. A visit to Vienna enabled him to hear the "Sun" quartets of Joseph Haydn, the influence of which he acknowledged by six of his own (K. 168–73).[15] Leopold tried to interest him more in the violin, having the opinion that had he chosen to practise he could have become a leading virtuoso of the instrument. Wolfgang responded to the extent of playing a concerto in public, and writing a number more in the next few years, but he always preferred to play viola in any string combination, escaping as soon as he could to his beloved keyboard. There was a break in the routine in 1774, when he was graciously allowed to accept a commission from the Elector of Bavaria, to provide an Italian *opera-buffa* for the Munich Carnival. The result was *La Finta Giardiniera* (The Pretended Garden-Girl), successfully produced in January 1775, and showing the first sparks of his mature dramatic vitality, as well as his first concerted opera-finale. Back at Salzburg the production of occasional compositions continued unabated. In the stream of symphonies the influence of Haydn was beginning to be felt, as in the bright A major example of 1774 (K. 201). The first mature clavier concertos were being composed, although still framed in the *rococo* spirit of J. C. Bach. Here we may note that all clavier works written before 1782 were, with a few possible exceptions, intended for harpsichord; those from that date for forte-piano. Among the numerous chamber works and *divertimenti* was the tuneful Haffner Serenade (K. 250 –1776), commissioned for a Salzburg wedding.

In 1777 Leopold, realising the stagnation of his son's prospects, asked permission for another joint tour. The Archbishop refused, but after some friction Wolfgang was told that he could depart alone. He departed, but not alone, for his placid mother was detailed to accompany him, their journey being fussily directed by the remote control of Leopold's letters from Salzburg. Both father and son hoped that the venture would end in the achievement of some well-paid post, but it was to prove an odyssey of disillusionment. At both Munich and Mannheim Wolfgang's playing was applauded, and he in his turn admired and learned from the performances of the Mannheim orchestra under Cannabich. But neither ruler had any employment to offer. Also, at Mannheim he complicated matters by falling in love with the young singer Aloysia Weber, one of an improvident family that was destined to play a large part in his future affairs, and actually proposed to accompany the Weber party to Italy, much to Leopold's horror. A peremptory letter from Salzburg arrived at Mannheim which propelled the travellers to Paris. Arriving there in March 1778 Wolfgang found that the child prodigy of earlier years was quite forgotten, and the interests of musical Paris centred for the time being on the war between the Gluckists and Piccinnists. The only commission of importance given him was for a symphony for the Concerts Spirituel, which produced his three-movement Paris Symphony (K. 279), with two clarinets in the score. It gained him approbation, but nothing more. Strangely enough, he refused an appointment as organist at Versailles at about £90 a year (perhaps he had Aloysia in mind), even though Leopold urged acceptance. Then came the sudden death of Frau Mozart. For two bewildered months the young man remained indolent in Paris, cheered only by the visit of his old friend Johann Christian Bach. Then the despairing Leopold ordered his recall. The Archbishop was relenting so far as to appoint him to the vacant post of Court organist at £40 a year. In January 1779 he arrived back at Salzburg (having found on the way that Aloysia had no further use for him) to take up his irksome Court duties and the more congenial tasks of composition. Among the large number of works belonging to this period is the lovely Symphony in C major (K. 338), the evergreen *Sinfonia Concertante* for violin, viola and orchestra (K. 364) and a concerto for two claviers (K. 365), written for Nannerl's co-operation in performance, and with a deliciously tuneful rondo subject.

1780 brought some encouragement. From the Elector of Bavaria came the commission for a Munich Carnival opera, on the old Metastasian theme of " Idomeneo, King of Crete ". Performed in January 1781, it was the first work of Mozart's operatic maturity. Opinions at Munich, including that of the Elector himself, were enthusiastic. It may be that the dignity and sincerity of *Idomeneo* owed much to the example of Gluck's *Alceste,* but its rich harmonies, intricate counterpoint and expressive instrumentation attained to heights beyond the reach of the older master. Nevertheless *Idomeneo*—a lovely, a monumental work—must be considered as belonging to an age that was fast fading, the greatest example of the moribund *opera seria.*

In the Munich-Salzburg correspondence between father and son at this time one learns first hand of Wolfgang's views on the theory and practice of opera composition, as well as of the trials of a producer. We find no tolerance for Gluck's ideas as to a subservient respect for the " poetry ". All through Mozart's mature operatic career is the insistence that the librettist (even da Ponte) should amend his text where necessary to the best interests, as the composer saw it, of the music. Mozart's major stage works were first produced under his own authoritative direction. He disciplined everybody, even the leading singers, who were not allowed their traditional Italian liberty with regard to unauthorised melodic ornamentations.

While still at Munich in March 1781 he received a sudden summons from the Archbishop, who was in Vienna. The latter wished to make use of his tame clavier player for his private social evenings at the capital. There were strange happenings in the next few months, for which we have only the accounts of one side. After all his Munich fêting the young man found himself relegated to the dining table of the cooks and lackeys, his scanty salary reduced, and himself forbidden to perform at any concerts where he might earn. Other humiliations followed. Mozart reacted with spirit and asked for his discharge. After some unseemly wranglings he finally chose to discharge himself. He declared to his father that he would have no trouble in maintaining an independent career in Vienna. Leopold's letters of the period were evidently censorious, the more so since Wolfgang was associating with the Weber family again. The father's worst fears were realised when next year his son told him of his intention of marrying the third Weber daughter, Constanze. For a while father and son were estranged.

During the winter of 1781–2 Mozart met Haydn again, and there began a friendship that ended only with Mozart's death. Haydn was in Vienna for the performance of his epoch-making " Russian " quartets. Once more Mozart marked and learned, but from this time on his own music had in return messages for the older master.

Among the many compositions of 1781–2 was the Haffner Symphony in D (K. 385), a reshaping of the genial Haffner Serenade of 1776. More important was a commission from the Emperor himself. Joseph had begun to take serious note of the mature Mozart and was persuaded that his scheme for the establishment of German opera might be aided by a contribution from this newcomer from outside the magic circle of the official establishment. The result was the *Singspiel, Die Entführung aus dem Serail* (The Flight from the Seraglio), the text being by the fashionable libretto writer Stephanie. It was something a great deal more than the usual *Singspiel,* being the first *German* comic opera by a great composer, and it established the respectability of the type. It is still performed, and is attractive not only for its delicious vocal and orchestral music, but for the composer's subtle characterisation of the comic figure of Osmin.[16*] In spite of the usual professional intrigues it was successfully launched in July 1782 and had fifteen more performances. Yet the Emperor (supported by Dittersdorf's opinion) could say to its composer : " Too fine for our ears, my dear Mozart, and a great deal too many notes ". Mozart retorted that there were as many notes as were necessary, but the fact remains that, strange as it may seem to us, many of Mozart's contemporaries held that his music was too involved and often too sombre for the tastes of the times. Dittersdorf's views were that he presented too many ideas, so that they confused the hearer's attention![17*]

In August 1782, after the success of " The Seraglio ", Wolfgang and Constanze were married. It appears to have been a happy union, but it was unfortunate that in matters of worldly wisdom the wife was no better equipped than the husband. Their household was set up on next to nothing, and for the rest of his brief life Mozart's normal existence was one of near insolvency.

Soon after his marriage Mozart was drawn into the musical circle of Baron van Swieten, the Imperial librarian who later translated and arranged the libretti of Haydn's oratorios. Van Swieten had previously been ambassador at the court of Frederick of Prussia of conservative musical tastes, and had developed an enthusiasm not only for the music of Handel but also for that of the almost forgotten J. S. Bach. He brought back to Vienna the printed Art of Fugue and certain manuscripts, including copies of the *Forty-eight Preludes and Fugues.* Thomas Attwood the Englishman, who was Mozart's pupil in 1785–6, said that the *Forty-eight* were always to be found on his master's piano-top. The impact of J. S. Bach upon Mozart was immediate and profound, and helped to bring about the last perfect synthesis of the " galant " and " learned " which was the quintessence of his own inimitable style. For van Swieten's private performances of the music of the old masters Mozart arranged several of the *Forty-eight* for strings, and wrote " additional accompaniments " for a number of the Handel oratorios, including *Messiah.*

His means of making a living in Vienna was by taking pupils (not very many; it was an occupation that he hated), by organising, composing for and performing in subscription concerts, and by accepting engagements for playing at the houses of the nobility. The enormous amount of labour that filled the years at Vienna can be glimpsed by realising that a typical subscription concert of his consisted mostly of his own compositions—a symphony, another orchestral piece of some sort, some arias, two piano con-

certos, often one of them new to the occasion, and—a favourite attraction—
an improvisation on a theme. The Emperor Joseph was sometimes to be
found in the applauding audience. " Un talent décidé ", was his opinion of
the composer, yet he did nothing towards giving some kind of fixed income
to the man who, as certain leaders of the nobility were beginning to say,
was of the stamp " that comes into the world once in a hundred years ".

To this period belongs the fine Quintet for piano and wind (K. 452), and
the " Linz " Symphony, written during a visit to Count Johannes Thun, one
of Mozart's admirers, at Linz. The latter work is a charming and mature
one, with an adagio introduction (a feature not often met in Mozart's
works), and some reminders of Haydn, especially in the merry finale. Early
in 1785 Mozart completed the masterly set of six quartets (K. 387, 421,
458, 428, 464, 465), which he afterwards dedicated to Haydn. The D minor
example (K. 421) is supposed to have been written down during the time
when Constanze was in labour with her first child, a remarkable example
of Mozart's powers of concentration. Leopold, now somewhat reconciled,
visited his son in February and heard the last three played by a quartet
party consisting of Joseph Haydn and Dittersdorf (violins), Wolfgang, viola,
and the popular Austrian composer Vanhal, 'cello. It was on this occasion
that Leopold received Haydn's famous declaration as to his son's calibre,
which must have come as some compensation for the long years of anxiety
and disappointment. When he returned to Salzburg in April 1785 he must
surely have believed that Wolfgang's fortunes were on the turn, in spite of
the domestic shortcomings, which were obvious to him. He lived long
enough to learn of the success of *Le Nozze di Figaro* at Vienna and Prague
and died in May 1787. Wolfgang, who had generous-hearted views as to the
brotherhood of man, and some mental scars concerned with the Age of
Patronage, had for some time (like Haydn) been attracted to Freemasonry.
In these Vienna years he wrote a number of compositions for use at various
functions of the Order.

To the years of concert-giving in Vienna posterity owes the gift of the
mature piano concertos. Mozart in the course of his career wrote about two
dozen, perfecting the classical concerto form in doing so, and achieving
originality of detail without bursting the seams. In the Vienna examples no
traces of earlier influences remain. Never before had such concertos been
written, each with its own character, its perfect balance of construction,
and its mutually tolerant partnership of soloist and orchestra. No adequate
notice of the sixteen or so Vienna works can be given here.[18] Let us mention
in passing the powerful and dark-toned D minor (K. 466) with its counter-
part the urbane and dignified E flat major (K. 482)—both of 1785 : the
bright and lyrical A major (K. 488) and the monumental C minor (K. 491)
—both of 1786. In the case of the C minor the presence of an unusual
number of corrections in the manuscript shows with what care it was
shaped and polished. It remains one of the world's greatest concertos, and
caused even Beethoven to have some very uncharacteristic self-doubtings,
communicated to his pupil Cramer as they listened to a performance.
The grim power of the close-knit first movement and the delicious series of

variations employed in the last will always keep it as a favourite in the concert hall. The final concerto, in B flat major (K. 595) was written in the last year of the composer's life. Something of the gathering darkness can be felt in its chromaticisms.

A fact that often escaped notice is that from 1785 onward Mozart the master organist possessed an independent pedal keyboard for use with his forte-piano, both at concerts and in private. Leopold mentions it, commenting on its weight but nevertheless its portability. From a description by a pupil we learn that it had the usual—but large-scale—hammers and dampers, and a range of two octaves, apparently from C_3 to C_1. This must be remembered when one tries to imagine what a Mozart piano performance sounded like, under the composer's own hands—and feet.

The commission for a short *Singspiel* late in 1785—*Der Schauspieldirektor* (The Impresario)—could have been but little help in his growing financial troubles. But some of the nobles who were becoming aware of his value now aided him by organising a private revival of *Idomeneo*. At the performance he met the well-known dramatist Lorenzo da Ponte, who instantly perceived his mettle. They were soon in agreement as to an adaptation of Beaumarchais' social satire *Le Mariage de Figaro*. The original play was political gunpowder, but the libretto, a judicious reshaping in Italian, gained the Emperor's grudging approval. The result of the partnership was the comic opera *Le Nozze di Figaro*, a work destined to endure as long as the art itself. Da Ponte's witty, satirical, crazily fantastic contribution was not only made plausible but altogether transfigured by Mozart's matchless music, which charmed the ear and at the same time limned the individual characters—Figaro, the Count, Cherubino, the Countess—with a wonderful veracity and clarity. The public receptions were so enthusiastic that encores had to be forbidden, yet after nine performances the work was withdrawn. The Italian " hidden hand ", unable after considerable effort to prevent the initial staging, soon found the excuse to substitute for it Dittersdorf's *Singspiel, Doktor und Apotheker* (see p. 232), which indeed ran very successfully, and when that faded, by Martin's *opera buffa, Una Cosa Rara*. Once again was heard the whisper that Mozart's music was too complicated, too clogged with detail. However, some good news came from Prague, a city of finer musical discernment, it would seem, than Vienna. Following its previous approval of " Seraglio " the population had gone wild to the tunes of " Figaro ". Mozart's good friend, Count Johannes Thun, invited him to the city in January 1787 as his guest, with the result that there occurred what must have been one of the happiest episodes of Mozart's life. He was present at a fine performance of " Figaro ", he was lionised everywhere, and the concerts that he gave were successful. At the first of them was heard the splendid " Prague " Symphony (K. 504) in three movements, in his most mature, close-woven style, and with a long and impressive introduction, a veritable opera *scena*.

While at Prague he undertook to supply Bondini the impresario with a work for the next season, the fee being a hundred ducats (? under £50).[19] Da Ponte and he were soon agreed upon a subject, the oft-told legend

Q

of Don Juan, and Mozart returned to Vienna to await his text. To this time, just before his father's death, belong two String Quintets (C major and G minor—K. 515–6) and the joyous Serenade, *Eine Kleine Nachtmusik* (K. 525).

In the autumn of 1787 he was back in Prague to complete his score and meet his singers. Several anecdotes have survived as to the care and authority with which he directed both the stage action and orchestra at rehearsals. Did ever another impresario get such value for a hundred ducats? The first performance was a triumph—unrehearsed overture and all. Its two creators called *Don Giovanni* a *dramma giocoso,* in spite of the stage demons and the flames of hell that finally caught up with the " hero ". It is something more than an Italian comic opera, and has even been proclaimed the greatest of all operas. Once again the musical characterisations were rich, varied and subtle, and the two act-finales were of dimensions and elaboration never before, and seldom subsequently, equalled.

Vienna was slow to take up the lead of Prague. Not until May 1788 was a performance of *Don Giovanni* given in the capital, and then without the success of the Prague performances. " No food for the teeth of my Viennese," said the Emperor, which remark was unfortunately true. Salieri, the Imperial *Kapellmeister,* had no difficulty in soon displacing it with an opera of his own, while Joseph Haydn raged against the neglect of " this unique genius ". There shortly followed the pitifully inadequate appointment as " chamber-composer " to the Court at £80 a year, no real relief for Mozart's financial position, which was becoming desperate. Constanze's confinements and illnesses, and the helpless impracticability of both of them in regard to money affairs, were causing him to make appeals to friends for aid. A number of begging-letters to his rich and generous fellow-Mason Michael Puchberg still survive. Yet in spite of this stress he could write down, between the end of June and mid-August 1788, his last three symphonies in E flat, G minor and C major respectively (K. 543, 550, 551), composed probably for occasions that never materialised, and never performed in his lifetime. They were his finest, each entirely individual and all perfect in workmanship. The last movement of the C major (the so-called " Jupiter ") presents successively five subjects :

Ex: 54

which are then woven one with another in increasingly complex combinations, leading to a climax in which all five are closely interlocked in so-called quintuple counterpoint—and all this while continuing to sound wholly spontaneous and charming as music. This finale is one of the miracles of the art. Julius Harrison has remarked concerning it : " I can only compare this amazing movement to a game of chess in which Mozart saw from the first every possible move on the board, no matter what combination of pieces might occur ". Did space permit, it would have been fitting to have given far more attention to these three great symphonies. Among their many felicities, there can be mentioned only the two splendid and original minuets of the G minor and the " Jupiter ", the brilliance of the finale of the E flat, founded almost wholly on a single merry theme, and the extraordinary ranges of the modulations found in it, as well as in the developments of the first and final movements of the G minor. This last-mentioned work must surely be one of the most wholly satisfying symphonies ever written.

In April 1789 Mozart accompanied his young patron Prince Karl Lichnowsky on a journey to Berlin. A brief halt at Leipzig enabled him to make his " discovery ", previously referred to, of the Bach cantatas. At Berlin he gained much credit but little else, although Frederick William commissioned some string quartets which were later written and paid for, (the " King of Prussia " set—K. 575, 589, 590). To this summer belongs the Quintet for clarinet and strings (K. 581). A revival in August of *Figaro* recalled him to the official mind, and he was given another *opera buffa* commission. The result, with da Ponte's collaboration, was the witty extravaganza *Cosi Fan Tutte* (" They all do it ", i.e. " All women like to deceive their lovers ".) It was produced in January 1790, but was soon halted by the sudden death of the Emperor Joseph. In any case it would probably have once again proved too tough meat for the Viennese. Later generations have shown a greater appreciation of its satirical subtleties, with the result that it seems destined for more frequent revivals than in the past.

At the beginning of 1791 Mozart's affairs seemed at their lowest ebb. There was little to be expected from the new Emperor Leopold II as a patron of music, and the composer's health was beginning to give anxiety, yet this his last year was one of his most prolific, and in the quality of the music, one of the most wonderful. Before we consider the major works there must be mentioned the String Quintet in E flat (K. 614), the last Piano Concerto in B flat (K. 618) and the lovely Clarinet Concerto (K. 622).

In March Emanuel Schikaneder, an old acquaintance of Mozart's, and the manager of a small suburban theatre, came to him with a libretto and a proposition. Schikaneder was a fellow-Mason; the libretto, a fantasy into which were woven allegories as to the brotherhood of man and a great deal of Masonic reference. Would Mozart set it as a *Singspiel* for his theatre? The composer hesitated and then undertook the task. Only he could have transmuted such material by the alchemy of his music. What was planned as a bourgeois entertainment developed into a unique work of art, and was indeed the foundation stone of German romantic opera. Simple melodies of the folk-song type, intricate coloratura arias, stately choruses, patter-songs, high dignity, humour approaching near to absurdity, together with moments full of a sense of the mysteries beyond man's comprehension—all these elements are met with and reconciled in *Die Zauberflöte* (The Magic Flute). The assimilation is so perfect that it comes as a surprise to learn that a great deal of older material was reshaped for the work.

While Mozart was working on the almost completed score in the summer of 1791 he received another commission. A stranger, a gaunt figure, brought him a letter which, enjoining secrecy, asked him to compose a Requiem Mass for an anonymous patron. Let it be said at once that this latter was an eccentric, a certain Count Walsegg, who was planning to have the work performed as his own, in memory of his late wife, the grave messenger being merely his house steward. Mozart, however, never learned this explanation. An even more urgent call succeeded this. The Estates of Bohemia demanded from him a full-scale *opera seria,* the text a modification of Metastasio's *La Clemenza di Tito,* to be ready for the coronation celebrations at Prague in early September—an almost impossibly short notice. The Mozart family, together with a professional pupil, Franz Süssmayr, hurried to Prague. With Süssmayr's help in the recitatives the work was somehow completed and performed. It could not be anything more than a hasty scrambling-together; the only wonder is that it has its finer moments.[20*] It was not warmly received, and Mozart, ill and discouraged hastened to return to Vienna and his two outstanding compositions. He was further cast down by the first reception, late in September, of *Die Zauberflöte,* but Schikaneder persisted, and soon citizen audiences were flocking to the small theatre for performance after performance, a success wildly exceeding that of any previous opera of Mozart's. Even Salieri came to applaud, seated in Mozart's private box. Though cheered by this change of fortune the composer found his sickness increasing as he struggled to complete the Requiem. The conviction grew upon him that he was writing it for his own obsequies, that the grey stranger was the messenger of Death, and that some enemy had poisoned him—(poor Salieri suffered that aspersion for the rest of his days). After a while he took to his bed, round which friends gathered to rehearse the numbers as they were completed. The opening bars of the *Lacrimosa* were his last, and he died on the 5th of December 1791. He had indeed been poisoned—by the years of overwork, nervous strain and disappointment, which had brought to his bloodstream the (then) deadly condition of uraemia. The circumstances of his funeral were such that the site of his grave soon became unidentifiable.

The Requiem was completed later by Süssmayr and the fee paid to his widow. Out of the 600 and more works that he produced only about 144 were in print while he lived, and of these a proportion were pirated. A typically flagrant example was the unauthorised piano arrangement of the "Seraglio", published (1785) before Mozart could complete his own version. The financial gains to the composer for the publication of his music can thus be counted as very small. Yet had he lived a little longer he might have found himself provided with what he had always sought, a stable income. Two separate subscription schemes were afoot for this end, by a number of Hungarian nobles and by a group of admirers in Holland. Another bitter irony is the fact that his leap to general fame came only a few years after his death. The wide public recognition of the worth of the German *Die Zauberflöte* followed by an almost equal appreciation of the previously neglected comic opera *Don Giovanni* led to a much increased printing of his works. Too late for him, the profits were to his widow and the publishers. He swiftly became Mozart " the divine ". We hear little more as to the " gloom " and " difficulty " of his music. Constanze married again in 1809, her Danish husband, von Nissen, becoming Mozart's first biographer. Of Mozart's two sons, the younger, Franz Xaver, took up music as a profession without, however, attaining eminence.

Conducting

A great deal has been said in this chapter concerning conductors and concertmasters. Let us now take some note of the methods by which generations of musical directors controlled the concerted efforts of their singers and instrumentalists. The need for such an overall discipline had been felt at least as early as the fifteenth century, a period when vocal polyphony was becoming more and more intricate. A leader, it seems, would stand before or among his musicians and direct matters with his raised hand, which sometimes grasped a tight roll of paper. A light wooden stick was sometimes used, if we accept as evidence a fifteenth century Italian painting depicting an angel conducting with such a baton—and holding it in a singularly modern fashion between thumb and two fingers. (See Plate 9.)

With the advent of the continuo age there grew up the practice of directing various types of musical ensemble from the keyboard—by gesture, and, when necessary by some kind of musical emphasis from the instrument. However, when considerable forces were being employed the older method, that of the standing, measure-beating conductor, sometimes brandishing the roll of paper, seems frequently to have been followed in all countries. France began to make use of a type of thick wooden baton, sometimes of formidable size. As early as in Lully's day it was in general and not always discreet use, since we read of complaints, continuing for decade after decade, that in churches choirmasters were drowning the sound of the music with their thumpings on desk and floor. This form of guidance by ear rather than eye earned for conductors the sobriquet of " woodchopper ". Indeed, the ulceration of Lully's foot which brought about his death was caused by a blow from the heavy staff with which he was pounding the floor during the performance of a Te Deum. As late as 1767 there is a mention by Rousseau of the " unbearable noise " made by the conductor of the Paris opera, who hammered with his baton and ruined the effect of the playing. Italy and Germany, generally speaking, showed a distaste for such methods, even though Leigh Hunt speaks of having heard in 1822 at Pisa Cathedral the " whip-crack " of a paper-roll beat. In Italian opera the larger establishments of the eighteenth century usually chose to have two harpsichords, one for the usual continuo player, and one for the *maestro* (normally the composer) who was directing the performance, taking care of the tempo by gesture and intervening with his instrument only when necessary. Even as late as 1782 Mozart controlled his " Seraglio " from the clavier.

Meanwhile the increased refinements demanded from orchestral playing were causing a growing importance to be given to the figure of the concert-master (Ger. *Konzertmeister*), the leading violinist, to whom most of the responsibility for the training of the instrumentalists was being delegated. The high efficiency of the orchestras at Mannheim (Stamitz), Berlin (J. G. Graun) and other great centres was maintained by the work of such instru-mental specialists, and the double rule of conductor and concertmaster was continued through the rest of the eighteenth century and into the nine-teenth. With the fading of continuo-playing in the 1770's the importance of the concertmaster increased. He expected to have the direction of the per-formance of symphonies, and even in operas and accompanied choral works he tended to assert himself by beating time with his bow or rallying his forces by emphasising a passage on his instrument. Rivalries and clashes between the two authorities were inevitable, and seem frequently to have occurred. However, during Haydn's visits to London in the 1790's the com-poser at the keyboard and that excellent leader of the orchestra Salomon exercised a dual control without any recorded friction. The direction of the first performance of Beethoven's Ninth Symphony in 1824 was similarly divided between a conductor at the pianoforte and a concert master, the orchestra being compelled to disregard yet a third presence, that of the deaf composer, who was also endeavouring to beat time. It is strange to think of the intrusion of pianoforte tone into the self-sufficient symphonic scorings of Haydn and Beethoven, occasional though the moments may have been.

An important forerunner in the more modern outlook was Johann Reichardt, who in 1776 became *Kapellmeister* to Frederick the Great. He was among the first to banish the harpsichord from the orchestral perfor-mance, and to assume sole direction from a conductor's stand. Yet his methods were heavily attacked in Germany, and dual control remained the normal method for many years. In London in 1820 the progressive Spohr found that he was expected to share his responsibility, and to direct from the pianoforte. He refused both demands and won his way. In 1829, in the same city, Mendelssohn was more complaisant, and remained at the key-board for a performance of Beethoven's Fifth Symphony. As late as 1846 when the same composer was conducting his *Elijah* at Birmingham (in modern fashion) the orchestral leader insisted on his privilege of " constantly beating with his fiddle-stick . . ."—to the annoyance of *The Times* critic. But a period had now been reached when the authority of a single conduc-tor, wielding a baton in front of the performers and endeavouring to inter-pret as well as indicate the measure, was far on the way to being every-where established.

Some English Musicians

In the period that we have been surveying the most frequent English name that we have met has been that of Dr. Burney, whom we have found in various parts of the Continent, indefatigably seeking out the great men of music, and earning the gratitude of posterity by putting on record all he heard and saw of musical Europe in the 1770's.

Charles Burney (1726–1814) came from a cultured family and received a thorough professional training as an organist, harpsichordist, string player (he was a violin pupil of Matteis) and composer. For a while he was the musical apprentice of Dr. Thomas Arne, and at times played in Handel's orchestras. He finally established himself as a fashionable harpsichord teacher in London, and was included in the best intellectual circles there, counting Dr. Johnson, Burke, Pitt, Reynolds the painter and Herschel the astronomer, as well as other famous men, among his friends. When he conceived his idea of writing a History of Music he saw the necessity of continental travel for the gathering of some of his material. His two Journals, which covered "The Present State of Music . . ." first in France and Italy, and then in the Germanic countries, were the results of the wide tours of 1770 and 1772.[21] His monumental History of Music, in four volumes, appeared between 1776 and 1789. Typical of his age is his poor opinion of the music of past centuries, including that of the English madrigal school, and his high regard for what nowadays is thought to be second-rate Italian music. The rest of his life was closely filled by other writings on music. He was much in Haydn's company during that composer's two visits. One of his daughters, Edith, was an outstanding harpsichord virtuoso; the other, Fanny (Madame D'Arblay) was the famous novelist.

An earlier figure must come in for mention, that of William Boyce (1710–79)—organist, composer, Master of the King's Music, and leading English musician (if we exclude Handel) of his day. Posterity owes him a debt for his collection and publication of three volumes of "Cathedral Music", which gave English church choirs a new and wider repertory. Though it may have included too many minor Restoration composers it made available also the Tudor masters—and in cheap scores, instead of the untidy manuscript parts generally used heretofore.

Besides many church compositions Boyce wrote a great deal of vigorous orchestral music, mainly in the shape of overtures ("symphonies") to specific works, and cast in the old suite form of several short movements. In the late 1750's the publisher Walsh issued a set of "Eight Symphonys in Eight Parts", which seems to have included the best of them. They belong almost wholly to the baroque world. A comparison between one of them and, say, a Mozart or Haydn symphony of a few decades later will afford quite startling evidence as to the complete change of symphonic outlook that was achieved in so short a span of years.[22*]

Thomas Arne (1710–78) also deserves mention as a leading English musician at a time of foreign domination. Most of his work was done for the London stage, where his English operas and masques, incidental music and songs made his reputation as a composer, even though his reputation as a man was never a high one. He was of course the composer of "Rule, Britannia" (from the masque of *Alfred*), and his arrangement of "God Save Our Noble King", produced during the 1745 troubles, is the first firm record that we have of a performance of our national anthem. One of his more ambitious works was his Italian-style opera, *Artaxerxes* (1762) with sung recitative, and the Metastasio libretto translated by the composer. It was a considerable success and received numerous performances. But he is best remembered for his Shakespearean songs and a few other incidental lyrics, such as " Now Phoebus sinketh " from an adaptation of Milton's *Comus*. He achieved in these simple vocal works a truly English quality of melody to which Handel was a stranger.

The well-known song, " The Lass with the Delicate Air " was written by his son, Michael Arne, himself a minor composer.

Maurice Greene (1695–1755), organist of St. Paul's, later Professor of Music at Cambridge and for a time friendly with Handel, composed a great deal of church music. He took the first steps in the collection of English cathedral music which was afterwards completed by his friend William Boyce.[23*]

Of late years the organ works of the blind composer John Stanley (1713–86) have had something of a revival. He wrote much organ and other instrumental music, as well as cantatas and oratorios, and succeeded Boyce as Master of the King's Music in 1779. The works of his which are heard nowadays bear out Burney's opinion that he was " a natural and agreeable composer ".

NOTES

Recordings of all the important works of Haydn and Mozart are readily available from one or another of the leading gramophone companies. For this reason the HMS VII recordings of the music of these two composers are confined to excerpts, mostly of lesser works, which afford comparisons or illustrate special points.

1* HMS VII has a recording of a performance of a 'Cello Concerto in G minor by G. M. Monn, cast rather in the baroque pattern.

2* HMS VII has a recording (complete) of a three-movement F major symphony by C. P. E. Bach, composed in 1776, and scored for two flutes, two oboes, two horns, five-part strings and harpsichord continuo. Also in the volume is a recording of a Fantasia in C minor for clavichord (1753), which illustrates well C. P. E.'s power of expressing in free form emotionalism of the *Empfindsamkeit* type. Another excellent recording of C. P. E.'s music is WLP 5040 (*Nixa*—three works). There is (a) a Symphony in C major for strings (1773), (b) one in D major for strings and wind (1780). Both show C. P. E.'s characteristic symphonic features— " fanfare " openings to the first movements, striking themes, dramatic contrasts of rhythm and orchestral colour, and bold modulations—yet being still experimental in form. The third work (c) has recently been discovered in the archives of the *Musik-akademie* at Vienna. It is a Concerto in A minor for keyboard and orchestra, and a very remarkable one, which when better known, must surely raise even higher the status of the composer.

3* HMS VII has a recording of the first movement of a keyboard Concerto in A by J. C. Bach (c. 1757). It represents an earlier stage in the evolution as compared with the C. P. E. concerto mentioned above, but there are suggestions of the sonata framework, including the so-called double exposition. Towards the end of the movement a six-four chord from the orchestra is followed by what afterwards became a familiar classical feature, a solo cadenza.

4   This quotation is a redaction from the full score of the movement as printed
    in HAM II (no. 294)—this taken from *Denkmäler der Tonkunst in Bayern*
    (*Leipzig 1900–1913*).

5* HMS VII has an excellent example of this type, a recording of the slow move-
    ment of Haydn's F sharp minor Trio for piano, violin and 'cello, published at
    the time of his second London visit. The 'cello part is particularly unambitious.

6* HMS VII has a recording of the Minuet and Adagio from Mozart's Diverti-
    mento in E flat (K. 289) for woodwind and horns, written in 1777 for the Salz-
    burg Court. Probably the best known nowadays of Mozart's numerous *diverti-
    menti* is the delightful Serenade, *Eine Kleine Nachtmusik* for strings (K. 525),
    recordings of which are always available. HMS VII also has a recording of
    three *German Dances* (precursors of the waltz) by Haydn, produced in 1792 for a
    Viennese ball.

7   The lively impact on their hearers of Haydn's frequently picturesque instru-
    mental works can be judged from the nicknames attached to a large number of
    them, for which, as far as we know, the composer had but little responsibility.

8* HMS VII has a recording of an interesting example of Haydn's use of the long
    neglected fugal device in instrumental music, the finale of the String Quartet in
    A, Op. 20, No. 6, labelled *Fuga con 3 Soggetti*. The Op. 20 group are known
    as the "Sun" Quartets, from the cover-decoration of the original edition.

9* HMS VII has a recording of the first and last movements of the Symphony No.
    31 in D, the so-called "Horn Signal"; an excellent example of Haydn's early
    symphonic technique. At the moment he had four horns at his command, at
    least one of them a virtuoso of his instrument. Throughout, the lower strings
    do little else but supply an accompaniment, the violas frequently doubling the
    basses.

10* HMS VII has a recording of Richard's famous air, "If the whole world forget
    me . . .", from Grétry's opera. One phrase seems to anticipate the opening bars
    of the *Marseillaise*, which appeared eight years later. Grétry makes striking use
    in the accompaniment of trumpets and muted drums. Elsewhere in the opera
    Blondel has a melody which, recurring frequently, appears as the germ of the
    leitmotif idea.

11* The attractiveness of Dittersdorf's opera may be judged by an excerpt recorded
    in HMS VII, an aria, "Lovers want no witnesses".

12 Mozart's sister 'Nannerl', who adored his genius, could yet say: "Outside music
    he was and remained something of a child, and that was a trait on the seamy
    side of his character. He always was in need of a father, mother or guardian.
    He could not cope with money matters, and against his father's will he married
    a girl most unsuited to him—and hence the great domestic disorder at the time
    of his death and after." Nannerl was perhaps prejudiced against Constanze,
    but her words concerning her brother suggest a certain fecklessness that was
    likely to be a handicap in the cut-throat battles for the higher musical posts that
    went on in Vienna and the leading German cities of the time. On the other
    hand, there is enough contemporary evidence to show that Mozart had some
    bitter enemies, particularly in the cases of the composers Peter von
    Winter and Leopold Kozeluch. Even the Imperial Kapellmeister, Salieri, intri-
    gued against him when he happened to get in the way. His operas were staged,
    his playing applauded, his instrumental music admired (with reservations) and
    he was fêted and given hospitality by aristocratic admirers. Yet when it was a
    matter of his being appointed to one of the long-term leading positions there
    came always the disappointment, except for the ill-paid and comparatively un-
    important post of Imperial chamber-composer awarded to him in 1788. Prob-
    ably there is no single reason that can explain the mystery; certainly not a one-
    sided one.
    Some interesting new lights are cast on Mozart's music and his career in A.
    Hyatt King's *Mozart in Retrospect* (*Oxford University Press—1955*).

13   The surviving letters of the Mozarts have been gathered in three volumes by
      Miss Emily Anderson—*The Letters of Mozart and his Family* (Macmillan). A
      selection, edited by Eric Blom (*Mozart's Letters*) is available in the Penguin
      series.

14*   HMS VII provides an excellent opportunity for comparisons in this matter of
      liturgical settings. A recording of an *Agnus Dei* by the eighteen year old Mozart,
      the third movement of a *Litany* composed for Salzburg (K. 195), and scored for
      solo, chorus, strings, oboes, horns and continuo, seems indeed operatic in its
      coloraturas and chromaticisms. A recording is also provided of a four-part setting
      with organ and strings of an Advent Gradual (*Prope est* . . .) by Michael Haydn.
      Haydn restored the liturgical settings of Offertories and Graduals which had
      previously been displaced by instrumental movements. These modest and appro-
      priate settings by Haydn eventually became widely known and employed.

15   Regarding the " K " numberings of Mozart's works—the German scholar Ludwig
      Köchel (d. 1877) was the first to supply a really systematic catalogue of them.
      Nowadays each work is usually mentioned with its " Köchel " number. Thus a
      clavier Minuet & Trio of 1761–2 is K.1. and the Requiem, unfinished at the
      composer's death, K. 626.

16*   HMS VII has a recording of the vocal quartet (*Ach, Belmonte* . . .) from the end
      of Act II of *Die Entführung*. Like the usual *opera buffa* finale the quartet is in
      several musical sections, differing in keys and tempi.
      One of the several friendly meetings between Mozart and Gluck was at a per-
      formance of *Entführung* in August, 1782, arranged specially for the old maestro's
      delectation.

17*   HMS VII affords a glimpse of the kind of operatic music that *did* move the
      Viennese public to enthusiasm, a duet from Act I of *Il Matrimonio Segreto* (The
      Secret Marriage), by Domenico Cimarosa (1749–1801). First produced in 1792,
      this lightweight work had a European fame.

18   The concertos are treated exhaustively in C. M. Girdlestone's *Mozart's Piano
      Concertos* (Cassell).

19   Mozart lived in an age without performing fees for composers. A composer
      was paid a sum down for supplying and helping to produce an opera. He might
      also get a " benefit night ", and apart from minor pickings that was that. If he
      were quick he might make a profit from a redaction of the score, but there were
      no copyright laws to prevent anyone else beating him to it with an issue if they
      got the chance. According to Leopold Mozart Italian copyists sometimes made
      more profit from a successful opera than did its composer, by selling separate
      copies of the arias.

20*   One of the finer numbers in *La Clemenza* . . . is Titus' aria *Se All' Impero*, in
      Act II. HMS VII has a recording of it.

21   A recent editing of Burney's accounts of his journeyings, by the late Percy
      Scholes, termed *Dr. Burney's Musical Tours in Europe* (*2 vols.—Macmillan*)
      makes fascinating reading. The editor restored many details and journey inci-
      dents noted by the author in his Journal and omitted by him from the original
      edition.

22*   HMS VII affords the material for such a comparison, a recording of all four
      movements of Boyce's Symphony No. 8 in D minor from the set mentioned in
      the text, and written for a meeting of the Three Choirs at Worcester. The
      printed score is for oboes, strings and continuo, but other instruments may well
      have been added in performance. It is fresh and vital baroque music, without
      any hint of the new formal principles already developing elsewhere. This work,
      like a great deal of Boyce's music, was written after he had become totally
      deaf.

23*   HMS V has a recording of a full anthem by Greene, " O, Clap Your Hands ",
      It is in motet style, somewhat old-fashioned for its period,

CHAPTER X

Beethoven and his Contemporaries

THE last decade of the eighteenth century witnessed a happening of the utmost importance historically, the social upheaval of the French Revolution and the establishment of the Republic. There followed the imperialistic expansion of France under Napoleon, succeeded, after the latter's downfall, by the attempts in various countries to put the clock back. These events and their social repercussions must be borne in mind as we follow the course of musical history through the early decades of the nineteenth century. One permanent result was the effective social emancipation of the middle classes, and their increasing influence on the course of cultural progress, for good and for ill.

Into these stormy times Music projected the most tremendous figure of all her chronicles. With the name of Beethoven are associated the qualities of indomitable strength and intellectual power, together with all that is heroic in the art. He was a child of the new age. In the full tide of aristocratic patronage Haydn had needed the aids of tact, deference and courtly good-humour to carry him to success and economic security; Mozart's battle for these objectives ended in defeat; Beethoven, insisting on his own worth to the pitch of arrogance, achieved the liberty that Mozart had failed to win, not only by professional ability but by the iron of his personality. He was indeed the first musician to be willing to stand *against* the world, an attitude soon to be imitated by certain " Romantic " composers. He condescended to accept the help of patrons (graciously or ungraciously as it suited his whim) but at the same time always stood for being treated as a social equal. It is a tribute to this enormous forcefulness and to the tolerance and artistic conscience of the Viennese aristocracy that such an " equality " was accepted, in the main, without question.

In their finest symphonies, sonatas and quartets, Haydn and Mozart had reached a classical perfection of beauty and logical construction. Beethoven was destined to expand the classical frame in a number of ways, e.g., in straightforward linear dimensions—the mature symphonic movements at his hands were twice, sometimes three times the length of those of the older

251

masters; in sonority—the sheer volume and depth of sound evoked in even the *Eroica,* not to mention the 5th, 7th and 9th Symphonies, were something new to music; in the wide range of his modulations (although indeed Mozart had done much pioneer work in that respect; one recalls the amazing tonal adventures in the first and last movements of the G minor Symphony, and in the last of the E flat); and above all in the intensity of the emotions expressed—the classical device of the " workings-out " of initial themes was carried to a new height of drama, to emotional tensions which seem at times actually to have frightened contemporary listeners. He swiftly became the dominant composer of the musical world, a paramount influence. The power of his music has never ceased to be felt by succeeding generations.

Ludwig van Beethoven (1770–1827) was born at Bonn, the eldest of the three sons of a drunken tenor singer in the employ of the Elector Max Friedrich, Prince-Archbishop of Cologne. At Bonn, the capital, the Elector maintained the usual Court *Kapelle.* Johann, the father, soon noted the unusual musical promise of the young child, and seeing himself as another Leopold Mozart, endeavoured to turn it towards personal profit. From an early age the boy was forced day and night to practise both keyboard and violin, the parental supervision being of the harshest. Fortunately, by the time he was eleven years old he had passed into better hands, those of the new Court organist, C. G. Neefe, an excellent musician, whose memory the mature Beethoven recalled always in terms of warm gratitude. Besides a general musical training, Neefe gave him a course of the " 48 " (Johann Sebastian was at last beginning to come into his own). At the age of twelve he could be safely left as Neefe's deputy. He also became cembalist to the orchestra, and at the age of fourteen, the salaried assistant Court-organist. The uncouth, untidy youth, ill-equipped in general education, gradually attracted good friends and admirers, including the cultured family of the von Breunings, and above all the young and generous Count Waldstein, a few years his senior. Meanwhile the new Elector, Max Franz, was proving an even keener patron of music than his predecessor. In 1787 Ludwig was sent to Vienna by him, probably at the instigation of Count Waldstein. Here he attracted the attention of Mozart by his skill in improvisation; Mozart may indeed have given him some composition lessons. However, the stay was brief, a matter of weeks, for he was recalled to Bonn by the death of his much-loved mother. Here he found himself responsible for the support of the family, for his deplorable father, soon to be dismissed, was no longer competent. His musical experiences were now widened through the establishment of a Court opera. Already an efficient string player, he was given a place in the theatre orchestra, and for a few years took an instrumental part in what was " modern " music, operas by such men as Mozart (*Don Giovanni*), Gluck, Cimarosa and Paisiello. The Elector had brought from Vienna, in particular, some exceptionally fine woodwind players. The skill and imagination which Ludwig showed later in his treatment of that department may have stemmed from the fact. In 1792, Haydn, passing through Bonn from London, saw and approved a cantata by the young man. In the same year Ludwig followed him to Vienna, never to return to Bonn. Johann Beethoven died soon after his going. Quite soon, owing to Napoleon, the Elector himself became a refugee in the Austrian capital.

Beethoven's first two concerns in Vienna were (a) to seek instruction in composition (b) to earn his bread. In regard to the first he went initially to the most famous musician in Europe—Haydn, but the association was broken by the latter's second journey to London. Beethoven transferred himself to the Court organist Albrechtsberger, and seems to have worked hard with him at counterpoint. Salieri, now Imperial Kapellmeister, and a leading composer of Italian opera (which was once more supreme in Vienna) instructed him for several years in matters of vocal music. Ignaz Schuppanzigh and Aloys Förster, leading figures in their day, also gave him lessons for a while—in string playing and quartet composition respectively.

Meanwhile he sought his own livelihood, at first primarily as a piano player and teacher. His great powers as a virtuoso pianist were soon recognised by Viennese society, a truly musical one. Certainly the Court opera was still an exotic, imported art, and was maintained largely by Italians, resident or otherwise, but the main artistic interests of these aristocratic patrons were in matters instrumental—keyboard, chamber and orchestral music. We read of private music-makings innumerable, and even breakfast-time quartet parties. Moreover, it was a practical interest. Some of the noble lords and ladies were really very competent players, and mingled with the professionals in their activities. Skilled teachers were in high demand. New compositions for keyboard and for various chamber-music combinations were always being called for. The attention and appreciation that such a society gave to Beethoven and his like was a discerning one.

He performed, for payment, in lordly halls and drawing-rooms, both as a soloist and (a favourite attraction of the age) in competition with other famous players. As a virtuoso he quickly established himself, being matched in general esteem only by Hummel, Wölfl and Cramer. In one feature he stood unrivalled, that of improvisation. He soon gathered a circle of rich patrons and admirers, the chiefs of which were the Princes Karl Lichnowsky and Josef Lobkowitz. Lobkowitz, who for several years gave him rooms in his house, possessed a musical establishment for the performance of choral and orchestral music. Lichnowsky maintained a string-quartet, whose leader was the famous Schuppanzigh, another of Beethoven's friends. Both units were soon to prove useful to Beethoven the composer, even though these patrons found it increasingly difficult to preserve such graces of the old aristocratic existence. Regarding orchestras, we may note that Vienna still lacked permanent professional bodies capable of maintaining regular *public* concerts, such as were to be found in Paris, for example. Single-handed public concerts (*Akademies*) were risky financial ventures for even the best of composers, as Mozart had previously learned. Beethoven did not attempt one of his own in Vienna until 1800, though on his tours between 1796–8, as pianist and composer, he seems to have given some in other German cities. The large public concerts in Vienna were usually composite affairs, organised officially for charitable purposes, and not very frequent. We shall note an improvement in the new century.

To read of the crudities of Beethoven's social behaviour during these early years of his "lionising"—the frequent instances of his rudeness and arrogance, his unchivalrous attitude towards defeated opponents, his ingrained boorishness and unpleasant personal habits, his apparent contempt for the vast majority of his fellow-men—is to wonder at the tolerance with which he was treated. Something of the inner worth of the man must have shone through all that was murky. Certainly women were aware of it. In his social contacts and as a fashionable pianoforte teacher he had much to do with aristocratic and attractive young ladies, and to a surprising proportion of these he paid court. Also surprising is the fact that quite a number chose to fall in love with him in return, in spite of his plebeian origin, his blunt, pock-marked features and general ungainliness. But none of these attachments had any permanence; Beethoven remained a lifelong bachelor.

As the decade of the '90's progressed his circle of supporters, and soon the rest of musical Vienna, became aware that he had claims to distinction other than in virtuosity. There began what is usually described as his "first period" of composition, which extended to a little beyond the year 1800, during which time his orchestral and chamber music clearly owed debts to the world of Haydn and Mozart, and his keyboard sonatas to the older master Clementi. There were, however, occasional and unmistakable signs of individuality, deemed eccentricities by some of his contemporaries, but which later generations, wise after the event, can perceive as portents of the future. No doubt some of the manuscripts came with him from Bonn, but early printed compositions were discarded. His Op. 1, a set of piano trios, and Op. 2, three piano sonatas, were first played in 1795 at Prince Lichnowsky's house, and were dedicated to, and heard by Joseph Haydn. A representative list of his "first period" compositions might include the following:

> Three Piano Trios (Op. 1—1793–5): the first dozen Piano Sonatas up to Op. 14 (including the two "easy" ones, Op. 49): the first two Piano Concertos—in B flat (No. 2—1795), and in C (No. 1—1797): two 'Cello Sonatas (1796): three String Trios (1797–8): six String Quartets (Op. 18—1798–1800): a Septet for strings and wind (Op. 20—1799–1800): and the First Symphony in C (1800).

As we have already seen in Mozart's case, publication was a very meagre and uncertain source of income to the actual composer in this age. Piracy could not easily be prevented, and publishers tended to pay parsimoniously and for complete ownership. Later, the established Beethoven was able to do better. In his turn he proved a shrewd bargainer, and not always a scrupulous one. But at first he was more inclined to use the "subscription" method, whereby he had copies printed at his own expense, and then sold them at his own figure to those who had undertaken to purchase. He was soon able to profit also by the device whereby a wealthy patron acquired the sole right of owning and controlling performances of a work for a limited period, having paid well for the privilege. The dedications that we still see printed at the head of various of his works were also usually sources of gain.

To comment on the above list of compositions. We may suppose that most of the piano sonatas mentioned will be known practically to the average student, who should surely not be without the complete set of the thirty-two, the " New Testament " of the musician's Bible, the " 48 " being the " Old Testament ". The mature Beethoven was not yet, but from the very start can be seen flashes of individuality—the terse first movement of the very first sonata, the depth of emotion to be found in a number of the slow movements, e.g., Op. 2, No. 2; Op. 10, No. 3. The composer had a lifelong admiration for Clementi, some of whose fine sonatas, it has been said, possess a Beethovenish atmosphere. The influence, in fact, first flowed the other way. The best of the " first period " group, the *Pathétique*, Op. 13, may be shown to contain a number of Clementi's already established characteristics.

It was in 1795 that Beethoven made his first appearance before the wider public, playing the solo part in his B flat piano concerto. Both concertos were masterly, but were still in the world of eighteenth century classicism, as were the Op. 18 string-quartets, inferior to the finer quartets of Haydn and Mozart. Altogether in the current mood was the Septet, Op. 20, a divertimento-like work that became immensely popular, a fact which later seems actually to have annoyed the composer, who regarded it in after years very much as Dickens did " Pickwick Papers ".

Not until 1800 did Beethoven venture on a symphony, and this on the occasion of his first independent concert. When it came, written for the normal late Mozart-Haydn orchestra, it must have suited the tastes of the day well enough, apart from the initial surprise of introductory cadences not belonging to the tonic key, and for an impetuous, whirlwind minuet, modulating to remote keys, the first of the true Beethoven scherzos. This movement was a glimpse of a new world, and must have impressed the more discerning of his hearers as much as it did a young lad by the name of Edward Elgar, in solitary exploration of things musical seventy years later. Belonging to this year also, and foreshadowing even more the greater Beethoven, are the C minor Piano Concerto (Op. 37) and the fine B flat Piano Sonata (Op. 22).

The Second Period

He was now at a time of supreme self-confidence. The world of musical Vienna was at his feet, and he trampled it. Already famed and fêted, he looked forward with certainty to a brilliant European career as virtuoso and composer. Never was the sin of pride more terribly and more appositely punished. Already in 1798 he had noticed some slight blunting of his powers of hearing, but had regarded the condition as temporary. By the turn of the century gnawing doubts had begun. He sought medical aid, but by 1802 he knew for certain that he was doomed to the musician's greatest affliction—deafness.[1] He withdrew from all society, and during the summer and autumn of 1802, at the little village of Heiligenstadt, fought a lonely fight with the utter despair which filled him. A document known as the "Heiligenstadt Testament", addressed to his two brothers and ostensibly his will, gives us a glimpse of the struggle. Most of it is in a mood of the deepest pessimism, yet he could say, finally: "Steadfast, I hope, will be my resolution to persevere." These words were easy to write; to implement them a very different matter. That he did so in such marvellous fashion represents a miracle of human courage and will-power. However inexplicable the fact, it is clear that soon after this time Beethoven was in command of new and higher powers in the art of musical composition. Had the blow not fallen he would doubtless have developed at a normal pace to become an outstanding composer, in what time was left him from his career as the greatest pianist in Europe. But the Second Period (c. 1802–12) represents an outburst of productive genius unique in the annals of the art. Hampered more and more in everyday affairs by his steadily increasing deafness, his inner imagination blazed forth in a series of works of unprecedented originality and beauty. He had accepted the challenge of Fate, and his victories, coming in rapid succession over the next decade, were expressed in the best-loved of his greater compositions.

He brought back from Heiligenstadt, where it had been composed, the score of his Second Symphony in D major. It had given him, it appears, infinite trouble, but its sunny spirit illustrates well the detachment that a great artist can show in his work. Of larger dimensions than the First, and with more colourful orchestration, it is usually held to belong to an intermediate stage between first and second periods, although the virile Scherzo (named as such in the score) and the merry, witty finale with its extended coda showed that full maturity was close at hand. "Intermediate" perhaps is also the Third Piano Concerto in C minor and the Op. 22 Piano Sonata, already mentioned. The great leap forward occurred with the advent of the Third Symphony, the *Eroica*, in 1803. Thereafter came the spate. In listing the leading masterpieces of the period 1800–12 we will include those termed above (no doubt controversially) "intermediate":

Third Piano Concerto in C minor (Op. 37—1800): Piano Sonata in B flat (Op. 22—1800): that in A flat (Op. 26—1801) with its celebrated first-movement variations: two Fantasy Sonatas (Op. 27—the second in C sharp minor miscalled the "Moonlight"—1801): the "Pastoral" Sonata (Op. 28—1801): and the group of three (Op. 31—1802): the Second Symphony in D (1802): then, the real landmark, the Third Symphony in E flat (Eroica—1803): the *Kreutzer* Violin Sonata (Op. 47—1803): two Piano Sonatas—the *Waldstein* (Op. 53) and the *Appassionata* (Op. 57), both of 1804: the first version of the opera *Fidelio* (1805—much revised later), and during the next few years its three *Leonora* Overtures: the Violin Concerto in D (1806): the Fourth Symphony in B flat (1806): the Fifth Symphony in C minor (1805–7): the Fourth Piano Concerto in G (1805–6): the three "Rasoumovsky" String Quartets (Op.

17. German brass players (mid- or early 16th century). The nearest instrument is a trombone, the other two slide-trumpets.

Radio Times Hulton Picture Library

18. "Family at Table" by the Flemish artist Jacob Jordaens (1593–1678). The practical devotion to domestic music by the ordinary citizen of the period is emphasised by the apparent sharing by a child in arms in the pipe playing.

Radio Times Hulton Picture Library

19. "Spanish Students" by Theodore Rombouts of Munich (1596–1637). There can be seen a guitar and the beautiful painting of the back of a lute.

59—1806): the *Coriolanus* Overture (1807): the Sixth Symphony in F (" Pastoral "—1807–8): the 'Cello Sonata in A (1808): the Fifth and last Piano Concerto in E flat (1809): the Piano Sonata in E flat—*Les Adieux, l'Absence et le Rétour,* and the one in F sharp (both of 1809): the String Quartet in E flat (the " Harp "—1809) and the one in F minor (Op. 95—1810): the Overture to Goethe's *Egmont* (with other incidental music—1810): the Piano Trio in B flat (the " Archduke "—1811): and finally two Symphonies, the Seventh in A and the Eighth in F (" the little one "), both of 1812.

—a formidable but nevertheless selective catalogue.

Back in Vienna late in 1802, Beethoven returned to society, to piano teaching and even to public playing, in which latter activity he persisted as long as he was able. Though by 1804 it was not easy to converse with him, it was not until 1808 that he bade farewell to solo concerto work at an *Akademie* of his own. The programme of this concert included the Fifth and Sixth Symphonies in first performances, as well as the Fourth Piano Concerto (notable for being opened by the solo instrument unaccompanied). There were also extracts from his Mass in C (Op. 86), a Piano Fantasia and the Choral Fantasia (Op. 80)—a gargantuan feast, and one highly profitable to the composer. We may note that by this time there had been established by a circle of music lovers the *Liebhaber* concerts. Vienna had at last some-thing that corresponded to the *Concert de la Loge Olympique* at Paris, even though the standard of orchestral playing left much to be desired. In 1807–8 no less than twenty of these concerts were given. For a number of years many of the greater works of Beethoven had their hearings in them—their chief attractions. There seems no doubt that the rising middle-class musical public readily accepted his compositions, whatever strictures professional opinion chose to make. When the fifth, greatest and last of his piano con-certos came for performance (the so-called " Emperor " in E flat) he felt himself compelled to hand over the solo part to his brilliant pupil Carl Czerny. In 1814 he took part in chamber music for the last time. There-after he became more and more of a recluse. Always naturally touchy and suspicious, the tendency grew with his disability. It is grievous to read of his recurrent and usually unjustified quarrels with even the most devoted of his friends.

Let us return to the year 1804, when the score of the Third Symphony awaited printing—" composed to celebrate the memory of a great man " (undoubtedly Napoleon) and having already had a private performance. Well authenticated seems the story of the angry Beethoven tearing away his first dedication on hearing that there was no longer a First Consul in France, but an Emperor instead. The work was first performed publicly in April 1805, a little more than six months before invading French armies entered Vienna.

With it a new page in the history of the symphony had been written. The dimensions of the " heroic " first movement are far greater than those of any previous symphonic essay; there is a new subtlety in the organisation

R

of the thematic material, both in presentation and development: any formality in the linking of subject groups which could justify the term " bridge " (" the clatter of dishes at a royal banquet ") forever disappears : finally, the extensive coda becomes in effect a second development, a feature often found in Beethoven's music henceforward. Regarding the last detail and to be fair to that great pioneer Mozart, we must recall that he had done very much the same thing in the finale of his last symphony, the " Jupiter ". This *Eroica* movement serves well to illustrate Wagner's contention that the classical plan of the presentation of themes followed by their dissection had been changed by Beethoven into the welding of initial fragments into a single mighty unity.

The spacious slow movement, the greatest of funeral marches, is followed by one of the most headlong of Beethoven scherzos—now a whisper, now a savage outburst—and a three-horn " fanfare " trio. In the finale he recalled another hero, the mythical defier of Zeus, borrowing from his own ballet, *Prometheus,* the theme from which he fashioned another tremendous movement in the form of a series of variations.

Beethoven's new dedication of the symphony was to Prince Lobkowitz, who for a time was its " owner ". Present at a private performance of it at Lobkowitz's country seat was Prince Louis Ferdinand of Prussia, nephew of the great Frederick. Though a professional soldier (he was killed in action in 1806), he was also an exceptional pianist and a well-trained composer. The work was new to him, and his appreciation of it was such that he asked for and was granted *two* more repetitions—with a necessary rest for an exhausted orchestra. Beethoven had the highest regard for him, and dedicated to him his C minor Piano Concerto.[2*]

A great deal of fruitless thought has been given to the question as to why Beethoven should kill off his hero before the second movement, leaving doubt as to what the third and fourth movements may " mean ". The problem arises only if we think of him as a romantic " programmist ", as he certainly was not, although indeed he pointed the way. In only one work, the egregious " Battle Symphony ", did he attempt throughout frankly to " paint " instead of " feel ". The *Eroica* is a study of heroism within the frameworks of logical musical structures, not, as in the case of Richard Strauss' symphonic poem, one fitted to a previously conceived literary programme. The theme was one to which Beethoven returned again and again. The overtures *Coriolanus, Egmont* and *King Stephen* (of Hungary) each had for its subject a hero of history. His single opera told of the actions of a heroine; while bracketed with the drama are the three *Leonora* overtures, successively abandoned as preludes, since their own effectiveness as heroic dramas in music tended to blunt the impact of the actual stage work following. His oratorio *Christus am Olberge* (1802) may have owed its lack of success in part to the fact that in it the Founder of our faith was pictured somewhat after the manner of a defiant Prometheus.

The opera *Fidelio* had been commissioned by the impresario Schikaneder. It told a romantic story of the rescue of a young nobleman from a tyrant's prison through the devotion of his wife, the courageous Leonora. The "rescue" theme had long been a favourite one in French *opéra comique* (usually serious, in spite of its name; we have already noted Grétry's *Coeur de Lion*). Moreover, Beethoven had always admired the music of Cherubini, the finest composer of that school, and had heard his famous "rescue" opera, *Les Deux Journées. Fidelio* followed the practice of *opéra comique* (and *Singspiel*) in having spoken dialogue instead of recitative : altogether, we may say that while its music could have been written by nobody except Beethoven, in the matter of operatic history the work broke no new ground. Its first production was unlucky; it was staged a week after the beginning of the temporary French occupation (Nov. 1805) and had but three performances. A revised version suffered a similar fate the next year. Its success had to await a further revision and a revival in 1814.

The Violin Concerto, after the passing of a hundred and fifty years, is still held to be unsurpassed of its kind. Of no great difficulty technically, as virtuoso technique goes, its inspired emotions demand the utmost from the performer in matters of interpretation. It is full of striking effects obtained by the simplest of means, as in the first few bars, where the alternation of solo drum taps with the gentle woodwind theme gives moments of pure poetry.

Similar immortality has been afforded to the "Kreutzer" Violin Sonata, the best of several fine sonatas which Beethoven wrote with such thorough understanding of the solo instrument. The set of variations which comprise the middle movement are among his most masterly in that form.

To return to Beethoven the symphonist— After the storm and stress of the *Eroica* came a more genial mood in the Fourth, with a long introduction out of which the opening subject of the first movement gradually builds itself. Notable is the slow movement, one of the loveliest of Beethoven's creations. Shaped during the same period is the mighty Fifth, an utterly original conception. Beethoven was probably hoaxing his gullible disciple Schindler when in reference to the four-note opening he told him "Thus Fate knocks at the door". The idea itself, heard for the first time, might well seem of small significance; it is what the composer did with it that is the miracle. The resultant movement, sweeping from start to finish with irresistible power and faultless logic, is probably the most widely known of all symphonic writings. The Scherzo, something more than a musical jest, is almost as famous. In the course of it we meet an early example of theme transference, when the horns blare the four-note subject from the first movement in a new rhythmic guise. This metamorphic version reappears in the last movement as a phantom-like foil to the triumphant march-music, the opening double-forte phrase of which might be considered as a transformation into the major key of the first pianissimo notes of the scherzo:

For this last movement Beethoven made some temporary additions to the normal classical orchestra that had served him (with occasional extra horns) thus far. Three trombones, new to symphonic scoring, were added, together with piccolo (he had learned how that smallest of instruments gives a culminating brilliance to the blaze of the full orchestra) and double bassoon. He used trombones again in his Sixth Symphony " thunderstorm ", and also occasionally in the Ninth, but their place in the symphony orchestra did not become firm until after his day.

Let us pause briefly to consider Beethoven's overall contributions to the art of orchestration. His symphonies called for no real extension of the constitution of the orchestra as shaped by Haydn and Mozart with the aid of previous pioneers, though, as we have seen, he demanded certain extra instruments on occasions. (He several times called for more horns in his overtures.) For his later symphonies greater *numbers* of string players were employed than would have been necessary for the works of the two older masters. His innovations were rather in the matter of treatment. Any section was liable to find greater technical demands thrust upon it than it had previously been used to, as did the double-basses in the middle section of the Fifth Symphony scherzo, or the horns time and again, with the celebrated passage for fourth horn in the Adagio of the Ninth as a culminating example. Both Haydn and Mozart had shown a tentativeness in their use of the clarinet; Beethoven settled it comfortably in the woodwind choir, which was treated with even greater artistry, particularly in the increased use of " conversations " between the solo woodwind voices. The violas also gained a further emancipation. The early classical practice of tying them either to the second violins or the basses in three-part harmony, relaxed by Mozart and Haydn, (the latter wrote: " in all my compositions . . . the viola rarely doubles the bass "), was continued to a complete freedom in Beethoven's later works. No longer could the viola section be thought of as " horn players who had lost their teeth ".

The " Pastoral " Sixth Symphony, the only one with more than four movements, recalls that the composer had a genuine love for the countryside. Most of his summers were spent in rural surroundings, at villages outside the city. Among fields and woods many of his greatest ideas came to him, scribbled into the famous notebooks. For all its bird-songs, thunderstorms, rippling brooks and rustic bands, models from which future " programmists " could learn, Beethoven did not intend a mere piece of programme music, saying very definitely, " More the expression of feeling than painting ". All the really significant material was treated with the usual symphonic logic.

The Seventh and Eighth, closely associated in time, represent another contrast in moods. Wagner's label for the gigantic Seventh—" the apotheosis of the dance "—suits well enough to describe the relentless and long-sustained rhythmic patterns of three of the movements. At a quieter level is the haunting second movement, an Allegretto in A minor, again one of the most famous pieces of music in existence. Some of the critics of the time had harsh things to say concerning the wild orgy of sound encountered in the finale. Such fury in terms of music was new to the art.

The Eighth brought a complete change of atmosphere; in the main, one of urbanity and polished wit. Many generations of concert-goers have chuckled over the conclusion of the first movement, where after a moment or two of pretended hesitation the opening phrase of the first subject suddenly reappears to bring about a perfect rounding-off :

In the second movement is heard, supposedly, the clack of Maelzel's primitive metronome. With the Minuet and Trio we are back in the eighteenth century again, but in a spirit of genial satire. The finale returns us to sudden surprises in the new manner, including the famous intrusive and explosive C sharp, and to a much extended coda. Beethoven called the Eighth his " little symphony ", but it is as great as any in merit. Thereafter for many years the composer's symphonic activities ceased.

The three " Rasoumovsky " string quartets of 1806 were naturally enough of the same intellectual temper as the mature symphonic works of the time. They have in fact been charged with being altogether too symphonic in style. A contemporary critic spoke of them as " very long and difficult . . . deep in thought and well worked out, but not generally comprehensible ". Even the urbane Schuppanzigh did not take to them at first, but they have long been, and still are, among the best-loved examples of string-quartet literature. The man who commissioned them was Count Rasoumovsky, the Russian Ambassador, long resident in Vienna and one of the Lichnowsky circle. The composer paid him the compliment of introducing " Russian airs " into Nos. 1 and 2. Rasoumovsky undoubtedly took part in performances of them, for, taught by Förster, he was an excellent amateur violinist.

In the " Harp " Quartet (the pizzicatos of the first movement account for the label) Beethoven returned to a truer string quartet style than is found in the more orchestral Op. 59. The slow movement is among his loveliest. He marked the last quartet of the decade, the F minor, as being " serious ", and justified the term with as grim and powerful a first movement as could be shaped in the medium.

Another fine chamber work of the period, the " Archduke " Piano Trio, reminds us that the person who received the great number of dedications from Beethoven was the Archduke Rudolph, youngest son of Leopold II and himself a polished pianist and all-round musician. He had for several years taken lessons in composition from Beethoven, and was a lifelong friend. Another dedication to him was that of the Piano Sonata, Op. 81a, and its subtitle a reference to his retirement from Vienna before the second French invasion and his subsequent return. Its near neighbour, the beautiful two-movement F sharp Sonata, was inscribed by the composer to the Countess Thérèse of Brunswick, a friend and former pupil; a noble woman indeed, and one whom he may well have hoped to marry.[3] The second-period sonatas affords wealth of artistic variety. In some the conventional four-movement plan was used; in others the composer's overall purpose was

achieved in two. Form and key schemes took on as new and original modifications as in the symphonies and quartets. Works like the mighty *Appassionata* called for a sonority that the pianofortes of the period were hardly
able to supply. Instrumental improvements however were coming fast.
Somewhat later (1818) Broadwoods of London sent Beethoven as a present
one of their latest products, of an advanced resonance.

After 1812, and lasting until 1817, came a period of comparative quies-
cence as far as composition was concerned. From 1812 onwards the composer grew more and more of a recluse as his deafness increased. In these
years his only significant works were the two 'Cello Sonatas (Op. 102—1815);
the cycle of six songs " To the Distant Beloved " (1816); a Piano Sonata
in E minor (Op. 90—1814) and another in A (Op. 101—1816). The flowing
E minor, in two movements only, is a " second period " work; the A major
far nearer the stature and style of the great " third period " examples.

The mention above of solo songs reminds us that although he wrote more
than seventy examples, song-writing was not an art to which he was much
attracted, or in which he excelled. The Italianate style is strong in many of
them (e.g. " Adelaide "), though in some of his later examples, particularly
in the " Distant Beloved " cycle, there are prophetic utterances which
caused Schumann to see his influence in the early *lieder* of Schubert.[4*]

To 1813 belonged that extraordinary composition " Wellington's Victory,
or " The Battle of Vittoria ", Beethoven's essay in popular programme music
which has been called " a piece of bombastic doggerel ". It was inscribed
fittingly enough to the Prince Regent, and was written in the first instance
for Johannes Maelzel, the inventor of the metronome, to be played by a
contraption of his called the " Panharmonicon ", a sort of mechanical wind-
band. The composer also scored it for concert orchestra, asking however for
four horns, six trumpets and three trombones, and in both forms it was a
considerable box-office draw. In 1813 it shared a programme with the first
hearing of the Seventh Symphony; in 1814 with the Eighth. That year
also saw another revival of *Fidelio,* further amended and with a new and
more appropriate overture. For several years following came the distractions
of a protracted lawsuit connected with the guardianship of his nephew
Karl. In 1820 Beethoven won his case against his brother's widow, but the
responsibility brought little else but all-round misery. In spite of his deep
affection for the lad he was entirely unsuitable as a foster-parent. Biographers
of late are showing more realisation as to what life with his eccentric
uncle must have been for Karl. In 1826 the unfortunate youth attempted
suicide, a shock for the composer that may well have hastened his end.
Karl in his mature years seems to have been a well-respected citizen.

The Third Period

In 1817 Beethoven braced himself once more for mighty tasks. The year
saw the first shapings of the gigantic Mass in D and the equally monumental Ninth Symphony. The following years, the so-called " third period ",
contained also the last piano sonatas and the final group of string-quartets.
As the evidence of the notebooks shows, his death prevented the fulfil-

ment of other projects. Listed below are the chief compositions of this final period :

The Piano Sonata in B flat—the so-called " Hammerclavier " (Op. 106 —1818); that in E (Op. 109—1820); that in A flat (Op. 110—1821); and the last, in C minor (Op. 111—1822) : the two great compositions mentioned above, the Mass in D and the Ninth Symphony (both taking several years for completion) : the Thirty-three Variations for Piano on a Waltz by Diabelli (Op. 120—1823) : thereafter between 1824 and his final illness, the last string-quartets—in E flat (Op. 127); in A minor (Op. 132); in B flat (Op. 130); the original extensive finale of this replaced by another movement, and detached and published separately as the *Grosse Fuge* (Op. 133); the C sharp minor (Op. 131); and the last, in F (Op. 135).

The composition of the " Hammerclavier " Sonata must have shared the composer's attention with work on the Symphony and the Mass, and like them, is of more than normal proportions and intricacy of thought. The slow movement is the longest found in the thirty-two. The finale is a kind of mingling of fugue and rondo form, the first of similarly original polyphonic movements used by Beethoven in his last works. The next two sonatas, though less in dimension, show the same logical and satisfying workmanship. The last, in C minor, is of only two movements, the first, one of storm and stress, the second closing peacefully as if in regions far remote. These final sonatas, written in a close-knit style of Beethoven's own, had no imitators. Piano composition was moving towards the romantic world of Chopin, Schumann and Liszt, whose sonorities depended much on the new techniques of the wide arpeggio and the sustaining pedal. It is worth noting that both early and late in his career Beethoven produced sets of short pieces, termed *Bagatelles*, which seem to represent brief mood-paintings, and thus anticipate the practice of Tomášek, Schumann, Mendelssohn and others, in their predilection for picturesque piano miniatures, often with fanciful titles.

The Mass in D (*Missa Solemnis*) was intended at first for use at the enthronement of Beethoven's benefactor Rudolph as Archbishop of Olomouc, in March 1820. Actually, the work was not completed until 1823, and by that time had grown to such gigantic proportions as to make its liturgical employment out of question. Only Bach's B minor Mass can be compared with it, and of the two Beethoven's possesses an overall unity absent from the older work. To use an oft-quoted phrase concerning it—" If you do not know the Mass you do not know Beethoven ". No quantity of words, and only a number of hearings can bring a full appreciation of its qualities.

The same comment applies to the Ninth Symphony. Like the Mass it was brooded over for years. Reshapings, rejections and rebuildings were characteristic of Beethoven's composition methods all his life. As the notebooks show, a theme, a melody, a sketch of a development section—fragments

large and small—suffered close scrutiny and frequent change until the
inevitable quintessence had been achieved. Though there was in Beethoven's
character a strain of vacillation which delayed important everyday-life
decisions, the uncertainties of the notebooks were due to his artistic scruples,
which in his greater works caused him to accept nothing less than what
he thought to be perfection. We have his own words for the processes.
". . . I change many things, discard others and try again and again until
I am satisfied; then in my head, I begin to elaborate the work in its breadth,
its narrowness, its height and its depth, and as I am aware of what I want
to do, the underlying idea never deserts me. It rises, it grows up, I hear and
see the image in front of me from every angle . . ." From this extract we
may gather in some small measure the reason for the impression of unity
which he created in his major works, whether the form employed is sonata,
variations, or that of his own original devising. Only Bach and Wagner
rival him in the invention of pregnant motives.

The first movement of the Ninth is a crowning example of such organic
growth. A foreshadowing of the powerful first subject is heard in the mysterious introduction. This theme rules the movement, not only at full
stature, but in the shape of its terminal fragment,

of which marvellous use is made. The daemonic movement which follows
is Beethoven's greatest Scherzo (although not so named). In it the timpani
make famous play, tuned to the octave interval. The slow movement reminds
us once more of his great gift of expressive melody (especially in the opening tune), and of his mastery of the variations form.

We come now to one of the most controversial pieces of music in history,
the finale in which the composer chose to add vocal forces to the orchestra
—soloists and chorus—whose task was to sing a setting of certain stanzas
from Schiller's " Ode to Joy ". This long and complicated movement, made
up of a number of sections each with its own tempo, cannot be dealt with
in detail here. Briefly we may say that, after a linking episode in which
instrumental recitatives prepare the use of a vocal one, the main themes
of the first three movements are briefly reviewed orchestrally and then
banished in favour of a new melody, one of the world's greatest tunes. This
is presented and expanded into variations by the orchestra, and eventually
proves to be the principal tune of the Ode, to be taken up and varied by
quartet and chorus in continual new combinations and even in the shape
of a double fugue. Interspersed are orchestral interludes, including a march
calling for the additions of bass drum, cymbals and triangle, the work concluding with a mighty *maestoso* choral passage.

In every generation there have been voices that have questioned the
artistic success of this finale, while others have expressed a positive dislike
for it. On the other hand, Wagner declared that from it his own works
had their derivation, Beethoven being his forerunner in the art of music

fertilised by poetry. The controversy still lingers, but one certainty is that the Ninth Symphony is a great and unique work. Its first performance took place in Vienna in May 1824, as the result of a petition to Beethoven for its production from a body of music-lovers in the city. It was warmly received, in spite of what seems to have been insufficient preparation. In connection with the occasion is told the moving story of the totally deaf composer being turned round to see the applause that he could not hear. Two days later came the unpleasant episode of his quarrel with some of his most devoted friends, his charge, totally baseless, being that he had been swindled out of some of the proceeds. Throughout his life Beethoven seemed never to understand that other people could have honest opinions in opposition to his. In his closing years his eccentricities of behaviour bordered close upon insanity.

After the Symphony he once more withdrew to the existence of a recluse, living in conditions of the utmost sordidness. In a remote world of his own he produced the last string-quartets, like no other music in spirit and in form. The works were viewed with considerable misgiving at the time, especially the *Grosse Fuge* movement, which was held to be unplayable. Opinions have changed with the generations; they now ' please ', as their creator had prophesied. He had long since ceased to write for a public, or to care for the voice of criticism.

Late in 1826 an injudicious coach journey in winter weather (concerned with Karl) brought him an attack of pneumonia. He never recovered his health. Devoted friends attended his bedside, messages and gifts arrived; the London Philharmonic, hearing of his illness, sent him £100. But a long-established cirrhosis of the liver proved fatal, and he died at the end of March 1827. A huge concourse of Viennese attended his funeral. One of the torch-bearers was a young composer, some of whose songs Beethoven had approved. His name was Franz Schubert.

The Beginnings of Romanticism

Beethoven, as we have seen, grew to maturity in an age of rapid social change. The French Revolution was but the most extreme manifestation of the general urge for liberation, which was concerned not only with social conditions but with all the arts as well. The so-called Romantic spirit in literature began to have a definite effect upon music, and that about the turn of the century. A romantic element is of course to be found in the music of every age. Josquin's *musica reservata* (see p. 97f.), the late Italian and English madrigal movements—all such orientations towards the future may deserve the term. It is only when this element becomes predominant, as was the case during the progress of the nineteenth century, that we can speak of a Romantic Age as beginning.

The following precise phrases regarding the word ' romantic ' are taken from the Oxford Dictionary :

imaginative, remote from experience, visionary.
(of music) subordinating form to theme, imaginative, passionate.

(of literary or artistic method etc.) preferring grandeur or picturesqueness or passion or irregular beauty to finish and proportion, subordinating whole to parts or form to matter . . .

Passionate emotions expressed in wholly individual fashion were manifest in the works of Beethoven, but these did not disturb the firm proportions of his musical architecture. Pondering the words quoted above ". . . subordinating form to theme . . . whole to parts . . ." we may well conclude that whatever emotional inspiration Beethoven's music may have given to the Romantic composers, whose works were " fertilised by poetry ", he cannot be counted among their number, in spite of all their attempts to claim him. Before considering these we must pause to speak of his greatest contemporary, who was more touched by the new spirit, but who, though a much younger man, survived him by only a year.

Franz Schubert (1797–1828), the youngest son of an ill-paid Viennese schoolmaster, grew up in a city that had experienced two harsh military occupations by the French, and after Napoleon's defeat, government by a reactionary and suspicious bureaucracy. Yet Vienna was still the musical metropolis of Europe. The aristocratic *Kapellen* which had played such an important part in the last century were gradually fading, the " Concerts of the Nobility " ceased after 1812, but the citizen classes, as we have already noted, were just as appreciative of the art, especially in its more homely and popular forms—the song, the part-song, piano and dance music, the domestic string-ensemble. In 1812 there was founded the " Society of the Friends of Music ", with a membership of four hundred, mostly of the stratum of more prosperous citizens, their object being to organise concerts among themselves. Innumerable were the family music-makings, and among these that of the Schubert circle. As a mere child Franz gained competence in violin, viola and keyboard playing from home and local teaching. In 1808 he won admission to the Imperial Choir, and, as a concomitant, to the Seminary (*Konvikt*), Vienna's most important boarding school. He stayed five years with the latter, receiving a musical and general education, together with valuable experience in the competent school orchestra, where he was soon the leading violinist and deputy conductor, and took part in the playing of such " advanced " works as Mozart's G minor Symphony and Beethoven's Second.

His boyish compositions, particularly the amazing *scena,* " Hagar's Lament ", earned him the privilege of lessons with no less a person than Salieri. There were overtures for the orchestra, piano pieces, numerous song-settings, mostly of Schiller, and before he left the school, a first Symphony. But the Age of Patronage was waning, and unlike Beethoven, he was not equipped for the career of virtuoso, although indeed a competent pianist. Thus in 1813, when his *Konvikt* days were over, there seemed only one profession open to him, a class-teacher's place in his father's school.

Yet it was already clear to him that the main purpose of his existence was to get down on paper the music that teemed incessantly in his brain. Except for Mozart no composer before or since has been gifted with such an apparently effortless ease, of the highest order. Yet in this matter too many false legends still exist. The enormous bulk of music achieved by him was as much due to his enormous industry as to his matchless facility. Contrary to popular belief he frequently sketched and re-sketched, wrote and revised, as surviving evidence proves. In 1815, in a period when he was occupied with class-teaching, he nevertheless accomplished six operatic scores, two symphonies, three piano sonatas and over a hundred and forty songs. Already in the previous year he had, unrealised by his contemporaries, made musical history by writing the first masterpiece of German romantic *Lieder,* " Gretchen at the Spinning Wheel ". He was destined to grope for several years yet before he gained a mastery of the instrumental forms, but his early achievements in song writing were something new to the art, and remain as one of its greatest miracles. His first boyish essays had shown the influence of men like the composer Zumsteeg (favoured by Goethe), a pioneer in his settings of the new German romantic poetry.[5*] *Gretchen am Spinnrade,* and many of the 1815 group, e.g. *Rastlose Liebe, Wanderers Nachlied,* and the dramatic ballad *Erlkönig* (all settings of Goethe), were already entirely individual and perfect, and are among his best loved. The romantic song was not a new phenomenon, but those that the young Schubert was writing were.

In 1816 he left his father's house. Thenceforward his life was spent mainly in lodgings, and always in near-penniless circumstances. The circle of friends devoted to him steadily grew. They were most of them young men of bohemian spirit and very little better off than himself—spare-time poets and writers such as Mayrhofer and Bauernfeld; von Schwind, a talented painter; von Schober, dilettante and man of the world, devoted to the composer but in some ways his evil angel. Schubert's existence was now one of incessant composition interspersed with social music-makings and the boon-companionship of Viennese café-life. Intermittently he made attempts to gain a permanent musical post, but always unsuccessfully, except for two summers as temporary music master to the family of one of the Esterhazys. He strove hard also for success as a writer of German operas (Salieri had at least trained him in the art of *opera buffa*), but only two of his dramatic works ever reached the stage. Even these were prompt failures, though they contained some of his loveliest music—mainly owing to their hopeless libretti, but also because Schubert lacked the true dramatic insight granted to many a lesser composer. Late in 1823 Vienna was charmed by his incidental music to " Rosamunde ", a worthless play by the eccentric Helmina von Chésy that quickly failed.

To return to the early days. Schubert's fame was beginning to spread to more influential circles. He was welcomed to the homes of well-to-do music lovers such as the Sonnleither family, both for his music and for his gift for improvising Viennese dances. Grillparzer, the famous dramatist, became an admirer, and even more important, Schober in 1817 introduced him to Vogl, the well-known opera singer, who recognised the quality of his songs and thereafter became an outstanding propagandist on his behalf. His friendship with von Gahy, a fine pianist, which began in 1817, gave him more insight into up-to-date keyboard music, and a fresh impetus to his production of piano sonatas.

There had begun the social meeting, known happily as the *Schubertiads,* when friends in increasing numbers gathered for evenings that were devoted in some measure to literary readings, but in the main to Schubert's compositions. We have been given more than one description of the modest but nevertheless dominating figure of the little man at the piano, accompanying Vogl in the singing of the songs that fascinated all hearers. Too much has been made of Schubert's gauchness, noticeable only when he mixed in formal society, which he did as little as possible. It contrasted with his cheerfulness, wit and ready conversation in the company of those congenial to him. Clearly, he had a remarkable gift for gaining devotion.

For all the *Schubertiads* and growing notice printings of his works were long delayed. The first publication by subscription of a score of his songs came as late as 1821, and only after the determined efforts of his circle (those of Spaun, a warm friend from the *Konvikt* days, in particular), and this out of the hundreds already in existence. One of these printings was the *Erlkönig* ballad, already widely known, thanks to Vogl.[6*] Thereafter publishers took a greater interest in him, though never much to his profit. Some items of his chamber and piano music, and even some church works, appeared in print in his lifetime. A not very distinguished set of variations for piano duet was dedicated to Beethoven (always their composer's chief hero), and was duly approved by the great man. Schubert had reached a chamber-music maturity in the " Trout " Quintet for piano and strings in 1819, but publishers passed it by, as they did the fine " Quartet Movement " of 1820. The latter is a masterpiece, an utterly original conception. Many orchestral pieces, e.g. a number of overtures and the charmingly melodious Fifth Symphony in B flat, had attracted favourable notices after public performances, but none of these was printed until long after the composer's death. Of his two symphonic masterpieces, the " Unfinished ", written in 1822 and remaining in the possession of one of his friends, lay unplayed and unknown, while the great C major Symphony of 1828 was tried, declared unplayable and forgotten. Songs were a different matter. 1823 saw a printing of a cycle of twenty fine songs, *Die Schöne Mullerin* (" The Fair Maid of the Mill "), the texts by a mediocre poet, Wilhelm Müller.

From 1824 onward production was maintained at what to a normal composer would be fever pitch. The torrent of masterly songs, which never abated, and the growing popularity of his keyboard and chamber music in citizen circles were bringing offers from publishers, usually shabby in amount. There were interludes, such as the walking tours with Vogl that spread his reputation. In many German cities favourable notices of his music, especially piano music, were appearing, but it was a quickly forgotten fame, to judge by the decades of neglect that his works were given after his death. Only in the last year of his life and under the urging of his friends did he venture on an *Akademie,* a successful concert of his own compositions—mostly songs (with Vogl singing them) and chamber music.

It won him 320 florins, which was temporary affluence, as he understood the word.

After 1822 his health had been undermined, for that year had been a fatal one for him. Round about that time he had been more than ever under the influence of the looseliving Schober, and had undoubtedly suffered a venereal infection that was never fully shaken off. Yet the last years saw many masterpieces—the finest piano sonatas; three great string quartets; the C major string quintet and a fantastic number of songs, including the *Winterreise* (" Winter Journey ") of twenty-four, the poems again by Müller. Then suddenly the end came. In November 1828, at his brother Ferdinand's home, his weakened body succumbed to an attack of typhoid fever. He was not yet thirty-two. His epitaph, by the dramatist Grillparzer, spoke of the art of music entombing " a rich possession but even fairer hopes "—which indicates how little realised, even by those who knew him best, were his actual achievements and real stature. A mass of his manuscripts came into the possession of Ferdinand, himself a minor composer, and through his efforts many more songs, together with piano and chamber music, secured publication. In 1829 there was printed the so-called *Schwanengesang* (" Swan Song ") group, which included settings of Heine and some of the composer's greatest songs. Schubert's supremacy as a song-writer had been recognised from the first, but in spite of the pioneer work of Schumann and Mendelssohn, and the first performance of the " Unfinished " in 1865 and its immediate and universal fame, it took most of the rest of the century to establish him as a master of every instrumental form, and one of the elect. The complete edition of his works, concluded in 1897, amounts to *forty* large volumes.

In the matter of the songs it was a case of the hour and the man. German romanticism of the late eighteenth century had produced an unparalleled outburst of lyric poetry, that of Geothe, Schiller, the brothers Schlegel and a host of lesser lights. Moreover, the pianoforte, the instrument of the small social circle to which the romantic *Lied* belonged, had now been perfected technically and was capable of illustrating and commenting in musical terms to a high degree of subtlety. The happy resolution of the age-old conflicting claims of poetry and music to be found in Schubert's songs was due to the composer's seemingly clairvoyant understanding of any text that he set, whether this was by a master or by one of his poetaster friends. His instinct for the most suitable musical form was almost always unerring. He knew when to employ the folk-song innocence of the single strophic melody repeated without change, as in *Haidenröslein*; when to modify such a pattern, as in *Du Bist die Ruh'*; when to " compose throughout " in response to the changing moods of the text, as in *Der Wanderer* (all these examples are taken from early songs); when to employ the *scena* with changes of tempo and main key and interspersed recitative, as in *Der Sänger*. He grasped with complete sympathy the meaning of a poem, its overall atmosphere and any picturesque details, and then illuminated it by its equivalent qualities in music, using the resources of striking harmony, of graphic figuration, of dramatic modulation in whatever proportions the situation demanded. In his finer songs he supplied not only an accompaniment but a revelation. The pictorial features of his accompaniments make a fascinating study. He possessed an inexhaustible store of devices with which to paint either the momentary thought or the whole atmosphere of a song. An early stroke of genius (at the age of seventeen) is the flying web of accompaniment which recalls the continuous hum of Gretchen's spinning wheel, and which breaks off suddenly at the most poignant moment of the singer's emotion, resuming as before only after a succession of falterings, as the lovelorn girl strives to regain control of herself. Often enough the composer chose wholly to disregard the individual details of a poem for the sake of the overall " affect ". Thus in *Versunken* the passionate swirl of the arpeggios is continuous, as is the murmur of the brook in *Wohin,* and the background storm in *Die jünge Nonne.* At other times the character of the accompaniment changes with each change of detail or mood in the poem, as in *Schafers Klagelied.*

Most dramatic of all Schubert's resources was his command of sudden and remote modulation. The two tremendous songs *An Schwager Kronos* and *Gruppe aus dem Tartarus,* together with *Der Atlas* and the subtle *Die jünge Nonne* already mentioned, contain stroke after stroke achieved by this means. In the last-mentioned the introductory " storm "-figure in F minor :

(which is in fact the germ of the whole song, melody and accompaniment), is almost immediately hurled directly into F sharp minor and then back again. The whole song abounds with such tonal adventures, as indeed do so many. Even that short and simplest of strophic songs *Jäger's Liebslied,* in D major, travels to F and B flat major.

In spite of the great part that the various devices of accompaniment play in the songs, they live also by the charm of their melodies. Schubert, as even the non-musician is aware, is one of the world's greatest melodists. Of these vocal lines P. H. Lang says : " (They are) such finished entities that they can be sung unaccompanied and will still give perfect aesthetic satisfaction. Only certain songs of Schumann and Brahms rise to such musical integrity . . ." (Op. cit., p. 781).

Whole books have been written on the subject of Schubert's songs. We must be content with one last reference—to *Der Doppelgänger,* in which,

exceptionally, the vocal setting is little more than a firmly rhythmic declamation. Heine's poem pictures a silent street at night, where a lover lingers
by the deserted house of his lost love. He sees another figure standing near,
seemingly torn by emotion, and in the moonlight recognises the ghostly
double of—himself! The poem is macabre enough, but Schubert reinforces
the atmosphere with the resources of his dramatic harmonies to a blood-
chilling pitch—bleak, hollow barrenness varied occasionally by agonised discords, the whole a piece of musical imagination which makes it one of the
greatest of all tragic songs.

Of the six hundred or more songs that he wrote only about one hundred
and eighty were in print in his lifetime. Only gradually did the world learn
of the remainder.

No adequate assessment of his instrumental music can be given in brief
space. Over all composers of the age loomed the mighty shadows of Haydn,
Mozart and Beethoven, and too many people were trying to write in imitation of those masters, especially of Beethoven. Yet in due course Schubert
escaped to become his own original self, and unknown to his generation
and even later ones, to achieve two last symphonies which can stand, without
fearing the comparison, with those of Beethoven. In the " Unfinished " and
the C major he produced felicities of orchestration (especially in his use of
woodwind, of horns and soft-toned trombones), rich harmonies and dramatic
modulations and an atmosphere of romantic beauty, which by an evil fate
remained unknown to the new generation of " romantic " composers, and
which they had to rediscover for themselves. He once asked : ' Who can do
anything more after Beethoven?' All unaware, he himself answered that
query with the ' Unfinished '. Two of his many " finger-prints " are his
subtle harmonic and modulatory use of the " Neapolitan sixth " (e.g.

—in A minor, stated baldly), and his love for the sudden swing from a minor
key to its tonic major, both devices found throughout his works.

Schubert was, to use Einstein's term, a classical romantic. In symphony,
sonata and chamber music work he continued to use the classical framework, not always, from the point of view of form, with complete success.
His greatest gift, that of spontaneous melody, sometimes led him to replace
a tense and logical working of his subject matter by charming but irrelevant
episodes, (' happy idlings '—to use Einstein's felicitous phrase). This is true
of many of the piano sonata movements, often of too great length and with
too much " adipose tissue ". It is otherwise in most of his latter and finer
works. No greater unity and terseness has ever been achieved than in the
first movement of the " Unfinished ", where drama and lyricism are ideally
combined. There is similar mastery to be found in the three last quartets,
A minor, D minor and G major, and in the three last piano sonatas. In a
freer style, in the " Wanderer " Fantasia for piano (named from the debt of
some of its material to the song) he foreshadowed the " cyclic " techniques of

Liszt and César Franck by using metamorphoses of the first-movement main subject as thematic matter for the later movements. It represented also an essay in the 'brilliant' type of keyboard writing being favoured by Weber, Thalberg and others of the new Romantic movement; too technically difficult, so the composer confessed, for himself to play satisfactorily. Apart from the score or more of piano sonatas he wrote an enormous quantity of keyboard music in lighter vein for 'success', i.e., with an eye to publishers and the amateur public, a great deal of it for four hands—dances of various kinds, marches, variations . . . Above all we must note the *Impromptus* and *Moments musicaux,* essays belonging to the romantic dawn. We have already seen an appearance of the keyboard " miniature " in Beethoven's *Bagatellen.* The type was continued in the poetic piano music of the Czech composers Tomášek and Worzischek, whose works may have served as models to Schubert.[7*]

Some Late-Classical Piano Composers

Mention has already been made of the admiration which the young Beethoven felt for the piano sonatas of his older contemporary, the cultured Musio Clementi (1752–1832). Clementi, trained in the tradition of Domenico Scarlatti and C. P. E. Bach, was influenced also by Schobert and J. C. Bach. Thanks to a patron he had tranquil years of early training in England, which became his adopted country, and his first concert triumphs were gained in London. He " contested " with Mozart in 1781 before the Emperor Joseph. The battle is supposed to have been drawn, but Mozart's own criticism was a hostile one. Nevertheless, the mature Clementi, by his finished playing, his keyboard compositions showing novelties of technique, and his skilled teaching of gifted pupils, laid the foundations of a true and distinctive pianoforte style. His hundred studies, the famous *Gradus ad Parnassum* (1817), his wholly classical concise and neatly written piano sonatas, and numerous short pieces which show touches of romantic promise—all these still live, if only for teaching use.[8*] Not so his many symphonies, which seem, however, very much to have impressed his contemporaries. He travelled widely as a virtuoso pianist and met Beethoven in Vienna in 1807. In London, where he settled permanently, he was not only a highly-paid teacher but also directed publishing and piano-manufacturing enterprises.

The German pianist and composer Johann Cramer (1771–1858), who also spent most of his settled life in London, studied under Clementi. He also met Beethoven, and gained approval for his playing, noted for its even cultivation of both hands, and for a musicianship not sacrificed to virtuosity. Of his many compositions it is only his piano studies which survive. Also surviving is his name in the publishing world.

Another remarkable Clementi pupil was the Irishman, John Field (1782–1837), who showed early promise both as virtuoso and composer. In 1802 he accompanied his master to Russia, where he settled for most of the rest of his life as a concert pianist and teacher, and where he died. His concertos and chamber music were much admired by his contemporaries, but he lives

20. "Allegoria dell 'udito" ("Allegory of the Sense of Hearing") by Jan Breughel (1569–1642) is a veritable museum of early seventeenth-century instruments. To the left are a chamber organ, a two-manual harpsichord, a drum, a trombone, viols of various sizes, a dancing-master's "kit" (a miniature violin), a cornett and a shawm. On the other side are several horns and a large harp. In the further room is a concert party—singers and instrumentalists—including a bass-viol player, a lutenist and a flautist

21. " Musical Pastime " by the Dutch painter Jan Molenar (d. 1668). The players are, respectively, handling a large lute and a cittern. The " hat stand " that the maid is trying to avoid disturbing is a bass-viol.

today by reason of his "Nocturnes", a piano type apparently of his own invention. In these the style, technique and very atmosphere of the Chopin nocturne—its flowing, gracefully embellished melodies, its pedal-sustained, widespread accompaniment figures—are foreshadowed in uncanny fashion. Field was closer to Chopin's age than he was to Clementi's.[9*]

Another player-composer linked with pre-Beethoven times was the Czech, Jan Dussek (1760–1812). He had clavier lessons with C. P. E. Bach, yet in his poetic playing (praised by Tomášek and Fétis) and virtuoso keyboard writing he looked forward at times, like Field, to a different age. It is remarkable how in certain passages of his music, admittedly music of no great permanent value, he has yet contrived to give prophetic glimpses of the technical 'finger-prints' of such composers as Schumann, Chopin and even, with a little stretch of imagination, Brahms. For a time he flourished in London, earning the praise of Haydn in 1792. For a time also he had as patron, pupil and friend, Prince Louis Ferdinand of Prussia, composer and admirer of Beethoven.[10*]

The Hungarian, Johann Hummel (1778–1837) was a major figure of his age. As a child he had a two-year training with Mozart himself, and afterwards toured with his father as a prodigy. In London he played at a Salomon concert, and was approved by Haydn, who actually wrote a sonata for him. Then for several years he studied with Clementi. Back in Vienna under Albrechtsberger for composition he had Beethoven as a fellow-pupil, and received some instruction from Haydn and Salieri. Thus equipped he launched into a career which varied between *Kapellmeister* posts and virtuoso tourings. In the art of extemporisation he was reckoned as Beethoven's chief rival. From 1819 until his death he was *Kapellmeister* at Weimar. His contemporary fame as a pianist rested on his enormous facility, but there is no doubt that he had a great influence as a teacher, building on the Clementi foundation and having more modern ideas regarding the techniques of fingering. His "Vienna school" produced such names as Hiller, Henselt and Thalberg. Czerny, who was with him for a while, found his playing a "revelation". The list of his compositions of every type is a formidable one, but very little of it has survived to modern times—a somewhat undeserved fate. Two of his chamber works still occasionally played are the Septet for piano, strings and wind, and the Op. 87 string quintet. His piano music undoubtedly influenced Chopin and Schumann. After much sonata writing in the classical manner he adopted a freer style, and, in particular, dazzled the young Schumann with his romantic Sonata in F sharp minor (1819).[11*]

The name of Carl Czerny (1791–1857) is a familiar one to most young pianists. A concert soloist at the age of nine, he impressed Beethoven to the extent of receiving many years' instruction from him and a lifelong friendship. He had also some teaching from Hummel and Clementi. In spite of his powers as a virtuoso (Beethoven chose him as soloist for the first performance of the "Emperor" Concerto) he strayed but seldom from Vienna, and early settled to a life of piano teaching—teaching of genius—and composition. His industry in the latter pursuit is terrifying to realise, his total of works

S

reaching the thousand mark, and including church music—everything, in fact, except operas. Among his many gifted pupils was "Nature's own pianist" Franz Liszt. As in Hummel's case, much fine music of his has been neglected and forgotten, but, in spite of gibes, the bulk of his technical studies will continue to survive. Liszt, in his old age, confessed to practising Czerny exercises for half an hour every day. What better testimonial could they have?

Opera—French, Italian and German

Some note has already been taken of the progress of French opera after Gluck, and the emergence of serious *opéra comique* (to use a paradoxical term) in such works as Grétry's *Richard Coeur de Lion,* the first of the "rescue" operas. With the coming of the Revolution, music became subservient to the State and its propaganda aims. Popular and gigantic choral performances of revolutionary songs in the open air with massed orchestras were the order of the day; matters of unprecedented noise and bombast. If the guillotine was busy so were the theatres, and the leading musicians of the time—Lesueur, Catel, Berton, Boïeldieu, besides those whom we have already noted, Grétry, Dalayrac, Méhul and Cherubini—found more than enough employment.

The "rescue" theme (as from the hands of aristocratic tyranny) was a favourite one for the opera composers of the Revolution. In those violent years a new type, the "horror" plot, supported by fantastic musical and stage effects, became popular, with Lesueur's *La Caverne* (1793) as the leading example. A remarkable feature of the Revolution and Imperial operas was the use made of the "recurring motive", a device of composition that we have already noted in Grétry's *Coeur de Lion* (see p. 231f.). Berton actually stated that in opera the Haydn art "of developing a motif and presenting it in all imaginable shades" should be employed. Wagner's *leit-motif* technique was being foreshadowed, however dimly. The best work of the period in Paris was being done by Cherubini, and by Méhul, whose *Joseph* (1807), founded on the Biblical story, was his masterpiece.[12*]

Luigi Cherubini (1760–1842), who was born and trained in Italy, spent most of his life in Paris. A learned classicist, a composer of every type of music and in due course head of the Conservatoire, he nevertheless was able to write successful operas for the French public and handle current types with a greater taste and mastery than most of his contemporaries. He commanded both intensity of feeling and superb craftsmanship, and exerted a considerable influence on the French opera of the time. His first outstanding work adapted to the French idiom, *Lodoiska* (1791), was an important event in the history of lyric opera. It was repeated 200 times and was surpassed only by his *Les deux journées*. The latter was a leading example of the "rescue" type, and *Médée* (1797—a shaping of the Greek legend) the best of the French "horrors". Cherubini's music was admired by leading European musicians, among them Beethoven, who used the same type of "rescue" libretto (derived from a French source) in *Fidelio,* and whose *Egmont* overture had an exemplar in the grim introduction to *Médée*.[13*]

Beethoven's heroic Leonora had counterparts in the several resolute women limned so vividly by the serious-minded Cherubini. In his later years he wrote much church music, some of which, particularly the two Requiems, Mendelssohn was glad to revive at Dusseldorf. He may perhaps be counted among those unlucky composers who in modern times have not received the quota of performances they deserve.

Cherubini's was too austere and independent a spirit to suit Napoleon. When the Emperor sought a composer-director of opera whose works would typify all the pageantry, the power and the glory of Imperial France he found him in the Italian, Gasparo Spontini (1774–1851). Neapolitan trained, Spontini had ventured on a French career and had fallen under the spell of Gluck. For his new style he chose historical themes which would yet hint at the triumphs of the existing régime. His stage works were shaped from a conglomeration of Gluckian dignity, features of Italian *opera seria* and the noise and sensationalism of French "horror" opera, all, be it admitted, of a high technical standard. The pomp and glitter, sound and fury of his sumptuously produced, sham-classical *La Vestale* (1803), followed by the even more strident *Fernand Cortez* (1809), laid the foundations of the pretentious French Grand Opera, whose high-priest in the mid-century was Meyerbeer. Thanks to Imperial support he was able to force his views and his stern discipline on his subordinates, and establish a stage pageantry and a high quality of performance which for a while overawed the rest of musical Europe.[14*]

The Italian *opera-buffa* export trade now produced a unique personality, Giaocchino Rossini (1792–1868). Trained at Bologna, and a child-composer for the stage, he was yet deeply versed in the music of Haydn and Mozart. He had outstanding gifts—an inexhaustible fount of sparkling melody, a thorough understanding of the art of singing, a mastery of colourful orchestration, and a sense of humour that was very vividly expressed in his music. His first success was actually in *opera seria*—*Il Tancredi* (Venice, 1813), but the several comic operas following established him as the leading composer in Italy at the age of twenty-one. In 1816 came the gloriously tuneful and satirical "Barber of Seville", probably the best-known comic opera in the world, and still frequently performed. Generations of concert-goers have become acquainted with the excerpt *Largo al factotum*. He continued to pour out opera after opera at an amazing speed, and these quickly found performances in every country in Europe.[15*] Few are heard nowadays, though of late there have been revivals of *La Cenerentola* (Cinderella) and the charming *Le Comte d'Ory*. Several of his attractively scored opera overtures have continued to hold a certain place in concert halls. He visited Vienna in 1822, at a time when there was a veritable Rossini furore everywhere. (He cashed in on this in England in 1823). At the Austrian capital he had several months of triumph, and even penetrated to Beethoven in his crabbed seclusion. The young Schubert flattered him by imitation, writing overtures " in the Italian manner ".

However, Paris was the Mecca of every opera composer of the time, and by 1824 Rossini was established there, favoured by the restored Bourbon government. His first post was that of director of the *Théâtre Italien,* where he produced some of his earlier operas and also introduced Meyerbeer to Paris for the first time (*Il Crociate*). Among the succession of his own French works which he produced was *Le Comte d'Ory* mentioned above. But his aim was not so much to continue with Italian *buffa* as to capture the very headquarters by writing French Grand Opera. In 1829 came his masterpiece, the grand opera " William Tell ", with a veritable symphonic poem for an overture. It influenced many of the great composers who followed, including Verdi, Wagner and Berlioz; also, at a lower level, Meyerbeer. It had an immediate success, but not the continued life that its composer had hoped for. Modern revivals of the work are handicapped by the fact that it is not easy nowadays to find a cast to face up to the high technical demands of the solo music. Incidentally, it should be noted that in Rossini we have once again a composer who, while catering for coloratura singing, yet disciplined his artists and *wrote out* all the *fioriture* that he intended to be sung in the body of an aria. Only slowly in his native land did the practices of individual display-vanity fade. It was after " William Tell " that Rossini made the " great renunciation ". Financially secure, during the remainder of his long life he wrote no other works for the theatre, unless, as some critics unkindly aver, we should include among them his *Stabat Mater* (1842). Except for this, a *Messe Solennelle* and some piano trifles the rest was silence. Perhaps the solution of the enigma was the emergence to Paris fame of Meyerbeer, whose pretentious pomposities Rossini disliked, and may not have wished to compete with. On the other hand, he had lived an over-full life, for which his health was now suffering. Whatever the explanation, he preferred indolence to further fame.

Meanwhile in the German operatic field the Italians were still very largely in command. Spontini at Paris had so impressed Berlin that he was offered princely terms in 1820 to direct opera there, and transferred his " imperial " works to the Prussian capital, astonishing it even more with his *Olympie* (1821). Vienna, Dresden and other large centres were also under Italian influence, to the detriment of all native composers who did not follow the prevailing fashion, while the impact of Rossini had everywhere been a resounding one. It took nearly the half-century to shake off the influence of foreign opera. But the zeal for a truly German art was kept alight, together with the desire to express it in terms of the new romanticism. With the example of the " Magic Flute " before them composers were writing *Singspiel* operas to German texts (many of these latter very bad ones), using native legends, fairy tales and fantasies, but with nothing particularly German or romantic in their music. Some moves in that direction were made by the writer-composer E. T. Hoffmann in his " magical opera " *Undine,* produced in Berlin in 1816. More important contributions came from Ludwig Spohr (1784–1859). Spohr, an all-round musician, was a figure of European importance in his day, a virtuoso violinist, a conductor and a most successful composer. His once popular symphonies and chamber music seem nowadays to be a curious and not always satisfactory mixture of the classical and romantic, written in a characteristically chromatic style, which over long stretches tends to pall.[16*] He made several visits to England, where his oratorios were particularly admired. Indeed, his " Last Judgement " is still not wholly moribund. He made two important contributions to opera in his *Faust* (1816), a *Singspiel* with a romantically novel " Witches' Dance ", and in *Jessonda* (1823). Both had romantic subjects, but in *Jessonda* his chromatic harmony (here well-managed), skilful and colourful orchestration, use of the recurrent motive and frequent " running on " of the musical scenes pointed the way to the true German romantic type.[17*]

The goal was fairly reached by Carl Maria von Weber (1786–1826), a cousin of Mozart's Constanze. Taught by Michael Haydn and the Abbé Vogler, and with great natural gifts, he had a somewhat dilettante existence for a number of years, as musician and opera-director at various princely courts; as virtuoso pianist and composer of concertos, symphonies and chamber music; even as writer and critic. Not a great deal of his romantically-inclined symphonic keyboard and chamber music has survived in the concert hall, but his impact on opera was vital. There were some early stageworks in a mixture of styles and of limited success before the arrival of his masterpiece, *Der Freischütz*. Given in 1821 at Berlin, to audiences which not long before had applauded Spontini's *Olympie,* it began a new chapter in the history of opera. Romantic emotions, especially German romantic emotions, were evoked as never before. All the ingredients that would be welcomed by a native audience were there—German village and deep mysterious forest, huntsmen's chorus, peasant dance and song, a shooting-match with the heroine as prize, magic bullets and a " Wolf's Glen " where lurked the Devil himself. To the story Weber brought his own magic—the haunting music of the horns, a truly symphonic orchestra that suggested atmospheres in vivid and colourful fashion, subtle uses of the recurrent motive, the association of characters with certain instruments—all tending to make the stage action really live and breathe. The opera was an immediate success, and holds the stage even today; the sinister " Wolf Glen " music can still chill our blood. Yet *Der Freischütz* is in point of form a *Singspiel,* for it contains a certain amount of spoken dialogue; in it also were debts owed to the French " horror " type. In his next stage work, *Euryanthe* (1823), Weber set out to establish German romantic grand opera. His collaborator was the alleged poetess Helmina von Chézy, of *Rosamunde* notoriety, and between the pair of them the libretto, a story of medieval chivalry, became such a farrago as to prevent the work having any permanent hold. However, it contains much fine music, the scenes " composed throughout " without spoken dialogue, and with an ever more evocative use of motives, finely dramatic recitative and a richly symphonic background. Technically, it was preparing the way for Wagner, but its dramatic faults were too manifold for its own survival.[18*] Weber's growing fame attracted an invitation from London to produce an opera at Covent Garden. Another " romantic " libretto (by a certain James Planché) was prepared for him, of the *Singspiel* type with spoken dialogue, and into *Oberon* he poured some of his loveliest music, full of picturesque strokes of genius. The overture, with its magic horn call, and its quite novel touches of orchestral colour is immortal. He was already far stricken with tuberculosis when he arrived in London in 1826, and died soon after the opera was launched. In all his greater operas Weber's background music was so striking and atmospherically successful that we can see in it the beginnings of the German tendency, later so manifest, of transferring the main interest away from the singer to the symphonic orchestra. With him a new art, the colourful and imaginative orchestration of the Romantic Age, began. It had begun also with Schubert, but that fact was not to be realised for many a year.

The Progress of Violin Technique

The later decades of the eighteenth century saw improvements in violin technique and method which paralleled those being made on the keyboard. The founder of the so-called Paris Classical School was Giovanni Viotti (1753–1824), trained in the traditions of Corelli, who spent much of his life in England and whose followers and admirers, P. Rode, R. Kreutzer and P. Baillot aided the establishment of a solid and modern style of virtuoso playing. Their more ambitious compositions are now neglected, but they all left valuable technical works. The "Forty Studies" of Kreutzer are still part of the everyday fare of the young violin student. Spohr's long career as a solo violinist also made its mark. All these, fine virtuosi and innovators as they were, were overshadowed by the sudden rise to European fame in the late '20's of a strange and unique figure, Niccolo Paganini (1782–1840). This Italian violinist, by dint of a natural genius independent of any "school" and years of concentrated practice, developed effects hitherto undreamed of— a superhuman facility in all of legato, staccato and pizzicato playing, the use of stopped harmonics by which he extended the accepted range of the instrument, glissandos, interspersed left-hand pizzicatos, together with tricks of showmanship on a lower level. He even revived the *scordatura* device of altered string-tunings which we have already noted in connection with the seventeenth century violinist Heinrich Biber. His concert repertoire was confined to his own compositions, these planned to display the infinite variety of his transcendent technique, in which improvisation seems to have played an important part. Thus equipped, he proceeded as a travelling virtuoso to astound and conquer musical Europe. Much of his music has proved ephemeral, but his Concerto in D (built on a quite classical framework) is still played. Of greater import are the Twenty-four Caprices for solo violin, which, for all their enormous difficulties, are of sound musical interest, and which fascinated such great composers as Schumann, Liszt and Brahms. Liszt, on the keyboard, was spurred to similar technical feats in his *Études d'exécution transcendante d'après Paganini* (1838) in which five of the Caprices were used as the bases for transcriptions of a technical difficulty never before approached. Schumann's two sets of studies founded on the Caprices, interesting and difficult enough, are somewhat milder in their demands.[19*] Brahms' two sets of fine variations are also for the piano. In more modern times (1934) Rachmaninov wrote a *Rhapsody* for piano and orchestra which is in fact a set of twenty-four variations on the last of the Caprices, indeed a beautiful work.

Paganini set a new and swollen standard of financial reward for the efforts of the " display " virtuoso. His concert earnings were fabulous, especially during his visit to England in 1831–2, when he netted something over £16,000. In some circles a sour view was taken of this, to judge from a London jingle popular at the time :

> " Who are these who pay five guineas,
>   To hear this tune of Paganini's?
>   —Echo answers—' Pack o' ninnies '."

Contemporary with him were a number of piano virtuosi—Thalberg, Herz and their like—who also reaped rich rewards for glittering displays of their less worthy music, but who were eclipsed by the coming of those composer-performers of genius, Chopin and Liszt.

NOTES

As in the cases of Haydn and Mozart, recordings of all the important works of Beethoven (and many of the lesser ones) are available from one or another of the leading gramophone companies. For this reason HMS VIII, while catering for some lesser composers of the period, gives no recording of anything of his. These remarks apply also to his younger contemporary, Schubert, except for one single example.

1   It has long been held that the decay of Beethoven's aural nerves was due to the inroads of syphilis, but some of the latest medical opinions are against this view.

2* Prince Louis, whom Beethoven himself allowed to be " a thorough, solid pianist ", studied with the Czech composer Dussek, and devoted most of his energies as a composer to chamber music with piano, music which charmed the young Schumann, full as it is of early romanticism. His best work is the Piano Quartet in F minor, of which HMS VIII records the first movement.

3   Was Thérèse the " Immortal Beloved " of Beethoven's famous and baffling love-letter? Other names well-known to biographers have also been speculated upon. However, the evidence recently offered (1954) by Dr. Siegmund Kaznelson points to a less familiar one, that of Josephine, Countess Stackelberg, sister of Thérèse. According to Dr. Kaznelson, Josephine in 1813 gave birth to a daughter, Minona, of whom Beethoven was the father.

4* The song-cycle An die ferne Geliebte (" To the Distant Beloved ") is remarkable for the novelty of the linking of the six numbers by piano interludes of varying length. There is a recording of the cycle on (HMV) ALP 1066.

5* The influence of Zumsteeg on the boy Schubert's first song-essays is well illustrated by the comparison afforded in HMS VIII of their respective settings of the poem Nachtgesang.

6* Zumsteeg was also the pioneer of the narrative " ballad ", with keyboard accompaniment, followed up by Schubert in his setting of Goethe's Erlkönig, and by Carl Loewe, who wrote a number of highly dramatic examples, including an Erlkönig (which Wagner preferred above Schubert's setting) and the blood-chilling Edward, the text a translation of the Scottish ballad of that name. HMS VIII has a recording of a fine rendering of this.

7* Regarding Vaclav Tomášek (1774–1850), HMS VIII has a recording of one of his poetic piano miniatures, an *Eclogue in A flat* (1813). He produced a number of sets of *Eclogues,* as well as *Rhapsodies* and *Dithyrambs.* His attempts " to transplant the various types of poem into the realm of music " make him a true pioneer of Romanticism.

8* HMS VIII has a recording of a Largo and Allegro from Clementi's Sonata in B minor, Op. 40, No. 2, and one of a short and lyrical dance movement, *Monferrina.*

9* HMS VIII has a recording of the first movement of Field's Divertissement No. 2 in A, for piano and string quartet (1818), rearranged and re-published some years later as Nocturne in A for piano solo.

10* HMS VIII has a recording of the slow movement of Dussek's piano sonata in F minor, Op. 77 (1810–11).

11* HMS VIII has a recording of the first movement of Hummel's F sharp minor sonata mentioned in the text. The figuration was clearly a model for some of the features of the young Schumann's piano music.

12* HMS VIII has a recording of an ensemble from Act I of Méhul's *Joseph.*

13* HMS VIII has a recording of a duet from Act I of Cherubini's *Les deux journées.*

14* HMS VIII has a recording of a recitative and aria from Act II of Spontini's *La Vestale.*

15* HMS VIII has a recording of an excerpt from Act III of Rossini's *opera seria, Otello,* written in the same year as the " Barber " (1816) but nowadays neglected, in spite of its containing much beautiful music. The portion given includes Desdemona's " Willow Song " and her brief " Prayer ".

16* HMS VIII has a recording of the introduction and first movement (Adagio & Allegro) from Spohr's attractive Octet, Op. 32 (1814).

17* HMS VIII has a recording of an excerpt from the Finale of Act I of Spohr's opera, *Jessonda.*

18* HMS VIII has a recording of the scena and aria which begins Act II of Weber's grand opera *Euryanthe.*

19* HMS IX has a recording of No. 6 of Paganini's Twenty-four Caprices for solo violin, together with Schumann's *Étude de Concert, Op. 10, No. 2* (1833), and Liszt's *Grande Étude de Paganini, No. 1* (1851), both piano pieces founded on the Paganini original. Liszt's set of *Grandes Études,* though of great technical difficulty, actually represent a modification of the " transcendent " demands of the 1838 versions mentioned in the text.

CHAPTER XI

The Romantic Period I

SOME note has already been taken of the new romantic spirit which found some stirrings in the music of Beethoven, and more particularly in the songs of Schubert and in the operas of Weber and others. There has also been attempted a brief definition of the new ideals which towards the end of the eighteenth century began to permeate certain European societies, particularly those of Germany, France and Britain, influencing many aspects of human thought—politics, philosophy and the arts. In literature, the earliest art to be so tinged, there appeared in Germany great names in poetry, drama and novel-writing—Goethe, Schiller, Tieck, the brothers Schlegel and " Novalis " (von Hardenberg) among them. The poet-novelist-musician E. T. A. Hoffmann (1776–1822) had some influence on his contemporary fellow-musicians. Britain played its own great part in the new literary movements, but the names in the period that seemed most to influence the Continentals (at least, the musicians) were those of Walter Scott and Byron. There was also a revived interest in Shakespeare. The French literary romantics—Lamartine, Victor Hugo, Vigny, Deschampes, to name but a few —were somewhat later in the field. Music was the last of the arts obviously to respond to the new spirit (being romantic in its very nature even in a classical age), but under the influence of the others it did so most completely.

A fundamental change from tradition can be seen in the professional outlook of the romantic composer. Musicians through the ages, from the jongleur in his guild to Haydn at Esterhaza, had held normally a somewhat lowly place in the social order. Usually of humble origin and frequently the sons of musicians, they worked under authority, being employed by the Church, or by princes, or patricians or even municipalities. They wrote to meet current needs and often to order, and were well enough satisfied so to do. Not for them art for art's sake. There were no misunderstood geniuses among them, composing for future comprehension in more enlightened ages. The truly exceptional and mighty free-lance of the mid-eighteenth century, the self-employed Handel, lived dangerously and found his final salvation only through the first appearance of a middle-class audience (for oratorio)

in an England that was at the time more advanced socially than the rest of
Europe. With the turn of the century the era of the free musician began to
dawn, but not soon enough to save Mozart from his bitter hardships.
Beethoven released himself from the bonds of the Age of Patronage, and
recognised the existence of a citizen public in the concert-hall. Ultimately,
he turned his back even on them, writing for himself alone, and in his last
quartets very definitely for the future. Yet even after 1800 there was still
plenty of employment for leading musicians in the *Kapellmeister* type of
post. This was more frequently a matter of the conductorship of a state
opera theatre than the older kind under direct and daily orders.

Weber, Schumann, Mendelssohn, Liszt and Wagner all held such positions for a while, under either princely or municipal control, but generally
speaking the leading creative romantic musicians, who came from higher
social strata than formerly, endeavoured to avoid such ties as far as they
were able, and to live by the production of their works. Many of them
could supplement these earnings by other free activities, not only as virtuosi
and conductors but also as *littérateurs*. Composers of the calibre of Spohr,
Schumann, Mendelssohn, Berlioz, Liszt and Wagner were, in the broadness
of their literary culture, independent-minded, able to express their opinions
in writing with force and distinction, and to demand treatment not as in
former times—as craftsmen carrying out the requirements of particular
employers—but as free agents, artists, tone-poets, uttering without inhibition
their inspired messages for mankind. Certain of them began to take on the
pretensions of prophets, with Richard Wagner as the most verbose and
egotistical example.

The task of finding definitions as to the basic principles and aims of the
musical romantics as conceived by such diverse personalities as, say,
Schumann, Berlioz, Liszt and Wagner is not an easy one. A burning desire
for " independence " was a common emotion. Their idol, Beethoven, had
set an example in achieving artistic liberty, and, musically, they wished
to be freed from the classical formality of the past age. Many believed
(mistakenly, as we have seen) that Beethoven had "broken the bonds of
form ", that he had revealed through his Ninth Symphony finale that
absolute music was not enough, that even the instrumental forms must call
poetry, in various ways, to their aid, and that in his symphonies and
sonatas (the "Pastoral" Symphony and the "Les Adieux" sonata would
in particular bear witness) there were hidden meanings and veiled programmes, to be revealed if only the keys could be recovered. In the *Eroica*
(as previously mentioned) Berlioz was convinced that he had found one.
Mendelssohn, in many ways the exception that proved the rule, was less
sure than most that the classical pattern of sonata form was done with, and
in his "Scotch" and "Italian" symphonies achieved impeccable architecture and, without labouring exoteric meanings, a truly poetic musical
content. Schumann followed very much the same path in his symphonies
with less satisfactory results, but the more fervent spirits (Berlioz and Liszt
the chief representatives) were moved to shape a purely instrumental work
in accordance with an admitted literary programme—dramatic emotions

or even events suggested in terms of music. They felt that the artist, moving directly from "feeling" to "expression", must not be hampered by any outmoded rules. While Berlioz, whose bizarre emotionalism usually derived from some declared literary source, succeeded at times in retaining the older symphonic framework in his works in recognisable fashion, he also used the method of the *idée fixe,* as depicting the chief personality of the instrumental drama that he was unfolding. Actually, this was a long realised resource, but was employed by him in a particularly striking fashion. The technique was further expanded by Liszt in his "transformation of themes" device, and the later Wagner in his (subtlest of all) *leitmotiv* development. Liszt, more revolutionary than Berlioz, produced new and more loosely constructed types of symphony and sonata, and highly skilled methods of presenting dramatic studies in his symphonic poems. Side by side with this latter and widely imitated new genre the more formally organised symphony lived on, at times somewhat revised, even distorted, in shape, but in the hands of men like Brahms, Bruckner, Dvorak and Mahler, achieving masterly syntheses of old and new. Hardly a new form but an interesting romantic development was that of the concert overture, again the product of the demand for a "literary picture". The overture as a prelude to a stage work has already concerned us from time to time. In the better examples of the late eighteenth and early nineteenth century overtures, not only the moods but the very essence of the drama to follow was captured, as in Cherubini's *Médée,* and Beethoven's *Egmont* and *Coriolan.* It was but a short step for the Romantics to substitute for a following drama the hinted programme of a story or experience. As items for the concert hall came such "overtures" as *King Lear* (Berlioz) and *Fingal's Cave* (Mendelssohn)—and a thousand more during the century. It will be recalled that many other romantic works of the same type, equally colourful, rounded in form and satisfactory in isolation, were nevertheless conceived in the first place to serve the original purpose. Mendelssohn can again supply an example in the immortal Overture to *A Midsummer Night's Dream.*

The normal outlook of the pre-1800 composer had been that his works must be comprehensible and acceptable to those who performed and listened to them. It is true that in the course of musical history there were original minds that had occasionally forged ahead (but not too far ahead) of the tastes of their times. We may recall the instances of some of the works of Monteverdi and Gluck, and Mozart's *Nozze di Figaro* ("Too tough meat for my Viennese . . ."). But on the whole, up to the end of the eighteenth century the composer wrote for immediate appreciation and reward. An opera was normally the result of an order, a symphony was written for a planned and forthcoming concert. Neither might survive the passing of the particular occasion. However, in the new era, and after Beethoven, "originality" of one sort or another became the fashion, and there was a great deal of writing *against* the age, rather than for it. A new purpose was to be seen in the printing of compositions. Formerly, the normal practice was that such a printing would take place only when there was likely to be a demand for it as the result of practical success. In the nineteenth century (and after) it would often be intended as a publicity device—to make known a composition the appeal of which might not be immediate. The later Beethoven's " take it or leave it " attitude was assumed by many a romantic composer, who was quite ready to be misunderstood by the majority of his listeners. It was a romantic gesture, anyway, to scorn the Philistine; as ever, there were " angry young men ". This isolation of the romantic artist, expressed so picturesquely in the journalism of Robert Schumann, had its dangers. If an earnest-minded and original composer did not succeed in soon convincing society as to the significance of his works he found himself, naturally enough, in a position of economic peril. This was certainly so in the cases of two of the leading figures of the time, Berlioz and Wagner, each of whom wasted long periods which might otherwise have been devoted to composition in counter-measures to the hostile opinions which threatened his very continuance as a creator. Many other leading composers also were perforce professional writers as well—both as a further means of livelihood and for the sake of their various causes and campaigns. All this was again in contrast to the practices of past centuries. Writers on music there had always been in plenty, as exemplified by such names as Anaxagoras, Guido d'Arezzo, Zarlino, Marcello, Morley, Couperin and C. P. E. Bach, but these in the main confined themselves to addressing their fellow-professionals on matters technical. The new composer-writers, with a considerable and interested middle-class public to appeal to, wrote not only from general aesthetic viewpoints, but took their share in a fast-growing professional activity, that of music-critic. Schumann, for one, did a great deal in setting a better example to the short-sighted pedantry and venal praise which frequently enough passed in Germany for criticisms of current music. Berlioz, the *enfant terrible* of musical Paris in the late '20's and the '30's, left published collections of his voluminous critical writings.

Another common feature in the music of the romantics was a far greater interest in sound (*per se*) than heretofore, and this as an aid to emotional and pictorial effect. To take a somewhat extreme illustration—in the art of J. S. Bach the marvellous content is clearly of far more importance, normally, than the nature and quality of the medium through which it is expressed. On the other hand, in Berlioz' works (largely orchestral or orchestra-accompanied) the instrumental colour is its very life-blood. Berlioz seemed to think most effectively in terms of orchestral sound, and even admitted that on occasion he aimed at a novel orchestral colour-effect first, and then set about finding the content to exploit it afterwards. We must remember always with admiration the pioneer originalities and the effectiveness of Haydn and Mozart in this art, and the innovations of Beethoven, but even so, there was a certain formality in the lay-out and employment of the classical orchestra that was due for change. Even in Beethoven's lifetime Schubert and Weber were obtaining colour effects never before dreamed of. The horn, the romantic instrument *par excellence,* came into its own in their hands as an instrument of pure poetry. Particularly haunting is the use made of it by the later masters, e.g. Mendelssohn and Brahms.

The early romantics chose largely to disregard the newly-invented valve-horn, which gave a completely chromatic range, and where necessary repaired the deficiencies of the natural scale by employing instruments crooked in several keys, being reluctant to lose the undoubtedly better tone which the natural horn gave. There was a similar tendency, and similar last-ditch tactics, in regard to the trumpet, but increasingly chromatic harmony was demanding an all-chromatic brass, and gradually valves won the day. Berlioz and Liszt began to give horn and trumpet prominent melody parts which did not always keep to the traditional austerities of the classical instruments. Wagner exploited their possibilities further, including the quiet and poetic use of chromatic harmony by the horns and the massed might of the whole chromatic brass choir. Another notable invention (perfected in 1810) was that of the Erard double-action harp, which gave another chromatic instrument and a rich colour-resource to the orchestra. Many innovations in the technique of instrumentation are to be found in the works of Berlioz, and these were quickly taken up by other masters. In due course attention will be called to some of them. In the new century orchestras tended to increase in size, since large public concert-halls were becoming the order of the day, for which the modest salon orchestras of Haydn and Mozart no longer sufficed. Yet it should be noted that the enormous " Ring " orchestra of the later Wagner came into being not primarily to obtain an overwhelming volume of sound, but rather to provide that resourceful composer with a palette of every known variety of colour. Even Berlioz, whose overheated imagination so often demanded huge choral and orchestral forces, a practice inherited from the Revolution period, and who was but the first of a number of romantic composers with a taste for the gargantuan and an airy disregard of its cost, achieved many of his most novel colour-effects with but modest means. In the first part of the century the techniques of scoring for orchestra had advanced to such an extent that it was now possible to assemble a lengthy text-book on the art, which was what Berlioz did in his *Traité d'Instrumentation* (1844). It can still be read with profit.

The development of new colour effects went hand in hand, as an emotional and pictorial resource, with a rapid expansion of the harmonic vocabulary. In this latter all the romantic composers, each in his own way, played a part, notably the two revolutionaries, Liszt and Wagner, and that great and original composer Chopin, from whom Liszt himself undoubtedly learned much. In his mature works Wagner carried the chromatic resources of major-minor tonality almost to their limits.

The name of Berlioz has loomed so large in this discussion of romantic sound that it may be fitting at this point to consider his career.

Hector Berlioz (1803–69), the greatest of the French musical romantics, was born near Grenoble in·S. France, the son of a physician of some standing. Like many another composer of his time he received a sound general education and learned enough Latin to have a lifelong passion for its literature. In spite of an early attraction to music, the only instruments he attempted to master were flageolet, flute and guitar, and these, appar-

ently, in little more than amateur fashion. He was never a pianist. Sent
as a young man to Paris to study medicine he met for the first time a brilliant
cultural life—drama, the Opera and orchestral concerts—which set even
more strongly aflame an already vivid imagination. Gluck, Beethoven and
Weber became his idols. As a lad he had acquired some theoretical knowledge of music and had attempted composition; in spite of parental objection he now determined to make this his career. In 1823 Lesueur, one of
the " Revolution " opera-composers and a professor at the Conservatoire, was
sufficiently impressed as to accept him as a pupil. For a while he saved himself from penury by teaching singing, flute and guitar, and himself singing in theatre choruses, while filling every spare moment with composition
and his own private study. During these years he gradually achieved his
unique command of the art of orchestration, not so much from instruction
as through score-reading, practical observation and (perhaps the greatest
factor) his own innate and sensitive genius in this respect. He himself said
that he had studied " the best modern masters of the art—Beethoven,
Weber and Spontini ". If the inclusion of the last-named should cause
surprise it must be recalled that Spontini's quite efficient music was far better
known in the Paris of that day than was Beethoven's.

Some of Berlioz' creative efforts in these years were aimed at winning the
Prix de Rome, the Paris Conservatoire's travelling scholarship in composition. After several abortive attempts he succeeded in 1830, but he seems
to have gained more stimulus from his wanderings in the Italian countryside
than from his stay at the Villa Medici, and long before the time was out
obtained permission to return to Paris. Even previous to his journey orchestral compositions of his had attracted performance and some notice—the
Francs Juges and *Waverley* overtures among them. (He was beginning to
appreciate Walter Scott.) But above all others the work of the period was
the *Symphonie Fantastique,* to which title the composer added parenthetic-
ally " Episode in the Life of an Artist ". It represented a sudden and highly
original flash of genius.[1*]

We have already noted from time to time examples of instrumental programme-music frankly intended as such, e.g. the *Nomos Pythikos* of Sakados
of Argos as the earliest known; the " Bible Sonatas " of Kuhnau; the
" Wellington's Victory " overture of Beethoven . . . Other instances will
be recalled readily enough, but the practice was only occasional, and usually
(to us at least) not very convincing. But to Berlioz music meant nothing
apart from literary ideas. Sounds were for the purpose of expressing these
ideas. Certainly he vivified a great deal of poetry in the normal way in his
various vocal settings (usually orchestrally accompanied) and in his three
operas, but his usual reaction to the reading of a poem, drama or story was
to relive his experiences in terms of orchestral sounds, coloured in his own
vivid and original way the better to make his meanings clear. Strictly
speaking, music can *depict* nothing; it can only suggest. A listener asked
to guess the " meaning " of a programmatic instrumental passage, and
lacking any kind of verbal clue, may well be very wide of the composer's
mark. Actually, a number of examples of Berlioz' pictorialisms can be shown

to have been taken from earlier works, where they seem to have meant something else. However, we must give him the credit for being the pioneer of an age of instrumental programme-music, when compositions were consistently written under some outside, non-musical influence, needing some explanation in terms other than sound for their full appreciation. In this practice he showed certain restraints, as will be seen, but later composers were to carry the idea to more extravagant lengths. That he realised the limitations of musical painting and the difference between feeling and the factual seems clear from the techniques used in his " dramatic symphony ", *Roméo et Juliette.* He decided that the quarrels of the rival families and the passionate emotions of the " Love Scene " could be expressed most fully and artistically by the colourful orchestra alone, but detailed expositions of happenings were left to soloists and a chorus. It was a strange and original essay in programme-symphony form, one which tried still to retain the old four-movement framework—which was an error on Berlioz' part. Liszt, in his later " Faust " and " Dante " symphonies, was more wary.

But to return to the 1829 *Symphonie Fantastique.* The " rejected lover " of its programme was Berlioz himself. In 1827 he had fallen violently in love with the Irish actress Harriet Smithson, whom he had seen with Kemble's company in Paris as " Ophelia " and " Juliet ". He listened to slander; hence the last movement of the Symphony in which his beloved is depicted as one of a foul and broomsticked company at a Witches' Sabbath. It might have been better for both of them if they had not met again, but there were second thoughts in 1833. The marriage brought but little happiness to either, and by 1842 they had parted. We may, however, associate Harriet with Berlioz' discovery and lifelong passion for Shakespeare, which afterwards inspired in him an overture, a symphony and an opera.

To appreciate what the composer of this new style *Symphonie Fantastique* had in mind, one must, according to his own statements, think of the five movements as being a series of opium-poisoned visions of a despairing lover who has attempted suicide. (We are truly in the Romantic Age!) Let us call them " scenes ", and note that in each of them there appears a melody, the *idée fixe,* a linking device, (a " leit melody " rather than a *leit motif*), which represents the " beloved " who has rejected him. It occurs in the first Allegro as the main subject, after the quite traditional employment of a slow introduction. The composer heads the movement with the words— *Reveries, Passions,* and though proceeding to depict the fluctuating and at times supercharged emotions of the lover, yet shows his respect for Beethoven by using a construction which imitates to some degree the traditional symphonic sonata-form. Later, he was to realise what an impossible problem the recapitulation presented to the composer of programme symphonies.

Here is the *idée fixe* as first stated, a forty-bar flute melody:

Ex:56

It is in some ways a typical example of the long-drawn-out tunes which Berlioz frequently used, called "sprawling" by his detractors. There are still critics ready to declare that attractive melody was not among Berlioz' major gifts. How alluring a picture of the lady this particular one brings to the listener must be a matter for individual opinion, but a curious fact is that the theme was a self-borrowing from an earlier work. Indeed, a great deal of the rest of the symphony has been shown to be a reshaping of material from abandoned previous compositions, but this was achieved with such skill and satisfactory result that the matter need not trouble us. It serves to show, however, on what shifting sands we base our interpretations of programme music.

The second scene, *Un Bal,* a graceful waltz movement, is coloured particularly by Berlioz' striking use of two harp-parts, chromatically written, as the new Erard instrument allowed. We note that the composer demanded two harps for each part, a typical Berlioz refinement, since softer passages were marked *Solo.* When his beloved appears, as she does twice, the *idée* merely conforms to the immediate rhythm, without any significant metamorphosis. This applies also to the appearances of the theme in the next two movements.

The central Adagio, a pastoral, is indeed an attractive piece of writing.

We are to imagine at the opening two shepherds piping distantly to each other, one using a *cor anglais* (an instrument employed with a new effectiveness by Berlioz), the other an oboe. The *cor anglais* call is used once more towards the finish of the movement, but this time—a dramatic stroke—the companion oboe makes no reply. Instead comes a distant and sinister mutter of thunder; *four* kettledrums using sponge-heads, and tuned to separate notes, a characteristic Berlioz originality. Between, is a long and mournfully beautiful piece of landscape painting, with, as ever, brief glimpses of the beloved.

The fourth scene is labelled " March to the Scaffold ". In his dream the frenzied artist has murdered his lady, and towards the end of the movement, after his last thoughts of her, pays the penalty to a full-scale orchestral crash. Actually the vigorous, jolly and rather commonplace tunes might have belonged to a festival procession (they came in fact from the abandoned *Francs Juges* opera), but the splendid scoring is in the best Berlioz vein.

The amazing finale is frankly programmatic—" Dreams of a Witches' Sabbath." Certainly no symphony audience had ever before encountered such strains : " bogy-man music ", John Russell has called it. The artist witnesses the gathering of a ghastly assembly among whom to his horror he presently distinguishes his lost love. She is limned by a distorted version of the *idée,* heard first on the normal clarinet and later rendered even more ignoble by the shrill tones of the smaller E flat instrument. There comes an interruption. A funeral knell of two bells is heard, and then the composer introduces on the brass the melody of the powerful medieval sequence, *Dies Irae,* equally daunting in another way. One might assume that this is a blasphemous burlesque of a funeral ceremony. The company gradually assume their more active preoccupations and the work ends with a *Hexentanz,* a wild orgy of sound through which towards the end there comes once more the thunder of *Dies Irae.* Nobody could have taught Berlioz how to write—and score—such music. It is an utterly original conception, but one is inclined to wonder with Schumann what kind of effect would be gathered by a hearer totally unaware of the " programme ", or even the titles of the movements. Certainly there is much, even in the finale, which has attraction as absolute music. On the other hand, without these external interests, the looseness of construction and the occasional banalities, both of harmony and melody, would become even more apparent.

The most striking feature of the work, apart from its being the pioneer of the dramatic trend of the symphony, is its orchestration. Not only is the colouring brilliant but it is so frequently " different ", owing to the originality shown in the treatments of the instruments. A close look at the printed score will reveal at times quite unfamiliar layings-out—that is, as far as the early nineteenth century is concerned. Perhaps it was not altogether a disadvantage that Berlioz had no piano-complex to consider when it came to scoring for orchestra. It is astonishing to recall that when these sounds were being imagined Haydn had been dead barely twenty years, and the Ninth Symphony was still " new music ".

T

Through the '30's Berlioz gradually built up his reputation as the leading romantic French composer. He was admitted to the circle of the romantics of the other arts—Victor Hugo, Balzac, Dumas, de Musset, Gautier, George Sand, Heine and the painter Delacroix among them, and was also friendly with the already famous young musicians Chopin and Liszt. The latter had a high admiration for the *Symphonie,* having made a piano transcription of it, which he played widely. But for a while the struggle merely to exist was a hard one for Berlioz.

His effort at writing a sequel to the Symphony, entitled *Lélio,* an untidy rehash of existing material and termed a monodrama, soon passed into neglect. His next important orchestral work was more successful. *Harold en Italie* (1834), another symphony with programmatic features, and with the addition of a prominent part for solo viola, was, according to the composer, commissioned by the great Paganini, who in fact expected a viola *concerto.* This story of its origin comes from Berlioz' frequently untrustworthy memoirs, and must be strongly suspect. The melancholy protagonist brooding over each of the four movements was the " Childe Harold " of Byron, and was represented by the device, once more, of the *idée fixe.* It was Berlioz' last symphonic use of the *idée,* and is played on each appearance by the solo viola. Again, we meet labels to the movements, but this time no detailed programme. Again, an almost classical first movement is succeeded by others of simpler construction. In his " March of the Pilgrims " Berlioz anticipated Wagner and all writers of " patrols " ever since, by moving the procession from and into the distance. For the finale we meet another " orgy ", this time of brigands. They are not, however, of the witches' quality. On the whole it was the mixture as before, with many felicities and originalities in the scoring.

When the work was heard by Paganini in 1838 he performed the " romantic " act of coming forward and kneeling at Berlioz' feet, and, of greater moment to the debt-ridden composer, presenting him two days later with a draft for 20,000 francs (c. £800), at the same time acclaiming him as Beethoven's true successor. Paganini was something of a miser, and the view has been advanced that regarding the whole affair he was under pressure from powerful journalistic circles. Anyway, the money gave Berlioz the necessary leisure to compose another major work, the " dramatic symphony ", *Roméo et Juliette.*

The previous years had brought him encouragement. He was now the hard-hitting critic of the influential *Journals des Débats,* and a storm centre; and had begun his reputation as an apostle of the gigantic by composing his Requiem (*Messe des Morts*) commissioned officially for a ceremonial occasion. He demanded, and obtained, huge forces of voices and instruments. The effect of the work, by all report, was overwhelming, and the composer, in later years still self-stunned, thought it the most worthy of his compositions. Posterity has not altogether agreed, though allowing once more novel and striking effects of instrumentation.

Berlioz was well aware that in the eyes of the Parisian public a composer was not at the summit until he had succeeded in opera. He had witnessed the storm of enthusiasm that had greeted Meyerbeer's *Huguenots* in 1836, and himself tried for several years to have one of his own staged, its subject another ebullient artist, Benvenuto Cellini. It was produced in 1838, but quickly failed, although the overture became a regular concert item, together with the *Carnaval Romain* overture, also based on material from the opera. Two months later came the balm of Paganini's draft. The next year saw that strange mixture of instrumental and cantata movements, *Roméo et Juliette,* which has already been noted, and which contained some of his best music. In particular the "Queen Mab" Scherzo shows some of Berlioz' most imaginative, delicate and original touches in its fairylike scoring. In complete contrast was the *Symphonie Funèbre et Triumphale,* the last of the four works to which Berlioz gave the name symphony, and which was to commemorate the heroes of the 1830 Revolution, being commissioned by the Ministry of the Interior. First performed (in open air) in July 1940, it was another of the composer's *colossi.* Even as arranged for an indoor performance Berlioz demanded a symphony orchestra of 130 and a military band of 120. The young Wagner, poverty-stricken in Paris at the time, heard both symphonies and other works of the composer, and admired the many felicities of orchestration displayed in them. He declared, with uncharacteristic modesty, " I felt truly like a student in front of him ".

By the beginning of the '40's Berlioz' position as the leading French romantic in music was fairly established, though not altogether safely in Paris, where he still encountered much indifference and many opponents, including Habeneck the well-known conductor. There now began the composer's periods of wanderings. During these years he undertook concert tours in many other European countries, conducting orchestras in his music, and making its novelties, particularly those of its instrumentation, known far and wide. On several occasions he came to London, conducting successful concerts but having another failure with *Benvenuto Cellini.* His two visits to Russia, in 1847 and in 1867–8, had a considerable effect on the young Russian school, and were particularly gratifying and profitable to the composer. In Germany he met Mendelssohn and Schumann, while in Vienna in 1845 he renewed his acquaintance with Liszt, and perhaps received from him the traditional tune which he worked up in his celebrated "Rakoczy March ". The March, which caused a patriotic sensation in Budapest, was dragged into the composer's *Damnation of Faust,* which episodical work he was putting together at the time. It was another vocal and instrumental hybrid, born of his preoccupation with Goethe's masterpiece, and with only the purely orchestral sections, e.g. the March, the delicate *Ballet of Sylphs* and perhaps the hectic *Ride to the Abyss* assured of much modern attention. Full performances tend to confirm the criticism that the work does not adequately belong either to stage or concert hall.

In France the new republic of 1848 was followed in 1852 by the Emperorship of Napoleon III. Berlioz planned for the coronation ceremony a mighty *Te Deum,* already brooded upon for many years, but the work was not performed until 1855. It contained some of Berlioz' most impressive moments —richer harmonies and more artistic modulations than the composer usually contrived—painted by a large orchestra, two choirs of a hundred each and another of six hundred children. The final section, *Judex crederis,* is one of the most thrilling movements for chorus and orchestra in the whole of romantic music. He was engaged also on another choral work at the time, to his own libretto. Begun with a short cantata *The Flight to Egypt,* and completed by two other parts, *The Dream of Herod* and *The Arrival at Sais* respectively, the complete trilogy *The Childhood of Christ,* was performed in 1854. It revealed almost a new Berlioz, with touching melody, effectively woven choral writing, and, as ever, magical scoring. Also, Berlioz had exploited the Dorian mode and made (for the time) striking use of the subtonal cadence.

During the '50's the composer had been heartened by the efforts of Liszt on his behalf at Weimar, where in '52 was held a week's festival of his works, including a revival of *Benvenuto Cellini.* The Princess Sayn-Wittgenstein, Liszt's bluestocking mistress, encouraged Berlioz to proceed with his plans for a Virgilian opera, *Les Troyens,* he writing both libretto and music. Meanwhile there was a German (Baden) commission for a comic opera (with spoken dialogue) on the Shakespearean theme of " Beatrice and Benedict ". This did not appear until 1862, and in spite of being a score of much charm, has not often been revived, after initial failure. *The Trojans,* a gigantic grand opera and completed around 1858, has had a not much better fate. Berlioz was now clashing with Wagner in more ways than one—even in Paris, where preparations for a *Tannhaüser* production were blocking the way for his own opera. He was forced in the end to bisect the huge work, and only the second part, *Les Troyens à Carthage,* was heard in his lifetime, and that as late as 1863. It has been treated with more respect nowadays, and in London among other places, performances of both parts have been achieved. There is nothing revolutionary in operatic method to be found in it. Opposing the tendencies of Wagner, Berlioz returned to the pattern of declamatory, accompanied recitative and set aria (while making some use of the " theme of reminiscence "), the whole in a formal and classical mood of great nobility and dignity.[2*]

He had no more works to write, except a revision of his " Memoires ", which modern research has decided contain a certain proportion of romantic fiction. Before his death in 1869 he had the solace of his last Petersburg visit, with its six concerts of his works and a unanimous homage from Russian musicians, including Balakirev and Tchaikovsky. For all the occasional extravagances of his actions and writings and the plentiful emotion expressed in his music, there were certain refinements that he always maintained in his art. One is never aware of the sensual element—of the Wagnerian eroticism. Perhaps because of this he was completely baffled by a hearing of the *Tristan* Prelude. Mendelssohn, who did not admire him very much, once uttered a shrewd comment to the effect that though he pretended to be mad he was actually thoroughly respectable. His stature is even yet not fully agreed upon, but modern opinion is inclined to place him in a much more exalted position than formerly. The crudity at times of his melodic and harmonic invention is manifest, yet there are many novel and inspired moments in regard to both with which to weight the other scale, especially in his later works. There is also the evidence of a number of enduring solo songs, including the early *La Captive*. He professed to despise J. S. Bach and all fugal invention, and though his own contrapuntal writing has been contemptuously dismissed as "rabbiting" he achieved with it many a well-knit climax. He could claim to have done much towards freeing rhythm from its traditional squareness, a lesson which his contemporary, Schumann, could have taken more to heart. Berlioz' asymmetries were original, calculated and effective. His experiments and innovations in regard to form, like his use of the recurrent theme, may not always have been completely convincing in his hands, but there were others who quickly profited by them. Above all he was the master-orchestrator. Every instrument of every group came under his scrutiny, and, while being treated with sympathy and understanding, had the range of its effects extended. We have already noted the composer's deep interest in the kettledrums, and the special and original effects that he obtained from them. We can here refer only to one more section, the strings, the normal tone-colours of which he varied in many ways—e.g. by multiple divisions, by the use of the highest registers, these made higher yet by the use of harmonics. Under his hand the violas continued their emancipation from being the Cinderellas of the orchestra, and rose at times to unwonted prominence. The double-basses frequently cut adrift from the 'cellos to have their own life, on occasion producing four-part chords of their own by division. For the rest, let us mention once again Berlioz' own "Treatise on Instrumentation", which is still available (in translation) and still of practical interest.

Whatever value may ultimately be assigned to Berlioz' music *as* music, there is no doubt as to his influence on composers as great and greater than himself. He must, even for that reason alone, be held to be of high importance in the history of the art.

Not only did the romantics develop the multi-coloured resources of the orchestra to a new pitch but they found new worlds of emotional possibility in the piano, which became perhaps the most characteristic instrument of Romanticism. Ready under the performer-composer's hands was a pliant means which could express his every mood, from wildest storm to calmest pensiveness, with greater resources of technique than previous ages had known. Mention has already been made of the early-romantic composer-virtuoso Hummel, whose rhapsodical F sharp minor sonata so fascinated the young Schumann. It has also been noted that Weber wrote much brilliant keyboard music with more glitter than content. In this period (as in most) virtuosity was a very paying pursuit, and there followed a generation of outstanding executants, e.g. F. Hunten, H. Herz, S. Thalberg (a pupil of Hummel's) and A. Dreyschock, who in the third and fourth decades reaped golden harvests not only from their virtuoso powers but from "display" compositions that have long passed into oblivion. On them Schumann turned the lash of his written criticism (Herz was particularly the object of his scorn), but a better weapon against this Philistinism was the fact that the great composers Chopin, Liszt and Schumann himself were able to show by example that brilliance in piano composition could be allied with worthwhile ideas. We have already noted that Schumann's and Liszt's aspirations towards virtuosity in composition had been kindled by a more worthy master than Thalberg and company (albeit in another medium)—Paganini.

The Romantics cultivated not only the effects of keyboard brilliance on a large scale but also the opposite extreme, the short and intimate piano piece, deriving from such sources as the Beethoven *Bagatelle,* the Schubert *Moment musical* and the miniatures of Tomášek and Clementi, and carried to higher degrees of charming fancifulness and poetry—as well as to the cloying and sentimental " pining for what is not " emotion to which even Schumann and Mendelssohn could lend themselves at times. In the case of each of these, one hastens to add, the poet overshadowed the sentimentalist. The work of Schumann, one of the greater poets of the romantic keyboard, will now be considered.

Robert Schumann (1810–56) had an early background that seemed almost perfectly designed to produce the new type of romantic composer. The son of a Zwickau bookseller and minor publisher, he lived amid stacks of books and volumes of music. As a child he read assiduously, early gained competence at the keyboard, and cultivated a gift for improvisation and sight-reading. In his teens, under the spell of Hoffmann and Jean Paul, Goethe and Byron, Beethoven, Hummel and Schubert, he expressed his romantic thoughts alternately in literary and musical composition. His general education was a sound one, and in 1828 he entered Leipzig University, where he neglected the study of law with great persistence but at the same time began a piano course with the famous teacher Friedrich Wieck. A move to Heidelberg brought him in contact with the law-lecturer and musical amateur J. Thibaut, who gave him an insight into long-past music, from Palestrina and Victoria to Handel and Bach. In 1830 he at last gained his widowed mother's consent for an attempt at a virtuoso's career, late in the day as it was. He had been impressed by the playing of Moscheles (the friend and piano teacher of Mendelssohn and a leading soloist), and was then overwhelmed by a hearing of Paganini. Back with Wieck, he found that the latter tended to neglect him in favour of the progress and concert-touring of his own gifted daughter, Clara. During that year he secured the publication of his Op. 1, the *Abegg* piano variations. In the next he began to take composition lessons with the fairly well-known Heinrich Dorn, made the acquaintance of the Op. 2 variations on " La ci darem . . .", of a new composer by the name of Chopin, and wrote for a leading musical journal his enthusiastic appreciation of them ("Hats off, gentlemen, a genius . . ."). His lessons with Wieck ceased in 1832. Continuing unaided his preparations for a virtuoso career, he devised a mechanism for strengthening his right hand, and with it succeeded only in crippling the hand permanently for any advanced work. Undeterred, he proceeded to develop his other two talents, those of a writer and composer. In 1834, he, Wieck and others joined forces for the founding of the *Neue Zeitschrift für Music* (The New Musical Journal). In 1835 Schumann became sole editor, and wrote of the importance of Berlioz' *Symphonie Fantastique*. Later in the year he met for the first time one of his idols, Mendelssohn, as well as Chopin and Moscheles. Mendelssohn ("Felix Meister") and the young Wagner each wrote contributions to the Journal.

Until 1840 all compositions published under opus numbers (Opp. 1–23) were for piano. During these years he devoted much time to solitary study, especially of matters contrapuntal—e.g. Bach's "Art of Fugue". There also seems to have been some sowing of wild oats. In 1839 he paid a visit to Vienna, where a fortunate meeting with Schubert's brother Ferdinand led to the unearthing (among other manuscripts) of the great C major Symphony. From 1835 onwards he was wooing Clara Wieck, already well known as a concert pianist. The father raised the strongest objections to the match, and maintained them for years, but failed to prove in the courts that Schumann was an habitual drunkard. The pair were married in 1840, the composer gaining a devoted helpmeet, who continued her distinguished career and who was the means, during his lifetime and after it, of making his music known all round Europe.

The piano music, Op. 1 to Op. 23, written between 1830–40, constitutes a landmark in musical history, one paralleled by the simultaneous appearance in western Europe of the early compositions of Chopin. In this truly romantic music, miniatures and fantasias for the most part, a new world of the keyboard was to be discovered. It was a graceful, lyrical art, essentially song-like and dance-like, the fitting together of short themes in mosaic fashion—contrasting movements often quite brief in duration and simple in form, but the texture often highly organised. In moments of greater emotion there might develop a polyphony of answering voices, appearing and disappearing, sometimes just hinted at, bound together in a variety and subtlety of rhythmic effects, a subtlety which Brahms admired and imitated. Neither Beethoven nor Schubert had paid much heed to the resources of the new sustaining pedal. Schumann (with Chopin) was among the first to develop its artistic resources and make its employment an essential part of the technique, using its colour effects, and writing passages that were only possible with its use.

In such works as *Papillons* (Op. 2), the *Davidsbundler* Dances (Op. 6), the suite-like *Carnaval* (Op. 9), the *Paganini* Studies (Op. 10), the *Fantasiestucke* (Op. 12), the "Scenes from Childhood" (Op. 15), the *Kreisleriana* Fantasies (Op. 16)—to name but some of the rich productions of the decade —are to be found a wealth of poetic touches, subtle allusions and esoteric meanings, together with such small riddles as "dancing letters" and cryptic "notes". The imaginative composer wove into the pieces episodes from his own life, as well as the fantastic personifications which haunted his critical writings—his own *Florestan* and *Eusebius* moods, and the *League of David*, which in his journal smote the musical Philistines. Hoffmann's demoniac *Kapellmeister Kreisler* appeared; there were the tone-pictures— *Chiarina* (Clara Wieck) and *Chopin*. Yet there was no actual programme element; poetic imagination had inspired the music, but it was music complete in itself.

To this period belong also the three piano sonatas, in F sharp minor, F minor and G minor (Opp. 11, 14 & 22) respectively. They are full of the lyric charm, but though the classical sonata framework is employed, the terse classical development technique is largely absent; instead, rather a remoulding of themes, the rhapsodical treatment of a born improvisator. In these sonatas also, as in other larger works, can be found the tendency to work to death a rhythmic pattern, and to present for too long phrase-lengths in steady successions of four bars.

The year of Schumann's marriage (1840) coincided with an almost complete preoccupation, creatively, with the solo song. It was a Schubert-like spate of sixteen sets—over 130 songs in all. His fondness for cycles continued from the piano works. After Schubert's death there was much immediate *lieder* writing to be found, but Schumann only was the true successor. His choice of poetry was fastidious, with Heine, Eichdendorff and Chemisso as his most successful collaborations. The 1840 songs remained his best, though he wrote many more during his later life. As in Schubert's case, there is a balance and intimate blending of voice and instrument to achieve the meaning and atmosphere of a poem. In some ways Schumann's piano plays a more prominent part, for time and again he makes use of the postlude— the closing commentary (as in the Heine song-cycle, *Dichterliebe*), as well as linking the items of a cycle by means of transitional passages, as Beethoven did before him. Anything like the same mastery of song awaited the coming of Brahms and Wolf. Liszt spared the time for some fine examples, and a contemporary "specialist" can be seen in Robert Franz (1816–92), who produced a very large number of charming but not particularly distinguished ones, mostly strophic. Peter Cornelius (1824–74), a better equipped musician and himself a good poet, also wrote songs that have lived. Hugo Wolf, a major figure in the art, will be given later consideration.[3*]

To return to Schumann. In 1841, with his gifted wife's encouragement, he began to seek wider horizons, in an attempt to reconcile the music of romance with the Beethoven traditions. One of his spurs was a hearing of the C major Symphony of Schubert's, the score of which he himself had salvaged. All the established forms were to be attempted. The year saw two symphonies, No. 1 in B flat, the so-called Spring Symphony, and the D minor, termed Symphony No. 4, since it was revised (to its detriment) ten years later. No. 2 in C major came in 1846, and No. 3 in E flat major (the "Rhenish", with its supposed tone-picture of Cologne Cathedral) in 1850. Even after more than a century critical opinion is far from agreeing as to the place that the works hold in the symphonic world. All must admit the harmonic richness and melodic charm of the music. Among the movements, especially the inner ones, there are those that are entirely rounded and perfect. But in spite of mottoes, thematic interrelations and cyclic plans (as in the C major) the overall effect is not of unity. In his sonata form movements the themes are manipulated rather than developed; they proceed to a point rather than grow from it. Like most generalisations this is not always true, as the opening movement of the E flat Symphony and some of the constructive features of the D minor will show. What is un-doubtedly a fact is that Schumann was not a natural writer for the orches-tra. He never broke himself of the habit of thinking *at* the piano, and in terms of the piano—the music first and something in the nature of routine scoring to follow, marred also by sheer clumsiness and (as in the case of his revision of the D minor Symphony) by nervous doubling of parts. Being a genius, however, even if an ill-trained one, he had his moments. In the inspired A minor Piano Concerto, completed in 1845, and the powerful *Manfred* Overture of 1849, the instrumentation is all that one could wish. As for the symphonies, in spite of their detractors, concert promoters decline to forget them. There are plenty of opportunities still afforded for hearers to judge for themselves.

In the same year he began a work (completed in 1843) for soli, chorus and orchestra—*Paradise and the Peri,* adapted from Thomas Moore's *Lalla Rookh.* It was the first, and is probably the best of a number of choral works, a genre in which Schumann did not shine.

1842 saw the beginning of his chamber-music contributions. First came three string-quartets. Though he prepared for his task by a close study of Haydn's and Mozart's works, even the best example, that in A major, is haunted by the ghost of piano technique. He was happier in his other chamber-music essays, all of which made use of the piano. Once again there is frequently employed the subtle transition of themes from one move-ment to another, once again there are attractive figurations and a rich har-monic vocabulary, yet in all of them—the fine quintet in E flat, the quartet in the same key, the three piano trios, the sonatas for solo instruments and piano—it is their lyrical rather than their constructional virtues which are to be admired.[4*]

Schumann's greatest triumph of the mid-forties was the Piano Concerto, the first movement of which began as a *Phantasie,* and had the later addi-tion of two equally meritorious movements. The first *Allegro affetuoso* is a completely satisfying experiment in (perhaps to coin a phrase) lyrical sonata-form. The piano sings and dominates, and the orchestra is content with its comparative subordination, while a single melody, in minor and major versions, rules the exposition. In the middle section we grow reconciled to a gracious world of song instead of the usual conflict of ideas. The deeply thought-out cadenza, far removed from the type of froth and display, is one of the most original of its kind. The *Intermezzo* is a brief and charming dialogue between soloist and orchestra, with a reminder of the A minor theme to link it with the joyous finale, where an ingenious rhythmic episode is provided by the second subject, a duple effect flung across the framework of a triple measure. The whole is the finest of Romantic piano concertos. In 1850 the composer wrote a 'cello concerto, and this with less success, though it still lives in the modern repertoire.

Mendelssohn became head of the Leipzig Conservatoire in 1843, and invited his friend to teach piano there. The appointment did not last long. The moody, introspective composer was not fitted for such a post; indeed, as the years passed overwork was bringing about nervous illnesses. There was more in it than that. Insanity was in the family, and Schumann knew it. Yet the production of works continued with but little relaxation. There came his one essay in opera, *Genoveva* (1847–50), but in spite of its containing much fine music it failed to hold the stage. Altogether, his epigrammatic and lyrical invention was more suited to intimate than to large-scale expression.

His fatal mistake came in 1850, when he accepted a fixed post that, in every way, he was quite unfitted for—musical director at Dusseldorf. He met much goodwill; a concert of his own music was given in his honour; he composed many new works there (mostly of a fading quality); he did useful propaganda work on behalf of the music of earlier times—among other things, helping to make better known Bach's "Matthew Passion" and B minor Mass. But he was no conductor at all, and after a while everyone was aware of the fact except the composer himself and Clara. Towards the end of 1853 he was compelled to give up. Earlier in the year he had met the youthful Brahms, had heard him play his own music, and had proclaimed in his former journal, "This is he who should come!" He toured with Clara for a time, but during 1854 more definite mental trouble set in, and from this he never recovered.

Born in the same year as Schumann was a composer who chose to confine himself almost wholly to the narrow field of the piano keyboard, yet whose influence not only on piano composition and technique but on the whole art of music is of the utmost significance. Frederic Chopin (1810–49) was born a Polish national, but his father, who held a language teaching post at the Warsaw *Lyceum,* had come from France as a young man. The child early showed his genius, and was taught the piano from the age of six, two years later playing a Gyrowetz concerto in public. Already making his own music, he was fortunate both in his parents and his teachers. The former imposed on him no infant prodigy career, but saw that he had an education of the broadest culture, and altogether the happiest of childhoods. The teachers, at first Aldabert Zywny and afterwards the well-known Józef Elsner, guided rather than attempted to modify his exceptional gifts. In 1826 he began a three-year course at the Warsaw Conservatoire, where Elsner was director, but already (in 1825) had published his Op. 1, a piano rondo. He was absorbing influences fast, and transmuting them into his own individual language. All around him was a music little known to Western Europe, that of Polish folk-song and dance. The native forms of the mazurka and polonaise made up a great portion of his early compositions. Warsaw heard much, perhaps too much, of the Italian operas of Rossini and his school, but from it the lad learned that the keyboard also could be made to sing, and express itself in delicate *fioriture.* Thanks to Zywny he early knew the Vienna masters and above all J. S. Bach. The latter remained his lifelong study. The nocturnes of Field he had noted and built upon long before he was friendly with the composer in Paris. In 1828 he heard Hummel, whose style, both as player and composer, had influence on him. Then in the next year came a far profounder experience, the visit to Warsaw of Paganini, which caused him to raise his virtuoso sights yet higher.

His reputation was already wide in Poland as concert pianist, improvisator and composer. Several piano pieces with orchestral accompaniment, including *La ci darem* variations and the *Krakowiak* Concert Rondo, had been written, and soon were added the two piano concertos in F minor and E minor, each employing a " Polish dance " finale. The first great " national " composer had begun to realise the value of this new colour element. He had a foretaste of the West in a concert visit to Vienna in 1829, where his audiences clearly appreciated the novel flavour of his music. In 1830 the time came for him to seek wider fields.

He left Warsaw for ever in November, and for several months travelled Germany giving concerts. A meeting with Thalberg showed him that he lost nothing by comparison as a virtuoso. While at Stuttgart he received the black news of the crushing of the Polish insurrection by Russia. His musical protest was the famous " Revolutionary " Study in C minor, the last of a group of twelve. He reached Paris in September 1831, his headquarters for the rest of his all-too-brief life.

His first public concert, though unsuccessful financially, gave him an instant reputation. Fétis, a power in Paris at the time, was favourable, noting his original ideas. He quickly won the admiration of such men as Mendelssohn, Berlioz, Liszt, Meyerbeer, Bellini and Ferdinand Hiller, the distinguished German pianist and composer, who was making the music of Bach and Beethoven better known in France. His circle of acquaintances came also to include such names as Balzac, Heine, Musset and Delacroix. He was even attracted to the austere and aloof Cherubini. Thanks to his brilliant playing, his undoubted charm of manner and the patronage of the Rothschilds, he was soon able to establish himself as a fashionable piano teacher among the " best families ", and save his rather frail frame from the wear and tear of the life of a travelling virtuoso. Fortunately for him he seems actually to have liked teaching. Throughout his life his solo playing was done far more in *salons* than in concert halls. As further social attractions he seems to have possessed a dry humour and a considerable gift for mimicry. Contrary to legend there was nothing effeminate in his make-up.

When he arrived in Paris he had already written his two piano concertos, the Twelve Studies (Op. 10), two sets of Mazurkas (Opp. 6 & 7), nine of the nocturnes, the Piano Trio (Op. 8), various lesser pieces for piano and the music already mentioned. Soon to be completed were the G minor Ballade and the B minor Scherzo. With these strikingly original works behind him he had already, at the age of 21, found himself as a composer. Thereafter he went his own individual way, influenced by none of the powerful personalities who were themselves developing around him. We discover in him no " three periods ", no long ascent as from *Rienzi* to *Ring*. At an early date he had accepted the models and the influences that he needed for the shaping of his own inimitable style and vocabulary. Composition from 1831 onward was but a process of deepening and enriching. If a single outside voice could be admitted to his later years, it would be that of J. S. Bach.

His teaching, composing and musico-social life in Paris continued for the next few years, with visits to Germany in 1834 and '35. At Leipzig Mendelssohn introduced him to Schumann and Clara Wieck, the latter's playing of his own music impressing him deeply. In 1837 he was in England, where many of his works were already to be found in print, some of them with quite unauthorised titles, much to the composer's disgust. Chopin's music will seem to most of us always to be full of tone-poetry, but he never indulged in fanciful labels for it, and no actual poems can be traced as backgrounds for his Ballades, though indeed he admitted that they were inspired by the poetry of his fellow-countryman Mickiewicz. His works live by their qualities as absolute music.

In 1838 began his association with the novelist George Sand (Aurore Dudevant) which continued for nine years and brought the composer a much-needed affection and care. The winter of 1838 saw the disastrous holiday in Majorca. Musically, the months brought the completion of the Twenty-four Preludes and the start of other fine works, but there were fatal consequences for Chopin's health, since the exceptionally bad weather and the primitive living conditions caused the first symptoms of tuberculosis to appear.

From 1839 onward, while continuing his lucrative teaching practice and his salon and (more occasional) concert playing in Paris, he spent the summers at George Sand's country-house at Nohaut, where (up to Op. 65) some of his finest works, and indeed his last of any significance, were written. Then in 1847 the pair separated. The state of Chopin's health was now becoming grave. Early in 1848 he gave his last concert in Paris, and soon after came the revolution against the government of Louis Philippe. Teaching as well as composition now ceased; Chopin travelled to Britain, where he found some good friends of former acquaintance and managed to give some concerts in both England and Scotland. His playing, so much subdued in power, was still clear and impeccable. He returned to Paris in November and in less than a year was dead.

His end came all too early, but both as pianist and composer his already wide influence was lasting. Liszt and other leading soloists of the time were quick to profit by the originalities of technique of the man whom Mendelssohn called " a truly perfect virtuoso ". He was by instinct an improvisator, a polished exponent of what is now almost a lost art, and a suggestion of the freshness and ease of this element is always to be found in his music —glittering, frequently highly chromatic passage work; charming melodies free from the squareness found in many of his contemporaries, and always ready to break into the little sprays of decoration which are part of their essential make-up. Both melody and harmony had been early influenced by the exotic-sounding minor and modal tones of Polish folk-music, and indeed he was the first (and greatest) of the so-called national composers; but whatever he may have absorbed, he spoke his own individual and quite unmistakable language. His chromatics, his novel and characteristic use of the appoggiatura, and his frequent and far-travelling modulations, while keeping within the conventional tonality of the day, were carrying convention to its limits, prophetic of the new world of chromatic harmony into which

Wagner entered with *Tristan und Isolde.* Undoubtedly Liszt, the link between Chopin and Wagner, won something from the rich vocabulary of this piano music. In a number of Chopin's later works the gains from his lifelong admiration for Bach can be seen in an increasingly rich contrapuntal texture. Death took him at a time when he might even more have influenced the course of musical history.

Composition for anything else than solo keyboard seldom attracted him. Only in his pre-Paris days did he make use of the orchestra as an accompaniment. He had no gift for colourful scoring, and the two Piano Concertos (of 1829 and 1830) suffer from this deficiency. The small amount of chamber music includes a piano trio and a late sonata (Op. 65) for 'cello and piano, the latter a beautiful and somewhat neglected work.

In the two early concertos, the three piano sonatas, the piano trio and the 'cello sonata Chopin made some gestures towards conforming to the established sonata framework, but his natural style was too rhapsodical, too episodical, to achieve a complete sense of overall unity. A contemporary critic, anent the concertos, complained of " a lack of continuous feeling " and posterity may perhaps have decided that he was right. Regarding the two mature piano sonatas, in B flat minor and B minor respectively, their attractive contents still cause them to be living works of art, the former (with its Funeral March) being the terser of the two. The brief, apparent formless, last movement of this sonata is one of utter originality, looking forward to the age of impressionism.

Chopin was indeed happier and more effective within the frameworks of his own devising—episodical, near-ternary, or dictated by his own fancy. He dared more than any other great composer to return again and again to a melody or episode, but so welcome is the reappearance of the material, often presented with some new decoration or elaboration, that his methods never pall. In the four great Ballades, particularly the A flat (Op. 47) and the F minor (Op. 52) examples, and the F minor Fantasy (Op. 49—actually another Ballade), extensive works are successfully shaped by these methods. With them may be grouped the Four Scherzos, with the splendid B flat minor (Op. 31) as a construction of more than ordinary fascination; also the highly original *Barcarolle* (Op. 60). Of lesser dimensions and emotional range are the four Impromptus and the score or so of Nocturnes, but containing some of the composer's loveliest singing melodies.

Throughout his life he remembered his native dance-forms, the Polonaise with its aristocratic formal connections and the more humble Mazurka. Both types Chopin developed in his own way; in his seven Polonaises expressing dignity, pageantry and a fiery patriotism, and in his forty-odd mazurkas a variety of graceful moods. Two resplendent Polonaises came in his last years, both in A flat, Opp. 53 and 61, the latter termed *Polonaise-Fantaisie,* and containing within itself a mazurka. There were various other dance-form publications, including eight Waltzes—salon music, slight at times, but polished and refined to the last degree. Further examples of each of the types mentioned, mostly representing early work, were printed posthumously.

His twenty-seven Studies present various technical problems, some of formidable difficulty, but each such problem also a musical germ to be expanded into a movement of beauty and significance. The maturity of the dozen examples making up Op. 10 must always be a source of wonder, as must be the final group of compositions of which we take note, the *Twenty-four Preludes* (Op. 28).[5] These are " preludes " only in name. Each is complete in itself, the painting of a mood, needing in some cases four-score or so bars for its expression, elsewhere a mere eight, but stated always in terms of pure poetry.

Contemporary with Chopin in Paris was one of the few native-born piano virtuosi and piano composers of the period, the enigmatic and un-deservedly neglected Charles Alkan (1813–88). His actual name was Morhange. Coming from a musical family and trained at the Conservatoire he was a well-known virtuoso at seventeen. He was admitted to the Victor Hugo circle, known and admired by Liszt and Rubinstein, and soon estab-lished as a piano teacher. Yet he chose in his maturity to retire to a life of seclusion from which he seldom emerged. There is no doubt as a player he approached the stature of Liszt. The comparison with Liszt holds in composition. Both wrote a certain amount of music of merely mechanical interest, sometimes approaching the trashy, but both produced works of startling and significant interest and originality. Unfortunately for Alkan he was one of those composers who somehow gets " missed ". But modern informed criticism is increasingly calling attention to the merits of the best of his piano music, macabre in tone though much of it is. In particular, his twenty-four Studies covering all the major and minor keys (Opp. 35 & 39) are of great importance in the catalogue of piano literature.

At a time when Schumann, Berlioz, Wagner and others of the romantics were busily campaigning against the Philistines another great musician had decided to accept the world very much as he found it, and was writing for the musical public of Germany and England in such fashion as to make him, among leading composers, probably the one most widely popular during his lifetime. Mendelssohn's stature under the searchlight of more modern criticism has been somewhat diminished, but it can still be granted that he had some measure of influence on the general progress of the art.

Felix Mendelssohn (Bartholdy), 1809–47, was indeed fortunate in the material circumstances of his youth. Grandson of the famous Jewish philo-sopher Moses Mendelssohn, and the son of a rich banker who had adopted the Christian faith, Felix had all the opportunities that a refined and affluent home-life in Berlin could give in matters cultural—with music as only one of the interests. But his special gifts were early recognised. He was taught the keyboard by excellent instructors, culminating with the famous Moscheles, and developed a command of the organ which in later years so much impressed the English professionals. Edward Rietz, a fine virtuoso, made a string player of him, while for composition he was under Goethe's friend, the distinguished Carl Zelter. He was composing systematic-ally from the age of twelve, and soon the Sunday morning family concerts, attended often by well-known musicians, were giving him the experience of hearing his own music regularly. In 1824 Zelter declared that his fifteen-year-old pupil was now fully fledged, with, among other works, Symphony No. 1 in C minor (really No. 12) to prove it. In the following year came the astonishing and original Octett, and then in 1826 the immortal " Midsummer Night's Dream " Overture. This work, a youthful miracle in its power of imagination and its complete mastery of the arts of construction and orchestration, represents a height of mature achievement such as not even Mozart had reached at the age of seventeen.

It is clear that had he so wished he could have gained distinction in ways other than music. In 1827 he matriculated at Berlin University in literature and classical philology, and in later years produced some elegant classical translations. His own writings showed him in command of an attractive literary style. He received a great deal of instruction in painting, and his water-colours were professional in standard. It was everywhere admitted that he had a charming social manner and was a brilliant conversationalist. But musician he chose to be. By natural genius, by unique early opportunity and by superb training he seemed all-prepared to become one of the greatest composers of all time. Yet in his maturity those heights were not achieved. His music—beautiful, graceful, perfect in form, easy in flow (his art disguising art), attracting appreciation everywhere, yet lacked some quality which would have put him among the very greatest, even though two of his symphonies appear to be evergreen and the Violin Concerto ranks with those of Beethoven and Brahms. There seems more than one reason for the absence of this ultimate quality. A pointer to a partial answer is that he died at the early age of 38 as the result of overwork and nervous strain. In his boyhood the routine discipline of his father Abraham had been severe. Felix himself mentions 5 a.m. as being the start of his usual working day, while his actor friend Devrient, in close knowledge of the facts, stated that his brain from early childhood had been taxed excessively. This drain upon his nervous energy continued throughout his life. Having a strongly developed sense of duty, he carried through the administrative tasks of his posts at Dusseldorf, Leipzig and Berlin time and again to the point of exhaustion and to the detriment of sufficient time for composition.

But this cannot be the full explanation. The fact is that although he faced his professional difficulties with an initial degree of resolution, a stage could be reached when, meeting with hamperings and opposition, as at Dusseldorf, he would choose to slip away and go elsewhere. He was not indeed formed to face up to anything but sunshine and the pleasanter aspects of life. There had been many fairies at his cradle, but the missing gift was the grit and determination of a Beethoven, a Berlioz or a Wagner. Again let Devrient speak : " He wanted to do only what was congenial to his nature and nothing beyond ". This rings true, since confirmation can be found plainly enough in his music. There was very largely absent from it any sense of conflict; his complete mastery of the art of composition which overcame without hesitation every technical difficulty may in itself have tended to reduce that sense of urgency and strain which must at times be present in all great music. Instead, we find it ruled very largely by the social instincts of politeness and good breeding. Passion, tragedy, strong emotions of any type he recoiled from; hence his neglect of serious opera. Only occasionally were his symphonic subjects those that would germinate, grow, contrast and create real conflict. Beautiful and polished as are his larger instrumental works his emotional caution in regard to the dramatic clash too often prevented his achieving a full reconciliation between classical form and romantic content.

One of his major services to posterity was early begun, the bringing once more into the full light of day the music of J. S. Bach and Handel. The basic position that these composers hold in modern times is due primarily to his pioneer work on their behalf in the face often of Philistine opposition. Thanks to his cultured mother, Lea, the boy, together with his gifted sister Fanny, had been nurtured on the keyboard fugues of Bach. In 1824 he had received a family gift of a manuscript score of the St. Matthew Passion (it had in fact been copied by Rietz). It took several years to convince an incredulous Berlin that here was an immortal work. Even Zelter was doubtful. There was in any case a personal antagonism in professional circles to overcome. But in 1829 a performance was secured. It was a hacked and distorted version, but it was the beginning of a revival which led eventually to the formation of the important Bach *Gesellschaft*. Throughout his career he sponsored and took part in revivals of various works of the great baroque pair. In 1835, for example, while he was conductor of the *Gewandhaus* concerts at Leipzig, he joined with Moscheles and Clara Wieck for a performance of the Bach Triple Concerto. Another instance was the revival of Handel's almost forgotten *Israel in Egypt*. Moreover he brought forward, both in Germany and England, the too-often neglected sonatas, symphonies and concertos of Beethoven and Mozart. To his credit, and Schumann's, was the revival of Schubert's C major Symphony.

In 1829 and over a period of more than three years, thanks to the silver spoon with which he was born, he was able to enjoy a Grand Tour of Europe like any eighteenth century aristocrat. He made the first of his many visits to Britain, and it was the enthusiasm and awe with which his piano playing and his compositions were received which helped much to spread his fame through Europe. Moscheles, established in London, was there to welcome him, and the Philharmonic Society became his devoted admirers. He met also Clementi and Cramer. The journey to Scotland gave him experiences which were afterwards recalled in the " Fingal's Cave " concert overture (1830–2) and the A minor (" Scottish ") Symphony (1842).

The Tour took him through Germany and Austria (where in Vienna he found ignorance of Mozart and Beethoven " rampant ") to Italy. At Rome he developed an admiration for Palestrina, for whose works he afterwards became a propagandist. The months in Italy inspired a high-spirited, highly polished youthful work that his later years never improved upon, the " Italian " Symphony, first performed by the London Philharmonic in 1832. There was much other composition, together with piano and organ playings and displays of improvisation that were widely admired, the time somehow snatched from his peripatetic social existence. Through Germany again, and Switzerland, he came to Paris, meeting Chopin, Liszt, Hiller, Meyerbeer and Heine the poet, among others, and giving concerts of his own works. He showed no liking for French music, and in return Paris was less enthusiastic about him than were other cities, and thought his new " Reformation " Symphony " dull ". Perhaps it is. In April 1832 he was back in London, conducting his compositions with the Philharmonic and giving a virtuoso pedal-display on the organ of St. Paul's. In all he visited England on ten occasions, always being given adulatory welcomes, and even penetrating to the drawing-room of Buckingham Palace. (See Plate 32.)

It was now time for the twenty-three-year-old musician, armed at all points, to settle down professionally. After a rebuff from Berlin (Mendelssohn and the musicians of that city were never great friends) he was offered the conductorship of the Lower Rhine Festival organisation, a considerable distinction. This was followed by his acceptance of an even greater responsibility, the general direction of the music of Dusseldorf—opera, theatre, and other musical activities. He found much to reform. His youthful zeal was perhaps over-vigorous; thus, after a couple of years of valuable concert-giving and profitless bickering, he gladly accepted an escape to the direction of the famous Gewandhaus Concerts at Leipzig. Here was a much more congenial world for him, and here much of his best work was done. He had as his *Konzertmeister* and firm friend the fine virtuoso Ferdinand David, who was also his adviser and soloist for the Violin Concerto of 1844, with another friend and awed admirer in Robert Schumann. Clara Wieck played for him, as did the visiting Chopin and Moscheles. There was more propaganda on behalf of Bach, Beethoven and Mozart in the concert programmes, and much composition of his own, including the completion of the oratorio, *St. Paul,* and the first sketches of *Elijah,* not finished until 1846.

He worked under conditions that the great Cantor would have envied; all the city's musical forces were under his unquestioned authority and it is pleasant to record that he always did his best to improve the lot of his humbler colleagues. He began to be highly regarded by the Saxon government, and ventured to propose a plan for the establishment of a musical Conservatorium at Leipzig. This materialised in due course, but not until 1843. In the meantime he had at last fallen sufficiently deeply in love to contemplate marriage, although characteristically he pondered the step awhile in calm deliberation before taking it. His bride was a Mdlle Cécile Jeanrenaud. Her mother being of an old and distinguished French stock there was enough of the spirit of *l'ancien régime* for local tongues to speak of the young lady's misalliance.

In 1840 the clouds began to gather, blown from the direction of Berlin. The new and cultured King of Prussia, Frederick William IV, had ideas for an Academy of Art, with Mendelssohn as head of the Music Department. For the composer, legally his subject, it was a difficult invitation to refuse. In May 1841 together with his family, he exchanged the congenial atmosphere of Leipzig for residence in Berlin. In the capital he found himself the King's *Kapellmeister* with very little authority, receiving commis-

U

sions for compositions but nothing concrete regarding the Academy. The King was well-meaning, but his officials were not, and the following years were full of bafflement and vexations, with the Academy post never materialising. For a first performance of the Scottish Symphony in March 1842 the composer preferred to use the Leipzig orchestra. Towards the end of the year he resigned his Berlin posts and moved back to Leipzig, but a year later was once more inveigled back, until it became clear even to Prussian eyes that the strain could no longer be borne. The only positive results of the Berlin episode were the works that he wrote at the King's order, e.g. the *Antigone* and *Midsummer Night's Dream* incidental music. With regard to the latter it is remarkable to note how its items blend in style with the youthful Overture, which we may take as being due either to a brilliant and deliberate effort of synthesis, or to the fact that the mature composer could effect no improvement on the music of his seventeenth year.

Meanwhile, the Leipzig Conservatorium had been started, with Mendelssohn as Director, and among others, David and Schumann to assist him. Later, those two stalwarts, Hiller and Moscheles, joined him and helped to lighten his tasks. The multiple responsibilities, the incessant labour and strain of routine, conducting and composition, his continual refusals to take the rest that his weakened health demanded were ageing him prematurely. Among his English commitments there was the long-laboured *Elijah,* due for Birmingham in the summer of 1846. That and other tasks were fulfilled at the cost of more overstrain, which was very apparent on his return to England next spring (1847) when the country saw him for the last time, conducting *Elijah* and others of his works, and giving organ and piano recitals. He went back to Germany in May a very sick man, and there cruel news soon met him, the sudden death of his devoted sister Fanny. Although he rallied and even wrote a string quartet to her memory only a few more months of life were left him. He was not yet thirty-nine.

Mendelssohn has been called a musical hedonist. He understood and sympathised with the new culture-seeking concert public which had grown up, and sought to give them pleasure in a music which reflected in the main the sunnier aspects of life. In this aim he had an overwhelming success. Thus for a generation and more there persisted, particularly in Britain, the belief that all musical evolution had moved towards the divine event of his appearance, and for some decades too much commonplace English music was written in imitation of his style, especially its weaker features.

Many of his solo songs were widely popular, but when they are placed beside those of Schubert and Wolf, the comparison is chilling. Again too much of his piano music must appear fragile when set against the rich and original work of his contemporary Chopin. Disregarding the *Songs without Words,* we may allow that some of the larger piano works, such as the *Variations Sérieuses,* are worthy of a great composer. There are matters of significance in his two published piano concertos. The not very important imitations of the Beethoven model produced by lesser men like Hummel, Field, Cramer and Moscheles had followed the so-called double exposition plan, with its delayed entry of the soloist. Mendelssohn struck out boldly for a single exposition, with soloist and orchestra sharing responsibility from the start. In the G minor Concerto, (played first in Munich in 1831), the earlier and better of the two, there are other notable features. The three movements are linked by a kind of motto-theme fanfare of trumpets and drums; and then in the last movement there comes a re-appearance of subjects from the first, a hint of the cyclic device. In the first movement of the immortal Violin Concerto there is seen once again the immediate participation of the soloist. The famous second movement, linked directly with the first, achieves a tender beauty of melody without betraying the banal streak of sentimentality which so often marred others of the composer's slow movements. Worthy of note, too, is the functional nature of the cadenza; no mere empty display but beauty and significance combined.

In chamber music Mendelssohn, like many another romantic composer, wrote charming single movements without often achieving that sense of overall unity which was the hall-mark of the great Viennese three. An exception is the string quartet in A minor (1827), a fine example of the cyclic treatment of themes, and an anticipation of César Franck's technique in this particular. The Op. 44 string quartets are also masterly, though neglected. The melodious D minor piano trio (1839) will no doubt always continue to be played where amateur chamber musicians foregather.⁹*

Of his symphonies the " Hymn of Praise " (with a choral cantata for a last movement), and the " Reformation " (which employs the " Dresden Amen " and Luther's " Ein' feste Burg " chorale with some sort of programme intention) are considered to be of much lesser moment than the " Italian " and the " Scottish ". These two show the composer at his best, each with its distinctive and cunningly contrived atmosphere. The joyous first movement of the " Italian " with its moments of real dramatic clash in the development, is one of the finest of its kind in all romantic music. The headlong *saltarello* finale is remarkable inasmuch, though of considerable length and entirely satisfactory, it is wholly in the minor mode. In the " Scottish " Symphony dramatic conflict is less evident, but the music, ranging from brooding melancholy to wild and rugged vigour, is another masterly piece of evocative writing, the pentatonic scale and the " Scotch snap " playing their parts. Although on one occasion Mendelssohn stated very firmly that music needed no words for its elucidation, and that a musical thought was altogether *per se,* yet in giving descriptive titles to these purely instrumental works, as well as to such others as the " Fingal's Cave " and " Calm Sea . . ." concert overtures, he was clearly admitting some degree of exoteric meaning. Indeed, on occasions, such as in the Midsummer Night's Dream Overture, he could not resist some moments of objective realism.

Already we have noted some of the debts that his contemporaries and successors owed to him. While not completely successful in his aim, he showed that some degree of artistic compromise was possible between the classical symphonic framework and the aspirations of romantic imagination. He made some contribution to the idea of the interlinking of movements, as well as the use of the motto-theme and the cyclic device : he effected reforms in the construction of the concerto, giving it a new life.

He was a master of the art of orchestration. Without being an innovator of the originality of Berlioz, his scores are models of clarity and poetic imagination, of the maximum of effect obtained by economical means— patterns for the student; even so gifted a one as Wagner. One of his greatest contributions to music as a composer was his invention (no less) of the fairy-like, merry-hearted Mendelssohnian *scherzo,* so very different from the sometimes heavy-footed movement inherited from the classical symphony. There are a number of such dainty movements to be found in his works, with the Scherzo from the " Midsummer Night's Dream " music as perhaps the supreme example.

From the fastidious and restrained imagination of a Mendelssohn we turn to a contemporary, only two years younger, whose mind was the most independent and revolutionary of all romantic musicians.

Franz Liszt (1811–86) once described himself as " half Franciscan, half gipsy ". This was putting it modestly. Busoni was blunter in designating the two warring elements as " Catholic " and " diabolic ". At an early age he laid the foundations of a keyboard technique which has probably never been equalled before or since. With this matchless equipment and an extraordinary command of the art of improvisation he toured the length and breadth of Europe for many years as the supreme showman, attracting everywhere large publics whose hysteria he deliberately exacerbated with his exhibitionism. For this purpose he wrote a large amount of piano music of no permanent value, e.g. elaborate fantasies and arrangements of operas popular at the time, the technical difficulties and brilliance of which were designed for the display of his powers. At the same time, especially in more exclusive circles, he was playing to understanding ears the almost unknown later sonatas of Beethoven, together with transcriptions of his equally neglected symphonies, and the larger organ works of Bach. We have already spoken of his good service to Berlioz in disseminating knowledge of his " Fantastic Symphony " through an extraordinarily effective piano arrange-ment. This kind of assistance, in an age before the gramophone record, was given to other contemporary composers. Quite a number of the songs of Schubert, too, were brought to the knowledge of a wider public through Liszt's brilliant transcriptions. We can say of him that he championed Berlioz in his young manhood, Borodin in his old age, and every composer of originality in between.

For all the vulgar streak which was an essential part of his make-up, his culture, basically French, was deeper and wider than that of most musicians of the time. Around 1830, in Paris, he speaks, probably without much exaggeration, of " devouring with fury Homer, the Bible, Plato, Locke, Byron, Hugo, Lamartine, Chateaubriand . . ." He was insisting at that time that the intellectual culture of musicians must be improved before a truly modern art could be launched. The practice of deep study—literary, philo-sophical and religious—continued through his life. Even as a youth he had shown a profound interest in religious matters, and twice had thoughts of entering the priesthood. Towards the end of his life he took minor orders as " the Abbé Liszt ". Yet meeting with, and enjoying, feminine adoration throughout his professional career his susceptibilities in that direction became notorious.

In contrast with the flesh and the devil must be set other characteristics —kindness, which amounted at times to a remarkable unselfishness; an un-failing generosity towards causes of charity especially if they touched on music, and a readiness to aid fellow-musicians in any way—monetarily, if necessary. Wagner, the arch sponger, took full advantage of this free-handedness. For over a decade at Weimar, while in charge of the ducal orchestra and theatre, he produced steadily works by contemporary com-posers, Berlioz and Wagner among them, which at the time were standing little chance of a hearing elsewhere, a practice which in the end helped to terminate his employment there. One of his finest services to music came in his later years, when, at Budapest, Rome and Weimar, in different periods of the year, he was training a new generation of brilliant young pianists, Weingartner, Lamond, Sauer and Rosenthal among them, and refusing all payment for the task.

Although born within the borders of Hungary he was of German stock. Adam Liszt, his father and a good amateur musician, was a land-steward to the Esterhazy family, the same that had employed Haydn. Thanks to the reigning Prince's discernment and patronage the nine-year-old boy and his father were sent to Vienna. There Franz was taught by Czerny, and, it is said, praised by Beethoven. After two years devoted to a Wolfgang-Leopold kind of tour the pair settled in Paris, which was Franz's spiritual home for the rest of his life, however far he sometimes moved from it. Study alternated with concert touring. " Le petit Liszt " became the " ninth wonder ". By the time he was fourteen he was held by some to be surpassed as a virtuoso only by Hummel. In 1827 his father died. For the next few years the young man concentrated at high pressure on perfecting his key-board technique, as well as making one of the most brilliant society of romantics to be found in Europe. 1830 was an important year for him. During it he first met Paganini, and resolved to equal his virtuosity in terms of the keyboard.[7*] He became friendly with Berlioz, and appreciated his attempts to fuse, in his own way, the arts of music and literature. Finally, there was a first encounter with the music of Chopin, with its novel chroma-tic harmonies, breathing its own inner poetry without the aid of any other art. At the gatherings of the circle Liszt's playing was a centre of attraction. We know that Chopin preferred, when possible, to entrust his compositions to Liszt's fingers. In 1833, at such a soirée of musicians, poets and painters, Liszt met the cultivated Countess Marie d'Agoult, the first of the two women (both separated from their husbands) who dominated his life. They left Paris together, and for several years lived in comparative seclusion in Switzerland and Italy. The serious-minded Marie encouraged Franz in " high thinking ", both in regard to culture in general and composition in particular. To this period belong, among other worthwhile works, the *Études d'execution transcendante* previously mentioned, and other brilliant studies and the many single piano pieces of impression and mood, gathered in the first two volumes of the *Années de pelérinage*.

The idyll could not last. In 1838 Liszt heard of the disastrous Danube floods, and went to Vienna alone to give concerts in aid of his fellow-Hungarians. The mission was a virtuosic and social success on an unprecedented scale; the fever of showmanship returned to his blood and the decade of concert-giving began which throughout Europe fixed him as the supreme pianist of the age. Marie was neglected, and they parted finally in 1844. One of the results of their association was their daughter Cosima, afterwards wife of von Bülow, one of Liszt's most famous pupils, and after that, mistress and finally wife of Richard Wagner.

It took until 1848 for the soberer Liszt to return. He was tiring of the virtuoso career; thus, when he was offered the post of musical director of the Ducal Court of Weimar he willingly accepted it. With him he brought from Kiev the formidable Princess Carolyne von Sayn-Wittgenstein, and with her settled in the city for the next thirteen years. In Carolyne was again a stronger personality than his. With her own literary ambitions there was her determination that he should prove himself a great composer. This was the period of his larger orchestral works—the symphonic poems, and the " Faust " and " Dante " Symphonies; as well as the piano Sonata in B minor and the final version of the E flat Piano Concerto.[8*]

At a time when musical Europe was being more than ever torn with faction Liszt maintained a gentle tolerance and broadmindedness in the friendships and assistances which he gave to visiting musicians. He received the fugitive Wagner in 1849, and gave a first production of *Lohengrin* in the next year. Carolyne was always Wagner's enemy. Perhaps she realised dimly who was the better composer. Liszt knew without question, and his continual and generous help to the self-centred Wagner is one of the finest chapters of his life. In the years of his stay Weimar became once again a leading musical metropolis to which, famous or amateur, all flocked. He took up piano teaching once more; free to those worthy of the privilege. Von Bülow and Tausig belong to this time, two among a number of brilliant pupils.

In 1858 he resigned his director's post, since official support was no longer warm. In 1861 the pair moved to Rome, with religion as an increasing interest; Carolyne (" that half-cracked religious blue-stocking ", as Ernest Newman has called her) to write enormous tomes on Church matters, Liszt for a while as the guest at a Dominican monastery. He contrived however to keep well in touch with the outside world and social life.

The writing of large orchestral works now ceased, and his mind turned more strongly to the long cherished idea of revolutionising church music, which, according to an essay of his young manhood, should be at once " dramatic and holy . . . ceremonious and earnest . . . stormy and restful . . ." Already he had written at least two Masses and a number of Psalm settings. To the years at Rome belong the completion of two extensive works, the *Christus* and *The Legend of St. Elizabeth* oratorios. There followed other Masses, further Psalm settings, (with *Psalm XIII* as the finest example), litanies and other works of various dimensions. This part of his output, though containing much beautiful music, has never met with much favour. Regarding the major works, prolixity, extravagant and unsuitable harmonies and modulations are some of the charges levelled against them.

In 1869 he was by ducal invitation made welcome at Weimar once more —by himself this time. He was concerned now only with the circle of piano pupils that he had formed there. Thus began the period, already noted, of the Rome—Budapest—Weimar piano *salons*. Composition continued, including much piano music, some of it of his best quality. A long breach with Wagner was at last healed, and he was present at the opening of Bayreuth in 1876. In 1886 he went on his last tour, which took him to Paris and on to England. Everywhere he was received with honour; London warmed to him as never before. Back in Germany the last music that he heard was that of *Tristan und Isolde* at Bayreuth. Within a few days he was dead.

In a number of ways Liszt was a prophet of the future; thus, whatever verdict may be passed on his achievements as a composer, he must occupy an important place in the history of music. With his invention of the one-movement symphonic poem he reconciled more successfully than Berlioz the partnership of music and literary ideas, and found a design that would replace to some degree the long established standard types of musical form. His principle was that the formal construction must be shaped by the poetic intentions of the music; content must not be ruled, as formerly, by pre-conceived patterns. Of the utmost importance was his use of the device of metamorphosis (or transformation) of themes. The idea was far from new : we have met something akin to it in Beethoven's Fifth Symphony, in Schubert's " Wanderer " Fantasia, and in the *idée fixe* of Berlioz (and indeed in the medieval and Renaissance Mass). But it was developed more subtly by Liszt, being more akin to the *leitmotif* scheme of Wagner. Most of his thirteen symphonic poems are based on actual literary ones. An idea or a character would be represented by a musical theme. As the poetic or dramatic background changed so a modification of the musical theme would take place. Normally, he aimed at creating a musical paraphrase of his subject, an evocation in a different medium of a similar state of feeling, and himself hotly denied that his purposes were objective, saying : " The poorest of apprentice landscape painters could give with a few strokes a much more faithful picture than a musician operating with all the resources of the best orchestra ". Even if in fact one does meet at times in his works vivid moments of direct representation, it must be admitted that of all the nineteenth century " programme " composers he seems to have given the greatest heed to Beethoven's words in connection with the Pastoral Symphony, " . . . more of feeling than painting ". He left the telling of a story, graphically and detail by detail, to such later composers as Smetana, Saint-Saëns and Richard Strauss. The best of the thirteen is possibly *Orpheus* (1854), which has no literary basis other than the legend in general. Wagner thought it to be Liszt's finest orchestral work. It can, in fact be appreciated as a piece of excellent music in the absolute sense. *Les Préludes* (revised

1854) meditates on some solemn lines by the French poet Lamartine concerning life and death, and has some fine themes treated in sincere fashion. *Hamlet* (1858), one of the briefest, succeeds in suggesting the vacillating moods of its subject. A work that was inspired by an actual picture is *Hunnenschlacht* (1857), the representation being of the hordes of Attila. In this the composer was more programmatic than usual in his tone-painting of a battle.

The principle of " free form " is to be found in his other major instrumental works. The " Faust " Symphony (1864) in three movements—(a) Faust, (b) Gretchen (Marguerite), (c) Mephistopheles, with a *Chorus Mysticus* for male voices with tenor solo to conclude, consists of musical studies of the principal characters on parallel lines with the poet's representations, and in contrast to Berlioz' treatment of the poem, which was to select from it dramatic " scenes ", to the neglect of Goethe. The first movement actually manages some kind of fusion of the *leitmotif* principle with symphonic structure. It employs at least five short motives, depicting apparently various aspects of Faust's character. The beautiful and peaceful " Gretchen " movement is in due course invaded by several of the Faust themes, and it would seem that some attempt is made to tone-paint the " flower scene ". The last (Mephistopheles) movement is the most original. The demoniac power is illustrated by the use of Faust themes transformed into mocking parodies. Gretchen's music only is proof against corruption, and in the end triumphs.

The two-movement " Dante " Symphony (1855)—(a) *Inferno,* (b) *Purgatorio,* with a concluding *Magnificat* for women's chorus (a distant glimpse of *Paradiso*)—is another interesting example of the composer's " free form ", with surely a great deal of colourful tone-painting intended in the first movement. The pity is that neither work is at all frequently heard nowadays for which their prolixities, one of Liszt's greatest faults as a composer, are doubtless to blame. Before the Weimar period Liszt, as a solo pianist, had had little to do with orchestration. Because of this lack of experience a great deal of the scoring of the earlier symphonic poems was done by such professional friends as Joachim Raff. But Liszt's apprenticeship was soon over. The " Faust " Symphony was one of the first of his works which he orchestrated wholly on his own, and a very colourful and competent business it is. At his best his imaginative scoring, admired by Wagner, had something to teach his successors.

The same principles, freedom of form and the transformation of themes, were observed in his two piano concertos, in E flat and A respectively, the latter a single movement work. The E flat Concerto, in three movements, has a second which combines the successive roles of the slow movement and scherzo. The main theme of the first movement is one of Liszt's most striking motifs :

Ex:57

It reappears in the following movements as does other material, in more than one transformed shape.

The famous one-movement B minor Sonata, with its main motifs set out in the first fifteen bars, its continuous developments and transformations of this material in the course of the changing moods of the work, showed him, as in the cases of the Concertos, applying his programmatic technique to absolute music. No hint came from the composer as to any literary interpretations to be read into either the Concertos or the Sonata.[9]

A similar rhapsodical spirit is to be found in his songs (about seventy in all)—settings of poems in a number of languages, and forward-looking in the harmonic subtleties of their accompaniments.[10*]

In harmony Liszt was definitely an innovator. A born improvisator, of infinite fluency, he experimented with new-seeming chords and cadences, and daring modulations, but generally speaking other hands made more effective uses of these innovations. In his old age there came some brief and remarkable piano pieces, such as the *Nuages gris* and the two *Lugubre Gondole,* Debussyan in their " impressionism ".

His position as a composer of major works still seems a matter of controversy. It may be thought that Liszt the composer was too much inclined to rely on Liszt the improvisator. His principal themes may at times seem undistinguished and their developments of very loose construction. While a Beethoven, a Wagner or a Brahms strides forward purposefully on a close-knit dramatic progress, giving always the feeling that he is " getting somewhere ", a characteristic of Liszt is the ebb and flow of his tempos; in his checks and restartings one is reminded of the virtuoso at the piano, pausing in his improvisations for fresh thought. In the concert keyboard works there are also frequent appearances of flowery cadences, pianistic " candy-floss ", attractive for the purpose of display but with the musical reason for their existence not always apparent. Probably he suffered from the lack of a thorough technical training in composition, especially in its contrapuntal aspects. One may question even the general success, as far as he himself was concerned, of the " transformation of themes " technique—as to whether even the keen listener might not often miss the point, and thus lose the unifying effect which the device was supposed to give.

After the experimental music of the Weimar years, a harvest of new and great instrumental compositions might have been expected to follow. But they did not come, and it is the best of the short and lyrically imaginative piano pieces, together with some of the brilliant concert studies, which of all his music seem likely for the longest survival. The restlessness and self-dissatisfaction which were so apparent in his last years may well have been due to his realisation that his chief service to the cause of neo-romantic music had been that of prophet and benevolent guide, and that the status of a supreme composer had eluded him.

The Progress of Opera

In the post-Revolution world Paris became more and more the main centre for live operatic activity, attracting to itself leading opera composers from other countries. Vienna was now passive, hearing operas but doing little to create them. Italy continued to pour forth its own brands, with *opera-buffa* on the traditional lines as popular as ever. But some change was taking place in Italian *opera-seria*, which was ceasing to be of the solo-aria type. An important factor in the change was the career of Simon Mayr (1763–1845). This Italianised German, with Mozart and Cherubini as his guides, gave the orchestra of his operas a far more colourful and significant share than heretofore (establishing the " finale " crescendo which Rossini, as " Signor Crescendo ", worked almost to death), and introduced choruses and massed scenes generally, features once belonging only to *opera-buffa*. The *da capo* aria tended to be more compressed, with more use of the *arietta* form, but vocal virtuosity and the use of elaborate *fioriture* were more than ever to the fore. These innovations were stereotyped by the prolific Saverio Mercadente and Giovanni Pacini, but the works of neither have lived. Rossini took this type, graced by his own individual genius, to Paris, where already Spontini had encouraged the French taste for spectacular pomposity. The monumental *William Tell*, as we have already noted, was Rossini's attempt to establish himself in the realm of the new Parisian and international grand opera, but the kingship was soon afterwards claimed by the German-born Meyerbeer, with his *Les Huguenots*, and Rossini wrote no more for the stage. It is characteristic of French serious opera that its chief exponents, from Lully onwards, should be foreigners, (it must be remembered that certain works of Bellini and Donizetti were popular in the Paris of the '30's and '40's). All the same, it was a native born composer, Daniel Auber (1782–1871) who in 1828 turned from his production of a long stream of *opéra-comique* works (e.g. *Fra Diavolo, Le Cheval de Bronze, Le Domino Noir* . . .) to write a masterpiece, *La Muette de Portico* (" Masaniello "), a most successful opera in the grand manner, with impressive choral effects and bold instrumentation. Another French composer writing meritoriously for the *Opéra Comique*, Jacques Halévy (1799–1862), also scored a single notable success in the supposedly higher form with his *La Juive* (1835). However, the establishment of the grand opera of the Parisian late twenties and onward was in the main the achievement of Meyerbeer, whose works were widely (too widely) regarded in his generation as the quintessence of the operatic art. This brand of grand opera was very much a compound, basically French but not lacking Italian and German ingredients, written for a public for whom " music " was synonymous with " opera ". Thus its chief aim was to obtain spectacular effects on a larger scale. As in most historical forms of opera the pattern was soon conventionalised. Einstein has summarised its main characteristics thus :

" Grand opera must have five acts, no longer three; it must include all the sensational features of operatic theatricality—especially the ballet, which in the Italian *opera seria* either was relegated to a position between the acts or followed the end of the opera itself. It must, in a fixed order, display a romance or a ballade, a few cavatinas and arias for the female and male leads, a passionate duet, and moving scenic effects at the conclusion of at least two acts, to the accompaniment of all available sources of musical power : soloists, chorus and orchestra. Indeed, the *chorus* began to play a greater and greater rôle, from that of mere decoration to real intrusion into the action."—(*A. Einstein: Music in the Romantic Era, p. 122: W. W. Norton & Company, Inc., New York.*)

The earlier career of Jakob Meyerbeer (1791–1864) was indeed one which prepared him for the niche he was to occupy. Born in Berlin of rich and cultured parents he was a brilliant pianist at an early age, and together with C. M. Weber became a pupil of the eccentric Abbé Vogler. Weber had a very great admiration for Meyerbeer both as a man and as a young composer, and always held one of his early *Singspiel* operas (*Alimelek*—1813) to be "genuine German art" and Meyerbeer to have "enormous creative powers". However, Meyerbeer disappointed him by moving to Italy, falling under the spell of Rossini and becoming quite a successful composer of Italian operas of the new *seria* type, culminating with *The Crusader in Egypt* (Venice, 1824). This accomplished work attracted Rossini's attention in Paris, and was produced at the Théatre des Italiens there, which was probably what the composer was aiming at. However, he took a long term view as to the next step, and, always a rich man, could afford to bide his time before attempting to storm the main Paris stronghold. It was characteristic of him that before embarking on this he made a comprehensive study of French operas through the ages, as well as reading French history.

In 1851 he was ready. He had taken the precaution of engaging as librettist the famous Eugène Scribe, to whom every audience-tickling trick of the operatic stage was known. The result was that *Robert le Diable* broke with an astounding effect on the Parisian public. The story was a "romantic" one, for grand opera had finished with classical and mythological subjects (*Les Troyens* stood alone). There were brilliant historical costumes, novel scenic effects and sensational situations, one of these being a ballet of ghostly nuns, rising from their cloister graves. The last feature outraged the more sensitive tastes, Mendelssohn's among the number. But the work showed more meritorious features—an attractive vein of ornate Italianate melody, vigorous declamation, and a closely detailed orchestral score put together with ingenious care and containing many striking effects, all this in contrast with the hurried and thinly-scored work of a great deal of contemporary Parisian opera. It brought huge profits to the *Opéra* itself, and performances quickly spread around Europe.

Meyerbeer was always a slow, hesitant, chop-and-change worker, often driving his partner Scribe to distraction. For this and other reasons it took another five years for him to assemble his masterpiece, *Les Huguenots* (1836). Opinion was lukewarm at first, for there were some variations of the basic pattern, but it quickly grew to even greater popularity than *Robert*, and has maintained a continuous if precarious existence into modern times, its main disadvantage for production being the enormous cost of its lavish staging.[11]*

Meyerbeer's operas have always been criticised as showing " effect without cause or reason"; the complaint being that a dramatic situation is frequently found projected into the action for the sake of its individual impact, without having been derived naturally from plot-development and character. This is certainly true, and although Scribe must take his share of the blame, Meyerbeer was both abettor and at times instigator. The charges of lack of taste, and at times, of sheer vulgarity, are also hard to refute. The desire at all costs to succeed with the audiences whose reactions he so carefully watched showed itself inevitably in a lack of that indefinable sense of integrity that is so apparent in the music of the dedicated composer; though his scores were far from being the " empty piles " of the ungrateful Wagner's denunciation. Berlioz and Wagner owed a great deal to his clever orchestrations, and that without acknowledgment; moreover, there seems little doubt that his melodic and dramatic innovations had considerable effect on the trend of nineteenth century opera.

In spite of German attacks on his music his fame brought him his appointment as *Generalmusikdirector* at Berlin, where he produced not only his own works but German operas in plenty. One of these was the young Wagner's *Rienzi*, the style of which owed much to the older man. Meyerbeer also pressed for a performance of the *Flying Dutchman*, and this took place in Berlin in 1845. Wagner's sense of gratitude may be measured by the poisonous attacks that he made on Meyerbeer in later years.

Meyerbeer's heart was undoubtedly really in Paris. In 1843, *Le Prophéte*, another long-brooded grand-opera, the text by Scribe, was produced there. Again successful, the work contained somewhat less of the element of display. Its " Coronation March " has, at a certain level, continued in remembrance, while the " skating " ballet still lives on at Sadlers Wells as *Les Patineurs*. Meyerbeer's eclectic knack, which enabled him to change his style so easily, gained him success when he ventured to invade the native preserves of the *Opéra Comique* with two three-act works, *L'Étoile du Nord* (1854) and *Dinorah* (1859). Meanwhile, the preparation over the years of his last and possibly most beautiful grand opera, *L'Africaine*, was continuing. The composer wrote and rewrote in his characteristic vacillating fashion, and having at last put it into rehearsal died in 1864 before the first production.

The Meyerbeer influence on French opera other than " grand " lasted long, as Offenbach was later to complain. We have already noted that although Auber was supreme in the field of *opéra-comique*, his *Fra Diavolo* being one of the finest of its type ever written, yet both he and Halévy felt compelled to attempt the " grand " form. Even so, *opéra-comique* was also taking over the cult of the sensational, exemplified by Hérold's *Zampa* (1831). To the name of Ferdinand Hérold (1791–1833) may be added those of Adolphe Adam (1803–56), Félicien David (1810–73) and Ambroise Thomas (1811–96) the latter managing to make *opéra-comique* material out of the figures of Hamlet and Goethe's Mignon. Thomas' *Mignon*, strangely enough was long popular in Germany.

Of more importance is the five-act opera *Faust* of Charles Gounod (1818–93), which still retains a world-wide popularity in spite of its weaknesses, that of false sentiment and at times a saccharine type of melody, which too often outweigh his gifts of dramatic effectiveness and skilled handling of the orchestra. He produced other operas, including the five-act *Roméo et Juliette*. Of these two leading operas Percy Scholes has remarked that those who love Goethe and those who love Shakespeare do not love Gounod. He wrote much church music, including two oratorios, *La Rédemption* and *Mors et Vita*, both once popular in this country, but their over-sentimentalised atmosphere no longer attracts.

A French opera of the period which still lives is the three-act *Samson et Dalila* of Camille Saint-Saëns (1835–1921), a musician of great general culture, at home in all periods. His eclecticism was reflected in the opera, mixed in style—new in what was considered its "voluptuousness" and its hints of Wagnerism, but retaining some of the Parisian conventions, including opportunities for ballet. Paris would have none of it at first, and London banned it until 1909. Liszt it was who arranged for a first performance at Weimar in 1877, although he himself did not direct it.

Of lesser French composers Leo Délibes (1836–91) is remembered chiefly by his *Lakmé* (1889) and for his two delightful ballets, *Coppelia* and *Sylvia*. Jules Massenet (1842–1912) wrote a number of lyrical operas the amorous sentimentality of which gained them wide acceptance. Any single work (say *Manon*) will display the essence of his facile art. His pupil, Gustav Charpentier (b. 1860) followed the same methods for stage success with *Louise*, a *verismo* picture of Paris working-class life, as his best remembered work.

The most significant French opera of the period, *Carmen*, romantic *opéra-comique* on the surface, with spoken dialogue, was the last work of the short-lived Georges Bizet (1838–75). Bizet's early career was full of the richest promise. A pupil of Halévy and Gounod at the Conservatoire, a brilliant young pianist who had actually been greatly praised by Liszt, he won the *Prix de Rome* in his turn, and seemed set for a successful career in what French composers of the time regarded as the highest form of musical art, opera composition. Surprisingly, he seems to have matured very slowly after Rome. There were no triumphs, but instead years of hack work. His *Pearl Fishers* (1863) and *Fair Maid of Perth* (1866) were both comparative failures, while in both of them there was too much of the influence of Gounod and Meyerbeer. (In discussing great musicians Bizet mentioned Beethoven and Meyerbeer in one breath.) Not until after the disaster of the Franco-Prussian war did he begin to find his true and original self. The *opéra-comique*, *Djamileh* (1872) was a stride forward—clever exotic colouring, real characterisation and harmonic originality, and at last a true personal style. Nevertheless, it failed, with a poor libretto partly to account for the fact. His incidental music to Daudet's play *L'Arlésienne*, of the same year, showed the same growing power, although only the more discerning of his contemporaries realised it. It is heard nowadays, frequently enough, in the form of two orchestral suites.

The *Opéra Comique* still persevered with Bizet, but the libretto upon which he engaged himself in the following year represented a new departure for that theatre. Based upon Prosper Merimée's story, "Carmen", the

opera became the first French example of the "veristic" type, which
painted everyday, commonplace life, still allowing romantic charm, but
admitting sordidness and vulgarity. In the wake of *Carmen,* which dared to
stage a murder as a dénouement and ring down the curtain on it without
any moralisings, there has followed a host of the same genre, *Cavalleria
Rusticana* and *Pagliacci* among them. But *Carmen* remains unique, one of
the immortal operas. It met with much hostility at first, even from the
Opéra management, which was concerned with Parisian public opinion and
the charges of critics as to the "repulsiveness" of the story and the
"obscurity" of the music. The composer was bitterly disappointed at its
initial lack of full success, and, his health impaired by years of overwork,
was dead within three months, unaware that his masterpiece was about to
spring to universal fame.

At a time when Wagnerism was spreading far, even in France, Bizet used
the "closed forms" with complete dramatic success, making but slight
use of the *leitmotif* device, but that with unerring effectiveness, as in the
instance of Carmen's "fate" theme :

The experienced pair, Meilhac and Halévy (nephew of Halévy the composer) were responsible for the excellent libretto, and gave opportunities
for characterisation that Bizet seized upon brilliantly. His rich harmony
and orchestral colourings were all his own, even though his few borrowings,
melodic and rhythmic, for his delicious tunes gave a romantic "operatic
Spanish" aura to the Spanish story. One captive of the opera's charm was
no less a person than Brahms. Nietzsche, having broken with his former
idol, declared that the music of *Carmen* should be used as a cure and
medicine against poisoning from Wagner's operas.

Besides the works already mentioned a charming orchestral suite, *Jeux
d'Enfants,* often used as a ballet, still survives, as does a youthful Symphony
in C, revived first in 1935.

Another feature of the French operatic scene must be noted, one concerned mainly with Jacques (Jacob) Offenbach (1819–80). To him in the
main was due the revival, under the name of *operetta* or *opéra-bouffe,* the
light musical stage-work that aimed at satire and parody. Such musical
mockery had been heard in the previous century in the Italian *intermezzi,*
the *Beggar's Opera* and other such *Singspiel,* and the farces performed at
French fairs and small theatres. Offenbach held that the *opéra-comique* of

Auber, Halévy and their like had forgotten its true purpose in trying to ape the methods of grand opera, and wished for a return to the lightheartedness of the late eighteenth century type.

He was German born, but coming as a youth to Paris and obtaining some Conservatoire training, he chose to make his way in the professional life of Paris as a writer of light music. In 1855 he managed to acquire a theatre of his own, *Les Bouffes Parisiennes,* where a number of his operettas were produced. In these, with the aid of clever librettists (including Meilhac and Halévy) he mocked at the pretentious features of serious French and Italian opera in music of great melodic charm and competent craftsmanship. His work (as Einstein puts it) belonged to the Romantic opera as the satyr play belonged to the Attic drama. Of his operettas, at least *Orphée aux Enfers* (1858) and *La Belle Hélène* (1864) are still alive. (The latter came out a year after *Les Troyens.*) We should perhaps have added others. His one *opéra-comique, Les Contes d'Hoffmann,* he failed fully to finish. The task of completion after his death was carried out by the Franco-American composer Ernest Guiraud, who had also been commissioned to add recitatives to *Carmen* in order to turn it into a " grand " opera !

In post-Weber Germany in spite of the continued desire for Italian opera of any kind, the taste soon to be extended to the Meyerbeer " grand " variety and the *opéra-comique* of Auber and other Parisian composers, there were a number of German musicians who continued to produce something of a native art. A very individual form of it was soon to come, and towards the mid-century lesser German opera-composers were " living under Wagner's shadow ", but they were affording their own gleams of light, nevertheless.

Heinrich Marschner (1795–1861) was for a time joint *Kapellmeister* with Weber at Dresden. Imbued with the ideas of German romanticism, in 1828 he produced at Leipzig with sensational success his " horror " opera *Der Vampyr,* which travelled to London and had a long run there. His masterpiece came in 1833 at Hanover—*Hans Heiling,* the libretto by Mendelssohn's friend, Devrient. Dealing again with a supernatural subject, Marschner brought to it some remarkably beautiful music, and displayed a striking command of modulation and refined orchestration.[12*]

A very different figure was Albert Lortzing (1801–51) actor, singer, poet and composer. He was no genius in any of these capacities, but writing his own libretti for a series of German comic operas he caught the public fancy with them. All very German in humour and general atmosphere, the best of them, *Zaar und Zimmermann* (1837), seems still to have survived in Germany. He also tried his hand in the field of romantic " fairy " opera in his *Undine* (1845), with some success.

A musician of higher calibre was Otto Nicolai (1810–49), *Kapellmeister* of the Court Opera at Vienna, for which he wrote a number of works. His masterpiece, produced shortly before his death, was a comic-opera version of *The Merry Wives of Windsor* (1849), an instant success and still holding its place in Germanic countries, its charming overture heard everywhere. Mention has already been made of Schumann's beautiful, dramatically com-

petent but somehow unlucky *Genoveva* (1848). Lesser lights such as von
Flotow (*Martha,* 1847) must be passed over, as we now come to one of the
most remarkable figures of the century.

Richard Wagner (1813–83), born at Leipzig, had an upbringing in which
drama and the theatre played a great part. His stepfather (some would
make the relationship closer) was the Jewish actor and painter Ludwig
Geyer; his elder sisters were on the stage; he himself was early writing
poetry and horrific tragedies, as well as taking an interest in Shakespeare
and ancient Greek literature (the latter in the original). Like the similarly
strong-minded Berlioz he *decided* to become a composer, the reason being
that he was in need of music of his own—of the Beethoven calibre—to
colour his dramatic work. The pattern of the man-to-be can be seen in the
self-assurance with which he plunged into musical composition with but the
slenderest help at first from others. Piano lessons he soon abandoned; again
like Berlioz he never desired to gain competence on the keyboard. When,
at 18, he did seriously seek professional help in composition he was fortunate
in coming under the guidance of Weinlig, cantor of the *Thomaskirche* (J. S.
Bach's old church—there was as yet no magic in the name). Weinlig, who
gave the young man plenty of counterpoint and his first real insight into
the greatness of Beethoven, realised the quality of the mind that he was
dealing with, and waived any payment for some very sound instruction.

Although at 20 he had written a great deal of instrumental music (now
best forgotten) the young composer's heart was in the theatre. In 1833
there began a six-year period of professional appointments with small operatic companies in various lesser German cities. As an ill-paid musical director
he gained an inside practical knowledge of the average German operatic
repertoire of the day, which contained more of the works of the " modern "
French and Italian composers than those of his own countrymen. At the
same time he made some attempts of his own, having learnt the tricks of the
trade, both *grand* and *comique,* and having the unusual advantage of
being able to shape his own libretti. *Das Liebesverbot* (The Ban on Love),
his working of Shakespeare's *Measure for Measure,* produced in 1836 at
Magdeburg, was a thoroughly competent *opéra-comique,* with much of
Spontini and Meyerbeer in its instrumentation. It had, however, but a single
unlucky performance. Undeterred by failure, he was soon planning a five-
act grand opera, *Rienzi,* in the most spectacular and flamboyant style of
Meyerbeer.

Throughout his life Wagner was a ruthless egoist. Convinced of his high
artistic importance to the world, he always took the view that the grateful
world should provide him not only with the necessities but also the luxuries
of life, luxuries being equally necessary for him as he pursued his career
of creation. Thus the years abounded with bilked tradesmen and sponged-on
friends. When he decided to go to Paris in 1839, with the idea of launching
Rienzi where its success would have the greatest effect, he was moved also
by the necessity of escaping an already well-established horde of exasperated
creditors. With him went his wife Minna, a former actress, with whom he
had made an impulsive marriage in 1836. She was a gentle, undistinguished,

oft-forgiving soul, no companion for an erratic and self-centred genius. Their life together was filled with quarrels, parting and reconciliations, until a final parting in 1862.

The journey (from Riga) was made by sea, a fearsome experience of weeks of tempest, later turned to account in the wonderful storm-music of the *Flying Dutchman*. At Boulogne he met Meyerbeer, and impressed him with the incomplete score of *Rienzi*. With a recommendation from the great man he travelled to Paris, where two years of disillusionment awaited him. Neither *Rienzi* nor the later completed *Flying Dutchman* could obtain a hearing, and only hack work for publishers, together with the usual loans extracted from kindly friends, saved the pair in their indigence. On the credit side it is clear that the composer heard much finely-played music, including the Beethoven performances of that conductor of genius, Habeneck, and, on his own admission, learned from the instrumental colour-innovations of Berlioz, whom he met, together with Liszt. Neither was particularly impressed by him, and he soon convinced himself, probably quite wrongly, that the far-too-prosperous Meyerbeer was his secret enemy. It was during the Paris years that he made acquaintance with the " Tannhaüser " and " Lohengrin " legends. Thus early in his artistic career began his devotion to those Germanic sagas that ruled the rest of it.

Then came a change of fortune. Midway through 1841 Dresden accepted *Rienzi* for performance, and early in the next year Wagner and Minna were able to leave Paris. The staging of the opera was a resounding success and gave the composer immediate fame. Next year, also at Dresden, the *Flying Dutchman* had its premiere, though with less favourable a reception. This is not surprising, for it was a very different work, one in which Wagner had taken a leap forward, both as dramatist and composer, even though French influences were not altogether shaken off, and there were still echoes of Weber and Marschner. But in Senta and the Dutchman were two living figures, and around them was the swirl and roar of the sea. The work attracted the critical Spohr, who praised it warmly and produced it himself at Cassel.

Meanwhile Wagner's new reputation brought him early in 1843 what was regarded as a coveted post, that of *Hofkapellmeister* to the Saxon Court. Creditors swarmed at the news, and debts were settled mainly by the establishment of new ones. For the next few years he achieved some valuable musical results, not only as an opera producer but as organiser and con-ductor of orchestral concerts. There was an historic performance of Beethoven's neglected Ninth Symphony; also he prepared two successful concerts for the visiting Berlioz. Meanwhile *Tannhaüser* had been com-pleted. Dresden heard it first in 1845, and it soon gained friends elsewhere, though Berlin and Paris would have none of it. Actually it represented no great artistic progress, and to the modern hearer its *longueurs* and crudities are apparent. By 1847 a new work founded on German legend was com-pleted, new in every sense of the word, for in *Lohengrin* Wagner had gone forward again, and reached his peak as a composer of romantic opera. Poetry and music were now linked in close accord, and even though the

x

traditional set numbers—aria, duet and ensemble—were still there, these were given some degree of continuity. What had happened was that Wagner the musician had at last overtaken Wagner the dramatist. The expressive melodic line is now unmistakably Wagner's own, the sonorous choruses make a real psychological contribution; above all the orchestration rises to new heights of achievement, giving distinctive colourings to character and scene. In this work he reached a climax in the art of lyrical romantic opera beyond which, he realised, he could not progress. In it, as in previous works, it was vocal melody which shaped the drama. The orchestra served to paint, to comment, to employ even the motive of reminiscence, but the singer was still dominant. There was now to begin a new and revolutionary style, in which more and more the " hundred-tongue " symphonic orchestra would assert itself, taking over the functions of the chorus and indeed providing the main means for the expression of dramatic emotion.

As it happened Wagner was not destined to hear a real performance of *Lohengrin* for many a year. In 1848 some of the political unrest that filled Europe at the time showed itself in Saxony. Wagner, already not wholly in favour at Court, became implicated in a revolutionary movement, and was compelled to fly the country. He took refuge at first at Weimar with Liszt. The latter's views on Wagner had now changed. With his usual discernment he recognised in him a composer of high promise, a fellow apostle preaching the cause of the " new music ", and thus one to be given every assistance. For the rest of his life Wagner turned time and again to the generous-hearted Liszt for tribute. But no part of Germany was safe for the fugitive at the moment, and Wagner soon moved to Switzerland, leaving Liszt to produce *Tannhaüser,* and later, *Lohengrin* at Weimar. The long-tried Minna eventually rejoined her husband at Zurich, and there began for the composer a period of exile, during which, until 1855, hardly a note of music was written, a six years' silence in that respect.

Up to 1861 his headquarters remained at Zurich, from which he travelled at times to " safe " regions such as Italy, Paris and London, employing his gifts as a conductor. He had now greater opportunities of brooding upon his theories concerning the future of opera, and how he himself would expand and reshape it into something of the highest cultural purpose. The result was a number of prose works, e.g. *Art and Revolution, The Art-Work of the Future,* and the monumental *Opera and Drama.* There was also the ugly and pseudonymously printed snarl, *Judaism in Music.* Wagner was always envious of the easy worldly circumstances of Meyerbeer and Mendelssohn.

At the time his dicta concerning the " universal art-work " were taken very seriously in Germany. Nowadays, with the advantage of looking back on events, we can afford to disregard most of the written verbiage and give our respect almost wholly to Wagner the musician. In many of his theoretical ideas he was but echoing what had been said before by Algarotti, Calzabigi, Gluck and others, although some of his practical reforms could never henceforth be wholly disregarded. According to him the " Art-Work of the Future ", of which he considered himself the high-priest, would be a partnership of all that was best in all the arts, for music could no longer stand alone. It must in future be "fertilised by poetry", as (thus he argued) Beethoven himself had shown in his Ninth Symphony. This "universal art-work" would have three main means of expressing itself—*Tanz, Ticht* and *Ton,* i.e. gesture, poetry and musical sound. Other arts would make contri-butions, e.g. architecture and painting. Only in the theatre, of course, could such a combination be achieved—and this in the new "music-drama". In future, said the poet and musician that was Wagner, the poet will not restrict himself for the sake of the music, nor the musician for the sake of the poetry. A true balance must be struck. For too long had poetry been subservient to music (an echo that rings all the way from 1600). He called also for a parallel unity, one of a spirit of devotion, binding together all who took part in this fellowship of the arts—singers, players, even the stage-hands. A similar devotion was demanded of the *listeners,* who should approach such a work in a very different mood from that of the normal audiences of the time, one of serious and absorbed attention (and, it went without saying, in a spirit of due reverence towards its originator).

As a competent and imaginative dramatic writer Wagner was enabled better than any other composer for the stage to achieve a unity between *Ticht* and *Ton.* In the works which followed this outpouring of theory, though the "poems" were written first, undoubtedly much of the thematic musical material was present in his mind and had some influence on the shaping of the text. What in the end brought about the ultimate fading of his "art-work of the future" dreams was the fact that while he was an effi-cient dramatist and a passable poet, he was as a musician, by contrast, a towering genius, and in the end it was the glorious symphonic flood of orchestral sound, ostensibly no more than the commentary, which became the predominant partner; so much so that excerpts from actual scenes from the music-dramas have been for many decades played in concert halls (e.g. Isolda's *Liebstod*) without the vocal parts being in any way missed. The composer himself sanctioned the partnership of the "Tristan" *Vorspiel* with the *Liebstod* as a concert item. It was Wagner, also, who said to the short-sighted Nietzsche at a performance of *Tristan* : "Take your glasses off ! You must hear nothing but the orchestra."

His first practical moves towards the building of this new art began in 1848 with his first poetic sketches of an episode from the German legendary epic, the *Nibelungenlied.* This episode he termed *Siegfried's Death,* the material of what is now *Götterdämmerung* (The Twilight of the Gods). He then discovered that some features of the story could only be fully under-stood through the writing of another poetic drama as prologue—*Siegfried.* Similar conclusions led to the creation of two more such linked dramas— *The Valkyrie* and *The Rhinegold.* Thus the poems of *The Ring of the Nibelung,* as the whole tremendous tetralogy came to be called, were written in an inversion of their natural sequence. This accounts for some of the wearisome stretches of explanation which occur from time to time. The texts of the whole of the *Ring* were completed in the summer of 1852, and represented an enormous act of faith as well as a new departure for Wagner the poet. Instead of the long rhyming lines of his earlier libretti (so often scanning as 11, 10, 11, 10, to the point of monotony) he adopted a metrical system founded on the short alliterative line of old German poetry. This blended well with the new musical style which began with the setting of *Rhinegold,* started in 1853.

The most striking feature of this style was his *systematic* use of the *leit-motif*. He had employed this device in less definite fashion in his earlier works, as indeed had many an operatic composer before his time, but with *The Ring* came a great and original expansion of the idea. These motifs, used with a new copiousness, are normally brief in dimension, always music-ally interesting and thus readily recognisable, and were altered, developed and even combined with each other during the progress of a work in a man-ner which achieved striking dramatic effects, and at the same time a sense of overall unity. His genius had so expanded that these contrapuntal weav-ings created simultaneously, when he so desired, the richest of harmonic effects. In innumerable ways the subtle references sounding in the orchestra added points to the drama. The instrumental commentaries, unlike those of a vocal chorus, were unceasing; they represented indeed the voice of the composer, ever talking, ever explaining his intentions and pointing the morals. By means of these motifs he limned characters, recalled previous events, hinted at the unspoken thoughts of his stage creations, and on occasion even reminded the listeners, in dramatic irony, of something that the figure on the stage did not know. The intentions and technical hand-lings of these motifs were far too subtle for them to be thought of as a collection of labels, the " lunatic's musical visiting-card " of Debussy's well-known gibe, which applied better to Wagner's imitators. This endless musical flow had a dramatic advantage inasmuch as it permitted no break in continuity from the beginning to the end of an act. For the old " closed forms " Wagner substituted his vocal system of " endless *melos* ", which came under attack as being no melody at all. Nowadays, no one would deny lyrical passages to *The Ring, Tristan* and *Parsifal,* but as we have already noted, in these works the musical interest is definitely more in the orchestral pit than on the stage. It would seem that he fashioned these music-dramas not in the usual manner, as vocally conceived operas, orchestrally accom-panied, but as symphonically developed and highly dramatic orchestral scores. At times it looks as if the vocal line has been the last consideration, shaped to fit into the orchestral scheme of the moment merely as one not particularly distinguished strand of the contrapuntal web. The new and masterly techniques used in the orchestral writing must of course be credited first to Wagner's own genius, but also to his study and assimilation of the " development " methods used by Beethoven in his symphonies, as well as to his close acquaintance with Liszt's symphonic poems, with their then new exploitation of the *leitmotif* device. Undoubtedly he made use also of some of Liszt's harmonic innovations, which often enough he turned to better account than did their originator. Nevertheless his mature harmonic style was altogether his own, unique and unmistakable. The rich and varied tone-palette which was the *Ring* orchestra contained some innovations; a third instrument was added to the normal wood-wind pairs, giving, if needed, a complete chord for each colour; a bass clarinet was obligatory; the (chromatic) horns had their number doubled, and new brass instruments, the bass trumpet and the Wagnerian tubas, made their appearance. The trend was set towards the gigantic orchestras of Mahler and Richard Strauss.

The steady progress in the composition of the " Ring " music was interrupted in 1857, at some point in *Siegfried*, and not resumed for another twelve years. The immediate reason was a domestic upheaval which led to a parting from Minna. Otto Wesendonck, a rich business man of Zurich, had not only lent Wagner money, but had rented the pair a pleasant house on his estate at a nominal charge. In return Wagner engaged in an intrigue with his impressionable young wife, Mathilde. To the credit side (if such a term can be permitted) of this episode is the fact that it triggered off in Wagner's mind the conception of one of the most wonderful art-works ever written, the music-drama *Tristan und Isolde.* It was finished in 1859, and (another fact of faith) the score accepted and engraved by Breitkopf & Härtel. It lay silent until 1865. It was Wagner's most fervent and romantic work, a drama of Dionysiac rapture; unified in style and mood, and expressed in music of a nature such as had never before been imagined, overwhelming in the tremendous erotic power of its chromaticism. " Evil ", " orgiastic ", " poisonous " it has been called, but none can doubt the force of its impact on the harmonic thought of the generations to follow. For all the static periods on the stage, the lapses into banality of the alliterative verse, the grip of the music never relaxes, from the first notes of the wonderful " Love Potion " theme in the Prelude :

to its final echo as the lovers lie dead :

During 1859–60 there occurred the episode of the attempted revival of *Tannhaüser* in Paris, for which the composer wrote a much improved version of the opening Venusberg music, but which was wrecked by organised rowdyism in the auditorium. Returning from France, he was at last allowed to enter Germany once more (thanks to Minna's efforts on his behalf). He wandered restlessly from place to place, eluding creditors and seeking chances for any further production of his works. He heard in the same year, and for the first time, a performance of *Lohengrin* at Vienna. He was now at the nadir of his fortune, yet such was the indomitable spirit of the man that, with long-laboured works, finished and unfinished, lying silent, he could yet turn to a new major project. Ever since 1845 he had had in mind a story which had for its background the sixteenth-century citizen "Mastersingers", whose leading figure was the cobbler-poet Hans Sach. He hastened to complete the poem, and early in 1861 the music was begun. There was little peace for such a task; his concert tours took him far and wide, until in 1864 the pursuit of his creditors reached a climax and his position became one of all-time desperation.

Then the miracle occurred. More or less in hiding in Stuttgart he received a message from the recently crowned, eighteen-year-old King of Bavaria, long a worshipper of his early romantic works, and somehow well aware of his present aims. Ludwig bade him come to Munich to be his friend and artistic adviser. Duly installed, Wagner summoned to his aid as conductor and Court pianist, Hans von Bülow, one of the circle of promising young musicians who had paid homage to him at Zurich. As von Bülow's wife was Liszt's daughter Cosima, already in love with the composer after his last visit to Weimar, here was a Tristan-King Mark situation which occurred more than once in Wagner's career. With ample musical resources to hand *Tristan und Isolde* was at last given performance in July 1865, under von Bülow's direction. But by the end of the year opposition, both public and official, to Wagner's influence over the somewhat unbalanced young king, was such that the composer was forced to retire to Triebschen in Switzerland, whence, however, Ludwig's munificence followed him. So also did Cosima, against whom at last the almost incredibly complaisant von Bülow had begun divorce proceedings. In the years at Triebschen the "Mastersingers" was completed, together with most of the remainder of the "Ring" music. Ludwig had been disappointed with Wagner the man, but against opposition continued to support the cause of his music. Others also seemed to be able to recognise the distinction between man and artist. When in June 1868 the genial comedy *Die Meistersinger von Nürnburg* received its first performance it was von Bülow who directed it, with Wagner temporarily in Munich to help in its preparation.

It is amazing to realise with what complete success Wagner was able to change his style in the composition of "Mastersingers". After the grimly serious gods and heroes of the mythological "Ring" story, and the hothouse atmosphere of self-centred erotic passion that dominated *Tristan,* we enter a fresh-air world of living human beings. For the poem Wagner returned to the normal-length rhyming line, and the vivid and various characters were drawn with the utmost skill—Hans Sach, the wise, kindly, understanding figure who dominates the work; an Eva of girlish charm; the young knight Walther, the re-creation of a chivalrous *Minnesänger,* and a background of honest German " masters " and high-spirited apprentices. It is an atmosphere of humour and tolerance, with the single foil of the querulous Beckmesser, Wagner's spiteful caricature of his chief music-critic enemy, Hanslick. In recalling scenes from mid-sixteenth century Nuremburg the composer returned to the older operatic techniques of choruses, processions, dances, occasional closed numbers—even a vocal quintet—as well as fugal movements, ancient chorales, lute playing and other musical devices to remind us of the past, even though the music is essentially his own. It is a changed music, though. There is plenty of flowing melody on the stage as well as in the orchestra, and the polyphony, though intricate (we may remind ourselves of the miraculous combination of the three main themes of the work at its climax) is, by comparison with *Tristan,* of a sturdily diatonic quality.

Minna had died in 1866. Cosima having at last been divorced, she and Wagner were married in 1870. On Christmas Day of that year came his tribute to her, the immortal *Siegfried Idyll* for small orchestra. Also in 1870 came the crushing of France and the emergence of the German Empire. Cured of his revolutionary ideals, Wagner planned to use the new chauvinistic spirit of German nationalism for the furtherance of his own aims—the erection of a theatre devoted to the production of his so-German music-dramas. During the next year he moved to Bayreuth, a small town in Bavaria, near to which a possible site had been found. To many the scheme must have appeared a crazy one, but backed by the composer's will-power and the money raised by admirers throughout Europe, the temple for his art was actually completed in 1876. The music of the " Ring " also having been finished, its performance began under conditions such as Wagner had long dreamed of—and written about—when everyone, on either side of the footlights, was disciplined into uninterrupted concentration upon the progress of the drama. Closed doors at the beginning of an act; a darkened auditorium; complete silence during orchestral prelude or interlude; a sunken, shielded area that hid altogether instrumentalists and conductor—these were some of the features unfamiliar to the opera-audiences of the day. If something of the same spirit of attention and decorum is observed in modern opera performance it is very largely to the Wagner tradition that we owe it.

Also at long last Wagner was gaining the patronage of the powers-that-be. Single-handed, a little German *Kapellmeister* had fought the whole musical world and won through, even though for a time there were financial razor-edges for Bayreuth. But Wagner was armoured against these situations and overcame them. Also, *The Ring,* being allowed to be performed elsewhere, won him considerable returns. In 1882 he completed at Bayreuth his last work, *Parsifal,* a subject, that of the Grail legend, upon which he had long brooded. The once militant atheist was now seen in the guise of a Christian mystic; the lifelong sensualist was now offering praise to chastity and putting upon the stage a scene which bore a close resemblance to the Roman Mass. But though there were outraged criticisms—Neitzsche for one saw materialistic motives in Wagner's change of heart—the power and beauty of the music, the style once more narcotically chromatic, gave a last triumph to the fast-ageing composer. It had its first performance in July 1882. Less than six months after came his death.

Far from establishing a " new art-work of the future " the effect of Wagner's music-dramas was very nearly to give the death-blow to *German* opera. His influence was so enormous as to encourage a swarm of second-rate imitations of a matter and method too individual and original to be successfully copied. The most satisfactory and longest lived of dramatic works based on Wagnerian technique and orchestral style was by Engelbert Humperdinck (1854–1921), who as a young man helped to produce *Parsifal*. In *Hänsel und Gretel* he attempted no heroic heights, but in charming and tuneful fashion dealt with no more than a children's fairy-tale; an instance, one might think, of historic irony. As for Wagner's own great works, they have long left their temple and have taken their places in the modern repertoire along with operas written before and after their advent. While the composer was yet living, the Italian, Verdi, was demonstrating in his own masterpieces that living characters and tense dramatic situation could still be painted in terms of the human voice with no more than subordinate assistance from the orchestra. As he himself said very reasonably : " Opera is opera, and symphony is symphony ".

Moreover, for all the Wagnerian impact, it was found that great music could still flourish alone, without of necessity being " fertilised by poetry ". In the year of Wagner's death, Johannes Brahms was planning the last and greatest of his four symphonies.

After Rossini's retirement the two most prominent Italians in the operatic field were Bellini and Donizetti, both of whom endeavoured to save the old Italian operatic ideals, while making use of the chorus in the new manner of the Mayr school. The short-lived Vincenzo Bellini (1801–35) relied almost entirely on his gift of rich and refined melody, so individual in its beauty, which charmed even Wagner, and had its influence on Chopin and Liszt. His harmony and instrumentation were no doubt commonplace, but his avoidance of complexity of any sort other than monodic was deliberate, the better to concentrate on the solo or duet (often with a soft choral background) with which he was able to paint quite convincingly living characters and dramatic situations. *Opera seria* lived on in *La Sonnambula* and *Norma,* both of 1831. He was for a while in Paris, encouraged by Rossini. There, in *I Puritani* (1835), he made some attempt to come to terms with French grand opera, but very much in his own way, that of an Italian romantic.

Compared with the refined Bellini with his hatred of noise, Gaetano Donizetti (1797–1848) was of coarser grain. Gifted with an enormous facility, he poured out a ceaseless stream of dramatic works (more than 60), giving himself but little time to ponder details. Being told that Rossini had composed his " Barber " in thirteen days, he replied : " Yes, yes, he was always lazy!" His own methods, as far as success was concerned, meant that at times hit alternated with miss. His *opera seria, Lucia di Lammermoor* (1835), with its brilliant *coloratura* writing (including the famous "mad-scene" and a remarkable sextet), still holds the stage in Italy. Like Bellini he was drawn to Paris, where he adopted a French guise for the still-played *La Fille du Régiment* (1840). His masterpiece was the *opera buffa, Don Pasquale* (Paris, 1843), a work certainly on a lower plane than that of Rossini's *Barber* and Verdi's *Falstaff*, but still compelling admiration and performance.[13] The overlordship of Italian opera was soon to pass to the last-named composer, the greatest master ever of the Italian art.

Guiseppe Verdi (1813–1901) was in most ways the antithesis of his great contemporary, Richard Wagner. He was born of humble peasant stock in the small village of Roncole in Parma, and in his boyhood lacked opportunities for either literary education, or even musical training of much consequence. Unlike Wagner, his character was one of basic simplicity and honesty, which later success never spoilt. Unlike him, also, he had no theories to air concerning dramatic art; he merely wrote opera after opera, steadily developing his natural gifts. " I am not a great composer ", he once said, with characteristic modesty, " but I am a very experienced one ". Thanks to the divine discontent which made him always build upon such experience, it was in his eightieth year that he was at the height of his powers! It was he above all others who showed in a world that was taking great note of Wagner's *leitmotif* symphonic works, that genuine opera must still remain in principle a vocal art.

There were those in Roncole and in the nearby small town of Busetto willing to help the gifted lad, in particular the music-loving merchant Barezzi, later his father-in-law. After some years as organist, pianist and local composer, he was sent at the age of nineteen to Milan, where, though the Conservatoire would not receive him, he gained more admirers and some competent private instruction. After some precarious years divided between Milan and Busetto there came the amazing acceptance of his very first opera by Merelli, the director of La Scala, and its printing by a young music publisher, Giovanni Ricordi, afterwards widely famous. Late in 1839 *Oberto* scored an immediate, if qualified, success. It was on the usual *opera seria* pattern, crude in many ways, and blatant in its instrumentation, but already the presence of a fresh and remarkable melodic gift was apparent. Merelli offered further contracts; then, as the young composer's path to success seemed open, his world crashed around him. His young wife (he had married in 1836) followed their two children to death, and, as might be expected, his next opera (ironically a comic one) failed completely. He declared that he would compose no more, but Merelli knew better. In due course he coaxed upon him a libretto of the Biblical story of Nebuchad-nezzar, and Verdi's musical instincts were aroused afresh. *Nabucco,* produced at La Scala in 1842, was a complete and widely hailed success, and the Italian public took Verdi to their hearts, once and for all. He was fortunate in more than one way. For one thing, Bellini being dead and Donizetti desperately ill, he stood out already as Italy's most promising composer. The music he was writing, though far from representing the mature Verdi, had already a fire, energy and sincerity not to be found in rival works. Moreover, the country was waiting for a politico-musical lead such as he was able to give. A conglomeration of separate states, it was seething with political discontent, and the hand of Austria lay very heavy on the north. The revolutionary movement was beginning, which, though defeated in 1848, eventually brought about unification under the native House of Savoy. The opera, that told of a captive race groaning under a tyranny, afforded analogies that the public throughout Italy seized upon with fervour. *Nabucco* was a work apart among Verdi's early operas, so vital that it can still hold the stage among his late masterpieces, even though we can no longer thrill to the double meanings of patriotic choruses. The next work, " The Lombards of the First Crusade ", was produced at Milan in 1843 before delighted Lombards, crusader-minded, and occasioned the first of Verdi's many clashes with the censor. *Ernani,* which followed next year, began Verdi's libretto links with French romantic authors, in this case Victor Hugo. Once again a patriotic chorus (*O mia patria . . .*) occasioned a public storm. With *Ernani* Verdi's reputation began to spread north of the Alps. A feature of the work is his first use of a recurring motive, associated with a character or mood, but not used structurally in the manner of a Wagnerian *leitmotif,* for which technique he had no use. A spate of further operas, mostly successful at the time with a public that dragged from them every impossible political implication, were nevertheless written too hastily for permanent life. There seems no doubt that Verdi during this time was a melancholy and disillusioned man, sickened of his career and planning to make sufficient money to retire from it to country life and solitude. However, by the late '40's his works were in regular demand at all the operatic centres of Italy, and Paris and even London were beginning to be interested. In 1847 he accepted an invitation to London, where he admired everything but the climate. The opera which he wrote for His Majesty's Theatre and Jenny Lind has passed into oblivion. Paris, which was his home on and off for two years, drew from him a French adaptation of *I Lombardi.* Earlier in the same year, in Italy, he had produced an opera of some greater significance. His cultural background may not have been deep, but he gave a life-long devotion to Shakespeare (in Carcano's translation). " The greatest authority on the heart of man ", he called him. *Macbeth* was the first practical sign of his devotion. The Italian-style text (by Verdi's usual librettist, Piave) would give but little satisfaction to a modern hearer, and was a travesty of the grim Northern tragedy with its atmosphere of darkness and blood. But in his setting Verdi was groping towards a more earnest and declamatory style at moments of high tension, and even urged his singers to study the dramatic situations more closely. However, Italian audiences and singers were far more concerned with *bel canto,* and Verdi himself was not altogether ready for the freer forms of his later years. The work failed, and in the somewhat undistinguished operas that followed close upon it he returned to the more popular style. He could not forget *Macbeth* however, and later in his career revised it. In 1848, " the year of revolutions ", he watched with grief the crushing of the risings at Milan and Venice. In the next year the production in Rome of his *Battle of Legnano* (the defeat of the Emperor Barbarossa by the Lombard League) roused a post-revolution popular frenzy.

Already he had bought an estate near to Busetto, Sant' Agata, which he gradually adapted as his permanent home. With him was Guiseppina Strepponi, the singer who had done a great deal towards the staging of *Oberto* in 1838, and whom he had met again in Paris. She was known as " Signora Verdi " long before they were at last married in 1859. Her influence on the composer was in every way for the good. She smoothed some of the rougher peasant edges, persuaded him to relax the tempo of his musical labours, did much to lift the cloud of his inveterate melancholy, and shared his delight in the country life of the estate, where Verdi became a patriarchal figure, employing at one time over two hundred people. She lived to see the final triumphs of his old age, dying only four years before him.

In 1851–3 all that had gone before was overshadowed by the appearance, close together, of three remarkable works. These, still written in the traditional *opera seria* framework of the closed forms, with cadenza-decorated arias liable, alas, to be " encored ", are even now high on the list of the most popular operas in the world—*Rigoletto* (Venice, 1851), *Il Trovatore* (Rome, 1853) and *La Traviata* (Venice, 1853). The libretti of all three were based on French romantic plays. Verdi was learning much from the French school, but it could teach him nothing in the matter of exploiting dramatic situations in terms of melody. Moreover, he was able to carry out what the Meyerbeer tribe so seldom troubled about, the justification of these dramatic highlights as arising from the human characteristics that he was learning to paint so vividly in terms of vocal music.

Rigoletto (founded on Victor Hugo's *Le Roi s'amuse*) is the best constructed of the three, notable among other things for its study of the complex character of the deformed jester, pander to the Duke, yet winning our pity in the end. There is a new care and depth in the orchestral accompaniment, which plays a greater part than the composer had yet allowed it. " La donna è mobile . . ." may not in itself seem a very subtle tune, yet subtle is the use to which its re-echo is put at the climax of the tragedy. The famous quartet is also well-known. It is generally allowed that *Il Trovatore* (The Troubadour) has an almost incomprehensible libretto, but the work sweeps the listener on from beginning to end by its irresistible vitality. Tune after fascinating tune occur in close succession—the " Anvil " and " Soldiers " choruses, the " Miserere ", the duet " *Ai nostri monti* . . ."—to name but a few. Technically *Il Trovatore* represented a recession in many of its features, particularly in the comparative crudity of its orchestral writing, but its lyrical power will always keep it alive. *La Traviata* (The Frail One—founded on *La Dame aux Camelias* by Dumas *fils*), unlike the other two failed on its first appearance, a matter in which, it seems, the singers were to blame, for it quickly became a favourite. With this, the tragedy of a high-minded courtesan, there was established the type of naturalistic

" everyday life " opera, eventually termed *verismo,* a (later) example of which we have already noted in *Carmen.* Ever since *Ernani* Verdi had made occasional use of the recurring motif; in *Traviata* the device is employed in particularly effective fashion. The scoring returns to the stand-ard of imagination shown in *Rigoletto,* with a striking passage for high divided strings, written long before the composer had encountered the *Lohengrin* Prelude.. The opera's greenest evergreen is probably " *Ah fors' è lui . . .*"

Paris was now more than ever interested in Verdi. After a period spent happily as estate owner at Sant' Agata, and less happily with a libretto of *King Lear,* a work that was never completed, the composer accepted a com-mission to write a five-act opera for the Paris Exhibition of 1885. It was through French grand opera (rather than from any contact with Wagner's music) that his outlook was being broadened. For something over a decade, until the advent of *Aïda,* he developed towards his mature style, altogether Italian and unique, and gradually got grand opera out of his system. The Exhibition work was *The Sicilian Vespers,* with Meyerbeer's partner, Scribe, as librettist and too much of Meyerbeer in the style of the music, which has survived chiefly in its overture. Back in Italy there came *Simone Boccanegra* (Venice 1857), another comparative failure, and *Un ballo in maschara* (The Masked Ball—Rome, 1857). The latter ran into grave trouble with the censor at Naples, where it should first have been produced. Assassination of rulers was not a safe subject. A further national upheaval was approaching, and the composer's popularity, expressed in the cry " *Viva Verdi!*" was intended also to imply " *Viva Vittorio Emmanuela Re D'Italia!*" In 1860, with the King and his minister Cavour established, Verdi was compelled to desert composition for a time to act as a parliamentary deputy.

A commission from Petersburg brought him back to music. *La Forza del Destino* (The Force of Destiny) was performed in the Russian capital in 1862, and has lived by its fine tunes, in spite of the extreme gloom and bloodshed of the story. Notable in the midst of tragedy is the figure of a comic monk, which, it is sometimes suggested, may have given Mussorgsky the idea of Vaarlem in his " Boris ". In the often-performed overture is heard the simple yet so effective three-note " Fate " motive. Returned to Paris (1864–5) the composer wrote his last grand opera, *Don Carlos* (founded on a Schiller play), in which deeper harmonic resources and enriched powers of orchestra-tion are apparent. There came a request from an unexpected quarter, Egypt, where at Cairo a large opera house was to be opened. Verdi twice refused a munificent offer, but was eventually attracted by the story devised by the Egyptologist, Mariette, shaped into a libretto (*Aïda*) which permitted a variety of dramatic and exotic scenes and much pageantry. Verdi seems to have intervened a great deal as the text was being shaped, as he had done in the case of many an earlier opera. He may have lacked at times an overall critical judgment, but he had a keen eye for a dramatic situation, or the lack of one. The much delayed performance of *Aïda* at Cairo in December 1871, followed by another at Milan soon after, revealed a Verdi master-piece, the first of the great four. Gone were any French traces; all was

Verdi, and moreover a new Verdi. It was spectacular Italian *opera seria*, with lyric arias, duets, trios, ensembles, marches—but combined with much dramatic declamation and with greater importance than ever given to the participation of the orchestra. It was all the result of a Verdian evolution; when the stupid gibe of " Wagnerism " was heard it aroused the composer to extreme anger. The instrumentation of his last works, as eloquent and plastic as Wagner's, was a world apart from Bayreuth.

The death of the great Italian writer Manzoni in 1875 was the occasion that roused Verdi once more to a work of high drama, but not one for the stage. In Manzoni's memory he composed a *Requiem* which used every resource of vocal and orchestral inspiration at his command. The *Dies Irae* movement is one of terrifying intensity; indeed, the whole work had to face at first, especially in Germany, the charge of " theatricality ". But it is now universally recognised for what it is—with Mozart's the greatest of its kind. It was soon being heard outside Italy; the composer himself took it to Paris, Vienna and even as far as London. Thereafter came over a dozen years of quiet life and musical silence before the advent of the first of the crowning achievements.

Chiefly responsible for the breaking of the silence was the poet and composer Arrigi Boito (1842–1918), a man of considerable culture, who had himself created an opera, *Mefistofele* (yet another working of Goethe's Faust) in 1865. This was unsuccessful at first, but has managed to maintain itself to the present day, even though, musically, Boito was far from being a Verdi, as he himself well knew. Whatever his merits as a musician, he was able to bring a knowledgeable and two-sided attitude to his responsibilities as librettist to a greater man. Some friends of both (Ricordi among them) engaged in an amiable conspiracy to bring them together, having the opinion that something remarkable might come of the partnership. Furthermore, they soon had a concrete proposal—that use might be made of Shakespeare's *Othello*. There was ice to be broken. Verdi had to overcome his suspicions of a man who had frequently expressed his enthusiasm for Wagner's music, which Verdi regarded as a deadly drug for Italian composers, while Boito had not always been an admirer of Verdi, though now thoroughly converted, and holding himself honoured to serve him. The project was a long while getting under way, but Boito gave a good lead by providing what is now admitted to be a text of extraordinary merit. He brought to his task an aesthetic judgment such as neither Verdi nor his previous librettists had been able to command. A compression of the original action was necessary, together with some transference of some of the details, and all this was done with the utmost artistry. The poetry was at a high literary level, as close to the original as was reasonably possible, and shorn of the word-repetitions that so often disfigured Italian operas (including Verdi's). Between them, the pair even dared to make a major inset of their own, the celebrated " Credo ", which enabled Iago to carry through a traditional feature of Italian opera, the " apron stage " confidential solo, addressed deliberately to the audience.

Verdi received the complete libretto in 1879, and expressed himself pleased with it, but the ageing composer was reluctant to commit himself, and there now began on his part an extraordinary series of evasive actions, including many months spent on revisions of two of his earlier operas. But the guileful persistence of his friends, abetted by Guiseppina, at last persuaded him to begin composition. Boito worked with him in the friendliest understanding, but Verdi refused to be hurried. It was in November 1886 that he was at last able to write a letter announcing that the score was finished. He concluded the sentence with seven exclamation marks; it was seven years since he had received the libretto. The first performance of the work at La Scala in February 1887 became in fact a festival of homage to Verdi. Musicians from all over Europe came to Milan to hear what the seventy-three year old composer had accomplished. They found something in the nature of a musical miracle. The gradual changes in method and style, the enriching of harmony and orchestral practice, begun with *Macbeth* and noticeable in *Rigoletto,* had reached their consummation. There are great set pieces—the powerful storm chorus with its raging orchestra, the love-duet, Desdemona's exquisite " Willow Song " among them, yet it is the nature of the dramatic recitative that is the most striking. There is a new plasticity in it, declamatory and yet as always melodious. The action flows on far more continuously than before, the obvious breaks for applause are gone, the points of repose are dependent on dramatic necessity, yet the composer is still distinguishing between lyricism and declamation. No use is made of leading motives; each character is painted by its own immediate music. But there are subtleties in plenty—such as the reminiscence, heard in the orchestra during the last terrible moments of the tragedy, of the lovely music of the first-act love-duet. The orchestra, while never dominating the voices, is handled with an insight and mastery never before attained by an Italian composer. As P. H. Lang truly says :

"The old form of the opera so contemptuously buried by Wagner and his apologists, returns here raised to undreamed of heights. And it presents us with a miracle : another *Othello,* not Shakespeare's, but one that is its equal; drama and opera, independent entities, and each the peak of its species."—*P. H. Lang; Music in Western Civilisation, p. 911: W. W. Norton & Company, Inc., New York.*

The acclamations over (Verdi hated publicity) he returned to what he termed approvingly the " loneliness " of Sant' Agata. But Boito had not done with him. Again with the connivance of Guiseppina he began the task of persuading the *maestro* to yet another effort. It was in his favour that the proposed subject was Shakespeare's *Falstaff,* and that Verdi remembered that Rossini had once said that he couldn't write a comic opera. In his libretto Boito matched his *Otello* skill. Basing it on the " Merry Wives " he also incorporated material from the much more satisfactory " Henry IV " picture of the fat knight. Convinced, Verdi began working on it in 1889, at leisure, and writing for his own enjoyment rather than for a public. It was produced at La Scala in February 1893, when the composer was eighty years old. What he had done for *opera seria* was now accomplished for *opera buffa*. It is not surprising that after the first rapturous reception the Italian opera public did not warm to *Falstaff* as to earlier works, for Verdi had gone forward once more along his own path. From the point of view of sheer technique *Falstaff* represents an even higher achievement of originality than *Otello,* while still keeping to the *opera buffa* framework that Boito had provided. The libretto itself is a work of genius, without doubt the finest in all Italian opera, full of brilliantly witty strokes, which the composer with incredible nimbleness of imagination matched in his music. The *speed* of the opera almost baffles a first hearing. The vocal pace has been described as a " frantic *parlando* ", the forms are freer yet, and the flow even more continuous than in *Otello,* arioso tending to replace clear-cut aria; but there is never any suggestion of bowing to the " endless melody " principle of Wagner. The swift-moving orchestra, still always subordinate to the vocal element, reaches a new pitch of technical subtlety; it sparkles and chuckles, and comments with an extraordinary flexibility, appositeness and wit. One delightful feature of the work, one that owes its inception to Boito, is the treatment given to the pair of young lovers, Fenton and Nanette (Ann Page). They have brief and stolen meetings, but their tender and charming love-passages are never allowed completion, cut off each time by the torrent of high-spirited comedy that roars round them. The rich stream of melody has its climax in the wonderful Windsor Forest finale, and the work concludes (of all things in Italian opera!) with a fugue. The wise old composer having, in the microcosm that is *Falstaff,* mocked the follies of mankind—gently and without malice, for all his disillusionment— now calls on his characters to leave their antics and sing to the audience, in a brilliant display of counterpoint : " All the world's a jest : Man is born a fool ". As Alfred Einstein remarks : " In a way opposite to Wagner, who overwhelmed Romanticism, Verdi reduces it *ad absurdum* "—in this his last mellow burst of laughter, the laughter of wisdom.

Falstaff is one of those works which for a time are too good for their public, and this accounts for a period of its comparative neglect. Musicians have always held it in high esteem. Richard Strauss, who should know, called it " one of the greatest masterpieces of all time ". Happily, there are signs that everywhere both it and *Otello* are gaining an increasing public. This is certainly so in Britain. In these two works Shakespeare received the greatest tribute ever given him by a sister art.

Verdi lived on for another eight years, writing only a few church pieces, a performance of some of these conducted by a promising young man named Arturo Toscanini. The new composers of the *verismo* school, Italian and French [note has already been taken of such men as Mascagni (*Cavalleria Rusticana*), Leoncavallo (*Pagliacci*), Massenet and Charpentier] were not favoured by the *maestro*. But before his death a young friend of his, Giacomo Puccini, had already established the claim to be his successor, albeit at a lower level.

NOTES

Since the British concert-going public continues to favour more than any others the romantic composers of the nineteenth century (together with Bach, Beethoven, Haydn and Mozart), and broadcast programmes seem to show the same tendency, there will be no lack of chances for hearing most of the works mentioned in this chapter without undue delay.

1* There are usually several different gramophone recordings of Berlioz' *Fantastic Symphony* on the market. The best that the present writer has ever heard is one that was conducted by the late Sir Thomas Beecham (HMV—ALP 1633). But alas, by the time these words are printed it may already be off the list.

2* HMS IX has a recording of a scene from the last act of Berlioz' *The Trojans at Carthage,* that of the despair of the deserted Dido.

3* HMS IX has recordings of single examples of songs by Schumann, Franz and Cornelius.

4* HMS IX has a recording of the first movement of Schumann's piano Trio in F major (Op. 80).

5 Usually printed with Chopin's "Twenty-Four" is the Op. 45 Prelude in C sharp minor.

6* HMS IX has recordings of the Scherzo from Mendelssohn's String Quartet in E major (Op. 44, No. 3) and the Andante from String Quartet in D major (Op. 44, No. 1).

7* Recordings of a Paganini violin caprice and piano studies by Schumann and Liszt based on it were detailed in the Notes of the previous chapter.

8* HMS IX has a recording of a Liszt piano work belonging to the late '40's, the programmatic Ballade in D flat major.

9 It is said that Liszt sometimes teased his listeners by singing to the first theme of the E flat Piano Concerto (quoted on p. 312) "*Das versteht Ihr alle nicht*" ("This none of you will understand").

10* HMS IX has a recording of a Liszt song ("How sweetly sings the lark") with a brilliant and atmospheric piano part that seems to dominate the setting.

11* HMS IX has a recording of the famous duet: *Tu l'as dit* from Meyerbeer's *Les Huguenots.*

12* HMS IX has a recording of the highly dramatic "melodrama and song" from Act II of Marschner's *Hans Heiling.*

13 In late years London has seen a successful revival of another of Donizetti's operas—*L'elisir d'amore.*

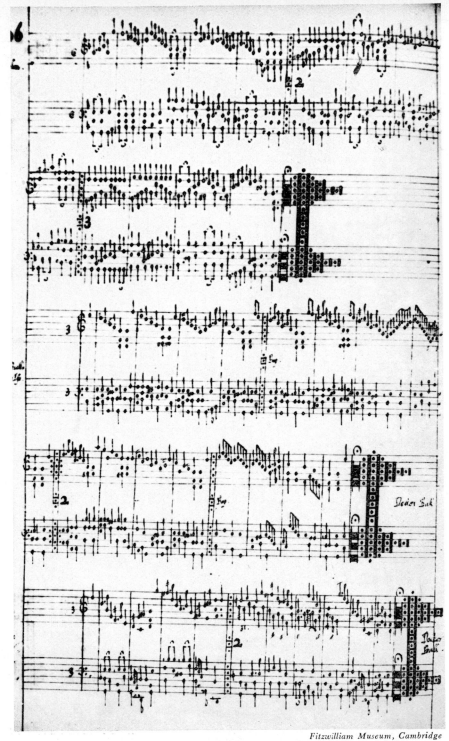

22. A page (306) from the Fitzwilliam Virginal Book, preserved in the Fitzwilliam Museum, Cambridge. The three pieces are (1) "Can shee" by Marchant; (2) "A Gigge, Doctor Bulls myselfe" by John Bull; and (3) "A Gigge", also by John Bull. The staves, it will be noted, are of six lines.

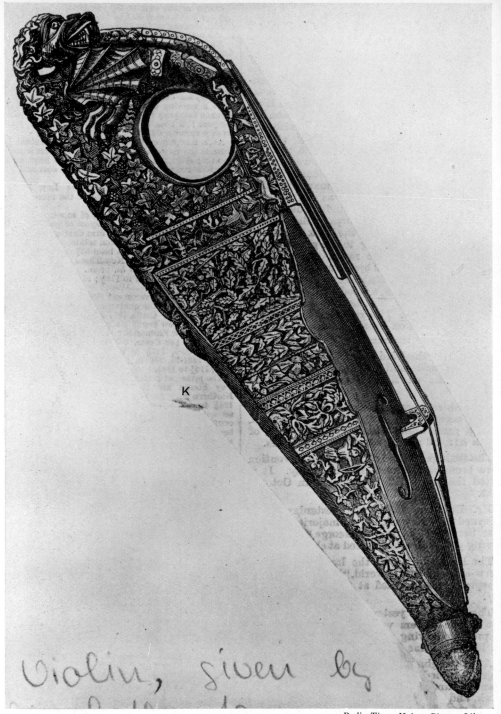

K

violin, given by [handwritten]

Radio Times Hulton Picture Library

23. A freak instrument, preserved at Warwick Castle. Originally a beautifully carved gittern, i.e. early guitar (c. 1330) it was re-bellied as a bogus violin in the sixteenth century.

CHAPTER XII

The Romantic Period II

The Continuance of the Symphony

IT has already been made clear that for all the tremendous impact of Wagner's mature art and the triumphant clamours of his following, the lyrical form of opera lived on, still dominated by the human voice rather than the orchestra. The highest form of absolute music, the orchestral symphony, also refused to be killed off by the "Art-Work of the Future". Among the composers living under Wagner's shadow, one of the first to demonstrate this was Anton Bruckner (1824–96). By one of history's ironies he was a devoted admirer of Wagner's. In antithesis to the master-egoist he was a meek and gentle soul, on whose piano-top there rested always the score of *Tristan*, but who nevertheless spent his life writing utterly individual music, including nine great symphonies wholly within the classical four-movement framework, and all " to the glory of God ", works of pure romantic " sound ".

He belonged to Upper Austria, peasant-born and bred, without the poise and assurance possessed by most of the leading romantic composers with their backgrounds of general culture. All his life he was markedly submissive to any form of authority; even willing (too willing) to allow his actual work to be influenced by the opinions of friends. As a youth he received a very sound practical training at the ancient religious centre of St. Florian, and grew up to be a magnificent organist. In his maturity he gave successful concerts at both Paris and London—these, with a similar trip to Switzerland, his only foreign ventures. Too much of his early career was spent in village schoolmastering, but from 1856 onward, after he had become organist of Linz Cathedral, he was enabled to study at Vienna under Simon Sechter (for whom Schubert had had respect) and then make acquaintance with the new world of harmony and orchestral colour opened to him by Wagner. He matured late. Not until 1864, when he was 40, did he as a devoted son of the Roman Church make his mark with his great Mass in D minor, a colourful and spacious work built on the Vienna traditions of Haydn, Beethoven and Schubert. In 1864 he was appointed professor at the Vienna Conservatoire, and later lectured at the University. Yet he remained always the shy, diffident soul upon whom his enemies were able to pour their contempt. It would have been difficult to quarrel with him personally, but unfortunately for him his admiration for Wagner, who patronised him in kindly enough fashion, drew him into the bitter atmosphere of the Wagner-Brahms controversies of the time—in the main a war of followers rather than principals. Thus his works were under attack during his lifetime for reasons other than their qualities.

Throughout his career he poured forth a wealth of beautiful Church music, but his reputation will always rest on his monumental symphonies, eight of which were produced between 1868 and 1886. The Ninth was left incomplete at his death. Even today these works are much better known and appreciated in German-speaking countries than elsewhere, though in Britain a cult of them, encouraged by broadcast and recording, is fast growing. In appraising them one is confronted by a factor which is unique in the history of music. It is firmly on record that Bruckner revised a number of them from time to time, and the whole body of them, involving these revisions, was duly published in what is known as the *Universal Edition*. But in the mid-'30's there came a rival series of issues, a printing of the symphonies in accordance with the composer's original manuscripts. The whole story is too complicated for much detail here. Let us record that battle was joined, in which one side maintained that Bruckner was notoriously meek about everything, even regarding the inviolability of his works, and that there was proof that the revisions were due to the suggestions of, among others, the conductors Nikisch and Löwe, Wagnerians both, Löwe having much to do with the U.E. publication-editing. Moreover, evidence was advanced purporting to show that these changes did not represent the true outlook of the composer, nor at times the true flavour of his scorings, and that secretly he resented them. The revisionists on the other hand contended that the amendments of the orchestration, and indeed the reshapings and prunings of design, had actually improved the symphonies as works of art, and of this the composer was well aware. He was certainly *not* aware of Löwe's drastic divergences from the manuscript of the posthumously published Ninth. The tendency nowadays is to go back to the original settings-down. Certainly in these the individualist which was Bruckner is most clearly seen. It was a seemingly unstudied originality. He loved Schubert's music, and like Schubert he gives the impression of innocent uninhibited creative power. All that he took from Beethoven (whose music he seems not to have looked at at all closely) was the pattern of that master's four movements, with perhaps the example of the mighty Adagio of the Ninth as the inspiration for his own slow movements. He employed all the resources of the mature romantic orchestra, including the Wagnerian tubas, but while he borrowed some of Wagner's tricks, such as his fondness for the string tremolo in accompaniment, on the whole his scoring was his clear and colourful own, based more than anything else on his consummate knowledge of the organ stops. He made use of the rich harmonic vocabulary of Wagner, but in order to create a very different world. One feature that he had in common with his idol was the deliberate and majestic pace of his long stretches of pure and beautiful sound. " Spacious " is the word that well describes his symphonic art—contemplation and landscape painting rather than drama. Richard Capell puts the case succinctly when he speaks of " the gulf between his rapturous symphonic visions and the action, variety and dramatic charge and release of the classical symphony ". He seems also to have been an unconscious nationalist. Austrian musicians tell us that the more rustic of his melodies " have a great appeal to listeners familiar with Austrian tone, accent and rhythm ". Such down-to-earth moments are found only in the scherzos, where indeed " one hears the heavy stamp of peasant boots ". In the main his music is cosmic in its contemplativeness, that of a mind which brooded ingenuously upon the mysteries of religion and the benignities of Nature, far removed from the wrangles of disintegrating Romanticism.

While the Fourth Symphony in E flat (the so-called " Romantic ") remains probably the best known, his finest music may perhaps be found in the Seventh, Eighth and unfinished Ninth. The enormous Seventh, now receiving more and more notice, was the one that really set the seal on his reputation in Vienna. Its famous slow movement was intended as a tribute to Wagner. The Sixth in A is less often heard but is quite characteristic. A recent (1961) recording of it by the Linz Bruckner Orchestra (Classics Club —X 141) represents a performance of the *original* score. It is interesting to compare it with the miniature score (long on the market) of the " revised " version.

Similar in avoiding the " programme "-haunted trend of the time and also finding an individual path to tread was another great composer whose work was chiefly concerned with Vienna. Yet the two were in hostile antithesis. To Bruckner it was enough that Brahms seemed the arch-enemy of Wagner; Brahms, on the other hand, though not such a rabid opponent of Wagner's music as is sometimes represented, had a very poor opinion of Bruckner's works, which to his orderly mind seemed too long-drawn-out, meandering and formless. It was his own life-task to bring back to absolute music the logic, conciseness and close-weave of the classical forms, with nevertheless many touches of romantic beauty and individual warmth and tenderness.

Johannes Brahms (1833–97), like Beethoven before him, came up the hard way. Born in Hamburg, the son of a poverty-stricken double-bass player, he was fortunate at an early age to come into the care of Eduard Marxsen, a musician of sound attainments, who taught him the piano and a certain amount of composition practice; and above all laid the foundations of that deep knowledge of Bach and Beethoven on which he was to build his own technique. Yet some years of his youth were frittered on the bread-earning necessity of playing the piano in the squalid sailor-taverns and dance-halls of the port. The rough experiences of his early days left a permanent mark on his social manners, which were frequently execrable and sometimes wounding. There is enough in his life to show, however, that an outward boorishness covered much that was honest and kindly. For all the nobility of his music, however, he was far from likeable as a man.

Emancipation came at the age of 20, when he undertook a tour as accompanist to the Hungarian violinist Remenyi, and, more important, met his future close friend the young violinist Joachim, who gave him the opportunities of making the acquaintance of both Liszt at Weimar and Schumann at Dusseldorf. Liszt, urbane as ever, expressed himself pleased with the awkward young stranger's piano sonatas and Scherzo in E flat minor, having read them at sight from manuscript.[1] Then in his turn he proceeded to play his own recently completed Sonata in B minor, only to find that his guest had fallen asleep during the course of it. It was Brahms' first, if involuntary, expression of his indifference to the " new music ". An even worse gaucherie was committed some years later (in 1860) by Brahms and Joachim in concert, when they drew up a manifesto against the extravagant claims of the " neo-German ", Wagner-Liszt party. Unfortunately, its terms leaked out amid ridicule before more than four signatures were on it, with Joachim's the best-known. The result was that Brahms gained lifelong enemies, though the generous Liszt was not among the number. A steady flow of partisan vituperation continued in print through the years, with the anti-Wagner critic Hanslick prominent on one side and Hugo Wolf on the other. Meanwhile Schumann's somewhat exaggerated backing (he spoke of Brahms' music in terms of " new paths ") did the young man's small reputation probably more harm than good for the time being. Brahms' warm relationship with the Schumanns became almost a filial one, and he was a sterling aid to Clara in the widowhood that came soon after. There was an enduring friendship between the confirmed and rough-tongued bachelor who spent his life in hired lodgings and the cultured and serious-minded Clara.

Schumann and Liszt were right in hailing the young Brahms as a rising star of romanticism. Romantic by instinct he always remained, but upon these emotional urges the more mature Brahms imposed an iron control. Before he was twenty-four he had done some very hard thinking. He had, as we have seen, no sympathy at all with the literary, pictorial or " character-study " programme-music of Liszt and his followers. Even in the early *Sturm und Drang* piano sonatas he had shown no trace of such elements. As it was, more and more his mind turned to the past, to the great art of the German masters of former times—Beethoven, Mozart, Haydn, Schütz, and beyond, to the Renaissance composers. Towards old German folk-song he had developed a similar veneration. No doubt he threw over these departed times the halo of his own romantic longings, sighing for what was not, but he considered that he had found in the classical masterpieces the sureness and serenity lacking in the wilful and experimental music with which he was surrounded. There gradually emerged the master technician who founded his art on the resources of thematic development as found in Beethoven, and on Bach's consummate command of counterpoint, taking delight in the old-time crafts of canon and fugue, and above all in that of variation writing. From his practice of this last he learned how to wring from his themes all that was musically latent in them, and to banish all that was irrelevant, economy of material being one of his outstanding characteristics. Economy of orchestral colouring was another. The brilliances of Berlioz' and Wagner's palettes held no attractions for him; but the symphonic scoring of his maturity was always masterly, even if greyer than that of some of his romantic contemporaries. There was no lack of imagination; it was the way he chose to have it. One predilection is very apparent—a love of cantabile horn-tone. His writing contains many a poetic passage in this medium.

To return to the days of his early '20's—for a time he earned a living as a touring concert-pianist and by teaching, with Hamburg as his base. Meanwhile composition continued and, as always, his study of the Masters. He actually exchanged exercises in counterpoint, canon and fugue with Joachim, the latter tiring of the discipline first. From 1857 to '59 he held a part-time " director's " post at the small court of Detmold. He seems for a while to have retained something of the old-world *Kapellmeister* outlook, for he was bitterly disappointed when in 1862 he failed to secure a permanent appointment in his native Hamburg. In the end he discovered that he had no vocation (including the tact and patience) for such employment.

Meanwhile the production of piano music continued, and included the four Ballades (1854),[2*] the Variations and Fugue on a Theme by Handel (1861) and the Studies (Variations) on a Theme by Paganini (1863), both the last two masterly and of great technical difficulty. Thereafter, strangely enough, except for the well-known Waltzes he wrote no more solo piano music (or at least, published none) for seventeen years. There was also a great deal of early chamber music with piano, including the Schubertian Trio in B major (1854—revised in his last years) and the Piano Quartet in A major, as well as the String Sextet in B flat major. With the loom of Beethoven's shadow over him it was many years before he dared publish a string quartet, though he tried what he considered his 'prentice hand at many, only to destroy them. His ventures into orchestral writing were limited to two Serenades in D and A major written for the Detmold court, and the Piano Concerto in D minor (1854–8), which began as a symphony and met with no success in its final shape, which has sometimes been called that of a symphony with piano obbligato. Many years elapsed before he ventured on another orchestral work (the " St. Anthony " Variations—1873).[3]

In 1862 he took a decisive step, and settled once and for all in what was his spiritual home, the Vienna of Mozart, Beethoven and Schubert. Except for travellings and holidays it was his abiding place for the rest of his career, which was illuminated by little more than the steady production of great works. For a while he conducted a *Singakademie,* whose members found themselves performing the newly-realised church cantatas of Bach, but this post he soon relinquished. His compositions were becoming better known, and with the production (1868) of a choral work, his German Requiem (in fact, a setting of texts drawn from the Lutheran Bible by the composer himself) his fame spread through Germany. Other choral works followed, e.g., *Schicksalslied* and *Triumphlied*, but none had the same stature as the Requiem.

He was now developing as a composer who like Beethoven strove for mastery in every branch of the art, (except for opera). He satisfied himself regarding the string quartet at last, and in 1873 produced a pair, in C minor and A minor respectively, works of the closest intricacy of thought and worthy to stand among the greatest. Even better loved is the B flat example of two years later, with its fascinating first-movement cross-rhythms; one of his most ravishing melodies in its second; a heaven-sent chance for the viola in the third; and the composer at his subtlest in the finale, when a set of variations is finally blended with material from the opening movement. There was much other mature chamber music—another string sextet (in G), more string quintets (that in G major of special note) and piano trios. His finest chamber work, one of the greatest ever written, came towards the end of his life, the immortal Clarinet Quintet.

As in the case of the string quartet Brahms seemed reluctant to tackle the problems of the sonata for solo instrument and piano, a genre which the romantic age had treated badly. His own examples—for violin, for 'cello and for clarinet—with one exception came late in his career.

His greatest mental struggles however concerned his approach to the symphony. The mighty past was ever-present in his mind, and not until 1876, when he was 43, did No. 1 in C minor appear. His very jest on the subject ("A symphony is no joke!") betrayed his grim sense of responsibility. He had after a long period resumed his handling of the orchestra three years previously in the charming Variations on the St. Anthony Chorale. The Symphony in C minor from its first hearing was received with profound respect. Von Bülow, turning from Wagner, and for the rest of his career doing much for Brahms' music, hailed it somewhat fatuously as the "Tenth", but the mature master in his symphonic writings was nobody but himself. In the four which he eventually completed he echoed the past in his close-knit and intellectually satisfying structures, but at the same time breathed into them his own originality, as well as the lyrical romantic spirit which for all his discipline persisted in breaking through. In the C minor, as in the next two, he made use of the motto-theme device. In all except the Fourth he avoided the headlong Beethovenish scherzo, harking back to the more minuet-like type. An effective Brahmsian trick, used in such move- . ments of his chamber music as well as in the *Allegretto* of the Second Symphony, was to shape a contrasting section by transmuting the first theme through a change of rhythm and a greatly increased speed. The effect in this latter work is a ravishing one, when

is changed to :

Ex:62

If the C minor was sternly serious in tone, the Second, in D major, which followed actually in the next year, was genial, almost pastoral, in contrast. The first notes of the first movement consist of a bass motto-phrase :

Ex:63

which in pervasive and masterly fashion haunts the whole symphony.

After these two works there again came a symphonic gap, filled by two concert overtures (the Academic Festival and the Tragic) and more important, two Concertos. The long-brooded Violin Concerto in D major, sponsored by Joachim, came in 1878, and did not find ready acceptance at first, its great technical difficulties earning it the gibe of being a concerto "*against* the violin". Nowadays it takes its place among the leading examples, and is seen to be a masterly blend of the lyricism and constructive genius of the composer, with a Hungarian folk-lilt in its finale. The Piano Concerto in B flat major, which was first heard in 1881, is the longest of all classical concertos and, exceptionally, in four movements, the composer having added a powerful scherzo before the slow movement. The solo part is a formidable one, yet Brahms, long retired from virtuoso playing, himself undertook it at its first hearing. His early technical attainments must have been high.

The first two symphonies came almost as a pair, and in emotional contrast. The case was the same in regard to the F major Third (1883) and the E minor Fourth (1885). The F major, heroic, passionate, yet generally happy in tone, opens with a motto-theme, heard recurrently. The splendid first subject of the first movement is similarly used with significance in the closing pages of the work, while the 'cello theme of the *Allegretto* third movement is among Brahms' finest romantic tunes.

The Fourth Symphony is surely the greatest of them, cast in a mood of fateful resignation and autumnal sadness. In the opening movement the long first subject gradually unfolds its possibilities, with every phrase a germ for future expansion, building up to some of the most subtly intellectual of Brahms' pages. Then comes the lyrical and stately slow movement, full of rich modulations, haunted by woodwind and horn voices and with a memorable second-subject tune. In complete contrast there follows his only symphonic *real* scherzo, very much of a rough-and-tumble. The famous finale sees him paying his last orchestral tribute to the departed world of the baroque, cast in the form of a monumental *chaconne*. From a Bach cantata he adapted the motif:

Ex:64

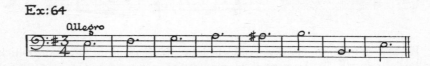

He repeated it *thirty* times (confined always to E minor or major) and above it built a superb set of variations. Only in the brief coda was he able to modulate further afield, yet such is the skill and variety of the treatment and its orchestration that the iron restrictions of the form are never apparent. The movement is one of Music's masterpieces. This tribute to an earlier age was also, as P. H. Lang puts it, " a Requiem Mass for the eternal rest of the soul of the symphony ".

There was only one more work with orchestra to come, the Double Concerto for Violin and 'Cello (1887). The unusual medium involved technical problems which Brahms overcame better than did Beethoven in a parallel work; nevertheless the Concerto has not even yet gained the appreciation given to his other major compositions.

Throughout his career, from Op. 3 to Op. 121, Brahms poured out solo songs, around 200 of them, and no Lieder singer can afford to neglect their existence. Once again in an art-form he chose to disregard the contemporary trend, that of the dominance of the instrumental part, and its insistence as a medium for commentary. Instead he founded his practice directly on that of Schubert's, with the voice well to the foreground, and his general approach musical rather than literary, the accompaniments, however highly organised, in due subordination. Always he had the resource of an unfailing spring of expressive melody. His sense of tradition gave him a predilection, whenever possible, for the strophic type, without his neglecting ternary, or even rondo form. Nowhere is he more moving than in his penultimate work, Four Serious Songs, when attuned once again to the baroque Lutheran composers, he made settings of texts from the Bible. He was always concerned with the preserving of actual folk-songs, collecting and setting a large number of them. A dozen or so opus groups were devoted to part-songs (duets and quartets) of various types, a proportion of them of folk-song flavour.

To turn to his keyboard production—after the Waltzes of 1865 there was nothing until 1878, when there began the types of brief romantic pieces which he labelled Capriccio and Intermezzo, followed in the next year

by two Rhapsodies on a larger scale. Finally in his closing years came
further sets of short lyrical pieces, concluding with a long and powerful
Rhapsody in E flat. His very last opus number, concluded when he was
mortally stricken, consisted of eleven Chorale Preludes for organ, his swan-
song thus being in terms of old German religious melody. Alfred Einstein
has summed up his career in these words :

" . . . the fiery beginning, the perception of the greatness and unaffected
happiness of the past, the sorrowful renewal of this happiness, and the
resignation of the man born too late. Along this road, the concentration,
the simplification, the masterfulness become greater and greater, right
up to those farewell works . . ."—*A Einstein: Music in the Romantic Era,
p. 154: W. W. Norton & Company, Inc., New York.*

What is his place in the hierarchy? Had he not lived, would the course of
musical history have been any different? Probably not; but the world would
have lacked many priceless treasures of musical beauty.

As the century progressed the art of orchestral conducting was treated
more and more seriously, both from interpretive and disciplinary points of
view. Liszt was a pioneer in the matter of conveying his own emotions to
his players by his gestures and facial expressions, together with an insistence
on every detail of phrasing and dynamics. Wagner followed in the same
spirit, and even wrote on the subject. There came a generation of masters
of the baton, who made conductorship a very specialised pursuit—von
Bülow, Hermann Levi, Richter, Seidl, Nikisch, Karl Muck (at Boston,
U.S.A.), Mahler, Richard Strauss, Bruno Walter, Weingartner and others.
To this distinguished list might be added towards the end of the century
the non-Germanic names of Toscanini and Henry Wood. The art of music
was no doubt the better for the greater refinements of performance that
these specialists brought, but the beginnings of a new peril was apparent
to the shrewd minds of two very different types of creator. Berlioz warned
composers that " the most dangerous of your interpreters is the conductor ";
Verdi complained that no sooner did he curb the absurd privileges of leading singers than he was faced with the problem of the high-handed conductor. This peril applied to composers dead as well as alive, for von Bülow,
Reger, Mahler, Weingartner, even Wagner busied themselves with improving the scoring of Beethoven and others of the great masters. As for the live
ones, we have already seen what happened to Bruckner during his working
career. A number of the great interpreters, Toscanini a shining example,
were scrupulously aware of their responsibilities. Yet the peril is still with
us of wilful " new " readings of established works.

The name of Mahler stands high among those who in the second half of
the century made the standard of German and Austrian performances the
finest in Europe. His other claim on history is as a writer of monumental
symphonies, the last Viennese exponent of romanticism in that field.

Gustav Mahler (1860–1911), an Austrian Jew who in his maturity turned
to the Church of Rome, early made his mark at piano playing and composi-

tion as a student at the Vienna Conservatoire, where he was influenced by his acquaintance with Bruckner. His course completed, he read history and philosophy at the University. It was thus a well-stored if highly emotional mind that faced the problem of late romanticism. A visit to Bayreuth in 1883 and a hearing of *Parsifal* had a profound effect on him. He first took to conducting as a means of earning a living rather than as a vocation, but soon made a reputation. For the next dozen years and more he directed operatic activities in various cities in turn, from Budapest to Hamburg, everywhere improving standards of performance and harrying his subordinates unmercifully in the process. He thus became a figure greatly admired by his audiences and, in the main, thoroughly hated by his professional musicians and singers. His fame went through Europe, and in 1897 he was appointed to be in charge of the Vienna State Opera, Brahms' high opinion of him weighing in his favour. Once again the new broom raised much dust, but raised immeasurably also were the standards, both musical and disciplinary. After ten years of devoted labour (and mounting friction with his staff) he resigned, now frail in health. For a few more years, until his death in 1911, he spent winter months with the New York Metropolitan Opera.

The wonder is, with all the storms and stresses of his executive career, he found time to compose (like Bruckner) nine large-scale symphonies, together with a symphonic song-cycle *Das Lied von der Erde* (The Song of the Earth). There is an unfinished Tenth Symphony. He wrote also more than forty songs, many with orchestral accompaniment, which nowadays are being performed with increasing respect. But (again like Bruckner) outside German-speaking countries his stature as a symphonist is still under dispute. He is certainly receiving more attention in this country nowadays than heretofore.

Like Wagner he brooded on high metaphysical matters, and saw himself as a philosopher giving expression in his symphonies to his love of nature, to his interest in man's everyday life and activities (expressed in his use of popular tunes and folksong, or imitation thereof), and even more to his preoccupation with the problems of suffering, death and eternity, endeavouring often enough in his blazing finales to preach hope and confidence. The kaleidoscopes of emotion expressed in his epic works meant huge canvases, welters of different themes, wonderfully varied and original orchestrations—also, say his detractors, lack of balance and logic, looseness of form, frequent stretches of banality marring much that is sublime.

Taking a great deal from Wagner, he followed the latter's view in employing symphonically the human voice, in solo and chorus. His symphonies came at more or less steady intervals, from 1888 to 1909. The First, Fifth, Sixth, Seventh and Ninth are for orchestra alone, albeit a very much expanded post-Wagnerian one. The Second, Third, Fourth and Eighth all contain one or more vocal movements (mainly religious in tone) with orchestra. No. 8 is in fact a monster " symphonic cantata " in two parts, the first containing a setting of the ancient hymn *Veni, Creator Spiritus,* the second using the text from the Final Scene from *Faust.* Popularly known as the " Symphony of a Thousand ", it is the supreme example of Mahler's titanism. Eight soloists, two mixed choirs, a boys' choir and a very much augmented orchestra (especially in brass and percussion departments) make up the magic number.

Mahler does not lack defence against the charges of looseness of form and banality of theme. Egon Wellesz, who knew him personally, maintains that in form he has broken away with success from the classical pattern to make some interesting experiments. He points out that while the classical symphony has its emphasis on the significance of the first movement, Mahler aims at a " spiritual development " from the first movement to finale, with the latter as the centre of gravity. Again, Wellesz argues that the " banality " of a theme may be intentional, its first appearance in that quality allowing again for " spiritual development " during its subsequent appearances. He quotes the second subject of the Sixth Symphony as an example, and uses the analogy of Berlioz' *idée fixe* in his *Symphonie Fantastique,* which suffers the reverse process of " blackguarding " in the Witches' Sabbath finale.

Whatever assessment may be made of Mahler, it must be recognised that a great mind was at work. But whether the huge frameworks, the rich textures, the masterly orchestrations—all the enormous labours—were worthwhile in regard to their intrinsic results, whether at heart he was not after all a lyricist, is not yet settled.

A weight of opinion holds that the Ninth Symphony and the splendid " Song of the Earth " (1908) represent him at his finest. Regarding the latter, perhaps he himself in this late and sorrowful lyrical work realised where his gifts best lay. In him died the last Viennese exponent of the romantic symphony. The great names in Vienna were soon to be those of Schönberg, Alban Berg and Webern.

Contemporary with Mahler in Vienna was another Austrian composer, similarly an admirer of Wagner, but employing his symphonic technique to a far different purpose, that of bringing the romantic *lied* to its last consummation.

Hugo Wolf (1860–1903) was given generous early opportunities for both musical and general education, but seems to have been one of the most crossgrained and difficult personalities in the history of the art. His schools' career was a series of expulsions, and his stay at the Vienna Conservatoire lasted only eighteen months. There, however, he attracted the encouragement of Bruckner; indeed, throughout his too-short career there seem always to have been good friends who, perceiving his genius, were willing to bear with his irresponsibilities of conduct. For some years after 1877 he maintained himself precariously in Vienna, profiting by the musical life of the city, and admiring the great masters together with Berlioz, Liszt and above all Wagner. At the same time he was reading voraciously in literature, and was pursuing composition with singular lack of success. Some kindness from Liszt encouraged him to launch into an orchestral tone-poem, *Penthesilea,* doomed to a fiasco performance in the hands of Richter, then closely identified with Brahms, who had previously snubbed the young man. When early in 1884 Wolf became music critic to the fashionable *Salonblatt* he used every opportunity for making vindictive attacks on Brahms, though writing otherwise much good sense during his three years' tenure of the post.

In 1888, through the efforts of a friend, he found publication for six of his songs. His main purpose in life now seemed revealed to him. In the ten years of production that were left to him he poured forth a wealth of utterly original songs for solo voice and piano with the feverish facility of a Schubert or a Mozart.[4*] No man made less money by his art; it was thanks to the generosity of friends that he was given the solitude for composition and the means to live. By the end of 1889 twenty settings of the poet Eichendorff and no less than fifty-three of Eduard Mörike were in print, followed in the next year by fifty-one of Goethe's. In 1891 appeared the Spanish Song-book, forty-four settings of poem-translations from the Spanish by Heyse and Geibel, as well as six of the poetry of von Keller. A set of twenty-two translations from the Italian by Heyse formed Part I of the Italian Song-book, and then the highly-strung composer struck a period of almost complete impotence regarding creation, but filled it with concert work concerned with his songs, the fame of which was spreading rapidly. He was also absorbed with plans for a projected opera, Der Corregidor, based on the Spanish story " The Three-cornered Hat ". Not until 1896 did the second part of the Italian Songbook find completion, when its twenty-four songs were written in little over a month. Soon after, Der Corregidor received its first performance with but moderate success. Merrily lyrical, with but little sign of Wagnerism, it has been revived in modern times, but the verdict is still that Wolf's genius does not burn brightly on the stage. One instrumental work of his that seems destined to endure is the Italian Serenade, written first for string quartet, and scored for orchestra in 1892. He wrote also a number of choral works, most of which were published only posthumously.

After the Italian Songbook, the climax of his life-work, only a dozen or so songs of lesser calibre remained to be written. Meanwhile the inroads of insidious disease were sapping his mental powers. From October 1898 until his death he was confined to a mental home, paralysed and insane.

Wolf's ideals and principles as a song-writer can be realised from his very title-pages, e.g.—" Hugo Wolf—Poems by J. von Eichendorff for solo voice and piano ". In other words—" the poetry's the thing ". The composer, out of his sensitive and conscientious regard for his poet, tried by means of his music to distil the last essence from the text—every shade of meaning and painting; moreover, it was not a matter of voice and accompaniment but the two factors hand in hand. Indeed, one may be forgiven for sometimes believing that the piano part is ruling the setting, since, inheriting all Wagner's vocabulary of chromatic and enharmonic harmony Wolf brought to the chamber-song resources of instrumental colouring such as had seldom before been imagined. Moreover, he made frequent use of Wagner's device of developing in symphonic manner one or more short themes. He was early employing this technique in masterly fashion, as in Das Standchen (1888) from the Eichendorff set, where the fragment,

in its first appearance not particularly distinguished, passes through a kaleidoscope of rich changes and rules the song. Other similar examples of this craftsmanship can be seen in his *Der Musikant* and *Verschwiegene Liebe* of the same period. Not that the voice was suffered to be eclipsed. If indeed at the moment there were matters of great import in the piano part it found its own expressive curves. Wolf (unlike Wagner) never allowed it to become instrumental in style. His vocal parts are never particularly difficult to sing apart from the musical perception needed to follow the frequent changes of key. Moreover, the composer never permitted the soloist to be blanketed by any ambitions of accompaniment, a frequent fault of his age. His care regarding the clear understanding of the words is seen also in his sensitiveness regarding prosody. There are no misplaced accents or other distortions of the text in his settings. Although in his mature songs he made more and more use of the motif-development device with modulatory and chromatic colourings, he could retract when the situation demanded to effective simplicity and diatonic harmonies. The range of emotion spanned by his song-poems is particularly wide and varied—from the religious lyrics of the Spanish Songbook (agonised as in *Mühvoll komm ich . . .*, or of heavenly tranquillity in Mary's cradle-song *Die ihr sehwebet . . .*) to the rough humour, say, of *Der Glücksritter* (Eichendorff).

He seems never to have attempted to set a poem which he considered had been adequately dealt with already. With his high regard for Schubert this led him to have to forgo many of Goethe's lyrics. However, his several "Wilhelm Meister" songs and his settings of *Prometheus* and *Ganymede,* among others, illustrated his contention that Schubert sometimes did not fully understand his poet. Nevertheless, the opinion is that Wolf did not always win the battle of comparative settings.

With him the romantic song with piano seems to have said all that it had to say. Mahler, his contemporary, tended often enough to transfer the chamber-song to the concert hall by adding the resources of orchestral colour, and losing a traditional intimacy in the process. If a true inheritor of Wolf's art is sought it may perhaps be found in the person of the Swiss composer Othmar Schoeck (b. 1886) in whose sensitive songs is expressed the same unity of spirit between poem and setting. As for Wolf, a glance at recital and broadcast programmes will show that his greater songs are more alive than ever.

Nationalism in Music

A late phase in the history of romanticism was the appearance in the art-music of a number of European countries of distinctive elements (i.e. of melody, harmony, rhythm, etc.) which were indigenous in origin and yet of sufficient worth as to merit international attention. Emerging mainly in the mid-nineteenth century these movements developed first in countries that had not previously made much impact on musical history, their leading musicians having been content to follow the stylistic patterns of the greater nations. In earlier centuries provincialism had counted for very little. Even though France, Italy and Germany had taken their turns in asserting them-selves, the main stream of mid-nineteenth century European music was sufficiently international in style for a French literary romantic like Victor Hugo to think of Beethoven solely as the greatest figure of a closely-bound sister art, one that was credited with "universality". An interest in folk-music had certainly been a preoccupation of some of the Romantic com-posers, but neither Schumann's and Brahms' concern with old German song, nor Liszt's and Brahms' flirtations with gipsy music and Mendelssohn's with Scotch snap made any real difference to the cosmopolitan and personal elements which comprised their individual styles. This is true of Domenico Scarlatti's previous absorption of some of the features of Iberian folk-music.

When the urge for self-assertion came to the countries concerned, what was needed were national composers of sufficient merit to make internationally acceptable the use of such autochthonous material. The many political stirrings of the mid-century had encouraged native composers inasmuch as such expressions represented not only art but patriotism. The case of Chopin has already been noted. Although there were strong Italian and German influences in his musical upbringing that of his country's music (together with his own original genius) was the strongest, this very deliberately empha-sised in his polonaises and mazurkas. After Chopin, Polish music, even Polish opera, continued to be cultivated, but not again impinging on the West now that its mainspring had been broken. The most significant name of the time is perhaps that of Stanislaw Moniuszko (1819–72), opera- and song-writer. Of no Polish implication was the career of the brilliant solo violinist Henri Wieniawski, who was French in training and interests.

Bohemia

The land of the Czechs and particularly its capital Prague had, ever since the days of Gallus and de Monte, been associated with great music. Prague held a warm place in Mozart's affections. Around the turn of the eighteenth century Czech composers such as Gyrowetz, Kozeluch, Reicha and Vanhal made their contributions to the Vienna school, while later, Tomášek was in his piano pieces an early romantic. But all this was not Czech *music,* though early in the nineteenth century attempts were made to write Czech-language operas, making use of native folksong. The emergence of a vital composer who could weave the Czech spirit and idiom into a worth-while art-music awaited the increased upsurge around the mid-century of political opposition to the Hapsburg rule and the advent of Smetana.

Bedrich (Frederick) Smetana (1824–84), the son of a provincial brewer, settled in Prague as a young man to earn his living as a piano virtuoso and teacher. He had been a child prodigy in both piano and violin playing. His idols, besides Beethoven, were Schumann, Chopin (the patriotic force of whose music he realised), Wagner, Liszt and Berlioz. Visits to Prague of the last two confirmed his taste for "programme" romanticism. Like many another young artist he received encouragement and probably even monetary help from the kindly Liszt. He spent several years as a musical conductor in Sweden (Gothenburg), where he wrote a trio of "literary" symphonic poems on the Lisztian pattern and in cosmopolitan style. When he returned in 1861 to Prague and a tense political atmosphere, his music began to identify itself more and more with the Czech spirit. He gradually established himself as Bohemia's leading composer in a series of operas, eight in all, which drew deliberately on Bohemian history, legend and country-life, folksong and dance—his own melodies and musical constructions, but impregnated with the spirit of old-time national music, and making spectacular use of the native *polka* and *furiant*. Of these *The Bartered Bride,* a sparkling comic-opera to a background of Bohemian village life, is now appreciated the world over, but others of his operas have failed to travel far from the land of their origin, handicapped possibly by difficulties of language. This is a pity, for among his serious stage works *Dalibor* and *Labuse* both contain much noble romantic music, and yet escape the shadow of Wagnerism.[5a]

In his later life he wrote a series of six particularly "Bohemian" tone-poems, under the generic title of "My Country", which painted in terms of sound landscapes and legends of his beloved fatherland, each with its detailed programme. Of them, *Vltava* (the "Moldau" river) and *In Bohemia's Meadows and Forests* appear to receive occasional British performances. Even more "romantic" was the purpose of his two late string-quartets, that of picturing the story of his own life—which ended so pitifully after the failing of his mental powers. It is an astonishing fact that a number of his later and excellent works were written under the handicap of total deafness. The last movement of the second quartet actually depicts the oncoming of this tragic infliction. He was followed as Bohemia's leading composer by a musician even more colourful nationally and famous internationally.

Anton Dvorak (1841–1904). Like Smetana, Dvorak as a youth was in danger of having to follow in his father's business, which in this case was that of village innkeeper and butcher. But the obvious high qualities of his musical gifts carried him to the Organ School at Prague, where he developed his keyboard and string playing and had some grounding in composition. Then came frustration and real poverty. For long years until he was thirty he made a living mainly through his orchestral viola-playing. But by that time he had come under the influence of Smetana, and had made acquaintance with his truly Bohemian opera music. He gave up orchestral playing in 1871 for the sake of greater opportunities for composition. His work, shedding a great deal of Wagnerism, now took on a more direct and clari-

fied style. He retained his early predilection in concerted instrumental work
for " absolute " music and classical form (with a certain naïvety new to the
art), but his rich natural gift for spontaneous melody and his infectious sense
of rhythm identified themselves more and more with Czech national music.
In both chamber and symphonic works are to be found examples of the
furiant, polka, styrienne and other Czech dances, together with the emotional
Slavonic *dumka,* with its alternating changes of mood.

In 1875 there came the welcome support of no less a person than Brahms,
who, on behalf of the Vienna government, judged some compositions
worthy of a small public grant. More than that, seeing their exceptional
promise the influential composer found a publisher for the Moravian Duets
(settings of folk-poems) and recommended that others of the young man's
works should be printed. The friendship remained until Brahms' death, a
remarkable circumstance when it is realised how surlily, and at times
savagely, Brahms behaved to other young composers. Dvorak studied the
scores of Brahms and listened to his advice, but showed no inclination to
follow any but his own paths. Now very conscious as a composer of his
duty to his country and the whole Slavonic race, he found fortune beginning
to turn. In 1874 the much revised *King and Collier* opera had convinced
Prague that he was in the Smetana succession. In the course of his career
other Czech-language operas followed, grave and gay, but these have never
received much international regard. The truth is that for all the delightful
music he put into these dramatic works a feeling for the stage was one of the
least of his musical virtues. His fame came otherwise. A setting of *Stabat
Mater* (1877) and even more his first set of Slavonic Dances in piquant
orchestral colour gained him European attention and led to his first invitation to England in 1884. London gave a cordial reception to, among others
of his works, the *Stabat Mater,* the Symphony in D major (the so-called
No. 1) and a Slavonic Rhapsody. The English success, which was followed
by later visits, was a happy augury for him, and helped to give him confidence (for there was always a streak of self-doubt in his nature) to continue
the production of large-scale works.

Concerning his five symphonies (there are also others, not regarded as
representative) the chronological details are as follows :
  (a) No. 3 in F major (1875)
  (b) No. 1 in D major (1880)
  (c) No. 2 in D minor (1885)
  (d) No. 4 in G major (1889)
  (e) No. 5 in E minor ("From the New World "—1893)
The discrepancy in the numbering is due to the composer having revised
his F major example in 1887. No. 5 in E minor, written in the United States,
is the most frequently played, and, like the " No. 5's " of Beethoven and
Tchaikovsky, has achieved a world reputation. Of the others the D minor is
outstanding, a very fine example of the symphonic art. As for the " New
World " Symphony, it abounds in charming and original melodies, but does
not make use of actual themes from negro or Indian sources, as is sometimes supposed. Dvorak had been introduced to " negro spirituals ", but how

24. One of Louis XIV's orchestra, playing a violin.

Radio Times Hulton Picture Library

25. "Lady at Spinet", c. 1685. A French painting by one of the Bonnart brothers.

Radio Times Hulton Picture Library

26. An 18th century "gentleman of quality" playing the
bass viol. The viol family was
being replaced by the violin
type, the bass-viol being the last
survivor. (After J. de St. Jean).

Radio Times Hulton Picture Library

27. From the cover of "Musick's Hand-maide" by John
Playford (1663), depicting a
violinist and a virginals player
performing one of the "new
and Pleasant Lessons" printed
within.

British Museum

much or how little of this music (itself largely derivative) he intended to reflect in his own is a matter of opinion. Certainly he was writing folk-dance syncopations and flattened-seventh minor cadences long before he saw America, and the E minor is Dvorakian and Czech through and through.

The symphonies are sometimes spoken of as " uneven ", but all Dvorak's striking qualities are to be seen in them—his fresh and novel melodic inventiveness, his rhapsodical adaptations of established form, his consummate command of orchestral technique and colour, in particular his magical use time and again of woodwind and horns. Purists have complained that his instrumental exuberance sometimes turns to blatancy, and that his symphonic constructions are inclined to creak at the joints (one feels that this is so in regard to the " New World " finale), but of a composer so rhythmically and colourfully vital much may be forgiven. An engaging gift, sometimes over-exploited, was his ability to invent ingenious rhythmic accompaniment figures, as well as counter-melodies almost as charming as their principals. There is no suggestion in his mature symphonies of any programme intent; his tone-poems came late in his career and have never been widely known.

His chamber-music is of major importance, a score or so of mature works (including ten string quartets). Outstanding among those of his mid-career are the " Slavonic " String Quartet in E flat (Op. 51) and the widely known Piano Quintet in A major (Op. 81). He concluded his chamber-music production with some of his best works, the so-called " Nigger " Quartet (Op. 96), where a " New World " atmosphere does indeed seem to make itself felt, the " American " String Quintet (Op. 97) and the last two string quartets in A flat and G major (Opp. 105 & 106). The " Dumky " Piano Trio (Op. 99) is often heard—six examples of the *Dumka* dance woven rather loosely into an extensive but attractive work.

His visits to England, where his music was warmly welcomed, were of great importance to his career, since, apart from their heartening effect on him, they led to the commissioning of choral and other works, the D minor Symphony for the London Philharmonic Society, the fine *Requiem* for the Birmingham Festival, 1891, the cantata *The Spectre's Bride* (1884) also for Birmingham, and the oratorio *St. Ludmilla* for Leeds (1886). But his greatest adventure was yet to come. In 1892 he accepted an invitation from New York to be Director of the newly-founded National Conservatoire of Music. It was a curious experiment. Dvorak seemed hardly cut out for an important executive post, for all his life he retained the characteristics of his simple peasant origin; innately intelligent but unsophisticated; " the soul of a child and the imagination of a poet ", as his chief biographer, a fellow-countryman, puts it. His real role in the United States was that of " great composer ", and conductor of his own attractive music. However, he seems to have made a definite impact as a teacher, although the aim of his developing a national school of composition founded on so-called indigenous music met with but little success. Nowadays, serious and gifted North American composers are writing major works which may be evolving towards something recognisably national—but it is along different lines. As for negro music,

z

the kind of "art" which commercial circles have developed from it would have astonished Dvorak considerably. The important result of the American episode was the fine music that he was able to write there. Besides the works already mentioned there was the beautiful 'Cello Concerto in B minor (Op. 104—1895), one of the few masterpieces in that genre.

In 1895 home-sickness won the battle against generous offers for a further contract. He returned to his native land and to composition with a new slant. He had previously written some picturesque concert overtures, with *Carnival* (1891) as the best known example; he now adventured wholly into the realm of programme music in a set of five symphonic poems based on Czech ballads, works that have been appreciated mainly in his own land. Two fine operas came towards the end of his life—*Rusalka* and *Cert a Káča* (The Devil and Kate), the latter sometimes heard elsewhere than in Prague.

His many songs and lyrical piano pieces are likely mostly to be mortal. One surviving item may well be No. 7 of a set of nostalgic *Humoresques,* written just before his return from America.

As with Poland, with the death of a master there was no one to take over his international position. Josef Suk (1874–1935) and Vítězslav Novák (1870–1949) were both pupils of Dvorak and fine composers but their music has not interested the rest of Europe. Very different is Leoš Janáček (1854–1928), who spent a musical life in such seclusion that the importance of his highly original work was not truly recognised until after his death. He was the last of the Czech nationalists, this trait apparent in his uncompromising insistence on the exclusive use of his native language in his vocal works, and his individual system of declamation founded on his study of the Czech language. Through his original harmonic style and his striking and unusual orchestration he is now proclaimed as a real modernist. His two best known operas, *Jenufa* and *The Cunning Little Vixen* (this with "animal" characters) have been receiving much notice of late.

Russia

Concerning the early days of Russia as a nation, it will be recalled that the conversion to Christianity of a pagan race by missionaries from Byzantium took place late in the tenth century (see p. 33). The Russian Church inherited all the Greek ecclesiastical forms including the majestic Byzantine sacred music, but in the course of centuries moulded it to its own national pattern, the form becoming known as the *znamenny* chant. This survived the three hundred years of Mongol conquest, which ended with the expulsion of the invaders in the fifteenth century. Though by then its language was Russian instead of Greek it still retained the Byzantine features of complete monophony (except for the occasional drone) and complete *absence* of instrumental accompaniment, even that of the organ. It was at its zenith as an art-form in the sixteenth century, particularly in the reign of Ivan the Terrible. It even lasted, a strange survival in a polyphonic world, midway into the seventeenth century, up to the time of the bitter struggle within the Orthodox Church between a reforming Patriarch and the sect of Old Believers, when it became one of the many casualties. Harmonised music

had already begun to penetrate from the West, and this affected the hurried
and confused attempts to produce a new chant. Worse was to follow. Italian
opera having entered Russia early in the eighteenth century (another of its
many conquests), the Imperial Court was persuaded in 1751 to send a young
native musician, Dmitri Bortnyansky, to study in Italy, where he remained
eleven years. On his return he took over the Imperial Chapel at Petersburg,
and while effecting immense reforms in regard to standards of singing he
thoroughly Italianised the Russian scene for a while through his Neapolitan-
style church music. However, by the middle of the nineteenth century the
Orthodox authorities succeeded in effecting a national reform. Simpler and
more dignified types of harmonised chant were introduced, more in keeping
with the ancient forms.

But Western secular music and Western composers, especially Italians,
continued to hold sway, and as yet the prodigious riches of Russian folk-
music remained unplumbed. During the second half of the eighteenth century the dilettante Russian aristocracy society welcomed such Neapolitan
opera composers as Traëtta, Galuppi, Sarti, Cimarosa, Paisiello and Martin.
Later, came the pianists Clementi and Field, and the French violinist, Rode.
But even the Italians became aware of the mutterings of an increasing
national artistic consciousness, and one of them, the Venetian Catteruno
Cavos, began to make some use of Russian peasant song in his operas. Native
composers like Alexis Verstovsky (1799–1862), who scored a mild success
with his singspiel-like Askold's Grave (1835) were but amateurish forerunners
of the real founder of Russian national music, Michael Glinka (1804–57).

Glinka, with his two operas, A Life for the Czar (1836) and Russlan and
Ludmilla (1842) together with orchestral pieces and songs, struck an authentic note that had been absent before. He began composing in a crude enough
fashion himself while one of a group of young Petersburg intellectuals, whose
number included the famous poet Pushkin. Then ill-health drove him to
Italy, where he was ravished by the art of Bellini and Donizetti, and had the
courage to realise his own tyro shortcomings. He moved to Berlin and spent
half a year on concentrated composition study under the well-known theorist
Siegfried Dehn, then returned to Russia with the avowed ambition to write
an opera that should be " absolutely national ". Ironically enough the
libretto, a story set in the seventeenth century of a young peasant who
chose death rather than betray his Emperor to the Polish invaders, was
shaped by a German, but Glinka's music set a firm pioneer example to native
composers. There was plenty that belonged to standard Italian procedure—
set numbers joined by recitative—the usual solos, choruses, duets and formal
dances, with some attempts at coloratura for the principals, but there was
also constructive use of Russian folk-songs, both as complete items and as
themes. The Polish enemies were given music of their own national colour,
and the whole was a work which for all its musical inexperience gave an
impression of unity and sincerity. There was a brilliant first performance (in
the presence of Czar Nicholas) and thereafter Glinka was held to be the first
composer of Russia, in spite of " cultured " views that he was writing
" coachman's music ".

For his second operatic essay he took as material Pushkin's satirical fairy
tale *Russlan and Ludmilla*. But the poet who might have partnered him had
been killed, and Glinka's amateur librettists were more than usually inept.
He took six years over the score, and when at last the work was performed
(1842) it was a total failure, and had indeed little public appreciation in his
lifetime.[6]* However, its musical values were soon realised by the new generation of Russian composers. Much more than before Glinka was endeavouring
to reconcile the modalities of Russian folk and Church music with the tonal
systems of the West. At the same time he was making use of Persian and
Tartar elements, that oriental flavour so often present in later Russian music.
This power of blending truly Russian characteristics with Western and other
more exotic elements made Glinka the earliest of musical eclectics in a
nation one of whose artistic strengths is its power of absorption. The failure
of *Russlan* seemed to discourage him from further serious effort. He travelled
to Spain where his eclecticism displayed itself in the wonderfully authentic
" jota " atmosphere of the *Spanish Overture* (1848). In the same year came
his other significant orchestral work *Kamarinskaya,* a Russian folk-wedding
piece. There was mutual admiration between him and Berlioz, whom he met
in Paris. One of the Frenchman's tributes concerned the Russian's gifts as an
orchestrator.

After Glinka's death there was a pause before worthy successors came, but
he had indeed blazed a trail for Russian music to follow. He had as contemporary the comparative dilettante Alexander Dargomijsky (1813–69),
who wrote one successful German-romantic type of opera, *Russulka,* with
indeed some Russian peasant elements, but after that a quite original work,
The Stone Guest, which embodied his own newly conceived theories as to
the setting of a libretto by continuous musical declamation—ideas which
Debussy developed. Like Glinka he also carried out experiments with un-
conventional harmonies and modulations, as well as with the whole-tone
scale. *The Stone Guest* was a failure, but it put thoughts into other Russian
composers' heads. Of greater artistic significance were the best of his solo
songs, where grim humour and realism played their parts, anticipating the
masterpieces of Mussorgsky in that genre.

In 1855 there came the death of the despotic Nicholas I, and with the
approach of the '60's a surge of musical development, part of the renaissance of all the arts which accompanied the newly awakened spirit of libera-
lism now abroad in Russia. German influence and German musicians had
already displaced the Italians, and now, owing to the work of the young
virtuoso pianist Anton Rubinstein (1829–94) the nation was given the opportunities of closer contact with Western music and of acquiring a better concert life and a higher musical education. He founded first the Imperial
Russian Music Society and then (in 1862) the Conservatoire of Music in
Petersburg. One of his first graduate pupils was Tchaikovsky. For all that
he was Russian-born Rubinstein was by training and inclination a German-
cosmopolitan. A pupil of Liszt and a consummate technician—almost his
master's equal, he was already famous in Europe and America before returning to Russia. He was a prolific composer of every form from opera and

symphony to song and piano lyric, all belonging to the school of Mendelssohn and Schumann, but his works have not lived. All the same, to him must go much credit for turning Russian musicians from dilettanti to true professionals.

Rubinstein was a cultured conservative with a thorough contempt for his native folk-music. The credit for the sudden emergence of a distinctive Russian art that could offer comparisons with masterpieces of the romantic West belongs very largely to one of the oddest groups of semi-amateurs ever to be encountered in the history of music. The spiritual leader of the " Mighty Handful ", as they were nicknamed, and the only one to whom (at least at first) the term " professional musician " could be applied was Mili Balakirev (1837–1910). He was an excellent pianist, sight-reader and improvisator, but even he professed to scorn scholastic courses in composition, claiming that the necessary light should be gained from the study of great works. He had been encouraged by Dargomijsky; and Glinka, close on death, had been impressed by him. His circle in their earlier efforts relied much on his guidance. His first disciple, who joined him in 1857, was César Cui (1835–1918), a young army officer of engineers. He was followed by Modest Mussorgsky (1839–81), another army officer, but after a decline in the family fortune a government clerk; Nicolas Rimsky-Korsakov (1844–1908) a naval cadet; and finally the oldest of the group, Alexander Borodin (1833–87), already established as a research chemist of distinction at the Medico-Surgical Academy at Petersburg. The group had the valuable support of Vladimir Stasov, writer, art- and music-critic, a man of wide cultural attainments.

The views of the " Five " were that in their techniques they followed the moderns—Berlioz, Chopin, Schumann and Liszt; what they learned from them was to be blended with their newly realised national material, which they maintained could be made a working basis for an intellectual art-music. At the same time they claimed the right to ignore academic rules when they chose; all was to be latitude and freedom. Their views on opera rejected of course the vocal displays of the Italian art, and called for a more serious treatment of all musical resources without Wagner's style of orchestral tyranny. From Dargomijsky they took the newest doctrine of realism, though only Mussorgsky was to make full use of this. Finally the conventions of the classical type of four-movement symphony came under their fire. With regard to the last point, several of them produced four-movement symphonies which at times skated suspiciously near the old procedures.

This was something of their avowed creed, though as individuals each diverged in his own way, in the end disagreeing often enough among themselves. There now began in the '60's a battle-royal in the press and in musical circles between the Five and the followers of Rubinstein. Balakirev tried to counter the Conservatoire by founding his " Free Music School ". The war of intolerance became a threesome when the influential composer-journalist Alexander Serov joined in. His only musical god was Wagner, although the three quite successful operas he produced were merely spectacular imitations of Meyerbeer.

The Five were handicapped at first by having very little to show in practice for all their theory. But in the end this hiatus was impressively filled.
The moody Balakirev, the man who knew how and who could show others
how, had himself strangely little of lasting value to contribute. His career
was interrupted by a long period of abandonment to religious mysticism.
Nowadays he is remembered only by his orchestral tone-poem *Tamara,* full
of oriental colour, and the extremely difficult piano fantasy *Islamey,*
founded on Armenian and Caucasian tunes. The output of César Cui causes
us to wonder how it was that his opinion weighed so heavily in the group,
for time has shown him to be no more than a salon composer, with little
sign of Russian or even individual characteristics. Rimsky-Korsakov's was
a very different case. He started as an amateur of amateurs, but alone among
the Five decided to acquire mastery of technical means by academic study
and exploration of the Western classical past. Previously, under Balakirev's
guidance he had had some success with early compositions (later much
revised), and in 1871 was, amazingly, offered a composition professorship
at Petersburg Conservatoire. He used the opportunity to teach himself as
well as his pupils, and for the rest of his life continued the practice of wide and
exhaustive study. His influence on his own and the next generation became
of increasing importance. Among his pupils are to be counted Glazounov,
Liadov, Arensky, and, notably, Stravinsky and Prokofiev. His greatest gift
was his unique command of the art of orchestration, particularly his power
of inventing novel and brilliantly colourful effects. In spite of his academic
leanings he was a romantic at heart. His neglected symphonies and chamber
music have small vitality as compared with the programmatic orchestral
works—the folklore tone-poems *Sadko* and *Antar,* the *Russian Easter Overture* and two world-famous compositions, the Arabian Nights' Suite,
Scheherazade, and the *Capriccio Espagnol.* Of his fourteen operas only the
fairy-tale *Snow Maiden* (1881) and *Golden Cockerel* (1907), with perhaps the
City of Kitezh, have survived to international acceptance. All have the
advantage of his picturesque orchestration, the last two showing signs in their
use of leading motifs and " symphonic " accompaniments of the impact on
the composer of Wagner's *Ring,* performed in Petersburg in 1889. In his
music there is to be found considerable distinction and originality yet
always charm and fastidious workmanship. He used Russian church modes
and oriental scales but he had no ambitions towards the harsh realisms and
declamatory methods of Dargomijsky and Mussorgsky. His powers as an
editor and master orchestrator were employed on behalf of posthumous
works of colleagues on a number of occasions, but not always wisely, for he
frequently thought that he knew better than the original composer, in
matters not only of scoring but harmony and structure. One of his most
valuable achievements was his autobiography, " My Musical Life ".

Borodin called himself a " Sunday " composer, and jestingly spoke of the
fact that he had no real time for composition except when he was too
unwell to give his chemistry lectures at the Academy of Medicine.[7] Thus
he wrote but few works, but the extraordinary fact is that most of these have
still maintained themselves in the international repertory. Almost by instinct,

but also by keen observation of the Western masters he obtained a firm command of structure and polyphonic texture in his symphonic and chamber music, being in fact the first Russian to succeed as a polyphonist, and the first to make a real impact on the West with his music. Like Glinka, he was a thorough eclectic, yet was still able to preserve Russian nationalistic elements in his works. These may be summed up as being two symphonies and an unfinished third; two string quartets; a tone-poem; an unfinished opera, and some original songs.[8*] (Piano music and lesser chamber works are unimportant.) The quantity is small but the quality out of all proportion by comparison. Regarding the first symphony, it is a wonder that it could have been composed at all considering Borodin's technical equipment at the time, but the wonder grows when the nature of the construction of the first movement is realised—the employment of a number of thematic fragments which are eventually, in the coda, reconciled to a melodic whole. It is the original appearance of a device used by twentieth century composers, including Sibelius. Borodin's masterwork was the fresh and powerful Second Symphony in B minor, now widely appreciated. One of the finest symphonies of the nineteenth century, it has a strikingly original first subject, strikingly treated :

Ex: 66

Liszt, whom Borodin met in Weimar, told him : " Your symphony is entirely new. Nobody has done anything like it ", and proceeded to introduce it and other works of Borodin's to Western Europe. The composer's symphonic poem *In the Steppes of Central Asia* showed him handling Russian and oriental themes in effective contrapuntal style. The opera *Prince Igor* was composed fragmentarily and in fits and starts. Dramatically the ancient tale was badly told, and the work achieves its high reputation principally through the series of musical pictures of a barbarous but colourful people, painted in the second act by solo, chorus and " Polovtsian " dance, examples of genuine and original musical romanticism. The opera had unfortunately to be completed by Rimsky-Korsakov and Glazounov, with certain amendments which, quite rightly, have been described as " editorial impertinences ". Neither of the two string quartets shows much sign of being particularly Russian, but both display much lyrical beauty and contrapuntal mastery, the second containing the famous Nocturne and still universally played.

The most original of the Five was undoubtedly Mussorgsky; the only one who never visited the West, and the only one who was the complete nationalist. He made far more penetrating use of Russian folk-music than his colleagues, and was the most violent breaker of technical conventions, professing to despise Bach and dismissing the great and original harmonist

Chopin as a mere salon composer. As an inheritor of the folk-speech methods of Dargomijsky, he was the only one who consistently practised the doctrines that had been preached of realism and naturalism, and thus the only one who brought to his music such an understanding of the life and spirit of the Russian masses as was displayed by such great writers of Gogol and Dostoyevsky. Gifted with a natural psychological insight he found his finest utterances in the drama of his fourscore solo songs and his operas. His professional employment and his dilatory habits cut down the hours for composition, and the increasing alcoholism that finally killed him shortened the years. He was an excellent pianist and a fine singer of his own music, but he failed to impress his circle as to his real status as a composer, and his harmonic and other innovations were too often thought to be ineptitudes. In contrast, when Liszt saw a handful of his songs, the only music of the composer to be known outside Russia in his lifetime, the old man was completely charmed by their originality.[9*] His greatest work was his setting of Pushkin's historical drama *Boris Godunov,* in which he showed how powerfully he could paint individual character, whether that of the conscience-stricken usurper or the various units of a really living Russian peasant crowd—no conventional chorus here. The work was accepted after various reshapings and had fifteen performances during Mussorgsky's lifetime. Then, after complete neglect, Rimsky-Korsakov in the new century produced an edition in which his old friend's bold harmonies and " ugly " but realistic melodic lines had been " corrected ", his orchestration rewritten and " brightened ", and actually new music composed. This is the version by which the work has long been known in Europe and America. Fortunately the original score has now been republished.[10*] Mussorgsky's only significant orchestral work, *A Night on Bald Mountain* (fantastic " witches' sabbath " music) also suffered mishandling, being heard only in Rimsky-Korsakov's version, recomposed to the latter composer's taste.[11] Rimsky-Korsakov even dared to " improve " a number of the songs. Of Mussorgsky's piano pieces the only one frequently performed is the highly original suite of impressions—*Pictures from an Exhibition.* Even this had not been allowed to remain as its composer left it; there is an orchestral arrangement by Ravel. Many of Mussorgsky's unfinished works were edited and completed after his death by contemporary hands, mainly Rimsky-Korsakov's. In the case of the opera *Kovanschina* this did indeed make a performance possible. Nowadays, republications of his major works, which make plain his own original intentions, are giving a truer picture of a highly individual mind.

Peter Ilitch Tchaikovsky (1840–93) was the composer who first put Russian music squarely on the world map. He started in the usual contemporary dilettante fashion as a fair amateur pianist and nothing more, and was already over twenty-two when he gave up a clerical post to enter the new Conservatoire at Petersburg, living in poverty until he had completed the course. He was then given (in 1865) a professorship of harmony at the Moscow Conservatoire, which was controlled by Nicholas Rubinstein, brother of Anton. There he stayed for twelve years, at the end of which time he had made his name. Early compositions were none too successful, but he came to something like musical maturity in 1869 with the concert overture *Romeo and Juliet* (revised however in 1880). Balakirev was in Moscow at the time, and there is no doubt that the work was written with the aid of his supervision. No bad thing, for even in his maturity Tchaikovsky was not a good critic of his own music. He admired Mendelssohn, Schumann, Mozart (the Mozart of the stage works), and the composers of French and Italian romantic opera. A first hearing of *Carmen* quite overwhelmed him. He spoke of his love for Russian folk-song, but his use of the native material, though picturesque, was in no way part of his musical make-up, as it was in, say, the case of Mussorgsky. He was indeed at heart a cosmopolitan, a highly emotional late-romanticist. Yet he had small sympathy for Liszt and Wagner and none at all for Brahms, whom he detested. Brahms returned the compliment. On the whole he kept on good terms with the Five, except for Cui, who wielded a poisonous pen, and Mussorgsky, to whose merits he was blind. From childhood to death he was neurotic to the extreme. Nervous depression and the blackest pessimism seem to have been his everyday moods, and there is every reason to believe that he was sexually abnormal. All his life he was ruled by emotionalism rather than cool judgment. His works up to 1877, the year he left his teaching in Moscow, included four unsuccessful operas. Of three early symphonies only the second, the "Little Russian", making use of a certain amount of Ukrainian folk-song, has survived to occasional performance. Like Dvorak he moved quite unconcernedly between symphony and orchestral fantasy. Indeed, in regard to construction there was often very little difference. The composer Taneyev complained that the Fourth Symphony gave the effect of a symphonic poem "with three more movements slapped on and called a symphony". After *Romeo and Juliet* there came other orchestral fantasies—*The Tempest* (1873) and the Dantesque *Francesca da Rimini* (1876). His first real success, and certainly the first of his works to be accepted outside Russia was the B flat minor Piano Concerto, which was fortunate in being taken up by von Bülow, who gave it its premier at Boston, U.S.A. in 1875. Its present form represents a revision, due to some stern criticisms of the original by Nicholas Rubinstein. In 1877, while the composer was engaged upon works that did much to establish him there occurred the amazing episode of his marriage, as the result of his weak-willed surrender to the importunities of a young girl student, who in fact finished her life in a mental home. The union lasted but a few weeks; Tchaikovsky, himself driven near to insanity, tried in a typically ineffectual manner to commit suicide and then fled to Switzerland. Almost immediately there came a happening that seemed also to belong to a world of fantasy. He received a letter from a certain Madame von Meck, a wealthy widow and an admirer of his music, offering him a regular and substantial annuity that would enable him to devote all the time he wished to composition. The single condition was that they should never meet. Tchaikovsky accepted gratefully, and in the year of recovery abroad completed *Eugene Onegin* and the F minor Symphony. (The allowance continued until within a few years of his death.) Freed from financial anxiety, but apparently none the happier for it, the rest of his life was filled with composition, relieved by travel. In 1885 he conducted his works in leading European cities as far as London, but even conducting was a severe nervous ordeal for him. In 1891 he visited New York, Baltimore and Philadelphia. The Tchaikovsky cult had begun.

Eugene Onegin, performed in 1878, was his first real stage success. He used the term "lyrical scenes" to describe the work, which still holds the stage, even though it is clear that opera was not his real métier. He made further dramatic attempts, of which *The Queen of Spades* (1890) seems likeliest to survive, with *Eugene Onegin,* out of a total of eleven. In 1878 came his only Violin Concerto, much criticised at first, but in its revised form now widely accepted among virtuosi. A Second Piano Concerto (1890), better constructed than the first, nevertheless does not have its vitality. Among the colourful orchestral works of this last period are the *Italian Caprice,* the well-worn "1812" Overture and the fantasy-overture *Hamlet.* Some of the composer's most attractive scoring is to be found in his three Suites for orchestra and his ballet music. To the early *Swan Lake* he added in his last years *The Sleeping Beauty* and *Nutcracker* ballets, all still vital. In 1888, after a ten-year gap, came the Fifth of his symphonies, one of the world's most popular. After fifty he aged quickly and prematurely, yet his last work was his best, the Sixth ("Pathetique") Symphony. It was given a first performance at Petersburg in October 1893. A few days later he contracted cholera and died.

Tchaikovsky was an extraordinarily uneven composer. In many ways he was a supreme master of beauty—of melody, of harmony, of instrumental tone-colour. But not of form, as he himself ruefully admitted. He could invent the most attractive and striking of themes, but they were too often without germinal power; they might oppose, but seldom did they interact. Time and again his emotions overcame the disciplines of musical design; he *felt* rather than *thought,* and expressed his feelings with an intensity that too often slipped from control. At his worst, and this is in several of his larger orchestral works, the construction is a matter of an alternation of episodes—a passion torn to tatters as it mounts in sequence-patterns to a climax of hysteria, followed by a luxuriant cantabile passage of tearful emotionalism, full-charged with self-pity. Such practices certainly continued to the end, but after the "anti-symphonic" Fourth Symphony, with a verbal programme as an afterthought and a last movement of noisy shapelessness (indeed the peasant-dance bedlam that its composer represented it to be), the Fifth and Sixth came as a considerable step forward in the organisation of symphonic material. In the "Pathetique" Sixth the composer was able to transmute his own pessimism, self-pity and sense of a relentless fate into something of great beauty, artistic value and wide appeal. Dramatically exaggerated and shamelessly emotional as the music may be in places, there are in this uneasy world many listeners (more perhaps than would admit it) to whom it conveys a sense of sympathetic fellowship with their own stresses, pinings and frustrations, and for that reason (and there may also be others) the Sixth Symphony is likely long to endure.

To some people the artistic best of Tchaikovsky is to be found in the ballets and the suites, where the very nature and purpose of the music places a curb on undue emotionalism, and his genius for the creation of rich and haunting melody set in superbly imaginative orchestration is expressed with such success. His mastery of the art of instrumentation occasioned the now well-worn gibe that his music "sounds better than it is", but certainly it was not always bolstering up inferior material. He has suffered much at the hands of the critics—his symphonies "mere suites", "useful perhaps as ballet music" (as indeed they have been), his melodies "over-sentimental", his orchestrations too often "blatant". Yet the fact remains that he possessed a clarity of thought and a directness of delivery denied to some composers usually held to be of greater stature. Clarity and directness are surely among the qualities that cause his music still to find ready appreciation.

There came now the second generation of Russian composers. The battle between the rival schools of thought had died down, music was now a respectable profession even for one of noble blood to follow, and the devoted work of the Rubinsteins and their staffs, including Rimsky-Korsakov and such famous executant teachers as Leschetizky (piano) and Auer (violin), had produced a number of highly trained, thoroughly professional musicians. Among these were Anatole Liadov (1855–1914), Sergei Taneyev (1856–1915), Michael Ippolitov-Ivanov (1859–1935), Anton Arensky (1861–1906), Alexander Grechaninov (1864–1956) and Alexander Glazunov (1865–1936). These on the whole were eclectic and unadventurous, capable of composing in any form and to any length, but without striking much fire. Some of them were as mighty drinkers as Mussorgsky or Tchaikovsky but they lacked the stimulus of the older men's genius. The incredibly indolent Liadov is remembered perhaps by his orchestral tone-poems *Baba Yaga,* and the *Enchanted Lake,* and by a few piano pieces, including the hackneyed *Music-Box.* Taneyev's was an extraordinary intellect. A virtuoso pianist, he yet became one of the most erudite of musical scholars, writing learnedly on contrapuntal matters and devoted to the music of past ages. Ippolitov-Ivanov more than his contemporaries showed oriental and national colouring in his music at a time when it was going a little out of fashion again, with the symphonic suite *Caucasian Sketches* as his best remembered work. Arensky, much influenced by Tchaikovsky, will be thought of for his tuneful Piano Trio in D minor and perhaps a few piano pieces. Gretchaninov, one of the several musicians who left Russia after the Revolution, wrote enormously, especially in the matter of choral music and songs, and gained some notice in America, where he settled. Glazounov's youthful ability was realised by Balakirev and Rimsky-Korsakov, who called him "the little Glinka". His first symphony, written when he was sixteen, was performed not only in Russia but by Liszt at Weimar. He went on to produce a steady stream of compositions, avoiding only opera. In 1906 he became head of the Petersburg Conservatoire. For a time his works were played in all the European capitals and in America, but for all their expert technique there remains in general regard only the charming Mendelssohnian Violin Concerto out of eight symphonies, a number of tone-poems and concertos, and much chamber and choral music. He expressed in turn a mild nationalism, the romanticism of Liszt and an innocuous classicism, and never found an altogether authentic voice. He left Russia in 1928 and retired to Paris. His greatest fame must be that of an influential teacher.

Following Tchaikovsky to international fame was Sergei Rachmaninov (1873–1943). After studying at Moscow he went for a time to Liszt at Weimar and early reached the highest levels as a piano virtuoso. He had ambitions as a composer as well, giving all homage to Tchaikovsky and the Teutonic West, from first to last remaining a nineteenth century romanticist at a time when music was undergoing revolutionary changes of outlook. At twenty he wrote a certain Prelude in C sharp minor for piano, that for better or worse spread his name round the world, but the total failure of his First Symphony soon after shocked him so profoundly as to affect his self-confidence as a composer for many years. He had gained world fame as a pianist and a certain reputation as a composer before the Russian Revolution drove him to settle in the United States. His Second Pianoforte Concerto in C minor (1900) with its sultry and nostalgic tunes was the god-child of Tchaikovsky's B flat minor, and as likely long to endure in popular esteem. Of more merit is the splendid Rhapsody on a Theme of Paganini for Piano and Orchestra, a late work (1934) where a virile and ironic quality replaces the nostalgic and sweetly lyrical, and a masterly series of variations is achieved. Rachmaninov (with Skryabin) filled a gap in the catalogue of Russian music, adding to the few worth-while compositions for piano with his numerous Preludes and Études, romantically individual for all their reminders of Chopin and Liszt. In one work he contrived to be wholly Russian and unique—in his *Vesper Mass* (1915), founded on ancient Ortho-dox chants. In 1931 his music was banned in Soviet Russia as " decadent " but after his death it was found after all fit to be performed.

Another late romanticist of Russian extraction was Nicolas Medtner (1880–1951). Moscow made him into a fine pianist, and he had something of a European reputation before finally quitting his native land in 1921. In the end he settled in England, where his music found staunch if limited support. There is an opinion that his piano works, " absolute music " in spite of some use of fanciful titles and firmly based on the older principles of tonality and form, deserve greater attention than they have so far received.

In a world of its own was the career of Alexander Skryabin (1872–1915), fellow-student with Rachmaninov, and like him early a virtuoso pianist. Recital travelling took him away from Russia, and for a time he settled in Brussels the better to pursue composition. The famous Russian conductor Koussovitsky did much to spread the knowledge of his orchestral works. As a composer he began with piano music which though individual had much affinity with Chopin in harmony and ornament, and was in a singu-larly beautiful keyboard style. Then came a Liszt-Wagner period of influence. Meanwhile he was developing his own fantastic brand of mysticism and pseudo-philosophy, expressed in a great deal of crazy prose-writing. Once again we hear that a union of the arts was to be " the transformer of life " and the composer " the teacher and redeemer of mankind ". He plunged into a jungle of harmonic experiment. In his piano sonatas from the Fifth onward, and in his gigantic orchestral works, *The Divine Poem* (1903), *The Poem of Ecstasy* (1908) and *Prometheus*—The Poem of Fire (1910) he developed his own harmonic and thematic system, based on a " synthetic " chord of superimposed fourths derived from the natural upper partials— C, F sharp, B flat, E, A and D. This idea haunted all his later works. To the immense instrumental score of *Prometheus* he even added a visual colour-scheme, to be thrown on a screen—a " keyboard of light ". There can be found high technical achievement, rhythmical subtleties and above all great originalities of harmonic *sound* in his works, but on the whole they have proved to be a musical dead-end. Some of his piano music is still played, and the last two gigantic orchestral works have an occasional revival. The " new paths " however seem to be those of the twelve-tone system and the " tone-row ". Except in his highly-charged emotionalism he showed no affinities with his country's music. The reaction in Russia against a decadent romanticism began in the work of Stravinsky, whose career belongs to the new age.

Scandinavia

Until well into the nineteenth century Sweden, Denmark, Norway and Finland had looked mainly to Germany for their musical guidance, but when the trend towards the cultivation of national traits began there was found in each country a bounteous wealth of native folksong on which to build. On the whole, however, their composers lacked the full-blooded energy of the Slavs, and produced no one of significant European stature, unless we make premature mention of Jan Sibelius, who began, late in the day, as a Finnish romanticist.

Sweden could indeed show a late-baroque native composer of considerable merit in Johann Roman (1694–1758) whose sonatas and concertos are in the process of being rediscovered as concert pieces. But musical style, whether in the hands of native or imported composers, continued to be very largely German until the advent of such men as Adolf Lindblad (1801–79) and Ivar Hallstrom (1826–1901). The greatest Swedish composer of the century was Franz Berwald (1796–1868). If not particularly " national " he wrote a great deal of symphonic music in a truly individual style, though it was not until long after his death that his countrymen awoke to his merits.[12] Another name of note to the Swedes is that of Johan Söderman (1832–76), a writer of dramatic music and large-scale choral ballads, as well as a *Missa Solemnis,* held to be one of the most important Scandinavian works ever created. The Swedish singer Jenny Lind (1820–87) was an international figure of highest reputation.

In Denmark the beginnings of a national element were to be found in the operas and opera ballets of Johann Hartmann (1805–1900). Better known Continentally was Niels Gade (1817–90), who studied at Leipzig and whose competent and picturesque Mendelssohnian music, so popular in his lifetime, has nowadays suffered eclipse. A pupil of his, Carl Nielsen, became a composer of eminence whose career belongs to the new century.

Norway had the advantage of a richer and more distinctive folk-music, the work of Ludwig Lindeman (1812–87) as a collector revealing an ancient wealth of peasant music, types that included the triple *springer* and the duple *halling*. But when (well past mid-century) Norwegian composers were struggling to find themselves, the shadow of Leipzig Conservatoire lay heavy on them also, as in the case of Johan Svendsen (1840–1911), his music largely cosmopolitan in spite of his " Norwegian rhapsodies ". The eccentric solo violinist Ole Bull (1810–80) did much to spread a knowledge of his country's folk-music through his own caprices and fantasias on such material—this throughout Europe and in North America, but the real architects of Norwegian nationalism in music were Richard Nordraak (1842–66) and Edvard Grieg (1843–1907). Nordraak, a composer of promise who died all too soon (his is the music of the Norwegian National Anthem) was an earnest patriot at a time when the political union with Sweden was an uneasy one. Bound up with his belief of his country's destiny was a similar enthusiasm for her folk-music. He began his friendship with the young pianist and composer Grieg at a time when the latter had returned from Leipzig, (where he had been sent on Ole Bull's advice), somewhat disillusioned by the shortcomings of his German training, and but little more satisfied with the coaching of Niels Gade. Grieg, instantly converted to Nordraak's views, determined that his music should henceforth express the soul of his country. He certainly succeeded in achieving his aim, but seldom by actual musical quotation. It was rather that he, like Chopin, was able to assimilate the characteristics of his native song, find the very essence of its rhythms and melodic turns, and then express its spirit in his own individual musical language. This was indeed one of great poetic charm, and it captivated hearers who, far beyond the borders of Norway, had never heard of a *slátter* or a " Hardanger fiddle ".[13] To the fascination of his folk-like melody he added some personal traits of harmony. Naturally enough there was a great deal of pedal drone in his dances, but he employed also a sophisticated vocabulary of chromatic harmony, which though no doubt derived ultimately from Wagner and Liszt, he made particularly his own. Though he wrote a few extended works in classical form, e.g. a String Quartet in G minor, three violin sonatas, and one of the best known piano concertos in the world, popular at every level and needing no further description, he was by nature a miniaturist. His greatest mastery is to be found in the sixty-six pieces for piano published under the general label of *Lyrische Stücke,* and to many of which he gave poetic titles suggesting small tone-pictures. There are instances when the originality of some of his harmonic thoughts suggests that, again like Chopin, he was one of the prophets of Impressionism.

The name of Christian Sinding (1856–1941) will be recalled nowadays only in association with a once very popular piano piece—*Frühlingsrauchen* (Rustle of Spring). His symphonies, concertos and sonatas, none of them showing any particular national colouring, seem more or less to have passed into oblivion.

As for Finland's emergence, the usual pattern is seen—the collection of folk-melodies, and the cultivation of national songs and choruses. Yet it was a German, Frederic Pacius (1809–91), a pupil of Spohr, who first gave a start to organised musical life in the country. A native composer, Robert Kajanus (1856–1933), produced rhapsodies and tone-poems that were given some measure of Finnish colouring. The music of Finland's greatest son, Jan Sibelius, will have later attention, since it belongs in the main to the twentieth century.

Spain and Portugal

It has already been noted that native Iberian music, for all its great Renaissance traditions, suffered the common European fate of an Italian dominance in the eighteenth and early nineteenth centuries. Spain shared a Rossini fever with the rest of the Continent, and also produced a composer, Vincento Martin Y Soler, whose (Italian) operas, the librettos of some by da Ponte, were successful in both Italy and Vienna. *Una cosa rara* was a greater attraction in its day than Mozart's *Nozze di Figaro*. However, a stand for truly Spanish music was made by Felipe Pedrell (1841–1922) who collected folk-tunes and made valuable researches in connection with the great Spanish musicians of the Renaissance. He also wrote several operas to Spanish texts, and altogether made Spanish composers of the twentieth century his debtors. Meanwhile the popular dramatic *zarzuela* (see. p. 159) had been kept alive, as well as the vivid music of the country's popular dances. Domenico Scarlatti, as we have already seen, had been happy to take over some of the characteristics of Spanish folk-music. In the nineteenth century there was an increasing awareness in other countries of the musical attractions of such dances as the *fantango, bolero* and *jota*. Leading European musicians, mainly Russian and French—Glinka, Rimsky-Korsakov, Borodin, Chabrier, Bizet (*Carmen*), and Lalo (*Symphonie espagnole*), made each his own particular paraphrases of what he had heard of Spanish music, while the famous Spanish violin virtuoso Pablo de Sarasate (1844–1908) played everywhere his Spanish Dances, and Gipsy Fantasies. The genuine article in the way of instrumental music awaited the coming of Albeniz, Granados and Falla. In dealing with these composers we shall be straying somewhat beyond what might be thought to be the limits of this chapter, but in their truly Spanish works all three were romantic-nationalists.

Isaac Albeniz (1860–1909), an infant prodigy as a pianist who later gained the approval of both Liszt and Rubinstein, had a fantastically adventurous and cosmopolitan early existence, until at thirty he more or less settled in Paris and became friendly with d'Indy, Dukas and Debussy. In spite of any French influence, a number of his piano works caught the genuine atmosphere of his native dance-music, especially in his well-known *Iberia,* a suite of twelve pieces, tone-pictures of Spanish life. There are other orchestral and piano pieces of national colouring. That he actually composed operas to the libretti of an English millionaire patron need not concern us here.

Enrique Granados (1867–1916) spent several years as a pupil of Pedrell, before completing his piano studies in Paris. He later became highly thought of in France as a pianist. Meanwhile he had returned to Barcelona and became a successful opera composer and teacher. His early piano music owed much to Chopin, Liszt and Grieg, but with his two books of piano pieces, *Goyescas* (1911), he swiftly gained a European reputation for individuality. They were inspired by the pictures and tapestries of the Spanish painter Goya, and in them Granados created something entirely Spanish in atmosphere, outdoing Albeniz in this respect. In 1916 he produced an opera in New York which, oddly enough, was founded on the same material and took over the same name. It was on his return from America that he was tragically drowned in the English Channel.

Manuel de Falla (1876–1946), though a pupil of Pedrell and a brilliant pianist, had a late emergence. He was nearly thirty when his opera *La vida breve* won a national prize. He also gravitated to Paris, and like Albeniz was friendly with Debussy and Dukas. *La vida breve* was produced in Paris in 1914, but the outbreak of war sent him back to Madrid. There came the two ballets, *The Three-Cornered Hat* and *El amor brujo* (Wedded by Witchcraft). In 1919 London gave a performance of a revised version of the former, and in 1921 a first hearing of three pieces for orchestra and piano, *Nights in the Gardens of Spain*, with the composer at the keyboard. Thereafter his production rapidly fell away, with a puppet-opera and a harpsichord concerto as the largest works. The latter, classical in design, recalls the spirit of Domenico Scarlatti. Falla also caught something of the modernisms of Debussy's impressionistic style, but his music remained quite individual, and he commanded all the effects, rhythmic, harmonic and orchestral, for creating the true Spanish atmosphere. He treated the guitar as an instrument capable of serious artistic achievement, as his *Homage* to the memory of Debussy, written for guitar solo, well shows. It was known that in his last years he was engaged on a large-scale choral epic, *La Atlántida* (Atlantis), but it was left unfinished. Portions have lately been performed and the work found to be of impressive quality.

Because of the insistent national spirit of these Spanish composers we must again stray deep into the twentieth century with the music of Joaquin Turina (1882–1949), who, though at Paris with Falla and friendly with d'Indy as well as Debussy and Ravel, was resolved " to fight bravely for the national music ". He followed the romantic trends of Albeniz and Granados in the Andalusian atmosphere of his symphonic poems, especially *La procesión de Rocio,* a picture of a religious festival with a background of dancing and the throbbing of guitars. His greatest work is perhaps his " cyclic " *Sevillian Symphony* (1920). He wrote also some notable chamber music and a wealth of piano pieces in the smaller and intimate forms. Oscar Esplá (b. 1889), more of Falla's temper, and more individual and symphonically minded than other Spanish composers, yet remained true to the spirit of his native regions, those of the Mediterranean coast rather than Andalusia, as in his *Don Quixote* tone-poem.

Portugal has made less impression on the musical world. Early in the century the name of Marcos Portugal (1762–1830) was known in Europe as a composer of Italian and Portuguese operas. A later and outstanding musician was Jose Viana da Mota (1868–1948), a pupil of Liszt and a pianist of high European reputation. He was a composer of Portuguese Rhapsodies and an influential teacher.

Hungary

The folk-music of Hungary was of ancient origin, and one untouched, at first, by Western and Northern influences. But the " Hungarian " music that attracted the attention of Haydn, Schubert, Liszt, Brahms and Joachim (himself, like Liszt, Hungary-born) was to some degree a popular synthesis accomplished by Hungarian gipsy-musicians, a far more cosmopolitan and conscious affair. Only recently, through the devoted researches of men like Bartók and Kodály (whose own music belongs to the twentieth century) has the distinction been analysed and demonstrated. The romantic composer Robert Volkmann (1815–83) settled in Budapest, and made efforts to incorporate Hungarian elements into his music. Native-born composers such as Franz Erkel (1810–93) were encouraged to attempt a national opera movement, but failed to impress the rest of the musical world as to the vitality of their dialect. Ernst von Dohnányi (1877–1960) spoke the language of Brahms rather than that of Hungary. Virtuosity was another matter. Liszt's is ever the greatest figure, but among world-famous violinists (besides Joachim) there are the names of Leopole Auer, Jeno Hubáy and Joseph Szigeti.

Rumania

Though Rumania has been proved to possess a store of attractive folk-music, thanks to the work of Georges Enesco (1881–1955), violinist, pianist and composer, his is the only significant name which has reached the outside world. The great violinist Yehudi Menuhin was one of his pupils.

Holland and Belgium

These possess mighty musical traditions that reach back to the triumphant days of the Netherland School, but like other countries exposed to the close influence of the greater musical nations of the later centuries, each was unable to find an authentic national voice, even though developing a vigorous musical life. Particularly distinguished was the Belgian school of violin playing, founded by the versatile Charles de Bériot (1802–70), virtuoso, composer, painter, poet and sculptor ! His concertos and studies are still in use. Just as famous was his pupil, the far-travelled Henri Vieuxtemps (1820–81), who played a Rode concerto in public at six. For a time he was a professor at the Petersburg Conservatoire. Some of his concertos, admirably written for the instrument, are, like de Bériot's, still played. In due succession for a high place among virtuosi came his pupil, Eugene Ysaye (1858–1931), to whom César Franck dedicated his Violin Sonata, and Debussy his String Quartet. Three Belgian names stand high in the world of musical scholarship. There is François Fétis (1784–1871), the author of the first encyclopedia of musical biography; François-Auguste Gevaert (1828–1908), among whose many works is a valuable treatise on orchestra-

2A

tion; and the modern Belgian musicologist of world fame, Charles van de Borren, in particular the authority on the music of Dufay.

The Belgian-born César Franck, an important and highly individual composer, chose to make his career in France, where he built up a following of his own.

France. The Revival of Instrumental Music

It has already been noted that French (= Parisian) music for a great deal of the nineteenth century was almost completely the music of the opera. The difficulties that Berlioz met in his single-handed efforts to create a public for his novel and picturesque orchestral works have also been described. Certainly the salon and the recital hall kept virtuoso playing in favour, but orchestral concerts were few and the practice of chamber music at a low ebb. Even the much revered Gounod, turning aside from the production of church music and operas to write a couple of symphonies in 1855, found them neglected, for all his instrumental skill. Then in the second half of the century, with the appearance of such men as Saint-Saëns, Lalo and César Franck, the scene gradually changed. Instrumental composers were greatly aided, moreover, by the devoted work of Jules Pasdeloup (1819–87), founder (in 1861) of the *Concerts Populaires*, which educated the Parisian public in the works of Berlioz, Wagner and the German classicists, as well as in the new native productions. In 1871 came the highly important *Société Nationale de Musique*, owing its existence to Saint-Saëns, Bizet, César Franck and his pupils d'Indy, Duparc and Chausson. Another important name is that of Charles Lamoureux (1834–99), violinist and conductor, who founded choral and chamber-music societies. Paris heard *Messiah*, *Judas Maccabeus* and the *St. Matthew Passion*, and even a string sextet of Brahms. In 1881 began the orchestral *Concerts Lamoureux*, which gave further opportunities for the increasing number of French instrumental composers. Lamoureux' enthusiasm for Wagner gradually reconciled Paris to that composer's works, with the ultimate triumph of a performance of *Tristan* in 1899. In 1894 another teaching institution was started, the *Schola Cantorum*, its inception due to d'Indy, Franck's pupil, Bordes, the choral conductor and the organist Guilmant. Though its original concern was with church music, its courses soon took on a broader basis, with d'Indy as its director, and " Franckism " as its creed.

Of the three pioneer composers mentioned above, the first to make his influence felt on the next generation was probably Edouard Lalo (1823–92), of Spanish descent. He was highly trained as a string player and had a career as a member of a professional string-quartet, but not until his late 40's did he gain success as a composer, when his Violin Concerto and *Symphonie Espagnole* for violin and orchestra found instant favour. Noteworthy also was his orchestral suite *Namouna*, arranged from a ballet. A late triumph was his tuneful opera, still performed, *Le Roi d'Ys*. Even though Beethoven, Schubert and Schumann were his idols his music is gracefully and individually French, and by its piquant harmony and colourful orchestration made a great impression on younger composers of the time.

Camille Saint-Saëns (1833–1921), born in Paris, was a prodigious pianist from an early age (at 11 he was playing Beethoven and Mozart concertos in public), and in his maturity was probably the most generally cultured musician since Mendelssohn. He was soon attracted to and noticed by Liszt, but his first prominence was as a church organist; for twenty years he held that post at the Madeleine. However, he soon began to make his mark as a composer. He wrote steadily throughout his career, and made contributions to every form and type, vocal and instrumental. For only a short time did he teach, and Fauré was one of his pupils. Of his symphonies, the third, with parts for organ and two pianos, has best survived. He was the first French composer to produce a tone-poem, following Liszt's lead with *Le Rouet d'Omphale* (Omphale's Spinning Wheel), still played, as is the celebrated *Danse Macabre*. Others of the genre have lasted less well. His concertos, five for piano, two for violin and one for 'cello; his chamber-music, which includes a piano quartet, a piano quintet, string quartets and trios, are all so admirably shaped, so skilfully written for the soloist, as to cause them occasionally to be revived. But the plain truth is that for all his great talent, sense of form and technical facility, his music lacks individuality and the power of conviction. He was the perfect eclectic; his study had ranged over the centuries and all the schools; he assimilated everything, and in the end remained a conservative French classical-romantic of impeccable workmanship whose music glittered rather than moved to any depth. In his later career French instrumental music had progressed past him, and he must be remembered most for his early championship of native composers, as seen in the foundation of the *Société Nationale,* and his stand for moderation and Gallic clarity at a time when Wagnerism was threatening the national character of French music. Note has already been taken of his one opera likely to live—*Samson et Dalila.*

César Franck (1822–90), Belgian-born, (he became a naturalised Frenchman only in 1871) was a major contributor to that upsurge of French instrumental music which finally broke the stranglehold of opera that Berlioz' fine symphonic works in earlier decades had failed to loosen. Yet Franck in the first fifty years of his life remained an obscure Parisian teacher and organist, deserving during that time but little better fate. Never did any other major composer leave his significant efforts to so late in the day, for his fame rests on the works of his last eighteen years. He was already sixty-eight, and within a few months of death, when the first real public recognition of his worth as a composer came to him, at a *Société Nationale* performance of his String Quartet.

In his boyhood he had already done much touring as a concert pianist under his father's commercial-minded supervision before entering the Paris Conservatoire at the age of fifteen. It was the period of the production of Berlioz' large orchestral works, and of Liszt's greatest fame as a piano virtuoso. He must have heard much of the music of both. During his five years of study he distinguished himself in piano and organ playing, and laid the foundations of his polyphonic style and mastery of variation form by his absorption of the music of Bach and Beethoven. Yet until 1846—until he broke away from his father's selfish control—his career was that of another aspiring Thalberg, the composition and playing in public of ephemeral piano pieces of the *fantasie* type. He had taken over many of the brilliant technical tricks of Alkan and Liszt. There was however an extraordinary exception to the designation of worthlessness that attaches itself to his early music—his Op. 1, three piano trios. Their merits were widely recognised, thanks to the distinguished list of musicians, Meyerbeer, Spontini, Liszt and Chopin among them, who subscribed to their publication. The interest of Liszt and von Bülow led to their being played even in Germany. In the first of them is very plainly seen two characteristics of Franck's mature style, his use of melodies which seem to circulate round a single note, and the "cyclic" device, whereby he employed some of his early material in later movements. Cyclic form, a characteristic romantic technique, has already been mentioned (p. 307), and the claim sometimes heard that Franck *invented* it does not hold water.

In 1851 he took up a post in which he continued for the rest of his life, that of ill-paid organist at the church of Sainte-Clotilde. There now began an uneventful and laborious period, over a dozen years filled with teaching work and routine composition of church music. Most of the organ and choir pieces of this period have little to recommend them to later generations. Written to need, they bear every sign of being born of hurried improvisation, and suffer from Franck's major fault, lack of self-criticism. Only the *Six Piéces* for organ (1862) are worthy of the master. But during that time he gathered round him a band of devoted pupils which eventually included such good musicians as d'Indy, Duparc, Pierné, Bordes and Chausson. Franck, like Bruckner, was a dedicated and unworldly son of the Church of Rome, and his simple honesty, goodness and gentle wit caused him to be termed " Pater Seraphicus " by his following, who knew, as others did not, what potentialities were there. All unwittingly he was founding a school.

In 1872 officialdom decided to notice him. He was given a professorship of organ at the Conservatoire, but was not welcomed by his colleagues, particularly as his organ classes soon turned into successful ones in composition. His own creative faculties were now awakened at a higher level. From 1876 onwards there came a steady succession of the works that have mattered, the orchestral tone-poems *Les Éolides*, *Le Chasseur Maudit* (The Accursed Huntsman) and *Les Djinns* (with a piano part), all owing much to Liszt's example; the splendid *Variations Symphoniques* (actually a piano concerto; only the middle part uses the variation form); a Piano Quintet; a three-movement and not very classical Symphony in D minor; a String Quartet; a highly original Violin Sonata; and two piano works of significance, *Prélude, chorale et fugue* and *Prélude, aria et finale*, all of them still holding their own with the concert-going public. During the period he completed his best but somewhat uneven sacred work, the oratorio *Les Béatitudes*. There came several fine organ works, of which *Trois Chorales,* his last compositions, are outstanding. These are of unique structure, truly poetic in atmosphere and with some splendid contrapuntal writing.

Yet through these years of production public indifference continued. A desperate effort at a Franck festival in 1884 by pupils, friends and Pasdeloup himself was a disastrous failure, mainly due to lack of rehearsal, and the Symphony was coldly received in 1889. Only in 1890, as already related, did the String Quartet win favour for the composer. A second success followed a few days later, when others of his chamber works were applauded; but this was at Tournai! Not until several years after Franck's death did France awaken to his worth.

When his music made its full impact the gain to the cause of French instrumental composition was considerable; it gave to it a new vitality and a new status. Yet strongly individual and attractive as it was, Franck's was not the music of progress. He had attempted to blend two irreconcilable elements—a highly chromatic harmonic idiom that was based on the Wagner-Liszt outlook, and a passion for classic German polyphony, this devoted to the purpose of establishing more firmly the symphonic form in French music. Apart from the traditional Gallic objection to *musique savant* the movement was already beginning towards emancipation from the heavy romanticism of the past century in the lighter atmosphere of Impressionism as expressed in the work of Claude Debussy. Yet Franck's music is as timeless as Bruckner's. The fervent idealism that he expressed and the richness and individuality of his harmonic vocabulary overshadowed in his best works the crawling chromaticisms, the too-frequent moments of banality, and the modulatory meanderings that replaced the firm tonal structures of the classic symphonic masters. Most of his characteristics can be seen (in their best light) in the A major Violin Sonata, one of his finest inspirations. In the *cantabile* opening movement are plenty of the luscious augmented sixths and consecutive sevenths and ninths to which he was so addicted. There are the usual " side-slipping " tonalities; a great deal of earlier thematic material reappears in succeeding movements; the stormy second is the only one the structure of which has any resemblance to sonata form; the third movement is little more than a leisured meditation on the main first-movement theme, and the principal subject of the finale is a strict but melodious canon between the two instruments, as delightful and masterly an example as was ever written. (See Ex. 67, which gives the first sixteen bars of the first movement.)

Franck had, historically speaking, attempted impossible reconciliations, yet left music likely long to endure. The same cannot be said for his pupils, who attempted to maintain his principles and the cause of German-tinged romanticism without the possession of his genius. His most intellectual follower was Vincent d'Indy (1851–1931), a man of culture, already acquainted with Germany and German music before becoming Franck's pupil and acquiring a taste for intricate counterpoint. In 1876 he heard the first performance of the *Ring* and never recovered from the experience. He helped Lamoureux in preparing for the initial performance of *Lohengrin* in Paris (1887), and his own operas were attempts to give a French slant to the basic principles of Bayreuth, with *Fervaal* and *L'Étranger* as the best examples. He had a considerable career as a conductor, reviving the music

Ex: 67

of Monteverdi, Bach and Rameau, yet performing the works of his rival in principles, Debussy. Thanks to the control that he gained of the *Société Nationale* and the *Schola Cantorum,* his own persuasive teaching and his impressive output of compositions of every type he was able to maintain the spirit of his own and his master's German-derived romanticism into the first two decades of the new century; this against the wholly unromantic atmosphere which then prevailed.

Folk-song had little to do with French nationalistic music, yet in his thirties d'Indy developed a sudden interest in the peasant tunes of his native Cévennes, and in due course made several collections of French folk-songs in general. One of the few works of his likely to survive is the *Symphonie cévenole* (1886) with an *obbligato* piano part and based on "a French mountaineer's song", with impeccable use of the Lisztian (and Franckian) metamorphosis of theme.

For all the weight of his chamber music, tone poems, symphonies, operas and choral works, opinions are still uncertain as to the intrinsic value of his music, which for all its fine and intricate workmanship seems lacking in vital musical inventiveness. Little of it seems to be heard nowadays except for the "symphony" mentioned above, and the symphonic variations *Istar*. Though he survived long into the twentieth century he belongs very definitely to the nineteenth.

Henri Duparc (1848–1933), particularly favoured by Franck, was at the opposite pole from his master in the matter of self-criticism, for he destroyed a number of major works that had already been favourably received. Then in his thirties a mental breakdown closed his career. But he is immortalised, at least in France, through the high quality of his fourteen or so surviving songs, which with certain of Fauré's and Chausson's, are held to represent the supreme heights reached by the French art-song.[14*]

Ernest Chausson (1855–99), more original that d'Indy, produced a Symphony modelled on Franck's that is held by some fully to equal it. It is without the latter's organ loft style of scoring, though containing something of the blare of *Tannhaüser* brass. Still heard is his *Poème* for violin and orchestra and an early Trio. His sensitive songs have already been mentioned. An accident cut short an individual art that was gravitating more and more towards that of Debussy.[15*]

Among the composers who stood independent of Franck (though not of Wagner) was Emmanuel Chabrier (1841–1904), whose brilliantly scored rhapsody *España* is still frequently performed. Through the vitality of his material, his striking harmony and orchestral colouring, his power of expressing wit in music, the latter feature well illustrated in his successful comic opera *Le Roi malgré lui,* he had a considerable influence on his own generation and the next, for his style at times foreshadowed that of Ravel.

Possibly the most progressive of the independent composers who preceded the Impressionists was Paul Dukas (1865–1935). Yet only one of his instrumental works has maintained itself, the imaginative and brilliantly scored symphonic scherzo *L'Apprenti sorcier,* a comment in sound on Goethe's well-known poetic legend, and played everywhere in the world. He had considerable dramatic gifts, and in his day the opera *Ariane et Barbe-Bleue* was considered his finest work. Like Duparc over-scrupulous in self-criticism, he ceased to compose in his early forties, and devoted the rest of his life to teaching.

Gabriel Fauré (1845–1924) is one of the instances of a composer who gains honour in his own country but singularly little appreciation elsewhere. As Eric Blom remarked, his art " reflects French civilisation at its most fastidious ". It is best appreciated in his sensitive song-settings (*Après un rêve* has certainly travelled beyond France),[16*] the flowing yet restrained style of his chamber music[17*] (the *Élégie* for 'cello and piano is a characteristic piece of Fauré lyricism), and the lovely *Requiem,* which took long to come into its own. He was never a master of the orchestra and wrote little such music, the scorings being mainly by other hands. His training was at a lesser Paris institution, the École Niedmeyer, but it was there that he experienced the interest and kindness of Saint-Saëns. He became an excellent organist, though his career was a long economic struggle until he was past fifty, when he became first organist at the Madeleine and a professor of composition at the Conservatoire. He succeeded to the directorship in 1905. Many of his devoted pupils, Ravel, Florent Schmitt and Roger-Decasse among them, had much to say in the new French music of the twentieth century, but his own style lay fixed in the romantic nineteenth. For all that, it is highly individual in the subtleties and originalities of its harmonic vocabulary. " Monotonous ", " mere *salon* music " are some of the criticisms that are occasionally heard regarding Fauré's *style souplisse,* but there is much that must be sought for below the surface.

Britain in the Later Nineteenth Century

The dominance of foreign, especially German, musicians in the musical life of these islands continued far into the century. Composers such as Weber, Spohr, Rossini, Mendelssohn and Dvorak; virtuosi like Paganini, Liszt and Joachim, came, conquered and were enriched by the welcome given them in this " land without music ". Mendelssohn's style as a composer had for a time an almost paralysing effect on any native originality, and Leipzig was the Mecca of most British musicians. The star of William Sterndale Bennett (1816–75—a composer highly thought of by Schumann) gleamed for a while and then faded. His smoothly competent concert-overture, *The Naiads,* is still occasionally heard. Two Irish men of the theatre, Michael Balfe and Vincent Wallace, gained fame with their respective operas, *The Bohemian Girl* (1843) and *Maritana* (1845). Both works were welcomed on the Continent and both still receive occasional revivals, but the rest of their stage-works are forgotten. Another worthy activity of the mid-century was that of Samuel Sebastian Wesley (1810–76) on behalf of Anglican Church music and high standards of organ playing. Several of his anthems, showing remarkable individualism in harmony and modulation for their time, are still in use. Other early Victorian church composers were Sir John Goss and Sir Frederick Ouseley, more influenced by Gounod than was Wesley. The vocal and instrumental works of men like Robert Pearsall,

James Loder, Henry Pierson, Sir Julian Benedict (German-born) and Sir George Macfarren (a Principal of the Royal Academy of Music and a worthy educational influence) have either passed into oblivion or have been given some single and infrequent revivals. The English choral tradition, Handelian and now with a strong admixture of Mendelssohn, was preserved in the continued production of undistinguished and unexportable oratorios and cantatas for musical festival consumption.

Then came a British renaissance, at the hands of a Scotsman, an English-man and an Irishman—Alexander Mackenzie (1847–1935), Hubert Parry (1848–1918) and Charles Stanford (1852–1924). Though Mackenzie wrote " Scottish " rhapsodies and a *Pibroch Suite* for violin and orchestra, Parry traditionally English choral works of Miltonic dignity, and Stanford an " Irish " symphony, the new atmosphere was one of improved musical quality rather than anything distinctive in nationalist colouring. Some excep-tion to this must be granted in the matter of Stanford's " Irish Rhapsodies ", some of his operas and those of his songs of Irish bent. He did indeed publish collections of the folk-songs of the land of his birth. Several decades passed before there developed a similar zeal for English folk-music.

All three composers were in due course knighted, one of the signs of a new regard for the art in Britain. There were a number of far less distin-guished musical knights in the period.[18] Mackenzie was a cosmopolitan, with the broad view given him by his residences in Germany and Italy. He was for thirty-six years Principal of the Royal Academy of Music, and in that and in other ways played a great part in British musical life. His academic work proved to be a decided brake on composition. He wrote one violin and one piano concerto, but neither symphony nor sonata. His colourful oratorio, *The Rose of Sharon,* is still sometimes heard, but most of his compositions, from operas to solo songs, from orchestral works to piano pieces, seem doomed to neglect, or, as in the case, say, of the *Britannia Overture* (1894), to very occasional notice.

Parry, with a background of Bach and Brahms, and to a lesser degree, Mendelssohn, yet developed a very characteristic style. He is remembered nowadays chiefly for the dignity of his choral writings, scrupulous in their accentuations and wedded to fine poetry. Among these can be mentioned the early *Prometheus Unbound* (Shelley), and the impressive Miltonic Ode, *Blest Pair of Sirens* (1887) for eight-part chorus and orchestra. Yet he possessed a vein of humour, apparent in a number of works, with the *Pied Piper of Hamelin* cantata as the best example. The six unaccompanied motets (Songs of Farewell) of his last years are sometimes recalled, as well as a few of his numerous songs. In covering every branch of the art he probably wrote too much, and his symphonic and chamber works are now largely neglected—the *Symphonic Variations* (1897) perhaps undeservedly so. As Director of the Royal College of Music and Professor of Music at Oxford, as well as by his cultured writings and through his sterling character he played a great and beneficial part in the musical life of his time.

Stanford, like Parry, had a powerful influence on the younger generation at the Royal College. Like him he attempted every form of composition, and like him pursued quantity sometimes at the expense of quality. In his younger days he studied in Germany, an admirer and later a friend of Brahms. As one of his (adopted) country's prophets he should be given his meed of honour, and in the case of at least two of his operas, some sympathy, for they have received less credit than they deserve. *Shamus O'Brien* (1896), a two-act *Singspiel,* Irish in every note of it, is a little masterpiece of nationalist writing and met with success for a time. Previously, in the other allegiance, the composer had in *The Canterbury Pilgrims* (1884) adapted himself to the Chaucerian scene, made use of the " Reading Rota ", and skilfully supplemented the poet's matchless character-drawing. The work needs a revival, such as was given to another of his operas, *The Travelling Companion,* in 1934.

He was at his best in the setting of words—the sound poetry that he and Parry were always scrupulous in choosing. The two Tennysonian " choral ballads " with orchestra, *The Revenge* and *The Voyage of Maeldune,* are among his best remembered works, redolent of the sea. In a few of his many solo songs he put himself among the masters by his power of capturing the atmosphere of a poem, and of blending voice and accompaniment into companionable alliance. *The Fairy Lough* is held to be his crowning achievement in this field.

His instrumental work, orchestral and chamber, has lasted less well. The " Irish " Symphony (with a very beautiful slow movement) and some of the Irish Rhapsodies are still played. The best of his concertos is that for clarinet. Stanford was himself a fine organist and wrote a great deal for the instrument. In church music his two Services, in B flat major and C major, still hold their own, and his *Stabat Mater* setting, a " symphonic cantata ", is the best of his larger choral works. Like Parry he was not among the first flight of composers, but like him also the sincerity and scrupulous workmanship of his music must always command respect.

Arthur Sullivan (1842–1900), London-born son of an Irish bandmaster, Chapel-Royal chorister, Mendelssohn scholar at the R.A.M. under Bennett, and for several years Leipzig-trained, was by all portents shaping to become very much of a " serious " composer. At twenty, his incidental music to *The Tempest* gave him an instant reputation. His career then became a more than strenuous one—professor at the R.A.M., organist, conductor and above all, serious composer indeed, answering calls from every direction for commissioned works—oratorios, cantatas, incidental stage-music, overtures and church pieces. Yet it is now abundantly clear that his place in musical history depends entirely on his genius as a composer of a particularly English form of light operetta, in partnership with another man of high ability, W. S. Gilbert. Covent Garden (" grand ") opera had continued to be devoted to foreign works, with foreign conductors and singers, and giving scant support to native composers, as Stanford and others found to their cost. However, the success of Offenbach's satirical operettas in Paris encouraged London impresarios to plan similar ventures. Through the '70's and '80's Sullivan and Gilbert, with D'Oyly Carte as business partner, poured out a stream of works (all but one with passages of spoken dialogue) that captured audiences of every degree of musical perception. The wit, satire and rhythmical variety of Gilbert's verses were matched in every way by Sullivan's freshly melodious and equally witty music. (Oddly enough he maintained that in music alone there was no such thing as humour.) Many of the finer points of his art probably remained unheeded by a good proportion of his hearers, e.g. his taste for satire and parody, not only of "grand opera" procedure, but the tricks of Rossini and the Italian *buffa* in general. His own technical subtleties—effective feats of counterpoint, charming surprises in orchestration and modulation, must always compel admiration. He was a lifelong student of Schubert, whose influence was reflected in his music. Indeed, he accompanied Grove on the famous Vienna pilgrimage that led to the recovery of the missing portions of the *Rosamunde* music. There is little need to offer a list of operetta titles, from, say *Trial by Jury* (1875) to *The Gondoliers* (1889), for most of the works are still widely known and are still performed in spite of the fact that Gilbert's Victorian humour tends at times to date. The partnership ended in 1896 after some less successful collaborations.[19]

Previously, in 1891, Sullivan had tried his hand at "grand" opera, but *Ivanhoe* proved a failure and deserved its fate, for most of it must be written off as dull. He was undoubtedly the most popular composer of his age in England and knew all the "best people". The inevitable knighthood came to him, but the pity is that both he and his circle of friends and admirers regarded the Savoy works as the pleasantly remunerative sidelines of a composer of high purpose, whose real vocation was to produce masterpieces of choral, symphonic and church music. These never came. He was too much of a social idler, too lacking in firmness of purpose to put himself among the greater names in this respect. To state it more bluntly, he just hadn't the ability. Ethel Smythe shocked him badly when she told him that of all his music *The Mikado* was his masterpiece. His best oratorio, *The Light of the World,* his best cantata, *The Golden Legend,* his best overture, *di ballo* (pure Savoy music), a few anthems and hymns, a few part-songs, *Orpheus with his lute* among the solo songs—these of his "serious" compositions may still occasionally be heard, but it is solely as a gifted composer of light opera, working in partnership with a stronger personality, that he is to be remembered. After his passing, this type of work, turning to "musical comedy", showed a progressive degeneration.

Two more musical knights of the period merit attention—Frederick Cowen (1852–1935) and John Stainer (1840–1901). Cowen, early an accomplished pianist, received most of his education at Leipzig and at seventeen established his reputation as a composer in England with a symphony and a piano concerto now long forgotten. He also became a leading conductor, connected among others, with the Philharmonic, Hallé and Scottish orchestras. Little of his own music has survived, though in his lifetime his *Scandinavian Symphony* made an impression both in Europe and America. His orchestral music was most successful when it dealt with fanciful and fairy elements, when the scoring usually showed a charming lightness and individuality. Of his cantatas, his setting of Collins' *Ode to the Passions* most deserves revival, while it may be that amateur societies still cherish *The Rose Maiden*. Stainer, organist of St. Paul's, Professor of Music at Oxford, educationalist and medieval scholar, must be remembered with honour, not for *The Crucifixion*, but for his research work which gave to the world the still valuable volumes on *Dufay and his Contemporaries* (1898) and *Early Bodleian Music* (1901).

In the period now reached two remarkable musicians were already writing, Elgar and Delius, the greatest native composers of the nineteenth century (or, for that matter, since Purcell). Their significant work, however, belongs to the present one.

The United States in the Nineteenth Century

Like Britain, the United States through most of the century was largely German-dominated, as indeed it had been in the eighteenth, beginning with the influence of the organist Karl Pachelbel at Boston. In the first part of the century Johann Graupner (1767–1836), who had played the oboe under Haydn, brought the music of Handel and the late eighteenth century Vienna masters to Boston, and founded the Philharmonic Society there. Other German-born musicians were active, until by the mid-century orchestral music of high standard was being heard in all the chief cities of the U.S.A. Boston and New York became influential centres, the New York Philharmonic being founded in 1842, the Boston Symphony Orchestra, which called on such famous German conductors as Georg Henschel, Nikisch and Karl Muck, in 1881. Visiting virtuosi, of course, swarmed, a fact that has been frequently noted. Meanwhile the native born and bred Lowell Mason (1792–1872) became the pioneer of general American culture in music, doing valuable work in establishing musical instruction in educational institutions. A truly American composer appeared in Stephen Foster (1826–64). His horizons were limited, but his unsophisticated songs have become part of the American heritage.[20*] The first native-born piano virtuoso was Louis Gottschalk of New Orleans, who was trained in Paris, where his technique was approved by Chopin. Though attempting to exploit the Creole music of Central America he was no more than a salon composer of the display type. More worthy efforts came from American musicians who, like the composers of the British revival, had a background of solid culture (generally that of New England) and of whom many had sought training in Germany. Lowell Mason's son William (1829–1908) continued and extended his father's good work, and serious composition was in the hands of men like John Paine (1839–1906), first Professor of Music at Harvard, Arthur Foote (1853–1937), George Chadwick (1854–1931), Edward MacDowell (1861–1908) and Horatio Parker (1863–1919). All made solid contributions to an impressive bulk of music which covered all the major vocal and instrumental forms, largely coloured by German romanticism, but having enough taste, technique and vitality to make a firm foundation for greater things to come.

Of these names the most significant is that of MacDowell, first Professor of Music at Columbia University, and the teacher of many of the following generation of United States composers. Early a brilliant pianist he was at Paris from the age of fifteen for three years. Then until 1887 he was domiciled in Germany, studying and later teaching and composing. His chief instructor in the creative art had been Joachim Raff, that prolific composer of the neo-German school. MacDowell was given respect in Germany both for his playing and his compositions, gaining Liszt's approval for his first Piano Concerto. After his return to America and settlement in Boston he soon made his influence felt. Unfortunately, like Sterndale Bennett and Mackenzie in London, he allowed the calls of academic duties to stultify his creative powers, and it was overwork that killed him. Some symphonic poems, two orchestral suites and two piano concertos represent the bulk of his major works. His main output was for piano, together with songs and part-songs. The shadows of Raff and Grieg lay on the romantically-tinged keyboard pieces, but in the *Indian Suite* for orchestra (1897) and in his *New England Idylls* (1902) there appeared elements that spoke of his native land.

Horatio Parker, organist, composer and Professor of Music at Yale, had some years as a student at Munich, and was the first American composer to be represented at choral festivals in England, with his oustanding oratorio, *Hora Novissima*. Major choral works were indeed the chief features of his output, and other such compositions of his were performed in England, while Cambridge conferred an honorary doctorate on him. Yet except for *Hora Novissima* his music has been unaccountably neglected even in his own country.

The important North American composers that were now beginning freely to appear, many guided by influences other than those of Germany, belong rather to the next century.

NOTES

1 Composer-pianists of the highest reputation as executants seem to have been so awed by the presence of Liszt as to excuse themselves from playing their own works, preferring to leave the task to him. Chopin affords an example.

2* HMS IX has a recording of Brahms' Ballade in D minor (the first of the four). The sombre and comparatively straightforward nature of the piano writing matches the grim and primitive Scottish ballad *Edward* which was its inspiration, and contrasts with the flamboyance of Liszt's Ballade in D flat (see Note 8). See also Chapter X, Note 6 regarding Loewe's powerful vocal setting of the ballad.

3 The Brahms Variations were known for long as being " on a theme by Haydn ", but it has been shown that Haydn was not the originator of the tune.

4* HMS IX has a recording of Wolf's *Er ist's* (Mörike), given in comparison with settings of the same poem by Schumann and Franz. Wolf's songs have been given plentiful attention by the gramophone companies, with leading artists performing them.

5* HMS IX has a recording of a solo from Act II of Smetana's *Libuse*.

6* HMS IX has a recording of an excerpt from Act I of Glinka's *Russlan and Ludmilla*.

7 Borodin's musical friends in their letters seem sometimes to have jestingly changed the usual courteous wish to " I do hope that you are quite ill!"

8* HMS IX has a recording of Borodin's *Song of the Dark Forest*.

9* HMS IX has a recording of Mussorgsky's highly original and realistic *Darling Savishna* . . . purporting to be the amorous and pitiful babblings of the "village idiot", hopelessly attracted to a peasant girl. Mussorgsky had actually overheard such an incident.

10* HMS IX has a recording of part of the opening scene of Mussorgsky's *Boris Godunov*, which illustrates very well the composer's down-to-earth realism in his treatment of the chattering, jesting, rather bewildered crowd of common people; a very different atmosphere from that of the conventional opera chorus.

11 Yet another version of *A Night on Bald Mountain* has come before the public, a highly coloured re-scoring by Stokowski for Disney's film *Fantasia*.

12 Recently (1961) the BBC broadcast a performance of Berwald's *Sinfonie singulière* (1845). It proved a skilled and attractive work in German romantic style, employing the device of transference of themes.

13* HMS IX has recordings of (a) a Norwegian folk-dance played actually on the high-pitched "Hardanger fiddle" (with four sympathetic strings besides the normal ones) and (b) Grieg's transcription for piano of the same little work.

14* HMS IX has a recording of Duparc's tense *Le Manoir de Rosemonde*, for voice and piano.

15* HMS IX has a recording of Chausson's *Les Papillons* for voice and piano.

16* HMS IX has a recording of Fauré's *Les Présents* for voice and piano.

17* HMS IX has a recording of the first movement of Fauré's Violin Sonata in A major (Op. 13).

18 The first knighthood to be given to a musician in England was that conferred on Henry Bishop by Queen Victoria in 1842. Certainly an English musician had been so honoured as early as in 1795, but in Ireland; the Lord Lieutenant had at the time the power to grant knighthoods in general, and had bestowed one on a certain Parsons, master of George III's band.

19 The success of the early Gilbert and Sullivan operettas was noted by the entertainment world on the other side of the Atlantic. As a result of the lack of any copyright protection, there were soon over a score of American companies performing unauthorised and distorted versions of *HMS Pinafore*, with not a penny coming to its creators. As the only way to counter this, the two took a company to New York to give the authentic version. While there they brought out the newly completed *Pirates of Penzance* in the capital with great success. However, the pirates of the U.S.A. soon turned their attention to that as well.

20* In recent years in the U.S.A. there has been a growing interest in the musical life of colonial America. Vocal works by spare-time composers such as Wm. Billings (1746–1800), Daniel Reed (b. 1757) and Jacob French (b. 1754) have been published and performed. There is no doubt that this choral music, if sometimes artless, yet gives the impression of vigour and sincerity. Examples can be heard on Brunswick, AXA, 4518 (*Five Centuries of Song*).

CHAPTER XIII

The Twentieth Century I

EVEN before the end of the nineteenth century signs were not wanting that a reaction had begun in many countries against the lush late-romanticism which had been so largely a German and German-influenced one. Many composers were seeking new modes of expression, and by the late '90's a strange and unique music, that of Debussy, had established itself. A decade later there began to be heard in Paris and elsewhere the first significant works of a revolutionary with quite another manner, Igor Stravinsky. These two were destined to have far reaching influences. But the most startling instances of the changes of technique which separate nineteenth century from modern music was the relinquishment by some composers of traditional tonality in favour of atonalism, followed by Arnold Schönberg's development in the early 20's of his " twelve note system of composition ", which abolished the idea of a tonic and treated all the chromatic notes of the octave as being of equal importance. This system was taken up and evolved further by an increasing number of disciples. " Serialism " served to enrich the resources of composers of the calibre of Alban Berg, Dallapiccola, Frank Martin, Matyas Seiber and Humphrey Searle, all of whom had not altogether renounced the past in their music.

Yet there were many voices that spoke the language of romanticism and that of firm major-minor tonality, far into the new century. Such were the German, Richard Strauss, whose production of operas continued to the second world-war; the Finn, Sibelius, whose last monumental symphony came in 1924; the Austrian, Mahler, most of whose symphonies belong to the first decade of the new century; and the Englishman, Elgar, who wrote not only full-scale romantic symphonies but oratorios of traditional pattern. All these composers handled the huge, late-romantic orchestra in consummate fashion. The chromaticisms of the English Delius and the Pole Karol Szymanowski, together with the very individual styles of the Frenchmen, Ravel and Roussel, remained still reconciled to traditional tonality. Basically traditional was the lively French school of the early '20's, Poulenc, Honegger and Milhaud among them. They showed their eclecticism by experiments in poly-tonality and astringent vocabularies of discord, all this while submitting to a key-signature. To these names could be added those of the Englishmen Arthur Bliss and William Walton and the Russian Prokofiev (together with the much later Shostakovich). The 'progressives' among them seem to have been more audacious at the beginning of their careers than later.

Even the resources of folk-music were given some employment in the new century in the hands of the Englishmen, Vaughan Williams and Holst, though the importance of their music depends rather on their own individual (yet tonal) styles. This applies to the outstanding and original Bela Bartók, who, late in the day, salvaged genuine Hungarian folk-songs. In the United States, with the emergence of an important school of native composers, American traditional folk-music has at times been drawn upon.

There remain a number more of outstanding composers who have sought to express themselves in a manner that strikes a note of great originality without abandoning consonance or needing the aid of serialism. Among them can be mentioned the German, Hindemith, the Englishmen, Benjamin Britten and Michael Tippett, together with the Czech, Janáček and the Hungarian, Bartók, previously mentioned.

After this somewhat incomplete sketch of the tendencies of the new century a consideration of the composers who shaped them will be given in more detail.

Two New Voices

The first of the two great figures destined to bring a provocatively new vocabulary and syntax to the art of music (the other being Stravinsky) came to the fore near the turn of the century. Claude-Achille Debussy (1862–1918), though of non-musical stock, early showed his gifts as a pianist, and was only ten when he entered the Paris Conservatoire. He stayed there for eleven years, though often in a state of rebellion against the conventions. This frame of mind, one of the bases of his genius, is well illustrated by the story of his being questioned as to the authority by which he was flouting, at the piano, the standard principles for the treatment of dissonance. He gave the defiant reply, " Mon plaisir ! " Fortunately Giraud was his composition master, a man of good sense and tolerance who guided his wilful pupil with a loose rein. Debussy himself, who strangely enough was for some years an admirer of Massenet's music, had sufficient discretion to curb his natural instincts to the extent of winning the Prix de Rome in 1884 with his cantata, *L'Enfant prodigue,* a somewhat Massenet-like composition.

Meanwhile, other and more fruitful influences were shaping his development. For three summers, from 1880 onward, he had been engaged by the much-travelled Madame von Meck, Tchaikovsky's millionaire benefactress, to act as her temporary family musician, teaching her children, playing scores (including Tchaikovsky's) for her delectation, and in general using his already remarkable gifts as sight-reader and accompanist. As a result of these European journeyings the young man met Wagner and other leading musicians, heard *Tristan* for the first time, in Vienna; and reaching Moscow, became attracted by the exotic music of the new Russian school, Mussorgsky's in particular. His official stay in Rome gave him no more satisfaction than it had given to Berlioz. With his return to Paris in 1887 there began his long search for the true light. His symphonic suite *Printemps* and the Rosetti cantata *La Damoiselle élue*, written to fulfil Prix de Rome conditions, were held by his Conservatoire judges to be too unorthodox for public performance. But settled in Paris as a professional composer, the early songs and piano music which he produced, including the much-loved two *Arabesques,* were characteristic of his mature style only in their Gallic grace and economy of means. There were visits to Bayreuth in 1888 and 1889, after which he expressed the opinion that Wagner was less an innovator than was generally thought, and that he saw no reason to imitate him. But he could not altogether escape the spell, and in later years Wagner became " Klingsor " to him, a powerful but evil magician whose influence must be opposed for the sake of the independence of French music. A new and absorbing experience was his hearing, at the Universal Exhibition of 1889, the pentatonic scales and sonorous gongs of the Javanese *gamelang* music. Dukas and Chausson seem to have been his only musical friends at the time; it was from the exponents of other arts that the strongest of all influences were coming to him, that of Impressionism, ultimately to make him the apostle of Impressionism in music.

" Impressionism ", a nickname, was first applied to the school of French painters, Monet, Manet, Degas, Renoir, Cézanne and others, who began to represent in a picture not the normal mass of detail which only repeated studies of the subject could take in, but rather the " impression " gained by one quick glance. In practice this amounted to concentrating less on the actual object than the momentary play of light upon it—" not the thing itself but the transitory phenomenon ". In poetry the " symbolists ", such as Mallarmé and Verlaine, pursued a similar elusive art with words, suggesting rather than stating. It was to these Bohemian circles that Debussy was attracted, and was moved to employ his own art for the same purposes. He endeavoured to express in sound something equivalent to the visual sensation, a matter of passive contemplation; not as in romanticism, the expression of human reactions. He himself spoke in unmistakable terms :

" I wish to write down my musical dreams in a spirit of utter self-detachment. I wish to sing of my interior visions with the naïve candour of a child."

Again :

" My desire is only to reproduce what I hear. Music was intended to receive the mysterious accord that exists between nature and the imagination."

Debussy was, of course, not the *inventor* of such a technique. As we have seen, romantics such as Liszt, Grieg, Wagner, Berlioz and Schumann all had their moments of tone-painting which approximated to Impressionism. But it is the thoroughness, originality, variety and subtlety of Debussy's exploration that place it in a class by itself. All his previous inclinations fitted him for the task. Thus there developed a music in which harmony was freed from

2B

many former sanctions. There were effects based on the composer's study of the natural series of overtones; with unresolved discords in plenty, chains of consecutive sevenths, ninths and elevenths used on every degree of the scale, chords deliberately employed, when necessary, as points of colour and not as items of a harmonic progression—and all this without abandoning traditional tonality. One of his devices, much exploited, for creating a temporary suspension of key and a consequent sense of vagueness or mystery was the use of the whole-tone scale (e.g. C D E F sharp G sharp A sharp), based as it is on the tonal neutrality of augmented triad harmonies. The pentatonic scale, too, played its part in this atmosphere of " otherness ". As the years went by the composer probed more and more into the past, exploring the realms of Couperin, Rameau and Claude le Jeune and eventually those of plainsong and medieval organum, and, by a miraculous synthesis, making all this material part of his resources. Rollo Myers' opinion is that he ended by producing " a series of masterpieces which were to change the whole course of music and usher in a new era of exploration and emancipation which has continued to this day ".[1]

All through the '90's Debussy's financial position was precarious. His works brought him almost nothing, he hated teaching, and he relied on hack work and the generosity of friends to gratify his somewhat expensive tastes. For a time around the beginning of the decade he seemed as a composer to be groping. The now well-known *Suite Bergamasque* and other small works were not the essential Debussy. Then in 1892 he began to find himself. There came the first Verlaine set of songs, *Fêtes galantes, I,* and, more important, he began the orchestral *Prélude à l'après-midi d'un faune,* founded on a poem of Mallarmé's, together with a setting as an opera of Maeterlinck's play, *Pelléas et Mélisande.* In the next year his only String Quartet was written. There was a great deal of traditional practice to be found in the Quartet, mingled with new-found techniques. The Phrygian mode theme—

Ex: 68

with which the work opens is used cyclically and in transmuted forms through three of the movements, which contain also plenty of harmonic surprises and uses of the whole-tone scale. The heaven-sent slow movement is one of Music's masterpieces. A greater work, however, is *L'Après-midi,* where, with the first notes of the solo flute playing, unaccompanied, the principal theme, a new world of sound was opened :

and the composer revealed as a master of delicate, elusive and original orchestral colour.

Although the famous Ysãye group performed his Quartet in 1893 and the Sociêté Nationale included *L'Après-midi* in one of their 1894 concerts, very little general notice was taken of them. Debussy continued quietly producing, writing among other works the orchestral *Nocturnes*. No musician will need introduction to two of the numbers, *Nuages* and *Fêtes*, impressionist pictures of great harmonic originality.

1900 was the composer's year of arrival. The *Quartet* and *La Damoiselle élue* were heard at the Paris Exhibition, *L'Après-midi* was becoming widely known and the *Nocturnes* had a very successful first performance. In 1902 the long brooded and much rewritten *Pelléas et Mélisande* at last reached the *Opéra-Comique*. As might be expected a large proportion of its hearers were bewildered. It became the centre of a storm of discussion, but there was now a solid core of Debussy enthusiasts. Within a few years it had established itself as one of the landmarks in the history of opera. It is unique and inimitable, indeed, the composer himself, for all that he tried, never succeeded in following it up. Debussy strongly approved of opera for the Wagnerian reason that it represented a mingling of the arts, and indeed something of " old Klingsor " is to be found in *Pelléas,* which would not in fact have been possible without *Tristan.* Debussy, who had previously made fun of the *leitmotif* device, employed it a great deal in the work, though always in unobtrusive fashion. Again, as in Wagner's music-dramas, most of the emotion of the dark and fate-ridden tragedy is expressed in orchestral terms, but, unlike Wagner's, it is an orchestra of restraint, of economy of means. " Rien de trop " was always the composer's principle. Debussy, in his opera as in his impressionistic pieces, was ever the detached observer. One of the most striking features of the opera was the composer's treatment of the vocal lines. In rhythmically simple recitative throughout, with only occasional suggestions of lyricism, he devoted himself to following the natural verbal cadences and bringing into relief the meaning of the words. It is characteristic of his art that at the climax of emotion when the two confess their love for each other the orchestra should be silent, and Mélisande's reply, " Je t'aime aussi ", a monotone.

It is strange that Debussy's music should be so filtered of passion and emotion generally, for he himself was a hedonist, ready at all times to fall into idleness and sensual pleasure. In 1899 he married Rosalie (" Lilly ") Texier, a young Paris dressmaker, who seemed to Debussy and his friends the living embodiment of Mélisande. She gave him a few years of complete devotion, but in 1904 the composer took a short cut to affluence by leaving her for a rich woman, Emma Bardac. There was a double divorce, the broken-hearted Lilly attempted suicide, and for a time Debussy lost most of his friends. If what he had aimed for was financial security he had now achieved it. He henceforward found himself, rather against his will, the leading figure in French music; he acquired the ribbon of the Legion of Honour, and, much to his annoyance, a large party-following which had declared war on the d'Indy faction. However, in the next decade important works were written. 1909 saw the first performance of the three symphonic sketches, under the overall title of *La Mer,* in which the play of sunlight, waves and wind on the waters is marvellously portrayed, and a more continuous melodic line employed than heretofore, in something approaching the older symphonic fashion. A still larger orchestral achievement was the triptych, *Images pour orchestre,* completed in 1912. Its three sections (*Gigues, Iberia* and *Rondes de printemps*) were supposed to depict the characteristics of three countries, England, Spain and France respectively, snatches of native music being used (England's was *The Keel Row*!). Of the three, *Iberia,* hailed by Falla as truly authentic, has best survived. A ballet, *Jeux,* written for Nijinsky at about the same time, is not often heard, but contains some delightfully delicate orchestration and some prophetic examples of poly-tonality. Another late large work, the incidental music to d'Annunzio's sacred drama *Le Martyre de Saint Sebastien* (1910) is little known in Britain. Opinions have been expressed that it contains some of his finest writing, re-creating a devotional medieval atmosphere.

During the first decade of the century there was a steady production of songs and piano music and a growing appreciation of their art. Among the late songs are the gentle, open-air settings of *Trois Chansons de France,* and the harshness and irony of two of the *Trois Chansons de François Villon,* which contrast with the pathetic remaining one, a prayer to the Virgin by an old woman, with its modal harmonies and fifteenth century atmos-phere.[2*] Some of his best known piano music is included in *Estampes* (e.g. *Jardins sous la pluie*); in the two sets of *Images* (e.g., *Reflets dans l'eau, Cloches à travers les feuilles,*[3*] *Poissons d'or*); in the two sets of *Préludes* (e.g. *La Fille aux cheveux de lin, La Cathédrale engloutie, Minstrels*), and the delightful *Children's Corner,* dedicated to his small daughter.

In his last years he turned to chamber music, planning to write a set of six sonatas, but completing only three, for 'cello and piano, for flute, viola and harp, and for violin and piano. They were not sonatas in the classical sense, but the melodic lines flow with a momentum seldom found in earlier works. Marc Pincherle says of them :

" The intentional conciseness of the writing and deliberate economy of means cannot, however, conceal their depth of poetic feeling and way-wardness, nor prevent us from detecting now and again an agonising undertone of melancholy—a secret which the music seems to be confiding to us, as if unwillingly."—*Marc Pincherle: An Illustrated History of Music, tr. by Rollo Myers, p. 181: Macmillan & Co., Ltd.*

The violin sonata was his swan-song. For some years he had been in the grip of cancer, and he died in 1918, at the time when the Germans were bombarding Paris. As regards productiveness Debussy's may have been " un petit art ", but the masterpieces that he wrote were as near to a new start in music as has ever been made, if we except serialism. Yet this novelty was due not only to his own " modern " originalities, but also to the revolutionary idea, soon to be taken up by others, of delving far back into the past and not merely *imitating* the music of earlier centuries but rather *absorbing* their techniques until they became part of his own language.

He left no " school ", and indeed never wished to teach anybody anything. His few strict imitators were of little worth, but of the great innovators who followed him there were a number who profited in their individual ways by his novel procedures, and all were indebted to him for the example he set for refusing so drastically to accept accepted ideas.

Meanwhile at the further end of Europe the other powerful challenge to German-derived romanticism was preparing. Russia had for a couple of centuries drawn her culture from the West, and had not long established her position of independence as a musical nation. Now, in the person of Stravinsky, the tide of influence was to flow the other way. Between them, Debussy and he changed the face of twentieth century music.

Igor Stravinsky (1882–) was born to an atmosphere of music and the theatre, for his father was a distinguished bass singer in the Imperial Opera at Petersburg and had filled the role of *Boris* in the early performances of Mussorgsky's work. The child was playing the piano from the age of seven, and acquainted himself at first hand with the scores of other Russian operas. Yet he was destined at first for the law, and indeed completed a professional course at Petersburg University, which took him to 1905. In the intervening years, however, he was discovering music for himself. Like Debussy, though he was willing to receive instruction, it was with the very definite determination of ultimately going his own way.[4] He became an excellent pianist, took some harmony and counterpoint lessons from a competent teacher, and then in 1903, late as it was, became Rimsky-Korsakov's pupil for three years, getting a thorough training from that master and inheriting from him his consummate skill in orchestration.

Besides absorbing Russian traditions he was already admiring the work of Debussy and Chabrier, and was now irrevocably committed to music as a profession. Some early compositions, such as the orchestral *Scherzo Fantastique* and a Glazounov-like symphony were but 'prentice efforts. In 1908 came his chance. The great Diaghilev, impressed by the young man's new work, the orchestral *Fireworks,* asked him to score two of the numbers of his ballet, *Les Sylphides,* founded on the music of Chopin. The story of the Imperial Russian Ballet, which began with the Paris performances of 1909, is an important chapter of art-history in itself. The beauty and originality

of the Diaghilev creations made an extraordinary impact on the West; and
with them on their journeyings went the music of Stravinsky, set to some of
the most famous of them.

His first independent score was *The Firebird* (1910). The ballet, founded
on a Russian folk-legend, was an immense Paris success; Stravinsky's name
was instantly made, and the concert suites derived from the work have gone
round the world. In the brilliance of the orchestrations he had already out-
glittered his master; also, harmonically, a real originality was beginning to
show. He was content to use Russian folk-tunes (in his own way) for the
human element in the story, but the two magical figures, the Ogre and the
Firebird, were each given characteristic chromatic music, derived in different
ways from the interval of the augmented fourth (or diminished fifth)
which divides the normal scale into two equal halves, and is anti-tonal in its
implications.[5] In 1911 came a masterpiece, *Petrushka*, the world-famous
ballet of the pathetic clown-puppet, magically brought to life at a Petersburg
carnival. The scenario, well enough known, is basically only a variant of the
traditional *commedia dell' arte* with its tragic figure of Pierrot, the unsuccessful lover. But the weird ambiguity caused by the juxtaposition of the earthy
atmosphere of the Russian fair with the fantastic world of the pseudo-
human puppets, and this linked to a completely original music, resulted in
an altogether unique dramatic work. Some would call it Stravinsky's finest.

The composer can be seen still haunted by the augmented fourth interval,
and the consequent link between the keys of C and F sharp. One sign of this
is the treatment in the second scene of Petrushka's characteristic fanfare,
where his dual nature seems to be underlined by the bi-tonal—

Ex: 70

In far more drastic ways than this the music of *Petrushka* struck a quite new
note in twentieth century music. The composer's style of " abrasive discord "
had established itself; basically diatonic, but, especially to its first hearers,
brutally harsh in its polytonality and its polyrhythm of violent impulses.
His style of orchestration also, took on features far removed from that of the
romantic age with its smooth blendings of instrumental colouring. In
Petrushka Stravinsky's was a bright " primary colour " scoring, solo instruments or sections standing out sharply and clearly.

If in some quarters the Petrushka music was held to be alarming and
revolutionary, a far greater shock was soon to come. The composer had
started a symphony that purported to depict pre-Christian Russian life.

Diaghilev and his assistants (including Nijinsky) seized on the idea, and there was shaped one of the most controversial works of the century. In 1913 *Le Sacre du printemps* (The Rite of Spring) was produced in Paris and immediately roused a violent storm of aesthetic disagreement. The dust has not even yet settled, but within a decade its music had been accepted as, if nothing else, a milestone in the history of the art, and in concert form played by all the great orchestras of the world. The programme of the ballet was primitive, barbaric, brutal—the savage ceremonies and ritual dances of an ancient fertility religion, culminating in the sacrifice of a human victim. To this choreography Stravinsky, handling a huge orchestra, brought a music as brutal and uncompromising as his subject. The themes were Russian folk-melodies or the composer's own imitations, but their treatment would have very much surprised Glinka. Normal conventions of harmony were now entirely banished; polytonality (that is, the use of different tonalities in counterpoint) ruled the whole work, combined with rhythmic schemes of great complication—perversely recalcitrant accents mingled with pounding ostinatos. Strident orchestrations in raw colours carried the sounds time and again to an extreme pitch of raucousness and seeming hysteria. Stravinsky was declaring war on all romantic beauty, yet in doing so using a romantic form, that of the orchestral tone-poem. Provocative as the work may sound on a first hearing the composer maintained that it was altogether " architectonic ", and indeed a closer examination reveals with what cool logic the tremendous structure was planned. As in many of Stravinsky's works one's first reaction is often a mingling of fascination and repulsion. Fascination was the effect on a whole generation of smaller composers; thudding rhythms and ear-splitting harmonic ugliness became the fashion among many who, unlike Stravinsky, had little else to offer.

Before the lights went out over Europe in 1914 there came another stage work, the long-pondered opera *The Nightingale,* the Hans Andersen fairy story set to a brilliant score that pleased Paris a great deal more than did the *Rite*. The music was rearranged as a ballet for Diaghilev, 1919–20.

With the coming of war Stravinsky took refuge in Switzerland. He had finished with the large canvases and swollen romantic orchestras of the three great ballets that had made his name. From now on came a new economy and conciseness of utterance. *The Soldier's Tale,* (Lausanne, 1918), founded on a Russian folk-story, broke new ground as a stage form—no singing, a narrator, two speaking parts, miming and dancing and an odd, almost " jazz " type of small orchestra.[6*] As a farewell to Russian folk-music he produced with Diaghilev in 1923 (again to the astonishment of Paris) the war-time *Les Noces* (The Wedding), a " choreographic cantata " which painted a Russian peasant festivity in musical terms as rhythmically barbaric and stridently discordant, almost, as the *Rite*. It was written for four soloists, a chorus, and an accompaniment consisting only of percussion instruments and four pianos, these latter used also in very percussive fashion.

After this work the composer seemed to have discarded primitive realism. Settled in France and introduced by his links with the Diaghilev company to the cosmopolitan world of French civilisation, he developed a complete change of outlook, while preserving always his intellectual independence and originality. He was entering now what is sometimes called his " neo-classic " period of a wide eclecticism. With his own very modern techniques he strove to express the spirit of the eighteenth century, anti-romantic in its objectivity, firm in his opposition to the idea that music should " express " anything other than its own sounds. These preoccupations with the past of a composer so thoroughly committed to a highly individual present resulted in a unique series of stylistic evocations of the spirit and practices of former times. At the same time he was continually experimenting in startling fashion with rhythm, harmony, instrumentation and form, his music throwing off sparks of suggestion and possibility for others to light what fires they could.

A Diaghilev ballet, *Pulcinella,* of 1920 was a deliberate echoing in the composer's own terms of Pergolesi's music. In the same year *Symphonies for Wind Instruments,* in spite of its grating harmonies, was meant to recall and do homage to a much later composer, Debussy, to whom Stravinsky owed much. The not very successful opera, *Mavra,* (one last glance at a Russian source, Pushkin) supposedly showed the superiority of Russo-Italian opera technique over that of the Wagnerian music-drama. After the Russian Revolution Stravinsky renounced his native land, and later became a French citizen. The Soviet authorities returned the compliment in due course by barring his music from the U.S.S.R.

There now came a period of absorption with the resources of wind instruments, as in the Octet of 1923, and with the keyboard style of the late baroque era. The Piano Concerto, performed in a number of American cities in 1925 with the composer as soloist, had no more than a wind instrument accompaniment. Its unique mixture of Bach's keyboard style linked with the harmonic dissonances and jaggedly irregular rhythms of Stravinsky's own techniques has caused it hardly to be a favourite, but its originality can never be in doubt. Other compositions of the period showed similar leanings.

A classical interest in quite another sense was shown in 1927. *Oedipus Rex,* called by the composer an " opera-oratorio ", and intended as a homage to Diaghilev, was a stage work in which the chorus remained static, and even the movements and gestures of the principals a good deal circumscribed. Masks were worn. The libretto, while founded on the Sophoclean drama-story, was written initially in French (by Cocteau) and then translated into Latin. The composer's idea was that only the dead language could express adequately the dignity and solemnity of the drama. A curious mixture of formal styles is apparent, with that of eighteenth century oratorio prominent, in impressive choruses, declamations and melismatic arias. Contrasted with these features are moments of Gregorian-like simplicity. The whole effect is one of a monumental dignity. On this occasion the composer's usual jagged and freakish rhythms are mostly eschewed, but the grinding tonal discords are there in full force. *Oedipus* has never been a popular work, but its immense power cannot be denied.

Classically Greek was his return to ballet, in *Apollo Musagetes* (1928). The work also recalled renaissance dance-forms—courante, sarabande and variation, and marked also his revived interest in the string orchestra for accompaniment.

The composer was now becoming quite a figure in the United States. His next major work, the *Symphony of Psalms* (1930) for chorus and orchestra was commissioned for the Boston Symphony Orchestra, and showed a new facet of Stravinsky's genius, for it was a religious one, a setting of Vulgate texts—three of the Psalms. The music was the inevitable Stravinsky mixture of past and very much present—chant, ground-bass, close-knit polyphony and double fugue, all expressed in the composer's own dissonant vocabulary. It is undoubtedly one of Stravinsky's greater works. For all its harshnesses, a truly religious atmosphere is apparent, and for once in a way in this period some warmth of emotion.

In the remaining years until the outbreak of the second world war Stravinsky was mainly concerned with instrumental music. An exception was the quite charmingly Gallic *Persephone,* a " melodrama " which called for speaking, singing, dancing and miming. More and more the composer's eyes were turned to the United States. The *Violin Concerto* (1931) was written for an American soloist, but its " man-trap " rhythms (as they have been called) and, some would say, a certain general bleakness, have caused it somewhat to be neglected. Best known from this period is the *Dumbarton Oaks Concerto* (1938), named from the estate of the American patron who commissioned it. It was a concerto in the Brandenburg sense, written for a chamber orchestra of fifteen wind instruments, and recalling in the composer's own abrasive terms that baroque style. Another " evocation " was the *Concerto for Two Pianos* (1936)—without other accompaniment. It was given a first performance by Stravinsky himself and one of his sons, and contained some suggestions of the styles of Beethoven, Chopin and even Liszt, with a touch of jazz thrown in.

When war broke out in 1939 Stravinsky moved to the U.S.A., eventually taking up nationality there. In this his " American " period the aridness to be detected in many of his past neo-classical pieces was gradually replaced by a new warmth and vitality, seen particularly in his *Symphony in Three Movements* (1945), in which there could be imagined almost the emotions of a romantic programme.

True to his capacity for bringing off the unexpected he produced in 1948 a setting of the Roman Mass—the usual five sections of the Ordinary, for small choir and ten wind instruments. The style evoked and modernised was this time that of the medieval Flemish school, with suggestions of even further distant organum—a study in scholarship as well as a work of dignity and austerity. In the same year he completed his trilogy of ballets founded on Greek mythology with *Orpheus.*

In what for most other people would be declining years, Stravinsky's imagination seems as vital as ever. In 1951 he brought out what is his most extensive work, the opera *The Rake's Progress,* with a libretto in English, founded on the famous series of engravings by Hogarth. If the usual " evocations " are sought they are to be found mainly in Italian opera and the eighteenth century lyric stage in general, with its secco and accompanied recitative, its arias and concerted numbers, all mingled with the unmistakable but more than usually restrained and urbane style of the composer himself. There are other works of the fifties, including a vocal *In Memoriam Dylan Thomas,* in which the composer toys with serial techniques (see p. 402ff.), again very much in his own way, as might be expected.[7] In all that Stravinsky has done, and no man has ranged further in vivid experimentalism, there is the stamp of a great intellect. It may be complained that on the whole his music is bleak, impersonal, lacking the warmth of the human touch, and that many works for that reason will not stand the test of time. But there is no doubt as to the tremendous force of his impact on the art, which took an intellectual "shot in the arm" as a result of his original thinking and practices.

Some Late Romantics

Even while such new paths as have been previously mentioned were in their early stages of exploration, there were still many great figures who desired to keep in closer touch with the romantic past. Among such was Richard Strauss (1864–1949), proclaimed by his many admirers as "Richard the Second". Indeed, in his hands the *leitmotif* device of the older master found utmost extension. Strauss, born in Munich, was the son of a horn-playing expert of very conservative views. From an early age the boy, revealed as a prodigy, was trained in piano and violin playing and in composition; and as a youth completed a general education at Munich University (1883). Meanwhile, he was already writing large-scale works in the classical, Mendelssohn and Brahms manner. By the time he was twenty his Symphony in F minor had attracted attention not only in Germany but in New York. Then a full appreciation came to him of the arts of Wagner and Liszt. There followed the famous spate of symphonic poems (*Tondichtung*—"tone-poem"—was his own term), which occupied the decade 1888–98, beginning with *Don Juan* and ending with *Ein Heldenleben* (A Hero's Life —himself the hero). These works, particularly *Till Eulenspiegel's Merry Pranks,* made him during the turn of the century the most widely known composer in the world, and they probably constitute his best work. Then in the first decade of the new century major symphonic composition ceased, except for the freakish *Symphonia Domestica* in 1903 and *An Alpine Symphony* in 1915, "symphonies" of a sort, but dependent on definite programmes. The composer's major works for the next thirty years or so consisted almost wholly of operas, the best of them having the beneficial collaboration of von Hofmannsthal, the well-known dramatic poet.

Salome (1905—founded on Oscar Wilde's play), and *Elektra* (1909—the Sophoclean story and the first of the Hofmannsthal texts) created a considerable and world-wide stir, owing to the brutality and violent emotions expressed in the libretti, underlined without restraint by the music of Strauss's huge orchestra. A more genial and classical note was struck by his fine comic opera *Der Rosenkavalier* (1911). Then came the interruption of the 1914 War. When he was remembered again after 1918 the new trends in music were passing him by, even though his production of remarkable operas in a more restrained and classical style, (notably the revised *Ariadne auf Naxos* and *The Egyptian Helen*), continued into the 30's.

In his last years he produced some mellow and masterly instrumental works such as the contrapuntal *Metamorphosen* for twenty-three solo strings, which while still belonging to an older world, were worthy of the greater Strauss.

A great deal of his busy life was spent as a conductor of his own and other masters' works (" A born conductor ", said von Bülow). Indeed, his routine activities probably did harm to his creative career. As a composer he was a thorough eclectic, a man of extraordinary vitality, but with an impulsiveness that was not sufficiently held in leash by self-criticism. No steady evolution in style can be seen in his output. Both melody and harmony could be highly original at times, but liable too often to sink to a level of banality. In the " Alpine Symphony ", for instance, while the great beauty of the " waterfall " music must be admitted, there are too many other stretches which fail to rise above the commonplace.

His chromaticisms could be extreme, but his art appeared always to be based on a classical sense of key. As an orchestrator he was among the world's greatest, master of every effect. In his tone-poems and earlier operas he demanded and controlled huge instrumental forces, but followed the fashion in being far more economical in his later works.

He carried the use of the *leitmotif* to extraordinary lengths. In *A Hero's Life* no less than seventy were employed, a special text detailing them being printed for the first performance. " Science ", " yearning ", " joy " were all musically present in his philosophical tone-poem *Thus Spake Zarathustra*. Similarly all others of the genre were sprinkled with themes that were supposed to be capable of exact material interpretation. He carried the " programme " idea far beyond Liszt's practice, and indeed every one of his tone-poems needs the printed explanation for its full appreciation. He claimed (at a time when the trend was turning against such an outlook) that his techniques for the expression of abstract feelings could indeed arouse these same emotions in the listener.

The most successful of his programme works were those which were shaped in long established forms. In *Don Quixote,* the adventure episodes were a series of variations, while his depiction of the career of the medieval rogue-jester Till Eulenspiegel took on the pattern of a rondo. Till's own beautiful motif :

—appears again and again from Introduction to Epilogue in a series of masterly transformations. Yet one still needs the written programme notes to reconcile the music with such incidents as the mock sermon, the debate of the pedants and Till's trial and hanging.

The composer undertook every type of composition except for the Church. His chamber-music, as well as a number of fine works for orchestra, with and without solo instruments, must perforce remain undetailed here. Among his hundred and fifty songs are many that are destined to live long— *Morgen, Caecilie, Blindenklage,*[8*] *Traum durch die Dämmerung*—to mention but a few.

Even more closely linked with the past was Strauss's younger contemporary Max Reger (1873–1916). He was in fact, like Brahms, a classical romantic. A highly trained contrapuntist and brilliant keyboard executant he developed an exceptional facility in composition which enabled him in the course of an all too short life to turn out more than a hundred and forty major works of every sort except opera and full-scale symphony. An unusually high proportion were for organ, which caused at least this facet of his art to be known in England. But on the whole his music has not travelled well; his close-knit, soundly constructed polyphonic style has found far more appreciation in Germany than elsewhere, which may be a pity. Owing to the one real weakness of his technique, an excessive and sometimes eccentric use of chromaticism, he was a long time living down the reputation of being a revolutionary. His music in fact had been built on a basis of Bach, Beethoven and Brahms. As well as his organ works, his sonatas for violin and piano are sometimes heard in this country, and of his comparatively few orchestral compositions the *Variations and Fugue on a Theme by Mozart.*[9*]

Another German neo-romantic much admired in his native land and Switzerland was Hans Pfitzner (1869–1949), but known elsewhere chiefly for his enormous opera *Palestrina* (of lofty spiritual aim and five-hour duration), although of late examples of his not particularly progressive chamber-music have been heard in Britain.

Another voice from the romantic era, but speaking in wholly individual tones, was that of the late-impressionist Frederick Delius (1862–1934). English-born, he was the son of a German immigrant, a hard-headed and in due course, very successful wool-merchant at Bradford. Frederick was also a grimly determined character—cynical and self-centred, an outspoken admirer of Nietzsche's harsh philosophy—yet the music which he created was of the utmost refinement, delicate sensuousness and wistful beauty. His harmonic genius seems to have been innate. He became an excellent amateur violinist, and cultivated a gift for keyboard improvisation. Hints of this latter practice are to be seen in his mature creative style. The first years of his manhood were spent in a struggle against being involved for life in his father's wool business. An " escape " to Florida to become, of all things, an orange grower, gave him some useful training with a competent American local organist. Eventually he got to Leipzig, formed a poor opinion of the academic instruction there, but heard much music, admiring above all that of Wagner and Richard Strauss. He became friendly with Grieg, another composer with whom he felt affinities. The latter's influence brought about the elder Delius' grudging acceptance of his son's true métier. The young man settled in Paris in 1888, his circles there including the painter Gauguin and the Swedish poet and dramatist August Strindberg. Apart from his travellings France held him for the rest of his life.

During the '90's he had written enough in a somewhat Straussian style to attract some attention in Germany. In 1889 he organised a one-composer concert of smaller works in London, a venture that was received at least with respect. The elder Delius read of it in his paper (" I see that Fred's given a concert "). There came eight years of comparative neglect. What notice he received was confined mainly to Germany, and included some performances of his opera *Koanga*. Meanwhile the composer, who for most of his life was in comfortable circumstances, settled at Grez-sur-Loing, near Fontaine-bleau, his permanent home, and there the production of his greater works began. He married the painter Jelka Rosen, who gradually sacrificed her career in caring for his.

The tone-poem *Paris* (Elberfeld, 1900) was the last evidence of the influence of Richard Strauss. Thereafter Delius was himself, with whatever faint tinges of Grieg and the later Wagner still remained in his chromaticisms. The opera *A Village Romeo and Juliet* (1901) had to wait six years for a Berlin performance. There followed in 1902 *Appalachia* (" Variations on an old slave song ") and *Sea Drift* (1903), both for chorus and orchestra, the latter thought by some to be the composer's most perfect work. *A Mass of Life* (1907), on a text derived from Nietzschian philosophy, was his most ambitious effort, but certainly not his best. The Piano Concerto (rewritten in 1906) has never met with wide acceptance.

Then in 1907 came sudden recognition in England, thanks to some pioneer work by Sir Henry Wood and others. Most valuable of all was the encouragement that the composer received from Sir Thomas Beecham, who in 1911 devoted a whole concert to Delius' music, and thereafter became its constant evangelist. *Brigg Fair* (1907), an orchestral rhapsody on a Lincoln-shire folk-tune, was soon generally well-known. Other major works before the 1914 War included *Dance Rhapsody* (1908), *A Song of the High Hills* (orchestra and wordless chorus) and the famous pieces for small orchestra *Summer Night on the River,* and *On Hearing the first Cuckoo in Spring* (1912). The war (in which he was not a bit interested) brought the composer into exile in England. In 1916 Sammons performed his well-written and (nowadays) somewhat neglected Violin Concerto. He returned to Grez after the war, where soon his tragedy began. Stricken by disease, the vital, athletic man gradually became blind and paralysed. Composition ceased, but in 1929 one great pleasure came to him, a six-day festival of his music in London, sponsored by Sir Thomas Beecham, with the composer present. Between 1928 and his death the devotion of Eric Fenby, a young musician-amanuensis, enabled a few more works to be completed.

There seems little doubt that some of Delius' music will live, for all the sameness of its nostalgic emotionalism, its continual harping on the theme of the transience of all beauty—" tout passe, tout casse . . ." Its chief virtue is undoubtedly the evocative power and flow of his chromatic harmony, matched to an unerring instinct for the appropriate, everchanging orchestral colouring. These two gifts served time and again to cover his deficiencies in the matters of rhythm and form and even of distinction in melody. Seldom is there much continuity of *melodic* flow, a criticism that must fail in the case of the Violin Concerto. Among the most successful of his larger works are those such as *Brigg Fair* and *Appalachia,* where the melodic material is already to hand and the variations pattern supplies a firm framework. Otherwise, his improvisatory methods and square-cut rhythms survive best in such shorter works as *On Hearing the First Cuckoo in Spring.* In this latter " impression " the Norwegian-derived melodic phrase—

—is re-harmonised again and again with ever-increasing poignancy until every particle of emotional chromatic resource has been wrung from it. In the harsh atmosphere of this modern world Delius' music is not widely congenial, but there are signs that at least in Britain appreciation is returning.

The greatest of the English late-romantics was Edward Elgar (1857–1934). As a consummate master of the large-scale, romantic orchestral canvas he stands on a level with Richard Strauss. As a symphonist and choral writer he created works that are likely long to endure. In him England produced her most significant composer since Purcell. Yet he was exceptionally late in emerging as a major figure, his first works of high achievement dating from the turn of the century. His long apprenticeship had been served at Worcester and Malvern, as organist, music teacher and highly competent violinist in local orchestras and Three Choir Festivals. He laid the foundations of his superb command of the art of instrumentation from his incessant study of scores and his experiments as conductor and arranger for incomplete local orchestras. In his craft as creator he was wholly self-taught. The English " festival " programmes of his earlier years being what they were, the influences of Mendelssohn, Spohr and Gounod were at first strong upon him. These he outgrew. It was less easy to escape from the Wagnerian spell.

After his marriage in 1889, to a wife who did much towards giving him a firmer concentration of purpose and belief in himself, there came ten years of steady production, which nevertheless brought him no more than a provincial reputation. Wise after the event, we can see in the concert overture *Froissart* of 1890 many of the signs of the mature Elgar, including a glittering instrumentation that no other British composer of the period could have approached. A number of choral works of the decade—*The Black Knight, Lux Christi, King Olaf* and *Caractacus*—are handicapped for modern performance by unsatisfactory and sometimes banal texts, together with shortcomings of the composer's own as regards word-setting, and even occasional lapses into musical banality.

Then in 1899 there came with unique suddenness a metamorphosis from talent to genius. Thanks to Parry and Hans Richter the quality of the newly written orchestral *Variations on an Original Theme* (" Enigma ") was swiftly realised, and almost overnight the composer became a national figure. The work was a series of tone-pictures concerning some of his friends, and included a brilliantly scored finale which was a self-portrait—not without touches of satire, for the composer knew something of his own idiosyncrasies. The " enigma " was in relation to his claim that a " larger tune " (never actually heard) went always with the variation theme, but it is nowadays reluctantly agreed that this is merely another Elgarian leg-pull. Of all the composer's major works the evergreen *Variations* are the most widely loved, and probably the most often played. His international fame followed with his next major composition, the great oratorio shaped to Cardinal Newman's poem, *The Dream of Gerontius* (1900), a vision based on the eternal theme of death and judgment, framed in highly emotional language, both verbal and musical, and making striking and subtle use of the *leit-motif* device after the Wagnerian pattern. The novelty, the white fire of Elgar's setting was somewhat beyond the grasp of both performers and listeners at its first hearing at Birmingham, but two renderings in Germany (in 1901 and 1902) made its true status clear. After the second Dusseldorf performance another great romantic, Richard Strauss, raised his glass to " *Meister* Elgar ". Britain swiftly made amends, but for the rest of his life the sensitive Elgar was always ready to imagine slightings and neglect of his music. Nevertheless, his position was now assured, even though two more oratorios, *The Apostles* (1903) and *The Kingdom* (1906), more episodical and less dramatic than the " Dream ", never achieved the same success. The truth is that Elgar was pursuing a form and style that was beginning to be outmoded, and in the end he recognised the melancholy fact. In the meantime he had become the country's musician-laureate, contributing in 1901 the *Coronation Ode,* which made use of the celebrated (or notorious) " Land of Hope and Glory " tune, lifted from its true and effective place as the trio of the first of his *Pomp and Circumstance* marches. Richter conducted an Elgar Festival in 1904, and soon after the composer was knighted. In the next year came one of his best-loved works, the *Introduction and Allegro for Strings*. It was for a quartet of soloists and *ripieno,* a revival in modern terms of the concerto grosso form, as rewarding for the skilled executants to play as for the listeners to hear. 1908 saw the appearance of the First Symphony, large in dimensions and orchestral demands. It is cast in the classical four movements, with a motto-theme that begins and ends the work,

and with two inner movements in which the scherzo first subject is transmuted to serve as the first melody of the *Adagio*. In the year of its appearance the symphony was given over ninety hearings. The Violin Concerto,
written by an expert in the finer techniques of the instrument, received
its first performance in 1910 at the hands of Fritz Kreisler, to
whom it was dedicated. Again a richly beautiful work, it has the original
feature of an accompanied cadenza, in which, while the themes are being
lovingly dwelt on by the soloist, there comes at times the novel background
of finger-thrummed string harmony. The opening theme of the first movement—

is one which dominates the whole of the concerto, its shadowy presence felt
in the construction of some of the later subjects. The first entry of the
soloist, who, instead of stating the theme, *replies* to it, is a stroke of genius.
The Concerto is a masterpiece, and stands on level terms with the greatest
of its kind. After years of comparative neglect it seems once more to be
regaining favour in the land of its birth.

In 1911 the Second Symphony appeared, using once again the four-
movement pattern, but with some constructional subtleties, particularly in
the handlings of the recapitulations. In its overall buoyancy and confidence,
held in leash only by the richly elegiac slow movement and a few dark
episodes, it seems to be the musical epitome of the Edwardian Age, an outlook and a way of life that was about to pass, but with which the composer
so fully identified himself. An exultant phrase, heard in the opening bars,
seems to summon the " Spirit of Delight " from the lines of the Shelley
quotation that precedes the score. It becomes a " motto ", reappears with
subtle modifications in the other movements, and takes the final curtain.
The last important composition before the outbreak of war was his major
essay in programme music—*Falstaff; a Symphonic Study* (1913). To it he
brought a penetrating literary understanding of his subject, and for all its
discursiveness it shows him at his best both as an orchestral technician and
as a character painter in terms of music. 1914 brought a drastic check in
production, but *Carillon* (a tribute to Belgium) and the choral trilogy *The
Spirit of England* (particularly *For the Fallen*) gave an answer to the charge
that he could express his patriotism only in terms of bombast.

Soon after the war came his last important work, the Violoncello Concerto
(1919). Its brevity and restraint caused disappointment at first to a public
who may have expected something of the opulence of the Violin Concerto,
but it is now recognised as among the few great examples of its kind. Casals,
Fournier and Tortelier, in particular, have set their seals upon it. None

28. An evening of Schubert's music at the house of his friend von Spaun. Schubert is accompanying. The figure on his right is Johann Vogl, the baritone opera-singer whose friendship and enthusiasm made Schubert's songs more widely known. The painter was Schubert's friend, Schwind.

UNE MATINÉE CHEZ LISZT

29. "An Afternoon at Liszt's," from a lithograph by J. Kriehuber, who is seated in the left foreground. On the right is the Moravian violinist, Heinrich Ernst. Berlioz, who owed much to Liszt's encouragement, and Carl Czerny, pupil of Beethoven and himself no mean pianist, gaze spellbound.

of the movements is developed to any length; the lovely Adagio is a matter
of a mere sixty bars. In spite of some high spirits in Scherzo and finale the
general mood of the work is lyrical, autumnal and nostalgic, but it contains
some of Elgar's greatest moments. One of these is the impact of the brief
return of the Adagio melody in the course of the last movement. The haunting tune for the lower strings which begins the first *Moderato*—

Ex:74

—was one of the composer's own favourites.[10]

Just previously he had produced three chamber works, a Sonata in E
minor for violin and piano, a String Quartet in the same key and a Quintet
in A minor for piano and strings. Only the last has retained much vitality.

In 1920 came the sudden death of Lady Elgar. With her, it would seem,
passed away most of the composer's desire to continue his art. In any case
he was very conscious of the new musical climate, and was fond of saying
that nobody wanted his work any more. Thereafter, only a few occasional
pieces appeared, but one of them was the brilliant transcription for orchestra of Bach's Fantasia and Fugue in C minor. Unfinished at his death were
sketches for an opera and a third symphony.

Elgar, like Brahms, is a tragic example of a composer born too late, overtaken and passed by the march of musical evolution. Nevertheless his greatness and individuality remain undeniable. His mature harmonic vocabulary
may have been evolved from Wagner and the German neo-romantic world
in general, but he used it in a highly distinctive fashion. His chromaticism
could be extreme; he could write long passages in which the precise tonality
would be hard to define, or such brief side-stepping moments as the brass
phrase from Part II of " Gerontius "—

Ex:75

—or the even better known progressions of " Go forth upon thy journey
. . ." from the same work. Yet he was a truly tonal composer, content to
place his own firmly individual stamp upon the traditional resources, with

2C

no time at all for folk-tune spicings, though contriving to write music that somehow has an authentic atmosphere of the English countryside. Some of his most effective harmonic moments are his purely diatonic ones, such as the simple sixths of the Prelude to Part II of *Gerontius* (" wandering in space "), or the muted strings in the slow movement of the Violin Concerto—

Ex:76

Most characteristic of all is his style of melody, so often the wide leap, the upward soaring, followed by the relaxed sinking down. The " lover's tune " from the early *Cockaigne Overture* gives a good example, as does the exquisite theme from the *Falstaff* " Dream Interlude ", and the principal subject of the Violin Concerto, already quoted. Yet at times he chose to use the " pattern " melody, the continued repetitions of a figure, as in the 'Cello Concerto theme already quoted, or the dignified opening of the Second Symphony Finale.

Many other characteristics could be spoken of—his use of the sequence, sometimes in subtle fashion, sometimes rhythmically overworked; his moments of harmonic and orchestral magic; his occasional lapses into blatancy. He remains one of those composers whose individuality and consistency of style enable a few bars of their music instantly to be identified. At times his art reflected a world that is now out of favour, and his own reputation has shared in the slighting; but the " Enigma ", the " Dream ", the Introduction and Allegro, the Concertos and the Symphonies will surely never cease to represent great moments of English music. As a recent writer has put it—" One may question his taste, but his invention, his uniqueness, his creation of immortal beauty—in short, his genius—never."—*Edward Elgar, by Diana M. McVeagh, p. 217: J. M. Dent & Sons, Ltd.*[11]

Yet another great sunset figure from the nineteenth century was the Finnish composer Jean Sibelius (1865–1957), a progressive in his own individual way but still a romantic, and still striving to give emotional meaning to instrumental music. As Elgar recalled often enough the English scene, so Sibelius's music is steeped in the spirit of the Northern sagas, and in the stark atmosphere of Finland's landscape of forest and lonely lake.

Finland had been too long oppressed politically by her mighty Russian neighbour, too long dependent on Sweden for her general culture, and on Germany for her musical outlook, but during Sibelius's early manhood she was beginning to seek independence in all things. Mention has already been made of Robert Kajanus, composer, and conductor of the Helsinki

Philharmonic Orchestra. He did much to aid the cause of native music and to encourage the early career of Finland's greatest son. One of the main sources of inspiration to the new generation of Finnish poets, painters and musicians was the *Kalevala,* a collection of ancient Finnish ballads and legends, made by Elias Lönnrot (1802–84). The young Sibelius steeped himself in this literature, from which he drew the material for most of his tone-poems, and which was in many ways the inspiration of his music as a whole.

His family was a cultured one, and as a youth he played both piano and violin. But like Stravinsky he came late to music as a professional, like him deserting the study of law for that purpose. But there was nothing amateurish in his approach thereafter. At the age of twenty-one he had a stern course at the Helsinki Academy under Wegelius, an avowed Wagnerian, and later studied at both Berlin and Vienna, amid the turmoil of the Brahms-Wagner civil war. Yet his early predilections were all for Tchaikovsky and Grieg, whose influences are plain in his first compositions, many of which he later disavowed. In 1891, at the mature age of twenty-six he was back in Finland, his apprenticeship complete, and determined, for all his Teutonic training, to be himself. For some years he taught and played the violin in Helsinki, but found time to produce such *Kalevala*-inspired tone-poems as *En Saga* and *The Swan of Tuonela,* together with the *Karelian Suite,* works which gave him national fame. This caused the unusually progressive-minded government to grant him a state pension, which enabled him to devote himself wholly to composition, and on occasion to travel widely. He retired to a country house near Helsinki, and in the main the details of his career were henceforward the productions of his compositions.

Of these the landmarks are the seven symphonies, for in them the intellectual progress of the composer is best seen. The First, in E minor (1898), though wholly mature in technique, is " dualistic " in the traditional fashion, using the classical conflict-of-themes device, and with much of the Tchaikovskian opulence in its make-up. The steady succession, the Second in D major (1902), the Third in C major (1907), the Fourth in A minor (1912), the Fifth in E flat major (1919), the Sixth in D minor (1923), and the Seventh in C major (*Fantasia Sinfonia*—1924) marked the evolution of entirely individual and novel methods of symphonic construction. He explored more and more thoroughly a technique (possibly first sketched by Borodin in his E flat Symphony—as we have already noted) whereby a movement, which began with what might seem mere rhythmic and melodic fragments, gradually coalesced them into ultimate full-grown subjects. In other words, the structure is frequently formed by the evolutionary nature of the material. This is not to say that Sibelius was committed inevitably to this technique. In many other ways he experimented with symphonic form. A recurrent mood of concision and economy of statement sometimes brought about a starkness which is terrifying—that of the bleakness of the Finnish landscape. The grimmest of his symphonies, the Fourth, seems dominated by the harshness of the augmented fourth interval which is heard in its first bars :

Ex: 77

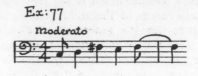

This tritone motive is metamorphosed in various ways, and makes its presence felt in each movement of this austere work.

Its successor, the Fifth, is by contrast genial and relaxed, ending in an instrumental blaze of triumph founded on one of his most widely-known themes, the bell-like :

Ex: 78

But the subtlety of the methods of construction are even more marked, progressing towards an inevitable goal, the presentation of a great symphonic structure with all its changes of tempo and mood within the scope of a single continuous movement. This was accomplished in his mightiest work, the Seventh.

A composition of less moment needs to be mentioned. The early tone-poem, *Finlandia,* though far from representing the mature Sibelius, made a considerable impact when produced by Kajanus at Paris in 1900. It was the composer's answer to a new wave of Russian oppression, and contained a nostalgic and folk-like melody that the Finns took to their hearts.

His Violin Concerto (1903), though highly original and showing all the characteristics of the greater Sibelius, has never been widely accepted by virtuosi, for all the brilliance of its solo part. A lack of balance is sometimes held against it—a monumental first movement followed by two others of smaller interest and much briefer duration.

After the Seventh Symphony of 1924 the whole musical world awaited its successor. The Eighth lived in rumour but never materialised. The United States (like Britain) always gave welcome to his music, and his final major work was commissioned by the New York Symphony Society—the greatest of the tone-poems, *Tapiola* (1925), of terrifying power and complexity. At a lower temperature came the last of *Kalevala* series, the choral and orchestral *Song of Väino* (1926). A few minor compositions followed, and then for the three decades before his death there was silence. Perhaps he knew, as Elgar had known, that the new musical climate was not for him. His place is among the last of the great tonal composers. His harmony could be harsh, even seemingly chaotic at times, but the prevailing key was always in the background, the tonal anchor never allowed to drag. His musical dialect, though wholly individual, still belonged to the world of the late romantics.

Among his Finnish contemporaries were his brother-in-law, Armas Järnefelt (1869–1958), widely known for two slight but popular orchestral pieces, and the pianist-composer Selim Palmgren (1878–1951). Later Finnish composers had the discouraging task of measuring up to a giant, yet Yrjö Kilpinen (b. 1892) has produced some masterly song-cycles in Finnish, Swedish and German; sadly neglected, it seems.

Another Scandinavian whose symphonies have made some impact is the Danish composer Carl Nielsen (1865–1931), born in poor circumstances but rising to be his country's leading musician. Like Sibelius, he was a late starter, and owed his academic training to the interest of Niels Gade. His First Symphony (1894) was Brahmsian in its outlook, but in the five more that followed a high degree of individuality was achieved. He continued to use " conflict " structures in the established manner, and his vocabulary was never markedly chromatic, but an increasing feature in them was the use of polytonality. One can speak of his polyphonic mastery and the power of his virile melody, but there remains a personal and unique quality in his music that appears inexplicable. He gave fanciful names to some of the symphonies, apparently without any programmatic intentions. In No. 5 (1922) there occurs the notorious passage where the progress of the music battles against the noise of an " extemporisation " by the side-drum player.

Atonal and Twelve-Note Music. The Viennese School

The practices evolved by the Viennese composer Arnold Schönberg (1874–1951), more drastically revolutionary than those of Debussy and Stravinsky, presented a phenomenon difficult to parallel in music, a sudden and complete break with all preconceived ideas of composition. His system has become known as " twelve-note music ", " dodecaphony " or " serialism ", for reasons that in due course will be made apparent.

Schönberg, born in Vienna, had no boyish ambitions towards music as a profession. He was given school lessons on the violin, taught himself the 'cello and played and composed in amateur fashion in chamber-music circles. Only when, in early manhood, he lost his post as a bank-clerk did he turn seriously to music. He received a few counterpoint lessons from the Viennese conductor Zemlinsky, who, with other discerning musicians, recognised the outstanding intellectual gifts of the young man, otherwise he can be counted as being wholly self-taught. These early musical experiences shaped him towards a linear, contrapuntal outlook, and this remained the chief characteristic of his creative methods. With the goodwill of Richard Strauss, Gustav Mahler, Otto Klemperer and the musicologist Guido Adler, as well as the ever faithful Zemlinsky, he occupied a series of teaching posts of increasing importance at Vienna, Berlin and other centres, and his early compositions began to be known. Among the pupils whom he attracted after 1900 were Alban Berg, Anton Webern and Egon Wellesz. Teaching and composition, together with travel as a conductor and lecturer occupied the rest of his days. In 1933, for racial reasons, he was dismissed by the Nazis from his post at the Prussian Academy of Arts at Berlin, and emigrated to the United States. There he was given academic employment of distinction, and there he died.

In his younger days he had managed to combine an appreciation of the chromatic richness of the *Tristan* harmony with an admiration for the counterpoint of Brahms. There were some innocuous early compositions, but already in 1899 he was carrying chromatic clashes to daring limits in his " programme " string sextet, *Verklärte Nacht*. In the choral and orchestral *Gurrelieder* (begun in 1900) and the tone-poem *Pelleas und Melisande* (1903) he used the gigantic orchestra of Wagner and Mahler with complete assurance, but in the *Chamber Symphony* for fifteen solo instruments (1906), he was tending towards the smaller combinations of his maturity. In this work, as in the String Quartets in D minor and F sharp minor, he was abandoning more and more the principles of tonality.[12*] In 1908, in some piano pieces (Op. 11) and in a set of songs (Op. 15), he adopted finally a completely atonal technique.

He arrived at this stage of " free chromaticism " as a result of his desire to find further and more intense ways of expressing emotion. The Viennese world of his time, belonging to the last years of the disintegrating Austrian Empire, was a decadent frustrated one, and overheated emotionalism was characteristic of its expression. Having decided that he could say nothing more within the major-minor key framework, however far stretched, he avoided in the music of his middle, " expressionist ", period every danger of key suggestion. Thus concords were banished (for the time being, at least) from his vocabulary. The immediate gain was a resource of highly charged sound-combinations such as had never been employed before, but this advantage had been won by destroying most of the resources that had made the traditional forms and structures possible—the tension and release of classical harmony, the effective contrasts obtained by well-chosen changings of tonal centres (modulation). He was compelled to grope awhile. Imitation, free or canonic, remained available, but the works of this period were in the main either brief, or assisted by words in their securing of musical shape. The *Five Orchestral Pieces* (Op. 16—1908) were widely played, but often against a great deal of clamour. In point of fact, through most of his career the composer found himself at loggerheads with a high proportion of his audiences, who were far less patient than the more thoughtful critics. However, *Pierrot lunaire* (Moonstruck Pierrot—1912), for speaking voice and five instruments, though atonal, has become one of his most successful works. The thinly scored accompaniment is held together by much canonic imitation.

Just before the 1914 War Schönberg had become an international figure, but during the conflict years creative work almost ceased. With the renewal of composition he resumed his search for a unifying principle analagous to the orthodox key-system that would put a backbone into the amorphous incoherence of free chromaticism. By 1923 he had found the way. The *Five Piano Pieces* (Op. 23) and the *Serenade* (Op. 24), for voice and solo instruments were his earliest " twelve-note " compositions.[13*]

The first principles of " composing with twelve chromatic notes only related to each other " (to use Schönberg's own description) can be stated in simple enough terms. From the twelve semitones of a chromatic scale, taken at any pitch, a composer chooses whatever succession of notes he happens to fancy. This is the *grundgestalt* (ground shape) or " tone-row ", the basic material for that particular work. Moreover, (an important point), it is the *total* notational material from which all melody and harmony must be derived—the reservoir, as it were. Lest this should seem a severe limitation of resource, it must at once be said that the tone-row can appear in three other forms, derived from old-time contrapuntal technique—in strict *inversion* of the note to note intervals;—in *retrogression,* the notes proceeding from 12 to 1—and in strict *inversion* of the *retrograde* form. Moreover, as each single note of this egalitarian musical republic can claim to start the series (the twelve-note equivalent of tonal modulation) it will be clear that these terms in themselves give altogether forty-seven ways of varying the original presentation of the subject matter, useful as one of the means of creating formal sections.

Let us suppose that the tone-row chosen is as follows:

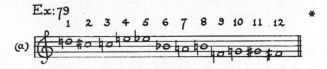

—The inversion would be :

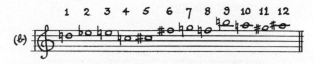

—the retrogression :

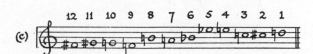

—and its inversion :

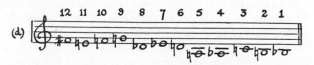

* These notes could be checked with the normal chromatic octave beginning on F—

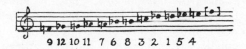

It should be mentioned that although " note-row " may be the more correct term, yet " tone-row " seems to be the established one.

The tone-row itself has laid down a certain melodic quality. In order to turn it into a *theme* the composer must now shape a rhythmic presentation of it. Here is such a one with its accompaniment, the beginning of a twelve-note composition. The theme follows the strict tone-row order, but the accompaniment is allowed some latitude, in that the row is broken up into shorter units of succession—as units sometimes forming chords, and as units not necessarily at their normal place in the tone-row :

Ex:80

It is impossible in short space to give details as to how this new basis for composition was developed by Schönberg and his followers. There can be mentioned that the idea of dividing the tone-row into segments for vertical presentation permitted passages that appeared purely " harmonic ", as in the first bar of the *Klavierstück*, Op. 33a :

Ex:81

Actually, as the technique developed the previously anathematised classical concord was allowed occasional toleration, while on the other hand the increased complications of the structures tended to conceal their " serial " bases. Not always in stating a subject was there horizontal insistence on the strict succession of the tone-row. For example, while the Fourth Quartet gives out its main theme in complete and orthodox fashion, in the Third the opening serialism seems far from rigid. Whole movements employed as subjects only a portion of the original row. One of Schönberg's later devices was to make use of the first half of his original twelve-note series together with its inversion at the fifth. This second group of notes in fact completed the particular chromatic series, though in different order from the original 7 to 12 succession. In any case, none but the keenest-eared of listeners was likely to be clearly aware of how the series was being manipulated. Indeed,

Schönberg himself stated that he did not seek aural comprehension in this respect.

He certainly gained none from the kind of hearer who judged the vertical results only in terms of traditional harmony. It is indeed its cacophonic, seemingly chaotic harmonic language which is the chief barrier to the general acceptance of twelve-note technique. The fact is that serial composition, like the thirteenth century motet, is primarily a linear art, each note conditioned to melodic and not harmonic relationships. In the building of a musical structure its chief resources are contrapuntal ones, including (as already noted) free imitation and canon; but in addition there is available the highly effective art of rhythmic variation writing. Several of Schönberg's mature instrumental works, including the important Variations for Orchestra (Op. 31) were cast entirely in that form. While his later major works, such as the Violin Concerto (1936), the Piano Concerto (1942) and his very last composition, the monumental opera *Moses and Aaron* were all written in his developed serial technique, he was never a fanatic in regard to methods of composition. The grounding he gave to pupils was on traditional lines, and one of his many pithy sayings was to the effect that " there is still a great deal of good music to be written in C major " (i.e. in tonal language). As for the method of composing with twelve notes, he said ". . . the accent does not lie so much on twelve notes but on the art of composing ". Not all his followers were so tolerant-minded in this respect.

His most faithful disciple was Anton Webern (1883–1945). Like his master spending a comparatively uneventful life in teaching, conducting and composing, he followed each phase of Schönberg's development through atonality to dodecaphony, and in fact kept more strictly to the latter creed than did his mentor. He was accidentally killed in 1945.

He was a past master of the quiet and subtly coloured orchestral effect, and, especially in his atonal period, produced works of the utmost brevity and economy of note-material, which at times seemed to reach to the limits of comprehensibility for anyone but the composer. The well-known *Five Pieces* (1913), for an orchestra of solo instruments, lasts altogether 10 minutes, No. 4 consisting of six bars only. In particular he developed a Schönberg trick of dividing the notes of a melody between various solo instruments, so that interval and colour varied together. His adoption of twelve-note technique brought longer duration and more comprehensible architecture to his works, now full of the most elaborate devices of serial counterpoint, including canons of every type and elaborate variations, together with ingenious attempts to reconcile sonata-form with the new art, as in the String Trio of 1927. His later compositions, always showing striking instrumental effects, included a String Quartet, Variations for Orchestra (of modest size), and two Cantatas, the second being his last work, and of more than usual stature. His art was specialised and, it might be thought, inimitable. Yet of the three pioneers it is he whom the later serialists seem to hold in highest regard. He is held to be the " purest " exponent of the twelve-note technique.

A book which explains in some detail various technical processes used by

Schönberg and Webern, with quotations from their works, is Leopold Spinner's *A Short Introduction to the Technique of Twelve-tone Composition* (*Boosey & Hawkes*). Another to be recommended is: Josef Rufer— *Composition with Twelve Notes*: trans. Humphrey Searle (Rockliffe— London, 1954).

Alban Berg (1885–1935), who was with Schönberg for six years and became the complete technician, progressed as did his master from the edge of tonality (in a beautiful Piano Sonata, Op. 1), through atonality to the twelve-note system.[14*] Finally, however, he seemed to be treating the new technique very much in his own personal way. He was early aware of the necessity of disciplining his over-romantic temperament, and throughout his career sought the counteraction of strict style in writing. He found fame in his opera *Wozzeck,* completed in 1921 in a Vienna of post-war misery and disillusion. The nightmare atmosphere of the tragedy of a wretched soldier driven to insanity and death was matched by a setting in the free chromatic style of, say, Schönberg's *Pierrot lunaire.* Yet the composer made use of the traditional *leitmotif* in regard to the characters, and though the vocal settings approximated most of the time to spoken speech there were still lyrical moments. Remarkable also is the fact that the music of each of the three acts followed traditional patterns of form—the first, the movements of a baroque suite (prelude, pavane, gigue, etc.); the second organised like a symphony; the third, six "inventions" in variations technique. These formal shapes, lacking the clues that tonality would have provided, are certainly never very apparent to the listener. Indeed, Berg did not wish that they should be so identified; the constructional disciplines were intended for himself. The work met with much hostility at first, but for all the strangeness of the music, at once original and decadent in its atmosphere, informed opinion nowadays is that a daring dramatico-musical experiment has proved to be an artistic success. Of the three pioneer serialists. Berg, with his lyricism and vivid musical imagination seems to have proved the most successful in shaping a difficult technique into living music. Sibelius, in his dry fashion, once named him as being " Schönberg's best work ".

The *Lyric Suite* (1926) for string quartet contained his first essays in actual twelve-note writing. His romanticism found expression, however, even in the shackles of the new style. These intentions are plain in some of the tempo indications—*andante amoroso, allegro misterioso, presto delirando,* etc.

The Violin Concerto (1935) is probably his most warmly human and best appreciated work. To him it was of the nature of a Requiem, for it expressed his deep sorrow at the death of a charming young girl, daughter of his friend Frau Mahler, by a second marriage. It was also his own requiem, for his unexpected death followed soon after. Though written in serial technique the programme nature of the concerto is quite apparent. The first two movements are intended to depict aspects of the heroine's attractive character, the third the catastrophe of her paralysis, suffering and death, the last a prayer for her eternal rest. A waltz rhythm and a Carinthian folk-tune are woven into the earlier part. The final movement makes considerable use of a Bach chorale, which begins (in tritone) :

Ex:82

Es ist ge - nug!

—whole-tone intervals, in fact. By a stroke of imagination, Berg works this phrase into his overall tone-row, thus the whole-tone fragment, with its association, makes great play in the work. The tone-row is also remarkable for the fact that, differing from the usual exotic successions employed, there is in it suggestions of the tonal system which Berg frequently enough proclaimed was altogether played out. Actually, the row uses (or could use) the four open strings of the violin, after the manner of some composers of the classical period, who so often employed the key of D in writing a violin concerto, thus obtaining tonic, dominant and subdominant on open strings. Whatever the reason for Berg's choice, there are some unusually tonal-seeming moments in the course of the work, apart from his use of Bach's own harmonies when the chorale is first presented.

Here is the tone-row of the Concerto, as presented complete by the solo violin at its first entry :

Ex. 83

Before the second World War the twelve-note technique was almost altogether confined to the Viennese trio, to which there might be added the name of Ernst Křenek (b. 1900), also of Vienna, who wrote much for the stage, including a jazz-influenced opera *Jonny spielt auf* before going over to twelve-note composition after 1930. From 1940 onward serialism was increasingly taken up by composers of many other countries, e.g. in Britain by the naturalised Matyas Seiber (1905–60) and by Humphrey Searle (b. 1915), who had some instruction from Webern. In Italy, Luigi Dallapiccola (b. 1904), was its chief early advocate.[15*]

Some of the more modern of twelve-tone composers and especially their followers, unhampered by anything resembling Schönberg's broadminded diffidence, are of the opinion that the new technique marks the beginning of a completely new epoch, that tonal composition must now be considered as dead, and that atonal serialism constitutes the music of the future. Yet it must be remembered that the dodecaphonic art is the result of a conscious, single-minded act of invention (as was Skryabin's harmonic system);

on the other hand, the principles of the fully developed major-minor tonal system which it purports to supersede were the outcome of centuries of evolution, and were based on the practices of a long succession of great composers. The history of the art of music has so far shown no signs of employing the customs of the priesthood of Nemi, and it may be that tonality may yet survive in some recognisable form. Certainly, serialism has produced some works of significance, but only time can prove whether this unusually artificial technique as at present practised has the qualities of permanence.

The third of Schönberg's leading Vienna pupils, Egon Wellesz (b. 1885) is a Renaissance-like figure of extraordinary versatility. He has a world-wide reputation as a musical scholar, being a leading authority of Byzantine music and having cast much new light on the subject of baroque opera. There are also other branches of musicology that have benefited from his researches. But in the opinion of the present writer his stature as a creative musician has been insufficiently recognised in this country.

In spite of his Schönberg training and his continued contact with that composer his early music came under the influence rather of Mahler and the classical Vienna tradition. The past has had an abiding fascination for him. The period of the 1914–18 War was for him one of research, baroque and Byzantine, the influences of these studies to be found henceforward in his own music, which continued to eschew dodecaphonic technique and to become increasingly individual. There came a series of operas, based on myths or classical legends, culminating in 1931 with *Die Bakchantinnen* (the text based on Euripides' *Bacchae*). The spirit of the ancient world dominated also a number of ballets written in this period. While making use of the dramatic power of modern dissonance the composer has shaped the structures of his operas on the baroque features of coloratura aria, ballet and chorus. The considerable amount of church music written in the '30's, (motets and three Masses), again strikes a balance between old and new, its polyphony recalling medieval and Renaissance atmospheres.

In 1938 Wellesz settled permanently in England, and has held various academic posts at Oxford. His later compositions have included another opera (*Incognita*), five symphonies, a fine chamber cantata (*The Leaden Echo and the Golden Echo—G. M. Hopkins*) and much chamber music, including four more string quartets, of which the last, No. 8, is an outstanding work. He seems to have succeeded in combining a modern harmonic idiom with a flowing and lyrically attractive contrapuntal style, needing no aid from twelve-note technique for the establishment of an individual voice. In 1961 the Austrian Government awarded him the Great Austrian State Prize, an honour not lightly bestowed.

A German composer who remained aloof from the twelve-note school was Paul Hindemith (1895–1964). In his maturity he produced a remarkable treatise *Unterweisung in Tonsatz* (Groundwork of Musical Composition—original, 1937; English version, 1945). He rejected the long-established theories as to the association of chords with the diatonic scale, their buildings-up by means of thirds, and the normal explanation of " inversions ".

At the same time he attacked atonality (which he had previously practised) as being arbitrary, and being the excuse for mental laziness. The harmonic system he expounded was based, he declared, on the natural laws of sound —on the chromatic scale derived from one fundamental note and the harmonics that it generates. He classified intervals according to what he held to be their " harmonic power ", while his theory as to chords and their inversions involved quite a revolutionary outlook. As J. S. Bach had proclaimed his belief in equal temperament by composing the " 48 ", so Hindemith demonstrated the tonal theories of his later career not only through his composition technique in general but by writing a special work for piano, *Ludus Tonalis* (1943). This consisted of a set of twelve fugues, linked by interludes and completed by a prelude together with its retrograde inversion as a postlude. Though academic in purpose it yet contains some fine music. The reader is referred to Vol. X of *The History of Music in Sound,* which gives a recording of the Fugue in D from the set. The accompanying *Handbook* (No. X—O.U.P.) contains on pp. 46–48 an exposition of the composer's " Groundwork " theories.[16*]

There was never a more practical theorist than Hindemith. He was a violin virtuoso at the age of thirteen, leader of the Frankfurt opera orchestra at twenty, and for many years the viola player in the well-known Amar string quartet, which took a leading part in the performances of the most modern music of the time. He was only twenty-three at the end of the First World War. Amid the political and economic stresses of a defeated Germany he began as one of the eclectic *avant-garde* in music. His revolt against romanticism eventually took a very individual form of neo-classicism, with, as in the case of Stravinsky, emphasis on the suppression of emotion. He had always leaned towards contrapuntal methods; he now developed a neo-baroque style of motor rhythms and melodic patterns, using old-time features such as canon and ground-bass but also a language of aggressively harsh harmonic clashes. The period 1923–30 saw the series of *Kammermusik* Concertos for solo instruments with chamber orchestra, and much other original chamber music of the same uncompromising temper. He wrote songs in which the voice relinquished its emotional function, its course depending on the music of the piano part.[17*] He produced a tragic opera (*Cardillac*— 1926) in which the instrumental music seems to disregard the details of the dramatic stage-action, and contents itself with overall moods in set forms, such as fugue. At the same time he joined with Křenek, Weill and other young composers in advocating the production of *Gebrauchmusik* (utility, objective music) for the masses—for community singing, for marching, for schools, etc. Some of his smaller chamber compositions were deliberately intended for amateurs. The " advanced " group to which he belonged proclaimed that they " indignantly protested against having their works regarded as art ". Music was to be thought of as one of the ordinary marketable commodities.

Enfant terrible or no, his fame both as a composer and viola virtuoso was growing fast. In 1927 he was given a professorship at the Berlin High School of Music. In 1929 he came to London to be the soloist in the first perfor-

mance of William Walton's Viola Concerto. By now the early ebullience had
cooled. From 1930 a change of outlook made itself more and more noticeable, an easing of the harshness of his harmonic vocabulary, a gradual
return from something like atonality to comparative euphony and a recognisable use of tonal centres. A violin sonata of 1935 was published as being
in E major; the last previous mention of key in a title was in 1922.

In the early '30's his music in general and his opera *Mathis der Maler* in
particular brought him into trouble with the Nazi authorities. The libretto
dealt with Mathias Grünewald, the famous and independent-minded German painter (c. 1530), and subjects concerned with rebellion against
authority were not in favour. Besides, the composer had committed another
crime in marrying a Jewish wife. In Berlin, what should have been the first
performance of *Mathis* was prevented, Hindemith was dismissed from his
teaching post and his music banned in Nazi Germany. He left his country
in 1935 and soon after settled in the United States, where he was given
academic welcome at both Harvard and Yale.

Mathis der Maler had its first performance in 1938 at Zurich, and has
since become recognised as a great work. In it, and in subsequent compositions Hindemith displayed a settled maturity, together with a greater harmonic euphony than heretofore. His counterpoint could now be seen as a
true and disciplined development in modern chromatic terms of the art of
Bach and the earlier German polyphonists. Even mellower than *Mathis*
was the ballet *Nobilissima visione* (The Conversion of St. Francis) produced
in London, also in 1938, a year after the original publication of the
" Groundwork " treatise. In 1945 came the *Ludus Tonalis* previously mentioned. Among his later compositions written in America were the well-
known *Symphonic Metamorphoses on a Theme by Weber* (1945), concertos
for violin, 'cello, piano and horn respectively and some outstanding chamber-
music.

Another German composer, Carl Orff, born in the same year as Hindemith, is mentioned here only in relation to a single work, the " scenic cantata " *Carmina Burana*. It is his most successful composition and has recently
been a good deal heard in this country. It embodies his theories regarding
stage-music, which, he holds, should break away from the elaborations of
established opera and return to the elements of the art. Thus the work is
built up of folk-like vocal lines based on strong and straightforward rhythms.
Forms are of the simplest, counterpoint largely avoided, harmony of primitive concordance apart from some rare clashes. As the name suggests, it consists of a series of settings of goliard poems taken from the thirteenth century
Benediktbeuern manuscript (see. p. 46), for three soloists and chorus, and
supported by miming and dancing. The work, half-barbaric, half pseudo-
medieval and using medieval German and Latin texts, makes an extraordinary impact on a first hearing, being unique in style. This uniqueness is
probably the greatest of its virtues. One of the most forcefully delivered of
the *allegro molto* choral tunes struck the present writer as familiar. He had
previously encountered it in a twelfth century French manuscript, where it
was sung by Mary Magdalen in expressive lament.

In quite another way did Kurt Weill (1900–50) make his mark in stage-music. A pupil of Busoni's, his light-opera style, modern yet based in Sings-piel traditions (he produced his own version of *The Beggar's Opera* in 1928) gained him a reputation in Germany, and was welcomed as a relief from the Wagner-Strauss domination. In 1933 he left Nazi-ruled Germany and eventually settled in the U.S.A. Here he resumed his career as a writer for the stage with even greater success. His music, though aimed at popular attraction, was that of a highly skilled craftsman. It made use of the idioms of the street and dance-hall, and could vary between the lyrical simplicity of the chanson and the blatant poundings of jazz. He could express in terms of music the deepest melancholy and nostalgia, which he used at times to bathe his scenes of city low-life in an atmosphere of pseudo-romanticism. His harmonic vocabulary contrived at once to be frequently novel, basically simple and dramatically effective. With these resources he succeeded in creating works which were not only appreciated by the less sophisticated listener but also had a considerable impact on the light-operatic art and the development of the Broadway " musical ". It was at the New York Broad-way Theatre that he gained a number of successes (e.g. *Street Scene, The Seven Deadly Sins*). He also showed the possibilities of " folk-style " opera in his *Down in the Valley* (1948).

At the beginning of 1963 performances were given in this country, for the first time, of the fantastic *Rise and Fall of the City of Mahagonny*, first pro-duced in Leipzig in 1930.

To the names of Stravinsky, Schönberg and Hindemith there must be added a fourth, that of a man whose intellectual power stands on a level with theirs and who brought new and unique resources to twentieth century music. Béla Bartók (1881–1945) was a Hungarian composer in the truest sense of the word. There had been the cosmopolitan Liszt, and also com-posers of more genuine Hungarian stock than he, but all had spoken the prevailing musical language of their times. From Haydn to Brahms and Liszt leading European composers had sometimes coloured their works by melodic and stylistic borrowings from the music of the Hungarian gipsy-bands and popular folk-songs. It was Bartók who first realised that this material, much of it superficial and sophisticated, was not the genuine article, and that among the Magyar peasants there still survived an ancient folk-music, non-European in many aspects of its melody and rhythm.

Bartók came from a musical home, and, trained at the Budapest Academy, early made his mark as a virtuoso pianist. In composition, his models had been first Brahms and the Brahms-influenced native composer Dohnányi. There had come a Liszt-Wagner phase, and then a complete but quite temporary surrender to Richard Strauss and his *Also Sprach Zarathustra*. These enthusiasms produced such works as a patriotic tone-poem, *Kossuth*, and a Rhapsody for piano and orchestra, but not until after 1905 did his true originality begin to show itself. It was then that he began his life-task of collecting, studying and publishing his country's age-old peasant music. The urge was something more than a patriotic and scholarly one; he was seek-ing an element that he knew to be necessary for his own full creative development. His was a highly individual mind, and around this time he had met the music of Debussy and had come under its liberating influence, while in due course he appreciated, without following too closely, the innovations of Stravinsky and Schönberg. But it was Magyar peasant-song, together with other Eastern-derived folk musics of S.E. Europe which most deeply conditioned his musical thought and speech. As a result there can be heard so often in his works the influence of archaic scales—pentatonic, modal or altogether exotic, frequent uses of the interval of the sharp fourth; even occasional quarter-tones (as a collector his garnerings included Arab music). A number of his solo vocal, choral and piano works consisted actually of arrangements of folk tunes; and even in the chamber music and the more ambitious concerted forms at least the flavour of the ancient heritage is to be found.[18*]

To exotic melody Bartók added Magyar complexities of rhythm which were far removed from the conventions of pre-Stravinsky Western Europe. These were joined with an eclectic harmonic system as harsh and uncompromising as that of Stravinsky or Hindemith, yet clearly in keeping with the primitive folk-art on which he was building. The result was that up to and including the period of the First World War, he obtained little more reputation than for being a "barbaric" composer. A piano professorship at Budapest kept him in daily bread. He gained some success in 1916 with a ballet, *The Wooden Prince,* and then in 1918 with the opera *Bluebeard's Castle,* Debussyan in its atmosphere. The *Miraculous Mandarin* ballet (1919) seems to represent him, musically, at his harshest. The subject also gave offence, and for a time his stock was once more low, particularly as at the same time he contrived to get himself into political hot water. His opinions were as uncompromisingly expressed as was his music.

In 1926 he began touring again as a concert pianist, and while in the U.S.A. actually won the Philadelphia Chamber Music prize with his Third String Quartet. A brilliant period of composition began, which lasted until the outbreak of the Second World War and included the *Cantata Profana* (1930), the Second Piano Concerto (1931), the Music for Strings, Percussion and Celesta (1936), the Violin Concerto (1938), the Concerto for Two Pianos (1938), and several string quartets culminating with No. 6 (1939). In 1940 he left to settle in the United States. His circumstances there turned out not as flourishing as he might have hoped, but his Concerto for Orchestra (1943) was well received, and a commission from the virtuoso Yehudi Menuhin produced a Violin Sonata (1944). He was, however, already in failing health, and managed only to complete his Third Piano Concerto. A Viola Concerto remained in rough and incomplete draft.

Two profound influences on the work of the composer remain to be mentioned, those of Bach and Beethoven. The young Bartók had learned from Debussy's music the new paths of harmonic possibility that existed, but his respect for the older masters was just as deep. Bach's counterpoint was for him of "transcendent significance", and he himself became a fine contrapuntist. Also, twentieth century musician though he was, he could speak of Beethoven as "one who had revealed to us the meaning of progressive

30. A French caricature of Wagner (*Figaro*, 1876). His reputation for noise is still being laboured. That Paris remembered the composer's chauvinistic outbursts against France after the 1870 war is recalled by the Prussian helmet.

The Mansell Collection

31. The young Chopin playing the piano at the home of Prince Anton Radziwill in Berlin. Radziwill (seated in front of the piano) was himself a creditable composer, and had befriended Beethoven as well as Chopin.

The Mansell Collection

32. The Prince Consort playing the organ at Buckingham Palace before Queen Victoria and Mendelssohn in 1842. The composer, whose own organ playing has made a profound impression in England, appears non-committal.

form ". Of the four outstanding composers of the mid-century (the others being Stravinsky, Schönberg and Hindemith) it was Bartók only who showed a warm sympathy for the traditional "sonata" principle of construction. In the larger works of his later years, when some of his harmonic acerbities had softened, the classical form is unmistakable, but blended at times with contrapuntal principles derived from baroque technique and always expressed in the terms of his very individual idiom. He was at heart a tonal composer, even though the exotic, frequently angular melodic material in which he dealt caused his music at times to stretch tonality to its limits, or to stray beyond. But in this late flowering of his art (belonging mainly to the '30's) there was, as in Hindemith's music, a more pronounced feeling for key and the traditional key-relationships. The frequently played Violin Concerto is perhaps the best example of his sunset mellowing. Though the material and the idiom are pure Bartók yet the first and last movements are quite recognizably in sonata form, with exposition, development (on individually Bartók lines) and recapitulation; and the middle movement an air and variations. The home key is clearly B minor-major, the overall scheme a cyclic one, and the general atmosphere one of great lyrical beauty.

Yet it is perhaps in the six string quartets that the essential Bartók is best to be found, and the intellectual power of his close-knit writing most fully appreciated. These, together with the Violin Concerto, the Music for Strings, Percussion and Celesta, the Second Piano Concerto, with perhaps the Dance Suite for Orchestra (1923), the *Cantata Profana* and the Twenty Hungarian Folk Songs of 1929, are probably his most outstanding works. It was his avowed aim as a composer " to make a synthesis of East and West " through his musical use of Oriental-derived material. How far he went towards achieving this purpose must be left in question, but the music that it invoked is without doubt strikingly individual.

Zoltan Kodály (b. 1882), Bartók's friend and collaborator in many of his folk-tune enterprises, was at once less distinguished as a composer and more successful in the worldly sense. He shared with Bartók an enthusiasm for Debussy—for him a permanent influence, and throughout his life his music has been popular in his native land. Unlike his friend he has managed to live at peace with authority throughout a long career and to be recognised as a father-figure in Hungarian musical life. Of his many attractive works his masterpiece is undoubtedly the choral and orchestral *Psalmus Hungaricus* (1923). The suite, *Háry János,* taken from his opera of the same name (1926), together with the folk-derived *Marosszek Dances* (1930) and *Dances of Galanta* (1933) for orchestra, are all internationally performed.

A brief return in time will be made to mention a remarkable international figure, Ferriccio Busoni (1866–1924). Italian-born, he spent most of his life in Germany or in world-travel. His first fame came as a virtuoso pianist, one of the greatest that ever has been, his technical powers enhanced by intellectual gifts of a high order. In spite of his nationality his musical sympathies were largely German. It was his Italian father, oddly enough, who early inculcated a love for the music of Bach, and throughout his life

2D

Busoni idolised the baroque master, and in slightly lesser degree only, Beethoven and Liszt. His mature development took place between 1894 and 1914, when Berlin was his main centre. He took a Baconian view of his art; he was to be the whole musician—not only a piano virtuoso of the highest flight, but composer and conductor as well. While producing a great deal of original music he sought also to build on the works of Bach—in formidable transcriptions of his major compositions for the concert grand piano and in original fantasies founded on themes of the master. His own command of all the resources of classical counterpoint was massive. His greatest work in this vein is the monumental *Fantasia Contrapuntista* for piano, in which he blended material from the Art of Fugue with his own into a gigantic composition of great technical difficulty. In his ceaseless search for new forms to be expressed in the classical manner he produced such works as the large-scale Concerto for Piano, Orchestra and Male Chorus (1904). There were several experiments in opera form in his attempts to create (like Wagner) a *Gesamtwerk*—*Die Brautwahl* (1910), a pre-Puccini *Turandot* (1917) and finally his *chef d'oeuvre, Doktor Faust,* medieval in its libretto derivations, and with the concluding scene left unfinished at his death. There is much noble music in *Faust,* but its success seems to have been confined to Germany, in spite of the fact that its style seems to be founded on that of Verdi's *Falstaff* rather than on Wagner. In general, while the quality of Busoni's music is consistently high, yet like that of many another all-purpose musician it is too eclectic and derivative to have had any effect on the course of the art.

Some background having been established as to modern international trends in music, it may be most convenient to conclude our survey by considering in turn the leading countries and their composers.*

Italy

The last outstanding figure in the great Italian opera tradition, Giacomo Puccini (1858–1924), outlived and far outshone his contemporaries Mascagni and Leoncavallo in the art of *verismo*—operatic realism. Perhaps the very melodramatic nature of his first successful work, *La Bohème* (1896), counted against him in some circles. Yet, beginning with Verdi, other great musicians up to Schönberg have admired the originality of his harmony and orchestration. His mastery continued in such operas as *La Tosca* and *Madame Butterfly* and the charmingly humorous *Gianni Schicchi,* to the climax of the final exotic masterpiece, *Turandot.*

Meanwhile Italy had awakened to a new interest in symphonic writing, oratorio and chamber music, thanks largely to the pioneer career of Giovanni

---

*To survey the vast international territory of actual contemporary music is matter for a large and single volume. Such efforts have been undertaken, mainly in symposium form. One thing is certain; many of the judgments that have been pronounced will in due course be drastically modified by Time's court of appeal, as has happened on many a past occasion. I have recoiled from the task to the extent of making but the briefest mention of any composer born after 1914—admittedly an arbitrarily-drawn line.

Sgambati (1841–1914), who campaigned for German and classical music generally in Italy, as composer, teacher and solo pianist. He had, at Rome, been a pupil of Liszt. His well-written orchestral, chamber and piano works became known in other countries. Significantly, he wrote no opera.

There followed a generation of younger Italian composers who, while often writing successfully for the stage produced works of value in other branches of the art. Ottorino Respighi (1879–1936), who actually went to Russia to become a pupil of Rimsky-Korsakov, showed, perhaps as a result, a strong liking for vivid orchestral colour, best displayed in his symphonic poems, *The Pines of Rome* and *The Fountains of Rome*.

More sensitive and more modern in outlook is the work of Ildebrando Pizzetti (b. 1880), with a large output in every form of composition to his credit, and with an individual lyrical style, tinged with modal influences, noticeable in his operas and choral works. Similarly Francesco Malipiero (b. 1882) achieves a compromise between past modality and a modern and imaginative style of his own in his symphonies, operas and chamber music and maintains a link with classical forms.

More uncompromisingly modern and less consistent in personal idiom was Alfredo Casella (1883–1947). His harmony could be harsh, with leanings towards polytonality and atonality, yet he attempted to revive the old Italian lyric spirit in such works as his instrumental *Scarlattiana* (1926) and *Paganiniana* (1942). As a teacher his influence on the rising generation was very strong.

Many worthy names, such as those of Petrassi and Castelnovo-Tedesco, will have to remain neglected, but some note must be taken of the singular Luigi Dallapiccolo (b. 1904), who succeeded in assimilating into his own personal lyrical style the twelve-note system of the Viennese School. Yet he has gone his own individual way in interpretations of the serial technique (see Note 15), and as a result several of his vocal works, particularly his opera *The Prisoner* has met with success in circles not usually enamoured with twelve-note music. As Marc Pincherle has remarked, he gives the impression of " a relaxed tonality rather than of an assault against tonality " (op. cit. p. 206). In approaching modern times one becomes aware of a considerable number of young Italian composers who are practising serialism in far more " advanced " fashion.

France

In dealing with modern French music some heed must be paid to the eccentric figure of Erik Satie (1865–1925), about whom musical opinion, especially in France, seems even yet not settled. Friend of Debussy, at once Bohemian and mystic, he is supposed to have claimed that the harmonic audacities of his early piano pieces had had an influence on that composer, an unlikely pretension. But owing to his contempt for all tradition, and his delight, musically, always in doing what was wrong in other people's eyes, he took on the appearance of elder prophet in the opinion of the generation of young French musicians who emerged in the '20's, full of neo-classical ideas built on Stravinsky, together with a taste for polytonality and atonality in general. Satie's influence was greater than his achievements, for his own satirical pieces, often with eccentric titles, seldom expressed any worthwhile innovation.[19*]

Contemporary with Satie was an independent of very different calibre, Albert Roussel (1869–1937). The contrapuntal training of d'Indy and the impressionism of Debussy are both evident in his early works (he was in fact a late starter) notably in the symphonic *Poème de la forêt,* but around the first World War he established himself with the famous ballet *Le Festin de l'araignée* and the less well-known *Padmavâti,* together with the choral and orchestral *Évocations.* In his maturity the impressionist element was banished, and he returned to the ideals of classical organisation, his polyphony ruled by a taste for both medieval and eastern modes (he had travelled in Indo-China). While never ceasing to be diatonic in principle he developed a characteristic boldness, even harshness of harmonic idiom that was his own rather than Stravinsky's. The Second and Third Symphonies (1930 and 1934 respectively) may represent his best achievements, works of classical structure and high musical content, and without any "programmes". He wrote in every genre, including a great deal of chamber music and some forty songs.[20*] His stage music consisted mostly of ballet, *Bacchus et Ariadne* being particularly successful.

Maurice Ravel (1875–1937), like Debussy, was thoroughly representative of Gallic art in its characteristics of economy, refinement and restraint. A pupil of the fastidious Fauré, his individual style early manifested itself. However, his " tranquil harmonic audacities " aroused reactionary opposition, and in 1905 a committee of the Paris Conservatoire refused to allow him to compete for the *Prix de Rome* at a time when several since-famous works—*Jeux d'eau, Miroirs* and *Sonatine* for piano, and the String Quartet in F major—had already been written and performed. This prejudiced behaviour caused a public outcry, but it was probably the most discordant happening of his otherwise tranquil bachelor existence, until the ill-health and mental collapse of his last years.

Most of his music was written in the smaller forms; like Debussy's, his was a " petit art ". Quite mistakenly it is sometimes actually bracketed with that of the older master, but as Alfredo Casella pointed out—" while Debussy created, and at the same time *exhausted* musical impressionism, Ravel remained faithful to classical forms, which he rejuvenated by his admirable innovations."[21*] His harmonic idioms, though personal, original and striking, were based on tradition, and he had no use for the whole-tone scale. His music, if less fluid than Debussy's, was clearer in outline, firmer in part-writing, more objective. This is not to say that it is of the same historical importance, or (could such comparisons be made) that it was in any way " better " or " worse ". Although he long maintained a friendship with Satie, their common outlook was probably only a hatred of the lingering influences of Wagnerism.

A remarkable trait of Ravel's was his extraordinary, instinctive command of colourful orchestration. A long acquaintance with, and admiration for Chabrier may have helped. Yet oddly enough, of his few orchestral works designed for the concert hall, only one was orchestral in its original form, this being the brilliant *Rapsodie espagnole* (1907). *La Valse*, and the repetitive *Bolero* ("orchestral effects without music"—as the composer himself called it), were both written originally for stage-dancing. Other colourfully scored works, the charming *Ma Mère l'Oye* (Mother Goose) ballet suite, the *Pavane pour une infante defunte*, and that glorious tribute to an earlier age of reticence and good taste, *Le Tombeau de Couperin*, were all at first written for the keyboard. In 1922 the composer made his celebrated orchestral version of Mussorgsky's *Pictures from an Exhibition*, a piano suite.

Of his piano pieces, where he is most characteristically himself, there must also be mentioned the *Gaspard de la nuit* suite, its first movement, *Ondine*, being another remarkable example of "water-music". Debussy himself may have learned something from the younger man's mastery of keyboard writing.

His chamber music, besides the String Quartet, includes a Piano Trio and a striking Sonata for Violin and 'Cello only—dedicated to the memory of Debussy. He wrote two piano concertos, one for left hand alone for the one-armed virtuoso Paul Wittgenstein—a war casualty.

His two stage-works *L'Heure espagnole* (1907) and *L'Enfant et les sortilèges* (1925) are both of such quality as to make it clear that he should have attempted more than he did in the matter of opera.

Mention should be made of the extraordinary Edgar Varèse (b. 1885 in Paris) who, after an orthodox training at the hands of d'Indy and Roussel and employment in Berlin and Prague, emigrated to the United States in 1916. There he turned to extreme modernity in composition, experimenting to extraordinary lengths in matters of harmony, rhythm and instrumental sound, and writing such works as *Ionization*, which needed neither melody nor harmony, being scored for percussion instruments with the addition of a couple of sirens. He appears to hold that music should be just *sound*, without the hindrance of any traditional associations.

Of the new generation of French composers already referred to, who emerged after the first World War, the most notable were a group known as *Le Six*. Actually the term was the invention of a journalist; the musicians concerned had no outstanding ties but those of friendship, nationalistic feeling, and in some cases a taste for satire. If historical significance is the test then the number really amounts to four—Darius Milhaud (b. 1892), Arthur Honegger (1892–1956), Francis Poulenc (1899–1963) and Georges Auric (b. 1899).

Of the four Milhaud is the most representative of the moods of the '20's. An eclectic and a restless experimenter who has included the writing of jazz movements among his techniques, he has probably published too quickly and too much. His output of works, these of every description, has reached the 400 mark. He was at the Paris Conservatoire for a while, and in his young days admired Debussy and Mussorgsky, loathed Wagnerism and was indifferent to Ravel. In his earlier compositions the anti-romantic quality was very marked, a stressed aggressiveness, a Stravinskian harmonic harshness, a taste for musical parody and a preoccupation with the problems of polytonality.

His handling of this latter technique was often so highly logical and lucid as almost to make it acceptable to ears attuned only to the nineteenth century.[22*]

He has travelled considerably, and from 1940–7 was in the United States. As is the case with many a neo-classicist his early dissonant moods have mellowed with maturity. He has shown that when necessary he can write in attractive and straightforward tonal style. He has always had a pronounced lyrical gift.

His enormous output includes the inevitably long list of ballets, and sets of incidental music. That written for Claudel's translation of Aeschylus' *Choephoroe* is singularly striking. Of his dozen or more operas *Christophe Colomb* (1928) stands out as a strange dramatic experiment—a series of tableaux, commentaries by a sort of Greek chorus, spoken texts, and assistance also from the cinematograph! Like all leading French composers of his day he has written much film music. Among his orchestral compositions are a number of small symphonic works and four full-scale symphonies. There are four piano concertos, and two each for violin and for 'cello. His friendship with the distinguished man of letters Paul Claudel produced a number of choral works. The long list of chamber compositions, which includes fifteen string quartets, is similarly impressive. In the matter of songs (about 180) and keyboard music he has also been very productive.

Milhaud holds the Jewish faith, but unlike Bloch, he has allowed an ancient tradition to impinge only lightly on his art. Whatever intrinsic value will eventually be given to his music, as an innovator he must hold a respected place.

A consideration of the work of Arthur Honegger discloses how loose were the links that bound *Le Six*. Honegger, born in France of Swiss parents and studying for a time in Switzerland, was thoroughly independent-minded, and as much German as French in his outlook. He had no time for the " fairground music " produced at times by his colleagues, and disliked Satie and his whole philosophy, for his own predilections were for serious and solidly constructed contrapuntal works founded on traditional forms. Although employing a harsh harmonic vocabulary, when he thought fit he had plenty of use for the plain common chord. There was a great deal of the romantic in his make-up, for in his five symphonies, his quartets, concertos and sonatas, all rigorously and logically constructed, there are at times flashes of a pictorial element. His best-known work—in fact the only one to gain international popularity—is the tone-poem, *Pacific No. 231* (he called it *Mouvement symphonique*), the orchestral equivalent of a great transatlantic steam locomotive stirring into life. To him this was not romantic picture-painting, but " descriptive realism ", as was his *Rugby*. His two most successful dramatic works, *Le Roi David* and *Jeanne d'Arc au bûcher*, took the form of concert- rather than stage-operas—types of dramatic oratorio. He wrote a large amount of ballet, incidental music and film music.

In Poulenc we again have a man handling Satie's weapons of parody and satire, highly gifted as a song writer, and willing to use the witty Parisian street-tunes as basic material. But his early frivolity and simplicity of line masked a solid and developing musicianship. He was a brilliant pianist, and wrote, besides keyboard pieces of distinction, several concertos, one well-known one for harpsichord, another for organ, strings and percussion. Apart from ballet and incidental music his orchestral writing was of the chamber type. For all his musical cynicism he had a sincere religious side to his character which expressed itself in a number of fine choral works, including an *a cappella* Mass (1937) and a *Stabat Mater* (1951). His greatest inspiration is perhaps to be found in his hundred or so songs. In 1957 there was produced in this country *The Carmelites,* a stage work actually in grand opera form, and in a French revolutionary setting. It was hardly a success. One of his last works was a clarinet sonata in memory of Honegger.

The music of Auric has some kinship with that of Poulenc in that his earlier work often made sardonic use of popular music. His humour and satire is if anything more acid. Though he studied with d'Indy the influences of Satie and Stravinsky were soon evident. In his maturity the harshness of his vocabulary has tended to relax. He is best known as a writer of truly musical ballets, and above all of film music, the most famous of his generation in the latter respect, and supplying English as well as French screens.

Of an even later group of French composers, termed *La Jeune France,* mention can be made only of Olivier Messiaen (b. 1908). Highly gifted, highly trained, virtuoso organist, scholar and composer, his two passions are his ardent Catholic faith which rules much of his choral and organ production, and his eager search for new means of expression. This latter has caused him to study Gregorian modes, Hindu scales and rhythms, micro-tonal intervals, exotic orchestrations including the use of electronic instruments, and last but far from least, bird-song. All these resources he has attempted in various ways to incorporate into his music, which has become increasingly experimental, especially now that his theories concerning rhythm are becoming so complicated. It must perhaps be left to the next generation to pronounce on the significance of his work.

Holland

Although Holland has developed a strong national musical life, there had been little sign in the last century of any great creative talent. An exception must be made in the case of Johan Wagenaar (1862–1941), for many years Director of the Royal Conservatory at The Hague and an immense influence for the good of Dutch music. He was a highly competent composer of the romantic school, and his orchestral music seems to be reviving in favour, both in Holland and elsewhere. One of his many pupils was Willem Pijper (1894–1947) who became a truly international figure. He wrote in all the larger forms, at first with elaborate textures and in polytonal and poly-rhythmic manner, but gradually evolving a simpler and more individual style. His influence as a teacher was very great. A pupil, Henk Badings (b. 1907) has become widely known as a versatile and original modern composer.

Switzerland

The list of eminent Jewish composers through the centuries is a long and formidable one. Ernest Bloch, born at Geneva in 1880, has been perhaps the most insistent in attempting to communicate in his music the exotic atmosphere of an ancient and enduring race-consciousness. This element is seen in his *Trois poèmes juifs* for orchestra, his *Schelomo* for 'cello and orchestra, his " Hebrew " pieces for various stringed instruments and piano and his *Israel Symphony*. However, he has not been obsessed with racial broodings. Two important orchestral works, the " epic rhapsody ", *America* (1926) and the " fresco ", *Helvetia* (1929), pay tribute to the land of his adoption and that of his birth. His music, so often rhapsodical rather than symphonic in form, shows adherence to no particular system, not even that of the twelve tones. Too much stress has sometimes been laid on his occasional use of quarter-tones.

Another Genevan composer, Frank Martin (b. 1890), a figure of considerable importance in modern music, graduated from romantic utterances reminiscent of César Franck to a highly individual and advanced modern style of his own. He uses twelve-note technique after his own fashion, often enough employing it as a foil to pure triadic harmonies. His *Petite Symphonie concertante* (1945) has now a world reputation. In 1948 came the remarkable oratorio *Golgotha,* proclaimed as a highly original conception. In his opera *Der Sturm* (founded on Shakespeare's *Tempest* and produced in Vienna in 1958) he differentiated between the various levels of dramatic action by the use of contrasting musical styles, e.g. Caliban and the comic characters were given serial music.

Another Swiss modernist of considerable individuality was Willy Burkhard (1900–55).

Czechoslovakia

The eminent Janáček was followed by a number of talented Czech composers, several of whom perished after 1938 under the rule of the Nazis. Among those who took refuge in the United States were Bohuslav Martinů (b. 1890) and Jaromir Weinberger (b. 1896).

Critical opinion seems to vary considerably as to the significance of Martinů's work. It certainly seems to show a great deal of fluctuation in quality, possibly owing to early shortcomings in training, and in spite of his becoming for a time a pupil of Roussel at Paris. However, his symphonies and concertos have gained him some standing in the United States, and eventually he was invited by the post-war Czech government to return to his native land.

The name of Weinberger is known generally only through one work, his comedy-opera *Schvanda the Bagpiper* (1927). Full of merry tunes, it found a swift welcome in many other countries, being the only other Czech stage-work to share world fame with Smetana's *Bartered Bride*. Nothing else of his music has proved of much significance.

Poland

Jan Paderewski (1860–1941) will always be remembered as one of the finest and most sensitive of piano virtuosi; also as a patriot who represented his government at the Versailles Peace Conference. As for the creative art, in Karol Szymanowski (1882–1937) there emerged a composer of European stature and a powerful influence on Polish music. Starting with an eclecticism that moved between Strauss, Debussy, Stravinsky and Schönberg he succeeded in developing an individual modernity in opera, symphony and chamber music. At the same time he was able to assimilate into his technique, as did Chopin before him, the rhythms and melodic idioms of the national folk-songs and dances. There is now a strong national school, though many Polish composers have made their homes elsewhere. The best known among them is probably Alexandre Tansman (b. 1897), resident in France.

Greece

From Timotheus of Miletus and Mesomedes of Crete to Nicos Skalkottas of Euboea (1904–49) is a far cry, but in this composer Greece once more found an international figure. He was for five years a pupil of Schönberg's, but his mature style was manifestly his own. His orchestral *Greek Dances* have been widely played, and lately a set of orchestral variations were broadcast in this country. With the formation after his death of a Skalkottas Committee, and a beginning made at printing those scores which remained in manuscript (the bulk of his work), interest has been growing in regard to his music. The list includes several concertos for various solo instruments and some chamber-music.

Russia

It has already been noted that the political atmosphere of the post-revolution years proved distasteful to the point of exile for a number of distinguished Russian musicians, including Stravinsky, Rachmaninov, Grechaninov, Glazounov, and, for many years, Prokofiev. The last-named went back to the Soviet Union in 1932, and took his place among the leading composers which the State had at its command. These included the veteran Nicolas Miaskovsky (1881–1950), the Armenian-born Aram Khachaturyan (b. 1904), Dmitri Kabalevsky (b. 1904) and perhaps the most famous of all, Dmitri Shostakovich (b. 1906); with of course the prodigal son returned, Serge Prokofiev (1891–1953). Before these musicians and their works are considered in more detail it may be as well to recall the conditions which ruled their art. Under the régime they were always subject to political and propaganda directives, and on more than one occasion the mailed fist came down very heavily indeed. This State control applied of course to all the arts. The case of the poet Pasternak will be fresh in the public memory. There can also be recalled the matter of the assembly of Soviet writers who in 1934 were addressed by the old revolutionary Maxim Gorky, friend of Stalin, on the subject of " Socialist realism "—the doctrine that was to rule Soviet art. Bourgeois concepts of " realism " in art were negative, destructive, decadent; " Socialist realism " was constructive, optimistic, with emphasis on the glories of proletarian existence. In other words, the writers' task was to extol the communist state and denounce all other philosophies. A word was coined which afterwards proved very useful against all types of music not approved by the hierarchy—" formalist ".

" Formalism " was art just for art's sake (instead of art with propaganda strings to it)—art that was experimental, individual or sophisticated; that was in any way technically beyond the ready comprehension of the masses. Or more simply stated—formalism = decadence = *Western* art in general. Up to this time Soviet composers had enjoyed a certain amount of freedom in their use of modern techniques, but in 1936 a crushing blow fell on Shostakovich, until then considered the music-laureate. His new opera, *Lady Macbeth of Mzensk,* which, like a number of his works in the '30's, had made use of polytonal and atonal effects, was suddenly denounced by the official *Pravda* as being full of " formalist " errors. Its production was stopped and the composer for a time ostracised. Other musicians hastened to take the warning to heart. A little later an even grimmer lesson was given to all creative artists, when the theatrical director Vsevolod Meyerhold, exasperated beyond caution, declared that the official policy would lead to the destruction of all Russian art and culture. He was immediately arrested and was never heard of again.

Then came the War, when composers found the task of writing patriotic and propaganda music congenial enough. Actually, " social realism " not being so loudly trumpeted for the time being, certain of them seem to have taken the opportunity also to write " below the desk " in their own preferred ways (? some of Shostakovich's chamber music of those years). But after 1945, with the Iron Curtain and the " cold war " in operation, the shackles again gripped all creative work. In 1948, Zhdanov, Stalin's lieutenant, assembled a conference of leading Soviet musicians at which he did most of the talking. He seems roundly to have denounced them for their formalist errors and imitations of the degenerate music of the West, and he also spoke of a coming Decree on Music that would tell them exactly the path that they had to follow. It came. All the prominent composers seem to have submitted and to have promised " reform ". With the fate of Meyerhold in mind one cannot blame them; but in appraising the characteristics of modern Russian music all this must be borne in mind.

Regarding Miakovsky, the oldest of the group, little is known even in Russia, for he was something of a recluse. He entered the musical profession late, was a pupil of Liadov and Rimsky-Korsakov and was friendly with Prokofiev. Like Rimsky-Korsakov his life was divided between composition and teaching. The most striking fact about him is that he wrote no less than twenty-seven full-scale symphonies, of which only the twenty-first, a beautiful but in no way original work, seems to have got across to the West. He appears to have kept to the romantic tradition and the classical structures, and to have had a considerable contrapuntal mastery, sometimes allied to a harmonic harshness. He showed a definite streak of Tchaikovsky-like pessimism, but was well able to build up the monumental type of large orchestral work likely to attract as a propaganda effort. Khachaturyan and Kabalevsky were among his pupils.

Prokofiev represented a very different outlook. A child prodigy who developed into a virtuoso pianist, he had a brilliant studentship at the Petersburg Conservatory, winning the Rubenstein Prize at nineteen with his First Piano Concerto. He quickly showed his anti-romantic leanings—aggressive rhythms, abrasive harmonies, parody and general musical grotesqueness —in such works as the piano *Sarcasms,* the barbaric *Scythian Suite* for orchestra (1914), and the *Buffoon* ballet for Diaghilev (1915). In 1911 he gave the first performance in Russia of Schönberg's epoch-making *Pieces for piano* (Op. 11). In 1921 while he was in the United States his satirical opera *The Love of Three Oranges* was produced in Chicago. In 1917, in complete contrast to his anti-romanticism and as an anticipation of one of Stravinsky's neo-classic devices, he deliberately evoked in modern terms the techniques and atmosphere of the eighteenth century in his *Classical Symphony,* probably the widest known of all his works.[23] While in the States (he had managed to get out of Russia in 1918) he also wrote his Third Piano Concerto, now considered to be among the best of its genre that the twentieth century has produced. Others of his works met with but little success in America. From 1923, for ten years, he based his movements on Paris, where he found greater appreciation.

It is difficult to discern in Prokofiev any continuous development. Even before he had made up his mind to return to Russia he had expressed himself dissatisfied with his early dissonant, atonal practices, and declared that he wished to cultivate " a simpler and more melodic style ". Thus he found it not particularly difficult after 1932 to conform to the aesthetic notions of the Soviet State. A great deal of his music in the mid '30's was of the incidental type, including the *Alexander Nevsky* film (very unrepresentative Prokofiev), and the ballet *Romeo and Juliet.* The latter has gained popularity in the West, but shows very little sign of his early radicalism. However, he did not escape the hierarchy's lash in either 1936 or 1948. In 1936 he showed his undoubted gift for writing children's music by producing *Peter and the Wolf* for narrator and orchestra. The charming if somewhat naïve little work has travelled the world. His compositions, through the War and beyond included much propaganda music (both choral and orchestral), together with a couple of symphonies and several piano sonatas. Much of his most imaginative work was done for the keyboard. His last ballet, *The Stone Flower* (1950), was televised in this country. An opera-buffa (1941) based on Sheridan's *The Duenna* has had some success in the West, but the more ambitious *War and Peace* seems to have been unsuccessful even in Russia. He was in his final period something of a neo-romantic, the former jagged angularities smoothed down. One of his characteristic tricks was that of modulating to extreme keys and then swinging back home again in sudden and unexpected fashion. However advanced his harmonic vocabulary was sometimes, in his larger instrumental works he tended to adhere to the classical forms. He had an abundant melodic invention, his lyricism being particularly attractive in the Second Violin Concerto (1935). His orchestral effects were often highly original and piquant. In all, he wrote seven symphonies of which the Fifth (1944) is possibly the most popular, a neo-romantic work strangely reminiscent of both Brahms and

Tchaikovsky. Of the piano concertos, the Third, dating from his *enfant terrible* period, seems likely to remain the most widely known. How he would have developed had he always been a free artist it is impossible to say, but even if the natural direction of his genius was diverted he still spoke with the imaginative voice of a major composer.

Like Prokofiev, Dmitri Shostakovich started with an enormous natural talent. When he entered Leningrad Conservatory in 1919 at the age of thirteen he so impressed Glazounov that the latter paid for the whole of his course there. He emerged as a highly trained, all-round musician, and at nineteen wrote his First Symphony, undoubtedly derivative, but so fresh and attractive that it was not only a great success at home but in Europe and America as well. It was a period in Russia (the late '20's) when the international climate had been allowed to warm a little. Shostakovich was able to hear and assimilate the music of Schönberg, Berg, Stravinsky and Křenek, together with that of Prokofiev. The result was apparent in his first Piano Sonata, strongly dissonant and in a keyboard style of dry percussiveness. His Second and Third Symphonies, with propaganda titles, fell rather flat, but he continued his polytonal and atonal methods in ballet (e.g. *The Golden Age*) and in the operas *The Nose* and the before-mentioned *Lady Macbeth of Mzensk*. The latter is very much of a *Wozzek* in both musical style and atmosphere. All these stage works were a success for a brief while, and then, as we have seen, the Kremlin hurled its thunderbolt.

To be fair to the composer, it does seem that before this time he had pondered the situation for himself and, like Prokofiev, decided to mollify his style somewhat. All the same, he expressed formal remorse, abandoned a Fourth Symphony and began a Fifth. This, like Prokofiev's identically numbered example, was just what the commissar ordered, for its plan and atmosphere was that of the "grand-opera" symphonic style of Tchaikovsky. From its first performance in 1937 it was an enormous success, and the composer was rehabilitated. It must be admitted that even if the technique was only very intermittently that of the twentieth century it was constructively a most impressive feat. He was to write better symphonies, even though these monumental works, together with numerous large-scale choral compositions, were always conditioned by their ideological aims. Successful internationally was the Seventh, a gigantic score, composed during the siege of Leningrad in 1941. He continued his taste for the monumental in the Eighth (1943), again very much of a "war" symphony. The two last of their genre are oddly different, the Ninth (1945) almost neo-classic, with touches of grotesque humour, the Tenth betraying a great deal of typical Slav melancholy, but showing that he had recovered his authentic, individual voice. However circumscribed he may have been for reasons other than musical, he yet shows himself a born composer of symphonies. One can think of the works as a Russian extension of Mahler's art. Between the last two symphonies came the 1948 castigation, which he was compelled to live down, or rather, compose down, with a particularly large and dreary choral piece.

Much of his finest work is to be found in his chamber music. Some examples are comparatively innocuous (he won a Stalin prize for a Quintet in 1940), but a Trio in E minor and a Third Quartet, during the War, as well as a Fourth and Fifth Quartet *after* 1948 are certainly full of vivid and modern-sounding " formalism ", for which somehow or other he escaped censure. Both his Violin Concerto (1955) and his 'Cello Concerto (1959), formidable works for their soloists, have met with success in the West.[24*]

Aram Khachaturyan had as one of his resources a command of his attractive Armenian folksong, of which he made skilful and highly coloured use. His Piano Concerto (1936) and his Violin Concerto (1940) have had favourable receptions in the outside world, together with a popular *Sword Dance* from one of his ballets.

Dmitri Kabalevsky, prolific in all types of composition from symphonies and operas to children's piano pieces, is known in the West for little more than his *Colas Brugnon* opera-overture, and perhaps a Second Symphony and a Second Piano Concerto. There remains a large number of lesser but clearly very competent Soviet composers who have plenty to do in providing the film music, ballets, patriotic operas and choral works, marches and songs —in general, " the music for the masses " that is always in official demand.

Although the Russian system of a strict control and direction of the arts must surely lead to the ultimate withering of all progressive creation, yet in the matter of the executive side of music the effect of strict system and discipline has been to produce a number of instrumental virtuosi of world standard. Moreover, the Soviet " people's music ", if not very modern, has, *qua* music, at least the elements of good taste and good workmanship, and affords a considerable contrast to the commercial swill that is fed to the English-speaking West under the name of " pop " music.

NOTES

1   The quotation is from *Twentieth Century Music, ed. Rollo H. Myers, p. viii* (*John Calder, London.*)

2* HMS X has a recording of this prayer-ballade.

3* HMS X has a recording of this " impression " for piano.

4   Here are Stravinsky's own words on the point, from his own *Chronicles of My Life* :
      " No matter what the subject may be, there is only one course for a beginner : he must at first accept a discipline from without, but only as a means of obtaining freedom for and strengthening himself in his personal method of expression."

5   One of the *Musical Pilgrim* series, *The Fire-Bird and Petrushka—Edwin Evans* (*O.U.P.*), discusses both these works and has an interesting analysis of their harmonic vocabularies.

6* HMS X has a recording of the *Marche Royale* from *L'Histoire du Soldat.*

7   In *In Memoriam Dylan Thomas* Stravinsky uses a succession of only five notes
    for his tone-row, and in rigid discipline derives every other note of the work
    from them. A tonal composer most of his long life for all his acerbities, Stravin-
    sky (in his eightieth year) has again turned to serialism in his latest work, *The
    Flood,* in cantata form.

8* HMS X has a recording of Strauss's *Blindenklage*.

9* HMS X has a recording of a movement from Reger's String Trio in A minor.

10 The late Sir Barry Jackson in a letter to the present writer in 1958 told the
    following story concerning the theme quoted in the text:
        "After Bernard Shaw had introduced us, Elgar and I became good friends
        and he frequently visited my house at the top of the Malvern Hills . . . One
        day there he began whistling the 'Cello Concerto melody, and, when he
        stopped, he said: 'If you hear anyone whistling that outside on the hills after
        I'm dead, don't be alarmed; it'll just be me.' "

11 Two other English composers of Elgar's generation ought perhaps to receive
    mention. Edward German (1862–1936) was once expected to prove a second
    Sullivan, and his light-opera music together with some orchestral essays in a
    more serious vein gained him a considerable popularity that now seems to have
    faded. Granville Bantock (1868–1946) had an impressive command of orchestral
    resource, but no distinctive style of his own. He wrote in many forms, with
    Omar Khayyam as his most important work for choir and orchestra, and with
    the *Hebridean Symphony* (1916) as probably his greatest accomplishment, since
    it shows a much greater constructional unity than others of his larger works.
    Both composers received knighthoods.

12* HMS X has a recording of a movement from Schönberg's String Quartet in F
    sharp minor (1907), a transitional work, which shows the composer balancing
    between an extremely chromatic yet still tonal idiom and a frank atonality.

13* HMS X has a recording of the March from Schönberg's *Serenade*. The move-
    ment is definitely atonal but the composer has not yet wholly evolved his
    dodecaphonic dogma.

14* HMS X has a recording of three songs by Berg that illustrate his harmonic
    progress from the somewhat unconventional to the near-atonal.

15* HMS X has a recording of Dallapiccola's *Goethe-Lieder* for mezzo-soprano and
    three clarinets. They show the composer being very strict in his handling of his
    tone-rows, which is not always his practice. The word-settings appear to present
    extremely difficult problems of intonation to any but the keenest-eared singer.

16* In regard to the recording of the *Ludus Tonalis* fugue in D in HMS X, it should
    be noted that Hindemith's "keys" are not major or minor, but include all the
    notes of the chromatic scale (See p. 47 of the Handbook).

17* HMS X has a recording of a song from Hindemith's cycle *Das Marienleben,*
    which well illustrates the point mentioned in the text.

18* HMS X has a recording of four of Bartók's eight *Improvisations on Hungarian
    Peasant Songs,* written for piano in 1920.

19* HMS X has recordings of three " anti-romantic " pieces by Eric Satie (*Trois
    petites pièces montées*), written for small orchestra; brief and quite effective.

20* HMS X has a recording of a Trio in A minor for strings (1937) by Roussel.

21 The Casella passage is quoted by Marc Pincherle, *op. cit., p. 184.*

22* HMS X has a recording of a movement from Milhaud's String Quartet No. 6,
    a good example of his effective use of bitonality.

23 There has been much earnest discussion as to the reason for Prokofiev's sudden swing to such a simple form of neo-classicism in this Symphony. His friend, Nicolas Nabokov, once supplied an explanation. He said that Prokofiev always composed at the piano, but decided that he would make a test of his "mental hearing" by writing a work under what might be described as "examination conditions". Says his friend: "But in order to hear the harmonies well and be sure of what he was doing, he adopted a simplified, conventional, so-called classical style! Thus he limited himself to the use of conventional chords."
This story is mentioned in Richard H. Leonard's *A History of Russian Music*, *pp. 299–300 (Jarrolds, London)*.

24° HMS X has a recording of the waltz movement from Shostakovich's String Quartet No. 2 (1944), music not very far removed from the Tchaikovsky tradition, and in no danger of being accused of "formalism".

CHAPTER XIV

The Twentieth Century II

Britain

THE increasing significance of the contributions that British composers were making to international music, first noticeable around the beginning of the century, happened more or less to coincide with an activity which most of the more important musical countries had carried through long before, namely, the revival of an interest in national folk-song. Certainly the surviving folk-music which had been gathered towards the end of the nineteenth century (the Folk-Song Society came into official being in 1898) had none of the widespread vitality of existence shown by, say that of nineteenth century Russia, to which Glinka and the new national school owed so much. But at least it made clear to British composers, long subservient to German and Italian melodic styles, that genuine native tunes evolved from the cadences of our own language had a distinctive flavour of their own. As a result, in the first decade of the century there appeared a multitude of "arrangements", rhapsodies, fantasies, suites and the like, founded on various rediscovered folk-melodies, which, attractive though the material might be, amounted in most cases to art-music of no particular significance. We have noted before that folk-song, however beautiful, cannot have any real international impact unless it can capture the imagination of a great composer (a Chopin or a Mussorgsky or a Bartók), who can assimilate its characteristics and make them part of his own utterances.

The first and possibly the only British composer at international level successfully to achieve this assimilation was the Gloucester-born Ralph Vaughan Williams (1872–1959). Fortunately for the cause of music private means enabled him throughout a long life to devote all the time he desired to deeply-pondered and unhurried composition. In the '90's there were years of studentship at the Royal College of Music with Parry and Stanford; at Trinity College, Cambridge (where he later took a Doctor's degree); and then back at the R.C.M. again. For a while he was at Berlin with Max Bruch,[1] and he even sought instruction (in vain) from Elgar. He was in fact in this period a musical pilgrim in search of a style, or rather the inspiration for a style. In 1905 he found the first gleam, not in London, Cambridge or Berlin, but in East Anglia, where, like Cecil Sharp and others in different parts of the country he had been busily engaged in seeking out tunes that were dangerously near falling into oblivion.

The direct result of these explorations were some *Norfolk Rhapsodies,* and a (later revised) *Symphonic Impression (" In the Fen Country ")*. In the *Rhapsodies* he made use of some of the best of his treasure-trove. In the *Impression* the thematic material was his own, but the source of its inspiration unmistakable. There was developing a personal melodic style of pentatonic and modal flavour which was at once unique and yet of English heritage. In the next few years came much song and part-song writing and then the first important works (for the Leeds Festival), settings of Whitman's poetry in the cantata *Towards an Unknown Region* and the hybrid *Sea Symphony.* For his old University he wrote the genial music for Aristophane's *Wasps* in a style manifestly his own and nobody else's. But the real landmark was the *Fantasia on a Theme by Tallis* for strings (1910) in which he can be said truly to have found himself. In it was made manifest the other abiding influence upon the shaping of his art, that of Tudor polyphony, again inherited from an English past. The language of folk-song had become his own language; the modal counterpoint of the Renaissance motet was absorbed in the same way, together with even more distant borrowings of chains of organum fifths and fourths; and all was moulded into a modern and personal idiom. The polyphonic strands were often enough unsparing of vertical clashes; pentatonic and modal themes associated with strident discords and abrupt modulations. Even the characteristic " false relation " device of Tudor part-writing was taken over, and used in effective modern fashion.

Throughout his career Vaughan Williams was preoccupied with symphonic form. Indeed, his problems were deeper than most composers who attempted to keep to the traditional pattern of the symphony, since the normal classical " conflict " procedures were not easily reconciled with a material derived from an age long antedating sonata form. Yet his first wholly orchestral essay in such a reconciliation resulted in a great and original work, now of international acceptance. *A London Symphony* (1914 —rev. 1920) was in late-romantic vein. For all the composer's claims to subjective intentions, he yet introduced, most felicitously, Westminster chimes, jingling cab-bells, " sweet lavender " and " mouth-organ " chords. Structurally, the blend of old and new was achieved in masterly fashion. " Old and new " can in fact be illustrated very economically by a brief quotation from the slow movement. The theme is pure modality, but the composer chose to make an abrupt switch of tonal centres. See Ex. 84, overleaf.

There are nine symphonies in all, the last two written when he was an octogenarian. In most the classical framework was preserved, with fugue and passacaglia also employed; he was a past master of all the traditional contrapuntal forms. Detailed note of these works cannot be given here, but there can be mentioned the Third in pastoral vein; the angry Fourth in F minor (1935)—the composer's harshest and most uncompromising, the date

2E

Ex: 84

explaining the mood; the D major Fifth, ten years later, the mellowest of them all, with its wonderful " alleluia " finale; and the Sixth, having a very different conclusion—an epilogue comprising some of the most original and *loneliest* sounds ever written.

One of his finest works, *Job, a masque for dancing,* was inspired by Blake's illustrations to the Book of Job. The several episodes gave full scope to every aspect of the composer's technique in his representation of the struggle between the forces of good and evil. The various themes evoke atmospheres that range from the purest serenity to the harshest of discordant stridence, yet it will be found that they are all subtly related, for the battle was for one man's soul.

The origins of Vaughan Williams' style ensured that his religious music would have the flavour of tradition. In any case his was a truly religious nature. The " Pilgrim's Progress " of Bunyan seems to have had a deep fascination for him. There are two long-pondered stage works founded on its episodes, and its atmosphere, as the composer interpreted it, permeates the Fifth Symphony. It was for him the spirit of Christian, with the harsh intolerance of Puritanism purged away.

Besides specific church works, which include a double-chorus *Mass* of Tallis inspiration, many of his choral works with orchestra were religious in intent and made use of biblical texts (e.g. *Flos Campi, Sancta Civitas, Dona nobis pacem*).

His excursions into opera were less successful. Probably his best appreciated stage-work is *Hugh the Drover* in tuneful ballad style, with a celebrated fisticuffs episode. For the Falstaffian *Sir John in Love* he used as interlude music his version of the Tudor folk-song *Greensleeves,* which, in various arrangements and as a recording, must have proved his " bestseller ".

Adequate justice cannot be done here to his devoted work for music in general, not only as a hymnal editor, but in a thousand other kindly ways. But above all he must be remembered as the man who revived true national music, expressed in twentieth century idiom, and with Elgar, put Britain on the European musical map once more.

Friend of Vaughan Williams, fellow explorer of folk tunes, and in a different way just as original in outlook was Gustav Holst (1874–1934). His stock was remotely Swedish and for four generations musical. He composed, played the village organ and conducted choral societies from an early age, and at nineteen came under Stanford at the Royal College. Neuritis drove him from the keyboard to the trombone, but gave him practical experience with first-class orchestras. Eventually he turned to teaching, and had years of association with St. Paul's Girls' School and Morley College. The *St. Paul's Suite for Strings,* with its " Dargason "-" Greensleves " finale is one of his best known minor works. He paid homage to folk-tune in his early *Somerset Rhapsody,* and in various songs and part-songs. This element tended to fade, but his music was often tinged by modal and organum influences, plain-song, free-rhythm effects and the use of *ostinato*—revivals in terms of modern technique indeed to be found in the music of Stravinsky, which he strongly admired. In much of his early composition he was pre-occupied with Sanscrit literature, producing some Rig-Veda *Choral Hymns* and the chamber opera *Savitra* (1908). But just before the 1914 War he had started on a work that eventually gave him international fame, the orches-tral suite, *The Planets.* He had always been interested in astrology, and in this series of wonderfully scored tone-poems each of the " seven " was given astrological rather than classical interpretation. Performances after the War caused its fame to spread abroad, especially to the U.S.A., where in succeeding years both Holst and his music were given warm welcomes. *The Hymn of Jesus,* for chorus and orchestra, first performed in 1920, con-firmed his reputation, although its harmonic acerbities startled some people. Like Vaughan Williams, he was less fortunate with his stage works. *The Perfect Fool* lives in its ballet music, the Falstaffian *At the Boar's Head* hardly at all.

His *Choral Symphony* (1924), like Vaughan Williams' *Sea Symphony,* was an attempt to fit vocal settings into all four movements of a symphonic framework. Holst chose poems of Keats for his material, but the work has never met with wide favour. The integrity of Vaughan Williams compelled him to confess " a cold enthusiasm " for it. An orchestral impression, *Egdon Heath* (founded on Hardy's description in his *Return of the Native* of a landscape of " swarthy monotony ") received even less general appreciation. Yet Holst himself declared that they were his two best works. Time must be the arbiter. Certainly he seems to have lacked the ability of Vaughan Williams to mould an individual language strongly tinged with modality into a truly progressive symphonic style. Yet a late *Scherzo* (1933) intended for another symphony is a finely shaped piece of orchestral writing. He was basically a tonal composer, for his experiments with bitonality were never extreme. In 1929 he wrote a two-violin *Concerto* for the sisters d'Aranyi, the solo parts supposedly in two different keys, but the result seems in no way startling. Another instrumental work, *A Fugal Concerto,* for flute, oboe, and strings (1923) continues in occasional performance. Whatever the ulti-mate assessment of his work may be it undoubtedly reinforced the impres-sion made abroad by Vaughan Williams, that British music was now speak-ing in terms of an assured independence.

There came some fine composers, not very much younger, whose indivi-duality needed little further aid from either folk-song or quasi-medieval

techniques. Among them was Frank Bridge (1879–1941), a writer of distinguished chamber music and a gifted teacher, and Arnold Bax (1883–
1953), who also gained an international reputation. Bax himself stated his
outlook very plainly: "A brazen romantic—by which I mean that my
music is the expression of emotional states". With all-round intellectual
gifts, he received a thorough musical training and was an exceptional pianist
and score-reader. His literary leanings caused him to identify himself with
the poetry of Yeats and the "Celtic revival" in general. Whatever effects
Wagner, Strauss and an experience in Russia of the new national music
(1910) had on him, he became a thoroughly individual composer, with great
lyrical gifts, a complicated chromatic style, and a mastery both of polyphony
and the large-scale romantic orchestra. Many of his compositions were
immediately successful and internationally played. Among them were the
tone-poems, *The Garden of Fand* and *Tintagel,* and from 1922 onward a
series of symphonies, seven in all. In them, in spite of a very great elaboration of texture, incessant chromaticism and very free modulation, a sense of
tonality is seldom absent. His gifts were rhapsodical rather than structural.
For that reason, and also perhaps because in him we have another example
of a gifted composer born too late, his frankly romantic symphonic music
has suffered comparative eclipse. He wrote much fine chamber music and
many songs. A large-scale carol for unaccompanied double-chorus, *Mater
ora Filium,* a work of great beauty, seems likely to endure. He was knighted
in 1937 and became Master of the King's Musick in 1942.

Bax was always well enough off to be free of musical routine. His friend
and fellow-composer John Ireland (1879–1962) was left orphaned in his
youth. Scholarships and small earnings kept him at the Royal Academy with
Stanford for some years, but afterwards composition had to be shared with
teaching and organ playing. His was an independent spirit. Though admiring the music of Ravel and Stravinsky, like Bax he had no interest "in
any modernist 'isms or factions". His classic-romantic inclinations developed
an entirely individual style—"diatonic with a tang", let us say, and with
a modal flavour that suggested the world of plainchant rather than folk-
song, but one capable of reaching out to near atonality if the stresses
demanded it. He had a predilection for the uncanny stories of Arthur
Machen, and a consequent interest in ancient pagan beliefs and ceremonies,
as his two orchestral works *The Forgotten Rite* and the *Mai-dun* Rhapsody (Maiden Castle—the Dorset earthwork) bear witness. Another of his
better known scores is a genial picture of quite another world, *A London
Overture* (1936). But the piano seems to have been his greatest love, whether
with orchestra, solo instrument or voice. There is the original and still
frequently performed Concerto (1930), in some ways classic, in some ways
Lisztian in its construction, but wholly Ireland. The *Legend* for piano and
orchestra is another fine work, with spectral moments that justify its dedication to Machen. The Sonata (1920) for solo piano is a high achievement,
a complex and important composition. Better known to the ordinary music-
lover will be the less ambitious tone-pictures e.g. *The Island Spell, London
Pieces, Amberley Wild Brooks.* It was with chamber music that he first

gained some attention; the Violin Sonata in A minor (1917), and the remarkable Violoncello Sonata (1933) were milestones in his maturity. He wrote over eighty songs, maintaining a high standard in choice of texts, and in some of them giving rein to his more advanced harmonic imagination.

In every age there are composers who start with high promise and then fail, sometimes inexplicably, to make the grade. That (Sir) Donald Tovey gained no wide fame as a creative artist is more than compensated for by the fact that the art of music has gained much enrichment from the shrewd scholarship of his writings. However, there is a 'cello concerto which fascinated Casals, and which has kept alive. Josef Holbrooke (b. 1878) also has a long list of works to his name, including an ambitious Celtic opera trilogy, *The Children of Don*, but his music seems to have faded into obscurity. Less explicable, or so it seems to the present writer, is the neglect of the refined art of Cyril Scott (b. 1879) whose piano pieces and songs were, decades ago, much cultivated in this country, but whose larger works (he has written in all genres) remain neglected in his native land, though having some well-deserved reputation in Germany and Austria.

E. J. Moeran (1874–1950) was the last English composer of distinction to be affected to any extent by the strains of folk-song, in his case East Anglian and Irish. A pupil of John Ireland, he made his reputation with his songs, some well-written chamber music, including a very individual quartet, a successful Irish-flavoured Violin Concerto, a less successful Symphony, and two well-received late works, a Sinfonietta (1944) and an orchestral Serenade (1948).

With the exception of Matyas Seiber all the British composers now to be considered are alive and productive, the senior being the veteran Sir Arthur Bliss (b. 1891), Master of the Queen's Musick. Like some of the leading composers on the Continent he began his creative career in vigorous, uncompromising anti-romantic style, and subsequently modified its asperities a great deal. Stravinsky and the younger school of French rebels clearly influenced his early music. This included *Rout,* for voice and chamber orchestra of solo instruments (and two other similar works—1919); *Conversations* for five solo instruments (1920);[2*] and *A Colour Symphony,* with " Purple ", " Red ", " Blue " and " Green " movements of heraldic connotations (1922, revised 1932). Later in the '20's there came a change of style, towards a more classical mood and a greater conciseness. It resulted in three notable works, the Oboe Quintet (1927), the Clarinet Quintet (1931) and the Sonata for Viola and Piano (1932), the last for Lionel Tertis, that great soloist whose playing inspired other fine viola compositions of the period. Like Vaughan Williams and Holst, Bliss tried his hand at a " choral " symphony —*Morning Heroes*: for orator, chorus and orchestra (1930). One of his best works is *Music for Strings* (1935), like Elgar's essay a revival in modern terms of the concerto grosso. For all his harmonic explorations he has always been a tonal composer, and in his later music has contrived to keep his individuality and at the same time create an atmosphere of immediate attractiveness that can be widely appreciated. This is true of the two successful ballets, *Checkmate* and *The Miracle of the Gorbals.* The reception of his first opera, *The Olympians* (1949) was not encouraging, but more will surely be heard of the televised *Tobias and the Angel* of 1960.

To the same generation belongs Arthur Benjamin, Australian-born (1893), the composer of much pleasant and competent, if not particularly "advanced" music; also Gordon Jacob (b. 1895), a specialist in the art of instrumentation, whose *Orchestral Technique* is a well-known textbook. He has written in most forms, and mainly in the astringent neo-classic manner of the 1920's, but his Second Symphony (1944) and *Bournemouth Suite* (1949) show more relaxed moods.[3]

Alan Bush (b. 1900) received instruction from John Ireland in composition and Moiseivich and Schnabel in piano. His early work soon gained him recognition, and he became known on the Continent, particularly for his "Dialectic" String Quartet. In 1938 his first Piano Concerto was performed at a B.B.C. concert, with the composer as soloist. In 1942 was heard his Symphony in C major. Up to the beginning of the second world war Bush had composed somewhat in the advanced Central European style of the period, practising an individual technique which had something in common with Schönberg but which was his own brand of melodic serialism. After the war it was clear that a gradual and deliberate simplification of style had taken place, a parallel to the principles that were eventually made obligatory for Soviet composers, to the effect that music must be such as could be appreciated by "the people". From this time on it was apparent that Bush's creative work was being very much intruded upon by his Marxist philosophy and his desire to propagate it. Two operas, *Wat Tyler,* which won an Arts Council prize (1950), and *Men of Blackmore* (1956) had their first performances in Eastern Germany. The Violin Concerto (1948) is held to be an excellent work, while among his chamber compositions the *Three Concert Studies* for piano trio (1947) are thought to be particularly skilful and original in style.

A number of very individual composers, all born in the century, continued to resist Continental trends and to find native inspiration. Gerald Finzi (b. 1901), whose production has been mainly of vocal music, is among the many behind whose word-settings can be perceived the spirit of Purcell. Late in development, but now an important figure in British music, is Edmund Rubbra (b. 1901). Trained by Holst and R. O. Morris and influenced by Vaughan Williams, he developed his characteristic vocal techniques through his absorption of English music of the sixteenth and seventeenth centuries. Even though he attracted attention by a number of striking vocal works, solo and choral, it was not until 1936 that his first Symphony was written, and a new phase begun. In turning to larger instrumental forms he faced a problem that has been noted before, that of a composer who has to reconcile lyrical and polyphonic methods with the principles of symphonic construction. His solution, not through the dramatic clash of contrasting subjects, but rather by the evolution and transfiguration of melodic phrases, took time to shape into a wholly convincing "monistic" style, but his Fifth Symphony (1948) has been generally accepted as an eminently satisfactory work, founded on his own original methods of "melodic generation". Other important instrumental compositions employing the same principles are the *Sinfonia concertante* for piano and orchestra (1934), and the *Soliloquy* for 'cello and small orchestra (1946). Rubbra's is again an idiom that can create fine music without renouncing tonal principles.[4*]

The name of William Walton (b. 1902) is likely to remain of permanent eminence in the records of British music. Though his early promise had been noted and encouraged by several well-known musicians (he won a Carnegie award at seventeen) he is an example of a composer very largely self-taught. He had a sudden leap to fame in 1922 with, in conjunction with the verse of Edith Sitwell, his highly original *Façade* music, cunningly scored for chamber orchestra. A similar instrumental mastery on a full symphonic scale was shown in the Overture *Portsmouth Point*. In 1929 came the triumphant success of the Viola Concerto, with no less a person than Hindemith as soloist. The style of the work, with its harmonic asperities and ambiguous tonalities, was fully modern, and Walton began to be called the "English Hindemith". The heaviest impact of all (in 1931) was the oratorio *Belshazzar's Feast*, for soloist, chorus, orchestra and two brass bands, one of the most sensationally dramatic of concert-room scores of the century. A long-awaited Symphony followed in 1934, the missing finale added in the next year. For all his original inventiveness Walton was a slow worker. Then came the beginnings of a change that has been noted in a number of twentieth century composers who have worked off their youthful exuberance in terms of near atonality. The Violin Concerto (1939), written to order for Jascha Heifetz, was quite frankly a romantic work, a great deal more tonal than much of the composer's previous music. The solo part, like Elgar's, is an extreme test for the best of virtuosi.

In company with most leading English composers of the period Walton made his contributions to film music. In his case concession to the appreciations of a wide public were matched with high musical qualities in the *Henry V* and *Hamlet* scores. The mellowing of the composer's style is noticeable also in his later serious works, which include a String Quartet in A minor, a large-scale *Festival Te Deum* for the Coronation of Queen Elizabeth II, a richly lyrical opera, *Troilus and Cressida*, a Second Symphony and (1956) a 'Cello Concerto. The composer was knighted in 1951.

Lennox Berkeley (b. 1903) was one of the several Anglo-Saxon musicians to seek instruction in Paris from the well-known teacher Nadia Boulanger. The influence of Stravinsky and Poulenc was obvious in his early works, but a gradual emancipation towards an independent and more lyrical style took place. He has written some most effective piano music, but his best works are probably his vocal ones, particularly the *Stabat Mater* for six solo voices and twelve instruments (1946) where echoes of a native choral tradition are apparent. He produced an opera, *Nelson,* in 1953.

Alan Rawsthorne (b. 1905) was another late starter, but made a swift reputation for originality in his early works. These included the *Symphonic Studies,* which were performed at the Warsaw Festival of 1939. For all his foreign reputation the composer belongs to no " school ", and his idiom is strikingly individual and basically instrumental (he has written but little vocal music). His harmony, apparently atonal, is notwithstanding never gratingly dissonant, and often appears to be on the edge of establishing key-definition. Normally his textures are comparatively thin and clear of any deep complexities. His busy, pattern-making style causes the variation form to be his most successful mode of expression. The straightforward and eloquent inventiveness of his music has given it, in spite of the unusual tang of its vocabulary, a considerable public appreciation. He has written two piano concertos, concertos respectively for clarinet, oboe and violin (the last betraying moments of quite " romantic " emotion), and two symphonies (1950 and '59).[5*]

Constant Lambert (1905–51), who studied with Vaughan Williams, might have had an even more distinguished career as a composer had he not chosen in the early '30's to devote much of his attention to concert conducting and to directing ballet. However, as a creator he early gained the attention of Diaghilev, for whom he wrote a short ballet, *Romeo and Juliet*. At intervals there were other examples, of which *Horoscope* (1937) represents him at his best in that sphere. His most widely known work is probably *The Rio Grande,* for chorus, piano and orchestra, a setting of a poem by Sacheverell Sitwell (1927). In it, in the Piano Sonata (1929) and in the Concerto for Piano and Nine Solo Instruments (1931) can be heard the jazz rhythms that the composer sometimes favoured. His *Music for Orchestra* (1927) was his only important symphonic work. Some of his finest music is to be found in his " Masque " for baritone, chorus and orchestra, *Summer's Last Will and Testament* (1935), based on the text of the Elizabethan poet, Thomas Nashe. Throughout his career Lambert wrote musical criticism, the finest example his trenchant book, *Music Ho!* (1934). Its subtitle was *A study of music in decline.*

Michael Tippett (1905) is one of the most serious and intellectual of composers, but the intricacies of his thinking have sometimes stood in the way of a full appreciation of some of his scores. Trained at the Royal College, his approach to instrumental music has seemed to be through the polyphony of the madrigal and through song and poetry, especially the poetry of Gerard Manley Hopkins. His first significant work was the *Concerto for double string orchestra* (1939). His reputation increased with the production of the oratorio *A Child of Our Time* (1941) in which he made use of negro spirituals after the manner of Bach chorales. His two Symphonies (1945 and '58) are characteristically of high intellectual content and considerable complexity. The same technical challenges are found in the now well-known song-cycle, *Boyhood's End.* Other instrumental works include a Piano Sonata, a Piano Concerto and *Variations on a Theme of Corelli for Strings.* His first opera, *The Midsummer Marriage* (1952) has not yet proved a success. Another, *King Priam* (1962), has been more fortunate.[6]

Benjamin Frankel (b. 1906) is exceptional in having gained considerable notice as a writer of very competent light music, including a great deal for films, before achieving a reputation as a " serious " composer. His best works to date seem to be his Violin Concerto (1950) and a Fourth String Quartet.

The remarkable Hungarian musician Matyas Seiber (1905–60) came to this country in 1935 and was in due course naturalised. He had been trained by Kodály, had known something of Bartók's outlook, had mastered the Viennese twelve-note technique and had explored historically from plainchant and Renaissance polyphony to jazz. Possessing a superb craftsmanship, he gained considerable notice in London musical circles both as a creative artist and as a teacher of composition. His natural eclecticism enabled him to absorb into his style the most diverse elements, from fifteenth century counterpoint to serialism. His cantata *Ulysses* (1947), a setting of some of James Joyce's extraordinary prose, is considered outstanding, together with some of his chamber-music, particularly the Third Quartet.

Of two notable woman musicians, Elizabeth Lutyens (b. 1906) has shared with Humphrey Searle a pioneer reputation for twelve-note composition in this country. Her works, mainly in chamber-music form, are known internationally. A Viola Concerto (1947) was favourably received. Similarly stark and concise is the music of Elizabeth Maconchy (b. 1907), also mainly in chamber form but not committed to serial technique.[7] In the case of Humphrey Searle (b. 1915), the present writer has felt compelled to waive his self-imposed " 1914 " limit to mention his Piano Sonata (1951) and Symphony (1953), both in one movement. In them the composer has displayed in successful fashion a technique that has assimilated the virtues of both Webern and Liszt.

The English composer best known abroad is undoubtedly Benjamin Britten (b. 1913). With all-round musical gifts and fortunate in his early training he possesses the broad outlook of the baroque *Kapellmeister,* ready to compose, direct, accompany or play a concerto keyboard part as the occasion demands. After instruction from Frank Bridge, and from John Ireland at the R.C.M. he dared to settle to make a living by composition alone, this work including film music, and incidental music for the B.B.C. His *Variations on a Theme of Frank Bridge* for strings was performed at the Salzburg Festival in 1937. After the interruption of the War he gained instant fame through his opera *Peter Grimes,* which is now known to all the leading opera-houses of Europe and the Americas. For all his production of fine instrumental music and his command of colourful orchestration, his imagination is at its most vivid when it is concerned with the setting of words. A recent (1962) vocal and orchestral work of large dimensions, *War Requiem,* may well prove Britten's greatest creation to date. In it, his settings of the ancient Latin Requiem Mass movements, for solo and chorus, are given full orchestral accompaniment, and are interspersed with poems by Wilfred Owen (killed in the first World War), the settings of which are accompanied by a chamber orchestra of solo instruments. A " distant " choir of boys' voices is also employed, with organ accompaniment. Early performances of the work have created a deep impression.

Several of the stage-works that succeeded *Peter Grimes—The Rape of Lucretia* (1946), *Albert Herring* (1947) and *The Turn of the Screw* (1954), were designed for a modest number of singers and a small orchestral ensemble—chamber-opera in fact. These attained wide appreciation, especially the macabre *Turn of the Screw*. Two full-scale, Covent Garden works, *Billy Budd* (1951) and *Gloriana* (1953) have made less impression. 1960 saw the first production of what seems to be proving a successful opera, a setting of *Midsummer Night's Dream*.

Although Britten has written some large-scale choral compositions, such as the *Spring Symphony* for solo, chorus and orchestra (the movements made up of settings of poems by a range of famous writers), some of the very best of his music is to be found in his smaller vocal works—*Les Illuminations* (settings of poems of Rimbaud), *Serenade* (miscellaneous poems), for tenor, horn and strings, and the voice and piano settings of sonnets by Michelangelo and Donne. Among his many gifts is his knack of writing for children's voices, always without condescension, yet effectively. In a number of his choral works use is made of choirs of boys; also there is that charming and original entertainment, " *Let's make an Opera* ". He seems less concerned with purely instrumental music, but the powerful String Quartet No. 2 and the world-famous *The Young Person's Guide to the Orchestra* stand out among his achievements.

He can be accused of no " 'isms ", for he owes allegiance to no system, and seems to create spontaneously. His harmonic vocabulary is modern, but unmistakable, and the interested observer will note the very novel effects that he sometimes achieves by the use of straightforward common chords—but in his own original contexts. Purcell has always been a guiding influence, and he has dealt much in traditional English song.

A composer who has come forward since the War as possessing a distinctive musical personality is Wilfrid Mellers (b. 1914), already well known as a musicologist. He has written a large amount of choral and solo-voice music, together with a truly dramatic opera, *The Tragical History of Christopher Marlowe* (1952). There are orchestral and chamber-music works, including a recent and unusual essay, *Cantilena e Ciacona* for unaccompanied violin (1962).

America—The United States

Music in the United States of the twentieth century reveals a very different scene from the one previously considered, when in the nineteenth century German influence constituted almost a monopoly, and American composers wrote works in the approved Leipzig-derived style. Yet in seeking signs of the growth of a musical independence one meets at a remarkably early date an extreme example indeed in the New England composer Charles Ives (1874–1954). Ives, though studying with Horatio Parker, composed only in his spare time from being an insurance partner; but finally discouraged, gave up creative work in the early '20's. In a provincial world of tough farmers and owners of small businesses with few cultural sympathies, he wrote music that reflected the everyday life around him, even if it was the out-of-tune singing at camp-meeting and chapel, or four different bands performing at once in the corners of the town square. Yet at the same time he held strong philosophical and religious views, which were also reflected in his compositions. As he saw it, art and everyday life (the life around him) must be indivisible in the struggle to reach out to a new and better world. With no musical inhibitions whatsoever he wrote, and published at his own expense, music of increasingly strange complexity, the harmonies atonal, seemingly chaotic; asymmetric rhythms and experimental techniques of various kinds. Actually, in his own fashion he anticipated many of the more advanced modern tendencies in Europe. It was long after he had given up composition that he first saw any scores of Stravinsky, Schönberg, Bartók or Hindemith, whose techniques he had in some way foreshadowed, even in his use of the tone-row. He was regarded by his contemporaries as nothing more than an eccentric, but in his later life there came some realisation of, at least, his originality of vision. In his very last year he heard for the first time a symphony that he had written in 1902. Originality does not of course imply high achievement, and a considerable proportion of his work is clearly experimental and even banal, but it is very apparent that he possessed an extremely acute aural imagination, and his fearless independence of mind has served as a beacon to the new school of native composers. Although he wrote four symphonies his most important work is probably the large-scale "Concord" Piano Sonata, with poetic and philosophical quotations from Emerson, Hawthorne and Thoreau; its movements, various aspects of the strife between two violently contrasted motives ("lyric" and "epic") and in the end their reconciliation.

In the '20's Carl Ruggles and Henry Cowell followed Ives' lead in unorthodox practice, and even outdid him in harmonic stridency. But a more significant generation of composers was now growing up, of all-round training. These included Walter Piston (b. 1894), Roger Sessions (1896), Virgil Thomson (1896), Howard Hanson (1896), Roy Harris (1898), Aaron Copland (1900), Elliot Carter (1908), Samuel Barber (1910) and William Schuman (1910). Of these, Piston, Thomas, Harris, Copland and Carter sought in their younger days to widen their outlook by gaining some of their training in Paris with the well-known composition teacher Nadia Boulanger.[8]

Piston, until recently Professor of Music at Harvard, exercises an important influence both as a composer and teacher. A neo-classicist, his output has been mainly instrumental and includes several symphonies. He is a master of counterpoint and logical structure, with his own brand of astringent harmonic vocabulary.

Sessions, Professor of Music at the University of California, is another whose influence as a teacher has been wide. Part of his training was received from Ernest Bloch, and he spent several years (1925–33) in Europe. His works, mostly instrumental, are few, but his Symphony No. 2, some of his chamber pieces, as well as the "Theocritus" cantata and the "Montezuma" opera, have become known internationally.

Virgil Thomson, widely known as music critic as well as composer of a formidable list of works of every type from opera to songs, had not only a student acquaintance with Paris but a much longer stay there (1925–32). It was then that he became friendly with some of the "Six", and with Eric Satie and Gertrude Stein. His music, in its aspects of wit and parody, reflects something of French sophistication. One of his best known works is the opera *Four Saints in Three Acts,* its libretto by Gertrude Stein. His mature works in the larger forms seem basically diatonic, and shaped to classical structures, though he seems to use chamber-music as an opportunity for experiments in chromaticism.

Hanson, of Swedish descent, by contrast to most of his contemporaries, is uncompromisingly " romantic " in outlook. His First Symphony (" Nordic ") and Second Symphony (" Romantic ") make clear his leanings. There are astringencies in his music that speak of affinities with the Danish Carl Neilsen. He has an impressive list of works covering most genres.

Roy Harris, born in " settler " society, continued as a young farmer until the first World War. He had very little instruction in music until he was twenty-five, and then with great concentration proceeded to make up for lost time. One of the travelling scholarships which abound in fortunate U.S.A. sent him to Paris for four years, but he returned with his innate American-ism unshaken by Gallic influences, for all his technical gains. In his early thirties he made swift progress to the forefront of American serious compo-sition. He has made much use of his country's traditional song-material (one of his popular works is the overture, *Johnny Come Marching Home.*) But for all his nationalism he is deeply studied in his art, basically tonal in spite of a few twelve-note experiments, and with a predilection for the old contrapuntal forms and for modal writing. His output, both in choral and instrumental works, is surprisingly large, and to judge by " national polls " he is one of the most popular of serious composers in the States. Like Ives he is intent on attempting to create a true " American " music. An extract from a 1943 writing of his concerning one of his symphonies will bear repetition :

> " I hoped to express qualities of our people which our popular dance music, because of its very nature, cannot reveal. Our people are more than pleasure loving. We also have qualities of heroic strength, determina-tion, will to struggle, faith in our destiny . . ."

Less single-minded is Aaron Copland. He received a sound early training in both keyboard and composition before spending several years in Paris (until 1924). Part of the time he studied with Nadia Boulanger, as a United States composer of the period almost inevitably did. He was thus equipped with all the clashing French " 'isms " of the early '20's, but in the struggles of his first professional years he toyed with an influence that had impinged on even the music of Stravinsky, Milhaud and Ravel, that of American jazz. The period produced the Dance Symphony (1925) and the Piano Con-certo (1927). He then proceeded to establish more firmly his own indivi-dual style, or rather, styles; one of an advanced modernism having some affinities with the later music of Stravinsky, with pounding rhythms and strong dissonances, the other apparent in works such as the ballets *Billy the Kid* (1938) and *Appalachian Spring* (1944), which uses American song-material and is a great deal more genial, as also is his radio and film music.

This dichotomy has continued—an apparent obligation to remain in the forefront of " progress ", together with his own proclaimed desire to follow the path of Hindemith and write *Gebrauchmusik,* in an effort to bring together the modern composer and the man-in-the-street.[8]* In his later " serious " works a certain compromise, some softening of acerbities, seems apparent. Most notable among his compositions are thought to be the piano Variations (1930), the Sonata (1941) and the Fantasy (1957), together with the Short Symphony (1933), the Piano Quartet (1950) and the Piano Concerto. The Third Symphony (1946) also made a wide impression. Copland has also a considerable reputation as conductor, lecturer and writer.

Another New York composer, Elliott Carter, has been gaining a growing international reputation. A pupil of Piston and later, Paris-trained, he has developed a controlled *avant-garde* style that is quite his own. There was a 1962 performance (and broadcast) in this country of his Double Concerto for harpsichord and piano with two chamber orchestras.

Samuel Barber shares with Aaron Copland the reputation of being, probably, the best known American composer in European capital cities. He received a very complete early training, with emphasis on contrapuntal skill, and even some instruction as a singer. In his early career a lyrical and romantic art emerged, made apparent to Europe through his well-known *Adagio for Strings* (1936). In 1937 his Symphony in one movement was the first American work to be played at the Salzburg Festival. But his development was towards a sterner idiom with something of a Stravinsky atmosphere. He had neither time for homespun " Americanism " nor jazz. His mature personal style was first made manifest in the Violin Concerto (1940). The *Capricorn Concerto* (1944) for flute, oboe, trumpet and strings (in something of a baroque framework), the 'Cello Concerto (1945) and the *Medea* ballet music (1946) added to his reputation. In his Piano Sonata (1951) he showed a liking for more extreme dissonances and chromaticisms.

William Schuman is nowadays fast establishing an international reputation. He actually had an early spell as a " Tin Pan Alley " composer, but developed other ambitions, won scholarships that took him eventually to Salzburg, and rapidly came to the forefront in the United States, not only as a leading composer but also as a well-known educator and organiser. He has long been President of the famous Juillard School of Music, and is also President of the Lincoln Center for the Performing Arts. Yet his list of compositions, choral, orchestral and chamber, is a formidable one. He seems to be at his most characteristic in his series of symphonies, of which No. 7 (1960), heavily scored, was given a recent broadcast performance in this country. His style, though not atonal and showing a taste for fugal and passacaglia forms, is definitely very trenchant in its harmonic vocabulary.[9]

There must always be borne in mind by the European observer, who may be inclined to dwell too much on the past, not only the enormous extent of the continent of 180 million people that is the United States, but also the enormous amount of private funds that are nowadays available for the furtherance of the cause of serious music. These support hundreds of musical institutions, aid the very many city symphony orchestras, and provide a large variety of prizes, grants, scholarships, foundations and the like which enable student-composers to complete their training under the most favourable conditions. In regard to the musicians already mentioned we have already noted how many of them benefited from such assistance. Although no further names can be considered here, there seems nowadays to be a spate of young composers all with works of major dimensions. The average European musician, reading of these in such leading United States journals as *The Musical Quarterly* may realise with perhaps some alarm that he knows little or nothing about them.

Europe stands in a far different situation in regard to what has been the U.S.A.'s most popular export—jazz, the brash attractions of which, in every country in the world, have captured the allegiance of a public not otherwise interested in music. It is usually supposed to have developed from primitive negro sources, but even though its rhythmic characteristics may have had such an origin, such features of its melody as the frequent flat seventh and pentatonic phrase are surely of international folk-tune flavour. Its somewhat circumscribed harmonic resources have even more certainly an ultimate European derivation. From hymn-tune level it has graduated nowadays into profiting by the vocabularies of (e.g.) Massenet, Delius and Debussy. The unsophisticated rhythmic abandon of the first American jazz bands in Paris after the first World War struck a sympathetic chord in the case of the composer of *The Soldier's Tale* and *The Wedding,* whose music was at the time full of the pounding ostinatos of his native Russian peasant music. Stravinsky began a use of jazz rhythm that was also practised for a while by musicians such as Hindemith, Milhaud, Honegger, Ravel, Křenek, Constant Lambert and Copland, together with others less distinguished, and it was thought that an important new influence had entered art-music. The last forty years have shown that this is not so. The rhythmic resources of jazz still remain its chief virtue, but its intellectual and emotional shortcomings have become apparent.[9]

Jazz is basically a short-breathed art, the brief communication of a single " affect ", its form almost entirely a matter of " variations on a ground "— music of the immediate moment with no feeling of development, of progress, and one, moreover, that with few exceptions cannot be studied in score. Its characteristics have been well and briefly summarised by Hugo Leichtentritt in his *Music of the Western Nations, p. 302, (Harvard University Press)* :

"It should be noted that jazz is not the achievement of one or of several composers, but rather a special method of ensemble playing that might be applied to almost any music. In fact, many classical compositions have been translated into the jargon of jazz. The notes are not meant to be played with rigorous exactitude; they serve as a general directive to the players, who decorate them with fanciful improvisations so that the same piece is never heard twice in quite the same manner. With this technique of improvised variation, the best jazz bands have obtained a high degree of efficiency. The inventiveness of talented players has also led to the discovery of many new tricks on almost every instrument."[10]

The vulgarities of jazz underwent certain refinements in the hands of George Gershwin (1898–1937), who, though at first earning a living in " Tin Pan Alley ", brought a better training in composition and a keener artistic conscience to this form of music. His *Rhapsody in Blue* represented an attempt to create some form of " symphonic jazz ". However, it is held by some that the mixture resulted in neither good Liszt nor good jazz. He tried the same experiment in opera. The result, *Porgy and Bess* (1935), proved a box-office success not only in the U.S.A. but in Europe. The only other United States composer so far to make anything of an international name in opera (apart from late-arrived immigrants) is the Italian-born but American-trained Carlo Menotti (b. 1911). Three of his stage-works, *The Medium, The Telephone* and *The Consul,* their well-constructed libretti by the composer himself, have received performances in London.

Canada

The English-born organist and composer Healey Willan (b. 1880) produced at Toronto in 1936 the first outstanding symphonic work composed on Canadian soil, his Symphony in D minor. He followed it in 1946 with *Deidre of the Sorrows,* the first full-length Canadian opera. Another prominent Canadian composer is Graham George (b. 1912).

Latin America

Something like a century has passed since movements for musical self-determination made themselves felt in such countries as Poland, Russia, Bohemia and Scandinavia. Many of the " national " composers who then emerged were able to assimilate the distinctive idioms of their particular country's traditional music, and themselves produce works worthy of being accepted internationally. A very similar process seems to have been in progress for the last few decades in the countries of Latin America. For too long these had been content to look to Europe, and especially to second-rate visiting Italian opera companies, for their musical " culture ". As for their own national resources, the main musical strain had been Spanish, with, however, some primitive Indian elements, and, in Central America and Brazil, a definite influence from negro music. Brazil, of course, has Portuguese rather than Spanish traditions.

The most progressive states so far have proved to be Brazil, Argentine, Chile and Mexico. In each case the processes seem to have been first, a generation or so of native professional musicians who sought their training in Europe, mainly in France or Germany. These, returning home, not only produced some commendable music in the larger forms, which attempted in most cases to reflect to some degree their own culture, but sought also to organise and educate. Each country mentioned above was fortunate in producing certain men of great vigour and understanding for the latter tasks. The further result was a new generation of home-trained and highly competent composers, together with musical conservatoires, symphony orchestras, and state organisations for the teaching of music in schools which compare favourably with many a European country.

Brazil's outstanding figure is undoubtedly Heitor Villa-Lobos (1887–1959), whose enormous output included works in every type. After an early career which included a great deal of bohemian travel in the remoter parts of his country, while studying at first hand Indian and other traditional music, he met at Rio both Darius Milhaud and Arthur Rubinstein the pianist. He was especially encouraged by the latter, and 1923 saw him in Paris, investigating the neo-classicism of Stravinsky, but also admiring Ravel's music. Moreover, while there he also secured some performances of his own works, the "brutalities" of which evoked both condemnation and support, but in any case caused his name to be noted in Europe. Rome and Barcelona also heard his music. Back at Rio his fame was now established as composer and conductor, and he continued his fluent creative production. Two types of composition very characteristic of him were more or less his own inventions. The *Chôros,* in "serenade" style, made artistic use of popular Brazilian music, written sometimes for solo instrument (piano or guitar), but also for various instrumental combinations up to full orchestra with "Brazilian" percussion. The orchestral suites, *Bachianas Brasilieras,* were, as the name implies, intended to combine Bach's contrapuntal style with Brazilian thematic material. Villa-Lobos overflowed with novel ideas, some less successful than others. As a composer he relied very largely on a background of colourful programme, and a great deal of his music may prove evanescent. However, he must be one of the most prolific composers who has ever lived, with over 3,000 works to his name.

But he has other claims to fame. In 1932 he was appointed General Director of Musical Education, and at once took vigorous action. One of the results was that under his supervision large numbers of music teachers were trained for the purpose of taking organised music to the national schools, with emphasis on choral singing. For this purpose he collected and arranged hundreds of Brazilian songs. His aim, he declared, was to make *everyone* Brazilian music-conscious. In many other educational ways he made powerful contributions to the national musical life.

Another prominent Brazilian composer was Oscar Fernandez (1887–1948), whose neo-romantic music has also become known outside Latin America. Another name to be mentioned is that of Carmargo Guarnieri (b. 1907).

In Argentina the father-figure of national music is Alberto Williams (1862–1952), of mixed English and Basque descent. Sent to Paris by the government in 1882 he spent seven years there, being trained in composition by César Franck. Back at Buenos Aires he soon abandoned a European classical style in favour of a skilful and individual use of the wealth of national folk-music, originating mostly among the Gauchos, that was available. Among his works are nine symphonies, the last dating from 1939, which can be considered truly "Argentinian" in their characteristic melodies and rhythms. As founder and director of the Conservatorio de Buenos Aires, and as teacher and conductor, he wielded a unique influence. He was poet and philosopher as well as musician. He wrote many songs; without exception it was his own poetry which he set. A prominent composer in Argentina today is Juan Jose Castro (1895), whose opera, *Prosperina*, won the Verdi prize offered by the Scala Theatre of Milan in 1951. Of growing fame is Alberto Ginastera (b. 1916).

Chile's sudden musical advance has been almost altogether due to the initial driving force of one man, Domingo Santa Cruz (b. 1899), although Pedro Allende (b. 1885) had already had some European successes, a 'cello concerto of his being played by Casals and praised by Debussy. Santa Cruz was Spanish trained, and after the first World War set to work with fiery energy to revolutionise all things musical in Chile—a Bach Society started, the Conservatorio re-formed, and in many other ways conditions created for sound musical training at every level. He has produced much music of his own in the neo-classical manner. The world-famous pianist Claudio Arrau (1903) was Chilean born.

Mexico has had a long history of devotion to Italian opera, which had been introduced by the famous singer Manuel Garcia in 1827. The move towards a national school began with Manuel Ponce (1882–1948) who had studied in Germany and Italy, and later with Dukas in Paris. Ponce was a collector of Mexican folk-songs, and though the influence of impressionism can be heard in his works, so can the scales and rhythms of Indian music. He was the teacher of Carlos Chávez (b. 1899), who, with Indian blood in his veins, was from boyhood steeped in native song. Chávez, the greatest figure in modern Mexican music, had the experience of international travel, and spent some years in romantic and impressionistic production; but he eventually developed his own individual style of austere neo-classicism, with which he blended the primitive Mexican elements which he knew so well how to handle. His appointment in 1928 as director of the National Conservatory and conductor of the Mexican Symphony Orchestra made him the leading musical influence in Mexico. For all his nationalism his students were called on to undertake a course that ranged from medieval plainchant and Indian pentatonic music by way of Bach and Beethoven to the most modern techniques. His own works cover all the usual genres, but include some interesting experiments based on native music, and the use of Indian instruments. Also to be remembered is Silvestre Revueltas (1899–1940).

Considerations of space forbid detailed mention of the musical progress of other Central and South American countries. In many of them there is apparent an increasing organisation and much professional competence. There are those who are convinced that Latin America promises to be one of the major forces in the progress of the art.

What of the Future?

Admittedly the music of today presents a situation in many ways unique in history; heterogeneous as never before in regard to techniques, purposes and even ideals—where these last exist at all. Thanks to various methods of mass-communication such as the radio and the gramophone, music of every kind is poured forth in a profusion beyond the dreams of earlier ages.

2F

We can, Glendower-like, summon it at will : there are other times when we seek in vain to escape its unwelcome penetrations. However, let us count our blessings. Thanks to a more enlightened facet of broadcasting policy there is a channel on which music, from the remotest of mediéval past to the most eccentric of *avant-garde* experiment can frequently be heard—music, that is, for the more specialised tastes; while in the normal programmes none of the enormous number of standard works remains unperformed for long. Gone are the days when, as those of us with grey hair will remember, it took some time and trouble before a young student could say with satisfaction that he had heard, for example, all nine symphonies of Beethoven, professionally rendered in a concert hall.

Yet the attitude that takes pleasure in listening to the music of days long past is one of comparatively recent development. It must be remembered that well into the nineteenth century the word " music ", to composer and listener alike, meant what we should now designate " modern music ", that is, the music of the actual time, with perhaps some backward glances at that of the not too distant previous decades—and always excepting the very special world of church-music. For Louis XIV Lully's style and that of his imitators was the only acceptable one. Burney regarded the contemporary music of the Germany and Italy through which he travelled (together with that of Handel) as being the art that really mattered. Frederick the Great was exceptional in sparing a little time from the music of Quantz and Graun to appreciate the contrapuntal but out-moded genius of J. S. Bach. But this could not prevent the great Cantor's music from passing into temporary oblivion. Only with the Romantics, and then but slowly, were the great works of the past rehabilitated and given the same status and appreciation as the most " up-to-date " music.

Yet nowadays we are presented with the phenomenon of the position in reverse. The works of modern composers—the productions of the present and the near past—are many of them far from being received with eagerness by the average cultured musical listener of today. The compositions of, say, Stravinsky, Bartók and Hindemith are undoubtedly approached with respect, and in a proportion of cases, with understanding, but the fact remains that many musical people tend to turn nostalgically to the " romance " of the nineteenth century, with some reinforcement from the Viennese masters and from Bach, perhaps as a refuge from the stresses and discords of modern social problems, so faithfully painted in so much of contemporary music. As far as the English scene is concerned confirmation as to this state of affairs can readily be obtained from the Saturday and Sunday pages of those national newspapers that advertise forthcoming public concerts. The aim of the promoter is, naturally, to build a programme that, in these days of broadcasting, will tempt from home the largest audience of normal musical culture. This is not to say that the three great moderns mentioned above together with others of the twentieth century, from Debussy and Vaughan Williams to Britten and Shostakovich, do not receive due measure of appreciation and performance, for indeed they do. There may be some significance in the fact that all these just referred to, for all their originalities of outlook, found it possible to write a great amount of fascinating music quite clearly within the framework of the tonal system.

But what of the revolutionaries for whom tonality is dead and damned, and whose prophet is Webern? The theories and practices of Boulez, Henze, Barraqué, Nono, Berio and Stockhausen, to name but a few, seem to have passed beyond both the interest and the comprehension certainly of most ordinary music-lovers, and probably of a large number of professional musicians as well. However, enlightenment to all has recently been offered by the French writer André Hodeir, in his book, " Since Debussy " (*Secker & Warner*). It is serialism of a new severity which is to save music for humanity, and this by breaking every link with the past. While the author concedes gratitude to Schönberg for the initial invention of the twelve-note row, and for dealing " the death blow to the tonal universe " (it has taken an unconscionable time over dying), yet the great pioneer is finally condemned for having " declined into academism ", a reference no doubt to his later lapses into occasional tonality. Stravinsky's and Hindemith's neo-classicism is dismissed with contempt: Bartók noted as having suffered a " final decadence ". It appears that of that generation only Webern saw the light. A curious juxtaposition occurs when the writer refers to " the forlorn little worlds of Britten, Menotti and their kind . . ." However, this remark is immediately followed by a blinding revelation . . . (they) " simply cannot hold a candle to Barraqué's splendid, shining universe." The truth is out; together with Boulez, Barraqué is to shape the new world-music. For M. Hodeir his Piano Sonata is " as brilliant and rigorous—I say this advisedly—as the last works of Beethoven ". The ultimate expression of the author's approval, it seems, is the use of the word " rigorous ". Unfortunately for him and the *avant-garde* the creations of every one of the composers whom he dismisses with such contempt still persist in attracting large audiences by their vitality. Undoubtedly the works of Barraqué and Boulez have something to say. But is it ever to prove comprehensible to the majority of those who, with cultured tastes, seek new voices that will give them the same aesthetic satisfaction as the music which still chooses to have some links with the past? So far, there has seemed little sign.[11]

Serialism is at present far removed from what must now seem the comparatively simple and single-minded principles of Schönberg, having diverged in various ways. Building on Webern's practices, the serialist *avant-garde* are creating a mathematical type of music, with not only linear succession but also rhythm and dynamics subject to serial control. Negation rules. Music is " non-tonal " and " athematic ", rhythm " irrational ", melody rejoicing in " dis-continuity ". Altogether, as a reaction against the radio and gramophone facilities which have made listening easier, the composers of the " ivory tower ", with no heed for normal taste and comprehension, have decided to make it as *difficult* as possible. Or so one might be forgiven for imagining.

It is sometimes argued that serialism is just another change of style, as from baroque polyphony to *galant*. I cannot believe this. Its basic principle, the equality of the twelve chromatic notes, strikes at the very foundations of the principles of music as we have known it. The inequalities of all the previous modes or scales have always made possible a mental sheet-anchor, whether Greek *mese,* plainchant *final* or major-minor *tonic*; sometimes with a reinforcement, whether *reciting-note* or *dominant.* Serialism was obliged to invent a new type of melody, lacking anything resembling the traditional bases. Will the ordinary music-lover ever find examples of it singable, or even memorable?

Serialism in some shape or other has clearly come to stay, but by now it has surely been realised that in its stricter forms it is too bloodless and dehumanised to evoke responsive warmth. It may be that its best employment is as one only of the devices of the creative artist, even if it has to be used in juxtaposition and contrast to its hated enemy, tonality. We have already noted that Berg at times made only partial application of the technique, in which practice he was followed by Frank Martin, Dallapiccolo and Matyas Seiber, to name but some. Eric Blom has somewhere remarked that serial music " must be a resource for the *wilful* use of great composers."

Brief note must be made of other innovations, e.g. the " prepared pianos " of the American, John Cage (1912), who has conducted other strange mechanical experiments, and the use made of that ancient resource, the microtone, by a number of modern musicians. These include the Moravian, Alois Haba (1893), advocate for and composer in quarter- and sixth-tones, practising also an " athematic " style of writing. Numbers of quarter-tone pianos and other such instruments have been constructed and music written for them, without however any great impact having been made.

More notable has been the evolution of two artificial systems of composition—*musique concrète* and electronic music. *Musique concrète,* as the adjective attempts to indicate, makes use of already recorded sounds; music or just noises. These are blended, distorted, played backward and otherwise manipulated as is thought fit to produce results that normally are used for accompaniment purposes—radio, film or ballet. The inventor was Pierre Schaeffer, who started to work on the idea in Paris in 1948. Experiments continue. Electronic music has been in the main a German preoccupation, and is wholly artificially produced—from electric frequency generators. By technical manipulation of the original sounds new timbres can be created. There are no scales to consider; thus intonation is wholly flexible, and it is possible to superimpose on the sounds every kind of complicated rhythm. Its leading exponents were recently Meye Eppler and Herbert Eimer of the West German Radio, but young serialists in both Germany and France have become interested, Boulez and Stockhausen among them. Like *musique concrète,* electronic music has had " background " uses. But now that the *avant-garde* on both sides of the Atlantic are developing it more ambitious results may be expected.

Thus far consideration of " divisions " has been confined to those which exist in what we have called " serious " music. Yet if the word music is understood in its comprehensive sense, then a much larger and more tragic dichotomy is to be admitted. This is the cleavage between on one hand " serious " or " art " music (given also such names as " classical ", " highbrow" and "square"), and on the other, "popular" music, the production and dissemination of which are highly profitable modern industries.

The flooding of the ether by the almost continuous sound of music of one sort or another has produced a kind of mass-receptivity on the part of a proportion of the listening public, whose sense of discrimination tends to be more and more blunted. Thus in modern times there has been an enormous increase in the number of people who are *hearing* music, but of them a smaller and smaller percentage who are really *listening*. One of the main uses of the art seems to have become that of providing a pleasant (or unpleasant, as the case may be) background to the normal activities of daily life. The facilities afforded by radio, television and gramophone have brought about an unprecedented expansion of the mechanised industry of music-manufacture, that of "pop" music, which provides entertainment at a new low level of culture. It is no spontaneous expression of creative art, but is imposed on a passive public with an eye to nothing more than a quick return of commercial profits. The public cannot altogether be blamed. It may be that some of them have found, after trial, that so much of modern "serious" music is to them incomprehensible. The music which is brought to them so readily is at least very easy to assimilate.

Once again we are presented with a state of affairs which is altogether peculiar to modern times. Returning in history to eras before the existence of commercial music, let us examine the point of view of say, the eighteenth century composer. As he understood it his music had but two functions, (1) to play its part in the worship of God, and (2) to provide enjoyment for that portion of humanity with which he was concerned. Thus Haydn and Mozart and their fellow-craftsmen got ahead with writing their Masses and motets, their symphonies, stage-works and serenades, but when called on to do so had not the slightest objection to turning out dance-music, of a quality that made them the most popular composers of that genre in Vienna. Schubert, with his swarms of keyboard pieces for dancing, was similarly unaware of the existence of any schism. This apparently also went for the ordinary citizen of Vienna—the man in the street. The story has come down to us of the summer evening practices of the Konvikt school orchestra, playing overtures and symphonies by such composers as Haydn, Mozart, the popular Czech, Kozeluch and the young Beethoven, with windows wide open, the street below so crowded with listeners as to be impassable, and an obliging householder opposite bringing out all his chairs for the sake of the ladies. And perhaps the boy Schubert leading the violins. Again, Schubert wrote "drawing-room" songs primarily for the social evenings with his friends, with no ideas as to their immortality. Indeed, in the first instance it was his friends who insisted that some notice should be taken of them by publishers. The story of "great composers" and "dance-music" could be continued with Weber and many others.

Only with the coming of the Romantics did the gulf commence to open. Serious composers began to cultivate high ideals as to their art, and to think of themselves as the movers and shakers of the world. The everyday trivialities of dance-music were not for them. When they chose to make use of the waltz it became a concert piece. A later glimpse of this attitude can be seen in the case of Sullivan, who was believed by many of his English well-wishers to be degrading his symphonic status by writing comic operas. He was inclined to think that himself. In the meantime another kind of composer had emerged, well-trained and competent. Men like Josef Lanner and the two Viennese so-called waltz-kings Johann Strauss, father and son, organised their own light orchestras and spent their lives in producing a wealth of attractive dance-music, venturing outside only into the realm of light opera, and having no symphonic ambitions whatsoever. The break was complete, and has so continued.

Ephemeral music in plenty there has been in past centuries, devised to catch popular fancy and with no expectation of anything more than may-fly existence. But never before this present time has there been such a weight and wide diffusion of trivial material at the lowest level of bad taste—and this encouraged by press and broadcast methods of publicity. It is a grave reflection on the standards of our general culture that nowadays the bawl-lings and clangour of " pop " music should bring to its exponents and their exploiters such disproportionate returns, as compared with those of the body of artistic and professionally trained vocalists and instrumentalists who spend long years in acquiring the advanced techniques and refinements of their art.

This division into two worlds has troubled many thinking musicians, who have rightly regarded it as no less than a tragedy. We have noted Hinde-mith's concern, and his efforts to establish a *Gebrauchsmusik*. Milhaud and Aaron Copland have also displayed their interest in the problem, but what has been done only touches the fringe of it. Can we believe that some real *via media* will eventually be found? The Russian answer surely cannot be the right one.

Meanwhile the ill-rewarded serious composer will continue in his art, not because he has any great hope of an amelioration of his lot in the immediate future, but because he feels that he has something significant to say, and must therefore say it.

NOTES

1   The German composer Max Bruch (1838–1920) has so far been neglected in these chronicles. His fame as a composer of symphonies and choral works was once much higher than it now is. In this country at least his name is chiefly recalled by the Violin Concerto in G minor and the *Kol Nidrei* variations for 'cello and orchestra.

2* HMS X has a recording of two of the movements of Bliss's *Conversations*.

3   Another English composer of the same generation, Eugene Goossens (1893–1962), though producing many works in modern style somehow failed to achieve the position as a creative artist that his early talents seemed to promise. Much of his career was given to administrative posts and conducting in the U.S.A. and in Australia.

4* HMS X has a recording of the *Sanctus, Benedictus and Agnus Dei* from Rubbra's *Missa Cantuariensis* (1945).

5* HMS X has a recording of a movement from Rawsthorne's Quartet for clarinet, violin, viola and 'cello (1948).

6 Several performances of Tippett's opera, *King Priam,* have resulted in a fairly unanimous opinion among the critics that a highly original score has been created, especially in the matter of the instrumentation.

7 Belated justice must be done here to Ethel Smythe (1858–1944), composer, writer and formidable feminist. She had a thorough German training and produced a remarkable early Mass (1893). Her operas, *The Wreckers* and *The Boatswain's Mate,* still receive occasional revival. Another mention should be that of Phyllis Tate (b. 1911), who writes gracefully, mainly in chamber-music and song forms.

8* HMS X has a recording of a movement from a Sonata for violin and piano (1943) by Copland, written in the idiom of deliberate simplicity referred to in the text.

9 A regrettable omission at this point in the text was the name of Wallingford Riegger (b. 1885), who, though growing up in a nineteenth century atmosphere, yet kept abreast with musical development to the pitch of an individual use of dissonance and twelve-tone procedures. He studied in Germany, with Max Bruch among others. Back in his own country he has given a long life to the production of choral, orchestral and chamber works of a vivid and contrapuntal quality. In particular, he has devoted much attention to "music for dancers", that is, for the theatre stage.

Opportunity will here be taken to mention a couple more United States composers associated with serialism and "advanced" techniques generally—Milton Babbitt (b. 1916), both musician and mathematician, early engaged in extending the serial system into the areas of rhythm, dynamics and tone-colour; and Arthur Berger (b. 1912), who is also a critic and a writer on music.

10 An article entitled *The Marriage Will Not Take Place,* by Martin Cooper, appeared in *The Daily Telegraph* for 27th May, 1961. This was a shrewd appraisal of a situation existing over the last forty years, when at times hopes were expressed that some artistic alliance could be effected between jazz and the historically established art of music. Mr. Cooper's opinion was foreshadowed in the title. Jazz had been tried, but for "transfusion" purposes had been found wanting.

However, opinion is not lacking that jazz has had a certain amount of *indirect* influence on serious composers on both sides of the Atlantic, some of whom, especially among the *avant-garde,* have been moved to greater rhythmic ingenuities and freedoms, and have made use of improvisatory techniques. In this matter I recall some opinions expressed to me by Mr. Eric Salzman, music critic of the *New York Herald Tribune,* whose remarks, relevant to the American scene, were somewhat in these terms:

"Recent experiments in modern jazz and in serious non-jazz improvisation have tended to assimilate the new jazz with other *avant-garde* ideas. Thus you find twelve-tone jazz, actually written in score, side by side with a new string quartet that uses chance, unpredictability and indeterminacy. Some of the music that combines modern jazz with *avant-garde* ideas is called 'third-stream' music; that is, it is a third stream which combines the two main streams of 'classical' and 'jazz'."

Whether this combined tributary will eventually be of much account to the mighty river of musical history only time will show.

11 M. Rene Leibowitz, in supporting *avant-garde* views, has declared that one should not expect music to provide either pleasure, distraction or relaxation.

INDEX